STATE AND LOCAL GOVERNMENT

Fourth Edition

Editor

Bruce Stinebrickner
DePauw University

Bruce Stinebrickner received his Ph.D. from Yale University in 1974. He has taught at Lehman College of the City University of New York and at the University of Queensland in Brisbane, Australia. He currently teaches in the Department of Political Science at DePauw University in Greencastle, Indiana. Dr. Stinebrickner teaches and writes about American politics and brings to Annual Editions valuable perspectives on the American political system gained from working and living abroad.

Annual Editions
A Library of Information from the Public Press

Cover illustration by Mike Eagle

The Dushkin Publishing Group, Inc.
Sluice Dock, Guilford, Connecticut 06437

The Annual Editions Series

Annual Editions is a series of over forty-five volumes designed to provide the reader with convenient, low-cost access to a wide range of current, carefully selected articles from some of the most important magazines, newspapers, and journals published today. Annual Editions are updated on an annual basis through a continuous monitoring of over 200 periodical sources. All Annual Editions have a number of features designed to make them particularly useful, including topic guides, annotated tables of contents, unit overviews, and indexes. For the teacher using Annual Editions in the classroom, an Instructor's Resource Guide with test questions is available for each volume.

VOLUMES AVAILABLE

Africa
Aging
American Government
American History, Pre-Civil War
American History, Post-Civil War
Anthropology
Biology
Business and Management
Business Ethics
China
Comparative Politics
Computers in Education
Computers in Business
Computers in Society
Criminal Justice
Drugs, Society, and Behavior
Early Childhood Education
Economics
Educating Exceptional Children
Education
Educational Psychology
Environment
Geography
Global Issues
Health

Human Development
Human Resources
Human Sexuality
Latin America
Macroeconomics
Marketing
Marriage and Family
Middle East and the Islamic World
Nutrition
Personal Growth and Behavior
Psychology
Social Problems
Sociology
Soviet Union and Eastern Europe
State and Local Government
Third World
Urban Society
Western Civilization, Pre-Reformation
Western Civilization, Post-Reformation
Western Europe
World History, Pre-Modern
World History, Modern
World Politics

Library of Congress Cataloging in Publication Data
Main entry under title: Annual Editions: State and local government.
   1. Local government—United States—Addresses, essays, lectures. 2. State governments—United States—Addresses, essays, lectures. I. Title: State and local government.
352'.000973'05   ISBN 0-87967-796-1

Fourth Edition

Manufactured by The Banta Company, Harrisonburg, Virginia 22801

Editors/ Advisory Board

EDITOR

Bruce Stinebrickner
DePauw University

Members of the Advisory Board are instrumental in the final selection of articles for each edition of Annual Editions. Their review of articles for content, level, currency, and appropriateness provides critical direction to the editor and staff. We think you'll find their careful consideration well reflected in this volume.

ADVISORY BOARD

Frank M. Bryan
University of Vermont

Steve Coleman
Rutgers University

Robert L. Delorme
California State University
Long Beach

Melvin Kulbicki
York College of Pennsylvania

Daniel J. McCarthy
College of New Rochelle

Melvin Oettinger
Coastal Carolina Community
College

James M. Penning
Calvin College

Craig Ramsay
Ohio Wesleyan University

Robert S. Ross
California State University
Chico

Carmine Scavo
East Carolina University

Thomas M. Scott
University of Minnesota

Herbert C. Smith
Western Maryland College

Nelson Wikstrom
Virginia Commonwealth University

STAFF

To The Reader

In publishing ANNUAL EDITIONS we recognize the enormous role played by the magazines, newspapers, and journals of the *public press* in providing current, first-rate educational information in a broad spectrum of interest areas. Within the articles, the best scientists, practitioners, researchers, and commentators draw issues into new perspective as accepted theories and viewpoints are called into account by new events, recent discoveries change old facts, and fresh debate breaks out over important controversies.

Many of the articles resulting from this enormous editorial effort are appropriate for students, researchers, and professionals seeking accurate, current material to help bridge the gap between principles and theories and the real world. These articles, however, become more useful for study when those of lasting value are carefully *collected, organized, indexed,* and *reproduced* in a *low-cost format,* which provides easy and permanent access when the material is needed. That is the role played by *Annual Editions.* Under the direction of each volume's *Editor,* who is an expert in the subject area, and with the guidance of an *Advisory Board,* we seek each year to provide in each *ANNUAL EDITION* a current, well-balanced, carefully selected collection of the best of the public press for your study and enjoyment. We think you'll find this volume useful, and we hope you'll take a moment to let us know what you think.

This collection of readings is the fourth edition in a series on state and local government. The book is designed for use in courses on state and local government and in state and local government segments of courses on American government. The educational goal is to provide a collection of up-to-date articles that are informative and interesting to students studying the area.

The 50 state governments and approximately 80,000 local governments in the United States have a great deal in common. They also exhibit remarkable diversity. The contents of the book as a whole inevitably reflect this theme of commonality *and* diversity. Some of the selections treat individual states or localities in considerable detail. Other articles focus on particular aspects of more than one state or local government. Still other articles explicitly compare and contrast regions, states, or localities. Taken together, the selections provide an overview of similarities and differences among state and local governments in the United States.

Keeping the idea of similarities and dissimilarities in mind can help students beginning their study of state and local governments. In many state and local government courses, a "home" state or region is given special attention. In such courses, the theme of commonality and diversity can serve to highlight what is and is not typical about the home state or region.

One cornerstone of Reagan administration policies was to cut national government spending on domestic programs. In response, many state and local governments took initiatives to help fill in the gaps. These developments bear continued watching during the Bush administration because they will probably affect the priorities and vitality of state and local governments for years to come.

The book is divided into eight units. Unit 1 is devoted to several eighteenth- and nineteenth-century commentaries on American federalism and state and local governments. Unit 2 treats relations among national, state, and local governments. Unit 3 covers voting, parties, and interest groups, and pays considerable attention to unusual features of state and local electoral arrangements. Unit 4 turns to government institutions and officeholders. Unit 5 focuses explicitly on diversity among regions and states. Cities and suburbs provide the material for unit 6, while unit 7 is devoted to finances and economic development. Unit 8 concludes the book with an examination of policies and policymaking in state and local governments, including the issue of privatization.

The book generally groups articles treating particular aspects of the governing process, be it state *or* local government, in the same units or sections. For example, unit 4 covers governmental institutions at both state and local levels, with sections 4A, 4B, and 4C treating state and local legislatures, executives, and courts, respectively. Unit 6, which treats metropolitan areas, is an exception to this rule in that it focuses primarily on issues involving *local* governments.

Deciding what articles to use in this revised edition was not an easy task. I tried to assess articles according to significance and relevance of subject matter, readability for students, and utility in stimulating students' interest in state and local government. Potential selections were evaluated not only as they stood alone, but also as complements to other likely selections.

The next edition of this book will bring another opportunity to make changes. State and local government is a particularly diverse field of study, and numerous newspapers and regional magazines across the country carry articles that might be suitable for use. I earnestly solicit reactions to this book as well as suggestions of articles for use in the next edition. In other words, readers are cordially invited to become advisors and collaborators in future editions by completing and mailing the article rating form on the last page of this book.

Bruce Stinebrickner

Bruce Stinebrickner
Editor

Contents

Unit 1

Early Commentaries

Five historical selections review the early bases of forming state and local governments.

The concepts in bold italics are developed in the article. For further expansion please refer to the Topic Guide and the Index.

Unit 2

Intergovernmental Relations

Five selections discuss the concept of "new federalism" as it affects the relationship between federal, state, and local systems.

Unit 3

Voting, Parties, and Interest Groups

Seven articles examine how voting, parties, and interest groups are affected by the electoral system, minority groups, initiatives, recalls, and special interests.

The concepts in bold italics are developed in the article. For further expansion please refer to the Topic Guide and the Index.

Unit 4

Government Institutions and Officeholders

Thirteen articles consider how legislatures, executives, courts, and other institutions influence the efficiency and functions of state and local government.

The concepts in bold italics are developed in the article. For further expansion please refer to the Topic Guide and the Index.

Unit **5**

Variations Among Regions and States

Five articles discuss how economic, historical, cultural, and geographic factors define the variations among regions and states.

Unit **6**

Cities and Suburbs

Five selections discuss some of the issues affecting suburbs and cities. The topics include the impact of business on the reshaping of America, the criteria that determine a well-governed city, and the relationship between poverty and crime in inner cities.

The concepts in bold italics are developed in the article. For further expansion please refer to the Topic Guide and the Index.

Unit 7

Finances and Economic Development

Six selections examine revenue generating methods in state and local governments and the problems and prospects of economic development.

Unit 8

Privatization and Policymaking

Ten articles review how state and local government policymaking affects education, criminal justice, public transportation, the welfare system, and public health. The impact of privatization on state revenues is also analyzed.

The concepts in bold italics are developed in the article. For further expansion please refer to the Topic Guide and the Index.

Topic Guide

This topic guide suggests how the selections in this book relate to topics of traditional concern to students and professionals involved with the study of state and local government. It is very useful in locating articles which relate to each other for reading and research. The guide is arranged alphabetically according to topic. Articles may, of course, treat topics that do not appear in the topic guide. In turn, entries in the topic guide do not necessarily constitute a comprehensive listing of all the contents of each selection.

TOPIC AREA	TREATED AS AN ISSUE IN:	TOPIC AREA	TREATED AS AN ISSUE IN:
Administration and Bureaucracy	11. Mixed Electoral Systems 22. Practicing Political Science 23. Change Masters for the States 26. "City Managers Don't Make Policy" 30. Technology Transfer 37. Snow White and the 17 Dwarfs 47. Privatization Crossfire 48. Privatization Presents Problems	**Education**	*See* School Boards/School Districts
		Elections and Electoral Systems	All selections in 3A 22. Practicing Political Science 34. The Two Souths
		Economic Development	All selections in 7B 32. An Economic Role Reversal 33. Halfway Home 36. How Business is Reshaping America
Cities	12. I Was a Chicago Ward Heeler 25. From Dreamers to Doers 26. "City Managers Don't Make Policy" 28. View From the Bench 36. How Business Is Reshaping America 37. Snow White and the 17 Dwarfs 38. Would We Know a Well-Governed City? 39. The Urban Strangler 40. Blacks in Boston Seek to Secede 46. Civic Strategy for Local Economic Development 56. The Myths of Mass Transit	**Environmental Policies**	54. The Battle Over Land Use
		Federalism/"New Federalism"	All selections in Unit 2 1. The Federalist No. 17 2. The Federalist No. 45 5. Nature of the American State 27. The Emerging Agenda
		Governors	23. Strategies for Leaders 24. Change Masters for the States 34. The Two Souths 44. The States' Global Hustlers
City Managers	26. "City Managers Don't Make Policy"		
Constitutions, State	27. The Emerging Agenda	**Initiatives**	*See* Referenda and Initiatives
Corruption	35. "Sweetheart, Get Me Re-Write."	**Interest Groups**	13. The Arms Race of Campaign Financing 14. Buying State Access 22. Practicing Political Science 40. Blacks in Boston Seek to Secede
Counties	4. Local Government: Observations		
Courts	All selections in 4C 28. View From the Bench 51. Bring Back the Orphanage		
		Mayors	25. From Dreamers to Doers 26. "City Managers Don't Make Policy"
Criminal Justice System	28. View From the Bench 39. The Urban Strangler 53. Drunk Driving	**Parties**	4. Local Government: Observations 19. Party Politics 20. Fifty Years Without a Conference Committee 34. The Two Souths
Diversity	35. "Sweetheart, Get Me Re-Write." 49. Safety Nets for the Poor *See also* Regions and Regionalism		

Early Commentaries

The American political system includes three levels of government—national, state, and local. Although not unique among nations today, this arrangement was unusual in the late eighteenth century when the United States became independent. Early commentaries on the American political system paid considerable attention to each of the levels of government as well as to relations among the three levels. These writings suggest the important role that state and local governments have always played in the United States.

Debate about the desirability of the proposed new Constitution of 1787—the Constitution that remains in force to this day—often focused on the relationship between the national government and the states. Some people thought that the states were going to be too strong in the proposed new union, and others argued that the national government would be. Three prominent supporters of the new Constitution—Alexander Hamilton, James Madison, and John Jay—wrote a series of articles in 1787-1788 explaining and defending it. Many of these articles, which came to be known as *The Federalist Papers*, treated the federal relationship between the national government and the states. So did many of the writings of other early observers. This shows the importance that was attached to the new federal relationship right from the start.

Local government was also the subject of considerable attention in early commentaries on the American political system. Alexis de Tocqueville, a French nobleman visiting the United States early in the nineteenth century, recorded his observations in a book entitled *Democracy in America* (1835). Tocqueville remarked on the extraordinary vitality of American local government institutions, comparing what he saw in the United States with European institutions at the time. Today American local government still plays a prominent role in the overall governing process, probably more so than in any other nation in the world.

Later in the nineteenth century, a second foreign observer, James Bryce, published another historic commentary on the United States, *The American Commonwealth* (1888). Bryce, an Englishman, discussed American federalism and American state and local governments. He described the similarities and differences among local government structures in different regions of the country, the nature of the states, and the lamentable performance of city governments. Like Tocqueville, Bryce was able to identify and analyze distinctive elements of the American system of government and make a lasting contribution to the study of the American political system.

Selections in this first section of the book come from *The Federalist Papers*, Tocqueville's *Democracy in America*, and Bryce's *American Commonwealth*. These historic observations on American federalism and state and local governments provide a baseline against which to assess the picture of contemporary state and local government that emerges in the rest of the book.

Looking Ahead: Challenge Questions

How does the picture of local governments provided by Tocqueville and Bryce compare with American local governments today?

Do you think that the observations of Hamilton, Madison, Tocqueville, and Bryce are out of date by now? Why or why not?

Students of politics frequently refer to the "historic" writings of Plato, Aristotle, Machiavelli, Hobbes, Locke, Rousseau, and others. Selections in this section are examples of early or historic writings on American politics. Why do you think that those who study politics so often look to the classics, even centuries after they were first written?

Do you find the arguments and logic of *Federalist 17* and *45* persuasive? Can you detect any "flaws" or "mistakes"?

Which author do you find most interesting and helpful—Hamilton, Madison, Tocqueville, or Bryce? Why?

THE FEDERALIST NO. 17
(HAMILTON)

To the People of the State of New York:

AN OBJECTION, of a nature different from that which has been stated and answered, in my last address, may perhaps be likewise urged against the principle of legislation for the individual citizens of America. It may be said that it would tend to render the government of the Union too powerful, and to enable it to absorb those residuary authorities, which it might be judged proper to leave with the States for local purposes. Allowing the utmost latitude to the love of power which any reasonable man can require, I confess I am at a loss to discover what temptation the persons intrusted with the administration of the general government could ever feel to divest the States of the authorities of that description. The regulation of the mere domestic police of a State appears to me to hold out slender allurements to ambition. Commerce, finance, negotiation, and war seem to comprehend all the objects which have charms for minds governed by that passion; and all the powers necessary to those objects ought, in the first instance, to be lodged in the national depository. The administration of private justice between the citizens of the same State, the supervision of agriculture and of other concerns of a similar nature, all those things, in short, which are proper to be provided for by local legislation, can never be desirable cares of a general jurisdiction. It is therefore improbable that there should exist a disposition in the federal councils to usurp the powers with which they are connected; because the attempt to exercise those powers would be as troublesome as it would be nugatory; and the possession of them, for that reason, would contribute nothing to the dignity, to the importance, or to the splendor of the national government.

But let it be admitted, for argument's sake, that mere wantonness and lust of domination would be sufficient to beget that disposition; still it may be safely affirmed, that the sense of the constituent body of the national representatives, or, in other words, the people of the several States, would control the indulgence of so extravagant an appetite. It will always be far more easy for the State governments to encroach upon the national authorities, than for the national government to encroach upon the State authorities. The proof of this proposition turns upon the greater degree of influence which the State governments, if they administer their affairs with uprightness and prudence, will generally possess over the people; a circumstance which at the same time teaches us that there is an inherent and intrinsic weakness in all federal constitutions; and that too much pains cannot be taken in their organization, to give them all the force which is compatible with the principles of liberty.

The superiority of influence in favor of the particular governments would result partly from the diffusive construction of the national government, but chiefly from the nature of the objects to which the attention of the State administrations would be directed.

It is a known fact in human nature, that its affections are commonly weak in proportion to the distance or diffusiveness of the object. Upon the same principle that a man is more attached to his family than to his neighborhood, to his neighborhood than to the community at large, the people of each State would be apt to feel a stronger bias towards their local governments than towards the government of the Union; unless the force of that principle should be destroyed by a much better administration of the latter.

This strong propensity of the human heart would find powerful auxiliaries in the objects of State regulation.

The variety of more minute interests, which will necessarily fall under the superintendence of the local administrations, and which will form so many rivulets of influence, running through every part of the society, cannot be particularized, without involving a detail too tedious and uninteresting to compensate for the instruction it might afford.

There is one transcendent advantage belonging to the province of the State governments, which alone suffices to place the matter in a clear and satisfactory light,—I mean

The Federalist, No. 17, Alexander Hamilton, 1787.

the ordinary administration of criminal and civil justice. This, of all others, is the most powerful, most universal, and most attractive source of popular obedience and attachment. It is that which, being the immediate and visible guardian of life and property, having its benefits and its terrors in constant activity before the public eye, regulating all those personal interests and familiar concerns to which the sensibility of individuals is more immediately awake, contributes, more than any other circumstance, to impressing upon the minds of the people, affection, esteem, and reverence towards the government. This great cement of society, which will diffuse itself almost wholly through the channels of the particular governments, independent of all other causes of influence, would insure them so decided an empire over their respective citizens as to render them at all times a complete counterpoise, and, not unfrequently, dangerous rivals to the power of the Union.

The operations of the national government, on the other hand, falling less immediately under the observation of the mass of the citizens, the benefits derived from it will chiefly be perceived and attended to by speculative men. Relating to more general interests, they will be less apt to come home to the feelings of the people; and, in proportion, less likely to inspire an habitual sense of obligation, and an active sentiment of attachment.

The reasoning on this head has been abundantly exemplified by the experience of all federal constitutions with which we are acquainted, and of all others which have borne the least analogy to them.

Though the ancient feudal systems were not, strictly speaking, confederacies, yet they partook of the nature of that species of association. There was a common head, chieftain, or sovereign, whose authority extended over the whole nation; and a number of subordinate vassals, or feudatories, who had large portions of land allotted to them, and numerous trains of *inferior* vassals or retainers, who occupied and cultivated that land upon the tenure of fealty or obedience to the persons of whom they held it. Each principal vassal was a kind of sovereign within his particular demesnes. The consequences of this situation were a continual opposition to authority of the sovereign, and frequent wars between the great barons or chief feudatories themselves. The power of the head of the nation was commonly too weak, either to preserve the public peace, or to protect the people against the oppressions of their immediate lords. This period of European affairs is emphatically styled by historians, the times of feudal anarchy.

When the sovereign happened to be a man of vigorous and warlike temper and of superior abilities, he would acquire a personal weight and influence, which answered, for the time, the purposes of a more regular authority. But in general, the power of the barons triumphed over that of the prince; and in many instances his dominion was entirely thrown off, and the great fiefs were erected into independent principalities or States. In those instances in which the monarch finally prevailed over his vassals, his success was chiefly owing to the tyranny of those vassals over their dependents. The barons, or nobles, equally the enemies of the sovereign and the oppressors of the common people, were dreaded and detested by both; till mutual danger and mutual interest effected a union between them fatal to the power of the aristocracy. Had the nobles, by a conduct of clemency and justice, preserved the fidelity and devotion of their retainers and followers, the contests between them and the prince must almost always have ended in their favor, and in the abridgment or subversion of the royal authority.

This is not an assertion founded merely in speculation or conjecture. Among other illustrations of its truth which might be cited, Scotland will furnish a cogent example. The spirit of clanship which was, at an early day, introduced into that kingdom, uniting the nobles and their dependents by ties equivalent to those of kindred, rendered the aristocracy a constant overmatch for the power of the monarch, till the incorporation with England subdued its fierce and ungovernable spirit, and reduced it within those rules of subordination which a more rational and more energetic system of civil polity had previously established in the latter kingdom.

The separate governments in a confederacy may aptly be compared with the feudal baronies; with this advantage in their favor, that from the reasons already explained, they will generally possess the confidence and good-will of the people, and with so important a support, will be able effectually to oppose all encroachments of the national government. It will be well if they are not able to counteract its legitimate and necessary authority. The points of similitude consist in the rivalship of power, applicable to both, and in the CONCENTRATION of large portions of the strength of the community into particular DEPOSITS, in one case at the disposal of individuals, in the other case at the disposal of political bodies.

A concise review of the events that have attended confederate governments will further illustrate this important doctrine; an inattention to which has been the great source of our political mistakes, and has given our jealousy a direction to the wrong side. This review shall form the subject of some ensuing papers.　　PUBLIUS

THE FEDERALIST NO. 45
(MADISON)

To the People of the State of New York:

HAVING shown that no one of the powers transferred to the federal government is unnecessary or improper, the next question to be considered is, whether the whole mass of them will be dangerous to the portion of authority left in the several States.

The adversaries to the plan of the convention, instead of considering in the first place what degree of power was absolutely necessary for the purposes of the federal government, have exhausted themselves in a secondary inquiry into the possible consequences of the proposed degree of power to the governments of the particular States. But if the Union, as has been shown, be essential to the security of the people of America against foreign danger; if it be essential to their security against contentions and wars among the different States; if it be essential to guard them against those violent and oppressive factions which embitter the blessings of liberty, and against those military establishments which must gradually poison its very fountain; if, in a word, the Union be essential to the happiness of the people of America, is it not preposterous, to urge as an objection to a government, without which the objects of the Union cannot be attained, that such a government may derogate from the importance of the governments of the individual States? Was, then, the American Revolution effected, was the American Confederacy formed, was the precious blood of thousands spilt, and the hard-earned substance of millions lavished, not that the people of America should enjoy peace, liberty, and safety, but that the government of the individual States, that particular municipal establishments, might enjoy a certain extent of power, and be arrayed with certain dignities and attributes of sovereignty? We have heard of the impious doctrine in the Old World, that the people were made for kings, not kings for the people. Is the same doctrine to be revived in the New, in another shape —that the solid happiness of the people is to be sacrificed to the views of political institutions of a different form? It is too early for politicians to presume on our forgetting that the public good, the real welfare of the great body of the people, is the supreme object to be pursued; and that no form of government whatever has any other value than as it may be fitted for the attainment of this object. Were the plan of the convention adverse to the public happiness, my voice would be, Reject the plan. Were the Union itself inconsistent with the public happiness, it would be, Abolish the Union. In like manner, as far as the sovereignty of the States cannot be reconciled to the happiness of the people, the voice of every good citizen must be, Let the former be sacrificed to the latter. How far the sacrifice is necessary, has been shown. How far the unsacrificed residue will be endangered, is the question before us.

Several important considerations have been touched in the course of these papers, which discountenance the supposition that the operation of the federal government will by degrees prove fatal to the State governments. The more I revolve the subject, the more fully I am persuaded that the balance is much more likely to be disturbed by the preponderancy of the last than of the first scale.

We have seen, in all the examples of ancient and modern confederacies, the strongest tendency continually betraying itself in the members, to despoil the general government of its authorities, with a very ineffectual capacity in the latter to defend itself against the encroachments. Although, in most of these examples, the system has been so dissimilar from that under consideration as greatly to weaken any inference concerning the latter from the fate of the former, yet, as the States will retain, under the proposed Constitution, a very extensive portion of active sovereignty, the inference ought not to be wholly disregarded. In the Achæan league it is probable that the federal head had a degree and species of power, which gave it a considerable likeness to the government framed by the convention. The Lycian Confederacy, as far as its principles and form are transmitted, must have borne a still greater analogy to it. Yet history does not inform us that either of them ever degenerated, or tended to degenerate, into one consolidated government. On the contrary, we know that the ruin of one of them proceeded from the incapacity of the federal authority to prevent the dissensions, and finally the disunion, of the subordinate authorities. These cases are the more worthy of our attention, as the external causes by which the component parts were pressed together were much more numerous and powerful than in our case; and consequently less powerful ligaments within would be sufficient to bind the members to the head, and to each other.

In the feudal system, we have seen a similar propensity exemplified. Notwithstanding the want of proper sympathy in every instance between the local sovereigns and the people, and the sympathy in some instances between the general sovereign and the latter, it usually happened that the local sovereigns prevailed in the rivalship for encroachments. Had no external dangers enforced internal harmony and subordination, and particularly, had the local sovereigns possessed the affections of the people, the great kingdoms in Europe would at this time consist of as many independent princes as there were formerly feudatory barons.

The State governments will have the advantage of the Federal government, whether we compare them in respect to the immediate dependence of the one on the other; to the weight of personal influence which each side will possess; to the powers respectively vested in them; to the predilection and probable support of the people; to the disposition and faculty of resisting and frustrating the measures of each other.

The State governments may be regarded as constituent and essential parts of the federal government; whilst the latter is nowise essential to the operation or organization of the former. Without the intervention of the State legislatures, the President of the United States cannot be elected at all. They must in all cases have a great share in his appointment, and will, perhaps, in most cases, of themselves determine it. The Senate will be elected absolutely and exclusively by the State legislatures. Even the House of Representatives, though drawn immediately from the people, will be chosen very much under the influence of that class of men, whose influence over the people obtains for themselves an election into the State legislatures. Thus, each of the principal branches of the federal government will owe its existence more or less to the favor of the State governments, and must consequently feel a dependence, which is much more likely to beget a disposition too obsequious than too overbearing towards them. On the other side, the component parts of the State governments will in no instance be indebted for their appointment to the direct agency of the federal government, and very little, if at all, to the local influence of its members.

The number of individuals employed under the Constitution of the United States will be much smaller than the number employed under the particular States. There will consequently be less of personal influence on the side of the former than of the latter. The members of the legislative, executive, and judiciary departments of thirteen and more States, the justices of peace, officers of militia, ministerial officers of justice, with all the county,

corporation, and town officers, for three millions and more of people, intermixed, and having particular acquaintance with every class and circle of people, must exceed, beyond all proportion, both in number and influence, those of every description who will be employed in the administration of the federal system. Compare the members of the three great departments of the thirteen States, excluding from the judiciary department the justices of peace, with the members of the corresponding departments of the single government of the Union; compare the militia officers of three millions of people with the military and marine officers of any establishment which is within the compass of probability, or, I may add, of possibility, and in this view alone, we may pronounce the advantage of the States to be decisive. If the federal government is to have collectors of revenue, the State governments will have theirs also. And as those of the former will be principally on the sea-coast, and not very numerous, whilst those of the latter will be spread over the face of the country, and will be very numerous, the advantage in this view also lies on the same side. It is true, that the Confederacy is to possess, and may exercise, the power of collecting internal as well as external taxes throughout the States; but it is probable that this power will not be resorted to, except for supplemental purposes of revenue; that an option will then be given to the States to supply their quotas by previous collections of their own; and that the eventual collection, under the immediate authority of the Union, will generally be made by the officers, and according to the rules, appointed by the several States. Indeed it is extremely probable, that in other instances, particularly in the organization of the judicial power, the officers of the States will be clothed with the correspondent authority of the Union. Should it happen, however, that separate collectors of internal revenue should be appointed under the federal government, the influence of the whole number would not bear a comparison with that of the multitude of State officers in the opposite scale. Within every district to which a federal collector would be allotted, there would not be less than thirty or forty, or even more, officers of different descriptions, and many of them persons of character and weight, whose influence would lie on the side of the State.

The powers delegated by the proposed Constitution to the federal government are few and defined. Those which are to remain in the State governments are numerous and indefinite. The former will be exercised principally on external objects, as war, peace, negotiation, and foreign commerce; with which last the power of taxation will, for the most part, be connected. The powers reserved to the several States will extend to all the objects which, in the ordinary course of affairs; concern the lives, liberties, and properties of the people, and the internal order, improvement, and prosperity of the State.

The operations of the federal government will be most extensive and important in times of war and danger; those of the State governments in times of peace and security. As the former periods will probably bear a small proportion to the latter, the State governments will here enjoy another advantage over the federal government. The more adequate, indeed, the federal powers may be rendered to the national defence, the less frequent will be those scenes of danger which might favor their ascendancy over the governments of the particular States.

If the new Constitution be examined with accuracy and candor, it will be found that the change which it proposes consists much less in the addition of NEW POWERS to the Union, than in the invigoration of its ORIGINAL POWERS. The regulation of commerce, it is true, is a new power; but that seems to be an addition which few oppose, and from which no apprehensions are entertained. The powers relating to war and peace, armies and fleets, treaties and finance, with the other more considerable powers, are all vested in the existing Congress by the articles of Confederation. The proposed change does not enlarge these powers; it only substitutes a more effectual mode of administering them. The change relating to taxation may be regarded as the most important; and yet the present Congress have as complete authority to RE-QUIRE of the States indefinite supplies of money for the common defence and general welfare, as the future Congress will have to require them of individual citizens; and the latter will be no more bound than the States themselves have been, to pay the quotas respectively taxed on them. Had the States complied punctually with the articles of Confederation, or could their compliance have been enforced by as peaceable means as may be used with success towards single persons, our past experience is very far from countenancing an opinion, that the State governments would have lost their constitutional powers, and have gradually undergone an entire consolidation. To maintain that such an event would have ensued, would be to say at once, that the existence of the State governments is incompatible with any system whatever that accomplishes the essential purposes of the Union.

PUBLIUS

The American System of Townships . . .

Alexis de Tocqueville

Why the writer begins his examination of political institutions with the township. There are townships in every nation. Difficulty of establishing and maintaining their communal freedom. Its importance. Why the writer has chosen the organization of the New England township as the main subject to examine.

It is not by chance that I consider the township first. The township is the only association so well rooted in nature that wherever men assemble it forms itself.

Communal society therefore exists among all peoples, whatever be their customs and their laws; man creates kingdoms and republics, but townships seem to spring directly from the hand of God. But though townships are coeval with humanity, local freedom is a rare and fragile thing. A nation can always establish great political assemblies, because it always contains a certain number of individuals whose understanding will, to some extent, take the place of experience in handling affairs. But the local community is composed of coarser elements, often recalcitrant to the lawgiver's activity. The difficulty of establishing a township's independence rather augments than diminishes with the increase of enlightenment of nations. A very civilized society finds it hard to tolerate attempts at freedom in a local community; it is disgusted by its numerous blunders and is apt to despair of success before the experiment is finished.

Of all forms of liberty, that of a local community, which is so hard to establish, is the most prone to the encroachments of authority. Left to themselves, the institutions of a local community can hardly struggle against a strong and enterprising government; they cannot defend themselves with success unless they have reached full development and have come to form part of national ideas and habits. Hence, until communal freedom has come to form part of mores, it can easily be destroyed, and it cannot enter into mores without a long-recognized legal existence.

So communal freedom is not, one may almost say, the fruit of human effort. It is seldom created, but rather springs up of its own accord. It grows, almost in secret, amid a semibarbarous society. The continual action of laws, mores, circumstances, and above all time may succeed in consolidating it. Among all the nations of continental Europe, one may say that there is not one that understands communal liberty.

However, the strength of free peoples resides in the local community. Local institutions are to liberty what primary schools are to science; they put it within the people's reach; they teach people to appreciate its peaceful enjoyment and accustom them to make use of it. Without local institutions a nation may give itself a free government, but it has not got the spirit of liberty. Passing passions, momentary interest, or chance circumstances may give it the external shape of independence, but the despotic tendencies which have been driven into the interior of the body social will sooner or later break out on the surface.

To help the reader understand the general principles on which the political organization of townships and counties in the United States depends, I thought it would be useful to take one particular state as an example and examine in detail what happens there, subsequently taking a quick look at the rest of the country.

I have chosen one of the states of New England.

Townships and counties are not organized in the same way in all parts of the Union; nevertheless, one can easily see that throughout the Union more or less the same principles have guided the formation of both township and county.

Now, I thought that in New England these principles had been carried further with more far-reaching results than elsewhere. Consequently they stand out there in higher relief and are easier for a foreigner to observe.

The local institutions of New England form a complete and regular whole; they are ancient; law and, even more, mores make them strong; and they exercise immense influence over the whole of society.

For all these reasons they deserve our attention.

Limits of the Township

The New England township is halfway between a *canton* and a *commune* in France. It generally has from two to three thousand inhabitants;[1] it is therefore not too large for all the inhabitants to have roughly the same interests, but is big enough to be sure of finding the elements of a good administration within itself.

Powers of the New England Township

The people as the origin of power in the township as elsewhere. They handle their principal affairs themselves. No municipal council. The greater part of municipal authority concentrated in the hands of the "selectmen." How the selectmen function. Town meeting. List of all municipal officials. Obligatory and paid functions.

In the township, as everywhere else, the people are the source of power, but nowhere else do they exercise their power so directly. In America the people are a master who must be indulged to the utmost possible limits.

In New England the majority works through representatives when it is dealing with the general affairs of the state. It was necessary that that should be so; but in the township, where both law and administration are closer to the governed, the representative system has not been adopted. There is no municipal council; the body of the electors, when it has chosen the officials, gives them directions in everything beyond the simple, ordinary execution of the laws of the state.[2]

Such a state of affairs is so contrary to our ideas and opposed to our habits that some examples are needed to make it understandable.

Public duties in the township are extremely numerous and minutely divided, as we shall see later on, but most of the administrative power is concentrated in the hands of a few yearly elected individuals called "selectmen."[3]

The general laws of the state impose certain duties on the selectmen. In administering these they do not require the authorization of the governed, and it is their personal responsibility if they neglect them. For example, the state law charges them to draw up the municipal voting lists, and if they fail to do so, they are guilty of an offense. But in all matters within the township's control the selectmen carry out the popular will, just as our mayors execute the decisions of the municipal council. Usually they act on their own responsibility, merely putting into practice principles already approved by the majority. But if they want to make any change in the established order to start some new undertaking, they must go back to the source of their power. Suppose they want to start a school; the selectmen summon all the voters to a meeting on a fixed day and place; they there explain the need felt; they state the means available for the purpose, how much it will cost, and the site suggested. The meeting, consulted on all these points, accepts the principle, decides the site, votes the tax, and leaves the selectmen to carry out its orders.

Only the selectmen have the right to call a town meeting, but they may be required to do so. If ten owners of property conceive some new project and wish to submit it to the approval of the township, they demand a general meeting of the inhabitants; the selectmen are bound to agree to this and preserve only the right to preside over the meeting.[4]

Such political mores and social customs are certainly far removed from ours. I do not, at this moment, want to pass judgment on them or to reveal the hidden reasons causing them and giving them life; it is enough to describe them.

The selectmen are elected every year in April or May. At the same time, the town meeting also elects many other municipal officials[5] to take charge of important administrative details. There are assessors to rate the township and collectors to bring the taxes in. The constable must organize the police, take care of public places, and take a hand in the physical execution of the laws. The town clerk must record all resolutions; he keeps a record of the proceedings of the civil administration. The treasurer looks after the funds of the township. There are also overseers of the poor whose difficult task it is to execute the provisions of the Poor Laws; school commissioners in charge of public education; and surveyors of highways, who look after roads both large and small, to complete the list of the main administrative officials of the township. But the division of functions does not stop there; among municipal officials one also finds parish commissioners responsible for the expenses of public worship, fire wardens to direct the citizens' efforts in case of fire, tithing men, hog reeves, fence viewers, timber measurers, and sealers of weights and measures.[6]

Altogether there are nineteen main officials in a township. Every inhabitant is bound, on pain of fine, to accept these various duties; but most of them also carry some remuneration so that poorer citizens can devote their time to them without loss. Furthermore, it is not the American system to give any fixed salary to officials. In general, each official act has a price, and men are paid in accordance with what they have done.

Life in the Township

Each man the best judge of his own interest. Corollary of the principle of the sovereignty of the people. How American townships apply these doctrines. The New England township sovereign in all that concerns itself alone, subordinate in all else. Duties of the township toward the state. In France the government lends officials to the commune. In America the township lends its officials to the government.

I have said before that the principle of the sovereignty of the people hovers over the whole political system of the Anglo-Americans. Every page of this book will point out new applications of this doctrine.

In nations where the dogma of the sovereignty of the people prevails, each individual forms an equal part of that sovereignty and shares equally the government of the state.

Each individual is assumed to be as educated, virtuous, and powerful as any of his fellows.

Why, then, should he obey society, and what are the natural limits of such obedience?

He obeys society not because he is inferior to those who direct it, nor because he is incapable of ruling himself, but because union with his fellows seems useful to him and he knows that that union is impossible without a regulating authority.

Therefore, in all matters concerning the duties of citizens toward each other he is subordinate. In all matters that concern himself alone he remains the master; he is free and owes an account of his actions to God alone. From this derives the maxim that the individual is the best and only judge of his own interest and that society has no right to direct his behavior unless it feels harmed by him or unless it needs his concurrence.

This doctrine is universally accepted in the United States. Elsewhere I will examine its general influence on the ordinary actions of life; here and now I am concerned only with townships.

The township, taken as a whole in relation to the central government, resembles any other individual to whom the theory just mentioned applies.

So in the United States municipal liberty derives straight from the dogma of the sovereignty of the people; all the American republics have recognized this independence more or less, but there were circumstances particularly favorable to its growth among the people of New England.

In that part of the Union political life was born in the very heart of the townships; one might almost say that in origin each of them was a little independent nation. Later, when the kings of England claimed their share of sovereignty, they limited themselves to taking over the central power. They left the townships as they had found them. Now the New England townships are subordinate, but in the beginning this was not so, or hardly so. Therefore they have not received their powers; on the contrary, it would seem that they have surrendered a portion of their powers for the benefit of the state; that is an important distinction which the reader should always bear in mind.

In general the townships are subordinate to the state only where some interest that I shall call *social* is concerned, that is to say, some interest shared with others.

In all that concerns themselves alone the townships remain independent bodies, and I do not think one could find a single inhabitant of New England who would recognize the right of the government of the state to control matters of purely municipal interest.

Hence one finds the New England townships buying and selling, suing and being sued, increasing or reducing their budgets, and no administrative authority whatsoever thinks of standing in their way.[7]

But there are social duties which they are bound to perform. Thus, if the state needs money, the township is not free to grant or refuse its help.[8] If the state wants to open a road, the township cannot bar its territory. If there is a police regulation, the township must carry it out. If the government wants to organize education on a uniform plan throughout the country, the township must establish the schools required by the law.[9] We shall see, when we come to speak of the administration of the United States, how and by whom, in these various cases, the townships are constrained to obedience. Here I only wish to establish the fact of the obligation. Strict as this obligation is, the government of the state imposes it in principle only, and in its performance the township resumes all its independent rights. Thus taxes are, it is true, voted by the legislature, but they are assessed and collected by the township; the establishment of a school is obligatory, but the township builds it, pays for it, and controls it.

In France the state tax collector receives the communal taxes; in America the township tax collector collects state taxes.

So, whereas with us the central government lends its agents to the commune, in America the township lends its agents to the government. That fact alone shows how far the two societies differ.

1. EARLY COMMENTARIES

Spirit of the Township in New England

Why the New England township wins the affection of the inhabitants. Difficulty of creating municipal spirit in Europe. In America municipal rights and duties concur in forming that spirit. The homeland has more characteristic features in America than elsewhere. How municipal spirit manifests itself in New England. What happy results it produces there.

In America not only do municipal institutions exist, but there is also a municipal spirit which sustains and gives them life.

The New England township combines two advantages which, wherever they are found, keenly excite men's interest; they are independence and power. It acts, it is true, within a sphere beyond which it cannot pass, but within that domain its movements are free. This independence alone would give a real importance not warranted by size or population.

It is important to appreciate that, in general, men's affections are drawn only in directions where power exists. Patriotism does not long prevail in a conquered country. The New Englander is attached to his township not so much because he was born there as because he sees the township as a free, strong corporation of which he is part and which is worth the trouble of trying to direct.

It often happens in Europe that governments themselves regret the absence of municipal spirit, for everyone agrees that municipal spirit is an important element in order and public tranquillity, but they do not know how to produce it. In making municipalities strong and independent, they fear sharing their social power and exposing the state to risks of anarchy. However, if you take power and independence from a municipality, you may have docile subjects but you will not have citizens.

Another important fact must be noted. The New England township is shaped to form the nucleus of strong attachments, and there is meanwhile no rival center close by to attract the hot hearts of ambitious men.

County officials are not elected and their authority is limited. Even a state is only of secondary importance, being an obscure and placid entity. Few men are willing to leave the center of their interests and take trouble to win the right to help administer it.

The federal government does confer power and renown on those who direct it, but only a few can exercise influence there. The high office of President is hardly to be reached until a man is well on in years; as for other high federal offices, there is a large element of chance about attaining to them, and they go only to those who have reached eminence in some other walk of life. No ambitious man would make them the fixed aim of his endeavors. It is in the township, the center of the ordinary business of life, that the desire for esteem, the pursuit of substantial interests, and the taste for power and self-advertisement are concentrated; these passions, so often troublesome elements in society, take on a different character when exercised so close to home and, in a sense, within the family circle.

With much care and skill power has been broken into fragments in the American township, so that the maximum possible number of people have some concern with public affairs. Apart from the voters, who from time to time are called on to act as the government, there are many and various officials who all, within their sphere, represent the powerful body in whose name they act. Thus a vast number of people make a good thing for themselves out of the power of the community and are interested in administration for selfish reasons.

The American system, which distributes local power among so many citizens, is also not afraid to multiply municipal duties. Americans rightly think that patriotism is a sort of religion strengthened by practical service.

Thus daily duties performed or rights exercised keep municipal life constantly alive. There is a continual gentle political activity which keeps society on the move without turmoil.

Americans love their towns for much the same reasons that highlanders love their mountains. In both cases the native land has emphatic and peculiar features; it has a more pronounced physiognomy than is found elsewhere.

In general, New England townships lead a happy life. Their government is to their taste as well as of their choice. With profound peace and material prosperity prevailing in America, there are few storms in municipal life. The township's interests are easy to manage. Moreover, the people's political education has been completed long ago, or rather they were already educated when they settled there. In New England there is not even a memory of distinctions in rank, so there is no part of the community tempted to oppress the rest, and injustices which affect only isolated individuals are forgotten in the general contentment. The government may have defects, and indeed they are easy to point out, but they do not catch the eye because the government really does emanate from the governed, and so long as it gets along somehow or other, a sort of parental pride protects it. Besides, there is no basis of comparison. Formerly England ruled the colonies as a group, but the people always looked after municipal affairs. So the sovereignty of the people in the township is not ancient only, but primordial.

The New Englander is attached to his township because it is strong and independent; he has an interest in it because he shares in its management; he loves it because he has no reason to complain of his lot; he invests his ambition and his future in it; in the restricted sphere within his scope, he learns to rule society; he gets to know those formalities without which freedom can advance only through revolutions, and becoming imbued with their spirit, develops a taste for order, understands the harmony of powers, and in the end accumulates clear, practical ideas about the nature of his duties and the extent of his rights.

Notes

1. In 1830 there were 305 townships in Massachusetts; the population was 610,014; that gives an average of about 2,000 for each township.

2. The same rules do not apply to the large townships. Those generally have a mayor and a municipal body divided into two branches, but a law is needed to authorize such an exception. See the law of February 23, 1822, regulating the powers of the city of Boston. *Laws of Massachusetts,* Vol. II, p. 588. [*The General Laws of Massachusetts,* Vol. II, Boston, 1823, p. 588 ff.] That applies to the large towns. Small towns also often have a particular administration. In 1832 104 such municipal administrations were counted in the state of New York. (*Williams's New York Annual Register.*) [*The New York Annual Register for the Year of Our Lord 1832,* by Edwin Williams, New York, 1832.]

3. There are three selectmen in the smallest townships and nine in the largest. See *The Town Officer,* p. 186. [Tocqueville refers here to a book by Isaac Goodwin, *Town Officer or Law of Massachusetts* (Worcester, 1829), which incidentally is to be found among the volumes of his library at the Château de Tocqueville.] See also the main laws of Massachusetts concerning selectmen:

Law of February 20, 1786, Vol. I, p. 219; February 24, 1796, Vol. I, p. 488; March 7, 1801, Vol. II, p. 45; June 16, 1795, Vol. I, p. 475; March 12, 1808, Vol. II, p. 186; February 28, 1787, Vol. I, p. 302; June 22, 1797, Vol. I, p. 539.

4. See *Laws of Massachusetts,* Vol. I, p. 150; law of March 25, 1786.

5. *Ibid.*

6. All these officials really do exist. To find out the details of all their duties see *The Town Officer,* by Isaac Goodwin (Worcester, 1829), and the *General Laws of Massachusetts* in 3 vols. (Boston, 1823).

7. See *Laws of Massachusetts,* law of March 23, 1786, Vol. I, p. 250.

8. *Ibid.,* law of February 20, 1786, Vol. I, p. 217.

9. See the same collection, law of June 25, 1789, Vol. I, p. 367, and March 10, 1827, Vol. III, p. 179.

Local Government: Observations

James Bryce

This is the place for an account of local government in the United States, because it is a matter regulated not by Federal law but by the several States and Territories, each of which establishes such local authorities, rural and urban, as the people of the State or Territory desire, and invests them with the requisite powers. But this very fact indicates the immensity of the subject. Each State has its own system of local areas and authorities, created and worked under its own laws; and though these systems agree in many points, they differ in so many others, that a whole volume would be needed to give even a summary view of their peculiarities. All I can here attempt is to distinguish the leading types of local government to be found in the United States, to describe the prominent features of each type, and to explain the influence which the large scope and popular character of local administration exercise upon the general life and well-being of the American people.

Three types of rural local government are discernible in America. The first is characterized by its unit, the Town or Township, and exists in the six New England States. The second is characterized by a much larger unit, the county, and prevails in the southern States. The third combines some features of the first with some of the second, and may be called the mixed system. It is found, under a considerable variety of forms, in the middle and north-western States. The differences of these three types are interesting, not only because of the practical instruction they afford, but also because they spring from original differences in the character of the colonist who settled along the American coast, and in the conditions under which the communities there founded were developed.

The first New England settlers were Puritans in religion, and sometimes inclined to republicanism in politics. They were largely townsfolk, accustomed to municipal life and to vestry meetings. They planted their tiny communities along the seashore and the banks of rivers, enclosing them with stockades for protection against the warlike Indians. Each was obliged to be self-sufficing, because divided by rocks and woods from the others. Each had its common pasture on which the inhabitants turned out their cattle, and which officers were elected to manage. Each was a religious as well as a civil body politic, gathered round the church as its centre; and the equality which prevailed in the congregation prevailed also in civil affairs, the whole community meeting under a president or moderator to discuss affairs of common interest. Each such settlement was called a Town, or Township, and was in fact a miniature commonwealth, exercising a practical sovereignty over the property and persons of its members—for there was as yet no State, and the distant home government scarcely cared to interfere—but exercising it on thoroughly democratic principles. Its centre was a group of dwellings, often surrounded by a fence or wall, but it included a rural area of several square miles, over which farmhouses and clusters of houses began to spring up when the Indians retired. The name "town" covered the whole of this area, which was never too large for all the inhabitants to come together to a central place of meeting. This town organization remained strong and close, the colonists being men of narrow means, and held together in each settlement by the needs of defence. And though presently the towns became aggregated into counties, and the legislature and governor, first of the whole colony, and, after 1776, of the State, began to exert their superior authority, the towns (which, be it remembered, remained rural communities, making up the whole area of the State) held their ground, and are to this day the true units of political life in New England, the solid foundation of that well-compacted structure of self-government which European philosophers have admired and the new States of the West have sought to reproduce. Till 1821[1] the towns were the only political corporate bodies in Massachusetts, and till 1857 they formed, as they still form in Connecticut, the basis of representation in her Assembly, each town, however small, returning at least one member. Much of that robust, if somewhat narrow, localism which characterizes the representative system of America is due to this originally distinct and self-sufficing corporate life of the seventeenth century towns. Nor is it without interest to observe that although they owed much to the conditions which surrounded the early colonists, forcing them to develop a civic patriotism resembling that of the republics of ancient Greece and Italy, they owed something also to those Teutonic traditions of semi-independent local communities, owning common property, and governing themselves by a primary assembly of all free inhabitants, which the English had brought with them from the Elbe and the Weser, and which had been perpetuated in the practice of many parts of England down till the days of the Stuart kings.

Very different were the circumstances of the Southern colonies. The men who went to Virginia and the Carolinas were not Puritans, nor did they mostly go in families and groups of families from the same neighbourhood. Many were casual adventurers, often belonging to the upper class, Episcopalians in religion, and with no such experience of, or attachment to, local self-government as the men of Massachusetts or Connecticut. They settled in a region where the Indian tribes were comparatively peaceable, and where therefore there was little need of concentration for the purposes of defence. The climate along the coast was somewhat too hot for European labour, so slaves were imported to cultivate the land. Population was thinly scattered; estates were large; the soil was fertile and soon enriched its owners. Thus a semi-feudal society grew up, in which authority naturally fell to the landowners, each of whom was the centre of a group of free dependants as well as the master of an increasing crowd of slaves. There were therefore comparatively few urban communities, and the life of the colony took a rural type. The houses of the planters lay miles apart from one another; and when local divisions had to be created, these were made large enough to include a considerable area of territory and number of land-owning gentlemen. They were therefore rural divisions, counties framed on the model of English counties. Smaller circumscriptions there were, such as hundreds and parishes, but the hundred died out,[2] the parish ultimately became a purely ecclesiastical division, and the parish vestry was restricted to ecclesiastical functions, while the county remained the practically important unit of local administration, the unit to which the various functions of government were aggregated, and which, itself controlling minor authorities, was controlled by the State government alone. The affairs of the county were usually managed by a board of elective commissioners,

and not, like those of the New England towns, by a primary assembly; and in an aristocratic society the leading planters had of course a predominating influence. Hence this form of local government was not only less democratic, but less stimulating and educative than that which prevailed in the New England States. Nor was the Virginian county, though so much larger than the New England town, ever as important an organism over against the State. It may almost be said, that while a New England State is a combination of towns, a Southern State is from the first an administrative as well as political whole, whose subdivisions, the counties, had never any truly independent life, but were and are mere subdivisions for the convenient dispatch of judicial and financial business.

In the middle States of the Union, Pennsylvania, New Jersey, and New York, settled or conquered by Englishmen some time later than New England, the town and town meeting did not as a rule exist, and the county was the original basis of organization. But as there grew up no planting aristocracy like that of Virginia or the Carolinas, the course of events took in the middle States a different direction. As trade and manufactures grew, population became denser than in the South. New England influenced them, and influenced still more the newer commonwealths which arose in the North-west, such as Ohio and Michigan, into which the surplus population of the East poured. And the result of this influence is seen in the growth through the middle and western States of a mixed system, which presents a sort of compromise between the County system of the South and the Town system of the North-east. There are great differences between the arrangements in one or other of these middle and western States. But it may be said, speaking generally, that in them the county is relatively less important than in the southern States, the township less important than in New England. The county is perhaps to be regarded, at least in New York, Pennsylvania, and Ohio, as the true unit, and the townships (for so they are usually called) as its subdivisions. But the townships are vigorous organisms, which largely restrict the functions of the county authority, and give to local government, especially in the North-west, a character generally similar to that which it wears in New England. . . .

It is noteworthy that the Americans, who are supposed to be especially fond of representative assemblies, have made little use of representation in their local government. The township is usually governed either by a primary assembly of all citizens or else, as in such States as Ohio and Iowa, by a very small board, not exceeding three, with, in both sets of cases, several purely executive officers.[3] In the county there is seldom or never a county board possessing legislative functions;[4] usually only three commissioners or supervisors with some few executive or judicial officers. Local legislation (except as it appears in the bye-laws of the Town meeting or selectmen) is discouraged. The people seem jealous of their county officials, electing them for short terms, and restricting each to a special range of duties. This is perhaps only another way of saying that the county, even in the South, has continued to be an artificial entity, and has drawn to itself no great part of the interest and affections of the citizens. Over five-sixths of the Union each county presents a square figure on the map, with nothing distinctive about it, nothing "natural" about it, in the sense in which such English counties as Kent or Cornwall are natural entities. It is too large for the personal interest of the citizens: that goes to the township. It is too small to have traditions which command the respect or touch the affections of its inhabitants: these belong to the State.[5]

The chief functions local government has to discharge in the United States are the following:—

Making and repairing roads and bridges.—These prime necessities of rural life are provided for by the township, county, or State, according to the class to which a road or bridge belongs. That the roads of America are proverbially ill-built and ill-kept is due partly to the climate, with its alternations of severe frost, occasional torrential rains (in the middle and southern States), and long droughts; partly to the hasty habits of the people, who are too busy with other things, and too eager to use their capital in private enterprises to be willing to spend freely on highways; partly also to the thinness of population, which is, except in a few manufacturing districts, much less dense than in western Europe. In many districts railways have come before roads, so roads have been the less used and cared for.

The administration of justice was one of the first needs which caused the formation of the county: and matters connected with it still form a large part of county business. The voters elect a judge or judges, and the local prosecuting officer, called the district attorney, and the chief executive officer, the sheriff.[6] Prisons are a matter of county concern. Police is always locally regulated, but in the northern States more usually by the township than by the county. However, this branch of government, so momentous in continental Europe, is in America comparatively unimportant outside the cities. The rural districts get on nearly everywhere with no guardians of the peace, beyond the township constable;[7] nor does the State government, except, of course, through statutes, exercise any control over local police administration.[8] In the rural parts of the eastern and middle States property is as safe as anywhere in the world. In such parts of the West as are disturbed by dacoits, or by solitary highwaymen, travellers defend themselves, and, if the sheriff is distant or slack, lynch law may usefully be invoked. The care of the poor is thrown almost everywhere upon local and not upon State authorities,[9] and defrayed out of local funds, sometimes by the county, sometimes by the township. The poor laws of the several States differ in so many particulars that it is impossible to give even an outline of them here. Little out-door relief is given, though in most

States the relieving authority may, at his or their discretion, bestow it; and pauperism is not, and has never been, a serious malady, except in some five or six great cities, where it is now vigorously combated by volunteer organizations largely composed of ladies. The total number of persons returned as paupers in the whole Union in 1880 was 88,665, of whom 67,067 were inmates of alms-houses, and 21,598 in receipt of out-door relief. This was only 1 to 565 of the whole population.[10] In England and Wales in 1881 there were 803,126 paupers, to a population of 25,974,439, or 1 to 32 of population.

Sanitation, which has become so important a department of English local administration, plays a small part in the rural districts of America, because their population is so much more thinly spread over the surface that the need for drainage and the removal of nuisances is less pressing; moreover, as the humbler classes are better off, unhealthy dwellings are far less common. Public health officers and sanitary inspectors would, over the larger part of the county, have little occupation.[11]

Education, on the other hand, has hitherto been not only a more distinctively local matter, but one relatively far more important than in England, France, or Italy. And there is usually a special administrative body, often a special administrative area, created for its purposes— the school committee and the school district.[12] The vast sum expended on public instruction has been already mentioned. Though primarily dealt with by the smallest local circumscription, there is a growing tendency for both the county and the State to interest themselves in the work of instruction by way of inspection, and to some extent of pecuniary subventions. Not only does the county often appoint a county superintendent, but there are in some States county high schools and (in most) county boards of education, besides a State Board of Commissioners.[13] I need hardly add that the schools of all grades are more numerous and efficient in the northern and western than in the southern States.[14] In old colonial days, when the English Commissioners for Foreign Plantations asked for information on the subject of education from the governors of Virginia and Connecticut, the former replied, "I thank God there are no free schools or printing presses, and I hope we shall not have any these hundred years;"[15] and the latter, "One-fourth of the annual revenue of the colony is laid out in maintaining free schools for the education of our children." The disparity was prolonged and intensified in the South by the existence of slavery. Now that slavery has gone, the South makes rapid advances; but the proportion of illiteracy, especially of course among the negroes, is still high.[16]

It will be observed that of the general functions of local government above described, three, viz. police, sanitation, and poor relief, are simpler and less costly than in England, and indeed in most parts of western and central Europe. It has therefore proved easier to vest the management of all in the same local authority, and to get on with a smaller number of special executive officers. Education is indeed almost the only matter which has been deemed to demand a special body to handle it. Nevertheless, even in America the increasing complexity of civilization, and the growing tendency to invoke governmental aid for the satisfaction of wants which were not previously felt, or if felt, were met by voluntary action, tend to enlarge the sphere and multiply the functions of local government.

How far has the spirit of political party permeated rural local government? I have myself asked this question a hundred times in travelling through America, yet I find it hard to give any general answer, because there are great diversities in this regard not only between different States, but between different parts of the same State, diversities due sometimes to the character of the population, sometimes to the varying intensity of party feeling, sometimes to the greater or less degree in which the areas of local government coincide with the election districts for the election of State senators or representatives. On the whole it would seem that county officials are apt to be chosen on political lines, not so much because any political questions come before them, or because they can exert much influence on State or Federal elections, as because these paid offices afford a means of rewarding political services and securing political adhesions. Each of the great parties usually holds its county convention and runs its "county ticket," with the unfortunate result of intruding national politics into matters with which they have nothing to do, and of making it more difficult for good citizens outside the class of professional politicians to find their way into county administration. However, the party candidates are seldom bad men, and the ordinary voter is less apt to vote blindly for the party nominee than he would be in Federal or State elections. In the township and rural school district party spirit is much less active. The offices are often unpaid, and the personal merits of the candidates are better known to the voters than are those of the politicians who seek for county office.[17] Rings and Bosses are not unknown even in rural New England. School committee elections are often influenced by party affiliations. But on the whole, the township and its government keep themselves pretty generally out of the political whirlpool: their posts are filled by honest and reasonably competent men.

Notes

1. Boston continued to be a town governed by a primary assembly of all citizens till 1822; and even then the town-meeting was not quite abolished, for a provision was introduced, intended to satisfy conservative democratic feeling, into the city charter granted by statute in that year, empowering the mayor and aldermen to call general meetings of the citizens qualified to vote in city affairs "to consult upon the common good, to give instructions to their representatives, and to take all lawful means to obtain a redress of any grievances." Such primary assemblies are, however, never now convoked.

2. In Maryland hundreds, which still exist in Delaware, were for a long time the chief administrative divisions. We hear there also of "baronies" and "townlands," as in Ireland; and Maryland is usually called a "province," while the other settlements are colonies. Among its judicial establishments there were courts of pypowdry (*piè poudré*) and "hustings." See the interesting paper on "Local Institutions in Maryland," by Dr. Wilhelm, in *Johns Hopkins University Studies,* Third Series.

The hundred is a division of small consequence in southern England, but in Lancashire it has some important duties. It repairs the bridges; it is liable for damage done in a riot; and it had its high constable.

3. In a few Western States the Town board has (like the New England selectmen) a limited taxing power, as well as administrative duties.

4. In New York, however, there is a marked tendency in this direction.

5. In Virginia there used to be a county feeling resembling that of England, but this has vanished in the social revolution that has transformed the South.

6. The American sheriff remains something like what the English sheriff was before his wings were clipped by legislation some seventy years ago. Even then he mostly acted by deputy. The justices and the county police have since that legislation largely superseded his action.

7. Or, in States where there are no townships, some corresponding officer.

8. Michigan is now (1888) said to be instituting a sort of State police for the enforcement of her anti-liquor legislation.

9. In some States there are State poor-law superintendents, and frequently certain State institutions for the benefit of particular classes of paupers, *e.g.* pauper lunatics.

10. New York had 15,217 paupers (of whom 2810 were out-door), Colorado 47 (1 out-door), Arizona 4. Louisiana makes no return of indoor paupers, because the parishes (= counties) provide for the maintenance of their poor in private institutions. (The accuracy of these returns has been questioned.)

11. Sanitation, however, has occupied much attention in the cities. Cleveland on Lake Erie claims to have the lowest death rate of any large city in the world.

12. Though the school district frequently coincides with the township, it has generally (outside of New England) administrative officers distinct from those of the township, and when it coincides it is often subdivided into lesser districts.

13. In some States provision is made for the combination of several school districts to maintain a superior school at a central spot.

14. The differences between the school arrangements of different States are so numerous that I cannot attempt to describe them.

15. Governor Sir William Berkeley, however, was among the Virginians who in 1660 subscribed for the erection in Virginia of "a colledge of students of the liberal arts and sciences." As to elementary instruction he said that Virginia pursued "the same course that is taken in England out of towns, every man according to his ability instructing his children. We have forty-eight parishes, and our ministry are well paid, and, by consent, should be better if they would pray oftener and preach less."—*The College of William and Mary,* by Dr. H. B. Adams.

16. The percentage of persons unable to read to the whole population of the United States was, in 1880, 13·4; it was lowest in Iowa (2·4), highest in South Carolina (48·2) and Louisiana (45·8). The percentage of persons unable to write was in the whole United States, 17; lowest in Nebraska (3·6), highest in South Carolina (55·4) and Alabama (50·9).

It has recently been proposed in Congress to reduce the surplus in the U.S. treasury by distributing sums among the States in aid of education, in proportion to the need which exists for schools, *i.e.* to their illiteracy. The objections on the score of economic policy, as well as of constitutional law, are so obvious as to have stimulated a warm resistance to the bill.

17. Sometimes the party "ticket" leaves a blank space for the voter to insert the name of the candidates for whom he votes for township offices.

Nature of the American State

James Bryce

. . . As the dissimilarity of population and of external conditions seems to make for a diversity of constitutional and political arrangements between the States, so also does the large measure of legal independence which each of them enjoys under the Federal Constitution. No State can, as a commonwealth, politically deal with or act upon any other State. No diplomatic relations can exist nor treaties be made between States, no coercion can be exercised by one upon another. And although the government of the Union can act on a State, it rarely does act, and then only in certain strictly limited directions, which do not touch the inner political life of the commonwealth.

Let us pass on to consider the circumstances which work for uniformity among the States, and work more powerfully as time goes on.

He who looks at a map of the Union will be struck by the fact that so many of the boundary lines of the States are straight lines. Those lines tell the same tale as the geometrical plans of cities like St. Petersburg or Washington, where every street runs at the same angle to every other. The States are not natural growths. Their boundaries are for the most part not natural boundaries fixed by mountain ranges, nor even historical boundaries due to a series of events, but purely artificial boundaries, determined by an authority which carved the national territory into strips of convenient size, as a building company lays out its suburban lots. Of the States subsequent to the original thirteen, California is the only one with a genuine natural boundary, finding it in the chain of the Sierra Nevada on the east and the Pacific ocean on the west. No one of these later States can be regarded as a naturally developed political organism. They are trees planted by the forester, not self-sown with the help of the seed-scattering wind. This absence of physical lines of demarcation has tended and must tend to prevent the growth of local distinctions. Nature herself seems to have designed the Mississippi basin, as she has designed the unbroken levels of Russia, to be the dwelling-place of one people.

Each State makes its own Constitution; that is, the people agree on their form of government for themselves, with no interference from the other States or from the Union. This form is subject to one condition only: it must be republican.[1] But in each State the people who make the constitution have lately come from other States, where they have lived under and worked constitutions which are to their eyes the natural and almost necessary model for their new State to follow; and in the absence of an inventive spirit among the citizens, it was the obvious course for the newer States to copy the organizations of the older States, especially as these agreed with certain familiar features of the Federal Constitution. Hence the outlines, and even the phrases of the elder constitutions reappear in those of the more recently formed States. The precedents set by Virginia, for instance, had much influence on Tennessee, Alabama, Mississippi, and Florida, when they were engaged in making or amending their constitutions during the early part of this century.

Nowhere is population in such constant movement as in America. In some of the newer States only one-fourth or one-fifth of the inhabitants are natives of the United States. Many of the townsfolk, not a few even of the farmers, have been till lately citizens of some other State, and will, perhaps, soon move on farther west. These Western States are like a chain of lakes through which there flows a stream which mingles the waters of the higher with those of the lower. In such a constant flux of population local peculiarities are not readily developed, or if they have grown up when the district was still isolated, they disappear as the country becomes filled. Each State takes from its neighbours and gives to its neighbours, so that the process of assimilation is always going on over the whole wide area.

Still more important is the influence of railway communication, of newspapers, of the telegraph. A Greek city like Samos or Mitylene, holding her own island, preserved a distinctive character in spite of commercial intercourse and the sway of Athens. A

Swiss canton like Uri or Appenzell, entrenched behind its mountain ramparts, remains, even now under the strengthened central government of the Swiss nation, unlike its neighbours of the lower country. But an American State traversed by great trunk lines of railway, and depending on the markets of the Atlantic cities and of Europe for the sale of its grain, cattle, bacon, and minerals, is attached by a hundred always tightening ties to other States, and touched by their weal or woe as nearly as by what befalls within its own limits. The leading newspapers are read over a vast area. The inhabitants of each State know every morning the events of yesterday over the whole Union.

Finally the political parties are the same in all the States. The tenets (if any) of each party are the same everywhere, their methods the same, their leaders the same, although of course a prominent man enjoys especial influence in his own State. Hence, State politics are largely swayed by forces and motives external to the particular State, and common to the whole country, or to great sections of it; and the growth of local parties, the emergence of local issues and development of local political schemes, are correspondingly restrained.

These considerations explain why the States, notwithstanding the original diversities between some of them, and the wide scope for political divergence which they all enjoy under the Federal Constitution, are so much less dissimilar and less peculiar than might have been expected. European statesmen have of late years been accustomed to think of federalism and local autonomy as convenient methods either for recognizing and giving free scope to the sentiment of nationality which may exist in any part of an empire, or for meeting the need for local institutions and distinct legislation which may arise from differences between such a part and the rest of the empire. It is one or other or both of these reasons that have moved statesmen in such cases as those of Finland in her relations to Russia, Hungary in her relations to German Austria, Iceland in her relations to Denmark, Bulgaria in her relations to the Turkish Sultan, Ireland in her relations to the United Kingdom. But the final causes, so to speak, of the recognition of the States of the American Union as autonomous commonwealths, have been different. Their self-government is not the consequence of differences which can be made harmless to the whole body politic only by being allowed free course. It has been due primarily to the historical fact that they existed as commonwealths before the Union came into being; secondarily, to the belief that localized government is the best guarantee for civic freedom, and to a sense of the difficulty of administering a vast territory and population from one centre and by one government.

I return to indicate the points in which the legal independence and right of self-government of the several States appears. Each of the forty-two has its own—

Constitution (whereof more anon).

Executive, consisting of a governor, and various other officials.

Legislature of two Houses.

System of local government in counties, cities, townships, and school districts.

System of State and local taxation.

Debts, which it may (and sometimes does) repudiate at its own pleasure.

Body of private law, including the whole law of real and personal property, of contracts, of torts, and of family relations.

Courts, from which no appeal lies (except in cases touching Federal legislation or the Federal constitution) to any Federal court.

System of procedure, civil and criminal.

Citizenship, which may admit persons (*e.g.* recent immigrants) to be citizens at times, or on conditions, wholly different from those prescribed by other States.

Three points deserve to be noted as illustrating what these attributes include.

I. A man gains active citizenship of the United States (*i.e.* a share in the government of the Union) only by becoming a citizen of some particular State. Being such citizen, he is forthwith entitled to the national franchise. That is to say, voting power in the State carries voting power in Federal elections, and however lax a State may be in its grant of such power, *e.g.* to foreigners just landed or to persons convicted of crime, these State voters will have the right of voting in congressional and presidential elections.[2] The only restriction on the States in this matter is that of the fourteenth and fifteenth Constitutional amendments, . . . They were intended to secure equal treatment to the negroes, and incidentally they declare the protection given to all citizens of the United States.[3] Whether they really enlarge it, that is to say, whether it did not exist by implication before, is a legal question, which I need not discuss.

II. The power of a State over all communities within its limits is absolute. It may grant or refuse local government as it pleases. The population of the city of Providence is more than one-third of that of the State of Rhode Island, the population of New York city more than one-fifth that of the State of New York. But the State might in either case extinguish the municipality, and govern the city by a single State commissioner appointed for the purpose, or leave it without any government whatever. The city would have no right of complaint to the Federal President or Congress against such a measure. Massachusetts has lately remodelled the city government of Boston just as the British Parliament might remodel that of Birmingham. Let an Englishman imagine a county council for Warwickshire suppressing the muncipality of Birmingham, or a Frenchman imagine the department of the Rhone extinguishing the municipality of Lyons, with no possibility of intervention by the central authority, and he will measure the difference between the American States and the local governments of Western Europe.

III. A State commands the allegiance of its citizens, and may punish them for treason against it. The power has rarely been exercised, but its undoubted legal existence had much to do with inducing the citizens of the Southern States to follow their governments into secession in 1861. They conceived themselves to owe allegiance to the State as well as to the Union, and when it became impossible to preserve both, because the State had declared its secession from the Union, they might hold the earlier and nearer authority to be paramount. Allegiance to the State must now, since the war, be taken to be subordinate to the Union. But allegiance to the State still exists; treason against the State is still possible. One cannot think of treason against Warwickshire or the department of the Rhone.

These are illustrations of the doctrine which Europeans often fail to grasp, that the American States were originally in a certain sense, and still for certain purposes remain, sovereign States. Each of the original thirteen became sovereign when it revolted from the mother country in 1776. By entering the Confederation of 1781-88 it parted with one or two of the attributes of sovereignty, by accepting the Federal Constitution in 1788 it subjected itself for certain specified purposes to a central government, but claimed to retain its sovereignty for all other purposes. That is to say, the authority of a State is an inherent, not a delegated, authority. It has all the powers which any independent government can have, except such as it can be affirmatively shown to have stripped itself of, while the Federal Government has only such powers as it can be affirmatively shown to have received. To use the legal expression, the presumption is always for a State, and the burden of proof lies upon any one who denies its authority in a particular matter.[4]

What State sovereignty means and includes is a question which incessantly engaged the most active legal and political minds of the nation, from 1789 down to 1870. Some thought it paramount to the rights of the Union. Some considered it as held in suspense by the Constitution, but capable of reviving as soon as a State should desire to separate from the Union. Some maintained that each State had in accepting the Constitution finally renounced its sovereignty, which thereafter existed only in the sense of such an undefined domestic legislative and administrative authority as had not been conferred upon Congress. The conflict of these views, which became acute in 1830 when South Carolina claimed the right of nullification, produced Secession and the war of 1861-65. Since the defeat of the Secessionists, the last of these views may be deemed to have been established, and the term "State sovereignty" is now but seldom heard. Even "States rights" have a different meaning from that which they had thirty years ago.[5] . . .

The Constitution, which had rendered many services to the American people, did them an inevitable disservice when it fixed their minds on the legal aspects of the question. Law was meant to be the servant of politics, and must not be suffered to become the master. A case had arisen which its formulae were unfit to deal with, a case which had to be settled on large moral and historical grounds. It was not merely the superior physical force of the North that prevailed; it was the moral forces which rule the world, forces which had long worked against slavery, and were ordained to save North America from the curse of hostile nations established side by side.

The word "sovereignty," which has in many ways clouded the domain of public law and jurisprudence, confused men's minds by making them assume that there must in every country exist, and be discoverable by legal inquiry, either one body invested legally with supreme power over all minor bodies, or several bodies which, though they had consented to form part of a larger body, were each in the last resort independent of it, and responsible to none but themselves.[6] They forgot that a Constitution may not have determined where legal supremacy shall dwell. Where the Constitution of the United States placed it was at any rate doubtful, so doubtful that it would have been better to drop technicalities, and recognize the broad fact that the legal claims of the States had become incompatible with the historical as well as legal claims of the nation. In the uncertainty as to where legal right resided, it would have been prudent to consider where physical force resided. The South however thought herself able to resist any physical force which the rest of the nation might bring against her. Thus encouraged, she took her stand on the doctrine of States Rights: and then followed a pouring out of blood and treasure such as was never spent on determining a point of law before, not even when Edward III and his successors waged war for a hundred years to establish the claim of females to inherit the crown of France.

What, then, do the rights of a State now include? Every right or power of a Government except:—

> The right of secession (not abrogated in terms, but admitted since the war to be no longer claimable. It is expressly negatived in the recent Constitutions of several Southern States).
>
> Powers which the Constitution withholds from the States (including that of intercourse with foreign governments).
>
> Powers which the Constitution expressly confers on the Federal Government.

As respects some powers of the last class, however, the States may act concurrently with, or in default of action by, the Federal Government. It is only from contravention of its action that they must abstain. And where contravention is alleged to exist, whether legislative or executive, it is by a court of law, and, in case the decision is in the first instance favourable to the pretensions of the State, ultimately by a Federal court, that the question falls to be decided.[7]

A reference to the preceding list of what each State may create in the way of distinct institutions will show that these rights practically cover nearly all the ordinary relations of citizens to one another and to their Government.[8] An American may, through a long life, never be reminded of the Federal Government, except when he votes at presidential and congressional elections, lodges a complaint against the post-office, and opens his trunks for a custom-house officer on the pier at New York when he returns from a tour in Europe. His direct taxes are paid to officials acting under State laws. The State, or a local authority constituted by State statutes, registers his birth, appoints his guardian, pays for his schooling, gives him a share in the estate of his father deceased, licenses him when he enters a trade (if it be one needing a licence), marries him, divorces him, entertains civil actions against him, declares him a bankrupt, hangs him for murder. The police that guard his house, the local boards which look after the poor, control highways, impose water rates, manage schools—all these derive their legal powers from his State alone. Looking at this immense compass of State functions, Jefferson would seem to have been not far wrong when he said that the Federal government was nothing more than the American department of foreign affairs. But although the National government touches the direct interests of the citizen less than does the State government, it touches his sentiment more. Hence the strength of his attachment to the former and his interest in it must not be measured by the frequency of his dealings with it. In the partitionment of governmental functions between nation and State, the State gets the most but the nation the highest, so the balance between the two is preserved.

Thus every American citizen lives in a duality of which Europeans, always excepting the Swiss, and to some extent the Germans, have no experience. He lives under two governments and two sets of laws; he is animated by two patriotisms and owes two allegiances. That these should both be strong and rarely be in conflict is most fortunate. It is the result of skilful adjustment and long habit, of the fact that those whose votes control the two sets of governments are the same persons, but above all of that harmony of each set of institutions with the other set, a harmony due to the identity of the principles whereon both are founded, which makes each appear necessary to the stability of the other, the States to the nation as its basis, the National Government to the States as their protector.

Notes

1. The case of Kansas immediately before the War of Secession, and the cases of the rebel States, which were not readmitted after the war till they had accepted the constitutional amendments forbidding slavery and protecting the freedmen, are quite exceptional cases.

2. Congress has power to pass a uniform rule of naturalization (Const. Art. i. § 8).

Under the present naturalization laws a foreigner must have resided in the United States for five years, and for one year in the State or Territory where he seeks admission to United States citizenship, and must declare two years before he is admitted that he renounces allegiance to any foreign prince or state. Naturalization makes him a citizen not only of the United States, but of the State or Territory where he is admitted, but does not necessarily confer the electoral franchise, for that depends on State laws.

In more than a third of the States the electoral franchise is now enjoyed by persons not naturalized as United States citizens.

3. "The line of distinction between the privileges and immunities of citizens of the United States, and those of citizens of the several States, must be traced along the boundary of their respective spheres of action, and the two classes must be as different in their nature as are the functions of their respective governments. A citizen of the United States as such has a right to participate in foreign and interstate commerce, to have the benefit of the postal laws, to make use in common with others of the navigable waters of the United States, and to pass from State to State, and into foreign countries, because over all these subjects the jurisdiction of the United States extends, and they are covered by its laws. The privileges suggest the immunities. Wherever it is the duty of the United States to give protection to a citizen against any harm, inconvenience, or deprivation, the citizen is entitled to an immunity which pertains to Federal citizenship. One very plain immunity is exemption from any tax, burden, or imposition under State laws as a condition to the enjoyment of any right or privilege under the laws of the United States. . . . Whatever one may claim as of right under the Constitution and laws of the United States by virtue of his citizenship, is a privilege of a citizen of the United States. Whatever the Constitution and laws of the United States entitle him to exemption from, he may claim an exemption in respect to. And such a right or privilege is abridged whenever the State law interferes with any legitimate operation of Federal authority which concerns his interest, whether it be an authority actively exerted, or resting only in the express or implied command or assurance of the Federal Constitution or law. But the United States can neither grant nor secure to its citizens rights or privileges which are not expressly or by reasonable implication placed under its jurisdiction, and all not so placed are left to the exclusive protection of the States."—Cooley, *Principles,* pp. 245-247.

4. It may of course be said that as the colonies associated themselves into a league, at the very time at which they revolted from the British Crown, and as their foreign relations were always managed by the authority and organs of this league, no one of them ever was for international purposes a free and independent sovereign State. This is true, and Abraham Lincoln was in this sense justified in saying that the Union was older than the States. But what are we to say of North Carolina and Rhode Island, after the acceptance of the Constitution of 1787-89 by the other eleven States? They were out of the old Confederation, for it had expired. They were not in the new Union, for they refused during many months to enter it. What else can they have been during these months except sovereign commonwealths?

5. States rights was a watchword in the South for many years. In 1851 there was a student at Harvard College from South Carolina who bore the name of States Rights Gist, baptized, so to speak, into Calhounism. He rose to be a brigadier-general in the Confederate army, and fell in the Civil War.

6. A further confusion arises from the fact that men are apt in talking of sovereignty to mix up legal supremacy with practical predominance. They ought to go together, and law seeks to make them go together. But it may happen that the person or body in whom law vests supreme authority is unable to enforce that authority: so the legal sovereign and the actual sovereign—that is to say, the force which will prevail in physical conflict—are different. There is always a strongest force; but the force recognized by law may not be really the strongest; and of several forces it may be impossible to tell, till they have come into actual physical conflict, which is the strongest.

7. See Chapter XXII. *ante.*

8. A recent American writer well observes that nearly all the great questions which have agitated England during the last sixty years would, had they arisen in America, have fallen within the sphere of State legislation.—Jameson, "Introduction to the Constitutional and Political History of the States," in *Johns Hopkins University Studies.*

Intergovernmental Relations

Three levels of government—national, state, and local—coexist in the American political system. They not only survive alongside one another, but they also cooperate and conflict with each other in carrying out functions.

Legal bases for relationships among governments in the American political system include the United States Constitution, 50 state constitutions, court decisions by both state and federal courts, and state and national legislation. But legal guidelines do not prevent complications from arising in a system of government with three tiers. Problems requiring attention overlap more than one state or local jurisdiction. Governments closest to the scene seem best able to handle certain kinds of problems, but at the same time higher, more "distant" levels of government are often more financially capable of doing so. Citizens give different degrees of loyalty and support to different levels of government, and competing ambitions of politicians at different levels of government obstruct needed cooperation.

The formal relationships between the national government and the states is quite different from that between the states and their local governments. The national-state relationship is formally "federal" in character, which means that in theory the states and the national government each have autonomous spheres of responsibility. In contrast, the state-local relationship is not a federal one. Local governments are mere "creatures" of the states and are not on equal footing with their creators and masters. In practical terms, however, the national government has gained the upper hand in its dealings with the states, and many localities are more nearly on equal footing with state governments than their inferior legal position suggests.

The three tiers of American government have often been likened to a layer cake: three layers in one overarching system of government. Still using the cake analogy, political scientist Morton Grodzins argued that a marble cake better represents the interactions of local, state, and national governments. According to Grodzins, these interactions are far less tidy than the model of a layer cake suggests.

It is easy to think, for example, that public schooling is a local government function. This impression is supported by the visible involvement of special-purpose local governments called "school districts" in governing public education. But, as Grodzins pointed out, such a view overlooks the powerful role that state governments play by providing financial aid, certifying teachers, prescribing curriculum requirements, regulating school safety and pupil health, and generally overseeing what school districts do. The national government is also involved in public schooling. In the last 30 years, the United States Supreme Court and lower federal courts have made numerous decisions aimed at ending racial segregation in public schools. In addition, national government grants finance various activities such as school lunch and special education programs. Even this brief review of local, state, and national involvement in one area, schooling, can show why Grodzins believed that a marble cake better reflects the reality of the American three-level system of government than a layer cake does.

Intergovernmental transfers of money are an important form of interaction among local, state, and national governments. "Strings" are almost always attached to money that one level of government transfers to another level. For example, when the national government provides grants to states and localities, requirements concerning use of the money accompany the funds, although the extensiveness and specificity of requirements vary greatly in different grant programs. Similarly, state governments aid local governments, and state money also brings "strings" of one kind or another.

Presidents often set forth proposals about the "best" way of structuring relations and dividing responsibilities among national, state, and local governments, and President Reagan was no exception. His "new federalism" was aimed at shifting greater responsibility back to the states and localities, thereby reversing a long-term trend toward greater national government involvement in providing an increasing number of services. The extent to which President Bush continues his predecessor's "new federalism" remains to be seen; however, given the size of the national government's budget deficit, a big increase in the national government's domestic responsibilities seems most unlikely.

Selections in this unit describe and assess "new federalism" and treat various aspects of relationships among national, state, and local governments.

Looking Ahead: Challenge Questions

Do you think that the current state of intergovernmental relations is satisfactory or unsatisfactory?

Which level of government do you think is contributing the most to the welfare of Americans? Why?

Under what circumstances do you think the national government should try to improve national standards on state and local governments? Under what circumstances do you think state governments should impose state standards on local governments?

Do you agree that states and localities should have responsibility for performing more tasks and for raising money to pay for them?

Federalism: The Linchpin of Liberty

A.E. Dick Howard

A.E. Dick Howard is the White Burkett Professor of Law and Public Affairs at the University of Virginia. This article proceeds in part from ideas developed in the author's Richard B. Russell Lectures, given at the University of Georgia, and is an adaptation of an earlier version that appeared in Intergovernmental Perspectives.

The concept of federalism was central to the Founding Fathers' philosophy of government. But the Supreme Court, by virtue of its Garcia decision, has apparently ignored the founders' intent, as well as the lessons of history. Garcia has raised fundamental questions about the role of the high court as the balance wheel of the federal government.

In 1987 Americans are marking the 200th year since the framers at Philadelphia put their signatures to the U.S. Constitution. During the bicentennial era, citizens are being asked to reflect on the fundamental principles of American constitutionalism—among them, consent of the governed, defined limits on government power, separation of powers and judicial enforcement of constitutional guarantees.

A linchpin of that constitutional order is federalism. One has but to read the text of the Constitution, which refers to the states at least 50 times, to realize how central the concept of federalism was to the founders' thinking. Indeed, it was a concern about the potential power of the new federal government that led to the adoption of the Bill of Rights.

In the 19th century, that perceptive French traveler, De Tocqueville, lavished praise on American federalism in his *Democracy in America*. On the link between self-government and liberty, he commented, "A nation may establish a free government, but without municipal institutions it cannot have the spirit of liberty."

As Americans commemorate the Constitution's bicentennial, the Supreme Court appears to have forgotten both the framers' intent and the teachings of the nation's history. In February 1985 the Court decided *Garcia vs. San Antonio Metropolitan Transit Authority*. Five justices joined in a majority opinion concluding, in effect, that if the states "as states" want protection within the constitutional system they must look to Congress, not to the courts. The "principal means," Justice Harry Blackmun wrote, by which the role of the states in the federal system is to be ensured "lies in the structure of the federal government itself."

The states and localities, to be sure, will survive the impact of *Garcia's* immediate holding, which involves the application of the Fair Labor Standards Act to a municipally owned mass-transit system. The holding undoubtedly will be both burdensome and expensive, but most local governments will find ways to adjust, as they have done to other fiscal and legal vicissitudes. But far more than labor laws and bus drivers' pay is at stake in *Garcia*.

Garcia raises fundamental questions about the role of the Supreme Court as the balance wheel of the federal system. The Court in *Garcia* abdicates a function that history, principle and an understanding of the political process strongly argue that the federal judiciary should undertake. For those who care about the health of American constitutionalism—including, but not limited to, federalism—*Garcia* should be an unsettling decision.

Although the ultimate reach of *Garcia* is unclear, the decision adopts a variation on a theme asking the Court to stay its hand when a litigant claims that a federal action is beyond the authority of the federal government in that the action encroaches upon some protected right of the states. Final resolution of such claims, this thesis runs, should be left to the political branches of the government.

Such a position reads an important part of the founders' assumptions out

Reprinted with permission from *State Legislatures*, Vol. 13, No. 5, May/June 1987, pp. 22-25. Copyright © 1987 by National Conference of State Legislatures.

of the constitutional order. One may debate—though the point has long since been academic—whether the founders intended the Supreme Court to have the power of judicial review. But assuming the legitimacy of that doctrine, it is hard to escape the conclusion that the founders assumed that limiting national power in order to protect the states would be as much a part of the judicial function as any other issue.

The principle of the rule of law adds force to what this history teaches. A basic tenet of Anglo-American constitutionalism is that no branch of government should be the ultimate judge of its own power. The principle that one cannot be a judge in one's own cause is of centuries' standing. This principle is stated by Sir Edward Coke in *Dr. Bonham's Case* (1610) and, in our own time, has been reinforced by *United States vs. Nixon* (1974). The principle is especially important in a system that, in addition to being federal, looks to checks and balances and the separation of powers to restrain arbitrary government.

A further flaw in *Garcia* is its resting upon erroneous suppositions about the ways in which the nation's political process actually works. Essential to any argument that the Court should abstain from adjudicating limits on national power vis-a-vis the state is the notion that the states have ample protection in the processes of politics.

This assumption has two dimensions. One is institutional—that the states play a major role in structuring the national government. The other is political—that the ways in which the process actually works (such as in the political parties and in Congress) focus on the states. In fact, neither argument reflects current realities.

There was a time when the states had considerable influence over the shape of federal politics. Under the original Constitution, U.S. senators were elected by the legislatures of their respective states. The Constitution did not set federal standards for congressional elections; the states controlled the franchise. And it was up to the state legislatures as to how to draw the boundaries of congressional districts.

All this has changed. The 17th Amendment (adopted in 1913) brought direct election of senators. Judicial decisions (such as that striking down the poll tax) and acts of Congress (notably the Voting Rights Act of 1965) have federalized much of the law respecting the franchise. The 1965 statute, for example, requires preclearance (by the attorney general or the district court for the District of Columbia) of voting changes in areas covered by the act. State power to apportion congressional seats has been circumscribed by decisions such as the Supreme Court's 1964 opinion in *Wesberry vs. Sanders,* requiring that congressional districts be based on population.

Accompanying these significant shifts in institutional arrangements has been a palpable decline in the "political" safeguards. Political parties, especially at the state level, are no longer the force they once were. Increased use of primaries and the impact of "reforms" have had the unintended consequence of encouraging the development of alternative institutions. Most striking has been the rise of political action committees (PACs), which now number in the thousands.

The "nationalism" of campaign financing has led to the weakening of the federal lawmakers' loyalties to constituents. Special interest politics has tended to replace consensus politics. Moreover, the explosive growth of the federal government in modern times has brought the emergence of the "iron triangle"—the convergence of bureaucrats, interested legislators (often powerful committee chairmen) and lobbyists to determine the shape of federal programs.

In defense of having the Court abdicate 10th Amendment questions, as it did in *Garcia,* one sometimes hears the argument that the Court cannot resolve empirical questions. Thus, it is argued, assessing the facts of a given case to "balance" competing state and federal interests requires the Court to undertake a mode of enquiry that more properly belongs to legislators. Yet in other areas of constitutional litigation, the Court resolves empirical questions as a matter of course. Every case involving claims that a state act burdens commerce requires the resolution of economic and other such data, but the Court does not shirk this task. Another objection to the Court's having a role in 10th Amendment cases is that the justices cannot draw workable distinctions, such as deciding (as precedents before *Garcia* had sought to do) what is and what is not a "traditional governmental function" and hence entitled at least to some presumptive measure of protection against federal intrusion. Such linedrawing, of course, is difficult. But its being difficult does not mean that it should not be undertaken, any more than the conceptual difficulties of deciding what constitutes "speech" or "religion"—the thorniest of problems—are grounds for not deciding First Amendment cases.

Whatever the tangles confronting the Court, there are even graver reasons to question Congress' competence or willingness to make considered judgments on constitutional questions, especially when the question is that of the limits of Congress' own power. The judicial process may have its flaws, but it aspires to a degree of rationality, including analytical reasoning, that one does not associate with the legislative process. The limits of time, the pressures of lobbyists, the temptations of expediency, undue reliance on staff and other distractions often have more to do with the final shape of legislation than any thinking about constitutional issues.

Still another argument for the Court's leaving the states and localities to the tender mercies of Congress is that the Court needs to husband its scarce political capital. This argument raises the spectre of a return to "dual federalism"—the *ancien regime,* before 1937, when the Supreme Court often derailed federal social and economic legislation in the name of states' rights.

Such a risk is chimerical. In the Court's 1976 decision in *National League of Cities vs. Usery* (overruled in *Garcia*), the majority played a role in protecting the states as states under the 10th Amendment. Such a role raises no question about Congress' power over the private sector.

As to keeping the Court out of unnecessary controversies, most of the debate over "judicial activism" in recent decades has involved such issues as school prayer, criminal justice and abortion. Federalism cases may provoke academic debate—and, of course, matter enormously to state and local officials—but they stir little outrage in the country at large. It is individual rights decisions that, by and large, stir passions. One doubts that the partisans of *Garcia* would be content to see individual rights matters, because they may be controversial, left likewise to the political process.

Garcia betrays a glaring disregard of a basic truth about American constitutionalism: that institutional rights, under our Constitution, are a form of individual rights. Even such basic guarantees as those in the Bill of Rights and the 14th Amendment do not secure absolute personal rights. The protection created is against governmental (that is, institutional) actions, not against infringements by private parties. Thus, to secure individual rights requires assurances as to the stability of the institutional safeguards explicit or implicit in the Constitution.

The individual American—as the heir to those who brought the Constitution into being—has a fundamental right to live under the form of government spelled out in the Constitution. The separation of powers is not to be abandoned simply because it may be inconvenient. Likewise, one of the tenets of the constitutional order is that the Supreme Court adhere to the values of federalism as manifestly implicit in the Constitution. Federalism may be an elusive idea, but it is no mere abstraction. And, while it was essential to the adoption of the original Constitution, it is more than simply a political compromise adopted to get the Constitution underway. Federalism is linked with individual liberty and with the health of the body politic.

It is through participation in government at the local level that the citizen is educated in the value of civic participation. A robust federalism encourages state and local governments as

schools for citizenship. Moreover, federalism both reflects and encourages pluralism, allowing individual idiosyncracies to flourish. One often hears Justice Louis Brandeis quoted on the states serving as laboratories for social and economic experiments. The states are more than laboratories; to the extent they encourage pluralism, they are handmaidens of the open society.

Ultimately, the case for federalism rests on a concern for preserving the right of choice—the essence of political freedom. State and local governments have, of course, often trampled this very right, for example, when they have denied the vote because of one's race. The remedies for such abuses lie in vigorous judicial enforcement of constitutional guarantees and in Congress' power to protect civil rights. But the need to guard against trespasses by states or localities on individual liberties does not undermine the conclusion that federalism as such can operate as part of the very matrix of protection for individual liberties.

In refusing to enforce the 10th Amendment—to play the role they regularly undertake in respect to other provisions of the Bill of Rights—the *Garcia* majority leaves an important constitutional sentry post unmanned. What recourse have those who care about the health of federalism?

There are other opportunities for courts to vindicate the underlying values of federalism. Federal statutes may be interpreted in light of their impact on state and local governments. For example, the Court's 1981 *Pennhurst* decision lays down the salutary rule that federal grant conditions, to be binding on state and local governments, must be clearly identified as such when grant funds are accepted.

Notions of comity can come into play when reviewing lower courts' use of their equity powers to reform state institutions (such as prisons) or when deciding how far a federal court may go in intervening in state court proceedings (as in the Court's 1971 decision in *Younger vs. Harris*).

Ultimately, one may hope for the undermining or demise of *Garcia*. The majority decision stops short of saying that under no circumstances could the constitutional structure impose affirmative limits on federal actions affecting the states. A more favorable fact situation than that in *Garcia*, one entailing a more serious intrusion on the states and a more marginal federal interest, might furnish the occasion to begin the movement away from the unfortunate decision in *Garcia*.

Early and outright reversal of *Garcia* should not lightly be predicted. Reversals typically come only after a precedent has been robbed of vitality.

Still, one can hope that eventually a majority of the justices will come to realize the mistake made in *Garcia*. Because federalism is an intrinsic component of the constitutional system— indeed, bolsters other constitutional values—safeguarding that process cannot be left to the unrestrained discretion of the political branches. It may be that the authority pronounced in *National League of Cities* (and renounced in *Garcia*) ought to be sparingly used. But it is salutary that the political branches know that the Court has power to step in when the facts point to intervention.

A Court that concerns itself with enforcing the Constitution and ensuring the protection of individuals should not neglect federalism. Federalism is part of the constitutional plan and a buttress of individual liberties.

The states make a comeback

Charlotte Saikowski

Staff writer of The Christian Science Monitor

Washington

THE states are bouncing back. From Massachusetts and New Jersey in the East to Washington and California in the West, state governments are experiencing a surge of vitality and self-reliance. The trend is breathing new life into America's federal system.

Industrial development, foreign investment, public schools, welfare reform – these are the nuts-and-bolts issues on the agendas of state and local communities.

Governors across the country capture the mood:

■ Thomas Kean of New Jersey: "The most important thing now is going on in the states, not in Washington. You now have a 'debating society' in Washington, so a great deal of power is devolving on the states because they are the units that can solve problems and are closest to the people."

■ Bruce Babbitt, former governor of Arizona: "Centrifugal, decentralizing forces are at work, and political and economic power has begun to spread outward in new forms. The action is now in state capitals."

■ Michael Dukakis of Massachusetts: "There clearly is a recognition that a good deal of what the country needs has to take place at the state and local level."

The trend would gladden the hearts of Alexander Hamilton, James Madison, and other Founding Fathers who sought to forge a strong national union without emasculating the states as political entities.

Until the Civil War the states were dominant in the federal structure. Proud and independent-minded, they were the principal actors in most domestic affairs. They educated the children, enforced the laws, built the roads. They were jealous of their rights. New England and the South enunciated the doctrine of nullification (the right of a state to declare a federal government action null and void). And the Civil War began when 11 Southern states exercised what they regarded as the right of secession.

Even in this early period, however, the national government began to assert itself. Under Chief Justice John Marshall, the Supreme Court upheld the right of Congress to establish a national bank. In McCulloch v. Maryland (1819), the court ruled that the Constitution and laws enacted by the federal government are the supreme law of the land and cannot be countermanded by any state.

With the Civil War came America's most severe test of federalism – a test won at terrible cost by the national government. When the fighting ended at Appomattox in April 1865, the doctrine of states' rights fell before the fact of national supremacy.

The Civil War, writes political scholar Everett Carll Ladd, was a watershed in federal relations, followed as it was by the adoption of the 13th, 14th, and 15th Amendments to the Constitution. The 14th Amendment, intended primarily to safeguard the rights of the emancipated Negroes, in time was construed as giving the Supreme Court authority to invalidate state statutes that infringed on individual rights.

The national government grew for other reasons as well, as Dr. Ladd recounts in "The American Polity."

Technological and economic development exploded in the late 19th and early 20th centuries, transforming an agricultural country into an industrial society with continental links. Telephones, trains, cars, and radios drew the nation together, and with the growth of cities and the rise of corporations, demands increased for a greater federal role. This period saw a growth of national regulatory laws – to protect food and drugs and to regulate railroads, shipping, and interstate commerce.

New Deal shifts the balance

BUT it was the New Deal that touched off a virtual revolution in federalism. In the midst of the Great Depression, Franklin D. Roosevelt launched the greatest planned expansion of national authority in history. He set up new regulatory bodies like the Securities and Exchange Commission to protect investors and the stock market and the National Labor Relations Act to help trade unions. He made the federal government responsible for smoothing out business cycles, keeping unemployment under control, and fostering economic growth.

Above all, the national government took on the task of welfare for the jobless and impoverished; previously this task was handled by private charities or state and local agencies. In 1935 the historic Social Security Act was passed. Between 1925 and 1941, writes Ladd, federal per capita spending jumped 400 percent. By the end of World War II, total state and local spending annually dropped below federal spending for the first time in US history – and has stayed below it.

As society grew ever more interdependent, what had been called "dual federalism" – the relative independence of the two levels of government – became a "cooperative federalism" in which Washington and the states shared responsibilities.

Not only technology and economic expansion fueled a growth of the federal government, however. In the 1950s the impulse toward individual rights gathered momentum as blacks launched a long struggle for equality and an end of racial discrimination. States'-rights governors like Orval Faubus in Arkansas and George Wallace in Alabama resisted the attack on segregation in the South. But the federal government prevailed as Americans came to feel that injustice as well as poverty were national problems.

As Washington undertook battles on other civil rights fronts and moved vigorously into such areas as public safety (in factories, on highways, in coal mines, in consumer products), consumer credit, and the environment, the role of the states waned. Supreme Court decisions making the Bill of Rights applicable to the states further expanded national power.

Washington came to be called "big government" and the states the "fallen arches" of federalism.

"The change was not incremental; it was a massive increase which qualitatively altered the national government's role," Ladd writes. "Let the end be legitimate, Congress was saying, and legislation on almost any conceivable subject is permitted, even required."

In the '70s a reaction began to set in against a bloated federal system. Lyndon Johnson's Great Society programs, the culmination of almost a century of gradual centralization, had vastly expanded the national government. In the view of many, Washington was trying to do too much; the states had become "federal junkies." Debate began on how to bring the federal structure into better balance and sort out the proper functions for each level of government.

State constitutions were modernized (for instance, giving governors a second term), and state governments were reformed. And with one-man, one-vote reapportionment, state legislatures became more powerful and assertive.

The White House also called for change. Richard Nixon, seizing on a Democratic idea, persuaded Congress to enact "revenue sharing," turning back to the states and cities a portion of the revenues raised by the federal government. Jimmy Carter launched a national urban program that reflected a strong federalism concept.

Reagan's 'counterrevolution'

IT is President Reagan, however, former governor of California and a longtime believer in states' rights, who set out to reverse 50 years of Rooseveltian growth in Washington's role. In his view, having to accept Washington's mandates and regulations was too high a price to pay for federal aid. Under his New Federalism plan of 1982, the federal government would become the chief provider of health care, the states would take over welfare programs, and taxes and grants would be restructured.

The plan was quietly dropped when it ran into opposition from Congress, the states, and the public. But during the Reagan presidency there has been a significant devolution of responsibilities to the states. The pendulum of federalism is moving away from Washington, driven not only by the Reaganites' antigovernment ideology (they seek to shrink government at every level) but also by huge federal budget deficits. States know they must increasingly go it alone.

"For 50 years – through the Great Depression, the New Deal, World War II, the Korean war, the Great Society, and Vietnam – the pendulum was swinging toward Washington because of its strengthened fiscal hand and national crises," says John Shannon, director of the US Advisory Commission on Intergovernmental Relations. "Now the pendulum is swinging the other way – toward the state and local governments and a 'do-it-yourself' federalism."

"The trend is rooted in history," comments Princeton University scholar Richard P. Nathan. "It's a kind of cycle – when the federal government is conservative, the action swings to the states. In the 1920s, in fact, it was the states that developed the innovations that became the New Deal."

Dr. Shannon thinks the trend will continue through the next decade. He sees the federal system being profoundly changed by three "semirevolutions":

■ The first is the tax revolt spawned by California in 1978, which signaled to state governments not to increase spending at a faster rate than taxpayers' growth of income. Some 19 states passed varieties of California's Proposition 13. As a result, spending by state and local governments flattened out and came into equilibrium with economic growth.

■ Second, there has been a turnaround in federal aid going to the states. Between 1954 and 1978, federal aid grew faster than state and local revenues. In 1953, federal aid accounted for a little more than 10 percent of total state and local outlays. By 1968, the figure had risen to more than 18 percent and by 1977, to 26 percent.

But President Reagan in 1981 drastically reduced federal-aid levels in entitlement programs. He cut back grants to states and localities for operating programs, and consolidated 80 categorical grants into nine general block grants under which federal funds went directly to states rather than to cities or nonprofit organizations. He also pushed through

> 'The federal and state governments are in fact but different agents and trustees of the people, constituted with different powers, and designed for different purposes.'
>
> —James Madison

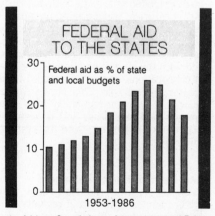

FEDERAL AID TO THE STATES

Federal aid as % of state and local budgets

1953-1986

Source: Advisory Commission on Intergovernmental Relations

legislation that gave the states the primary role in job training and gave them new flexibility in managing medicaid, enabling them to control costs.

Total federal aid to the states – especially medicaid – continues to grow. But as a result of these measures, in 1983 the aid dropped to 21.5 percent of local and state expenditures and by 1986 it had declined to an estimated 18 percent. Now that revenue sharing has ended, it is expected to drop further.

"This has had a bracing effect," Shannon says. "States no longer look to Washington to set the domestic agenda."

■ Third, the tax overhaul passed by the 99th Congress will intensify interstate competition for tax wealth. High-tax states worry about a loss of jobs

> 'Centrifugal, decentralizing forces are at work and political and economic power has begun to spread outward in new forms. The action is now in state capitals.'
>
> —Bruce Babbitt, former governor of Arizona

and upper-income taxpayers. So, to reduce their vulnerability to interstate competition, they will have to cut rates and pay for this by broadening the tax base.

Shannon believes these trends reflect the self-correcting forces in American society. "Uncle Sam bit off too much and had to be pulled back," he says. "The decentralization of our system is one of our weapons – the fact that we have 50 states and 20,000 local governments, each making its own decisions. States now know there is no more candy in Washington."

This is not to say that all 50 states are doing well economically. Many, especially those in the Northeast, are experiencing a resurgence. Others – Oklahoma, Texas, Iowa, Wyoming – are in distress. Most have gone through a painful process of shrinking programs and increasing taxes in order to balance their budgets. And because many legislatures did not make up for the loss of federal welfare benefits, poverty has grown across the nation.

Nor has the federal government shrunk as a result of the shift to the states. Deficits and debt notwithstanding, the national government keeps growing. This year's federal budget runs a trillion dollars – 24 percent of America's gross national product and more than the combined budgets of all the states.

Washington cannot abdicate responsibilities that can only be borne at the federal level: defense, entitlements, scientific research, and management of the economy. The Supreme Court, moreover, has enhanced the power of the federal government to regulate state activities, such

Recently state governments have been experiencing a surge of vitality and self-reliance. This is having a positive effect on America's federal system.

as requiring that minimum-wage and work-hours laws cover public employees.

And although the national government often finds itself stalemated – on the budget deficit, for instance – it can and does produce breakthrough legislation. "Tax reform shows that the federal government can still work," says Margaret Kunin, governor of Vermont.

New vigor in state capitals

SOME scholars also see national government as a check on strong local economic interests and corporate power. "Ultimate power has to reside somewhere in a democratic polity," writes Arthur M. Schlesinger Jr. in "The Cycles of American History."

"If that power is not exerted by the public government, then national policy is seized by self-serving private interests. Government off the back of business means business on the back of government."

"We have come to recognize over one-half century that certain things are national and require national action," comments Governor Dukakis. "But good creative states can do more at the grassroots to be effective."

The new vigor of the states is much in evidence. A meeting of the National Governors' Association in South Carolina last fall reflected the states' robust efforts, not only to deal with problems within their own boundaries, but to cooperate with one another – and with the federal government. Governors debated issues from education and environment to law enforcement and the use of National Guardsmen in Central America.

"The tide is turning toward more responsibility and a greater role for the states," observes Richard Thornburgh, former governor of Pennsylvania. "The reasons are a recogni-

tion that our resources are finite and that you can no longer provide the enormous sum of federal support for a lot of programs. Also, there is a sense of alienation from a government that has become remote and Washington-centered."

"The devolution is not faddish, it'll be sustained," says former governor of Florida Bob Graham, now a US senator. "And it's possible that government is best that's closest to the people's desires and to the problem that government is intended to impact."

Out of today's state capitals are emerging thinkers and innovators, searching for modern-day answers to modern-day problems. Daniel J. Evans, a US senator and former governor of Washington, and Charles Robb, former governor of Virginia, head up the Committee on Federalism and the National Purpose, which seeks to promote a federal system that is more humane and efficient and to end the great disparity in wealth between the states.

States are becoming aggressive in promoting private business at home and economic ties abroad. Today governors fly off to Africa, Asia, and other corners of the globe to forge trade links. When he was in office, Governor Thornburgh traveled to China, Japan, Africa, Israel, and Egypt to "plant the flag of Pennsylvania so people will think not only of dealing with the federal government but with the states."

Federal-state partnership

STATES have even established overseas offices to attract foreign investment and tourism. "A governor could be pretty laid back 15 years ago," says John Carlin, former governor of Kansas. "But come 1990, because of world competition, a governor will be judged on whether he has followed through on economic development."

Today's urgent problems at home and abroad appear to demand not only a heightened role for the states but greater cooperation between the states and Washington. "We need a shared federal-state partnership where we work hard on development," says Governor Dukakis. "If you're concerned about our competitive posture or drug abuse or infrastructure, there has to be more cooperation at all levels."

The role of the cities and counties in the federal system is also changing.

During the heyday of federal largess in the 1960s and '70s, mayors hightailed it to Washington to lobby for sewer grants, jobs programs, and money. Now, as federal programs have been phased out or as responsibility is transferred to the states, the cities again have to deal with state capitals. And they are becoming more self-sufficient, raising their own money to meet local needs.

Counties, which once represented rural populations, also are involved in gritty urban problems, and they seem to be gaining in political power.

As Robert Kerrey, former governor of Nebraska, comments: "You see much more direct participation by citizens at the local level. Cities, counties, and school districts are being controlled by nontraditional politics because of rights for women and blacks, and economic changes."

Lamar Alexander, former governor of Tennessee, says: "Twenty years ago the national government began to support things it had never been involved in, and local officials began to do an end run around the states. But the states have become stronger and different entities for the cities to deal with."

The federal system, in short, is alive and well in 1987. There will continue to be a shifting back and forth of responsibilities between the states and the national government as times and demands change. Each American generation will sort out for itself the trade-offs of federal and state functions.

Governor Alexander capsules the thinking of many politicians of this generation when he says: "The best job in the United States has to be the governor of his or her state."

Further readings:

"The Changing Politics of Federal Grants," by Lawrence D. Brown, James W. Fossett, and Kenneth T. Palmer: The Brookings Institution (1984).

"American Federalism," by Richard H. Leach: W. W. Norton & Co. (1970).

"Federal Grants: Giving and Taking Away," by Richard P. Nathan and Fred C. Doolittle: Political Science Quarterly (Spring 1985).

"Storm Over the States," by Terry Sanford: McGraw-Hill Book Company (1967).

T his Constitution, and the laws of the United States which shall be made in pursuance thereof; and all treaties made . . . under the authority of the United States, shall be the supreme law of the land; and the judges in every state shall be bound thereby; any thing in the Constitution or laws of any state to the contrary not-withstanding."

Article VI, U.S. Constitution.

A more favorable court
States fare better on preemption

Carter G. Phillips

Mr. Phillips is a member of the legal firm of Sidley & Austin in its Washington D.C. office, and a member of the advisory board of the State and Local Legal Center.

Independence Hall, where the Declaration of Independence and the Constitution were adopted, will be the center of pageantry and parade throughout the Bicentennial year.

T he 200th year of our Constitution is occasion to reflect upon political doctrines such as federalism, which although nowhere mentioned by name in the Constitution was central to the constitutional plan.

The President's Task Force on Federalism last year suggested that after 200 years "the states appear to be relegated, with respect to national policy-making, to little more than another special interest group."

This gloomy assessment was based in large part on the Supreme Court's announcement that the Constitution provides little, if any, protection for states against direct congressional action. But the issue of direct constitutional restraint of federal authority has long been of more symbolic than practical concern.

More important to the practical workings of federalism is the extent to which state and federal government can operate concurrently. This is in contrast to when the federal regulatory presence precludes the states from exercising their police powers. Because the federal government is ubiquitous,

the potential for such conflict is great.

Fortunately, the news from the Supreme Court on the eve of our Constitution's bicentennial is heartening for states.

Preemption and the supremacy clause

The legal term for deciding whether federal regulation precludes state regulation is preemption and the legal basis for the preemption doctrine is the supremacy clause of the Constitution. Article VI declares that the laws of Congress are the supreme law of the land. Preemption questions typically center on whether Congress intended in a particular statute to exercise its authority to regulate exclusively without any state involvement.

When Congress intends to impose exclusively federal standards upon a particular subject, it is said to "preempt the field." In that situation, even state regulation which complements federal law is unconstitutional.

In addition, preemption is required whenever state law

From *State Government News*, July 1987, pp. 10-11. Reprinted by permission of The Council of State Governments.

actually conflicts with a federal statute. A conflict exists if (1) federal law and state law impose inconsistent duties making compliance with both impossible, and (2) state law is an obstacle to the full achievement of Congress' purposes.

Legislation by Congress does not exhaust the sources of federal law under the supremacy clause. Federal administrative agencies, such as the Interstate Commerce Commission, often have authority to adopt rules which have the effect of law. When state law directly conflicts with an agency rule, the federal regulation prevails just as if it were a federal statute. In addition, agencies have power similar to Congress' to preempt the field by declaring expressly a subject to be a matter of exclusive federal concern.

Good news for states

Now for the good news. The Supreme Court in the last three years has shown a genuine reluctance to hold that state law is preempted implicitly by federal action or that there is a conflict between federal and state law absent clear evidence of a problem. What this means is that the states are being permitted to continue exercising their powers unless Congress expressly speaks to the contrary.

For instance, in a case involving a Florida county's efforts to regulate the selling of blood to commercial blood banks which were challenged as preempted by federal Food and Drug Administration regulations, the Supreme Court ruled, "If an agency does not speak to the question of preemption, we will pause before saying that the mere volume and complexity of its regulations indicate that the agency did in fact intend to preempt."

Thus, the court indicated that implicit preemption by administrative agencies is clearly disfavored. This means that federal bureaucrats will have to state their intentions clearly if they wish to stop the states from regulating in an area.

Similarly, last year the court rejected claims by the Federal Communications Commission that it had authority to preempt certain facets of intrastate rate making by state regulators of telecommunications. The court declared that "an agency literally has no power to . . . preempt the validly enacted legislation of a sovereign state, unless and until Congress confers power upon it."

Earlier this year the court upheld state environmental permits for national forest lands in the state. Even though the federal interest in such lands is evident, the court refused to assume preemption of state law. Instead it examined the "almost impenetrable maze of arguably relevant federal legislation" and concluded that nothing clearly precluded the state from imposing reasonable environmental protections through a permit system.

In another early 1987 decision, the court upheld a California law providing special protection for female employees who seek to return to work after taking pregnancy leave. The court rejected a claim that the special benefits conferred by the state violated Title VII's prohibition against sex discrimination. In upholding the state law, the court noted that "Congress failed to evince the requisite 'clear and manifest purpose' to supersede" the state statute in question.

These cases all indicate that preemption is disfavored by the court. Indeed, the court's reluctance to strike down state laws is also reflected in other recent holdings. Examples are the court's decisions that rent control statutes are not superseded by federal antitrust laws, that some state securities laws are not preempted by federal securities laws and that certain statutes protecting workers from plant relocations are not preempted by federal labor laws.

These positive developments indicate that state and local governments are holding their own in the federalist system.

Favorable tax decisions

There is particularly good news for states and localities in tax disputes. On three occasions in the last two years the court has upheld state and local taxes against preemption claims.

The court upheld (1) a North Carolina property tax against a challenge under certain U.S. Customs regulations; (2) a South Dakota airline flight property tax challenged as conflicting with a federal airway improvement act; and (3) a Florida sales tax on airplane fuel challenged under the Federal Aviation Act.

While the court does not give special treatment to state tax laws, the power to tax is vital to states and localities. The court's recent decisions indicate a particular unwillingness to interfere with taxing power absent clear proof of congressional intent.

States better represented

In the last three terms, states and localities have fared unusually well in the Supreme Court. Moreover, the law seems to be moving in a direction distinctly favorable to states. One explanation for this is the work of the State and Local Legal Center in Washington, D.C. The center presents *amicus curiae* briefs to the Supreme Court on behalf of state interests for The Council of State Governments and other organizations representing states and localities.

While there is no substitute for states and localities having the best attorneys represent their interest directly, their efforts are bolstered by the center.

The days are gone when state and local interests were consistently overpowered by private and federal government legal resources. Instead, with limited resources, the State and Local Legal Center has effectively advocated in favor of state and local governmental interests.

Its role is most clearly evident in the preemption area. In part because of the center, states and localities will enter the next century under our Constitution with a supremacy clause that fairly recognizes their interests. These interests include the exercise of police powers and the right to maintain state laws absent very clear indications that federal law and policy require a uniform national approach.

THE NEW FEDERALISM HASN'T MEANT LESS GOVERNMENT

Commentary/by Aaron Bernstein

Sometimes getting what you ask for is the worst thing that can happen to a politician. That may be just how conservatives feel about President Reagan's New Federalism campaign. Many true believers thought that his push to shift power from Washington to the states was a sign that their day had finally arrived: Big government was on the way out and states' rights were coming in.

Seven years later, Reagan has indeed turned many issues over to the states. But instead of the anticipated laissez-faire, New Federalism has spurred the states into action on everything from the minimum wage to parental leave (table). What's more, the decisions they've made tend to be the type that liberals endorse, such as the law Massachusetts Governor Michael S. Dukakis backed that requires companies to provide health care insurance for most employees. "New Federalism has worked in rather ironic ways," says Norman Ornstein, policy analyst at the American Enterprise Institute.

New Federalism had its roots in the conservative belief that government actions often constitute unjustified interference in voters' lives. Reagan hoped that allowing the states to make decisions would mean many decisions just wouldn't be made at all. Instead, dozens of states have initiated experiments to reform the welfare system or to overhaul public schools, for instance. To the horror of some conservatives, a few states have even raised taxes to fund new programs. As a result, New Federalism has had the effect of affirming the role of government, not denying or reducing it.

LIBERAL MOVES. Conservatives have seen their cherished power-to-the-states principle backfire in other ways, too. One example: State after state has embraced the liberal concept of comparable worth. This is the idea that sex discrimination is to blame for keeping the pay of jobs typically held by women below that of comparable jobs held by men. So far, 20 states and 93 cities, counties, and school districts have begun to raise the pay levels of public-sector jobs primarily held by women.

The states have been flaunting plenty of other liberal moves in the faces of New Federalists. Tired of waiting for Congress to raise the $3.35-an-hour federal minimum wage, 10 states and the District of Columbia have raised it on their own. And 15 states have passed laws requiring employers to provide parental leave. "The states are usually more liberal than Reagan thought they would be," says Paula Roberts, a lawyer at the Center for Law & Social Policy in Washington.

Why have so many states turned out to be full of liberal activists? In part,

STATES TAKE THE LEAD

Issue	State action
COMPARABLE WORTH	20 states and 93 localities have begun to raise pay levels of public-sector jobs usually held by women
EDUCATION	Dozens of states and school districts have initiated reforms such as giving teachers more involvement in setting school curriculums
HEALTH CARE	A Massachusetts law will require employers to provide health care for most employees. Four other states are testing insurance subsidies
MINIMUM WAGE	10 states and the District of Columbia have raised the minimum above the $3.35-an-hour federal level
PARENTAL LEAVE	15 states have passed laws mandating parental-leave policies in the private sector
WELFARE REFORM	47 states are experimenting with programs that train welfare recipients for work or help them find a job

DATA: BW

they may have been attracted by the new opportunities. When the feds called the shots, many ambitious politicians saw state capitals as little more than way stations on the road to Washington. But talented people became more interested in state-level jobs as opportunities arose to create original programs. "I don't think that states looked to recruit liberals or conservatives," says Stuart Butler, a policy analyst at the Heritage Foundation. "They just wanted to hire people with good technical skills. But they ended up with more liberals than conservatives."

Some conservatives say the New Federalism hasn't been a complete disaster. Butler points out that one aspect of the idea was to let domestic issues be handled by those most closely involved. By pushing decision-making down to the states, he says, voters have been given more control. In addition, at least some state actions seem conservative. Last year, for instance, Oklahoma passed a law that requires an absent unemployed father who can't pay child support to take a job the state finds for him or enroll in a job-training program. Under the law, which hasn't yet been implemented, a judge can charge a father who resists with contempt of court and ultimately jail him, says Robert Fulton, secretary of social services in the Oklahoma governor's office.

Overall, however, conservatives might be better off without New Federalism. According to plan, when the Reagan revolution put their power in Washington at its peak, they started giving it away. But that giveaway is now coming back to haunt them at the federal level. With the Democrats in control of the Senate again, a more liberal, interventionist attitude has been taking hold in Washington. Congress is considering raising the minimum wage and may also pass laws on parental leave, welfare reform, and even mandated health care. Action on these issues by so many states has put pressure on Congress to follow suit.

SOCIAL LABORATORY. There's one outcome of New Federalism that may prove attractive to political pundits of all stripes. Social programs made in Washington typically are put into place throughout the country. As a result, everyone suffers from the same legislative defects. But now that the states are taking the lead, many ideas are being tested at once.

Thus, Massachusetts can experiment with liberal approaches to health care while Oklahoma tries something at the other end of the spectrum. Because the states function as a kind of social laboratory, Congress can choose the ideas that work best. "Even if liberal ideas become more widespread, the diversity will allow us to end up with better policy," says Butler. That's something that all sides may find worthwhile.

The State of State-Local Relations

Steven D. Gold

Steven D. Gold is director of fiscal studies for NCSL.

Cutbacks in federal aid are inducing changes in state-local relationships but they're still more adversarial than cooperative.

Paternalism or indifference from state officials. Distrust and frustration from local officials. Hostility and disrespect on all sides. Too often, these seem to be the reigning attitudes among the leaders of state and local governments.

But casually perceived attitudes and rhetoric can be misleading. What's really happening in state-local relations? Are things getting better, getting worse, or staying about the same? Difficult questions. Princeton University's Richard Nathan, one of the leading scholars of intergovernmental relations has observed, "So much happens at the state and local levels across this vast nation that it is very hard to generalize about broad trends."

This is particularly true about state-local policies. Comparing one state to another is hampered by the incredible diversity in state and local systems. A critical problem in one state may not even exist in another. To make matters worse, state-local relations is one of the less glamorous issues around. As former Virginia Governor Charles Robb used to say, "There is no faster way to clear out a room than to begin talking about federalism."

John Shannon, until recently the boss of the U.S. Advisory Commission on Intergovernmental Relations (ACIR), has coined the term "fend-for-yourself federalism" to describe the current period. One of the main reasons for this development is the enormous cutback in federal support for state and local governments. According to the budget presented by President Reagan last winter, federal aid for state and local government operations was slashed 37 percent in real terms between 1980 and 1987. As a percentage of the gross national product, grants fell from 2.2 percent to 1.2 percent in those seven years.

In part because of this shrinking federal role, NCSL's* Task Force on State-Local Relations has predicted that "we are on the brink of a period of significant change in the way state and local governments interact." Federal cutbacks "create a vacuum that forces states to reassess their policies."

There has not been enough time in the two years since the task force approved this statement to expect major policy changes, but it is worth inquiring about the development of state-local relations in the past few years. Unfortunately, no comprehensive survey is available on this issue. Still, the fragmentary evidence available does reveal that the winds of change are beginning to pick up force in state capitols around the country.

One of the most tangible impacts of the task force is increased interest in creating state ACIRs. The task force

*National Conference of State Legislatures

placed heavy emphasis on the role such groups can play in providing a forum for discussion of intergovernmental issues and for doing research on solutions to state-local problems.

Jane Roberts, assistant director of the U.S. ACIR, reports that there has been more discussion of establishing such bodies in the past several years than ever before. A new ACIR in Utah last year and one expected to be created this year in Rhode Island are directly attributable to initiatives by legislators who served on the NCSL task force. Representative Bob Bianchini of Rhode Island explains, "State and local governments should work together to solve problems before they reach the critical stage. The task force discussions convinced me that a state ACIR can play an important role in fostering that kind of cooperation."

As the rubric "fend-for-yourself federalism" implies, local governments may have to bear much of the burden of raising revenue to finance their services. If they are to do this, however, they must have sufficient flexibility. Several states have relaxed constraints on the ability of local governments to raise revenue. California, Iowa, Nevada and Utah are examples of states where limits on property taxes or spending have been liberalized. California, for example, amended Proposition 13 to allow localities to raise their property tax rate to pay off newly-issued general obligation bonds, even if this means having a tax rate of more than 1 percent. Utah replaced a 6 percent limit on property tax increases with a strong full-disclosure process—notices explaining why taxes are going up must be sent to taxpayers before the increase. Moving in the opposite direction, Wisconsin this year imposed a new set of limits on local governments (and on the state as well).

Another important trend is the loosening of restrictions on local sales taxes. Among the states to grant new sales tax authority are Florida, Georgia, Iowa, Minnesota, Missouri, North Carolina, Tennessee, Texas and Wisconsin. Local income taxes have not been as popular, but they are an integral part of a sweeping local tax-reform program approved by the Pennsylvania House earlier this year. That state's Senate was considering a different approach as this article went to press, and some major reforms were given a good chance of passage this year. South Carolina is another state where a far-reaching reform of local finances (developed by its ACIR) has been working its way through the legislature.

Cities and counties often have an ambivalent attitude toward the way in which states allow them greater latitude to raise taxes. Doug Peterson, a senior policy analyst for the National League of Cities (which last year published a good report on local revenue

Local Tax Effort

Counties are making a greater effort to raise tax revenue while municipalities and school districts have a falling tax effort, at least for the period from 1980 to 1986. Per $1,000 of personal income, county tax revenue increased from $9.74 in 1980 to $10.29 in 1986. At the same time, municipal tax revenue dipped from $16.19 to $15.37, and school district tax revenue fell from $15.16 to $14.51.

These are national averages, and the patterns for individual states might well differ because of a variety of factors. Cities and counties have been relying more heavily on user fees and charges, and counties were hit the hardest by the cutbacks in federal aid. Other explanations for the relative increase in county taxes are that they have been assuming more municipal functions, and pressure has been intense on social services provided by counties. Legislators who are considering whether to pump more aid into local government budgets might consider whether effort is increasing or decreasing—as well as the reasons for the changes.

—*Steven D. Gold*

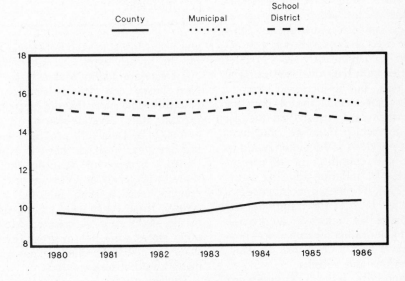

LOCAL TAX REVENUE
PER $1,000 OF PERSONAL INCOME

County Municipal School District

Source: U.S. Census Bureau

diversification), says that sometimes cities are appreciative and consider it a genuine help, but frequently it is an "empty offer" because states generally have been requiring that voters approve sales tax increases in referenda that are difficult to pass. This boils down to "removing one hurdle but creating another," he said.

Some states are helping local governments to raise revenue by reducing some of the "rough edges" of the property tax, the mainstay of local tax systems. Maine and Vermont expanded their property-tax circuit breakers last year, reducing the heavy burden of this tax on the poor. Oklahoma this year is making a major effort to improve property tax administration.

Another important trend for both state and local governments is the use of impact fees that require developers to help pay for the costs that arise when new development takes place. A state can pave the way for such fees by enacting legislation that spells out how and when they can be employed. Assemblyman Dominic Cortese, who authored such a bill passed by California last year, wanted "to make sure that local governments have the tools to allow development to go forward and to ensure that fees are not exorbitant." California has also created new kinds of special taxing districts to pay for such construction as highway interchanges.

Even in an era of "fend-for-yourself federalism," states have not been placing the entire burden of paying for services on local governments. State aid to cities and counties was relatively depressed in the early 1980s as states wrestled with their own serious fiscal problems, but it increased strongly after fiscal year 1983, the low point for state finances. In fiscal 1986 (the last year for which data are available), states provided $50.6 billion in aid to cities and counties, an 18 percent increase in inflation-adjusted terms from 1983. The biggest recent increases have not been in the traditional aid categories like highways and revenue sharing but rather for categorical programs to help with transit systems, corrections and housing.

When the federal government abolished general revenue sharing in 1986, many local governments turned to their states in hopes of obtaining a replacement for the $4.5 billion that

New York's State-Local Commission Is Making a Difference

New York's Legislative Commission on State-Local Relations is perhaps the best example of how a small investment in organization-building can contribute to the solution of state-local problems. Established by the Legislature in 1981, this bipartisan commission has some solid accomplishments and is playing an important role in elevating the consideration of local issues in that state. Here are five examples of its activities that other states might want to emulate:

- In 1985 it played a key role in breaking a deadlock that had for years prevented any increase in New York's revenue-sharing program for local governments.
- It facilitated the creation of the New York Municipal Council, a group of local government organizations that advises the Legislature on local priorities. Senator James H. Donovan, the Commission's vice chairman, says that the inability of local governments to agree on common positions used to detract from their ability to influence the Legislature, but the Council has helped to overcome that problem.

- It developed a computer-based model of all state and federal aid programs that makes possible instant analysis of changes in formulas and the size of programs. Few if any other legislatures have such detailed information readily available.
- It commissioned a major study by Cornell University researchers to identify which services local governments are providing and how they are being financed. State officials elsewhere frequently don't know what's really happening in local government.
- It surveyed state and local officials to determine their perceptions of the state of state-local relations. The responses revealed a big difference in views, with local officials much more pessimistic.

Commission chairman Assemblyman Joseph T. Pillittere urges legislators in other states to learn from New York's experience. "Our commission has done a lot of solid work," he says. "State-local issues are so important that a legislature ought to single them out for special attention."

—Steven D. Gold

was lost. Most states did not step in to fill the breach explicitly. Connecticut, Delaware, Idaho, Massachusetts, New Jersey and Rhode Island are among the few states that did create or expand state revenue-sharing programs. (The Delaware program was for one year and has been discontinued.) Except for Idaho (which shared with localities a portion of the revenue from a state sales-tax increase), these states were among the fiscally strongest in the country. Most other states were not in great fiscal shape and concluded that local governments could absorb the loss.

To keep matters in perspective, it is important to recognize that nearly every state already has at least one aid program that provides general support to local governments. According to the

U.S. Census Bureau, such programs provided $13.4 billion of aid in 1986. In addition, states spent another $34.6 billion that year on categorical aid to local governments not including school aid. Many of these aid programs are regularly expanded either by increasing appropriations or automatically because they are financed by ear-marked state taxes.

Another way that states assist local governments financially is by assuming responsibility for functions that used to be paid for by local taxes. The most important area where this has been occurring recently involves financing the courts. According to the National Center for State Courts, Iowa, Michigan and Oregon are among states that have assumed greater responsibility for court costs in recent years. Illinois, New Jersey, Ohio, and Pennsylvania are other states where this is a hot topic. Last year California set up a program expected to cost about $500 million to relieve the counties of most of the expense of supporting the trial courts. In 1988 Wisconsin approved a plan for state to assume the costs of local district attorneys.

Other examples of increased state responsibility include Nebraska's and New York's increased assumption of local Medicaid costs and New York's takeover of the City University of New York.

One of the most contentious areas of state-local relations centers around unreimbursed mandates. States often add to local burdens by requiring local governments to provide services or meet certain standards without helping them pay the bill for these actions. One response to this problem has been to increase awareness of mandates by requiring fiscal notes on bills that impose significant financial costs on local governments.

Fourteen states have legislative or constitutional requirements that states reimburse localities for new mandates, but some of these provisions are honored more in the breach than the observance, since the legislature may suspend their operation in specific cases. When a mandate reimbursement requirement is embodied in the constitution, like California's Proposition 13, states have been more successful in slowing the growth of new mandates, according to a new report by the U.S. General Accounting Office (which studied selected state programs to help Congress consider what to do about federal mandates on states and localities).

California, Massachusetts and Rhode Island are among the states where mandate reimbursement programs have been somewhat successful in restraining new mandates. California is one of the few states where mandates have actually been repealed. But Allan Burdick of the California County Supervisors' Association points out that it may be difficult to terminate an existing program just because the mandate for it has been eliminated. An unusual feature of Massachusetts' law (which derives from Proposition 2-1/2) is that local governments do not have to abide by a mandate if the state does not pay for it.

While a lot has been going on in state-local relations, we still seem to be in the early stage of a major long-term shift. Illinois Senator Dawn Clark Netsch, who chaired the NCSL State-Local Task Force last year, puts it this way: "My impression is that we've certainly raised the level of consciousness about state-local issues. How much that gets translated into action remains to be seen."

This year's task force chairman, New York Senator Charles Cook, goes a step further. "We're still living pretty much in a traditional mode, but that's going to change," he says. Cook, who chairs the New York Legislature's Commission on Rural Resources, foresees a major reorganization of local governments in New York and other Northeastern states, with counties assuming some new functions and towns taking on more municipal activities. The state has an important role to play as a catalyst for these changes, which he thinks will take decades to unfold.

If there is going to be major change in our state-local system, attitudes are going to have to change radically. The Task Force called on states "to stop considering local governments like just another special interest group and to start treating them like partners in our federal system of providing services to citizens." This may already be occurring, but progress seems rather slow. While legislators and local leaders in many states have begun to place a higher priority on state-local affairs, the executive branch of state government has been notable by its silence. Until governors decide to make local issues a top priority as they did the discussion of school improvement, reform of state-local relations will tend to remain on the back burner.

Proponents of state-local reform may be tilting at windmills unless they can convince more people of the importance of the issue. A fundamental problem is that this area is not exactly sexy. In the words of essayist Calvin Trillin, "Government tends to be boring, and local government bores absolutely."

There may be a way to overcome this formidable hurdle. We are living in an age when nothing is more important than competitiveness, and efficiency in government is highly prized. Improving the state-local system can bolster both. When that becomes clear, a new age for state-local relations may actually emerge, confirming the proclamation of Mayor Joseph P. Riley of Charleston, S.C., that the recommendations of NCSL's Task Force of State-Local Relations would be seen as a watershed in the history of this issue.

Voting, Parties, and Interest Groups

- Elections and Interest Groups (Articles 11-14)
- Referenda, Initiatives, and Recalls (Articles 15-17)

The American political system is usually classified as a representative democracy. Top officials are elected by the people and, as a result, government is supposed to be responsive and accountable to citizens. Both the theory and practice of representative democracy are of interest to students of American politics. Political scientists study various processes that seem essential to the functioning of representative democracy: parties, interest groups, election laws, campaigning techniques, and so forth. Attention is not limited to the national government; state and local governments are also examined to assess responsiveness and accountability.

State and local governments operate under somewhat different circumstances and institutional arrangements than the national government. In many states and localities, voters can participate directly in the policy process through mechanisms known as *initiative* and *referendum*. In addition, many state and local voters can participate in removing elected officials from office by a procedure called *recall*. In some localities—most notably in the New England states—an open meeting of all local citizens, called a town meeting, functions as the local government legislature. These mechanisms provide additional avenues for citizens trying to influence state and local governments.

Generally speaking, party organization is strongest at the local level and weakest at the national level. Party "machines" are a well-known feature of the local political landscape in the United States, and colorful and powerful "bosses" have left their mark on local political history. While the heyday of "bosses" and "machines" is past, noteworthy examples of contemporary political machines still exist.

National elections, especially for the presidency, are usually contested vigorously by the two major parties and, over the long haul, the two parties tend to be reasonably competitive. This is less true of states and localities, because voters in some states and many localities are decidedly oriented toward one party or the other. We can generally expect Democrats to control the governorship and legislature of states such as Massachusetts and Georgia as well as city governments in Chicago, Philadelphia, and elsewhere. Republicans, on the other hand, are good bets to hold power in most suburban localities. Thus, in some states and localities, closer and more significant competition can occur within the nominating process of the dominant party than between the two parties in general elections.

Party labels do not appear on the ballot in many localities, and this may or may not affect the way elections are conducted. In "nonpartisan" elections, candidates of different parties may in fact openly oppose one another just as they do when party labels appear on the ballot. Another possibility is that parties field opposing candidates in a less than open fashion. As yet another alternative, elective offices may actually be contested without parties or the political party affiliations of candidates playing any part. One cannot assume that formally nonpartisan elections are accompanied by genuine nonpartisanship; nor can one assume that they are not.

One last feature of state and local political processes deserves mention here. While members of the Senate and House of Representatives in Washington, D.C., hold well-paid, prestigious positions, their state and local counterparts often do not. Many state legislators are only part-time politicians and earn the bulk of their livelihoods from other sources. This is also true of most general-purpose local government officials. In addition, almost all local school board members are unpaid, even though many devote long hours to their duties. That so many elected state and local officeholders do not get their primary incomes from their positions in government may well affect the way they respond to constituents. After all, while they and their families typically live in the community that they are representing, their livelihoods do not depend on being reelected.

Selections in the first section of this unit focus on elections and interest groups. The second section treats referenda, initiatives, and recalls—three procedures that give voters in many states and localities a direct role in determining policies and overseeing the performances of elected officials during their terms in office.

Looking Ahead: Challenge Questions

If you were the head of an interest group, would you use different techniques in trying to influence a state govern-

Unit 3

ment than in trying to influence a local government? What would the differences be?

Do you think there is much difference between running for office in a small town and running to be a member of Congress?

Do you think people are more or less knowledgeable in voting in state and local elections than in national elections? Why?

In your opinion, which is (are) more responsive to citizens—the national government or state and local governments?

Do you think citizens should be allowed to participate in policy-making through the initiative and referenda processes? Why or why not? What do you think about allowing citizens to "recall" officials during their term in office?

Mixed Electoral Systems: The Newest Reform Structure

Susan A. MacManus

Susan A. MacManus is director of the Ph.D. Program, College of Urban Affairs, Cleveland State University.

Mixed electoral systems are those in which some council members are elected at large and others from single-member district seats, with the latter usually being the larger number. Mixed systems have gained in popularity as at-large systems have declined, being accepted by traditional good government or reform groups and by minorities and their advocates.

Mixed systems are attractive to reformers who are unwilling to go so far as to endorse exclusively single-member districts, which they regard as merely "wards in sheep's clothing." At the same time, they are increasingly reticent to defend exclusively at-large councils when they appear to have the effect of diluting minority representation. For reformers, mixed plans are an acceptable compromise which "not only furnish representation to specialized interests concentrated within particular geographic areas but also ensure the election of some representatives who will direct their priorities toward the needs of the entire city."

A lesser-known fact is that mixed systems are also being embraced by those whose primary interest is greater minority representation on city councils, school boards and county commissions. Civil rights groups, the courts and the U.S. Justice Department are more and more accepting mixed systems as mechanisms to increase and enhance levels of minority representation, whether defined in a physical sense or in a broader policy sense. In addition to electing minorities to governing bodies, they are concerned about a government's responsiveness to minority needs and priorities. Perhaps the best statement of the various types of minority representation has been made by Rufus P. Browning, Dale Rogers Marshall and David H. Tabb in *Protest Is Not Enough: The Struggle of Blacks and Hispanics for Equality in Urban Politics* (Berkeley, University of California Press, 1984). In addition to representation of minority persons on councils, the authors identify two other aspects of political equality: policy responsiveness of government (responsiveness to the interest of minority groups in the distribution of benefits); and the degree of incorporation of minority groups into the political system (measured by assessing the extent to which they are represented in coalitions that dominate city policymaking on minority-related issues). Many studies have reported that mixed systems can provide these different types of representation (see bibliography).

The purpose of this article is to examine the growing popularity of mixed systems, focusing primarily on the features which promote minority representation. It should be noted, however, that these same features can also characterize the more traditional electoral arrangements (at-large or single-member district) depending on the political, demographic and socioeconomic setting in which they exist.

Frequency of Usage

Mixed systems are not unusual electoral arrangements, being in use in 773 (19 percent) of all U.S. cities over 2,500 population, according to the 1982 *Municipal Yearbook* (see Table 1), and in more than half of the largest cities. Using 1976 data, two studies found that 37 (35.2 percent) of the 105 central cities with more than 15 percent black population had mixed systems, as did

TABLE 1
TYPES OF ELECTORAL SYSTEMS

Classification	No. of cities reporting (A)	At large system No.	At large system % of (A)	Ward or district system No.	Ward or district system % of (A)	Combination system No.	Combination system % of (A)
Total, all cities............	4,089	2,721	66.5	595	14.6	773	18.9
Population group							
Over 1,000,000	3	0	0.0	1	33.3	2	66.7
500,000–1,000,000	12	4	33.3	2	16.7	6	50.0
250,000– 499,999	25	13	52.0	3	12.0	9	36.0
100,000– 249,999	95	48	50.5	15	15.8	32	33.7
50,000– 99,999	226	134	59.3	20	8.8	72	31.9
25,000– 49,999	463	294	63.5	61	13.2	108	23.3
10,000– 24,999	1,012	662	65.4	122	12.1	228	22.5
5,000– 9,999	1,048	706	67.4	151	14.4	191	18.2
2,500– 4,999	1,205	860	71.4	220	18.3	125	10.4
Geographic division							
New England	185	100	54.1	22	11.9	63	34.1
Mid-Atlantic...........	625	455	72.8	109	17.4	61	9.8
East North Central......	857	463	54.0	152	17.7	242	28.2
West North Central	467	203	43.5	132	28.3	132	28.3
South Atlantic	555	425	76.6	43	7.7	87	15.7
East South Central......	243	202	83.1	12	4.9	29	11.9
West South Central	451	300	66.5	62	13.7	89	19.7
Mountain	223	146	65.5	41	18.4	36	16.1
Pacific Coast	483	427	88.4	22	4.6	34	7.0
Form of government							
Mayor-council	2,111	1,199	56.8	438	20.7	474	22.5
Council-manager	1,878	1,422	75.7	157	8.4	299	15.9
Commission	100	100	100.0	0	0.0	0	0.0

Source: Heywood T. Sanders, "The Government of American Cities: Continuity and Change in Structure, *"The Municipal Yearbook 1982*. Washington, D.C.: International City Management Association, 1982, Table 3/3:180.

Reprinted with permission from the November 1985 issue of *National Civic Review*, pp. 484-492. National Civic Review, 1601 Grant Street, Suite 250, Denver, CO 80203.

75 (31.4 percent) of 239 central cities of all population sizes. Another study of 80 southern cities over 10,000 showed 14.5 percent had mixed systems, and, of these, 54.5 percent had at least one black city council member. A 1978 study of 264 cities over 25,000 with at least 10 percent black population reported 64 (24.2 percent) with mixed systems. Finally, a 1985 survey of all southern cities over 25,000 population found that 51 of 222 (23 percent) used mixed systems.

There is evidence that if cities change electoral setups, the choice of a mixed system is not uncommon. For example, of 41 Texas local governments that made such changes between 1970 and 1979, almost 20 percent switched to mixed systems. Likewise, 44 southern cities changed their election systems between 1970 and 1981, 43 percent to a mixed system and 57 percent to single-member districts. Between 1975 and 1985, of 50 southern cities, 38 percent changed to a mixed plan and 52 percent to a single-member district system. The overwhelming majority of those adopting a mixed system changed from a pure at-large system (see Table 2).

In 22 percent of the cases the change to a mixed system occurred because of Voting Rights Act litigation. The fact that such a plan was accepted by the plaintiffs and/or the courts confirms our contention that mixed systems may facilitate greater minority representation.

TABLE 2
ELECTION SYSTEMS ABANDONED BY SOUTHERN CITIES CHANGING TO MIXED SYSTEMS: 1975-1985

System Abandoned	% Changing to Mixed (N=19)
Pure At-Large	56%
At-Large, from Seats or Positions	11
At-Large, Residency Requirements; posts. geographically-based	22
Single member district	11
	100%

Source: Telephone survey of city clerks in cities over 25,000 population, November 1985-March 1985.

Attractive Features

Enhancement of Minority Representation on Governing Bodies

The popularity of the mixed plan is attributable to a number of features. One of the most prominent is its success at increasing and enhancing minority representation and influence on city councils. Every scholarly investigation of black representation (proportional representation) has found that *average* black equity scores are considerably higher with mixed systems than with pure at-large plans, and not significantly lower than in single-member district systems. For example, in the study of black representation among southern cities changing electoral structures between 1970 and 1981, representation under mixed systems adopted was .70. (Equity is defined as a ratio: percent minority on council divided by percent minority in city population. Absolute proportional representation would yield an equity score of 1.00.) For southern cities changing to single-member district systems, the equity score was .87; for cities maintaining at-large systems, it was only .39. Another study found slightly greater minority representation in mixed systems than in wards.

Broadening of Impact and Influence Points

Another attractive feature of mixed systems is that they may increase minority impact and influence on a larger number of council races than possible under a single-member district system. The mixed plan offers the potential for blacks to influence the outcome of each at-large race in addition to determining the outcome of contests in minority-majority districts. The opportunity to influence at-large positions has become more significant in recent years in light of the dispersion of the minority population, a higher incidence of black bloc voting, and higher turnout rates among blacks than whites. These trends hold true even in the south, especially in urban areas. Migration patterns have brought in persons with more liberal racial attitudes, but several studies have found that even older native southerners have become more racially tolerant.

The Case of Sarasota, Florida

The growing tolerance on the part of white southerners may partially explain the success of a mixed plan recently adopted by Sarasota and upheld by the courts. The city adopted a $^2/_3$ plan: two at-large and three district-based seats. The city has a black population of only 16.3 percent (12.6 percent voting age population), which is gradually spreading into white areas adjacent to predominantly black neighborhoods. The plan created one predominantly black district (50.1 percent of total population; 42.6 percent of voting age population; but only 43.3 percent of registered voters). In drawing the district, the city placed whites of lower education and income with blacks, thereby creating a more socioeconomically homogeneous district than the rest of the city. This strategy was not new. Albert Karnig and Susan Welch had earlier suggested that black candidates have better chances of winning when placed with white voters of lower socioeconomic status.

When it came time to file to run, one white candidate (a former city commissioner and mayor) and two blacks did so. Skeptics forecast a highly racially polarized election in which the white candidate would win when blacks split their votes between the two black candidates and white voters turned out in record numbers to bloc vote for the white candidate. The underlying assumption was that the whites were likely to be extremely racist. Quite the contrary occurred: 47.2 percent of the blacks turned out, compared with 18.6 percent of the whites. This demonstrates that socioeconomic indicators are much better predictors of white political participation than black. In addition, there was a much higher incidence of white crossover voting than had been projected. The white candidate received only 15 percent of the vote. The two black candidates received 85 percent, with more than 55 percent of the whites voting for a black candidate.

The higher than expected white support for the black candidates might have been the result of personal contact between the candidates and their white constituents in the course of campaigning. Or it might have been the result of whites living in fairly integrated neighborhoods which increased their racial tolerance. Whites in this area had traditionally given more support to black candidates than had whites in the rest of the city. Regardless of the reason, the result was a more equitable level of representation for the city's black population both in the short term and in the long term, as the mixed system protects the opportunity for the growing number of minorities who live outside the district to coalesce with those living in the district to influence the outcome of the at-large races.

Minority Occupancy of At-Large Seats

Another very important point to note about black influence on the at-large seats in mixed systems is that blacks often capture these seats, sometimes after serving an apprenticeship as a district-based council member. For example, in a study of Buffalo, New York, three of the six at-large representatives were black. In Houston, two of the five at-large seats are held by blacks; one previously served as a district council member. These are not isolated observations. Karnig and Welch reported that in 22 percent of 50 mixed systems they studied, the at-large seats provided greater black representation than the district seats; in 28 percent, the at-large seats provided at least some black representation. The author's 1985 survey showed that blacks held at-large seats in 35 percent of the 51 southern cities over 25,000 with mixed systems.

Protection of Geographically Dispersed Minorities

Mixed plans are also effective where minority groups are geographically dispersed. This allows minority votes "lost" in creating minority-majority districts (votes of those living outside such districts) to be "saved" through bloc voting for at-large seats or coalescing with sympathetic whites to influence at-large seat outcomes. This is an especially attractive feature if there is evidence that the minority population is spreading beyond what had been the city's traditional black enclave (as was the case in Sarasota) and where the minority population is not sufficiently concentrated to draw a majority-minority district, often more of a problem for Hispanics than blacks.

Relatedly, if the minority population is too small *and* dispersed to capture a district-based seat, the at-large posts maximize its capacity to swing vote. In *Your Voice at City Hall* (State University of New York Press, Albany, 1984) Peggy Heilig and Robert Mundt state that "a minority population must comprise about 30 percent of the total and be geographically concentrated for a [pure single-member] district plan to result in increased representation depending on the number of districts." When the minority population is small, mixed, at-large and single-member district systems produce similar levels of minority representation.

Attention to Neighborhood and Citywide Issues

A more racially neutral advantage to mixed systems is the provision of simultaneous attention to specific neighborhood-oriented and citywide issues. As noted by Francine Rabinovitz and Edward Hamilton: "A mixed system yields some natural division of labor between district-based and at-large representatives. . . . The smaller electorate demands and receives greater attention to more localized 'backyard' problems from the district-based than from the at-large representative. . . . The at-large councillor is expected to take a broader perspective on citywide policy, and to balance off the parochial concerns of their district-based colleagues" (see the REVIEW, July 1980, page 385). Indeed, several studies have shown that district-based council members get more calls from constituents regarding day-to-day problems.

But the fact that district-based and at-large council members represent different constituencies causes a wider range of policy issues to be discussed at council meetings. This means that council members "have a better grasp of the diverse problems and concerns of residents throughout the city" (see the REVIEW, July-August 1983, page 380). It also increases citizen participation—at council meetings and at the polls, although some studies have found that changing to a mixed system is no consistent guarantee that turnout will be higher. A more probable outcome of the diverse representational perspectives is to increase the likelihood of policy responsiveness through council coalition building, especially in cities where minority voters cast the swing vote in the at-large and mayoral contests.

Summary

In summary, there is a number of reasons why mixed electoral systems are often attractive to minorities and traditional good government proponents. In a sense, mixed systems represent the American political system's tendency toward compromise; theoretically they offer something for everyone, although in certain instances so do the more traditional systems. Mixed electoral systems:

- Are not unusual; they are commonly used alternatives to at-large or single-member district systems throughout the U.S.;
- Often result in higher levels of minority representation than the traditional systems which they replace;
- Increase the number of council seats which can be captured and influenced by minorities, thereby expanding their representational opportunities;
- Enhance and protect the chances of electoral impact for geographically dispersed minorities;
- Promote representation of neighborhood areas and citywide concerns, operating much like a bicameral legislative body encouraging coalition building; and
- Encourage broader discussion of a wider range of policy issues.

Of course, no plan can produce the same outcome in every jurisdiction. Structure almost always takes a back seat to political, demographic and socioeconomic patterns in terms of explanatory power. But, in the right setting, mixed systems can be effective mechanisms for enhancing minority representation.

Bibliography

Bullock, Charles S., III. "Feasibility of Electing a Black under Sarasota's 3-2 Plan." Report prepared for the City of Sarasota, Florida, 1984.

Browning, Rufus P., Dale Rogers Marshall, and David H. Tabb. *Protest Is Not Enough: The Struggle of Blacks and Hispanics for Equality in Urban Politics.* Berkeley: University of California Press, 1984.

Cohen, Jeffrey E., Patrick R. Cotter, and Philip B. Coulter. "The Changing Structure of Southern Political Participation: Matthews and Prothro 20 Years Later," *Social Science Quarterly* 64 (September, 1983): 536-549.

Combs, Michael W., John R. Hibbing, and Susan Welch. "Black Constituents and Congressional Roll Call Votes," *Western Political Quarterly* 37 (September, 1984): 424-434.

Davidson, Chandler, and George Korbel. "At-Large Elections and Minority Group Representation: A Reexamination of Historical and Contemporary Evidence," *Journal of Politics* 43 (November, 1981): 982-1005.

Engstrom, Richard L., and Michael D. McDonald. "The Election of Blacks to City Councils: Clarifying the Impact of Electoral Arrangements on the Seats/Population Relationship." *American Political Science Review* 75 (June, 1981): 344-354.

———. "The Underrepresentation of Blacks on City Councils: Comparing the Structural and Socioeconomic Explanations for South/non-South Differences," *Journal of Politics* 44 (1982): 1088-1099.

Haselwerdt, Michael V. "Voter and Candidate Reaction to District and At-Large Elections: Buffalo, New York," *Urban Affairs Quarterly* 20 (September, 1984): 31-45.

Heilig, Peggy, and Robert J. Mundt. "Changes in Representational Equity: The Effect of Adopting Districts," *Social Science Quarterly* 64 (June, 1983): 393-397.

———. *Your Voice at City Hall: The Politics, Procedures, and Policies of District Representation.* Albany: State University of New York Press, 1984.

Karnig, Albert K. "Black Representation on City Councils: The Impact of District Elections and Socioeconomic Factors," *Urban Affairs Quarterly* 12 (December, 1976): 223-242.

Karnig, Albert K., and Susan Welch. "Electoral Structure and Black Representation on City Councils," *Social Science Quarterly* 63 (March, 1982): 99-114.

———. *Black Representation and Urban Policy.* Chicago: The University of Chicago Press, 1980.

Latimer, Margaret K. "Black Political Representation in Southern Cities: Election Systems and Other Causal Variables," *Urban Affairs Quarterly* 15 (September, 1979): 65-86.

Lyndon B. Johnson School of Public Affairs, The University of Texas, Local Government Election Systems Policy Research Project. *Local Government Election Systems.* Austin, TX: The University of Texas, Report No. 62, 1984.

MacManus, Susan A. "City Council Election Procedures and Minority Representation: Are They Related?" *Social Science Quarterly* 59 (June, 1978): 153-161.

MacManus, Susan A., and Carol A. Cassel. "Mexican Americans in City Politics: Participation, Representation, and Policy Differences," *The Urban Interest* 4 (Spring, 1982): 57-69.

Rabinovitz, Francine F., and Edward K. Hamilton. "Alternative Electoral Structures and Responsiveness to Minorities," *National Civic Review* 69 (July, 1980): 371-401.

Robinson, Theodore P., and Thomas R. Dye. "Reformism and Black Representation on City Councils," *Social Science Quarterly* 59 (June, 1978): 133-141.

Robinson, Theodore P., Robert E. England, and Kenneth J. Meier. "A Closer Look at Mixed Electoral Systems," paper presented at the annual meeting of the American Political Science Association, September 3-6, 1981.

Sanders, Heywood T. "The Government of American Cities: Continuity and Change in Structure," *The Municipal Yearbook 1982.* Washington, D.C.: International City Management Association, 1982): 178-186.

Sheffield, James F. Jr., and Charles D. Hadley. "Racial Voting in a Biracial City: A Reexamination of Some Hypotheses," *American Politics Quarterly* 17 (October, 1984): 449-464.

Stewart, Alva W., and Phung Nguyen. "Electing the City Council: Historic Change in Greensboro," *National Civic Review* 72 (July/August 1983): 377-381.

Taebel, Delbert. "Minority Representation on City Councils: The Impact of Structure on Blacks and Hispanics," *Social Science Quarterly* 63 (June, 1978): 142-152.

Vedlitz, Arnold, and Charles A. Johnson. "Community Racial Segregation, Electoral Structure, and Minority Representation," *Social Science Quarterly* 63 (December, 1982): 729-736.

Zimmerman, Joseph F. "The Single-Member District System: Can It Be Reformed?" *National Civic Review* 70 (May, 1981): 255-259.

———. "The Federal Voting Rights Act and Alternative Election Systems." *William and Mary Law Review* 19 (Summer, 1978): 621-660.

*Tearing down posters, packing press kits,
and other campaign adventures*

I Was a Chicago Ward Heeler

John Eisendrath

John Eisendrath is a former editor of The Washington
Monthly.

The cop savors the possible headline. "Candidate's brother arrested tearing down opponent's posters," he says. When he pulled the squad car to the curb moments earlier and asked for my driver's license, I contemplated gift-wrapping it in a twenty. *That* would be a headline.

Six weeks earlier I had been a political journalist in Washington. Rarely leaving the office, I opined about how the government was mismanaging its finances and whether certain politicians were presidential material. I have never worked in government and had long since given up trying to balance my checkbook. My experience working for a politician was limited to a month-long Capitol Hill internship, which consisted primarily of carrying the congressman's golf clubs from his office to his car. No matter: I was an editor, a pundit. I was paid to educate readers about how Washington really works.

Now it's two a.m. and I'm the one being educated. It's February in Chicago, about ten degrees outside, and my pockets are filled with crumpled posters of The Opponent. At one point there were four people running against my brother for an open seat on the city council, but now, in a runoff, there is only one. I hate The Opponent. I hate the people who work for him and am convinced they are all child abusers. I hate the local reporters who seem unable to grasp that my brother is the greatest political prospect since Abe Lincoln grew whiskers.

I am, in a word, possessed. More people—reporters in particular—should learn what it's like inside a campaign. The fear and insecurity. The all or nothing gamble. The hope. The experience engages voters and provides reporters with the insight to be incisive and tough.

There is knowledge: how to build a precinct operation; what to say when knocking on doors; little things like picking campaign colors and big ones like deciding on campaign themes. There is also perspective: I've done a dozen stories about negative campaigning, for instance, but I never understood what it feels like to be low-balled. As a reporter, I was disengaged from such stories, finding them dull and unimportant. As a campaign manager, I responded venomously, until cooler heads prevailed.

We spent $280,000 on the election. The Opponent spent $250,000. This is a grotesque amount and it underscores how daunting it is to run for even the most rudimentary public office. Both candidates have quick smiles and, with a little well-placed gel, nice hairdos. This matters, but plain speaking, a solid message, and knocking on doors play an equally large role. Even in local Chicago, political character is an issue.

Begging for (and thankfully receiving) the forgiveness of a patrolman in the middle of the night is one way of glimpsing democracy in action, as are a number of other humbling experiences: going door to door during the dinner hour, for instance, or trying to chat up the candidate to a bunch of freezing commuters at a bus stop. As a way of understanding how our system works, there is no substitute.

Teacher candidate

Sure I am biased. But there is really no arguing with my brother's credentials. First, Edwin has never been indicted. For a candidate running for city council in Chicago, that in itself is a pretty good platform. The number of indicted council members frequently hovers around 10 percent. Second, he has no experience dipping into the public till. This too makes him stand out: after approving a $296 million municipal bond issue for infrastructure repairs recently, 15 aldermen designated part of the money to repave streets in front of their homes. By not having a rap sheet, Edwin was a potential juggernaut.

But there is more. Edwin, who was 28 when the campaign began, went to Harvard. He graduated at the beginning of the "go-go" eighties, but opted against pursuing greed and glory on Wall Street and took a teaching job in Chicago's public schools. For four years, he taught elementary school children in a predominantly Hispanic west side neighborhood. His community involvement was extensive and had been cited by the mayor.

Edwin didn't become a teacher in order to become a politician. He actually enjoyed sharing his knowledge with a group of unruly ten-year-olds. Edwin had been undeterred by the obstacles that keep so many talented people from becoming public school teachers. When he first applied to become a teacher, for instance, Edwin was told that his degree in psychology from Harvard did not qualify him to teach in the public schools. To become "qualified" he dutifully wasted a year of his life getting a master's degree in education at a local teacher's college.

He believes in public service. Still, life as an educator in a big-city public school bureaucracy is frustrating. No books. No chalk. Standardized lessons. Low pay. At the beginning of three of the four years he taught, Edwin and his colleagues went on strike. To do something about it, Edwin twice applied to become a member of the Chicago Board of Education. He was rejected both times. Denied access to those areas within the bureaucracy that would allow him more say in improving Chicago's schools, he began exploring the possibility of running for public office.

This was in the summer of 1986. It was seven months prior to the election, and, although the incumbent had not yet decided to step down, a changing of the guard seemed likely. The 43rd ward in Chicago is located along Lake Michigan just north of downtown. A primarily white community, it's known as home to the city's "Lakefront Liberals."

Over the years, the ward has become increasingly affluent. Gentrification has turned bungalows into showplace homes and urban renewal has transformed a number of factories into parks. Of Chicago's 50 wards, the 43rd is the second most affluent, with a median family income of more than $30,000.

Not surprisingly, the ward's politics have grown more conservative. The incumbent alderman, a liberal ideologue first elected in 1975, pondered these changes as well as the deep deficits he had racked up during two unsuccessful attempts at higher office and decided in August 1986 to retire to his law practice.

The H word

The following day my brother announced he was a candidate. A less momentous occasion can scarcely be imagined. To prepare for the big event, we combined the collective wisdom of a number of experienced political advisers with about $20,000 of consultant's advice and campaign materials to package Edwin's blue chip credentials. Slogan: "For the Basics, Back the Best." Poster: the candidate, jacket slung over his shoulder, smiling. Campaign literature: a heartfelt letter from Edwin decrying politics-as-usual. Image (wholly unintentional): Frankie Valli in his prime.

Intuitively we knew Edwin's strengths were his knowledge of the public schools and his study of the city budget. However, what came through was that too many members of his family were involved in the packaging process. We love him, it all shouted, you'll love him, too. (And right away some did: several high school girls stopped by the campaign office asking for copies to hang on their closet doors. A teen idol craze was averted only because beyond about three feet the posters, printed black on grey, were unreadable.) Blinded by our family affection, we failed to notice some of the rougher edges, like the wrinkles in Edwin's pants or the belt loop he missed. Voters beyond adolescence were less likely to be impressed.

The Opponent, motherless no doubt, projected an image as slick as oil. His slogan ("Effective. Experienced. Independent.") was supported in his campaign literature with lists of accomplishments. He looked God-like, born to lead. His message, printed in blue and orange against a white background, jumped off the page like it was in 3-D. Plastered side by side on El platforms throughout the ward, The Opponent's posters, fresh and colorful, made ours look like a run for the student council. Certainly our explanation for why Edwin should be alderman wasn't simply that he was a nice guy. But that was the message our initial efforts conveyed. I remembered Ted Kennedy's incoherence in 1980 when Roger Mudd asked why he should be president. Like most people, I laughed at the time. Never again. Those questions, which seem like softballs, are doubtless the hardest questions to answer.

Back at the drawing board we ditched the slogan, hid the posters, printed legible literature and decided to let Edwin be Edwin. Above all, he was a teacher. Lousy public schools mean a lousy workforce. Improve them and you've taken a big step toward ensuring future prosperity. Who better to do that than someone who understands the system?

Only one problem remained: in a ward populated by yuppies and DINKS (double income no kids), public school teachers are about as respected as a bear market. It's a perception that no amount of white papers on education reform can change. Fortunately, there is one word that can make a yuppie respect a public school teacher running against an attorney, one word that could have evened the playing field between my brother and The Opponent: Harvard. A Harvard-educated public school teacher is to so many people an oxymoron that it shatters their preconceptions. It had, we hoped, just the ring of intelligence and sacrifice to make even the most doubting DINK think. Budget reform and community matters were part of the package, but if voters knew just one thing about Edwin it was going to be that he had the longest job title in Chicago: a Harvardeducatedpublicschoolteacher.

Press kit blues

Like every campaign, we hoped to get our message out through the press. But reporters didn't exactly hang on our every pronouncement. When we held a press conference to unveil Edwin's position paper on the city budget, only one reporter showed up. Our disappointment was compounded when the reporter, who worked for a local wire service, evinced more interest in my knowledge of possible newspaper jobs in Washington than in Edwin's mastery of the city's finances.

When we released Edwin's school reform package, in many ways the intellectual centerpiece of the campaign, we had the same confidence-building turnout. Hoping some good visuals would draw TV coverage, we held the press conference in front of a local school. When no camera showed, Edwin held the press conference in the confines of the lone reporter's car to escape the sub-zero temperature.

We weren't naive enough to expect a large turnout. One important reason for putting together detailed position papers was to influence editorial board members of the *Chicago Tribune* and *Chicago Sun-Times*. Their endorsements were important, and to get them Edwin needed to address significant city-wide issues. Still, before each press conference we prepared dozens of press kits, just in case a miraculously slow news day led all the political reporters in town to our office.

A press kit is a horrible, demoralizing thing. Nothing better exemplifies how desperate campaigns are for publicity. On the bottom of the press kit goes the position paper. It has about as much chance of being read as an article in *Playboy*. On top of that goes the summary of the position paper. This serves to thicken the packet so that even in tossing it out unopened a reporter will know he's dealing with a candidate of substance. Next up is the press release, which assumes either that no one will show or that the

reporters who do make an appearance will be too bored to take notes. When, as expected, the press conference bombs, the press kits are schlepped over to all the newspapers and TV stations on the theory that if you're persistent enough, some editor might give you mention on page 65.

Eventually, of course, the campaign does get coverage. With 49 other alderman races to write about, as well as a bitter campaign for mayor, all the press has time for is the basic "who's who" piece. One by one the reporters come by the office, which we conveniently over-staff for the occasion, and get down to the business of parachute journalism. Invariably they neither know nor care about the issues. Their interest is strictly money (as in "Aren't you buying the election?") and the mayor's race ("Who do you support?"). When pressed about issues, most reporters, in a discouraging chorus, reply: "Do you have a press kit?"

There were several candidates running for mayor, but as far as the press was concerned it was Harold Washington vs. the "regulars." Considering Chicago's political heritage, it's no surprise that the term regular—as in regular Democrat—is synonymous with "hack." It's applied principally to members of Mayor Daley's machine and their political heirs. Politicians who broke ranks with Daley and those allied with him are "independents." It's a sign of Daley's lingering influence that more than ten years after his death local politicians are still judged in relation to the Boss.

The press likes it this way. It makes it easy to categorize candidates and handicap races. Either you're a hack or you're not. In a racially polarized city like Chicago there is an implicit message as well: if you're not with Mayor Washington, you're a racist. Although the mayor made no formal endorsement, everyone knew he supported The Opponent. That made Edwin the regular. It only made matters worse when Edwin suggested such preconceptions were dated. In the *Sun-Times*'s "who's who" piece, Edwin was reviled for insisting he was not a mouthpiece for the machine. To this "boast of independence," the *Sun-Times* replied that Edwin "fit snugly inside political webs."

Besides running a series of tabloid-style overview pieces (the recurring headline during the runoff: "The battle of the bluebloods"), the media focused primarily on making the candidates look as foolish as possible. Without any proof, the *Tribune* wondered aloud if The Opponent actually lived in the ward. Edwin, who had lived in the same neighborhood for 23 of his 28 years, was chastised by the paper for having the chutzpah to allege he was a lifelong ward resident. Items like these, which the gossip columnists love, appear in every campaign and rarely, if ever, affect the outcome. Still, they reflect the patronizing attitude of so many political reporters who believe that, on the evolutionary scale, can-

Behind the office we found garbage bags full of Edwin's posters. Three days later our phone lines were mysteriously snipped.

didates are to used car salesmen what baboons are to the rest of us. Their attitude seems to be: whatever you're selling, we're not buying.

A certain press skepticism is, of course, warranted. Campaigns are wars with each side looking for any advantage; to get it, both sides try to manipulate the press. One week before the runoff, for instance, I turned on the evening news and was shocked to hear that my favorite deli, an extremely popular spot in the middle of the ward, was going to be torn down in favor of a high rise. Shock turned to panic when The Opponent, his cursed face now getting precious air time, told the reporter he was fighting the fat-cat developers who supported Edwin and wanted to make money at the neighborhood's expense.

Not only were there no plans to tear down the deli, but both Edwin and The Opponent supported the pending city council ordinance that would prohibit the construction of a high rise on the property. The issue was phony, but coming up on election day the press, desperate for some hot political news, turned it into a cause celebre. Advantage: The Opponent.

While we were never able to land such a glorious sucker punch, we did manage a few slick jabs. When Edwin received the endorsement of a prominent public interest group, we made sure that in reporting the story the press mentioned that The Opponent was on the organization's board of directors. Our most shameful moment —one that more than any other, shows the strain campaigns place on people—occurred less than a week before the election when, after a long illness, my grandmother died. The day after she passed away, we called a local columnist who had known my grandmother. He ran the following item in the *Sun-Times*: "Popular Ada Rosenberg succumbed without realizing her ambition to campaign for her grandson, Edwin Eisendrath, 43rd ward alderman candidate." Advantage: Eisendrath.

At one level ward races are turf battles. The 43rd ward, with about 60,000 people, has an area of about four square miles. There are six major streets and only a handful of corners where they intersect. The number of busy El stations and bus stops is equally finite. A well-organized campaign should control these spots. For much of the time before the election, The Opponent, his 3-D posters at the ready, was firmly in command. He gazed from every lamp post, his blond hair and

aquiline nose making him look all too much like Robert Redford.

Before working in a campaign, I never paid the slightest attention to political posters. Most people probably don't, and the impact they have in larger contests is almost certainly negligible. Posters don't mean much, for instance, in a contest with lots of TV ads. We had none, however, and so visibility on the streets became an important way of reinforcing our name recognition. The Opponent knew this all too well. The ward was smothered with his smiling mug. Looking at a lamppost was like gazing into an eclipse. I was so self-conscious about The Opponent's posters that after passing one, I felt like shouting: "He's been airbrushed! In person he looks more like Gumby."

Our counterattack consisted of ordering thousands of hooker-red posters so big that, once up, a passerby who couldn't immediately make out the name Eisendrath emblazoned in white might think he'd wandered into China on flag day. On a Friday night ten days before the February election we gathered together a group of high school buddies and, with visions of the Sharks battling the Jets, set out to reclaim the neighborhood. That Saturday was sunny and unseasonably warm. The streets were packed with people, and everywhere they looked and as far as the eye could see, there was the name Eisendrath.

For a day anyway. On Sunday a political gadfly working for The Opponent came by to inform us that we would get a good lesson in Chicago politics if we went out back and looked in the alley. Behind the office we found garbage bags full of Edwin's posters. Three days later our phone lines were mysteriously snipped. It wasn't too long before the cop with the knack for a good headline had me quivering in the back seat of his patrol car.

Campaigning in tongues

Since the days of the machine, elections in Chicago have been held at the end of February. The theory was that in the middle of winter the only people who will work the precincts are patronage employees whose jobs depend on how well they turn out the vote. With few exceptions, however, the days of the ward heelers are over. A first-time candidate has to build from scratch a precinct operation based solely on volunteers.

This is a daunting task for a political neophyte running in an upscale ward with constituents who, if the stereotypes are to be believed, think of volunteerism in terms of joining the local health club. What Edwin needed was credibility. On paper this is hard to come by as a 28-year-old elementary school teacher. Matters certainly weren't helped any when, reporting on the campaign's first fund-raiser, one local reporter noted that it was "organized by the candidate's mother."

We combatted the image of Edwin sitting in a high chair four ways. First, we ran him ragged. At bus stops every morning. In front of high rises every evening. Knocking on doors every night. Sure, some people treated him like a Hare Krishna, but most were open-minded and willing to hear him out. During the Super Bowl he pressed the flesh in the neighborhood bars; on Valentine's Day he played the piano in homes for the elderly. On many a Sunday my nice Jewish brother sang the Gospel and made his pitch in one of several all-black churches in the ward. After one church address a lady suddenly began speaking in tongues. Though most people weren't quite so moved upon first meeting him, many of our best precinct captains were total strangers who happened by Edwin one morning on their way to work.

Second, we sought numerous endorsements. Like most campaigns we started with a citizens' committee. This list, which at the outset is the only proof the candidate has that he's not going to get shut out, consists of every third cousin and high school acquaintance you can remember. Edwin and I have no other siblings, yet we managed to find 40 relatives for the citizens' committee.

Edwin and The Opponent each fielded an all-star roster of political endorsements. The first public official to back Edwin was the ward's Democratic committeeman. Edwin had for several years been a volunteer in her organization. A former alderman who had known Edwin for years also signed on. From there the committeeman and former alderman turned to other public officials they knew and convinced them of Edwin's merits. Pretty soon three state legislators and the attorney general were having their pictures taken with Edwin and saying in press kits and in letters to constituents that they hadn't seen a political prospect like him since, well, Abe Lincoln grew whiskers. Just prior to the February election the *Tribune*, citing the position papers that its reporters found so dull, also endorsed Edwin. (The *Sun-Times*, which in February endorsed one of the candidates who failed to make the runoff, backed Edwin in April.)

Third, we contacted voters through the mail and over the phone. In four months we mailed more than 200,000 letters and pieces of campaign literature to ward residents. If someone moved into the ward, he or she got a letter from Edwin.

If someone registered to vote, a letter was sent. Three times we mailed letters or campaign newspapers to every household in the ward. Everyone over 65 was informed by the attorney general that in the city council Edwin would champion senior power; in case they forgot between the first election and the runoff the attorney general sent them a reminder letter. About half the ward residents live in high rises that don't allow volunteers to go door to door. Almost all of them received five phone calls and at least four letters. A 65-year-old newly registered Democrat who had just moved into a lakefront high rise in the ward would have received 13 letters and five phone calls—probably enough to get a pretty good sense of where Edwin stood on the issues.

Even at the ward level this is extremely expensive, underscoring that with rare exception the key to becoming a credible candidate is money. You can get endorsed by the Pope and still lose the Catholic vote if you don't have the money to let people know it. Likewise, no candidate, no matter how tireless, can come into contact with even a small percentage of the voters. In this respect Edwin was lucky. He had a network of family and friends willing to make generous financial contributions. He also had enough standing in the community to generate a large number of modest contributions. Edwin's good fortune extended to his having a best friend who's a fund-raising genius. The three candidates who failed to make the runoff were all badly outspent. Undoubtedly that helped cripple their campaigns. In the runoff, however, Edwin and The Opponent went at it practically dollar for dollar.

There is no such thing as raising too much money, because in a campaign there is no such thing as overkill. This is especially true in a campaign like ours where, because of the expense, no polls were taken. As far as we could tell, the bundles of letters we sent out each day were providing voters with free bathroom wallpaper. So tenuous was our sense of progress that we treasured every positive comment and any slipup haunted us for weeks. At a bus stop one morning, after about 30 minutes of tucking Edwin's campaign literature leper-like into the overcoat pockets of people too cold to reach out their hands, let alone talk, one woman approached me with a big smile and her arm out. She said she was thinking of voting for Edwin but wanted to know more. Seeing a bus approaching in the distance I launched into my two-minute offense.

Harvardeducatedpublicschoolteacher, I said. Plans to cut city spending. She teed the ball up for me and asked how. Knowingly I replied: pensions and health benefits of city workers need to be trimmed. Her eyes narrowed, and just before boarding her bus she told me what I already knew: she worked for the city. As sure as I was standing there I knew the election had just been lost.

The only tangible evidence that we were moving forward was the growth of the volunteer operation—the fourth leg of our campaign strategy. Faced with the two coldest months of the year, people were actually coming forward and volunteering to knock on doors: accountants, people who were unemployed, lawyers, doctors, policemen, bankers. Out of nowhere came a real estate broker who, in addition to becoming a terrific precinct captain, managed to get the waitresses at a popular neighborhood restaurant to wear sweatshirts with Edwin's name on them. Another precinct captain who would have done the Boss proud was a bus driver who, whenever his bus took him through the ward, laid out Edwin's campaign literature on all the seats.

The DINKS deliver

We had little to offer these people except ideas. No money, no jobs, and certainly no glamour. And neither during nor after the campaign did any of our workers come asking favors. Yet most of those who got involved (measured either in time or money) were the young urban professionals so often bashed by pundits for having no vision beyond the edge of the nearest bond pit. Of the more than 400 people who helped out, only a handful had ever been involved in a campaign before. Together we learned the tricks of the campaign trade: how to canvas neighborhoods to find out where people stand; how to "run voters" on election day to make sure the people who said they would vote for Edwin actually went to the polls. For a group that will be remembered for making the eighties a decade of avarice, it was a moving display of selflessness. The new generation of precinct captains may never be as dogged as their machine predecessors, but in the clutch they were no less enthusiastic. There are 72 precincts in the 43rd ward. On election day, each captain had to be at his or her precinct by 5:30 a.m. When I called at 5 a.m. to make sure everyone was getting ready, not a single one was still in bed.

Edwin beat The Opponent. They raised and spent about the same money, matched endorsements coattail for coattail, and got an equal amount of publicity. The Opponent is four years older and his resume—which includes a stint as

counsel to the local Better Government Association and as a legislative aide to former Rep. Abner Mikva—would do George Bush proud. Yet Edwin got 65 percent of the vote.

Why the rout? One reason was The Opponent's association with Harold Washington. Washington's lack of popularity in the 43rd ward and The Opponent's association with him hurt. The Opponent also suffered from the where's-the-beef phenomenon. His resume was so gold-plated that he decided to run on it. Edwin, by contrast, ran on an agenda: school reform and city finances. Voters received equal amounts of literature from the candidates, but the messages couldn't have been more different. The Opponent talked about what he had done; Edwin talked about what he was going to do.

Another reason was that, despite my urgings to the contrary, cooler heads did prevail. In debates and in the literature we distributed, Edwin was monotonously positive. In community forums he talked about what he planned to accomplish. The Opponent, by contrast, was negative. For months, he thumbed Edwin more times than a lousy club fighter. Six days before the runoff election The Opponent mailed out an "Urgentgram" to most ward residents. In it he accused Edwin of "desperation tactics...a vicious whisper and smear campaign...'Hit' pieces in local media." Mistaking an overzealous reporter for one of our campaign workers, the Urgentgram declared: "Days ago, two people were caught ransacking garbage at my house, taking pictures through my mail slot." Yet on election day, Edwin won 71 of the ward's 72 precincts.

Running a clean campaign helped Edwin gain voters' trust. The Opponent, bless his slickness, was too smooth. In the 43rd ward lawyers outnumber public school teachers probably 100 to 1. Many parents send their children to private schools. Yet a public school teacher whomped three attorneys. In the end, the yuppies and the DINKS did think, and in doing so they came to appreciate the value of sacrifice and working for the common good. No one traded in his BMW, but many came out and volunteered, and almost all ended up with a far less cynical view of the political process.

I know I did.

The Arms Race of Campaign Financing

Worried that political races are becoming so expensive that soon only the wealthy will be candidates, states are restricting campaign funds, coming in and going out.

Sandra Singer

Sandra Singer is a principal research analyst in NCSL's Legislative Management program.

"Afool and his money...are soon elected." So says one of the buttons for sale in a local gift shop. Those who hold elective offices may know better, but the button illustrates the public's perception that money exerts too much influence on the outcome of elections.

When Representative Fran Carlton first ran for the Florida House of Representatives in 1976, she spent $7,000 to beat an incumbent in a six-member district of a half million people. Ten years later, after Florida had changed to single-member districts—a move that was supposed to decrease the cost of campaigns—Carlton spent $140,000 to win in a district of 82,000 people. The costs, she says, are putting public office "out of sight for some folks. To be a successful politician, you must be a successful fund-raiser."

Campaign costs have risen dramatically in recent years. Although the most startling numbers come from populous states like California or New Jersey, costs in smaller states are also making great leaps. California has the most expensive legislative races in the country—Senate and Assembly seats average over $500,000. In 1986, $57 million was spent on legislative races, up $8 million from 1984. And in 1990, with legislators fearful of losing seats under the new reapportionment plan,

the California Commission on Campaign Financing predicts that $100 million could be spent on the 100 seats up for election.

New Jersey's 1987 legislative campaigns exceeded $11.3 million, more than double the amount spent in 1983. Costs in nine separate districts topped $500,000. In Washington, between 1976 and 1986, the average Senate race jumped from $10,226 to $54,322, and campaign costs for House seats went from $7,490 to $23,074.

Costs are also going up in North Carolina where winning candidates raised an average of $6,396 for a House seat in 1984 and $11,671 just two years later. Representative Walter Jones Jr.'s staff predicts that unless these trends are stopped, House candidates could be raising as much as $30,000 in 1990 and as much as $48,000 in 1992. Senate war chests could be as high as $85,000 in 1992.

States have been taking action in recent years to combat both the perception of undue influence from large contributors and the rising cost of campaigns, passing laws to limit contributions and expenditures and provide for public funding. Limitations on contributions broaden a candidate's base of support and lessen the appearance of undue influence from special interests, but they don't lower campaign costs. The only way to do that is through expenditure limitations, which must be coupled with voluntary public funding

to be constitutional.

Florida, Ohio and Oregon have recently enacted public funding and Arizona has added contribution limits which go into effect this year. The Rhode Island General Assembly, directed by an initiative passed in 1986, is putting into motion a new system of public funding with contribution and spending limits. The states of Connecticut and New York have commissions studying the issues.

New York City recently enacted public funding with limitations on contributions and expenditures in city council races. (And although this is "only" a city, its $28 million dollar program is bigger than that of many states.) In 1987 Sacramento County in California became the first county to enact public funding with contribution and expenditure limits.

Other state legislatures have made attempts at reforms. Bills providing for public funding have passed in California, Illinois and, most recently, Iowa, but were vetoed by their governors. And early this year, in the Washington House a public funding bill died in conference committee.

Why are so many people worried about our systems of campaign financing? Says Representative Jones of North Carolina, "When the average-income person can't afford to run for office, our democratic process is suffering. We're becoming an elitist form of government in which only the well-to-do or retirees will be candidates."

What makes it difficult for those average-income challengers is that they are up against political action committee (PAC) money (almost 99 percent goes to incumbents) and wealthy candidates who may spend as much of their own money as they wish unless limitations are imposed. In fact, the incumbents have such advantages that the nationwide re-election rate is staggeringly high. In 1986, California incumbent senators outspent challengers by a ratio of 62 to 1, and incumbent assemblymen outspent their challengers by 35 to 1. Not one single incumbent lost in that election. And in preparation for the 1988 election, California incumbents already have raised $25 million during the non-election year of 1987.

PAC money is a serious issue in itself. New Jersey Assemblyman Bill Schluter claims that "contributions have bought access, good will and availability." Alan Rosenthal, director of the Eagleton Institute of Politics at Rutgers University, says "the environment is getting a little tainted. It gives an unseemly appearance because it looks like people are buying influence, or more. Although it's difficult to demonstrate, legislators are aware and concerned about contributors. I don't know what that buys, but certainly it buys a sympathetic ear." If nothing else, the PAC situation is "more of a perception problem. But as long as it's there, it has a negative effect on voters and may be one of the reasons they don't turn out to vote," says Representative Jones.

"PACs have too much influence on incumbents," says Robert Stern, general counsel for the California Commission on Campaign Financing. "One PAC gave at least $500 to all but one of the 117 incumbents that were up for re-election last time, regardless of their political philosophy. When we pointed that out, they said they must have missed that one and they would get some money to him, too. They give to people in power, not on philosophy."

Dr. Joseph Hatch, chairman of the board of the American Medical Political Action Committee (AMPAC), disagrees. "PACs will support someone they think is philosophically in line with them. We're very interested in people's past voting records. That's how we know who to support." He explains that this is why studies show a correlation between contributions from PACs and members' voting records on those PACs' issues; it's not because PACs are buying votes.

Rosenthal doesn't think PACs have excessive influence. What bothers him more is the emphasis that legislators have to give to fund-raising. The preoccupation with financing campaigns means too much time spent on fund-raising and not enough time working on significant bills.

In a number of states, fund-raising is an important function of the legislative leadership. They raise large sums of money and dole it out to candidates. Prohibiting or restricting transfers between politicians is a coming trend, according to campaign finance reformers. Ed Feigenbaum, legal counsel for the Hudson Institute in Indianapolis, says the practice allows leaders to support loyal incumbents or recruit challengers. "It is undue influence," he says, "and it's the elected official who's buying the influence."

Rosenthal, on the other hand, thinks it would be harmful to deny leadership the ability to raise funds. "It's like a 'share-the-wealth' plan whereby safe, secure legislators can give up something to the least safe and secure." Although Stern is against transfers, he says one good thing about them is that it helps competition by funneling some of the money to challengers.

Some argue that transfers strengthen the parties by making individual legislators more accountable to leadership. But Stern counters that it's really only the individual leaders who are strengthened. Herbert Alexander, director of Citizens' Research Foundation in Los Angeles and an expert on campaign finance, points out that banning transfers could affect parties differently. For instance, in California, Republicans can raise more at the local level, whereas Democrats raise more through leadership. Alexander doesn't object to transfers in general, but he prefers that they come from the parties. That would strengthen the parties and leave less power to personality.

An alternative view espoused by the Citizens League in Minneapolis is that leaders need such power to enable the legislative process to work as intended. "Caucus leaders, to the degree they can mobilize members' votes, have access to the one thing needed to pass laws: a majority vote. Few other individuals can get this to happen," states a report "Power to the Process," published by the League. As for abuse of that power, the report notes that leaders "are chosen by their peers when the legislature organizes every two years ...and therefore must be directly responsive to membership concerns." Furthermore, "if members are unhappy about leadership choices, they are free to vote against the leaders."

Bill Kelly, director of government relations for Norwest Corporation in Minneapolis and co-chairman of the Citizens League study, argues that leaders need tools with which to lead. The traditional methods of leading have eroded, he says. Legislators now have personal staff and no longer depend on leadership for staff help. And the increased percentage of funds coming from special interests lessens the importance of caucus funds. A bill was introduced in Minnesota's 1988 session that would prohibit individual fund-raisers during the session. Caucus fund-raisers would be allowed, and leaders could distribute the money raised.

How do contributors feel about all these changes? Many say they want to continue being able to give as much as they choose to whomever they choose. But stories also abound of lobbyists who are tired of the "shakedowns" and being "expected" to give. Contributions are being sought these days, all year long, every year—not just before elections. "It's not 'campaign contributions.' It's just 'money' they're giving. It's irrelevant to the election," Stern says.

"People are becoming professional politicians these days. Politics is their livelihood, and they must raise money to fend off opponents in primary and general elections."

Twenty-three states have contribution limits of various types (individual,

PAC, single donation, aggregate donation, etc.) ranging from $250 to $150,000. Twenty-three states prohibit corporate contributions, and 13 limit the size of their contributions. Nine states prohibit labor union contributions and 17 more limit them. Two states limit off-year contributions. Texas prohibits all contributions during the 120-day session and the 30 days preceding it. Minnesota merely lowers the contribution limits by a very large percentage during the off year.

According to the the U.S. Supreme Court in the case of *Buckley vs. Valeo,* the only way to use expenditure limits without impermissibly restricting freedom of speech is to couple them with voluntary public funding.

Stern feels that the Court was probably incorrect on *Buckley* and predicts that Congress will pass a constitutional amendment within the next 15 years that will essentially overrule the decision. Feigenbaum agrees. He feels that "the Court has come down less hard on commercial speech and other areas that have less impact than campaign finance." U.S. Senator Ernest "Fritz" Hollings of South Carolina and U.S. Representative Charles E. Schumer of New York have already introduced such bills in their respective houses. From Representative Jones' point of view, if campaign finance laws open up the process to those who can't raise big money, "that's what freedom of speech is all about."

Twenty-two states have enacted some method of public funding. Twenty of these raise money for the programs through the tax system. Twelve use a tax check-off on the state income tax form similar to the federal system. Eight use tax add-ons (which increase the taxpayer's liability) in a similar fashion. Florida, with no state income tax, provides legislative appropriations. Oklahoma passed public funding in 1979, but it never went into operation.

The tax system can also be used as an incentive for individual contributions. Alaska allows full tax credits for campaign contributions, and four states and Washington, D.C. allow partial credits. Five states allow tax deductions.

Twelve states give public funding money to the parties, while eight give it to candidates' committees. Some states require the parties to distribute

Q&A

How can campaign expenditures be limited?

Various ceilings can be set on contributions depending on whether the contributor is an individual, PAC, party or caucus. There can also be aggregate limits per contributing entity for each election. A New Jersey bill would prevent organizations from avoiding limits by creating a number of affiliated PACs. Limits can apply to election years only, or off-year contributions can be limited or prohibited. Loans can be viewed as contributions and be limited.

What about transferring money?

Transfers of funds can be prohibited from all entities or allowed only from certain types such as caucuses.

Are there ways to hold down campaign costs?

Yes. Spending caps can be set for the general election or can include the primary as well. They can be set at specific amounts or with an equation. A North Carolina proposal would set limits for legislative races at the number of votes cast for the highest House and Senate vote-getter in the last presidential election times $1.

What are some new approaches to matching funds?

A California initiative would set the match at three state dollars for every $1 in contributions of $250 or less and increase it to a 5:1 match for contributions inside a candidate's district. A Washington bill would have increased spending limits and matching funds for a candidate if his opponent raised more than the limits or did not apply for the program.

What about independent expenditures?

They could be regulated by capping the amount a contributor can spend independently in support of a candidate (or in opposition to his opponent) after that contributor has given more than a certain amount to the candidate.

How are states dealing with fraud?

Fraud can be attacked in a number of ways. A New Jersey bill, for instance, prohibits corporate and union officers from accepting a salary increase in order to give it to a campaign.

some of the money to candidates, and some states prohibit it. When parties use the money mostly for party operations, it strengthens the parties, but it doesn't help the candidates much or keep down the costs of campaigns.

Seven states limit expenditures as a condition for receiving matching funds. Three of these, Hawaii, Minnesota and Wisconsin, provide funding for legislative campaigns. The others provide only for gubernatorial or other races for statewide office.

The effectiveness of these programs depends upon a number of factors. Alexander says, "There's a lot of nostalgia for the low cost of campaigns, but it's not realistic." There are reasons why some costs simply aren't controllable in direct terms, he says. "The first is inflation. The second is the professionalization of politics. There are so many people to hire—professional campaign managers, advertising specialists, computer specialists, election lawyers, and more. The third is job security. People are becoming professional politicians these days. Politics is their livelihood, and they must raise money to fend off opponents in primary and general elections."

Other factors come into play in setting up public financing programs. First, enough funds must be generated for a successful public funding program. The tax add-on states often have a problem because even though the added tax liability is only $1 to $5, citizen participation is extremely low, averaging 1.6 percent. Participation rates vary greatly in the tax check-off states, but are generally much higher and have gone as high as 54 percent in Hawaii in 1983.

For states with voluntary expenditure limits, it's essential to set the limits at a reasonable level. If they are too high, they won't do any good. But if they're unrealistically low, candidates won't agree to the voluntary programs because they know they won't be able to wage an effective campaign without spending more. This was the case in Minnesota, where candidates were not participating in the program until the matching funds and the spending limits were brought up to higher levels. Low spending limits also tend to favor incumbents, who don't need to spend as much as challengers to get their messages out. Even in such cases though, public funding can sometimes do more help than harm to challengers by providing funds that they might not otherwise be able to raise.

"Loopholes" can also eat into a system's effectiveness. But as Alexander says, "What is a loophole to one is a constitutional right to another. They are legal mechanisms enacted by incumbents to protect themselves and their parties' interests."

Independent expenditures and "bundling" are common mechanisms. Independent expenditures are funds spent by an individual or organization for or against a candidate but without any coordination with any candidate. It has been ruled that independent expenditures cannot be restricted, as a function of freedom of speech.

Bundling is used by PACs to get around the contribution limitations. Instead of collecting money from individuals and then disbursing that money in the name of the PAC, the organization tells individual contributors to make out their checks to specific candidates. Then the PAC takes a stack of individual checks, which might well add up to more than the PAC could contribute itself, and

delivers it in a bundle to the candidate. Only Arizona prohibits the practice. To date, neither independent expenditures nor bundling have been used extensively at the state level, but both are becoming problems at the federal level and could increase in the states as well.

To make any program work, a state needs a commission that is alert and well-funded to enforce its provisions. To have any effect whatsoever, disclosure reports must be collected, analyzed and disseminated to the public on a timely basis. Likewise, to mean anything, contribution and spending limitations must be monitored and enforced. Feigenbaum notes that thresholds for reporting contributions must be realistic as well. It's impossible for candidates and commissions to keep track of every $25 contribution. He feels that a coming trend is to require reporting of last-minute contributions and expenditures within 24 hours because that information is useless for purposes of informing the public if it isn't disclosed until after the election.

Campaign funding isn't a problem in every state. Bill Russell, chief counsel for Vermont's General Assembly,

claims that in Vermont "you can run on as much as it takes to put gas in your Volkswagen to drive around knocking on people's doors." But for the vast majority of states, campaign finance problems will become increasingly serious unless steps are taken. Despite initial difficulties, more and more states are both undertaking reforms and making adjustments to them as they learn to make them workable.

The more comprehensive programs —Michigan, Minnesota, New Jersey, Wisconsin, the city of Seattle and the federal system—are working well. "Very few inclusive laws have been repealed," says Stern. And, in fact, Seattle first enacted its public finance system in 1979, allowed it to sunset in 1981 and then re-enacted it in 1984. The reforms won't solve all the problems. Candidates in hotly contested races will usually opt out of the public funding systems so they can fight with as many resources as they can lay their hands on. But the money can be used in the safer districts to lessen the burden of fund-raising, reduce the appearance of undue influence and hold down the cost of campaigning.

Buying State Access

Who cares who wins a state treasurer election? Wall Street does: The investment banks that underwrite bond issues are heavy contributors in state and local races.

W. JOHN MOORE

Utah state treasurer Edward T. Alter faces a dilemma. A recent *Salt Lake Tribune* poll shows him trailing his likely Democratic opponent in November by almost 40 percentage points. Up against a challenger who has better name recognition in the state than he does, Alter, who is well respected in New York City financial circles and is a former president of the National Association of State Treasurers, recognizes the need to build a campaign war chest. He also realizes that it is almost certain that most of his campaign money will come from Wall Street, from the very industry that he conducts state business with virtually every day.

The thought of soliciting money on Wall Street clearly bothers Alter. Yet, he estimates, up to 80 per cent of his campaign contributions in 1984 came from bankers and bond lawyers. He predicts the same percentage this year, mainly because the state treasurer's race hardly excites the public's fancy and produces grass-roots campaign dollars. "It's a tough sell when you're talking about revenue floats and cash mobility and all the other things treasurers do for a living," he said. "None of these are sexy or eye-catching" to the public.

But Wall Street thrives on just such matters, which can make or break an investment banking firm's public finance department. "You come back to the people who know who you are and might have some appreciation for the job you've

Research assistance by William Berezansky

done," Alter said. "I wish I could say I found another way and that I could tell you I don't need those guys, but it is just not true."

Other politicians share Alter's need for campaign money but not his reservation about taking it from Wall Street—or from any other industry that thrives on doing business with state and local government. And of course there is the perception that Wall Street investment banks have the money. "They have the largest arteries: It is easier to get the needle in," said Maine treasurer Samuel Shapiro (who is elected by the Legislature).

The indications are that Wall Street is not hesitant about making campaign donations. Unencumbered by many of the contribution limits and disclosure requirements that apply to federal election campaigns, Wall Street bankers and lawyers have splurged at the state and local levels, where there is often a bigger bang for the buck.

At the federal level, contributions by political action committees (PACs) are limited to $5,000 per candidate for a primary election and $5,000 per candidate for a general election, and contributions by individuals are limited to $1,000 per candidate per election. In many states and localities, no such restrictions apply. Information from some key states suggests that individual Wall Street firms are probably spending hundreds of thousands of dollars nationwide electing their favored candidates to state and local offices.

It is impossible to determine the full extent of these contributions because many states don't require the disclosure of

campaign contributors, and those that do require such disclosures use different reporting systems. And contributions to state and local officials are not required to be filed with the Federal Election Commission (FEC), although some details can be gleaned from FEC reports. And leading Wall Street firms declined to discuss their total campaign outlays.

Based on information from FEC reports, state campaign finance offices, state branches of Common Cause, the self-styled citizens' group, newspaper accounts and *Institutional Investor,* which revealed Wall Street's concerns over the contributions, it is clear that campaign dollars flow to almost every state from virtually every Wall Street bond underwriter.

Contributions from these investment bank PACs to individual state and local candidates sometimes run into tens of thousands of dollars. Many of the firms have contributed to lesser-known state officials such as auditors, comptrollers and treasurers, who have the power to determine which Wall Street banks will share in lucrative state financial business.

For example, Smith Barney, Harris Upham & Co. Inc. contributed $30,000 in 1985–86 to the late California Treasurer Jesse Unruh, who once called money "the mother's milk of politics." The firm also served as underwriter for $1.9 billion worth of California state and local bonds sold over that period and ranked among the state's top seven underwriters both years. *(See table, p. 58).*

In New York City, Merrill Lynch & Co. Inc. was the biggest contributor to Mayor

Edward I. Koch during an 18-month period ending on Jan. 15, according to figures compiled by state Sen. Franz S. Leichter, a Manhattan Democrat who issues periodic reports on New York campaign finances. Last year, Merrill Lynch ranked second in the underwriting volume for New York City bonds, as it did in 1986. Figures compiled by the New York State Commission on Government Integrity also showed that almost 60 per cent of State comptroller Edward V. Regan's campaign contributions came from investment banks that conduct financial business for the state. (See chart, p. 60). Chemical Bank, one of the banks that holds the city's deposits, contributed $9,000 to Koch during that 18-month period.

Wall Street firms also contribute big bucks to gubernatorial campaigns. As an example of what the Chicago Tribune dubbed "the big bucks of pinstripe patronage," 13 investment banking firms contributed nearly $100,000 to Republican Gov. James R. Thompson Jr.'s 1986 reelection campaign and later handled the sale of highway bonds that brought those firms $8 million in total fees. The top seven out-of-state contributors to that campaign were Wall Street firms, according to Common Cause/Illinois. The 10th was the New York law firm of Hawkins Delafield & Wood, which does financial work for the state. Merrill Lynch, the leading out-of-state contributor and the fifth-biggest contributor over all, gave $24,000 to Thompson's 1986 campaign. Shearson Lehman Brothers Inc. ranked eighth over all, with $20,000, followed by Bear, Stearns & Co. Inc., Salomon Brothers Inc. and Kidder, Peabody & Co. Inc. Meanwhile, Smith Barney was the fourth-biggest special-interest donor to Democrat Adlai E. Stevenson III's gubernatorial campaign. According to Common Cause/Illinois, underwriters and banks gave almost $200,000 more in the 1986 election than they did in 1982.

During New Jersey Gov. Thomas H. Kean's reelection campaign in 1985, five investment banking concerns that had collected fees of $4.8 million on bond issues since 1982 gave a total of $257,250 to the state Republican Party. Bear, Stearns topped the list with $85,050 in contributions, according to New Jersey Democratic Party officials.

Smith Barney also gave $10,000 in 1986 to both New York Lt. Gov. Stan Lundine and Texas Gov. William P. Clements Jr., according to FEC reports. Donaldson, Lufkin & Jenrette Securities Corp. contributed $10,000 in 1986 to losing gubernatorial candidates in Kentucky and Pennsylvania, and last year, it opted for a $1,500 contribution to the winner of the 1986 Pennsylvania gubernatorial race, Robert P. Casey.

Philadelphia mayoral candidate Frank L. Rizzo, a blue-collar kind of guy, received a $5,000 contribution from Dillon Read & Co. in 1987. That Wall Street investment house also gave $1,000 to Denver Mayor Federico Peña and $2,500 to Houston Mayor Kathryn T. Whitmire. The New Jersey Republican state committee collected $5,000 from the firm. Another $1,000 went to the Republican majority in the New Jersey Assembly. Dillon Read also contributed $3,000 in 1987 to New Yorkers for Koch 1989.

The issue of special-interest campaign contributions intruded briefly into this year's Democratic presidential campaign. Annoyed with the attention shown by rival candidates and by the news media about the money he received from PACs, Richard A. Gephardt questioned Massachusetts Gov. Michael S. Dukakis's campaign contributions. "An analysis of Federal Election Commission records shows that Gov. Dukakis has received hundreds of thousands of dollars from an all-star cast of special interests doing business with the commonwealth of Massachusetts," a Gephardt campaign press release said in February.

More than $450,000 of the $2.1 million raised by the Dukakis campaign in the second quarter of 1987 came from lawyers and law firms doing business with the state, according to the Gephardt campaign. Twenty-four lawyers with the Boston law firm of Mintz, Levin, Cohn, Ferris, Glovsky and Popeo, bond counsel for the state and the Massachusetts Convention Center Authority, contributed money to the Dukakis presidential campaign. Ninety investment bankers from nine firms that manage state bond issues contributed $44,000, The Boston Herald has reported. (See NJ, 4/23/88, p. 1068.)

Investment banks are hardly the only entities that are dependent on government business and give campaign contributions to state and local officials. Architects and engineers with an eye on lucrative road and bridge contracts have become active givers in some state and local races. Advertising agencies with state contracts sometimes give campaign contributions. Bozell, Jacobs, Kenyon & Eckhardt Inc., a New York City agency that was awarded $3.2 million worth of no-bid contracts to promote New Jersey tourism, gave $19,000 to Republican candidates in 1985, according to a New Jersey Democratic Party report. Computer contractors and companies pushing privatization schemes have started giving money.

WALKING A FINE LINE

Despite questions raised about the propriety of some campaign contributions, Wall Street giving is legal. And Wall Street executives deny that they have bar-

tered bucks for business. In fact, both state officials and investment bankers expressed distaste for the system. Nevertheless, numerous examples suggest that campaign contributions are considered good business. "You give to get," a New York City investment banker conceded.

"The welfare state has been turned into a business," William Stern, a New York business executive and former campaign manager for Gov. Mario M. Cuomo, told the New York state integrity commission.

"Those who are dependent on government decisions like to have people in office with whom they have a relationship and, at the margin, will be favorably disposed to them," Edwin M. Epstein, a professor of business and public policy at the University of California (Berkeley), told the commission.

The evidence about money going from Wall Street firms into the political arena gives at least the appearance that the game might be rigged for the rich and powerful. "Public confidence in the honesty and integrity of government can be shattered by the staggering sums of money contributed by those doing business with government," John D. Feerick, chairman of the New York state integrity commission and dean of the Fordham University Law School, warned during a March hearing on campaign money.

In an interview, Feerick said there is an appearance problem when a private company contributes to government officials and then turns to government for assistance or benefits. "The public," Feerick said, "is suspicious where there is a connection between a subsequent benefit and an earlier campaign contribution."

"The contributions may be legal and aboveboard, but it undermines the system. I would term it legalized corruption," said Gary Snyderman, managing director of Common Cause/Illinois. "We have not seen allegations that contracts have absolutely been bought for campaign contributions. . . . But if this is allowed to continue, there is the increasing danger that one of these days we will find that the money has gotten too much and someone has given in to temptation."

Wall Street can ill afford another attack on its reputation. Allegations of insider trading abuses, the stock market's plunge on Black Monday and the decisions by some banks to disband their municipal bond departments have created an industry whose credibility is shaky at best.

According to many investment bankers, the growing financial dependency of investment banks on state and local government for underwriting business in an era of cutthroat competition, coupled with the soaring costs of state and local campaigns, creates an unhealthy situation. "It has gotten a little out of hand."

New Rules of the Game in Louisiana

Money and politics have been as much a combination in Louisiana as cold beer and hot food. But as a gubernatorial candidate, Democratic Rep. Buddy Roemer served notice that the times are changing. He eschewed large campaign contributions from special interests, including Louisiana bond lawyers and Wall Street bankers. Even before he was sworn in as governor in March, Roemer trekked to New York in January and told the investment community that "Louisiana is not for sale."

Now Roemer has implemented some of his promised reforms. Before selecting a six-member underwriting team to manage an expected $1 billion financing by the new Louisiana Recovery District, state officials interviewed 28 firms, quizzing the bankers on their fees and their technical qualifications for the job. "Before, there was no interview process, there was no 'request for proposal,' there were no requirements to present your credentials," a Wall Street banker said. "It sent a strong signal that this guy means business."

"This was a good-faith effort to professionalize operations and level the playing field," state treasurer Mary L. Landrieu said. "In the past, politics reared its ugly head and decisions were made behind closed doors. While no process is perfect, this is clearly superior to any that went on before."

Law firms have learned the same lesson. After Roemer required law firms to submit sealed bids for the $1 billion deal, the New Orleans firm of Foley & Judell won with a $60,000 bid. A year ago, the firm collected fees of $820,000 for handling a similar-sized bond issue. "Now is the time for all good men to come to the aid of their country," said William H. Beck Jr., a Foley & Judell partner, who said the firm's fee was basically a donation to help the impoverished state government. The next-lowest bid was $120,000.

"It adds to the competitive juices to do it this way," Roemer explained in an interview, acknowledging that the closed bids from bond counsel and close scrutiny of underwriters symbolize a new direction for Louisiana. "In years past, this has been a big business with a lot of special-interest overtones in a state that has had, as part of its government philosophy, the use of bonds. And that has led to some abuses," Roemer said. "There were some relationships between politicians and investment types that meant large political contributions running into six digits."

Some underwriters suggest that the old system was a little fishy. "All I know is that there are times when the [state] issuers don't select the people who have done the best job of buying bonds for localities on the competitive bids," said Edward Roddy, a vice president with the banking firm of Scharff & Jones in New Orleans. "If somebody has a great track record with competitive bidding but is not considered worth hiring for a negotiated issue, it makes you wonder."

The influx of Wall Street money into state political campaigns coincides with an increase in negotiated bond sales compared to competitive bond sales, said James C. Brandt, executive director of the Bureau of Governmental Research, a public-interest group in New Orleans. Brandt, executive director of the Bureau of Governmental Research, a public-interest group in New Orleans.

According to the *The Times Picayune* in New Orleans, investment bankers and law firms contributed more than $300,000 last year in 12 state races involving officials who traditionally decide the allocation of the bond business. Donaldson, Lufkin & Jenrette Securities Corp., which helped underwrite $2.69 billion worth of bonds in 1987 and established a Baton Rouge office headed by a former assistant state treasurer, led the way with contributions of $56,800 in 1987, twice the amount given by any of its competitors. The contributions included $20,000 to state Sen. Sammy Nunez. Six months before, Nunez, a member of the state bond commission, recommended that Donaldson, Lufkin & Jenrette get the business for a $1.1 billion refinancing of Louisiana general obligation bonds. The commission approved the selection of the firm on a 9-4 vote.

Donaldson, Lufkin & Jenrette "has made campaign contributions and will continue to make them in the future. It's the American way," James A. Cooper, a senior vice president of the firm, told the *Times Picayune*.

Other Wall Street firms also gave last year in Louisiana, a state with no campaign contribution limits. Shearson Lehman Brothers Inc. contributed $21,000; Bear, Stearns & Co. Inc. and E.F. Hutton & Co. Inc. gave $10,000 each. Lesser amounts came from Drexel, Burnham & Lambert Inc., Kidder, Peabody & Co. Inc. and Merrill Lynch Capital Markets.

Cranston Securities Corp. of Washington contributed $26,500. A New Orleans banker, Hattier, Sanford, & Reynoir, was third with $26,000. The biggest amount in 1987 came from individual attorneys in the Foley & Judell firm: Their lawyers' total contributions were $59,337.

Roemer, who is readying a campaign finance reform package, and Landrieu ran for office last year without much help from special interests. Former Gov. Edwin W. Edwards collected $53,000 from underwriters and lawyers; Roemer received $3,000. Landrieu's opponents, Claude (Buddy) Leach and Thomas Burbank, got $22,500 and $17,000, respectively. Landrieu received $5,500 out of total contributions of about $750,000, according to state reports.

said Carol Bellamy, a vice president at Morgan Stanley & Co. Inc. and a former deputy mayor of New York. And Iowa state treasurer Michael Fitzgerald said, "The fact is, if it is not a blood relative, it's reaching to think that contributors are just interested in good government and your office."

Call it Gucci giving or political panhandling, investment banks and state officials seem to be enjoying an ever-cozier relationship. State and local officials and the municipal bond fraternity have forged an alliance in opposition to tough federal restrictions on tax-exempt financing, for example. Few state officials or bankers question the right of Wall Street firms to contribute to state and local campaigns, despite worries that the amounts in some cases may be excessive. "There is a fine line between raising money from Wall Street and making sure that it doesn't influence your job, but the line is there," said Michigan Treasurer Robert A. Bowman, an appointed official.

"The test is one of scale," Bellamy said, rather than a question of contributing or not contributing to a campaign.

Only in the rare case of actual corruption does anyone insinuate that a political contribution was exchanged for a specific government favor. In many cases, bond underwriters are selected on the basis of sealed bids. Even in those instances in which bond issues are negotiated, rather than awarded by competitive bids, public and news media scrutiny ensure a fair price, many bond experts emphasize. "You don't buy business anyplace," said Joseph M. Giglio, a managing director for public finance at Bear, Stearns.

But others argue that the contributions are designed to provide access to the appropriate state and local officials. To some public finance experts, political contributions are simply an entrance fee, letting the company into the game but hardly guaranteeing a victory. Many state officials and investment bankers maintain that the fact that virtually all Wall Street firms give to most campaigns means that the best choice will be made. Under the existing system, treasurers and comptrollers can choose the best banker and maximize their campaign donations at the same time, a state official joked.

The rising cost of state and local campaigns is widely blamed for officials' willingness to squeeze Wall Street for more money. An Arizona legislative race now costs seven times more than it did in 1974, according to a recent study, "Money and Politics 1988," by Arizona Common Cause. According to the 1987 Common Cause/Illinois report, Thompson received more special-interest money in his 1986 gubernatorial campaign than both he and his Democratic opponent got in

Underwriting, Check Writing

Wall Street firms and California underwriters have contributed thousands of dollars in state political campaigns. The charts below show the top 10 underwriters of California state and local bonds in California in 1985 and the political contributions by the same firms to Republican Gov. George Deukmejian and the late Democratic treasurer Jesse Unruh in 1985-86.

Top 10 Underwriters

Firm	Volume (in millions)
Merrill Lynch Capital Markets	$3,609.3
Goldman, Sachs & Co	2,107.5
PaineWebber Inc.	1,716.6
E. F. Hutton & Co. Inc.	1,549.6
Salomon Brothers Inc.	1,547.8
The First Boston Corp.	1,492.0
Smith Barney, Harris Upham & Co. Inc.	1,129.3
Bank of America NT&SA	1,122.7
Shearson Lehman Brothers Inc.	964.3
Miller & Schroeder Financial	915.0

SOURCES: Securities Data Co.; *The Bond Buyer*

Contributions to Deukmejian

Firm	Amount
Merrill Lynch Capital Markets	$30,000
Goldman, Sachs & Co.	0
PaineWebber Inc.	2,00
E.F Hutton & Co. Inc.	11,000
Salomon Brothers Inc.	10,000
The First Boston Corp.	10,000
Smith Barney, Harris Upham & Co. Inc.	0
Bank of America NT&SA	36,500
Shearson Lehman Brothers Inc.	9,000
Miller & Schroeder Financial	2,500

Contributions to Unruh

Merrill Lynch Capital Markets	$26,000
Goldman, Sachs & Co.	0
PaineWebber Inc.	20,500
E. F. Hutton & Co. Inc.	34,500
Salomon Brothers Inc.	19,700
The First Boston Corp.	18,500
Smith Barney, Harris Upham & Co. Inc.	30,000
Bank of America NT&SA	24,000
Shearson Lehman Brothers Inc.	30,000
Miller & Schroeder Financial	3,000

SOURCE: California Fair Political Practices Commission

1982. Total campaign spending in all Colorado statewide races jumped from $1.7 million in 1974 to $7.8 million in 1986, according to a recent Colorado Common Cause study. When Koch ran for mayor of New York City in 1977, when he had a tough primary fight, he spent $1.7 million; in 1985, with little opposition, Koch spent $7.5 million in the primary, according to state Sen. Leichter.

SPREADING THE BOUNTY

The financial community plays an in-

creasingly important role in New York's state and local politics. Although the state commission on integrity's hearings focused on campaign contributions by real estate developers, the commission also produced documents showing Wall Street's pervasive influence. No banker's contributions were illegal. But some investment bankers certainly developed intriguing twists to campaign financing.

For example, commission documents showed that in 1985, William N. Loverd of the Kidder, Peabody Group, using a technique called "bundling," sent 12 letters with checks from associates to New York City comptroller Harrison J. Goldin's campaign committee. According to Goldin's spokesman, the comptroller has declared a moratorium on fund raising and strongly supports strengthened campaign finance reform proposals.

Other documents obtained by the commission showed that despite a corporate campaign contribution limit of $5,000, Shearson Lehman Brothers in 1985 was legally able to send $25,000 to Goldin's campaign committee. Three separate Shearson entities sent $5,000 checks, and 11 Shearson executives sent personal contributions to Goldin. Five separate Drexel Burnham Lambert Inc. companies did much the same thing a year earlier, according to a Dec. 28, 1984, letter from Drexel, Burnham senior vice president Joel R. Mesnick to the Goldin campaign.

"What is offensive here," Leichter said, "is the large amount of the contributions and the fact that the money was clearly dedicated to officials who had a direct impact on the contracts that the firm gets." According to Leichter's figures, Wall Street money has become the norm in New York state and City politics. His figures show that Bear, Stearns gave $286,857 since 1971 to members of the city's Board of Estimate and the Republican and Democratic county committees, more than all but five other companies and individuals. Three other investment banks were listed among the top 25 givers.

Although the amounts may be higher in New York, Wall Street contributions have provoked controversy almost everywhere. In West Virginia, Donaldson, Lufkin & Jenrette was selected as lead manager for a $123.5 million bond deal for which no competitive bids were invited. The firm had contributed $10,000 to Gov. Arch A. Moore Jr.'s 1984 campaign. There were also allegations that the firm made an unreported in-kind contribution to Moore's campaign because Donaldson, Lufkin & Jenrette did some campaign consulting work for Moore, according to Charleston newspapers. Secretary of state Ken Hechler investigated the charges but never acted on them.

In a series of 1986 articles, *The Courier-Journal* of Louisville revealed that bankers at Donaldson, Lufkin & Jenrette and Cranston Securities Co., a Washington-based firm, had invested in real estate and racehorse partnerships with the husband of then-Gov. Martha Layne Collins. Donaldson, Lufkin & Jenrette's PAC also contributed $12,000 to the Kentucky Democratic Party shortly before Collins's election in 1983. In the following three years, those two firms were put in charge of seven bond issues worth more than $1.4 billion. In the three years prior to the in-

Staying Out of Disfavor

Once upon a time, oil lubricated virtually every political deal cut in Texas. Real estate still serves that function in New York. During two days of hearings in mid-March, the New York State Commission on Government Integrity underscored the role that real estate plays in Big Apple politics, and vice versa.

Over a repast in the Plaza Hotel's Edwardian Room, New York City comptroller Harrison J. Goldin sought a campaign donation of $50,000 from Joseph Bernstein, a lawyer, real estate magnate and front man for deposed Philippine President Ferdinand E. Marcos. In another instance, City Council president Andrew Stein let a real estate developer repay a $25,000 loan from his 1985 campaign. And Mayor Edward I. Koch collected millions of dollars from fund-raisers at the Metropolitan Club and the 21 Club and a birthday bash at the Metropolitan Museum of Art.

"There can be no question," John D. Feerick, commission chairman and dean of Fordham University Law School, said at the hearings, "that New York's mix of big-money interests and politics is unhealthy."

The hearings produced New York dialogue worthy of an ode to 1980s greed. Herewith a sample, from a transcript of the proceedings:

Commission member and former Secretary of State Cyrus R. Vance: And is it because you're fearful that if you don't contribute, that you're going to be punished in some way, or that the corporations you were involved in will be punished?
Bernstein: That's the good, plain English way of saying it, yes.
Vance: So that is the fact, is it?
Bernstein: Yes. The contributions that I make are not to get a favor but to avoid disfavor.

Committee investigator: What happened when you arrived at the Plaza Hotel?
Bernstein: I guess we ordered some food, and started talking, and [Goldin] made a mention a little bit about running for mayor, and that it would be nice if I were to support him.
Q: And what else did he say?
Bernstein: He thought that a contribution of $50,000, $25,000 for each of the two years, would be appropriate.
Q: Isn't it a fact that you were shocked by the manner of this approach?
Bernstein: I thought it was a bit excessive.
Q: Mr. Bernstein, did you comply with the city comptroller's request?
Bernstein: Yes.

Vance: Are you aware of any real estate developer in New York City who conducts their business in New York City without making campaign contributions to a large number of members of the Board of Estimate?
Real estate developer Donald Trump: I really don't know.

vestments and contributions, neither firm had been lead manager for any Kentucky bond issues, according to a May 1987 *Institutional Investor* article on underwriters' campaign contributions. A spokesman for the company, now Cranston-Prescott Securities Co., denied any connection between the contribution and the bond business, adding that the newspaper charges were never corroborated.

Wall Street firms may attract notoriety, but other investment bankers who deal with states also face increased scrutiny. Arkansas state auditor Julia Hughes

Jones, a member of the state retirement board, recommended that pension fund money be invested in a real estate project. Four days earlier, the *Arkansas Gazette* reported last August, the company sponsoring that project had helped host a fund-raiser for Jones. Jones said the fund-raiser was not related to the investment proposal, but the proposal was dropped.

Such problems are certain to continue, investment bankers and state officials say. Even a new round of campaign finance reform could founder on other factors. In an era of financial complexity, some in-

Shaking the Money Trees in New York

According to the New York State Commission on Government Integrity, more than half of New York state comptroller Edward V. Regan's campaign contributions came from investment banks doing business with the state. The commission also found that New York City comptroller Harrison J. Goldin got nearly half of his campaign donations from financial, real estate and legal interests.

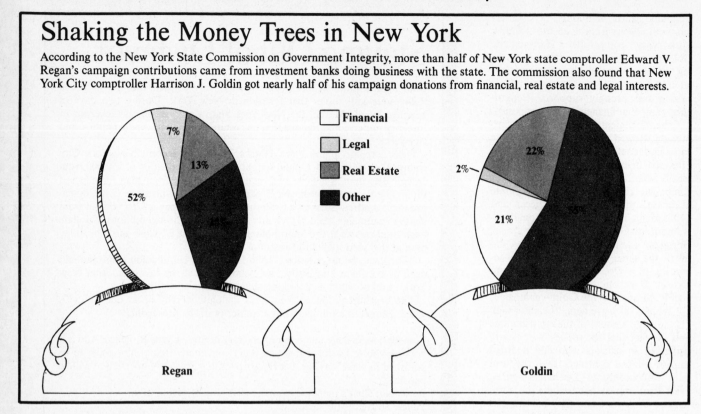

vestment bankers noted, bond financings are more likely to involve negotiated deals between government and banker. And greater competition between investment firms for business typically increases campaign contributions. In New Jersey, for example, more underwriters participate in bond dealings than during the previous administration, but at the same time, underwriters' campaign contributions have soared.

And other state officials may face Utah treasurer Alter's dilemma. Asked why Regan received more than half his contributions from the financial industry, Lawrence Huntington, Regan's former campaign chairman, told the New York commission that few voters even knew the comptroller's duties.

Huntington blamed himself for failing to get Regan known in a wider circle. "But when you get outside the financial business," he said, "people say to me, 'What is a comptroller?'

Populism Revived

Joseph F. Zimmerman

Joseph F. Zimmerman is professor of political science at the State University of New York at Albany.

The referendum, the initiative, and the recall were promoted by many governmental reformers in the 1890s and early 1900s as mechanisms for restoring popular control of state and local governments dominated by business corporations and/or bosses. The employment of direct legislation since 1978 to limit property taxes in California (Proposition 13) and Massachusetts (Proposition 2½) and the recall to change political party control of the Michigan Senate, highlight the need for an assessment of these popular control devices in terms of their impact upon representative government.

The origin of the first two devices is traceable to the colonial period. The referendum, based upon the concept of shared decision-making, is a natural extension of the New England town meeting and allows voters to determine whether referred matters are to become parts of the state constitution, state statutes, local charters, or local ordinances. Not surprisingly, the first referendum was held in the Massachusetts Bay Colony in 1640.[1]

The initiative, the process by which citizens by petitions place questions on the referendum ballot, dates to 1715 when the Massachusetts General Court (legislature) enacted a law requiring the selectmen to include in the warrant calling a town meeting any item accompanied by petition signed by 10 or more voters.[2]

The practice of submitting proposed state constitutions to the electorate became well established in the early decades of the 19th century and, commencing with the Rhode Island Constitution of 1842, provisions were incorporated in many constitutions forbidding the legislature to borrow funds or levy property taxes exceeding constitutional maxima without the sanction of the state's voters.

Citizen law-making entered a new era in 1898 when South Dakota voters amended the state constitution to provide for the statutory initiative and referendum by stipulating they "expressly reserve to themselves the right to propose measures, which measures the legislature shall enact and submit to a vote of the electors of the State" and "to require that any laws which the legislature may have enacted shall be submitted to a vote of the electors of the State before going into effect. . . ."[3] In the same year, San Francisco freeholders adopted a new city-county charter providing for the initiative and the referendum.[4] South Dakota's and San Francisco's leads were followed by other states and local governments, and the use of the initiative and the referendum became relatively common during the subsequent two decades.

Whereas the referendum and the initiative allow voters to make the final decision on proposed laws, the recall is designed to remove public officers—legislators, executives, and judicial officers—from office prior to the expiration of their terms. In common with the other devices, the process of removing an officer is commenced by the circulation of petitions for voter signatures. The recall first was adopted by Los Angeles in 1903 when voters ratified a new city charter providing for the device.[5]

The Referendum

The Delaware constitution is the only constitution which does not provide for a referendum on constitutional amendments enacted by the state legislature. In the other states, the size of the legislative vote and referendum vote required for approval of a constitutional amendment varies from state to state.

From *State Government*, Winter 1986, pp. 172-178. Reprinted with permission from The Council of State Governments.

Thirty-six state constitutions currently contain provisions for referenda on certain laws enacted by the state legislature such as ones pledging the "full faith and credit" of the state. In addition, voters in 25 states may petition for a referenda on a law enacted by the state legislature. The filing of the required number of signatures on petitions suspends the law, except appropriations and emergency ones in several states, until the electorate determines whether the law should be approved.

Mandatory Referenda. A relatively long list of state and local governmental actions—adoption of state constitutions and local charters or amendments, incorporation of municipalities, calling of a constitutional convention, annexation of land, mergers of local governments, and pledging the "full faith and credit" of the government—are subject to a compulsory referenda in many states.

Serious objections are raised by many governmental observers to mandatory referenda on bond issues because such a requirement has led to more expensive ways of financing large governmental projects. The plebiscite requirement can be evaded by creating public authorities empowered to issue "moral obligation" bonds and by entering into lease-purchase agreements. Authorities are not subject to constitutional debt referenda requirements and a number of such authorities have been created in various states with the power to issue bonds backed by a "moral obligation" or "indirect" guarantee that a future state legislature will appropriate funds to meet interest and principal payments should the issuing authorities be unable to meet their financial obligations. These bonds carry a higher rate of interest than "full faith and obligation" bonds and, consequently, place a heavier burden upon taxpayers.

Lease-purchase agreements involve a state or a local government entering into an agreement to purchase large capital equipment or facilities on the installment plan. In other words, a government signs a long-term contract providing the government may use a facility constructed and financed by another government or a private firm with title to the project passing to the former government on a specified date. In common with "moral obligation" financing, lease-purchase financing is more expensive than "full faith and credit" financing.

The Citizens' Veto. The petition referenda, also known as the protest or direct referenda, provides for a citizens' veto by allowing voters by petitions to stop the implementation of a law until a referenda determine whether the law is to be repealed. This type of referenda is similar to the initiative in that action to place a law on the referenda ballot originates with the voters. Successful collection of the requisite number of signatures results in a mandatory referenda.

The protest referenda may be employed in 24 states. However, in eight states—Alaska, Idaho, Massachusetts, Michigan, Missouri, Montana, South Dakota, and Wyoming—the petition referenda may be employed only against an entire law whereas in the other states the referenda may be used against part or all of a law. The constitutional provision authorizing this type of referenda typically excludes certain topics—religion, appropriations, special legislation, and the judiciary—from the referenda.

States lacking the petititon referenda at the state level authorize its use at the local level. New Hampshire statutes, for example, authorize the owners of 20 percent either of the land area or lots to petition for a referenda on a change in land use regulations adopted by a town.[6]

The protest referenda can be employed by conservative or liberal groups, or by integrationists or segregationists. Whereas business groups typically do not employ the initiative to achieve their goals, such groups use the protest referenda to annul statutes. In 1982, the Massachusetts Soft Drink Association filed petitions for the first referenda in the nation on the subject of repealing a mandatory bottle deposit law enacted by the Massachusetts General Court. Although voters defeated a proposed bottle deposit law by a small margin in 1976, they rejected the repeal proposal in 1982.

There is no evidence that "conservative" groups make more use of the referenda than "liberal" groups, but there is evidence that voters take both a "conservative" and a "liberal" stance on different propositions on the same ballot. Massachusetts voters in 1982 approved a death penalty proposition, generally considered to be a "conservative" issue, and a bottle deposit proposition and a nuclear freeze proposition which are considered to be part of the "liberal agenda."

The Initiative

The constitutions of 23 states contain provisions from one or more types of initiatives. In 17 states, the initiative may be employed in the process of amending the state constitution. And in 21 states, the initiative may be employed in the process of enacting ordinary statutes.

Initiatives may be classified as (1) state, (2) local, (3) constitutional, (4) statutory, (5) direct, (6) indirect, and (7) advisory. The first four categories are self-explanatory.

Direct Initiative. This type circumvents the entire legislative process as propositions are placed directly on the referendum ballot if the requisite number and distribution of valid signatures are collected and certified.

The state legislature in five states—Maine, Massachusetts, Michigan, Nevada, and Washington—is authorized to place a substitute proposition on the referendum ballot whenever an initiative proposition appears on the ballot. Although the constitution of Alaska provides only for the direct initiative and contains no provision for an indirect initiative, a section of the constitution allows the state legislature to enact a substitute which voids the initiative petition provided the substitute is "substantially the same."

On the substate level, the direct initiative commonly is employed to place local charters or charter amendments on the referendum ballot as illustrated by voters in Summit County, Ohio, in 1980, successfully placing on the ballot a proposed home rule county charter which was ratified by the voters.

The major objection raised against the direct initiative is the fact initiated measures often are drafted imperfectly, violate the federal or state constitution, or produce unintended adverse effects. Opponents and proponents of a 1978 California proposition limiting smoking in public places agreed the proposal was defeated because of technical defects, including prohibition of smoking at jazz concerts but not at rock concerts.

Indirect Initiative. Employed in eight states, the indirect initiative involves a more cumbersome process as a proposition is referred to the legislative body for its consideration upon the filing of the required number of certified signatures. Failures of the legislative body to approve the proposition within a stipulated number of days, varying from 40 in Michigan to adjournment of the Maine legislature, leads to the proposition being placed automatically on the referendum ballot. In three states, additional signatures must be collected to place the proposition on the ballot as follows: one-half of 1 percent and 10 percent

of the votes cast for governor in the last general election in Massachusetts and Utah, respectively, and 3 percent of the registered voters in Ohio. Only the Massachusetts constitution authorizes the indirect initiative for constitutional amendments and an amendment proposed by the initiative is not placed upon the referendum ballot unless the proposal is approved by at least 25 percent of the members of the General Court in two consecutive sessions.[7]

Relative to proposed statutes, Maine, Massachusetts, and Wyoming provide only for the indirect initiative. Michigan, Nevada, Ohio, South Dakota, Utah, and Washington authorize employment of both types.

The indirect initiative can have the salutary effect of prodding the legislature to take action to solve a major problem. Within a fortnight of the filing of 145,170 signatures on initiative petitions prohibiting the use of cats and dogs from pounds for medical research, the Massachusetts General Court in 1983 enacted the petition.

Advisory Initiative. This type of initiative allows voters to circulate petitions to place a nonbinding question on the ballot at an election and is a mechanism citizens and groups can employ to pressure legislative bodies to take a certain course of action.

Until the late 1970s, the advisory initiative was employed relatively infrequently and attracted generally only local notice. The growth of the environmental and nuclear freeze movements, along with movements opposing United States involvement in Central America, has resulted in national attention being focused upon such referenda as national and regional groups employ the initiative to place questions on election ballots. In 1983, for example, voters approved advisory initiative Proposition 0 directing the mayor and the board of supervisors of the city and county of San Francisco to notify President Ronald Reagan and Congress the voters favor the repeal of the provisions of the federal Voting Rights Act requiring the city and county to provide ballots, voter pamphlets, and other materials on voting in Chinese and Spanish as well as in English.

The Recall

The concept of the recall was incorporated into Article V of the Articles of Confederation and Perpetual Union which provided that states were authorized to replace their delegates to Congress. However, the voters only indirectly participated in this type of recall since the state legislature possessed the power of the recall.

The recall was a product of the populist and municipal reform movements which were in sympathy with the early 19th century Jacksonian distrust of government officials. Jacksonian democracy attempted to keep public officials continuously responsible to the electorate by providing that most public officers should be elected and their terms of office should be short; i.e., six months to one year.

The constitutions of 14 states authorize the employment of the recall to remove state officers from office. These states also authorize, by statute, all or certain local governments to employ the recall against all or specified local government officers. In addition, 17 states authorize the recall of local officers by general law, special law, or a locally drafted and adopted charter.[8]

The reasons for the use of the recall in most states are not limited to a scandalum magnatum as the recall can be employed for any reason, including disagreement on a policy issue. The Michigan constitution stipulates "the sufficiency of any statement of reasons or grounds procedurally required shall be a political rather than a judicial question."[9] On the other hand, the Washington constitutional provision requires petitioners to recite "that such officer has committed some act or acts of malfeasance or misfeasance while in office, or who has violated his oath of office, stating the matters complained of, . . ."[10]

Restrictions on Use. Constitutional, statutory, and local charter provisions typically place restrictions on the exercise of the recall by the voters. The constitutions of Alaska, Idaho, Louisiana, Michigan, and Washington exclude judicial officers from the recall.

The Montana recall law is the only one that provides for the recall of appointed as well as elected state officers.[11] In addition, a number of local charters authorize the recall of appointed as well as elected officers. The city of Greeley, Colorado, has an unusual charter provision authorizing voters at an election held every six years to terminate the employment of the city manager.[12]

Constitutional and statutory provisions authorizing employment of the recall often prohibit its use during the first two months (Montana) or year of an elected officer's term of office and a second recall during the same officer's term of office unless the petitioners pay for the cost of

the preceding recall election. Louisiana law prohibits a second recall attempt within 18 months of the previous unsuccessful recall election.[13]

There are no restrictions on the use of the recall, other than time period or frequency, in California, North Dakota, Ohio, South Dakota, and Wyoming. Kansas law enumerates the grounds for recall—"conviction of a felony, misconduct in office, incompetence, or failure to perform duties prescribed by law."[14]

Petition Requirements. The recall is similar to the petition referendum and the initiative in that action originates with the voters. The first step in initiating voter removal of a state officer in eight states—Alaska, Arizona, California, Georgia, Idaho, Kansas, Oregon, and Washington—is the filing and publishing or posting of a notice of intent to circulate a recall petition.[15] A filing fee of one hundred dollars is required in Alaska, but the fee is refunded if verified signatures equal to 25 percent of the votes cast for the office in question at the last election are filed by the deadline for petitions.[16] Kansas also levies a one hundred dollar filing fee.[17]

Each recall petition must contain a declaration by the circulator that each signature is a genuine one.[18] Petitions must be filed within a stated number of days—ranging from 60 days in Wisconsin to 270 days for state officers in Washington—after the certifying officer notifies proponents that the form and wording of the filed proposed petition are correct.[19] Successful collection of the required number of certified signatures results in a special election to determine whether the named officer(s) shall remain in office until the expiration of the regular term of office. The most common petition requirement is signatures equal to 25 percent of the votes cast for all candidates in the last general election for governor in the involved unit or the officer whose recall is sought.[20] In some states, there is a geographical requirement relative to the minimum number of signatures for the recall of an office elected on a statewide basis.

The Recall Election. The typical recall provision stipulates the process is terminated should the public officer against whom the petitions are directed resign the office. Should the officer resign, the vacancy is filled in the manner provided by law.

The reasons advanced in support of the recall are printed on the recall ballot, but the number of words is limited; 200 is the most common limit.[21] The officer whose recall is sought may submit a statement of justification of conduct in office.

In nine states, voters in a recall election simply vote on the question of whether the officer should be recalled. A majority affirmative vote ipso facto removes the officer from office in most jurisdictions. The vacancy resulting from an affirmative removal vote may involve a second special election to select a successor. If an officer is recalled, Montana law directs that "the vacancy shall be filled as provided by law, provided that the officer recalled may in no event be appointed to fill the vacancy."[22]

A separate election on the question of recalling an officer has the advantage of allowing voters to concentrate on the question of the removal without having their attention diverted by the claims of other candidates, but suffers from the disadvantage of increasing governmental costs if a special election is held to fill the vacancy.

Proponents of the recall typically recruit and endorse a replacement candidate and campaign for his or her election. In the only judicial recall election in Wisconsin, recall proponents in 1977 did not endorse a replacement candidate for fear of dividing voters favoring the recall of Judge Archie Simonson of Dane County.[23]

Campaign Finance

State corrupt practices acts regulate the financing of election and referenda campaigns. Historically, these acts required the reporting of campaign receipts and expenditures, and limited the amount that may be contributed to or spent in campaigns.

In 1976, the United States Supreme Court in *Buckley v. Valeo* examined the Federal Election Campaign Act of 1971 and its 1974 amendments, and upheld the individual contribution limits, disclosure and reporting requirements, and public financing provisions, but held "the limitations on expenditures, on independent expenditures by individuals and groups, and on expenditures by a candidate from his personal funds are constitutionally infirm."[24]

Two years later, the Court invalidated a Massachusetts statute restricting corporate contributions to referendum campaigns by ruling a corporation was protected by the First Amendment to the United States Constitution and could expend funds to publicize its views relative to a proposed state constitutional amendment authorizing the General Court to levy a graduated income tax.[25]

Statewide initiative, referendum, and recall campaigns are expensive because of the difficulties of obtaining the requisite number of certifiable signatures on petitions and the high cost of persuading the electorate to support or reject ballot propositions, or remove an officer. Proposition 15 on the 1982 California ballot would have placed controls on hand guns and resulted in approximately $10 million being spent by interest groups to secure its approval or defeat with the largest contribution, approximately $2.5 million, coming from the National Rifle Association.

The danger of "moneyed" interests employing the petition referendum and the initiative for their own benefit has been increased by the Court's decisions, yet evidence to date reveals that the side spending the most money in a campaign does not invariably win.

Populism Revived

Few question whether citizens are sovereign or the desirability of submitting proposed organic documents—state constitutions, constitutional amendments, local charters, and charter amendments—to the voters for a final determination. Strong objections, however, have been raised by many observers to the protest referendum, the initiative, and the recall on the ground that these devices undermine representative government.

The petition referendum is a form of citizens' veto designed to correct legislative sins of commission and should be available to voters as a safety valve to be employed to reverse unrepresentative legislative decisions. This type of referendum has not weakened representative government by discouraging many able individuals from seeking or continuing in legislative office, or by encouraging legislative bodies to shirk their responsibilities by employing the optional referendum (legislative placement of a proposition on the ballot).

One of the auxiliary advantages of the protest referendum, in conjunction with the initiative and the recall, is to encourage the electorate to revise state constitutions and local charters to make them short documents confined to fundamentals and readable by removing detailed restrictions since direct legislation and the recall provide the citizenry with mechanisms to ensure that legislators do not abuse the trust placed in them by the electorate.

Consideration should be given by states to a new type of petition referendum which, upon the filing of the requisite number of certified signatures, would suspend a law and require the legislative body to consider the repeal or amendment of the law within a stated number of days. Should the legislature fail to adopt the proposal contained in the petition within a specified number of days regardless of whether the legislature is in session on the day the petitions are certified, a referendum automatically would be held on the proposal. At present the filing of the requisite number of signatures results automatically in a referendum where voters are limited to a "yes" or "no" choice on the question of repealing the referred law. The proposed new type of petition referendum would encourage the legislative body to amend or repeal the law in question, thereby obviating the need for a referendum and its attendant expenses.

On balance, the indirect initiative strengthens the governance system. This type of initiative has the benefit of the legislative process, including public hearings and committee review, study, and recommendations. Should the legislative body fail to approve the proposition, voters have been advantaged in their decision-making capacity by the information on the proposition generated by the legislative process.

The indirect initiative can be an effective counterbalance to an unrepresentative legislative body and no more undermines representative government than the executive veto and the judicial veto. A major advantage of the initiative is the fact it makes the operation of interest groups more visible in comparison with their lobbying activities in a state or local legislative body. Furthermore, the availability of the initiative increases the citizen's stake in the government.

Support for the indirect initiative does not suggest that it should be employed frequently. It should be a reserve power or last resort weapon and the relative need for its use depends upon the degree of accountability, representativeness, and responsiveness of legislative bodies.

A model constitutional provision for the initiative should contain the following elements: (a) the attorney general and/or community affairs department should be directed to provide petition drafting services to sponsors of initiatives; (b) upon submission of a certified petition, a confer-

ence should be held at which the attorney general or community affairs department explains initiative wording problems, if any, to sponsors and suggests amendments if needed; (c) if a defeated proposition is resubmitted to the voters within two years, sponsors should be required to obtain additional signatures on petitions equal to 2 percent of the votes cast for governor in the last general election in the affected jurisdiction; (d) the state constitution should authorize the employment of the initiative for purposes of placing the question of calling a constitutional convention on the ballot.

The question of adopting the recall has been the subject of controversy in many states and local jurisdictions, but not in most jurisdictions that have adopted it, when measured in terms of voluntary abandonment. Because citizen-initiated recall appears to be an application of modified direct democracy to representative democracy, philosophical arguments about it have abounded. State laws providing for the automatic vacating of a public office by an incumbent convicted of a felony have not generated controversy.

The recall possesses the potential for abuse unless the authorizing provision restricts its employment to cases involving malfeasance, misfeasance, or nonfeasance. If there are no restrictions upon the use of the recall, it may be employed by the losing candidate in the previous election in a second attempt to gain office or the charges may be the result of a grudge or philosophical differences of opinion on issues. Experience reveals that the dangers of the unrestricted recall are small and are outweighed by its associated advantages.

The recall seldom has been used at the state level; only one governor—Lynn J. Frazier of North Dakota in 1981—has been recalled. Nevertheless, the recall can produce a major political change on the state level. Two Democratic state senators were recalled by Michigan voters in 1983 and replaced by Republicans, giving the Republicans control over the Senate.[26] The recall generally has been used on the local level to remove members of a city council who voted to fire a popular city manager.

To a certain extent, the infrequency of the use of the recall may be due to its restraining effect upon officers who recognize its existence is a threat to their continuance in office if they step out of line with majority opinion.

The recent and more frequent use of the direct initiative and the petition referendum should not obscure the fact that most representative governments have been responsive to the citizenry. Most citizens are interested chiefly in the delivery of quality public services at a reasonable cost. If legislative bodies ensure these two goals, use of direct legislation and recall should be uncommon.

No system of representation is perfect. Per consequens, a quadrivium of correctives—voting in regular elections, the direct initiative, the petition referendum, and the recall—should be available to the electorate, but preferably triggered only by gross misrepresentation.

Notes

1. Nathaniel B. Shurtleff, ed. *Records of the Governor and Company of the Massachusetts Bay in New England* Vol. 1, (Boston: From the Press of William White, Printer to the Commonwealth, 1853), 293.

2. *The Acts and Resolves of the Province of the Massachusetts Bay* Vol. 2, (Boston: Wright and Potter, 1874), 30.

3. *Constitution of South Dakota*, Art. III, Section 1 (1898).

4. *Charter for the City and County of San Francisco*, Art. II, Chap. 1, Sections 20-22.

5. Frederick L. Bird and Frances M. Ryan, *the Recall of Public Officers: A Study of the Operation of the Recall in California* (New York: The Macmillan Company, 1930), 22.

6. *New Hampshire Revised Statutes*, Section 31.64 (1983 Supp.).

7. *Constitution of the Commonwealth of Massachusetts*, Articles of Amendment, Art. XLVIII.

8. Arkansas, Florida, Georgia, Hawaii, Massachusetts, Minnesota, Mississippi, Missouri, Nebraska, New Jersey, New Mexico, Ohio, Pennsylvania, South Dakota, Tennessee, West Virginia, and Wyoming.

9. *Constitution of Michigan*, Art. II, Section 8.

10. *Constitution of Washington*, Art. I, Section 33.

11. *Montana Laws of 1977*, Chap. 364, and *Revised Code of Montana*, Section 2-16-603 (1983).

12. *Greeley Colorado City Charter*, Section 4.3.

13. *Louisiana Acts of 1921*, extra session, No. 121, Section 9 and *Louisiana Revised Statutes*, Section 1300.13 (1956).

14. *Kansas Statutes Annotated*, Section 25-4302 (1981).

15. For an example of a statutory requirement, see *California Elections Code*, Sections 27007 and 27030.5 (1977 and 1984 Supp.).

16. *Alaska Laws of 1960*, Chap. 83, and *Alaska Statutes*, Section 15.45.480 (1982) Supp.).

17. *Kansas Laws of 1976*, Chap. 178, and *Kansas Statutes Annotated*, Section 25-4306 (1981).

18. For an example, see the *Constitution of Arizona*, Art. VIII, Section 2.

19. See *Revised Code of Washington*, Section 29.82.025 (1965 and 1984 Supp.).

20. For details, see *The Book of the States, 1980-81* (Lexington, Ky.: The Council of State Governments, 1980), 198.

21. For an example, see *Michigan Public Acts of 1978*, Public Act 533, Section 1, and *Michigan Compiled Laws Annotated*, Section 168.966 (1984 Supp.).

22. *Montana Laws of 1977*, Chap. 364, and *Revised Code of Montana*, Section 2-16-635 (1983).

23. "Winner in War Over Judge's Words," *The New York Times*, September 9, 1977, B1.

24. *Buckley v. Valeo*, 424 U.S. 1 at 143 (1976).

25. *First National Bank v. Bellotti*, 435 U.S. 765 (1978).

26. Candace Romig, "Two Michigan Legislators Recalled," *State Legislatures*, January 1984, 5.

Civic Strategies
for Community Empowerment

JOSEPH F. ZIMMERMAN

Joseph F. Zimmerman is a professor of political science at the State University of New York at Albany, and editor of the NATIONAL CIVIC REVIEW Metro Trends department.

The past two decades have seen a serious erosion of "dynamic" democracy in many parts of the United States as eligible citizens vote less frequently and withdraw from other key aspects of local political life. Instead, we increasingly find a disturbing brand of "reluctant" democracy in which formal rights to participate are widely ignored in practice.

Among the explanations given for this phenomenon is a spreading sense of political impotency which discourages involvement. In many communities today, one routinely hears that "you can't fight city hall." While this theme is not new, when juxtaposed with a growing number of "private" preoccupations (e.g., multiple jobs to support the family or the explosion of recreational opportunities) and residential mobility, it provides good reason to keep out of the public arena.

However many communities (including larger jurisdictions) have effectively used certain structural mechanisms to combat feelings of political powerlessness and thus stem the potentially dangerous slide toward "reluctant" democracy. In this article we examine the record of such devices in three critical areas: the election system; ethics and openness in public affairs; and the degree of local discretionary authority. These areas offer future avenues for greater citizen participation.

Election Systems That Invite Participation

To encourage involvement, the formula used for electing officials must be generally perceived as fair. The criteria for measuring systems include effectiveness of ballots cast, responsiveness of elected officials, maximization of access to decision makers, equity in representation, and legitimization of the legislative body.[1] These canons can be used to evaluate six electoral structures: at-large; combined ward and at-large; limited voting; cumulative voting; and proportional representation.[2]

If an electoral system produces accurate community representation, government may satisfy voter needs. Unfortunately, no means for selecting officials accurately represents the views of all citizens on all issues at all times. The law making process can foster the illusion that each measure is scrutinized carefully and fully prior to its approval, amendment, or rejection. However, elected representatives—whether ethical or unscrupulous—are to a greater or lesser extent "trustees" who take many of their cues from non-constituent sources, thus producing results that never fully reflect voter consensus (if, indeed, there is one).

Three Mitigating Devices

Three devices can mitigate the problem: initiative, the referendum, and recall. Ideally, these mechanisms should be available on a standby basis as circuit breakers to be triggered only by gross misrepresentation of the electorate.

The Binding Initiative. This approach allows the electorate to place proposed laws on the referendum ballot. It can be traced to a 1715 Massachusetts law and to an 1898 constitutional amendment with respect to other areas of the United States.[3] Today 23 state constitutions authorize its use. Seventeen provide for constitutional and 21 for statutory initiatives. Placing a measure on the ballot requires petitions signed by a certain number of registered voters (from 3 to 15% of votes cast for Governor in the last election). Measures approved by the voters are not subject to gubernatorial veto. State statutes and municipal charters often authorize local initiative.

> *... elected representatives—whether ethical or unscrupulous—are to a greater or lesser extent "trustees" who take many of their cues from non-constituent sources, thus producing results that never fully reflect voter consensus ...*

This direct method for circumventing the legislative process attracts criticism. Opponents argue, for example, that elected representatives produce better laws or that popular measures are often poorly drafted, confusing to voters, and not coordinated properly with other statutes.[4]

An alternative, the indirect initiative, available in eight States including Massachusetts, empowers voters (with requisite signatures) to refer measures to the legislature for its consideration (akin to submitting a bill). If that body fails to approve the proposition within the stated time limit, in five states it is automatically placed on the ballot. In three states, sponsors of the proposal must collect additional signatures to force a popular vote. Five states authorize their legislatures to place a competing proposition on the ballot.

Advisory Initiatives. Non-binding questions may be placed on the referendum ballot to place pressure on law-making bodies to enact certain measures. The theory supporting this type of initiative suggests that elected representatives will act in accordance with the clearly expressed desires of the voters. In the late 1970s, the environmental and nuclear freeze movements often used such means to influence public opinion and law makers.

The Referendum. Plebiscitarian techniques in the United States are traceable to the Massachusetts Bay Colony where the General Court (legislative body) in 1640 authorized the use of the referendum.[5] However, this democratizing tool did not become established in most parts of the country until the early 1800s when state legislatures and constitutional conventions began to submit proposed constitutions for

Reprinted with permission from the May/June 1988 issue of *National Civic Review*, pp. 202-212. National Civic Review, 1601 Grant Street, Suite 250, Denver, CO 80203.

voter appoval. The first New York State Constitution of 1777, for example, was adopted in convention without popular vote.

In the late 19th century, several state legislatures, including New York's, so abused their powers that the public demanded (and won) the right to approve constitutional changes and a class of "conditional" laws which do not become effective unless approved by the voters. These restrictions are contained today in many state constitutions, including New York's, and typically involve taxation and the borrowing of funds.

A more dramatic development occurred in South Dakota in 1898 when voters amended the state constitution to authorize the electorate to employ the petition or protest referendum and the initiative.[6] This device allows voters to veto most laws enacted by a legislature. Exempted are laws designed to preserve "the public peace, health or safety, [and] support of the State Government and its existing institutions."[7]

The petition referendum, when signed by two to 15 percent of those voting in the last general election, suspends a law until a mandatory referendum on it can be held.

In 24 states, the protest referendum is authorized by the state constitution. In eight cases, it may be employed only to repeal an entire law while in the others it can be used like a line-item veto.

Specified topics (e.g., appropriation of funds, the judiciary, statutes applying to a single local government, and religion) usually are not subject to the petition referendum. The Commonwealth of Massachusetts excludes the largest number of items.[8]

Twenty states require a majority vote for repeal; the balance require from 30 to 50 percent of the vote in the last general election. Six constitutions forbid the state legislature to amend or repeal the voters' decision.

Local government charters and state statutes often allow for petition referenda to overrule municipal laws. The procedures are typically identical with those at the state level.

The Recall

This tool for popular involvement is a natural extension of the others. The recall or "imperative mandate" concept appeared in the Articles of Confederation and Perpetual Union, the national platforms of the Socialist Labor Party in 1892 and 1896, and the platform of the Populist Party in several states during the same period.[9] It was first authorized in the 1903 Los Angeles charter.[10] Currently, 14 state constitutions allow recall of state and certain local officers.[11] Also, 17 states authorize the recall of local officials by general law, special law, or a locally drafted and adopted charter. Although the California Constitution directed the State Legislature to provide for the recall of local officers, this provision does not affect cities and counties with "home rule" charters.

In Massachusetts, 52 locally drafted city and town charters allow recall. The Billerica town charter, for example, stipulates "any person who holds an elected town office, but not including an elected town meeting member, with more than six months remaining of the term of office, may be recalled from office by the voters"[12] The Oxford town charter simply states that "any elective officer of the town may be recalled and removed from public office by the voters of the town as herein provided."[13]

Charters of professionally managed cities typically include similar provisions to counterbalance the authority of that non-elected official. Although managers are theoretically accountable to the council, it is widely felt that intra-governmental politics can insulate them from popular opinion, thus requiring such protection.

In a few states, the recall ballot is also used to elect a replacement. If there is no prohibition, the target incumbent may simultaneously seek reelection (which, ironically, can occur if the other candidates split the opposing vote).

Like the initiative and the protest referendum, the recall process is launched by petition (usually requiring signatures equal to 25% of votes cast in the last election for governor or the position in question) and concluded by a special election.[14]

Several states require that recall petitions for statwide elected officials contain a geographical spread of signatures. California, for example, stipulates 1% of the last vote cast for the office in each of five counties.[15]

Typically a short justification for recall and defense appear on the ballot. San Francisco publishes a voter information pamphlet containing a sample ballot, the proponents' statement of reasons for the proposed recall, the officer's reply to the reasons, and paid advertisements. The 1983 pamphlet relative to the special recall election of the Mayor contained 49 paid advertisements (37 favoring the Mayor and 12 supporting recall).

In nine states, the electorate simply votes on the question of recalling an officer. In most jurisdictions, a majority affirmative vote *ipso facto* vacates the office which is then filled according to law, and may involve a second special election to select a successor.

In a few states, the recall ballot (e.g., Arizona) is also used to elect a replacement. If there is no prohibition, the target incumbant may simultaneously seek reelection (which, ironically, can occur if the other candidates split the opposing vote).

Arguments for and against the recall resemble those aimed at the initiative and petition referendum.[16] Not surprisingly, many elected officials oppose all three corrective devices. Yet it appears that their availability often promote dynamic democracy by enhancing governmental legitimacy and reducing feelings of political impotence.

Open and Ethical Government

These conditions are essential for effective, participatory democracy because citizens possess substantially fewer political resources than elected and appointed officials. As Aristotle insisted:

> If the citizens are to judge officers according to merit, then they must know each other's characters; where they do not possess this knowledge, both the election to office and the decision of lawsuits will go wrong![17]

Information and resulting citizen inputs alone, however, generally do not provide a sufficient antidote to unethical official behavior. Other, complementary mechanisms are needed.

So long as ethical problems remain clear-cut, the venerable English common law approach which relies on precedent-based judicial decisions may suffice. Nonetheless, today's issues often assume more subtle form, creating gray areas that require different treatment.

Codes of Ethics

While no one mechanism can ensure that governmental actions will be ethical, strong ethics codes and boards for rendering advisory opinions represent a critical first step.[18] Such codes establish essential guidelines for governmental officers, facilitate self-regulation, and bolster public confidence. Publication of advisory board opinions, with appropriate deletions to preserve the privacy of those making the requests, will in time build a case inventory to guide other elected governmental personnel contemplating similar actions.

Sunshine Laws

Sunshine laws are designed to throw light on governmental actions, the decision-making process, and attempts by individuals and interest groups to influence it. They include mandatory financial disclosures by public officers, open meetings of public bodies, and citizen access to public records.

Financial Disclosure. Requirements that public officers publish information about their personal and family finances are related closely to conflict-of-interest laws and codes of ethics. Manditory disclosure preferably should be restricted to a listing of income sources rather than specific amounts, and also might be limited to specified sources of income exceeding a stipulated amount. The required statement should contain the name and address of each creditor to whom a minimum amount is owed, due date, interest rate, date and original amount of the debt, existing special conditions, and a statement indicating whether or not the debt is secured. Mortgage debt on a personally occupied home and retail installment debt might be exempted from the disclosure requirement.

A thorny question is whether financial disclosure should apply to all part-time citizen officers in small municipalities who serve without compensation or receive only minor stipends. There is no denying that service on a non-paid board of commission represents a sacrifice of time and money, and may also subject the officers to abuse and criticism by the public. A mandatory disclosure requirement for all officers might discourage candidacies—something to be avoided when the aim is to encourage wider participation by qualified individuals. Thus, in the case of part-time positions, it seems wise to limit disclosure requirements to candidates for bodies with regulatory powers such as planning boards.

A thorny question is whether financial disclosure should apply to all part-time citizen officers in small municipalities who serve without compensation or receive only minor stipends . . . A mandatory disclosure requirement for all officers might discourage candidacies—something to be avoided when the aim is to encourage wider participation by qualified individuals.

Open Meetings. Informed citizen participation is hindered by *in camera* decision-making. Many local governments and state legislatures have enacted open meeting laws designed to throw light on the policy process while, at the same time, permitting closed-door executive sessions for certain sensitive issues as property acquisition, disciplinary action, salary negotiations, or matters that could prejudice a government's position in a law suit.

Care must be exercised in defining the term "meeting" when adopting such laws. The Council of State Governments recommends that the concept refer to "the convening of a governing body for which a quorum is required in order to make a decision or to deliberate toward a decision on any matter."[19] It is also important to require that adequate public notice be given to interested persons and organizations of the place and time of meetings, and to specify exceptions to the open meeting requirements. In addition, complete and accurate records of meetings should be kept so that citizens unable to attend can examine proceedings.

Freedom of Information. A third type of "sunshine" law attempts to ensure that citizens will have ready access to most official records of government. Such devices are desirable because excessive confidentiality can shield unethical or prejudicial actions from cure. Yet the matter of what information should be released and under what conditions raises delicate questions which should not be addressed haphazardly. In 1977, the New York State Legislature addressed this problem by creating the Committee on Public Access to Records, charged with developing guidelines for the release of official information by state and local government agencies, and providing advice in cases of disputes.[20] The Committee's performance of its duties has been excellent.

A conflict can exist between freedom of information and privacy laws. The Federal Privacy Act of 1974, for example, requires executive agencies to keep confidential personal information, yet the Federal Freedom of Information Act requires agencies to make executive branch records available for inspection or duplication except "to the extent required to prevent a clearly unwarranted invasion of personal privacy."[21]

Balancing these two elements is a challenge for which no universal solution exists, indicating that communities must experiment with alternatives within the current legal framework until they find one which serves local needs.

Local Discretionary Authority

As suggested earlier, citizen participation tends to increase as communities gain greater control over their own public policy process. Historically, the legal relationship between states and their political subdivisions was governed by the *Ultra Vires* (beyond powers) concept, also know as Dillon's Rule, which denied inherent powers of local self-government and emphasized the plenary authority of the state legislature.[22] Fortunately, most states have modified the *Ultra Vires* Rule and provided for increased local discretionary authority by the adoption

of provisions for an *Imperium in Imperio* (empire within an empire). New York State employs the three approaches simultaneously, thereby producing considerable confusion relative to the legal powers of various local jurisdictions.

Clearly, local governments that deliver most public services and operate on a relatively small scale offer greater participatory opportunities. When these institutions lack substantial autonomy, citizen interest obviously wanes.

Retention of broad powers over local governments makes the state legislature a target of interests unable to achieve their goals at the grass roots. In general, state legislatures have been responsive to such demands, enacting many laws that mandate courses of action for more accessible political subdivisions.

The only national survey of this phenomenon reveals that most states have imposed numerous mandates upon their local governments, with New York in the lead. There, the legislature imposed its will in 66 of the 76 functional areas studied.[23] In contrast to the national government which still provides most financial assistance to subnational units with conditions attached, New York State is generous in sharing its income tax revenues with its political subdivisions with few conditions attached. However, the separate enactment of state mandates by the New York State Legislature over the years has reduced significantly the discretionary authority of the local units.

To what extent do states reimburse local governments for mandated expenditures? Currently, 12 provide full or partial support. California's Initiative Proposition 4 of 1979 and Massachusett's Initiative Proposition 2-1/2 of 1980 make this a requirement.

Mandates fall into 11 categories: entitlement; structural; service level; tax base; personnel; due process; equal treatment; ethical; good neighbor; informational membership; and record-keeping. A strong case can be made that the states should not be forced to reimburse costs associated with the last six types, since these are relatively inexpensive functions which (in spite of state intervention) should remain under maximum local control.

Conclusion

This review reveals that a substantial range of formal, participatory instruments have been devised to make state and local governments more responsive and accountable to their electorates. Unfortunately, not all of these mechanisms are everywhere available. Moreover, legal and other impediments often prevent their best use to overcome widespread feelings of political impotence and achieve "dynamic" democracy.

Given their greater authority and scope, state legislatures remain the prime key to establishing broader participatory "rights." They are still in the best position to initiate statutes and constitutional amendments for corrective devices to expand potential citizen influence on the governance process. They can increase the discretionary authority of local governments and establish general mechanisms for furnishing ethical advice to public officials. While not sufficient by themselves, such democratizing actions would set the stage for enlarged, more satisfying citizen participation.

Notes

[1]For details, see Joseph F. Zimmerman, "Electoral Systems and Direct Citizen Law Making." A paper presented at the University of Wurzburg, Federal Republic of Germany, July 1, 1987.
[2]Joseph F. Zimmerman, *The Federated City: Community Control in Large Cities* (New York: St. Martin's Press, 1972), pp. 65-79.
[3]*The Acts and Resolves of the Province of the Massachusetts Bay* (Boston: Wright and Potter, 1874), vol. II, p. 30, and *Constitution of South Dakota,* art. III, I (1898).
[4]Joseph F. Zimmerman, *Participatory Democracy: Populism Revived* (New York: Praeger Publishers, 1986), pp. 91-95.
[5]Nathaniel B. Shurtleff, ed. *Records of the Governor and Company of the Massachusetts Bay in New England* (Boston: From the Press of William White, Printer to the Commonwealth, 1853), vol. I, p. 293.
[6]*Constitution of South Dakota,* art III, I (1898).
[7]*Ibid.*
[8]*Constitution of the Commonwealth of Massachusetts,* Articles of Amendment, art. XLVIII, The Referendum, 2.

[9]*Articles of Confederation and Perpetual Union,* art. V.

[10]Frederick L. Bird and Frances M. Rayan, *The Recall of Public Officers: A Study of the Operation of the Recall in California* (New York: The Macillan Company, 1930), p. 22.

[11]Alaska, Arizona, California, Colorado, Georgia, Idaho, Kansas, Louisiana, Michigan, Nevada, North Dakota, Oregon, Washington, and Wisconsin.

[12]*Town of Billerica* (Massachusetts) *Charter,* art. VI, pp. 6-4.

[13]*Town of Oxford* (Massachusetts) *Charter,* chap. VII, p. 6.

[14]For details on signature requirements, see *The Book of the States* (Lexington, Kentucky: The Council of State Governments, latest edition).

[15]*Constitution of California,* art. II, p. 14 (b) and *California Elections Code,* p. 27211 (b).

[16]For details, see Zimmerman, *Participatory Democracy: Populism Revived,* pp. 122-26.

[17]Benjamin Jowett, trans., *Artistotle's Politics* (New York: Carlton House, n.d.), p. 288.

[18]Joseph F. Zimmerman, "Preventing Unethical Behavior in Government," *Urban Law and Policy,* vol. VIII, 1987, pp. 335-56.

[19]*Guidelines for State Legislation on Government Ethics and Campaign Financing* (Lexington, Kentucky: The Council of State Governments, 1984), p. 4.

[20]*New York Laws of 1977,* chap. 933 and *New York Public Officers Law,* pp. 84-90.

[21]*Freedom of Information Act,* 88 Stat. 1986, 5 U.S.C. p. 552 (a) (2).

[22]For details on the legal relations existing between state and local governments today, see Joseph F. Zimmerman, *State-Local Relations: A Partnership Approach* (New York: Praeger Publishers, 1983), pp. 15-48.

[23]Joseph F. Zimmerman, *State Mandating of Local Expenditures* (Washington, D.C.: United States Advisory Commission on Intergovernmental Relations, 1978).

Electoral Accountability: Local Recalls

CHARLES M. PRICE

Charles M. Price is a political science professor at California State University, Chico.

In the first half of 1987, 18 Nebraska local elected officials—five, mayors, six council members, four school board members, and three village board members—were forced into recalls by petition campaigns directed against them. Of these 18, eight were removed by voters, four were able to retain their positions, and the others await their elections. Is this unprecedented local recall outbreak in Nebraska merely happenstance, or is it part of a larger pattern?

Significance of Local Recalls—Prevailing Sentiment

Most local recall elections are unique events occurring mainly in isolated, rural communities. While recall elections are usually bitter and divisive within a community, they rarely generate interest outside the immediate locale. A recall of a small-town mayor or rural county supervisor is unlikely to be considered prime news by a state's major metropolitan newspapers or television stations. Additionally, because no statewide recalls have successfully qualified for the ballot in over 50 years, scholars and journalists have tended to pay scant attention to this removal technique[1]

To complicate the picture further, no state has a central repository for the aggregate data, making it difficult to study local recalls systematically. Local recall election results are kept at various sites—offices of the county or city clerk, school administration offices, or special district offices. Finally, even when prominent local politicians are targets of recalls (such as former Cleveland, Ohio Mayor Dennis Kucinich in 1978, or Passaic, New Jersey Mayor Robert Hare and former San Francisco Mayor Dianne Feinstein in 1983) the media tend to treat the campaigns as aberrations based on either off-beat incumbent personalities or fluke issues.

The conventional wisdom among scholars and political experts is to downplay the recalls' significance. Charles Adrian argued in 1967 that there was a trend away from recall elections and "the question of recall use is no longer very important."[2] In 1983, Austin Ranney concurred, expressing "a strong impression that the use of the recall has dwindled somewhat from what it was in the early years of the century."[3] Also in the late 1960s, Duane Lockhard maintained that the recall was little used in the various states except in California.[4] Most recently, Randy Arndt of the National League of Cities, commenting on the Nebraska recall outbreak, stated "There is no national trend toward more recall elections. It's a pretty rare phenomenon where one instance sets off another."[5]

Extent of Recall Use

As reported in the April 1983 issue of the NATIONAL CIVIC REVIEW, recalls of local officials do take place with some regularity in at least eight recall-prone states (Oregon, Nebraska, Alaska, Idaho, Michigan, Nevada, California and Washington) and less frequently in the other 29 states allowing for some form of local recall. In fact, some modest indications suggest an increase in local recall use over the last several decades. This upsurge can be attributed to a growing population (more new jurisdictions and thus more recallable officials); declining confidence in government fueled by the failures of the Vietnam war, Watergate and the resignation of president Richard Nixon, and more recently, the Iran-Contra scandal; and a growing willingness on the part of the public to engage in petition politics.

Clearly, local recalls are more commonplace in some states and communities than others. Part of the explanation for variations in recall use hinges on procedural provisions—that is, how easy or difficult it is to qualify a recall petition in a particular community. In Pennsylvania, Minnesota, and Virginia, local recall advocates must prove "misfeasance" or "malfeasance" to remove an official. Not surprisingly, few local officials there have had to face recall campaigns. In 15 states, local recalls can only take place in home rule or charter counties and cities, or can be directed against only certain local elected officials, not all. In some local settings, the signature threshold level needed to qualify a recall is set so high that attempting to qualify a recall petition is only remotely possible (Chattanooga requires 50 percent plus one of city voters to sign a mayoralty petition; in Kansas all state and local recalls require 40 percent of votes cast for that office at the last election). In some communities the signature circulation time is very short, which also complicates recall qualifying.

On the other hand, in Paradise, California, a gold-rush, rural community with a large retired population, recall petition drives are constantly under way or threatened. Resorting to recalls is not an extraordinary feature in the gold country of northern California; it is a normal, almost expected facet of the region's local election process. In a similar vein, a former (recalled) mayor of Pequannok, New Jersey stated; "What's happening now is that people are using (recalls) so that if they lose an election, they start a recall drive and hope they win the second time around." In New Jersey some incumbents lose their recall and then shortly afterward get reelected to their former posts.

Local recall issues of the 1970s-80s have run the gamut, but overall many have involved scandals and allegations of impropriety, responses to tax increases proposed by local officials, the firing of popular local administrators (a city manager, police or fire chief, or school superintendent), economic discontent, school financing problems, or planning dilemmas.

Recent Recall Epidemics

While most local recalls are indeed isolated, idiosyncratic events, several examples of recall outbreaks indicate that on occasion one recall can indeed trigger another. That is, on occasion, "epidemics" of local recalls promoted by "copycat" recall proponents occur. Proposition 13, the late Howard Jarvis's and Paul Gann's *Property Tax Relief Initiative* of June 1978, sparked a host of new tax-cutting initiatives in California and other states in much the same way.

Some examples of recent rashes of recalls from some of the more susceptible states follow.

Nebraska. The well publicized recall of Omaha Mayor Mike Boyle in early January 1987 appears to have provided the impetus for recall drives launched against other local officials across the state. Former Wymore Mayor Rolly Salts (he was recalled from office) argued that the Omaha recall results cast a pall on other local officials. Many of the recalls occurring in the Cornhusker state dealt with the firing of a local administrator, with the fired official's friends in the community launching recalls against those who voted for the firing.

New Jersey. The mid-1980s saw a rash of recall drives directed against several well-known mayors. In 1983 a recall of Passaic Mayor Robert C. Hare came close to qualifying. In 1984 Atlantic City Mayor Michael Matthews was recalled and replaced by James L. Usry. And in 1986 Hoboken Mayor Thomas Vezetti became the target of a recall effort.

Michigan. In 1983 the Michigan state legislature and governor supported a proposal to increase state income taxes by 38 percent. Some 15 state legislators and the governor had recall petitions filed against them in a well-organized drive by angry Michigan taxpayers. Eventually, two Democratic state senators were removed from office in recall elections. This in turn switched majority control in the Michigan upper house from Democratic to Republican hands.

Oregon. Between 1970 and 1974 only eleven local recall elections (approximately 2 per year) took place in Oregon, a state famous for its heritage of direct democracy. But from 1975 to 1983 some 205 Oregon local officials, about 60 percent of them school board members, had recalls successfully qualified against them (approximately 23 per year). Many of those Oregon school board members had become entangled in the local school finance problems which plagued the state during this period.

California. Dozens of local recalls have been waged in the Golden State over the last several decades, mainly in mushrooming suburban communities whose political leaders have had to deal with one central issue: planning decisions. Environmental and "old settler" interests have fought for planned—or as their detractors contend, "no-growth"—policies against developers, realtors, business interests, and labor unions. As with Nebraska, Michigan, and Oregon, in California too there appears to be a recall spillover from one community to another. California counties with the greatest recall activity in the 1970s and 1980s tend to share borders with other counties with substantial numbers of recalls, while more distant parts of the state had virtually no recall activity. This suggests that there may be some sort of contagion effect operating.

Even in the most recall-prone states many citizens know little or nothing about the recall mechanism. However, succesful use of a recall in one community can inspire others nearby to give it a try. Debbie Christlieb, the successful leader of the recall drive to remove the mayor of Wymore, Nebraska, admitted that she had never heard of the process until stories of the Mayor of Omaha's recall had become news.

The examples cited above in Nebraska, New Jersey, Oregon, Michigan and California suggest that local recalls are not always isolated aberrations. The removal of a controversial local politician in one community can alert others in the area to the recall's feasibility. Thus the much-discussed recall effort directed against Governor Evan Mecham of Arizona could inspire recalls directed against a number of local Arizona officials.

Final Thoughts

Is the local recall process a good or bad feature? Does the recall process promote democracy? Are recalls unfair to incumbents? Does the recall mechanism discourage able citizens from seeking local office? Does the threat of a recall encourage some incumbents to forsake elected office? Are voters equipped to cast a ballot on emotionally charged recalls? Is voter turnout in recalls truly representative of the electorate? Are the frequently bitter, long-term divisions engendered within a community by a recall campaign worth the benefits?

Not surprisingly, a great many local officials, particularly those who have had to weather a recall campaign, have strong misgivings about the recall process.

There are a host of good arguments that can be made for and against the recall. Recalls can and do polarize communities. Charges levelled against an incumbent are sometimes flimsy, political and/or mean-spirited. Costs of the recall special election can be high, and turnout low. Many believe that recalls also encourage single-issue politics. Yet, notwithstanding these valid criticisms, the local recall serves a vitally important role at the local level in the American democratic system. It helps enforce accountability of local officials to the electorate.

At the local level, citizens can get directly involved in government. City council meetings are accessible, and it is possible to monitor local government leaders. Those citizens who have an interest in an issue and who have the time and energy (frequently the retired) can have an immediate impact. And one of the most effective tools to enforce leadership accountability, at least in some communities, is the petition process and recall election. While incumbents' concerns about the potential abuses in the local recall process are understandable and not without substance, and while citizen input can be misguided, the recall provides citizens at the local level with an important accountability tool. In fact, would it not be healthier to have our state and federal officials more responsive to the public by making them all subject to recall too? In the local recall states, citizens don't just have to take it; they can fight city hall—and sometimes win.

Notes

[1]Very few state officials have ever been recalled, and of this handful only one or two were *statewide* officials. The number of signatures needed to qualify a recall petition against a statewide elected officer is very high. While successful statewide recalls are extremely rare, greater opportunities exist for the process to be employed these days than in the past. Though expensive, the use of the direct mail firms with the ability to send mailings to hundreds of thousands of targeted voters persuading them to sign the enclosed petitions and return them with a campaign contribution means more potential for successful statewide recalls. In addition, even unsuccessful recall campaigns waged against statewide officeholders can have a negative impact on the incumbent. In the late 1970s and '80s former California Chief Justice Rose Bird had several different recalls filed against her. While none qualified for the ballot, they weakened the Chief Justice politically, a circumstance exploited by her opponents which contributed to the loss of her confirmation election. Also, the strength of the recall campaign against Arizona's Governor Evan Mecham may have contributed to the state senate's willingness to impeach him.

[2]Charles Adrian, *State and Local Governments,* New York, McGraw-Hill, 1967, p. 39.

[3]Quoted in *Herald-News* story by Matthew Moser, April 7, 1983, p. B-1.

[4]Duane Lockhard, *Politics of State and Local Government,* London, MacMillan, 1969, p. 254.

[5]Quoted in Associated Press story by Steven Wine in *Sacramento Bee,* May 26, 1987, p. A-3.

Government Institutions and Officeholders

- Legislatures (Articles 18-22)
- Executives (Articles 23-26)
- Courts (Articles 27-28)
- Other Institutions and Related Matters (Articles 29-30)

Government institutions are to state and local political systems what skeletons are to people. They shape the general outlines of policy processes in the same way that bones shape the outlines of human bodies. For state and local governments, as well as for the national government and most governments everywhere, institutions are critical factors in the governing process.

There are important institutional differences among the states. In "strong governor" states, chief executives hold substantially greater appointive, budgetary, and veto powers than in "weak governor" states. The roles of parties, committees, and leaders differ among state legislatures, as does the degree of "professionalization" among legislators themselves. The roles of state court systems vary according to contents of state constitutions as well as state political and judicial traditions. In some states, the state's highest court plays a role that may be roughly comparable to that of the United States Supreme Court at the national level. The highest courts in most states, however, are generally less prominent. Finally, the devices of initiative, referendum, and recall, already mentioned in the overview for unit 3, are available in some states but not in others. Structural details of state governments are spelled out in each state's written constitution, although state constitutions generally do not play as prominent or symbolically important a role in state government as the United States Constitution does in national government.

Local governments do not incorporate the traditional three-branch structure of government to the extent that state and national governments do. Legislative and executive powers are often given to a single governing body, with the members choosing one of themselves to be the nominal chief executive. For example, school boards typically elect their own board "president" to preside over meetings, but they hire a professional educational administrator, called a superintendent, to manage day-to-day affairs. What is true of school boards also applies to many other local governments. In contrast, the structures of some "strong mayor" cities do resemble the executive-legislative arrangements in national and state governments. The traditional notion of an independent local judiciary as a "third branch" does not easily apply at the level of local government. Local courts, to the extent they

exist, do not restrain the other branches of local government in the way that state and national courts are empowered to restrain their respective legislative and executive branches.

Despite the complications noted above, this unit on institutions is organized along traditional legislative, executive, and judicial lines. The first section treats state and local legislatures, which include town meetings, city and town councils, school boards, and, of course, state legislatures. The second section turns to governors and local government executives. The third section treats state and local courts, and the last section considers miscellaneous institutions and related matters that appear in the state and local landscape.

Looking Ahead: Challenge Questions

Compare and contrast the positions of president of a school board, elected chief executive of a small town, city manager, mayor of a large city, state governor, and president of the United States.

Compare and contrast the positions of school board member, member of a town meeting, town council member in a small town, city council member in a large city, state legislator, and member of the United States House of Representatives.

Get a copy of your state constitution and read it. How does it compare and contrast with the United States Constitution—in length, subjects covered, ease of reading, and familiarity?

Attend a meeting of your local school board. What was the meeting like?

How many state governors and state legislators can you name? Do you feel you know enough about your own state governor and your representatives in your home state legislature to evaluate their performance?

Is it better to have well-paid and prestigious elected positions as in the national government, or less well-paid, part-time elected posts as are common in local governments and many state legislatures? Which makes for better government?

Do you think that it is a good idea to let citizens participate directly in the policy process by means of initiatives, referenda, or town meetings? Or is it better to leave legislating to elected representatives? Why?

Unit 4

Reinventing the Legislature

State legislatures have changed and progressed more than any other governmental institution over the past 20 years. Stimulated by increases in staff and other resources, the "first branch of government" has now established itself as a powerful political entity.

William T. Pound

William Pound is director of NCLS's Denver office and a former political science professor at the University of Denver.

Each one is unique, yet they are all strikingly similar. Each has diverse responsibilities, yet they all share common problems. State legislatures—"the first branch of government"—are the most revitalized, changed and challenged governmental institutions in America and today they have a vastly increased capacity to govern.

Interested citizens, legislative staff, lobbyists and even lawmakers themselves may take the resources and capabilities that have fostered this change for granted, but state legislatures in 1986 have progressed more than any other governmental institution over the past 20 years. As recently as the 1950s, a national study referred to state legislatures as "19th-century institutions." But by the early 1980s, futurist John Naisbitt called state and local governments "the most important political entities in America." Legislatures had been transformed in a number of ways to make them equal partners in state government.

The reapportionment revolution of the mid-1960s was the catalyst for the modernization of state legislatures. State and federal courts handed down the one-man, one-vote rule, requiring equality of population in all representational districts. But the impetus for change had already begun.

The beginnings of the modern legislature can be traced back to 1901 when Wisconsin established the first permanent legislative staff by creating the legislative reference bureau. Prior to that, administrative functions in the legislatures were limited to the clerk and secretary, two positions derived from English parliamentary tradition. During the middle third of this century, a majority of states established legislative councils (the first council was established in Kansas in 1933) to allow the legislature to function during interim periods and give it some permanent research and legal capability—independent of the executive branch or outside resources.

After World War II, specialized legislative staffing began to emerge, particularly in the fiscal area. California and Texas were among the first legislatures to establish a strong, independent budget development and analysis capability. Previously, legislatures merely ratified executive budgets—still the case in some states—or depended entirely on the executive branch for budget analysis.

Modernizing the state legislature, however, involved not only the growth of staff capacity, but the removal of many limits on sessions and salaries, and on matters legislatures could consider. As recently as 1941 only four legislatures held annual sessions. That number grew to 19 by 1962, to 35 in 1972 and to 43 today. Only Arkansas, Kentucky, Montana, Nevada, North Dakota, Oregon and Texas retain biennial sessions.

Adequate pay for legislators was an important element in legislative modernization. Constitutional restrictions on legislators' salaries were removed. Today only nine states establish legislator salaries in their constitutions. In the remainder, statutes control, often with some type of compensation commission to make binding or advisory recommendations. Those states retaining salary limitations tend to provide the lowest levels of legislator compensation. Current salaries range from $100 per year in New Hampshire to $46,800 in Alaska. The average legislative salary in 1986 was slightly above $17,000. In fact, though, this figure understates actual legislative compensation due to the widespread payment of vouchered and unvouchered expenses to legislators and additional compensation paid to leaders (and sometimes committee chairmen) in 42 states.

The removal of restrictions on sessions has been accompanied by a continuing discussion as to how much time legislatures should spend in session and

Competitive Legislatures Seek Stronger, Specialized Staffs

The increasing volume and complexity of issues confronting state legislatures have contributed to growth and specialization of legislative staff. But the fundamental catalyst behind most major staff changes is "competition."

When state legislatures decided to compete for a stronger role in policymaking, they confronted the very formidable resources of the federal government, the governor's office and the expanding ranks of lobbyists and special interests. As state legislatures succeeded in gaining power and influence, internal competitions between parties, chambers and candidates also heightened.

In all of these contests, legislators have sought to strengthen their position with the aid of more and better information provided by more and better staff.

The most recent major reorganization of staff occurred in Louisiana and Oklahoma about six years ago. In each case, a more traditional legislative council system was abandoned to create separate, bipartisan staffs for each house. According to Alan Yates, legislative director of the Oklahoma Senate, the old centralized arrangement was not able to satisfy the divergent needs of the two chambers. "In Oklahoma there is not as much of a power struggle between the two parties as in other states," comments Yates, "[but] we have more of a routine, ongoing battle between the House and the Senate. It was difficult for staff to be between both of them." Similarly, the catalyst for Louisiana's staff split was leadership's mismatched expectations of necessary staff roles and functions.

Being caught between competitive parties also can be difficult for staff. Not surprisingly, states with more party competition and relatively larger staffs tend to employ a more decentralized, partisan staffing pattern.

In Indiana, where the parties are moderately competitive, small caucus staffs provide speech writing, press relations and constituent services. All other major staff functions are provided by a central Legislative Services Agency, whose executive director, Chuck Harris, believes that the caucus staffs provide essential insulation between the agency and the legislature's partisan activities. "We will remain effective as long as we're bipartisan," says Harris. "We [also] feel there is a need for a strong partisan staff."

Washington's more politically competitive atmosphere has lent support to the creation of very active caucus staffs that perform research and provide substantial assistance to leadership. And in the very large, very political states like New York and Pennsylvania, few staff members operate outside the realm of the party caucus.

The trend toward the creation of specialized staff units has slowed and state fiscal stress has caused some of these units to be cut back or eliminated. A variety of interesting examples, both technical and political, of staff specialization continue to thrive, however.

Florida's Division of Economic and Demographic Forecasting lends new and sophisticated information to the legislature's fiscal debates. The Illinois legislature supports a unique Chicago-based science unit that, due to its location, is able to draw information from a vast pool of technical resources.

California, Illinois and New York—states with large urban/industrial populations that are particularly sensitive to federal policy shifts—operate full-time staff offices in Washington, D.C.

Jeff Wice directs the New York Assembly's Washington office that is a joint venture of both houses. According to Wice, beyond providing a liaison between the speaker's office and the state's Congressional delegation, he and his staff monitor federal funds, identify energy issues, handle basic research and interact with other states that are active on state/federal issues of mutual interest.

Two areas of specialization continue to be popular—budget analysis and program evaluation. Both functions give legislators new tools (some might say "weapons") in their struggle to control fiscal policy and program effectiveness.

Decentralization of legislative staff, especially where personal staff and staff activities respond primarily to the partisan needs of individual members, is a trend that has fostered considerable debate within the state legislative community. Critics argue that the "congressionalization" of state legislatures threatens to diminish the integrity of the legislative institution in favor of the short-term priorities of individual members.

This debate recently flared in Nebraska in the wake of criticism that the legislature's "scattered" staff arrangement inhibits effective information sharing and long-term research. One sentence from a *Lincoln Journal* editorial commented on the argument about personal staff: "This is the staff which some senators believe has become vital to the performance of senatorial jobs: research, scheduling and 'constituent services'—especially constituent services."

Whether providing constituent service, research, program evaluation, fiscal analysis or one of dozens of other services, it is likely that state legislative staff will continue to grow, although at a cautious pace. Some states faced with severe revenue shortfalls, such as Oklahoma and Texas, have had to freeze or reduce staffing levels.

All state legislatures are confronted with a renewed challenge to squeeze additional services from existing resources. "There will be more people, more issues, more growth and more pressure for services," predicts Nevada's Don Rhodes.

Indiana's Harris speaks for many legislative staff directors when he adds, "The only way we've been able to improve our services is through better planning and by providing better tools to our staff . . . in other words, by becoming more efficient."

Jeff Wice, right, with Congressman Charles H. Schumer of New York

—Brian Weberg, senior staff associate, Legislative Management, NCSL

what is the most effective use of legislative time. Should the legislator's role be considered "full time" or "part time"? Can a legislature operate with fairly limited sessions and still maintain an active policy and oversight role through effective use of the interim?

The argument about limited sessions is often couched in terms of preserving the "citizen" nature of state legislatures as opposed to developing "professional" or full-time legislatures on the congressional model. There is no question that the amount of time spent in session and the level of compensation affect the composition of the membership of legislative bodies. Many argue that it is desirable that the predominant occupation of members of legislatures not be that of legislator, but that legislative bodies represent a broad spectrum of vocations. However, the growing demands on state legislatures and the greater legislative role in initiating policies, budgeting and overseeing programs have increased the pressure on legislative time.

There is no limit placed on the length of sessions in 12 states. Of 32 states that constitutionally limit legislative sessions, two limit only the second year and the remaining six states have statutory or indirect limitations based on cutoffs in salaries or per diem expense payments.

During the 1960s and 1970s, limits on legislative sessions were eliminated or relaxed. Recent years have brought a mixed response to the question of session length. Alaska adopted a 120-day limit in 1984, replacing its previously unlimited sessions. Colorado adopted a second-year session limit of 140 days in 1982, and Washington set session limitations when it went from biennial to annual sessions in 1981. Utah lengthened its sessions by 10 days per biennium in 1984 when it changed from a 60-day first year/20-day second year system to 45 days per session. New Hampshire adopted annual sessions effective in 1985. Several legislatures, notably Arizona and Iowa, have limited their sessions by legislative rule or statute. Movements to adopt more restrictive session limits surface periodically, particularly in the states having the longest sessions.

Whether a legislature is full time in nature can generally be measured by time spent in session, level of compensation and occupational self-definition of the members. The legislatures of California, Illinois, Massachusetts, Michigan, New Jersey, New York, Ohio, Pennsylvania and Wisconsin have lengthy sessions, relatively high legislator salaries and many members whose primary occupation is that of legislator. None of these states have constitutionally imposed session limitations, though both California and Wisconsin adopt a systematic schedule of committee and floor activity, as well as recess periods, at the beginning of each biennium. Many of the legislatures that have longer sessions meet only two or three days per week, while in other states with more restricted sessions, five- and six-day workweeks are common. Several of the medium-size states actually spend as many days in session as do the full-time legislatures. Full-time legislators are likely to spend considerable time in district offices and place a high priority on service to constituents. More than two-thirds of the legislatures

were in session more than 100 legislative days each biennium during the 1980s.

Legislators who define their occupation as "legislator" are increasing in number. A recent survey of state lawmakers conducted by NCSL found that more than half the legislators in New York and Pennsylvania define their occupation as "legislator." This study also indicated that the number of "business owners" who are legislators in the larger states is much smaller than in the states with more limited sessions. Lawyer legislators exist in greatest numbers in the South, but their numbers are decreasing. In a number of states persons engaged in "education" outnumber as legislators those coming from any other professional background. Persons engaged in "agriculture" are still found in every legislature, but serve in greatest number in the rural Midwestern and mountain states. Women and minority representation continues to increase each biennium: There are now more than 1,100 women and nearly 400 minority members among the country's 7,461 state legislators.

Women and minority legislators are gradually moving into leadership positions. There are currently two black speakers (California and Pennsylvania) and a female speaker and senate president (Oregon and New Hampshire).

A continuing preoccupation of legislatures is the management of time during sessions. Most legislatures have adopted some type of committee and floor scheduling systems, and deadlines for bill filing and legislative action. The practice of prefiling bills and allowing the carry-over of bills to the second session has become more prevalent in legislatures in the past 20 years. Forty-four states allow prefiling today; fewer than 10 used this procedure 20 years ago. In the mid-1960s, only nine states had bill carry-over provisions; in 1986, 25 legislatures carry over bills to the second session. Limitations on bill introductions are gaining favor in a few states. These limitations often do not apply to prefiled bills and thus allow a fast session start and the scheduling of an even flow of legislation.

Other factors contributing to the modernization of state legislatures include stronger committee systems and procedures, and a greater emphasis on interim committee activities. While committee strength varies from state to state, committees in most legislatures have been reduced in number, have greater substantive expertise than in past years and are more influential in the shaping of legislation. In many legislative bodies today, most bills are killed in committee, not on the floor. Money committees have become increasingly powerful, corresponding with the assertion of legislative budget authority.

Legislatures have also become more active during the interim period between sessions. Florida and Washington use committee weeks or weekends to get interim work done while minimizing time demands on legislators. They concentrate all interim committee meetings within a three- or four-day period each month.

The effectiveness of interim committees varies widely. A

New Rules, Procedures: Speeding up the Process

The business of state legislatures has grown more complex over the past three decades, increasing the number of bills considered and debated by legislators. To handle the flow of bills, various mechanisms have been instituted to save session time and expedite the processing of legislation.

The most common time-saving techniques are deadline systems setting cut-off dates for drafting requests, bill introductions, committee action in the house of origin, final action in the house of origin and similar steps in the opposite house. The deadlines are designed to spread the work flow throughout the session, reduce end-of-session logjams and help leaders better manage the work load.

Seventy-nine legislative bodies establish deadlines for introducing bills and 46 have cut-off dates for requesting bill drafts. Over half of the houses indicate that deadlines are suspended routinely, or often fall late in the session and make little difference.

Colorado, Iowa and North Dakota all have successful deadline systems that regulate the flow of work throughout the session. The Iowa General Assembly schedules by weeks. For example, all bills must be introduced by the seventh week of the session, floor consideration of bills in the house of origin must be completed by the 11th week and bills originating in the other house must be considered by the appropriate committee by the 13th week. At the final cut-off, the two houses consider only the bills that have passed both houses, "exempt" bills and unfinished business.

Exempt from the deadlines are appropriations, ways and means and finance bills, bills co-sponsored by the majority and minority floor leaders, companion bills sponsored by the majority floor leaders of both houses, bills introduced by members of the administrative rules review committee, and bills in conference committee. Iowa uses "exempt" bills to handle emergency situations.

In addition to managing legislative work flow, each of the deadlines stops a certain number of bills from proceeding any further during the session. This helps the rank-and-file members explain to constituents why their bills have failed. On the other hand, the deadline system reduces the bargaining power of members, who can no longer withhold their votes from leadership in exchange for votes in support of other pieces of legislation that may miss the deadline.

Another time-saving device is limiting the number of bills a legislator can introduce.

The Nebraska Unicameral and the Colorado General Assembly are the only two legislatures that have attempted to set absolute limits.

In Nebraska, however, the limits were often circumvented and proved difficult to enforce. As a result, the absolute limit was abandoned at the start of the 1981 session.

In 1984, Colorado began limiting members to four bills in even-numbered years of a session, but it is too early to draw any conclusions about its effectiveness.

A more successful strategy limits the number of bills a member can introduce once the session starts, but permits unlimited prefiling. This rule, implemented by both houses in Colorado, Indiana, Montana, and North Dakota, the Florida House and the South Dakota Senate, encourages prefiling of bills so that legislation is drafted early and is ready for committee consideration.

Legislatures employ a variety of committee-scheduling techniques to help minimize conflicts for members and increase time for committee meetings. All states now schedule floor and committee meetings at separate times. Seventy-nine of the 99 state legislative bodies set the committee schedule at the start of the session and almost half set a specific day and time for weekly committee meetings. Kentucky, the New York Assembly and the Pennsylvania House use computers to help scheduling of committee meetings.

One of the more successful techniques states use is to divide committees into categories, with members serving on only one major committee within each category. However, a member may serve on more than one minor committee. One-third of the legislative bodies use this procedure.

The Hawaii House, for example, uses an "A" and "B" bracketing system, with the "A" bracket composed of the major committees. The standing committees are grouped by subject matter into six program areas, three within each bracket. Members serve in only one program area in a bracket, but sit on all of the standing committees contained in the program area. The system has reduced absenteeism and eliminated conflicting meeting schedules for members. It also confronts the problem of overlapping jurisdiction among committees, and provides for legislative deliberations on the basis of related subject matter.

—Jan Carpenter, principal staff associate, Legislative Management, NCSL
Further details on rules and procedures are available from the NCSL Denver office.

growing trend is to use standing committees during the interim. In states with strong interim or legislative council traditions, interim committee bills often have a high rate of passage. Even where no direct legislation results from interim work the interim may have a substantial educational effect on subsequent legislative action.

Other results of the reduction in constitutional restrictions and the changing operating environment of state legislatures are seen in the ability of 29 legislatures to call themselves into special session and the increased frequency with which special sessions have been held. An emerging practice in some states without constitutionally limited sessions is to recess subject to the call of the leadership rather than to adjourn *sine die*. This practice allows the legislature to act at any time and react immediately to changing situations rather than reposing interim authority entirely in the executive branch.

Legislatures also override gubernatorial vetoes with greater frequency than in past years. In part this is due to the development in some states of veto sessions that provide the legislature greater opportunity to consider the governor's action on bills. But in a number of states it is primarily due to increased independence in the legislative branch and to split partisan control of the branches of government. There are states, such as New York, where until recent years, more than a century passed without a veto override.

These changes have been accompanied by continual expansion of legislative capacity through staffing, facilities and information resources. The permanent staff of state legislatures totals more than 16,000 employees, with another 9,000 temporary or session staff. Nearly all this staff growth has occurred since 1969, with the development of specialized staff in areas such as fiscal, legal services, auditing and program evaluations, administrative rule review, computer services and committee staff. There has been a similar growth, particularly in the past decade, of personal staff for legislators and of caucus staff.

Legislative staff was at one time largely organized in central agencies, under leadership direction. Recent years have seen the decentralization and specialization of legislative staff. Louisiana and Oklahoma have most recently moved to separate House and Senate staffs from a centralized structure. Individual members now employ staff in many legislatures and committee staff is used extensively in California, Florida, Pennsylvania and New York.

Staff decentralization may be an irreversible trend, but both Illinois and Nebraska have recognized management problems with a fragmented staff situation and moved to assert more centralized leadership control.

Legislative facilities have been improved in nearly every state. At the beginning of the legislative reform movement, few states provided more to legislators than their desk on the floor. Committee rooms were non-existent or inadequate. Legislatures have gradually moved other governmental offices out of capitol buildings, increasing the space available to the legislature and providing the opportunity to construct offices for legislators and modern committee and staff facilities.

In a like manner, the information resources available to legislatures have expanded steadily. Increased staff resources have meant greater independent information and support for state legislatures. As recently as the 1950s, the majority of legislatures were primarily dependent on the executive for information and support services. Computers are having a significant impact on the legislative process. Modern word processing and information systems facilitate electoral tasks and communication with constituents. Such systems also can develop models of the possible implications of legislation and track appropriations and can contribute to more effective legislative oversight. Computers have made legislative bill processing and record keeping much faster and allow both legislators and the public to have more information about bills and bill status.

Legislatures have undertaken many new functions. They have become aggressive in the oversight of programs, though legislative oversight is sometimes performed badly and inadequately linked to the ongoing legislative process. Some legislatures have created some mechanism for the review and/or veto of administrative rules. Program evaluation units have been established in many legislatures. Constituent services, district offices and public information efforts have been developed by a number of legislatures, particularly in the larger states.

Changes in state legislatures have not occurred at the same pace in all states. In states that are dominated by one political party, such as Kentucky, Louisiana and Tennessee, the catalyst for development of legislative independence and expansion of the legislative role has often been the capture of the executive branch by the other party. The last few years have seen a consolidation of earlier legislative reforms and their gradual spread throughout the states. Legislatures are again paying more attention to their own procedures and staff structure, as evidenced by the number of studies of rules, staffing and operations during the mid-1980s.

One result of legislative independence has been constitutional confrontation between legislature and executive, often over legislative assertions of authority. Considerable variation exists in the role and power of the legislature in budgeting but, in general, legislatures are playing a much more assertive role in fiscal policy. The legislature dominates the budget process in states such as Colorado, New Mexico, and Texas and is at least an equal partner in others.

State legislatures are dynamic, ever-changing institutions. The environment in which they function is changing as the relations and responsibilities of our various governmental levels change. With the responsibility for most domestic programs becoming centered in the states, there is increased lobbying pressure on state legislatures and the cost of legislative election campaigns is rapidly rising. The number of registered lobbyists in many states has more than doubled in the past 10 years. And the costs of state legislative election campaigns have risen to the hundreds of thousands of dollars in the larger states, with proportionate increases in the smaller states. These pressures no doubt will result in continued changes in state legislatures.

The role of the state legislator has not necessarily become easier, despite the increased resources available. Programmatic, budget and constituent demands will continue to grow. As John Bragg, a veteran Tennessee legislator, commented, "Have you noticed that all those funny stories we told about the legislature happened more than 10 years ago? Things are more serious and difficult now. Then it was all fun and frivolity; either you were with the governor or against him, and that was all you had to know."

Party politics:

The new chamber game

Alan Rosenthal

Dr. Rosenthal is director of the Eagleton Institute of Politics at Rutgers — the State University of New Jersey.

Partisanship and the growing electoral pre-occupation of legislative parties is stimulated by the concern of leaders and rank and file with retaining or acquiring party majorities and leadership positions.

One of the most significant developments in state legislatures today is the expanded political role of the legislative party caucus and of legislative leadership. In earlier years, legislative parties and leaders focused on legislation and the legislative process, devoting relatively little attention to campaigns and elections. Now they are immersed in campaigns and elections, displacing party organizations at state and local levels and taking over the electoral function. With state and local parties becoming weaker, legislative party caucuses are filling the vacuum.

Re-election was always a principal concern of individual legislators, and it remains so. But now, it is also a principal concern of the legislative parties, at least in those states where parties are organized in the legislature and where competition is sharp between Democrats and Republicans. Thirty years ago, only a dozen or so states had competitive parties. Now half of the states have substantial competition in the legislative as well as the executive branches, and in most other states, competition is increasing.

Some legislatures are still dominated by a single party, such as those in Maryland and Kentucky where few Republicans have seats. But overall, partisanship has increased, especially in states where competition has been keen for some time, such as California, Michigan, New Jersey and Wisconsin. Partisanship has also increased in states such as Florida and Texas where a single party has ruled until quite recently.

Partisanship and the growing electoral preoccupation of legislative parties is stimulated by the concern of leaders and rank and file with retaining or acquiring party majorities and leadership positions. Competition arises when for one party, there is the opportunity of winning a majority, and for the other, the possibility of losing a majority. Parties engage in three major types of electoral activity: campaign fund raising, staffing, and managing issues for their party's advantage and to their opponents' disadvantage.

Leaders in more than half the states have taken on the job of raising funds and allocating them to members and challengers alike. Speaker Willie Brown in California sets the pace. Not only has he raised millions for Democratic assembly candidates, but he has intervened in primary races as well. In 1986, Brown's candidates won in five of the six primaries where the speaker played a significant role (while Minority Leader Pat Nolan's candidates lost in three out of five primaries). Although most legislative leaders steer clear of primaries, Brown justifies his involvement on the grounds that the party needs to nominate candidates who can win the general election. To do otherwise is a "good way to lose your job," he maintains.

From *State Government News*, April 1988, pp. 22-23. Reprinted by permission of The Council of State Governments.

As in California, in those states where political parties compete vigorously in legislative elections, one of the principal jobs of the leader has become that of campaign manager. This is the situation in Connecticut, Illinois, Michigan, Minnesota, New York, Ohio, Pennsylvania, Washington and Wisconsin, among others.

The experience of Chuck Hardwick, who had been majority leader in the New Jersey Assembly, is illustrative. For a full year, he spent part of every day working for the Republicans' 1985 legislative campaign. His efforts (and Gov. Tom Kean's coattails) paid off: the Republicans won control and Hardwick became speaker. Later on, in discussing his new role, Hardwick put preparing for the next campaign first among the various tasks of the speaker. The order of priority was no accident, for if Hardwick neglected maintaining his majority, he would not have to concern himself with most of the other tasks. His work, and that of his majority leader, Robert Franks, was effective. In the 1987 elections, the Republicans kept control of the assembly, by 42-38, a smaller margin than they had before, but control nonetheless. And Franks took over as chairman of the State Republican Committee, symbolizing the ascendancy of the legislative party.

Partisan staffing is on the rise in many legislatures. In Illinois, for example, the size of partisan staffs has tripled or quadrupled over the last 20 years. Today, house Democrats and Republicans each have about 80 professionals on the payroll, while senate Democrats have 60 and senate Republicans somewhat fewer. Most of Michigan's 900 staff professionals are organized along partisan lines.

Another example is Connecticut where until 1987, the General Assembly's nonpartisan central staff easily outnumbered the partisan staff. However, in 1984, the Republicans won the Legislature from the Democrats. In 1986, the Democrats regained their majorities. At the same time that partisan competition was increasing, a new legislative office building was completed, allowing room for more staff. As a consequence, the number of partisan staff positions was increased nearly four-fold in 1987.

One of the purposes of expanding partisan staff is to improve the party's electoral prospects. New York is a prime example. Traditionally, some people carried on the New York legislative payroll have political campaigning as their principal, or even exclusive responsibility. In 1986, eight Democratic candidates, of whom six were challengers, were assisted in their campaigns by workers on the senate minority's payroll. This prompted the Manhattan district attorney to bring an indictment for grand larceny and conspiracy against the senate minority leader and one of his colleagues. The case is still pending.

Elsewhere, campaign activity by partisan staff is more circumspect. Officially, partisan staff does not get involved in campaigns as such — that is, staff will take leave from their jobs if they are going to work in the districts or go door-to-door. But unofficially, staff work to help maintain or achieve their party's majority, or to simply add to party numbers. As one partisan professional described things, "We don't do anything *on* a campaign, but everything we do is *for* the campaign. The first year, we set them [members] up legislatively; the second year, we work their constituencies."

Today more than before, the competition between the parties for electoral advantage is being waged in the legislative process. Partisanship is becoming more intense. When Democrats and Republicans are poles apart ideologically, partisanship will be strong, as is the case in California. But whatever the ideological split, issues are being raised and used as vehicles in the parties' quest for power. While there is nothing new with legislative parties taking into account the potential effects that their positions vis-a-vis a bill will have on their electoral prospects, today they go further. They raise and exploit issues to secure an electoral edge, to establish a record that will help themselves and embarrass the opposition. Floor amendments, requiring record votes, are conventional devices to achieve such ends.

Partisan positioning, by one means or another, appears to have become routine in states like California, Connecticut, Illinois, Iowa, Michigan, New Jersey and Wisconsin. The floor session is managed with the next election in mind, and the maneuvering between the parties often bears a striking resemblance to guerrilla theater.

The new electoral role of legislative leaders and legislative parties is probably unavoidable, given the increasing competition and high stakes of the game. And this legislative electoral machine has its critics. One of them, Sherry Bebitch Jeffe, writing in the *California Journal* (January 1987), describes the California Legislature as "politicized and corrupted by the pervasive influence of money in politics and government," [viewing] politics as a career orientation, [and] lack[ing] time to consider policy because time must be spent raising money [for re-election]."

Proponents, however, see greater leadership and caucus involvement in elections as a needed unifying force. Tom Loftus, speaker of the Wisconsin Assembly, defends the practice, but he, too, recognizes some of the risks involved. At a conference on The State of the States, sponsored by the Eagleton Institute of Politics in December 1987, Loftus sounded a cautionary note: "I understand how the party functions have moved into the legislature. . . . It's when it's overdone that I think it's of some concern. What happens is that the leaders then become expected to raise money for candidates, the system gets out of control. . . . And it may not bring a caucus together, it may not strengthen leadership, it may indeed give leadership an additional job and be a distraction."

Nebraska's Unicameral

Fifty Years Without a Conference Committee

Nebraska embarked on a legislative experiment in 1937 that has become a tradition there after half a century, but so far no other state has copied it.

Pat Wunnicke

Pat Wunnicke is assistant editor of State Legislatures.

Times were tough in Nebraska in 1934, drought and Depression taking their toll, the Legislature doing nothing effective about either. An appealing aspect of one proposal for the November ballot was the promise that a new one-house legislature would be cheaper to operate than two, and might be more effective.

The idea of a unicameral legislature, like the idea of non-partisanship and citizen initiative, grew out of the Progressive movement at the turn of the century, and had been kicking around in Nebraska as well as other states in the Midwest and northern plains for a good many years. In fact, the proposal had been defeated by only one vote in the Nebraska constitutional convention of 1920, after being repeatedly quashed early in the century by legislators perhaps understandably reluctant to sacrifice their own seats.

But now the proposal had the backing of beloved George Norris, longtime U.S. senator and Nebraska hero. First elected to the U.S. House of Representatives in 1902, Norris spent 40 illustrious years in the Congress before he died at 83. The summer and fall of 1934, however, he spent travel-

Photos: Nebraska State Historical Society

U.S. Senator George Norris spent the summer of 1934 traveling Nebraska, expounding on the evils of the bicameral system and extolling the virtues of unicameralism.

ing the dusty back roads of Nebraska —"wore out two sets of tires and two windshields," recalled his widow three decades later—speaking at every opportunity on the evils of the bicameral system ("illogical and clumsy"), extolling the virtues of unicameralism and pleading with the voters to support it.

A one-house legislative body was not unheard of. It had been adopted, in various guises, by almost all cities and counties, and in modified form

was (and still is) a feature of Canadian provincial governments. During Revolutionary times, Georgia, Pennsylvania and Vermont experimented with a type of unicameralism, but abandoned it early, Georgia and Pennsylvania before the turn of the 19th century, and Vermont in 1836. For a century thereafter, the two-house state legislature prevailed throughout the United States. (Among the territories, Guam and the Virgin Islands use the unicameral system.)

But years of legislative experience had convinced Norris that the conference committee, inevitable with two bodies, was an unmitigated evil, distorting or even thwarting legislation that had been approved by a majority. In addition, he disapprovingly traced the two-house method of organization back to the English class system that produced the House of Commons and the House of Lords. He said, "...in this country we have no such classes and the constitutions of our various states are built upon the idea that there is but one class. If this be true, there is no sense or reason in having the same thing done twice, especially if it is to be done by two bodies of men elected in the same way and having the same jurisdiction."

Norris was ahead of his time. His comments were on firmer ground 30 years later, after the reapportionment decisions did ensure that both bodies of a legislature were "elected in the same way and (have) the same jurisdiction."

The question of one house or two and the merits of each had been discussed at length 150 years before. Madison wrote worriedly (in The Federalist, #38) of the Confederation's "Congress, a single body of men,... the sole depositary of all the federal powers." Salvaging the Constitutional Convention in 1787, the Great Compromise setting up a two-house legislature put to rest the fears of the delegates from the smaller states that their interests would be overlooked by a national legislature dominated by representatives from the large states.

Although low on the list of national priorities, unicameralism is still being debated. At an Eagleton Institute of Politics conference for state legislators in the 1960s, the late Jess Unruh, fabled California politician and sometime speaker of the California Assembly, called unicameralism "the wave of the future," asking rhetorically, "Does any corporation have two boards of directors?" He called the two-house system "a costly and inefficient anachronism" and said, "I do not believe that increased salaries, new facilities and professional staff will be more than temporary palliatives for the ills that it is hoped they will cure. These reforms in themselves

only make a more efficient horse and buggy. I take little comfort from the fact that legislatures can be the fastest horse and buggy in the jet age."

Unruh's disciples have kept the discussion going in California, but it has yet to make its way to the ballot box. In recent years, several other states have looked at the unicameral option with more than curiosity: Hawaii and Mississippi have considered it in constitutional conventions, and petition efforts were made but failed to gain enough signatures in Michigan and Montana. Alaska voters, invited by the Legislature in 1976 to cast an "advisory vote" on whether an amendment to the state constitution should be offered future voters, obliged with 58,782 yeas and 55,204 nays, but the following years' sessions ignored the advice.

Minnesota Speaker David Jennings proposed a unicameral setup in 1985 as a way of dealing with conference-committee problems, but the Minnesota Citizens League disagreed. Its report, "Power to the Process," published in September 1985, found "no compelling evidence that the unicameral structure is superior to the two-house model." The report, while admitting that the two-house arrangement requires additional work and extra staff, suggests that it brings the advantages of different ideas and policy approaches to the policymaking process, and introduces "a major check into the legislative process."

However, a report in the University of Minnesota's Humphrey Institute *Future of the State Legislature* series, published in March 1986, takes a more positive view of the unicameral option, although it stops short of explicitly advocating the change.

Robert Sittig, professor of political science at the University of Nebraska (Lincoln), and author of *The Nebraska Unicameral After Fifty Years*, believes that only in the 14 states with the initiative has the system much of a chance. He points out that "the greatest drawback often is the one which frustrated the original unicameral proponents in Nebraska: The legislature itself is the prescribed starting place for constitutional amendments; however, legislators are disinclined to approve proposals which would alter substantially the body in which they serve."

Norris and his cohorts in 1934 used

that powerful new tool, the initiative, which had been adopted by Nebraska 22 years before. He and John P. Senning, professor of political science at the University of Nebraska, drafted the language of the initiative that was to amend the state constitution that fall. It would save time, talk and money, they said. (It did save money. The cost of the first unicameral session in 1937 was about half that of the last bicameral in 1935.)

The battle might have been easier if Norris had not insisted that the members of the new body be nominated and elected on a non-partisan ticket. That feature earned the proposal the enthusiastic opposition of both political parties and most of the state's newspapers. Even among ardent supporters of the unicameral idea, feelings were, and still are, mixed about the question of allowing partisan representation. Nevertheless, nearly twice the needed number of voter signatures were collected that summer, and with the issue on the ballot, the proposal was handily approved in November of 1934 by a vote of 286,086 to 193,152.

Senator Jerome Warner, who has served in the Nebraska "Unicam" for 25 years, as speaker and most recently as chair of the Appropriations Committee, says that "non-partisan-

The beloved senator used his influence to persuade thousands of voters.

84

How the Nebraska Unicameral Works

Nebraska's thinkers have managed to prevent the kind of hasty legislative action that the two-house arrangement was said to avert, by bringing the public into the process at every stage. A nine-member "reference committee" refers all bills either to a standing committee or directly to the general file; and the reference committee sets all bills for hearings. Every bill must receive a public hearing, preceded by at least five days' published notice of date, time, place and subject. After the hearing, when the standing committee goes into executive session, media representatives must be allowed to attend and report on the proceedings.

Introductions are limited to the first 20 days of the session. A minimum of seven days must elapse from introduction to final enactment of any measure. Assuming committee approval, three floor votes are necessary for passage. The constitution requires that at least one legislative day pass between correct engrossment and a final vote.

About a dozen committees deal with the 600 or 700 bills introduced or carried over in each annual session. Each member typically serves on two committees, with a few on three and Appropriations members on no other. Committee membership is structured by four geographic regions, with each region entitled to two seats per committee. The lieutenant governor presides.

On final reading and passage, all bills are read through in full by the clerk, with senators required to be present and seated.

For what it's worth, a look at Nebraska's proportion of enactments to introductions during the 1985 session compared to a half dozen other part-time legislatures show that Nebraska is on the low end of a range of numbers of introductions (728 compared with numbers commonly above 1,000) and also in the low range of percentage enacted (34 percent compared with ranges from 37 to 59 percent).

Members' terms are four years, staggered so that about half are elected every other year.

ship wasn't all that strange" to Nebraskans, who had a long history of support for the idea. A Non-Partisan League was active in the state at the turn of the century, and a number of offices at the local level were stripped of party labels. Historically, says Warner, as in many other states there was "a far stronger geographic division in alignments than partisan division, even when it was a two-house legislature. It was whether you were north or south of the Platte [River]."

Commenting on the fateful 1934 election, Warner notes that there were two other proposals on the ballot with the initiative, one to allow pari-mutuel horse racing and another to repeal Prohibition. "The advertising was to vote yes on all three," says Warner, "and there are those who think that may have been a factor."

But it may have been simply the force of George Norris' personality that got the thing passed 3-2 in the face of powerful opposition. Bob Sittig thinks so. "It *was* George Norris. He deserves nearly all the credit for pushing it over the top, after people had been working on it for 20 years." After it passed, Norris went back to Washington and Professor Senning, soon to be officially named consultant

to the Legislature on the unicameral, began drawing redistricting maps. The last bicameral legislature in 1935 looked over, and quarreled over, nearly three dozen different maps before finally passing one on the last night of the session.

The amendment called for between 30 and 50 members, to be designated senators; the 1935 session settled on 43; there are now 49. And it provided that "the aggregate salaries of all the members shall be $37,500 per annum, divided equally among the members..." Considering that sessions were biennial, and lasted for only about 100 days, that wasn't too bad a wage with bread at a dime a loaf.

The voters of Nebraska thought it was plenty for 23 years. In 1960 they finally approved a raise to $2,400 a year per member. Today it is $4,800 plus per diem, for annual sessions that run 90 days in odd-numbered years, 60 in the even numbered, unless extended by a four-fifths vote of the members. Nebraska is one of the few states whose constitution specifies a salary amount for legislators.

Three-quarters of the members of that first unicameral in 1937 were the same partisans, now under a non-partisan banner, who had previously

Senator Norris and President Franklin Delano Roosevelt at a campaign stop, 1936.

Norris and his friend, University of Nebraska Professor John P. Senning (above), together drafted the language of the unicameral initiative. Later, Senning was named official consultant to the Legislature on the unicameral. Left, Norris at home in McCook after 1944.

served in the traditional legislature. Jerome Warner's father, Charles J. Warner, was the first speaker under the new regime that began Jan. 5, 1937. First elected to the statehouse in 1900, the year after he graduated from the University of Nebraska, he spent 26 years, off and on, as a member. "We're a political family," says the younger Warner, who adds that, although an active Republican, he wouldn't change the Nebraska system. He said that the lack of party requirements leaves members free to oppose or support both legislation and people for leadership positions, and he believes that that is an advantage, not a detriment. "Like

any other legislator," he confesses, "I suppose I like the system because I'm used to it."

Who does lead in a non-partisan body? With whom does a governor, or a lobbyist, deal? Jerome Warner says it's a "one-on-one" situation. Professor Sittig says, "If there's one thing I'm critical of, it is the rather ill-defined areas of authority that result from non-partisanship. Power seems to drift toward the speaker, and though there

has been some strengthening of the standing committees, basically it's a fairly unstructured, collegial sort of operation." Collegial wasn't what Nebraska Governor Roy Cochran called it more than 40 years ago. He said, "There is no formal leadership. It's just like a Mexican army, all generals."

"The lobbyists like it," said Sittig, "and that makes me a little uneasy." He went on to say that the Unicam, as it has come to be called, gets good media coverage, and since fully a third to a half of the first half of the session is devoted to open committee hearings, any citizen who's interested can participate.

Although there are rural-urban and geographic splits without partisanship, "there's a lot less acrimony and animosity," says Dick Hargesheimer, director of the Nebraska Legislative Research Division. "With only 49 members, they get to know each other pretty well." He contends that although lobbyists have fewer people to deal with, without formal political caucuses and with fluid coalitions that change frequently, "it's harder for them to get a handle on it." Interestingly, Minnesota had a non-partisan bicameral legislature up through the late 1960s, but that is another story.

Non-partisanship is only a feature of the Nebraska system, not its essence. Says one-time Wyoming treasurer Shirley Wittler, a Nebraska native and former president of the Lincoln League of Women Voters, "I grew up with the [one-house] system, so it didn't strike me as unusual until I started looking at [other states]. For the citizen, it's much easier to track legislation, and the processes are methodical and unhurried. There are open sessions every morning, and committee hearings in the afternoon, with times and subjects published in advance."

It has also been suggested that access to a single chamber is easier for the unsophisticated lay person, while the sophisticated find it impossible to play the kinds of games between the bodies that is possible in the other 49 states.

But if Nebraska's legislative system, now an established tradition there, is the wave of the future for other states, it's a mighty slow-moving wave.

The Decline and Fall of Town Meeting

John Pierson

A former reporter in the Washington bureau of *The Wall Street Journal*, JOHN PIERSON helps run his family's dairy farm in Vermont.

SEVEN KINDS OF PIE? I would count: lemon meringue, coconut cream, apple, blueberry, mince, pecan, pumpkin.

Yes, seven!

With these and other small timbers, the Ladies Circle braced our spirits in the hour between Town Meeting and School Meeting.

To this prodigal son, come home to Vermont after seventeen years of newspaper reporting in Washington, D.C., those seven kinds of pie seemed reason enough why Town Meeting was still, as Jefferson said, "the wisest invention ever devised by the wit of man for the perfect exercise of self-government, and for its preservation."

There were other reasons, that bright March day, for feeling good about Town Meeting: the full house, the fight about salting the roads, the sun reaching through the old glass windows of the Pomfret Town Hall, Doric columns white against the white snow, blue star quilt raffled (dollar a chance) for the kindergarten's benefit, the Declaration fixed firmly to the wall, the stage framed in red velvet, Moderator Jillson's dark suit and tie, tiny scraps of paper scrounged from anywhere for a secret ballot.

And yet—if seventeen years among the bureaucrats had failed to dim the artist's eye for color, neither had it dulled the reporter's habit of digging. I dug. What I found was a kind of self-government much fallen away, in form and substance, from Jefferson's ideal.

The thing that attracted Jefferson, the thing that makes Town Meeting different, is its democracy. Most other forms of government in this land are representative. We elect a city council, a state legislature, a national congress to write our laws, and a mayor, governor, or president to carry them out. Not your traditional New Englander. He goes to Town Meeting to write his own laws, then picks selectmen to carry them out.

Take Pomfret:

WARNING

The legal voters of the Town of Pomfret are hereby warned and notified to meet in the Town Hall in said Town on Tuesday, March 3, 1981, at 10:00 A.M. to act on the following articles:

1. To elect a Town Moderator for the ensuing year.
2. To elect a Town Clerk for the ensuing year.
3. To act on Reports to be submitted. . . .

Seventeen articles later—with time out for lunch and the School Meeting—the legal voters of Pomfret have elected the rest of their officers. They've appropriated money for cemeteries, the library, the regional planning commission, the kindergarten, the visiting nurse, the fire department, a new snowplow, highway repairs, and a new grader/loader. They've agreed to keep the furnace on and let the kindergarten keep using the Town Hall, so long as no other place can be found. They've agreed to levy taxes and by when. They've refused to appropriate money for mental health. They've decided to spend revenue sharing money on the salt shed rather than the Town Hall kitchen, but they've also voted to cut the budget for road salt in half.

In doing all this, Pomfret voters are behaving pretty much as voters do in 236 other Vermont town meetings that first Tuesday in March, and as voters do in hundreds of other towns across the land on at least one day each year. Town forms of government exist in at least twenty states and town meetings in thirteen of these: the six New England states, Illinois, Michigan, Minnesota, Nebraska, North Dakota, South Dakota, and Wisconsin. Only in New England, however, are towns and town meetings the dominant form of local government. Elsewhere, government is more apt to be organized by county.

In Illinois, Minnesota, North Dakota, South Dakota, and Wisconsin, counties have more power to write ordinances than towns. Nebraska's towns can't write ordinances at all. In Illinois, Michigan, and South Dakota, town budgets aren't set in Town Meeting, according to a study by James W. Beutler,

an expert on public administration with the staff of the Michigan State Senate. And in Illinois, Michigan, Minnesota, the Dakotas, and Wisconsin, a city or a village has power to deal a neighboring town the last indignity: The city or village can expand its own boundaries until, amoebalike, it ingests the town—Town Meeting, selectmen, and all.

Thus, any survey of Town Meeting comes to rest finally on New England, where Town Meetings began. A century and a half ago, the French traveler and historian Alexis de Tocqueville, after visiting the United States, praised Town Meetings as being "to liberty what primary schools are to science; they bring it within the people's reach, they teach men how to use and how to enjoy it." When Tocqueville wrote those words, early in the 1830s, Town Meeting was already 200 years old. In 1622, two years after the Pilgrims landed at Plymouth, they took action "at a general meeting" to transact the settlement's business.

Scholars can't agree about the remoter origins of Town Meeting. Some say it came from ancient Germany, where farmers met in their fields to parcel out land and regulate crops. Others say it came from English parish meetings. I prefer Edward Channing's conclusion that New England towns and their government simply "grew by the

exercise of English common sense combined with the circumstances of the place."

The circumstances of the place are plain enough to see from town records of the seventeenth and eighteenth centuries. Acting through their officers (selectmen, constables, tithingmen, fence viewers, pound keepers, herdsmen, raters, surveyors of highways, hog reeves, drummers, perambulators, sealers of leather, procurers of wood), the citizens of New England towns disposed of public land, set the pay of clergymen, regulated the height of fences, impounded stray pigs and cows, sold firewood and lumber, set tax rates, abated taxes, admitted new inhabitants, regulated the sojourn of strangers, built wharves, erected windmills, fined householders whose chimneys caught fire, caged Sabbath-breakers, apprehended Quakers, and warned the healthy away from the funerals of smallpox victims. In short, during the first two centuries, Town Meeting busied itself with public things in a community of farmers who took life, including religion, seriously.

During the American Revolution, Town Meeting became an engine of sedition and military activity against the Crown. In fact, its seditious heritage went back at least a century earlier, to the time when Sir Edmund Andros, the new royal gover-

nor of the short-lived Dominion of New England, declared there to be "no such thing amongst you as a Town." In 1689 Sir Edmund was merely jailed by his subjects for so cavalierly dismissing what they took to be their proper authority. But during the Revolution, town meetings formed committees of correspondence and safety, voted bounties for army volunteers, and provided arms and ammunition for the rebels.

By the time Tocqueville arrived in 1831, New England town life and the New England Town Meeting had reached their apogee. But starting in about the third decade of the nineteenth century, Town Meeting began to decline. New immigrants were landing in increasing numbers, and with rapid population growth came rapid growth in manufacturing (shoes, ships, soap, candles, shovels, spades, plows, iron castings) and in communications (turnpikes, steamboats, railroads, telegraph). The towns found themselves unprepared to handle this kind of diversity and this kind of expansion.

Larger communities gave up their town governments and became cities. Boston was the first, in 1821, to trade in its town meeting and selectmen for a mayor and council. Meanwhile, the state began to tread what had been, until then, mostly town paths: poor relief, health, police, the schools. In 1838 there came a Massachusetts Health Commission, in 1853 a Board of Agriculture, in 1855 an Insurance Commission, and so on. By 1892 historian Charles Francis Adams was ready to pronounce Town Meeting "a relic, though always an interesting one, of a simple and possibly better past."

Our century has seen still more changes destructive of town life: the arrival of additional millions of people, their concentration in cities, national roads, the telephone, radio and television, the expansion of state economies into a national economy, the decline of the farming population, two world wars, a great depression.

My own informal survey finds the traditional town meeting form of government surviving in only 261 of Massachusetts's 351 municipalities, and these the less-peopled ones. In Connecticut, 92 of 169 communities keep to the old ways; in Rhode Island, 14 of 39. In northern New England, where change tends to come slower, Town Meeting has held on longer. In Maine, 430 of 498 communities still have it; in New Hampshire, 221 of 234; in Vermont, 237 of 246.

When towns abandon Town Meeting, what do they put in its place? Some, like Boston, become cities with mayor and council. Others remain towns in name but use a council to write their laws and a town manager to carry them out. Many towns that have retained Town Meeting have nevertheless debased the coinage, hiring full-time managers to run the town, electing boards of finance to write budgets, empowering selectmen to write laws as well as execute them. Unable to fit all eligible voters under one roof, some larger towns have switched to a "representative town meeting," where all may speak but only a few deputies, elected by districts, may vote.

Meanwhile, towns that have kept the traditional form have trouble maintaining citizen interest. Frank M. Bryan, professor of political science at the University of Vermont, has found that, on the average, only 25 per cent of eligible voters bother to attend their town meeting. Because Vermont's employers aren't required to give employees time off to vote, some towns have scheduled their meetings in the evening. But attendance is even lower at night, Bryan says.

Other towns have separated the talk from the voting. Last March, Woodstock, Vermont, where I vote, held a meeting the night before Town Meeting Day to discuss the forty articles in the warning. Then we quit until the next morning, when the polls opened at 10 A.M. and stayed open until 7 P.M. Entering the elementary school gym, we were handed, instead of seven kinds of pie, seven different paper ballots—white, green, blue, yellow, dark pink, light pink, and off-white—which we marked in the mortuary quiet of curtained voting booths.

Proponents say that this so-called Australian ballot system increases participation. (One in ten Woodstock voters came to the talk session the night before, but one in three cast a ballot the next day.) Proponents say that with separate, secret balloting, the inarticulate "little guy" is less likely to be intimidated by the "better people" or swayed by a demagogue's passionate oratory.

I didn't find the little guy inarticulate or intimidated in Pomfret, where my wife and I own land. Rising in support of the road crew and salt, Wesley Luce, a retired farmer, said simply: "As long as they keep 'em safe for us, I believe we ought to go along with 'em."

As for the person who shuns talk and merely votes, what he may gain in dispassion he loses in information. The night before Town Meeting Day, our lister, Edwin Thompson, carefully explained why, for the fourth time, he had requested money for a tax map. The town's property appraisals were out of date and unfair; the map was the first step toward setting them right. If the money wasn't forthcoming, Mr. Thompson said, he didn't see how he could, in good conscience, continue serving. Some 200 of us heard Ed Thompson that night. The next day, 429 voted against the tax map, while 331 voted for it. In all, Woodstock voters rejected 21 of 33 special articles, including one to fund our police. Surely there's more to democracy than scratching a mark on a piece of paper. Woodstock's system, in which Town Meeting Day is for voting only, neglects the responsibility of voters to inform themselves about the issues before them. (Arguments like these apparently have had an effect on the citizens of Woodstock. Last fall they voted to go back to the traditional Town Meeting format for budget items that exceed $2,000.)

But why should a citizen of Woodstock, or any other town, attend Town Meeting, learn about the issues, vote even, when so much of the cloth of local government is cut in his state capitol, and in Washington?

THE STATE OF VERMONT HAS taken over completely the funding and administration of welfare. Overseers of the poor, renamed "town service officers," nowadays do little more than provide bed and breakfast for an occasional transient. The state police enforce the law in all Vermont towns, except the few that have established their own police departments. Even these must meet state standards. Vermont towns provide for schools, but the schools, and hence the towns, must comply with hundreds of state and federal rules about everything from square feet per pupil in the library to number of pupils per English teacher. Many roads that used to be town roads are state roads now. And in Vermont the state regulates what until recently was thought to be beyond the reach even of local government: use of land, air, and water. If you own fifty acres and want to sell, say, seven, you need a state permit. The state can force you to repair your septic tank. State law says you may not burn your garbage.

The trend toward state control is strong throughout New England. G. Ross Stephens, professor of political science at the University of Missouri, says that the six New England states, where Town Meeting pretends to flourish still, are among the most centralized in the country. Vermont ranks third, after Alaska and Hawaii, in letting state government perform what used to be local functions, and the other five New England states aren't far behind.

Air and water know no political boundaries. So state and national, even international, government may be needed to keep these elements clean. But a strong case can be made for local handling of poor relief, police, schools, roads, and land use. Centralization is corrosive of the spirit of local citizenship. One hundred fifty years ago, Tocqueville wrote, "the township in New England possesses two advantages which strongly excite the interest of mankind: namely, independence and authority. . . . Without authority and independence a town contains good subjects, but it can have no active citizens."

One comes, then, upon the dead or dying corpse of Town Meeting. What, if anything, can be done to make it leap upon its feet again?

I see three counterforces to the decline of towns and Town Meeting: a small but growing band of intellectuals from left and right who preach that small is beautiful, the back-to-the-land movement, and no-strings revenue sharing. Yet I doubt these combined forces are strong enough to stop the march of bigness and save Town Meeting.

Revenue sharing is a possible loser in the fight to balance the federal budget, if not this year then some year soon; certainly there's little prospect of the kind of expansion of revenue-sharing programs that would give local governments ample wherewithal to meet local respon-

sibilities. The back-to-the-landers don't appear to be turning out in great numbers at Town Meeting; perhaps they have little use for government at any level. And the prophets of smallness have yet to devise a practical plan for reversing society's centripetal rush.

So maybe the time has come to bid goodbye to the town as a unit of local government and to make it over into something—forgive me—into something bigger. In Vermont, that something might lie between the town and the county in area and population. It would have to be large enough to achieve economies in snow plowing and the like and to afford a good high school and a professional manager, but small enough to be governed by a body like the representative town meeting. With this kind of local government, the lawmakers in the state capitol might be willing to share large hunks of state revenue, without strings. To this kind of local government a citizen might attach his mind, if not his heart.

The mind tells us that Town Meeting is a government whose time, in this space age, has passed. Towns just aren't efficient enough to be worth saving. But let's not fool ourselves about what we're giving up.

Nothing—and that goes for the new form of town/county government I've proposed—nothing can replace a town's and Town Meeting's rich sense of history, community, and close human association. These are the things that give life to social arrangements. These are the heart.

AND THIS CITIZEN'S HEART? Well, it is still up there in Pomfret, where the late afternoon sun is pouring through those old glass windows, turning our company to gold. Salt has just lost, but a moment later someone makes a motion to thank the road crew "for its fine work in keeping the roads open this winter."

Now, if seventeen years as a Washington reporter have taught me anything, they've taught me that the press never applauds anyone, not even the president. We'll stand for the president, but we'll clap for no one simply out of obligation. Point of professional chastity, I guess.

But when someone moved to thank the Pomfret road crew, and the motion was seconded and approved, friends and foes of salt applauded with a roar. As for me, I dropped my pen and notebook and banged my hands together as lustily as my neighbors.

You see, they *are* my neighbors.

Practicing Political Science on a Local School Board

Gerald M. Pomper
Eagleton Institute, Rutgers University

Gerald Pomper is professor of political science at Rutgers and director of the Center on Political Parties at the University's Eagleton Institute of Politics. Normally engaged in research on American politics, including the forthcoming *The Election of 1984,* he is now preoccupied with the most critical current campaign—winning voter approval of the annual school budget.

If politics is the art of the possible, political scientists have much to learn through the practice of government. Accepting this premise, many political scientists, following the example of Charles Merriam, have taken on political and governmental jobs. In this informal article, I want to report on my own experience.

My involvement is minor—one member of a nine-person school board, in a small community of 14,000 people and 1,600 students, with an annual budget of $8 million. The scope is relatively small, but I still find the lessons I have learned widely applicable. I have been particularly gratified to find that political science *is* relevant. The small matters that constitute the work of a small political entity have been illuminated by the generalizations of the discipline. In turn, these experiences have deepened my knowledge of political science—and provided good illustrative material for my courses.

I will briefly deal with four subjects: elections, interest groups, bureaucratic politics, and the political community. Inevitably, this is a personal report, but still, I hope, one that will be of more than parochial interest.

Getting Elected

School boards are voluntary and unpaid bodies. There are few "self-starters" and political parties usually refrain from involvement. "Recruitment," in this case, is not only a category of analysis, but a reality. Probably like most candidates, I was asked to run, and had to be persuaded.

Once committed to the race, however, the campaign becomes as personally absorbing and important as a contest for offices with far greater power and personal rewards. It almost seemed as if I were running for president—but in an alternate universe in which every political variable had been compressed to microscopic size. Fundraising and spending limits were important, even though the legal limit on expenditures was only $1,000. We considered gender balance, and concluded that I had an advantage over my female opponent when five of the other eight positions on the Board were already filled by women. Discussions of means to attract the "black vote," the "Catholic vote," etc. were as earnest as any in the Democratic National Committee. The difference was that we were talking about how to win support from 50 blacks, or 500 Catholics, not millions.

> *Once sworn into office, I found myself in still another universe, a pluralistic world apparently designed by David Truman.*

These small numbers underlined the truth of the old adage, "All politics is local." One of my unofficial "campaign managers" persuasively argued that every campaign is an effort to establish a personal tie between the candidate and each voter. Presidential candidates must do this artificially, by bogus personal letters and media messages. In a school board campaign, where 800 ballots would probably win, I could realistically hope to reach every voter. On the strategic level, this fact meant targeting specific individuals. Tactically, it led to an hour of telephoning every night for a month, holding 20 informal coffees for groups of as few as three people and no more than 15, and shaking hands for hours at the local supermarket, our functional equivalent of the traditional general store.

Personal contact is more important than I had believed. Early in the campaign, I went to a meeting of parents favoring an all-day kindergarten, one of the most visible school issues. By attending and declaring my support, I hoped to win the support of this group of voters—and to counter the appeal of my opponent, who had been one of the prime advocates of the program. The next day, however, I learned that I had lost rather than won votes, despite my being scored "right" on the issues. My mistake was in leaving the meeting at its formal end. What the parents had wanted was not only my programmatic support, but personal contact, the opportunity to "schmooz," and "press the flesh.' After that, I never left a meeting until the hostess began yawning.

In these meetings, I deepened my understanding of the impact of issues on voting behavior. Educational issues are quite specific, proximate, and personal. Parents are often the true experts when it comes to the needs of their children, and parents of schoolchildren (and resident teachers) are the essential constituency in a school election. As a result, public opinion is highly informed, and a candidate must be both knowledgeable and ready to learn. At the same time, the voters I met seemed to me to be realistic in their expectations. They knew that no elected official could solve even the small problems of one school district and were willing to allow discretion and to follow leadership. In short, I found no "democratic distemper" but a healthy dialogue.

The effective place for citizen control is the budget.

Most generally, I came to value elections in a personal way that reinforced my academic appreciation. We have long known about the "arrogance of power," and academicians often have inflated egos. But in the voting booth, all women and men are equal—and you, as a candidate eagerly want their approval. I spent four hours one evening listening to three people tell me about the decline of morality in contemporary society (i.e., beer bottles on the high school football field) and the extravagance of government (i.e., the cost of lettuce for home economics classes). Yet, despite the fact that I held a Ph.D. and have taught for 25 years, I listened respectfully to them. Once elected, I was eager to support policies to bar drinking from school grounds and to reduce food purchasing bills. On large as well as trivial matters the dependence of elected officials on their constituents makes them responsive to their democratic masters. Mill, I found, was right: "Rulers and ruling classes are under a necessity of considering the interests of those who have the suffrage; but of those who are excluded, it is in their option whether they will do so or not."

Interest Group Politics

Once sworn into office, I found myself in still another universe, a pluralistic world apparently designed by David Truman. Decisions often depended on the resolution of conflicts between self-interested groups. Intensity and proximity made some groups more influential than their numbers warranted, but considerations of the general public interest did have an impact.

One example is provided by our biennial negotiations for a teacher contract. Despite the decline in the national rate of inflation and despite a comparatively high salary schedule, the premise of our negotiations was that a settlement would require at least an annual seven percent increase in teacher salaries. The teachers were the only organized interest group involved. Moreover, many of their members were local voters, and their cooperation was obviously central to any improvement in the schools. Parents, the only other obvious interest group, typified Walter Lippmann's "phantom public"—wanting a resolution of the conflict and unwilling to deal with specific issues in dispute. The "general interest" may have been that of the taxpayers, who were already typically paying $3,000 annually in property taxes for the schools, but it was not represented specifically. Speaking for this interest, the Board was able to win some concessions that would effect future economies—but at a price.

A second case involved the sale of a school building closed as the result of declining enrollment. Two alternatives were possible—selling to a developer who would convert the building to condominium apartments or tearing it down and selling subdivided lots for single-family homes. The first option would produce the most revenue for the schools, but the loudest demands came from a handful of persons near the school, who favored single-family homes on many grounds, including the resultant increase in the value of their own property. A majority of the Board was prepared to listen to this limited public, until—following Schattschneider—the "scope of conflict" was changed. A federal mandate to equalize girls' athletic facilities suddenly required the Board to find a large new source of revenue. Forced to concentrate on the schools' own needs, the Board decided to sell to the highest bidder.

Bureaucratic Politics

Most of a school board's time is spent with professional administrators. Working full-time, versed in the educational lore and jargon, regulated and protected by state laws their colleagues often have drafted, the staff has immense advantages in any conflict with a volunteer and amateur Board. Not surprisingly, scholarly studies have found that these boards exercise relatively little real authority over the professionals. School governance sometimes is undiluted symbolic politics, a la Edelman, as boards go through impotent rituals of power. All appointments

are formally made by roll-call votes, even when they involve tenured personnel who could be removed only for the most flagrant moral abuses. Similarly, each new course and each financial transaction requires a roll-call, even though the members must necessarily follow staff recommendations in almost all details.

The effective place for citizen control is the budget. As representatives of the taxpayers, who in many states vote directly on the school budget, Board members attempt to hold down spending to limit tax rates. School bureaucrats have their established routines to counter these economy drives, many of them resembling the techniques used by the Pentagon to resist cuts in defense spending. "We can't fall behind the Russians" is a slogan that can be employed to buy either multi-warhead missiles or the newest science texts. "Most of the increase is due to inflation" can explain expensive tanks or new $45 basketballs. As we know from Wildavsky, bureaucrats build budgets incrementally, assuming that past expenditures are unquestionable, and that only new spending for the coming fiscal year requires discussion.

The best technique to use in this situation is to make the professional educators directly aware of the tradeoffs inherent in any social policy, including a school budget. This cannot be done by asking abstractly, "Which programs are of lower priority?" The answer will inevitably be that everything is indispensable, whether it is sewing in the fourth grade, calculus for a handful of advanced students, or separate whirlpools for girl and boy athletes. Instead, there must first be a total limit placed on spending, forcing prioritizing among programs and, not incidentally, providing a defense against the many particular interests that will want a "small" increase for their pet programs. Seeing the process at work, I am now far more sympathetic to such proposals as mandatory ceilings on taxes. Imposing real, even seemingly arbitrary, limits prods administrators to think creatively and to question past assumptions. When there is no new money for math courses, an additional secretary becomes less indispensable. In the end, school administrators will usually make the choices that are best for the children—but they can use some encouragement.

This strategy is particularly necessary in education policy, for school spending is likely to rise annually, whatever the level of inflation or the school enrollment. Spending groups are identifiable and organized. The basic object of this spending, our children, are the embodiment of our dearest hopes. The natural generosity we feel toward their education inherently cannot be tested against any measures of cost-effectiveness. Still more is this the case when the nation has become alarmed over "a rising tide of mediocrity" (or at least a "rising tide of reports") in the schools.

Budgets have the advantage for the citizen Board member of being tangible and precise. More difficult to control are the curriculum and administrative matters that come before the Board. On such matters, professors are likely to be misled by analogies to higher education. They believe that universities are, or at least ought to be, governed and collegial, while public schools are administered and hierarchical. Other Board members' experience may be even less relevant. In their efforts to improve the schools, most representatives follow two very different strategies—suggesting "grand ideas" ("back to basics") or dealing with very specific grievances ("Why do the buses come late on Third Avenue?"). These interventions can be very valuable, but they typically miss the middle range of activity, such as program development and implementation that comprises most of the actual management of any bureaucracy, including schools.

This pattern leaves school administrators free to shape most policy, unless a school board member is unusually pointed and persistent. (But, as Neustadt asked of presidents, how often does a Board member ask three times about the same issue?) Even then, it is hard to "command" such desired outcomes as "creative thinking" (and Neustadt reminds us how rarely direct command is used). If challenged, administrators use some common bureaucratic defenses. Delay, as I have just suggested, is one. A second is to argue that law or practice will not allow innovation, e.g., "the state (union/commissioner/insurance company) won't permit it." Lacking expertise and time for research, the Board member must usually accept the answer. Another defensive technique is over-compliance. A new policy is followed to a logical absurdity, so that the Board member learns to mind his own business. A request for information is dutifully answered by reams of paper, the mass of detail burying the Board member's original thought. In dealing with academicians, like myself, a particular variant is to cite the research literature in education. As you might guess, the reference is not necessarily enlightening.

Political science suggests some ways to deal with these problems. Here are a few recommendations. Create competing interests within the bureaucracy. Thus, if dissatisfied with the results of English in-struction, establish a new "writing across the curriculum" program. Provide incentives, such as competitive awards for new teaching techniques. Rotate administrators, so that undesirably entrenched patterns are necessarily disrupted. Define issues so that the Board sets the terms of the agenda, rather than the school hierarchy. For example, reduce the time devoted to woodworking by emphasizing additional language instruction, rather than debating the merits of ripsaws. Perhaps most important, remember that organizations are not simply goal-oriented groups, but are natural systems in which individual needs and interpersonal relationships must be nurtured.

The Political Community

Much of this essay suggests that school board membership is frustrating and that the idealistic goal of educating our children faces great obstacles in voter resistance, interest group parochialism, and administrative routines. All of that is true.

Nevertheless, it is a rewarding experience, and I suspect the rewards are even greater in positions of greater responsibility. It is a learning experience, and professors can and should always learn. It is a real experience, more so than most of what we do in the classroom or research center. In our academic work, we may talk about the relative desirability of spending public money for an MX missile or a food stamps program, but we are only talking theoretically. It is quantitatively much less important, but qualitatively more meaningful, actually to find means to reduce the cost of health insurance by $50,000, so that you can begin to teach computer literacy to 1,600 students who are your friends' children and your neighbors. It is also an enlarging experience. The office-holder necessarily becomes conscious of acting, however inexpertly and bounded, on behalf of larger interests, and this feeling may be most satisfying when acting for a powerless group, such as children.

The benefits of political involvement go beyond these personal satisfactions, toward the discovery of public life in a deeper sense. As de Tocqueville warned us early, the greatest defect in American life is likely to be the lack of community, the absence of personal ties which gain meaning in common enterprises. That defect is even more apparent today, when we have necessarily delegated much of the work of government to distant sites, when we live in transient communities, when material and emotional demands force a concentration on our personal well-being.

Political life counteracts this absence of community. In holding even a minor public office, your relationships to others in the community change. Conversations are more likely to be on the general issues with which you deal. Neighbors talk not only about the weather or the grocery prices, but about the desirability of revising the science curriculum. The relationship is not less friendly or less egalitarian (there is no "power" involved), but it is more *public,* more concerned with your common lives.

That talk educates both the public official and his or her constituents. After my election, I fulfilled a campaign pledge to go back monthly to some of the homes where I had campaigned and to discuss school developments. It is a sad commentary on the trust voters have in politicians that my hosts were surprised that I bothered to return, and one assumed, incorrectly, that I was running for a new term. Otherwise, these were heartening evenings. We discussed not theories of education, but classroom instruction in the fourth grade. While I tried to explain our new program budget, I also was taught the realities of raising children in single-parent families. Amid the fun and the coffee cake, all of us learned. Madison was right in thinking that the election of representatives would "refine and enlarge the public views," but he neglected to mention the same effect of community activity upon the representatives themselves.

My experience has convinced me that there is still great potential for a public life, at least in small localities. Residents have a vast reservoir of knowledge about their towns; on one occasion, I found that there was cumulative local experience of over 200 years among ten householders on a single street. Schools —and other issues—do matter to the voters, whether they view them as past or present students, parents or grandparents, or taxpayers. And there is a desire, inexpert but warm, to "do good," for children and for the community.

Democratic political theorists have based their philosophies on such optimistic premises. In current political dialogue, however, they are often forgotten, as both academicians and electoral candidates stress self-interest and group competition. As political scientists, we might do better to teach these other lessons, not only in our schools, but to our national leaders.

Strategies for Leaders Who Do Not Have a Lot of Power

A governor's power and influence may hinge more on the governor's use of management and leadership than on the actual powers of the office. So-called "weak" governors have mastered the forces of change in their states by first mastering the art of governing.

Regina K. Brough

Regina K. Brough is executive director of the Governors Center at Duke University.

Although many people think of a governor as the president of a state, most governors do not possess presidential-like powers. For the last 20 years, however, the presidential model of power has persisted as the basic guide for executive branch reform (Bowman and Kearney 1986, 52).

Power Shift from Legislature to Governor

The cautious architects of the original state constitutions limited the power and authority of the executive branch. Checks and balances on the governor's office prevented the incumbent from taking charge. This form of government worked so well for the original colonies that the Philadelphia convention incorporated similar principles into the new federal constitution.

At both the state and national levels, the dominance of the legislative branch lasted throughout the 19th century. Not until the terms of Theodore Roosevelt and Woodrow Wilson did the power, prestige and influence of the modern presidency emerge. But, in the state capitols, governors lagged behind.

For governors, no radical shifts in power occurred until 1918. The turning point came when Gov. Al Smith of New York commissioned a study on the reorganization of state government. Resulting reforms proposed by Smith which were adopted included a four-year term for the governor; gubernatorial appointment of all statewide officials except the lieutenant governor, attorney general and comptroller; and preparation of an executive budget by the governor for submission to the general assembly.

The supremacy of the state legislature had previously been insured by a two-year term for the governor, an elected cabinet and a budget prepared by a commission or board presided over by the governor.

Variations on the Theme

The strong executive form of government adopted in New York was used as a model for 21 other states, but was not universally accepted. Many states still limit the power of their governors. Vermont, New Hampshire and Rhode Island, for example, limit the length of the governor's term to two years, while allowing incumbents to seek re-election indefinitely. Kentucky and Virginia bar their governors from immediate succession, but not from seeking an additional four-year term after an interim. Delaware, Missouri and North Carolina have two-term limits. Oklahoma, Alaska, Arkansas, Indiana, Nebraska and 16 other states restrict their governors to two consecutive terms of four years each but allow them to seek the office again after a sabbatical.

Likewise, the appointment and budgetary authority of the governor varies greatly among the states. State cabinet systems, in many instances,

From *The Journal of State Government*, July/August 1987, pp. 157-161. Reprinted by permission of The Council of State Governments.

differ significantly from the presidential cabinet model. Some states do not even have cabinet systems. For example, South Carolina agencies are run by independent boards or commissions whose members are appointed by the governor with state senate approval.

Neither does New Hampshire have a cabinet reporting to the governor. Instead, a unique executive body — the executive council, comprised of five members voters elect biennially from separate districts — is charged with "advising the governor in the executive part of government." The governor and the council can each veto nominations and appointments of state executives, thereby requiring unanimity in these choices.

When the National Governors' Association (NGA) recently ranked the formal powers of governors, it concluded that Maryland and Massachusetts have the governors with the strongest formal powers.

By contrast, Massachusetts has a cabinet structure resembling the presidential model. The governor appoints the 11 cabinet secretaries who manage the major executive offices. Under them are the state's various departments, commissions and boards. The governor is constitutionally strong and directs the cabinet.

The power to appoint and remove the heads of state agencies, boards and commissions is fundamental to the governor's formal managerial and policy-making powers. Without that authority to hire and fire, a governor lacks the leverage required to effectively direct executive agencies. Consequently, those agencies may respond to other interests than those the governor interprets as the public interest.

Although reformers prefer unilateral gubernatorial appointment power, department heads in many states are appointed by independent boards or commissions. This dilutes the governor's influence even if the governor appoints the members of these boards or commissions because, among other things, rarely can the governor remove these appointees.

For example, the Missouri Constitution provides that the governor each year will appoint eight members to the state Board of Education which then selects a commissioner of education. In practice, the commissioner dominates and controls the board members and is relatively far removed from the influence of the governor.

Texas's boards and commissions are legendary. The governor appoints several thousand individuals to a constellation of state boards, which range in size from three members to more than 20. Most of these appointments must be approved by the state senate, and most are appointed on a staggered basis so that it usually

takes the governor two four-year terms to appoint all the members. Many of these boards, such as the ones that oversee the Department of Human Resources and the university regents, select chairpersons or executive directors to run their agencies (Brough 1986, 60).

In strong governor states like New Jersey and New York, governors submit executive budgets reflecting gubernatorial priorities. But in South Carolina the budget control board, chaired by the governor, submits the budget to the legislature. This five-member board is composed of two elected executive officers (the state treasurer and controller), two elected legislators (the chairman of the Senate Finance Committee and the chairman of the House Ways and Means Committee) and the governor. The board, equipped with the power to veto line-items in appropriations bills, controls the budget process from beginning to end.

Where Are the Strong Governors?

From time to time, researchers have examined gubernatorial power, chiefly from the viewpoint of achieving passage of the governor's legislative program. The formal powers of governors were compared by Joseph A. Schlesinger in a study published in 1965 (207-236). He used four measures of formal power: veto, budget, appointment and tenure. Thad Beyle (1968, 540-544) added other measures of formal power in his exhaustive study of governors.

When the National Governors' Association (NGA) recently ranked the formal powers of governors, it concluded that Maryland and Massachusetts have the governors with the strongest formal powers. New York and West Virginia share second place. Utah, Louisiana and Connecticut were tied for third.

Strong governors have a substantial degree of formal constitutional power at their disposal. Governors who do not possess a significant amount of formal power must rely on informal tools to achieve success. These governors depend on their leadership skills to excel.

Modern Executive Branch Reform

As Larry Sabato (1978, 71) has pointed out, executive branch reform since 1965 has sought to strengthen the office of governor — to increase the authority of the governor to match the responsibilities thrust upon the office from the fast-changing environment.

One influential study of executive reform was published in 1967 by The Committee on Economic Development (CED). The study, *Modernizing State Government*, recommended specific reforms to strengthen the managerial and policy-making powers of the governor. For proponents of increased gubernatorial powers, the CED work has been the guiding authority. The CED recommendations include:

- **The Short Ballot.** The governor and lieutenant governor should be the only elected executive branch officials, and they should be elected as a team rather than on separate ballots.

- **Appointment and Removal Power.** The governor should have the power to appoint all department and agency heads and likewise to dismiss them for failure to perform. Boards and commissions, with the exception of higher education and regulatory bodies, should be advisory only.

- **Budgetary Power.** The governor's office should prepare and execute the state budget.

- **Term of Office.** Governors should be permitted to serve an unlimited number of four-year terms.

- **Veto Power.** The governor should have the power to veto bills passed by the legislature and to veto line items in expenditure bills, subject to a two-house override.

- **Reorganization Power.** The governor should have the power to initiate and to carry out administrative changes and limited reorganizations of the executive branch.

Management and Leadership Techniques

Despite the constitutional and statutory restrictions on gubernatorial authority and action in every state, some governors have been remarkably successful in achieving their agendas. What management techniques have been employed by these public CEOs to accomplish the goals they have set forth? Four techniques can be used by any governor:

1. Intellectual dominance of the subject,
2. A strong gubernatorial staff,
3. Mobilization of outside influences and
4. Exhaustive use of the bully pulpit to hammer the issue.

Mastery of these techniques greatly enhances a governor's ability to govern. For the weak governors, however, the command and clever use of these skills are critical to the successful implementation of their policies. The following describes some examples of how governors with weak formal powers have successfully used these techniques.

- **Intellectual dominance of the subject** has made John Sununu of New Hampshire a master of fiscal affairs. Sununu purposefully limited his first-term agenda to just one item. In fact, argues Sununu, to succeed a governor must "resist all efforts to broaden his agenda." The public CEO must concentrate on a small number of objectives and avoid being enticed to take on additional goals. Pressure to broaden the

gubernatorial agenda comes from all quarters — the governor's own staff and constituencies who helped elect the governor want "to make their own particular interest as much a priority as other items." Consequently, according to Sununu, limiting the gubernatorial agenda is "one of the tough lines that has to be drawn" (Behn and Brough 1986, 16).

Despite the constitutional and statutory restrictions on gubernatorial authority and action in every state, some governors have been remarkably successful in achieving their agendas.

During his first term, Sununu sought "to reestablish the fiscal integrity of the state" as one "that was very proud of its fiscal structure; a state that had always maintained a triple-A bond rating; a state that had always operated with a solid budget surplus." Yet, when Sununu first took office, New Hampshire's bond rating had been downgraded twice and it faced a budget deficit of $35 million (Behn and Brough 1986, 17).

In order to gain control of the state budget, Sununu first had to master the budget cycle. The strongest tool for a governor to do this, he said, "is to know more about what is going on in every department than the department heads, and secondly, to require those department heads to know more about what is going on in each of their divisions than their division directors." In the few months between his election and his inauguration, Sununu learned everything there was to know about the state budget. He became so conversant with budget details and was such a dominant, controlling presence in the budget preparation process that he personally presented the budget to the legislature, handling questions on his own rather than deferring to his budget staff.

This master-of-the-details continues to use intellectual dominance to run New Hampshire. Equipped with a computer terminal in his office, the governor has precise, up-to-the-minute information on all aspects of the state's financial system — a calculated effort on his part to remain continuously informed without the helpful intervention of his staff. The staff members, in turn, hold their boss in awe.

- **A strong gubernatorial staff.** By contrast to Sununu's go-it-alone approach to managing New Hampshire state government, former South Carolina Gov. Dick Riley relied heavily on his bold, strong gubernatorial staff. With his staff, Riley achieved an overwhelming success with the passage of the Education Improvement Act (EIA) of 1984.

Governors, according to Martha Weinberg (1977, 58), have three types of management resources: personal, situational and enabling. Enabling resources include staff assistance, funding for the governor's office, access to information and time.

For Riley, the seven staff members of the Governor's Division of Education were especially important during the EIA campaign. They understood what Riley wanted and possessed the technical expertise and professional standing to provide knowledgeable support. Riley's relentless and successful harnessing of this staff expertise helped give one of the country's weakest governors one of the South's greatest legislative victories.

The public CEO must concentrate on a small number of objectives and avoid being enticed to take on additional goals.

Indeed, South Carolina is very much a "weak-governor" state. The executive directors and commissioners of the 147 executive branch agencies do not report to the governor. Rather, the governor appoints the members of boards or commissions for staggered terms (of usually six years), which in turn, select their agencies' full-time executives. A newly-elected governor discovers that appointees from the previous governor hold most of the state's appointed leadership positions. A current governor's appointees only begin to have influence on boards and commissions during the latter half of the governor's first term.

It might take a governor more than one term to fill most of the appointive positions with people who reflect the governor's executive style and priorities. Fortunately, during Riley's first term of office, the legislature and voters amended the state constitution to permit a governor to serve two consecutive terms. In his second term, Riley found his influence greatly enhanced through his appointments to state boards and commissions.

The story of the passage of the Education Improvement Act is complex and fascinating, and is more fully described in another article in this volume. But a brief description illustrates the importance of the management techniques listed earlier. At the heart of the story is an extraordinary governor. Described by *The Washington Monthly* (October 1986, 41) as "the best governor in America," Dick Riley is not a household name outside of South Carolina. In a *Newsweek* (March 24, 1986) poll of governors, his peers ranked Riley as the third most effective governor in the nation.

Riley's attitude toward education reform was driven by his response to the question, "What is the purpose of state government?" He answered that the purpose is to "attempt to give the proper opportunities to all the people out there as best you can . . . . You can't turn salt into sugar but you can move things in the right direction." According to Riley, if your goals are always to move toward improvement of the state, or toward a better life, "in my judgment you're doing what you're supposed to be doing in your job."

Among the many opportunities to make a difference in South Carolina, Riley chose public education as his passion. Knowing that the entire system could not be changed in one fell swoop, Riley focused on early childhood education. His primary objective was for South Carolina to become "first in first grade." South Carolina might not be first in education immediately, Riley conceded, "But we were going to improve more every year than any state in this nation" (Behn and Brough 1986, 23-26).

- **Mobilization of outside influences.** Riley failed in his first attempt to get education reform passed. However, the governor and his staff learned from their mistakes. For the second effort, the governor mobilized two task forces.

The first task force of educators, legislators and private sector representatives was charged with developing a program for excellence in public education and determining the best way to pay for the program. The second task force, comprised of industrialists, business leaders, educators, the governor's staff and legislators, critiqued the first group's work and garnered political support for the final recommendations.

The task forces' recommendations were authoritative because they were the result of penetrating and thorough research by persons of stature. Throughout the study process, Riley kept up the pressure, meeting continuously with the members of the task forces to sustain the momentum. He never let anyone off the hook.

Riley's commitment to the program was total and he demanded the same devotion from everyone involved. He conducted the drive for the EIA like an election campaign that required the staff's single-minded dedication. The staff devoted little time to other policy issues. Riley set the tone for the campaign by informing his staff that his sole interest in the days ahead would be education — all other issues would receive little or none of his attention (Kearney).

For almost an entire year, the governor focused the state's attention on education. "What I told people then with the EIA, the key word was 'improvement'," Riley recalled. "People started talking about first-place instead of talking about tying for 50th with Mississippi" (Behn and Brough 1986, 23-26).

The dedication of Riley and his staff, as well as a core of supporters in the legislature and among the public, took on "the aura of a religious mission" (Kearney, 9).

It became apparent that little of the state's business would get done until the education issue was resolved.

- **Exhaustive use of the bully pulpit.** Riley excelled in his use of leadership techniques to overcome his limited formal authority. He commandeered the bully pulpit and would not surrender it. His public relations work was all-consuming from his first appearance on state-wide television to announce the EIA campaign. He campaigned for education reform at forums throughout the state attended by an estimated 13,000 South Carolinians. Paid television, radio, and newspaper advertisements appeared in support of the education package and its proposed sources of funding. The ads were attention-getters and poignant, centering on the theme of "a penny for their thoughts." The "penny" was a one-cent sales tax increase appropriated separately from the general fund and sufficient in size to finance a $213 million overhaul of South Carolina's backward public school system.

Leadership, Not Mechanics

Brilliant management of state government can be accomplished despite the absence of formal help from the state constitution. Consider Sununu's and Riley's effective use of management and leadership techniques. Managing state government, according to Riley, is "more a question of leadership instead of mechanics. The mechanics . . . work well if you have leadership that works well. You can spend a lot of time talking about whether it is better to have the budget initiated by the governor or the legislature. But, in my judgment, what is really important is hard work and leadership" (Behn and Brough 1986, 5). □

Sources

Behn, Robert D. and Regina K. Brough. 1986. "Governing the States — Reflections of Duke University's Gubernatorial Fellows," *Capital Ideas* (National Governors' Association), (November 1).

Thad L. Beyle. 1986. "The Governor's Formal Powers: A View from the Governor's Chair," *Public Administration Review*, 28 (November/December).

Bowman, Ann O'M. and Richard C. Kearney. 1986. *The Resurgence of the States.* Englewood Cliffs, New Jersey: Prentice-Hall.

Brough, Regina K. 1986. "The Powers of the Gubernatorial CEO: Variations Among the States," *The Journal of State Government*, 59 (July/August).

Committee for Economic Development. 1967. *Modernizing State Government: A Statement on National Policy*, 20-75. New York.

Kearney, Richard C. The Weak Governor as Policy Maker: Governor Dick Riley and the South Carolina Education Improvement Act. Department of Government, University of South Carolina.

Newsweek. 1986. "How Governors See It: A Newsweek Poll." March 24.

National Governors Association. Washington, D.C. The NGA study, in progress, uses the Schlesinger factors plus an additional factor: whether the party of the governor has a majority in the state legislature.

Sabato, Larry. 1978. *Goodbye to Goodtime Charlie: The American Governorship Transformed, 1950-1975.* Lexington, MA: Lexington Books.

Schlesinger, Joseph A. 1965. "The Politics of the Executive." In *Politics in the American States*, edited by Hubert Jacob and and Kenneth N. Vines. Boston: Little, Brown and Co.

Weinberg, Martha W. 1977. *Managing the State.* Cambridge, MA: MIT Press.

Change Masters for the States

In a fast-moving society, governors are the state leaders most able to master economic, social and political changes and lead their states in new directions. But even governors endowed with vision cannot do it all alone. Top state administrators, gubernatorial staff and even leaders outside of government can provide the spark needed to propel a state into the future.

Dan Durning

Dan Durning, a Research Associate at Duke University's Governors Center, is on the Faculty of the Institute of Policy Sciences and Public Affairs at Duke University. He worked for two years in Arkansas state government, and was a consultant to state and local governments for five years.

Francis Cherry would no longer recognize his old job. When he was governor of Arkansas 34 years ago, his chief tasks were to administer the on-going functions of state government: he made certain taxes were collected, highways paved, welfare checks written, the state universities and hospitals open, and the state police alert. He headed an organization with a $100 million dollar budget and about 14,000 employees.

Today, the person sitting in Cherry's old seat, Gov. Bill Clinton, is chief executive officer of a state government with a budget exceeding $2.5 billion and 35,000 employees. Although Clinton still oversees the administration of the traditional functions of state government, he does much more: he manages the state's response to economic and social changes, and he coaxes the state toward his vision for its future.

Clinton and other modern governors do not just administer large organizations, they manage ideas and innovations that can transform their states. The best of them are "change masters" — leaders who excel at persuading their states to adopt new ideas and innovations (Kanter 1983). These governors convince the public and a majority of state legislators to accept major changes that will alter the state's future. Governors who are masters of change create and sell visions that — if enacted into law — will affect the lives of everyone in the state.

The Governors Center at Duke University, in cooperation with the National Governors' Association, has worked with The Council of State Governments to prepare this special issue of the *Journal of State Government*. The articles examine how change has been managed recently in several states. Some articles tell the story of how change masters — usually governors — have fostered important ideas and innovations, have convinced the public to embrace these changes, and have pushed them through sometimes quarrelsome state legislatures. Other articles focus on how governors (with the help of others) have changed their state governments to make them more efficient, responsive or innovative. The diverse articles in this issue are tied together by the idea that states must adapt to constantly changing economic, social and political environments, and that change masters overcome resistance to make needed changes happen.

Governors: The States' Best Change Masters

Rosabeth Ross Kanter (1983, 13) in researching corporate innovation and change found that

From *The Journal of State Government*, July/August 1987, pp. 145-149. Reprinted by permission of The Council of State Governments.

Governors who are masters of change create and sell visions that — if enacted into law — will affect the lives of everyone in the state.

the nation's best corporations have change masters, managers who are "adept at anticipating the need for, and leading productive change." Like major corporations, states are organizations that need change masters to push them in new directions. A governor is the person most likely to fill the role of change master for a state: the governor has both the motives and resources to stimulate changes in state laws and state government.

A governor has two chief motives to press for changes in the state. First, the governor must determine the state's response to crises and problems. The governor is held accountable for the state's responses to problems regardless of the origin of the problems. If a state's overcrowded prisons are declared unconstitutional, the governor must take the lead to solve the problem. If a tornado or blizzard hits, the governor must see that all pertinent state government agencies respond to the emergency. If the state loses a large number of jobs because a plant closes, the governor is expected to help relieve the short-term suffering and to propose programs to address the long-term economic problems of the state.

In summary, the governor is expected to take charge when major problems arise. The governor must shape the state's response to problems whether it requires changes in the operation of a state agency, a reallocation of money or a new public policy. The governor has to supply the leadership that makes state agencies do what is needed — even if it disrupts bureaucratic routines. It also takes the governor's leverage to dislodge the needed funds and create new programs.

A governor has another important motive to manage change: the opportunity to influence the future of the states and to leave a legacy through innovative programs. Few governors would turn their backs on the long-term problems facing their states; they are elected to solve problems. Governors have the opportunity to leave a lasting mark on their states with major new policies.

These two motives for governors to manage change are reflected in the observations of Richard McClure and Duncan Kincheloe in their article ("Issues Management") on how governors should manage policy issues. McClure and Kincheloe differentiate between "offensive" and "defensive" issues. Offensive issues are those that a governor chooses for his or her agenda and are part of the governor's vision for the state. Defensive issues, on the other hand, are

problems thrust upon the governor from the outside that demand a response.

McClure and Kincheloe suggest that a governor strive to stay on the offensive, to select issues that the public will associate directly with him or her. These issues move the state toward a worthwhile objective and will become the governor's legacy, but also require extended attention and a major public relations effort. As a result, according to McClure and Kincheloe, they should dominate the governor's time.

Not only are governors motivated to manage change in their states, they have the resources to take on both offensive and defensive issues. They are in a unique position to overcome resistance to change that may exist both inside and outside state government. Terry Sanford, a superb master of change when he was governor of North Carolina, observed (1967, 185):

> "The center of the state system, and its chief proponent in the eyes of the people, is the governor. The governor's prestige and his power to move people and ideas within his state are the strongest weapons in each state's arsenal . . . It is the governor who must ask the people to do more. He must prod the institutions of state government to the service of the people."

Governors on the Offense: Changing the State Through Major Legislation

Two articles in this issue describe how former Gov. Richard Riley of South Carolina convinced his state to adopt a major education reform financed by a penny sales tax increase. These two articles are case studies of how a governor with few formal powers, a "weak" governor, can produce major changes against determined opposition.

Richard Kearney ("How a 'Weak' Governor Can Be Strong") found that Riley succeeded in getting his school reform legislation, the Education Improvement Act of 1985, enacted by exploiting two informal powers of his office — access to the media and the prestige of his office — and his personal characteristics, including popularity, skills in consensus building, public relations abilities, ambition, energy and devotion to a cause. Regina Brough ("Strategies for Leaders") attributes Riley's success to use of a strong staff, mobilization of outside influences, and "extensive use of the the bully pulpit" to hammer the issue into the public mind.

Riley's story represents the experience of many other governors who in the past few years have pushed their states to adopt important policy reforms. A review of Riley's education reform and other major reform initiatives shows how a governor operates as a change master: the governor believes deeply in a vision, has a strategy to communicate the vision to the public and to legislators, and possesses persistence.

The Policy Vision

Change starts with a vision. Warren Bennis (Bennis and Nanus 1985, 30) wrote that vision "animates, inspirits, transforms purpose into action." U.S. Sen. Bob Graham during his eight years as governor of Florida often talked about the need for a "magical vision" that was large enough to inspire action. Henry Kissinger has stressed this theme: The task of the leader is to get his people from where they are to where they have not been. . . . Leaders must invoke an alchemy of great visions. Those leaders who do not are ultimately judged failures, even though they may be popular at the moment (Peters and Waterman 1984, 282).

Governors chose their own visions. Riley's vision was embodied in a slogan, "A penny for their thoughts." He saw South Carolina's future tied to the quality of education offered its citizens. Many other governors have brought similar visions to their states by proposing restructured educational systems. Other governors have offered other types of visions. Gov. John Ashcroft of Missouri (like several other governors) proposed that the welfare system be restructured and formulated a "learnfare" program to replace welfare. Graham as governor inspired action with his call to Save the Everglades. Gov. Gerald Baliles of Virginia tied the economic future of his state to a $12 billion program to improve the state's transportation system. Gov. John Sununu pursued a vision concerning the need to ensure energy supplies for Northeastern states.

Selling the Vision

But visions alone are not enough. Governors have to sell their visions to get the changes that they want. When former Gov. Lamar Alexander of Tennessee promoted his vision of improved state education, he — like Riley — sold it with singleminded purpose. Alexander acknowledged spending 70 percent of his time selling his proposal. He told a reporter, "I've run for office three times. But nothing compares to this. It's by far the most difficult thing I have ever been through in my life" (Aldrich 1984, 49).

Governors use their communication skills and their unique access to the media to sell their visions. Like Riley, they have taken their visions directly to the citizens of the state, campaigning for their ideas on television talk shows, at press conferences, with paid advertisements, through rallies, and by phone calls and personal appeals.

Governors have the opportunity to leave a lasting mark on their states with major new policies.

Governors often try to influence public opinion to accept their vision — and the associated policy proposals — because they want to force the proposals through the state legislature despite opposition from powerful interest groups. A governor can use enthusiastic public support of a reform to convince legislators that it is in their self-interest to vote for the reform.

When trying to sell their visions, governors wisely use their most precious resource: their time. As Gov. Michael Dukakis of Massachusetts has suggested, they allot their time to reflect their visions: their schedules reflect their priorities. Governors use their time to communicate their visions by carefully selecting the people they see, the speeches they make and the content of their speeches.

Persistence

Gubernatorial visions may not be immediately embraced, especially if strong interest groups oppose the changes they would bring. Thus, governors often must persist in selling their visions. Former Gov. Lamar Alexander says that a governor who selects an issue and "leans into it in a compelling way" can wear down everyone else. Gov. Thomas Kean maintains that a governor can "outlast" everyone else: since a governor cannot always win in the state legislature right away, he or she will have to stick with a vision in the long run to get his or her way.

Helping the Change Masters

While governors have many resources to promote important state changes, they need help to turn their ideas into law. As Kearney and Brough point out, Riley relied on his knowledgeable staff and two task forces, consisting of educators, business people and legislators, to advance his education reform. The expert staff and task forces provided the research and knowledge on which the reform was based. The task forces permitted diverse groups to be involved in the education reform process and thereby to share ownership of the reform proposal.

Paula King and Nancy Roberts ("Policy Entrepreneurs") describe the essential roles of another outside group in the process of creating innovative changes in education. These authors tell how a group of eight "policy entrepreneurs," who were not employed in state government, proposed creation of a market for education in Minnesota and helped enact a portion of their proposals into law. These entrepreneurs

While governors have many resources to promote important state changes, they need help to turn their ideas into law.

proposed that students be allowed a choice of schools and that state aid to school districts follow the students. With this "choice" system, the good schools would attract students and thrive while poor schools would improve or disappear.

The entrepreneurs convinced Gov. Rudy Perpich to adopt the "choice" idea as his own. The governor proposed legislation, called Access to Education, to create a market for education by implementing the "choice" proposals, and campaigned hard for the proposal. The policy entrepreneurs devoted substantial time to an effort to convince the state legislature to adopt the governor's proposed education reform. Despite opposition by Minnesota's education establishment, parts of the proposal were enacted into law.

Just as change masters can be assisted by the active participation of groups inside and outside of government, they also can be helped if other state policymakers are fully informed. Because most state policy results from state legislation, state legislators determine which major changes become law. To make these important decisions, legislators should fully understand the issues and their impact on the state.

John Martin, speaker of the Maine House of Representatives, describes a program in his state to help legislators better understand economic concepts so they can make informed votes on complex issues affecting the state's economy ("Adapting to a Changing Economy"). The nonprofit, bipartisan Institute on the Maine Economy provides legislators with workshops and seminars on economic issues, and takes legislators to different regions of the state for a hands-on economic tours. In these tours, state legislators talk to people involved in different aspects of the state's economy.

The institute's program for legislators is supplemented by a program to help business people understand more fully how the legislative process works and how pressure is imposed on state legislators. By helping legislators to understand better the business economy and giving business leaders insight into how and why state laws are made, the institute promotes a public-private partnership that helps state leaders better manage Maine's response to its economic challenges.

Changing State Government

A governor depends on the state bureaucracy to administer state programs. As the manager at the top of the state's organizational chart, the governor is responsibile for ensuring that the state is implementing its programs as well as possible.

Often a governor (or kibitzers) may desire to change state government operations. The governor may perceive that state government is not as efficient as it should be or that the state government structure no longer is adequate to meet changes in the economic, political or social environments. Because state governments are large organizations that adhere to standard operating procedures and organizational routines, they resist change. Sometimes governors must provide the push for state governments to change for the better.

Three articles in this issue deal with efforts to change state bureaucracies. Two articles focus on changes in organizational structure, and a third tells how a state is trying to improve its effectiveness by creating a managerial culture that encourages state employees to propose innovative ideas.

The article by James D. Carney ("Downsizing Government") describes how Iowa Gov. Terry Branstad responded to a budget crisis by proposing to downsize and restructure the state government. In 1986, Branstad found that the state faced a large deficit despite previous large budget cuts and the enactment of a sales tax. So, he initiated a crash effort to reduce the size of state government to reflect new economic realities, to eliminate unneeded programs, to impose budget controls and to make the government structure easier to manage.

The main elements of the governor's plan were formulated in nine weeks. The governor hired a management consulting firm to help prepare the plan. The consultants worked with two advisory committees, made up of members of the governor's staff, some top private-sector managers and key state government managers, to prepare recommendations for the governor.

The governor's downsizing and restructuring plan took up much of the time of state legislators during the 1986 session. Most of the governor's plan was adopted into law, including elimination of some 50 departments and 42 boards and commissions. Also, the governor for the first time was empowered to appoint many department and agency directors.

Branstad overhauled the structure of state government through intense work over a short time. He was assisted by many people both inside and outside of government who helped him prepare his plan and sell it to the legislature. His plan reshaped Iowa state government in a way that put the governor in a better position to manage the state government and be accountable for its operation.

But reorganization does not mean that state government will automatically be improved. Les Garner ("Managing Change Through Organization Structure") recounts the reorganization of Florida's Department of Health and Rehabilitative Service (HRS). The HRS was created in 1969 by combining various social service programs that had been administered by independent agencies. In 1975, in a further reorganization the state assigned the responsibility for the delivery of social services to HRS district offices. HRS kept a central office only for program planning, monitoring and evaluation.

The main purpose of the reorganization was to integrate the social services: the districts were supposed to provide packages of services to clients rather than administer each service individually, unrelated to other social services. However, Florida's social services are not integrated; the reorganization did not accomplish its key objective. Garner writes that states find it extremely difficult to improve their operations by changing organizational structure. Garner maintains that services can be integrated by using other basic management tools. He concludes that often there are easier ways for states to make desired changes in program operation than to change the structure of the organization.

Rather than change the structure of Minnesota's state government, Gov. Rudy Perpich's administration is improving state operations by changing its managerial culture. He and Commissioner of Administration Sandra J. Hale have tried to improve the quality and cost-effectiveness of state government by unleashing the innovative potential of state employees.

Michael Barzelay and Robert Leone ("Creating an Innovative Culture") describe how Perpich, rejecting the traditional approach of using private sector experts to tell state employees how to be more efficient, asked Hale to propose a strategy for improving the management of state government. Hale decided to try to create a climate of innovation, experimentation and performance improvement. She wanted state employees to have control over the innovation process, but also to use private expertise and resources to help employees innovate.

Barzelay and Leone tell how Hale formed a coalition of prestigous private sector chief executive officers, union leaders and political leaders who believed in her idea of empowering

state employees to improve the management of the state. A high-powered steering committee was designated to evaluate state employees' ideas for improving state government. When a proposal for an innovative idea is approved by the committee, it has the informal stamp of approval of the governor, the state business elite, top state managers and public sector unions.

The authors conclude that Hale's approach to change has been successful. Many innovations have been implemented through the program. More importantly, they write, the program has created an environment in which good ideas can "percolate to the top, are championed by public entrepreneurs, and are politically accepted. . . ."

Conclusion

In the past three decades, the job of governors has changed as the responsibilities of state governments have increased and the pace of economic and social changes has accelerated. The Francis Cherrys were mainly administrators who saw themselves with limited power and a limited mandate to influence the future of the state. Now, the Bill Clintons — the aggressive governors — view themselves as leaders of not only state government, but the state. They, as Ashcroft says, "redefine the possible."

Past studies have noted that governors serve many different roles: they are the state's chief administrator, the chief legislator, the leader of the party, the ceremonial head of government and the chief ambassador to other governments. Studies of today's governors should note that many governors now devote large portions of their time to a role not on the traditional lists: they function as change masters, leaders who get important ideas and innovations enacted into law. □

Sources

Aldrich, Hope. June 1984. "The Day the PTA Stayed Home," *The Washington Monthly*.

Bennis, Warren and Burt Nanus. 1985. *Leadership: The Strategies for Taking Charge*, New York: Harper & Row Publishers.

Kanter, Rosabeth Ross. 1983. *The Change Masters*. New York: Simon and Schuster.

Peters, Thomas J. and Robert Waterman, Jr. 1984. *In Search of Excellence*. New York: Warner Books Inc.

Sanford, Terry. 1967. *Storm Over the States*. New York: McGraw-Hill Book Co.

From Dreamers to Doers

A new generation of black mayors has arrived after the crest of the civil rights movement. Facing nitty-gritty tasks, they call themselves problem solvers, not crusaders.

W. JOHN MOORE

BALTIMORE—Call Kurt L. Schmoke ready. The first black elected mayor of Baltimore, Schmoke prepped for success at all the right places: Yale University, Harvard Law School, Oxford (as a Rhodes Scholar) and the White House, followed by stints at Baltimore's oldest law firm, as a prosecutor in the U.S. Attorney's office here and as elected state's attorney for the city. Behind his desk in City Hall are rows of trophies and plaques, visible reminders of those past successes. *Life* magazine plans a photo spread on the new mayor. Once a star quarterback in high school, Schmoke has run up the score in his resumé.

Ivy League in style, methodical in manner, Schmoke could hardly differ more from the irrepressible William Donald Schaefer, who served 16 years as mayor and is now Maryland's governor. Schaefer once plunged into Baltimore's National Aquarium garbed in a bathing suit and straw boater, accompanied by his rubber duck. Belly flops hardly fit Schmoke's image.

Nor does Schmoke, by background or outlook, resemble many of the pioneering black mayors who came to power in the aftermath of the civil rights movement. Instead, he symbolizes a new generation of black mayors—sometimes young, typically well-educated, politically pragmatic.

"The first-generation mayors were pioneers," said Roger Wilkins, a history professor at George Mason University and a senior fellow at the Institute for Policy Studies. "For the first generation, it was a leap of faith that they could be mayor. The second generation is closer to conventional urban politicians."

A beneficiary of the civil rights movement, Schmoke readily acknowledges its import. But his generation's politics were not forged in that crucible. "We come into power at a time when the laws have been changed, the legal barriers are down," he said in an interview. "Now we have to deliver the goods and talk more about economic empowerment than traditional civil rights issues."

Schmoke's victory over Mayor Clarence H. "Du" Burns last November capped an extraordinary two years of ferment in black politics that signaled a changing of the guard.

Five black mayors known for their clout and charisma no longer run their cities. Just before Thanksgiving and just as he had begun consolidating power, Chicago Mayor Harold Washington died: He was succeeded by Eugene Sawyer. Last May, Thomas V. Barnes toppled Gary (Ind.) Mayor Richard G. Hatcher, the nation's longest-serving black mayor, who was first elected in 1967. And in 1986, Sharpe James defeated another veteran black leader, Newark Mayor Kenneth A. Gibson. Also, in 1986 Sidney J. Barthelemy, relying on overwhelming white support, succeeded Ernest N. "Dutch" Morial as New Orleans mayor after defeating another black, state Sen. William Jefferson. And Charlotte (N.C.) Mayor Harvey Gantt, the epitome of the new black official, was upset by Republican Sue Myrick, who is white.

Philadelphia Mayor W. Wilson Goode narrowly won reelection last November by less than 1 per cent of the vote over former Mayor Frank L. Rizzo. Richard Arrington Jr. was elected mayor of Birmingham, Ala., for the third time.

And in 1989, Michael Lomax, the 39-year-old black chairman of the Fulton County (Atlanta) Commission, is expected to run for mayor against his former boss, Maynard H. Jackson, for the job that Mayor Andrew Young must vacate after two terms.

"What we see as a general shift in the new generation is a much more conscious articulation by racial coalitional appeals for votes," said David J. Garrow, a political science professor at City College of New York and the author of a 1987 Pulitzer Prize-winning study of Martin Luther King Jr., *Bearing the Cross* (William Morrow & Co.).

Each of these new mayors faces distinctly local problems. But many of them are linked by background, priorities and style. And they differ more from their predecessors than from each other. More pragmatists than pioneers, professionals than preachers, coalition builders than confrontationists, they came to power during a period of drastic cutbacks in federal money for cities, and they are hawking economic progress and managerial expertise.

"The new breed of black mayors tend to be different in terms of their focus on citywide development efforts as opposed to even running on a banner of change for minority and poor communities," said Linda F. Williams, associate director of research at the Joint Center for Political Studies, a Washington organization that tracks black political trends. "New black mayors have consciously shaped their images so as not to be threatening to middle-class blacks or to white America," she said.

Style is only one difference between the first and second-generation black mayors. Performance counts far more now than it did in the early days, when pride helped black leaders through tough times. "Those leaders were held with a certain reverence because they were first," New Orleans Mayor Barthelemy said. "And I think more was tolerated by the people from them than will be tolerated from us because having a black mayor is no longer a novelty."

BIG-CITY NORM

Since 1970, the number of black mayors has jumped more than fivefold, with blacks now controlling about 300 City Halls. *(See chart, this page.)* And black women now govern upwards of 50 cities. *(See box, next page.)* But black Republican mayors remain a rare species.

Much of that increase occurred before 1980. "There has a been a steady increase, not a surge in any one year," said Michelle D. Korouma, executive director of the Atlanta-based National Conference of Black Mayors Inc.

But future gains may be much slower, in part because of black success stories. Two-thirds of the cities with black majorities already have black mayors, according to the Joint Center for Political Studies. "And it is getting more difficult to attract a large percentage of the white vote" for a black candidate, Williams said.

In the South particularly, the numbers tell an intriguing story of political strength—primarily in rural hamlets, many of which have had black-majority populations since the Civil War. There are black mayors in towns rich in both black education and history, such as Grambling, La., and Tuskegee, Ala. Alabama has the most black mayors, 30, of any state; Arkansas follows with 26. In Virginia, blacks control City Hall in Richmond, Roanoke and Newport News, three of the state's biggest cities.

Blacks' most important and publicized gains were achieved in major cities in the South and the North. Starting in 1967 with Cleveland and Gary, followed by Newark, Atlanta, Los Angeles, Washington, Detroit, New Orleans, Philadelphia, Chicago and Baltimore, black mayors became the big-city norm rather than the exception. Indeed, of the nation's top six cities, only New York and Houston *don't* have black mayors.

Changing demographics have played a crucial role. The concentration of black electorates in the cities, combined with white flight to the suburbs and beyond, created cities in which blacks became the majority. And like the Irish, the Italians and the Poles before them, they elected their own as mayor. In Chicago, City Hall passed from Richard J. Daley to Michael A. Bilandic to Jane M. Byrne to Harold Washington.

Black political success also owes a debt to the civil rights struggle and its key political achievement, the 1965 Voting Rights Act.

"It is the ultimate realization of what the march from Selma to Montgomery was all about," said Washington lawyer Vernon E. Jordan, Jr., a former president of the National Urban League.

The mayoral victories for blacks "signaled the shift in the nation from the civil rights struggle, which had accomplished its major legislative goals, to the political arena, which would dominate the efforts of black Americans for the foreseeable future," Cleveland's Carl Stokes, the nation's first big-city black mayor, said in an interview.

"MORE MAINSTREAM"

The first black mayors were often veterans of the civil rights movement and activists in black churches or black political organizations who were propelled to power with calls for racial solidarity and social change. Even mayors such as Atlanta's Young or Washington's Marion S. Barry Jr.—or, in some ways, Chicago's late Mayor Washington—fit part of that profile. Obvious differences exist among them. But they are much closer in background and outlook to one another than they are to the new mayors such as Barthelemy and Schmoke.

Atlanta's Young, for example, who is 55, graduated from a traditional black school, Howard University, and from the Hartford Theological Seminary and worked with King. Coleman A. Young of Detroit was a veteran of the labor movement. Many second-generation leaders are professionals with advanced degrees and fast-track careers. Schmoke has the most glittering credentials, but former Charlotte Mayor Gantt is an architect out of Clemson University, and Philadelphia's Goode has earned degrees in public administration.

Many of the new mayors have long experience in government, and for them, the job of mayor caps a career in the public sector. Goode was city manager under former Mayor William J. Green and before that, head of the city's public utility commission. Barthelemy, a onetime social worker, had more than 12 years' experience in city government and was brought in by former New Orleans Mayor Moon Landrieu. Before beating Hatcher in Gary, Barnes was county assessor for nine years.

"Politically, they're more sophisticated and technically much better equipped than were the mayors in the late '60s or '70s," said Robert McAlpine, coordinator of policy and government relations at the National Urban League in Washington.

Along with government backgrounds, management skills now are touted as keys to a mayor's success. The first-generation mayors weren't usually in that mold: Even Chicago's Washington wasn't considered a particularly good administrator, despite his political genius and his success in repairing the city's finances. Washington wasn't enamored of "the homely, fundamental tasks of civilization" such as garbage collection or street cleaning, said Eugene Kennedy, a Loyola University (Chicago) psychologist and veteran observer of that city's politics. "Under Harold Washington, the city is beginning to look uncared for and overgrown, like an old estate whose gardeners take the money and don't mow the lawns," Kennedy wrote in *Chicago Times* last year.

"This is not only a new generation but a group of people with a new, somewhat different agenda, one that is much more mainstream, much less oriented toward a specific segment of the community," said William Davis, director of policy analysis and development at the National League of Cities and head of its Election '88 project. The issues today, he said, are less "black" issues such as poverty and welfare and more such typical urban concerns as envi-

Black Mayors and Their Constituents
(combined population of cities and towns with black mayors)

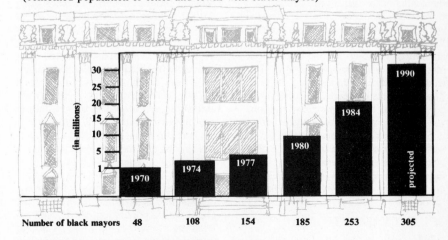

| Number of black mayors | 48 | 108 | 154 | 185 | 253 | 305 |

SOURCE: National Conference of Black Mayors Inc.

Black Women Climbing Up to City Hall

Rosa Parks ignited the civil rights movement when she refused to budge from the front of a Montgomery (Ala.) bus. Fannie Lou Hamer toiled long and hard as a civil rights worker in Mississippi. Shirley Chisholm was the first black woman whose name was placed in nomination for President at a major party convention.

Black women have struggled mightily to achieve political clout in city government. But until recently, few succeeded in transforming their civic activism into control of city hall. Now that is changing. Almost 20 per cent of black mayors are women. And their numbers are growing at a faster rate than the number of black male city officials, according to the Joint Center for Political Studies, a Washington think tank.

But only three black women govern cities with populations of more than 50,000, noted Linda F. Williams, the center's associate director of research. Lottie L. Shackelford in Little Rock, Ark., and Jessie M. Rattley in Newport News, Va., were appointed mayor by their city councils in 1987. Carrie Saxon Perry in Hartford, Conn., is the only black woman elected mayor of a big city, Williams added—and that post has limited powers. "It is more important symbolically that there was finally an election of a black woman mayor" in a city of Hartford's size, Williams said. "It serves as encouragement for other black women running for office."

Long political apprenticeships are the norm for most women mayors. Elected in 1970 as the first black and the first woman city council member in conservative Newport News, Rattley said that she had to convince a somewhat skeptical citizenry that the city "would not sink into the river" if she became mayor. Perry served in Connecticut's legislature for seven years before becoming mayor. Shackelford first ran for the city council in 1974: She lost but was appointed four years later.

In background and philosophy, many black women mayors have demonstrated a strong interest in expanding social services. Perry, for example, has a degree in social work, worked as an administrator for the Greater Hartford Inc. community renewal team and was director of a day care center. At a strategy meeting during her 1987 mayoral campaign, Perry recalled in an interview, she decided to address the problem of declining social services despite warnings from her advisers that as a black women, she might be too closely identified with welfare issues. Her first major achievement in office was to meet with gang leaders who had terrorized part of Hartford.

During her 18 years as council member and mayor, Rattley of Newport News said, she has focused much of her attention on drug abuse, the homeless, hunger and "those issues that many white males in particular just never seem to address."

But as is the case with their male counterparts, economic development takes first place as a government priority for these women. "My goals have been to forge partnerships with the business community so we could work on our overall goal, and that's continued, steady and quality growth for our city, with some development earmarked for the inner city, Shackelford said.

No matter how similar their goals are to those of other mayors, black women in City Hall run the risk of being stereotyped. "I'm a two-fer," Rattley said. "Everybody looks upon me as being a representative of women or a representative of the black community. I see myself as representative of the entire city."

But Veronika E. Shepherd, the Republican mayor of Urban Crest, Ohio, said the mostly black residents in her town of 1,100, near Columbus, have no problems accepting a black woman. Last November, she defeated the black male incumbent in a nonpartisan election. In 1971, the town was the first in the country to elect a black woman mayor. Now black women dominate Urban Crest's public life: Four of the six council members are black women, and so is the city clerk.

Shepherd, a veteran state government employee, said that economic development was her theme, especially new programs to support light industry. That message may sound like ideal, small-town Republican politics. But Shepherd, a Jesse Jackson supporter, has no time for national Republican leaders, especially President Reagan. "My motto for Urban Crest is that we will no longer take the skim milk—we want the cream."

---

ronment, finance and transportation.

Yet there are holdouts to the trend toward making management a top priority. Washington Mayor Barry scoffed at the notion that managerial skills determine a mayor's success. "I'm not a manager—I'm an elected official with a vision," he said. "You can be the best manager in the world, but if you don't have a progressive vision, you might as well not even be there. I don't like to use this kind of analysis, but we've had some white mayors who were racists but who were excellent managers. . . . All the progressive mayors who are making things happen did not go to the Wharton School."

GREAT EXPECTATIONS

Differences in age, background and style account for only part of the distance between these generations of black mayors. The times have changed far more than the mayors. Some of them—Gibson in Newark, Young in Detroit and Hatcher in Gary, for example—inherited economically troubled cities that were beginning steep slides: Gary lost more than 10,000 steel-industry jobs in the 1970s, and more than half of Detroit's businesses have departed since 1967. Reagan Administration budget cuts, the loss of revenue sharing and reduced federal spending on housing programs also hurt.

But the black electorate also grew tired of repeated excuses, especially from mayors who had held power for two decades. Gary, with a population of 145,000, suffered an average of 60 murders a year during Hatcher's tenure, and unemployment reached 20 per cent. In many cities, voters replaced one black mayor with another and demanded better performance. "The symbolic aspect of ethnic politics recedes as there is only so much the voters can take," said Harvard University government professor Martin Kilson.

Barnes pledged during Gary's May 1987 primary to fight crime by hiring more police. Interviewed at the recent U.S. Conference of Mayors midwinter meeting just after his inauguration, Barnes acknowledged that he will judged by tougher standards. "We were allowed a very long honeymoon, an extremely long honeymoon, and that won't happen anymore," he said, noting that many criticisms of Hatcher were ignored as racially motivated. "We will be judged on performance, not hype," he stressed. As a first step, Barnes said, he planned to hire a chief administrative officer to bolster the city's finances.

Black politicians have noted the change in voter emphasis. "When I was elected mayor of Birmingham in 1979, blacks were overjoyed that they got a black mayor," Arrington recalled. "Some of the glitter of having a black mayor wore off by 1983, when I ran again, but I still benefited from it. I was just reelected in November, and I spent a great deal of time explaining to blacks, especially young blacks, what I was doing in terms of an economic agenda for blacks. And they asked why weren't blacks getting any more of the business from Birmingham, both the public and private sectors. That was their main focus."

Arrington added that black voters readily acknowledged their pride in having a black mayor and in the fact that police brutality, in a city where Bull Connor was once police chief, was no longer an issue. They also conceded that blacks had obtained a fair share of government jobs and contracts, he said. What black voters want now, he said, is a chunk of the city's commercial and economic development boom: "That's where the thrust is today."

The black electorate demands political change because some black mayors have often ignored lower-class blacks, according to critics. "With the exception of police brutality complaints, lower-tier blacks have not gotten much help from black elected officials," said Adolph L. Reed, Jr., a black political scientist at Yale. In terms of public employment gains, he added, the impact appears small, except in professional and managerial jobs, even though more government contracts go to black and other minority businesses than used to be the case.

Research also shows, Reed maintained, that during periods of fiscal woes, black mayors are more willing than white officials are to force a black electorate to swallow unpalatable austerity measures.

The decline in federal dollars streaming into the cities obviously hurt. Hatcher and Gibson, among others, proved to be masters at getting federal grants: In his first term, Hatcher tripled Gary's federal aid, and Gibson did almost as well. But actually running the city on empty proved a tough task for many first-generation black mayors. Their successors have emphasized economic development to counter a declining tax base and cuts in financial aid. During James's first 18 months in office, Newark snagged a $55 million U.S. courthouse, a major office complex near the airport, a $300 million cultural complex and even an $83 million medium-security prison.

But some black mayors have promised a renewed commitment to social welfare

Jackson and the Mayors

For many black mayors, Democratic presidential candidate Jesse Jackson remains the candidate of choice, still able to instill pride and hope. Jackson represents "new hope and a new vision for a better America," Newark Mayor Sharpe James said when he endorsed Jackson last October. The mayors of New Orleans, Oakland, Calif., and Washington are among the 93 black mayors who have also announced their support for Jackson. But Tom Bradley in Los Angeles, Andrew Young in Atlanta and Coleman A. Young in Detroit have not endorsed him.

Some black mayors view Jackson as a problem, even a test of political clout. In an interview, Mayor Richard Arrington Jr. of Birmingham, Ala., who sided with Walter F. Mondale in the 1984 Democratic presidential primary but has now endorsed Jackson, acknowledged the dilemma Jackson's candidacy poses for black elected officials: "We must redefine what our role is as politicians from the black community. It is not as simple as always saying we will always support a black candidate. Yet we are still in a stage where most black officials will support, say, Jesse Jackson, and are not willing or not courageous enough, in a public setting, anyway, to talk about the need to assess what his chances are, what supporting him means and whether there should be alternative strategies."

For a nuts-and-bolts politician such as Baltimore Mayor Kurt L. Schmoke, electability also matters. Although impressed with Jackson, he has not endorsed a candidate yet. Schmoke said that he doubts whether it is possible to have a color-blind presidential election. "I am looking at these candidates to determine whose views I am closest to and who has an ability to win," he added.

Among the new black leaders, commitment to Jackson is based on more than race. For example, New Orleans Mayor Sidney J. Barthelemy, who endorsed Jackson early, applauded his position on urban issues. "Jesse Jackson has been the only candidate [who] has truly been committed to the cities," Barthelemy said. Jackson, he added, talks about drug abuse, the cities' lack of financial resources, unemployment and poor housing. "He is trying to make the nation aware that they have to address these issues."

Jackson probably hurt his chances by committing political gaffes. He supported some losing mayoral candidates: former Gary (Ind.) Mayor Richard G. Hatcher, for example, who lost to Thomas V. Barnes and later joined Jackson's campaign. (Barnes has yet to endorse a candidate.) And in Chicago, Jackson's hometown, he wanted Alderman Timothy Evans to succeed the late Harold Washington, but the city council voted for Eugene Sawyer.

Although black mayors wield some clout, it is questionable in many cases whether their endorsement counts for much. Washington Mayor Marion S. Barry Jr. noted that Jackson carried several cities in 1984 Democratic primaries despite black mayors' endorsements of other candidates; Atlanta Mayor Young's support of Mondale, for example. "Harold [Washington] was lukewarm, and he carried Chicago," Barry said. "He got a significant black vote in Los Angeles, and Bradley was not for him."

Jackson's ultimate accomplishment may be to open the door for another black on the Democratic ticket—if not this year, perhaps in 1992. "It will not be Jesse Jackson," David J. Garrow, a political science professor at City College of New York, predicted. "I think that the best the Jackson campaign can achieve is Bill Gray for Vice President"—a reference to Rep. William H. Gray III, D-Pa.

causes. "Economic growth is more than office towers, ports, expressways, airports and skyscrapers," Philadelphia's Goode said on Jan. 4 in his second inaugural address. "As we boast about breaking through the skyline," he added, "too many have stood in the soup line." To aid blacks, Goode called for a new affirmative

action hiring program for private real estate development. He also asked for increased adult job training and new programs to curb drug abuse and reduce school dropouts.

Nor does the focus on growth impress some critics. Abraham L. Davis, a political scientist at predominantly black

Morehouse College in Atlanta, believes that only a few black mayors—Chicago's Washington or Atlanta's former mayor, Jackson, for example—helped middle or lower-class blacks by giving black businesses a share of the contracts and concessions at Atlanta's airport. Under Mayor Young, Davis complains, Atlanta has focused its development efforts in the predominantly white, northern part of the city rather than in the middle-class, black neighborhoods in the southwest. "For some reason, whether consciously or subconsciously, black mayors do not respond to the black community in proportion to the number of blacks who supported him or her to victory," Davis said.

In New Orleans, where white voters swung the election to Barthelemy, they will get many of the benefits, Davis added. "That is the irony of the black predicament as far as the election of mayors is concerned."

BLACKS V. BLACKS

As blacks move up the political ladder or battle each other for political jobs, coalition building typically replaces racial polarization. The recent contest in New Orleans showed that when two black candidates square off, white votes may determine the outcome. Barthelemy easily defeated Jefferson, winning 58 per cent of the vote: Only 35 per cent of the black voters supported Barthelemy, but 85 per cent of the white voters backed him. Barthelemy is the first mayor since 1969 who got less than half of the black vote.

Edward F. Renwick, director of Loyola University's Institute of Politics in New Orleans, said Barthelemy collected white votes because he was so different from former Mayor Morial, who had become increasingly unpopular in the white community. Long-standing rivals from the middle-class black ward, Morial and Barthelemy had frequently clashed, and Morial supported Jefferson. "Morial was perceived as an aggressive, feisty politician, who would decide his position on an issue and fight for it," Renwick said. "Sidney is more of a consensus politician."

In office, Barthelemy has tried to appeal to a broad group, a difficult strategy given the $30 million budget deficit that greeted him. He has added parking, business and inheritance taxes, has frozen pay increases for a number of city workers and has cut back some services.

But Barthelemy concedes that governing is difficult for a centrist who's seeking coalitions. "It is easier when you have one homogenous group of constituents so you know where you stand on each policy issue and you know who you are trying to please," he said. "My approach is to reach across the board and impact everyone."

That strategy can be risky. Appealing to moderates of both races can leave a candidate without strong support from either group. "You can win," Barthelemy said, "if you ride the tiger and you stay up. But the danger is that you slip off and get devoured."

Coalitions can fall apart, as Gantt discovered in November. An architect who was comfortable with elites of any color, Gantt in 1963 was the first black to enroll at Clemson. Defeated in his initial bid for the job, he became Charlotte's first black mayor in 1983, even though the city's population is 70 per cent white. Five years ago, he received 36 per cent of the white vote, and two years later, his percentage increased to 46. But in 1987, Gantt's percentage dropped to 34. The only real issue in the contest was traffic, which Myrick, the winner, said Gantt failed to address.

Theodore S. Arrington, chairman of the political science department at the University of North Carolina (Charlotte), attributed Gantt's defeat primarily to the 6 per cent growth in the number of registered Republicans, most upper-income whites who voted for Myrick. Turnout among registered black voters, meanwhile, which is normally high, dropped slightly.

"Very simply, the bottom line here is that blacks did not vote for Harvey as strongly as they have in the past, and whites went out and voted for me," Myrick said. But race wasn't an issue in the campaign, she said.

Julius L. Chambers, a former Charlotte attorney now with the NAACP Legal Defense and Educational Fund in New York, disputed her assessment. "We have not gotten to the point where whites were able to vote for him based on his contribution to the community," he said. But Chambers acknowledged that some blacks wanted Gantt to be more of an advocate for their interests. "Harvey had the problem of developing positions that cut across racial lines." he said.

BEST HOPE?

"Gantt's loss," said King's biographer Garrow, "leaves open the question [of] what new-generation black mayor could symbolize this new, biracial coalition."

Many believe that Baltimore's Schmoke has become a leading contender for the title. With a large base of black support, Schmoke can follow his predecessor in emphasizing downtown development while aiding his black constituents, too. "You don't ignore your base," he stressed. Among his immediate goals are forcing the city to live up to minority business set-aside laws and establishing a housing program that encourages low and moderate-income people to own homes.

Recent studies have noted the limitations in Schaefer's approach. From 1980-86, Baltimore had a net loss of 7,700 jobs, according to a recent study by the District of Columbia government that compared the prospects for growth of Baltimore and Washington. And *Baltimore 2000*, a study by a Baltimore civic group, offered a grim vision of the city's future despite the rebirth downtown.

During the mayoral campaign, Schmoke talked about satisfying unmet needs. Yet he remains cautious about what can be accomplished immediately. "I know that expectations are high," he said. "But I don't fuel it by making unrealistic statements about what I can accomplish."

Schmoke sounds more like a pragmatist than a populist. His political heroes include former Democratic Rep. Parren J. Mitchell, for opening up Baltimore politics, Los Angeles Mayor Tom Bradley and Rep. William H. Gray III, D-Pa., for his role in the federal budget process. But Schmoke first mentioned Mario M. Cuomo because the New York governor's diaries recount the difficulties of maintaining a private life while holding a public office.

Nor is Schmoke's philosophy a surprise. "I used to tell people when I was a state's attorney that my criterion in hiring was a liberal who had been mugged," he said. "That is, people with a sense of compassion for people less fortunate than them and a belief that government can make a difference—but who also realize that we have to pay our bills."

"City Managers Don't Make Policy": A Lie; Let's Face It

DAVID N. AMMONS and CHARLDEAN NEWELL

David N. Ammons is a Research Associate at the Carl Vinson Institute of Government at the University of Georgia. Charldean Newell is Professor of Public Administration and Associate Vice President for Academic Affairs at North Texas State University.

Spoils, graft, and corruption in U.S. cities had 19th century reformers clamoring for change. In 1899 the National Municipal League adopted "A Municipal Program" (soon dubbed the *Model City Charter*) as a blueprint for reform.

Model City Charter: Democracy + Management

Now in its sixth edition with a seventh in preparation, the League's model charter has been broadly distributed and widely adopted, though commonly with local modifications. The purpose of the model is to provide a plan of municipal government that is "(1) democratic—that is to say responsive to the electorate and the community—and at the same time (2) capable of doing the work of the city effectively and translating the intentions of the voters into efficient administrative action as promptly and economically as possible."[1]

Since 1913, that prescription has been interpreted by the League as a call for the council-manager plan. That plan assigns to the city council responsibility for municipal legislation and policy formulation and to the city manager, appointed by and answerable to the city council, responsibility for carrying out policy directives and managing the delivery of municipal services. In a single stroke, the reformers believed they had preserved democracy in local government while removing undue political influence and enhancing managerial expertise in the "business" of local government.

The six versions of the *Model City Charter* reflect the concerns of their times and, to a lesser degree, the concerns of the times that came before. Remedies designed to address issues in the era of one edition became embedded in the next. Over the years the focus has moved from the elimination of blatant corruption and political spoils, and the introduction of scientific management practices and local "home rule," to professionalizing the public service, instituting modern budget procedures and state-of-the-art planning and zoning practices, and enhancing positive intergovernmental relations.[2]

Changing Attitudes in the Model Charter

Although the model charter has continued to prescribe the council-manager form of local government, its most recent versions, as well as deliberations for the seventh edition, suggest an increasing willingness to accept the "strong mayor" alternative. In part, such disposition is no doubt attributable to the passing of time since the worst excesses of turn-of-the-century political machines. More favorable consideration of the strong mayor alternative may also be attributable to the recognition that, in practice, city managers are less insulated from politics and more active in policy processes than originally envisioned. In other words, the idea that administration can be divorced completely from policy and politics is a myth...a lie.

The fact is, the politics vs. administration dichotomy presumed to be established through the council-manager plan has proven to be far less absolute than at least some of the reformers had originally thought.[3] Furthermore, anecdotal evidence regarding more than a few strong mayors suggests that even elected officials may be managerially as well as politically progressive and that many, in fact, concern themselves with managerial issues more commonly than caricatures of the mayor as a perpetually wheeling-and-dealing political broker would suggest.

This article explores the evolving roles of chief executives in reformed and unreformed cities (i.e., city managers in council-manager cities and mayors in mayor-council cities). The implications of that evolution are examined not only as they relate to the philosophical underpinnings of the council-manager plan but also more concretely as they relate to the prescriptions of the *Model City Charter.*

Mayors vs. Managers: Perceptions vs. Reality

A role-perception and time-allocation survey of chief executives in the 418 U.S. cities having 1980 populations of 50,000 or greater was completed during the spring of 1985. Responses were received from 226 executives for a response rate of 54 percent. The total included 153 city managers and 73 mayors.[4]

Respondents were asked to indicate the amount of their time that they devote to each of three roles identified by Deil Wright in his pioneering work on the role perceptions of city managers, published two decades ago.[5] The three roles identified by Wright are the "management role," the "policy role," and the "political role." Mayors and city managers were asked to report how their time was spent, and which role they perceived to be most important to their job success.

As expected, city managers reported devoting higher percentages of their time to the management role than did mayors. Surprisingly, however, given the rationale of the council-manager plan and the assumptions of its proponents regarding strong mayors, the management role commanded less of the city managers' time and more of the mayors' time than expected. City managers reported spending 51 percent of their time on the management role—much less than might be expected of an administrative technician. By comparison, mayors reported 44 percent—much more than expected of a politician (Table 1).

Reprinted by permission from the March/April 1988 issue of *National Civic Review*, pp. 124-132. National Civic Review, 1601 Grant Street, Suite 250, Denver, CO 80203.

TABLE 1
Mean Percentage of Time Devoted to the "Management," "Policy", and
"Political" Roles by Chief Executives in City Government

	Mayors[a]			City Managers[b]		
	Management Role	Policy Role	Political Role	Management Role	Policy Role	Political Role
Jurisdiction Population (1980)						
50,000 - 74,999	48.6%	24.6%	26.8%	51.7%	30.1%	18.2%
75,000 - 100,000	48.8	24.2	26.9	49.5	34.1	16.4
Greater than 100,000	37.8	27.2	35.0	50.6	33.4	16.0
Mean	44.2	25.6	30.2	50.8	32.2	17.0

[a]Mayor-council or commission form of government.
[b]Council-manager form of government.

Average time allocations to the management role differ little across the mayor and city manager groups from cities of 50,000 to 100,000 population. Among chief executives of larger cities, those greater than 100,000 population, substantial differences in role expectation become evident. While city managers in large cities report devoting 51 percent of their time to the management role on average, their mayoral counterparts report devoting only 38 percent of their time to that role.

City Managers: 32 Percent Policy Makers

Perhaps even more surprising to the council-manager purist expecting the overwhelming allocation of time by city managers to the management role is their substantial involvement in the policy-making process in local government. City managers reported devoting 32 percent of their time on average to the policy role, clarified on the survey instrument to include council relations, compared to a reported 26 percent average allocation by mayors.

Stereotyped views of the mayor and city manager would suggest heavy allocation of time to the political role by strong mayors and virtually none by city managers. Neither expectation is borne out by the survey results. Mayors report spending an average of 30 percent of their time on the political role, associated on the survey instrument with community leadership; city managers, 17 percent.

Images Behind the Mayor vs. Manager Dichotomy

These results suggest a rather clear break from the images supporting local government distinctions promulgated by naive partisans of one form of government or another. Somewhat paradoxically, the images conveyed by each camp are fundamentally similar. Both pretend that the strong mayor is a political leader unencumbered by managerial minutiae—a condition viewed by one group as positive (i.e., "providing political leadership") and by the other as negative (i.e., a management "amateur" whose guiding principle is political gain). The city manager, on the other hand, is imagined to be an expert administrator unencumbered by policy responsibilities or political incursions—again, viewed positively by one camp (i.e., free to make rational decisions regarding the "business" of local government) and negatively by the other (i.e., "insulated," "unresponsive," "insensitive").

What differ, of course, are the values assigned to particular roles. Advocates of the council-manager plan consider the management role most essential and base their support of that plan on the assumption of greater expertise in and devotion to the management role by the city manager. Advocates of the mayor-council form place a higher priority on political leadership—i.e., the political role and the policy role—and suggest that the city manager is ill-equipped to fulfill that need, and moreover is precluded by city charter from doing so.

Reality: A Mix of Roles

Reality suggests something much different from stereotyped images. Although degrees of emphasis differ substantially, mayors *do* manage and city managers *do* engage in policy and political roles. This assertion is not to suggest that mayors and city managers are indistinguishable from each other; such an assertion would be far from truth, as city managers tend to emphasize the management role, and even the policy role, to a greater degree than strong mayors, while mayors tend

to emphasize the political role to a greater degree than do the city managers.

But suggesting that the approaches taken in fulfilling their obligations are so different as to have virtually nothing in common would be just as inaccurate. Differences exist and they are perceptible; but they are differences in emphasis and degree, not absolutes.

Mayors who ignore their management responsibilities are rarely reelected. Their background may be partisan politics and they may perceive themselves to be local visionaries, but somebody has to cope with service problems and somebody has to resolve the interdepartmental quarrels.

Similarly, the city manager cannot and should not be insulated from the policy processes of local government. Policy proposals, expert advice, and policy interpretation and implementation are all crucial aspects of the policy process that often turn on the talent, shrewdness, and integrity of the chief executive. The maintenance of council relations is interwoven in that role. Without policy adeptness, the city manager may also have a short tenure. Even the political role, when its meaning is softened to exclude partisan involvement and instead to imply community leadership, has been territory occupied by many city managers, perhaps to the degree that elected officials left it vacant or even overtly encouraged city managers to assume it.

Although they differ in time allocations, mayors and city managers acknowledge involvement in all three of Wright's roles. Each of the three roles, in fact, is designated by some members of each fraternity as most important to job success. That is an important finding for those who fail to see any common ground between the jobs. For others the evolving perspective of city managers and the contrasting perceptions of mayors are equally important.

In 1965 Wright surveyed 45 city managers in cities of greater than 100,000 population and found that 37 percent perceived the management role as most important to their job success, while 22 percent accorded that status to the policy role and 33 percent to the political role (Table 2).[6] City managers form cities of similar size surveyed in 1985 placed similar priority on the management role but substantially different priority on the other two. The management role was considered most important to job success by 39 percent of the 1985 city managers, the policy role by 56 percent, and the political role by only 6 percent. In contrast, only 23 percent of the mayors thought the management role was most important to their success; 35 percent, the policy role; and 42 percent, the political role.

TABLE 2
City Managers and Mayors' 1985 Designation of Most Important Role
Compared with Wright's 1965 Findings (Populations Greater than 100,000)

Role Perceived as	Wright's Study of City Managers	City Managers	Mayors
Most Important to Job Success	1965[a]	1985[a]	1985[b]
Management Role (administrative activities)	37%	38.5%	23.1%
Policy Role (and council relations)	22%	55.8%	34.6%
Political Role (community leadership)	33%	5.8%	42.3%

[a]Council-Manager form of government.
[b]Mayor-council or commission form of government.

Implications for the Model City Charter

The *Model City Charter* informs and influences choices affecting fundamental aspects of local governance across the country. Reliance on the model by countless city charter commissions bears out that point. However, as its drafters have acknowledged, the model is influenced by its times. It molds views on good government, but its drafters have also attempted to reflect prevailing sentiment and realities. Insistence on a particular city council size, at-large elections, explicit procedures for planning and budgeting have already, or will eventually, give way to more flexible prescriptions and language. The model in its current form even attempts to accommodate the possibility of an elected chief executive, albeit as an appendix to the prescription of the preferred local-government structure.

A model charter informs and influences, but it does not, and should not be expected to, dictate what local government structures will be adopted across the nation and what division of responsibilities will be deemed acceptable. The role of local government itself has changed dramatically since the sixth edition of the *Model City Charter* was adopted. Local officials, in wrestling with complex policy issues such as environmental pollution, civil rights, and welfare services, have inevitably seen more blurring of traditional lines of responsibility. Role changes among city managers from 1965 to 1985 have occurred during an era covered by only one edition of the model charter, and the increasing "policy role" priority of modern city managers is hardly prescribed by that model. It is safe to assume that actual roles and activities commonly depart at least to a degree from those prescribed in actual, adopted city charters. Still, copies of the *Model City Charter* are in considerable demand; the model does appear to influence the intent, at least, of those who would reform their local government.

Differences in form of government are important. The selection of a particular form says something about the values of a community—the aspects of governance that it thinks most important, that it wishes to have emphasized. The selection of a particular form should not exclude the chief executive from roles necessary for functioning—regardless of formal declarations in the city charter. Perhaps as important as any of the formal effects is the influence that the choice of a particular form of government has on the types of people—their orientations, backgrounds, and specialties—that are drawn to the key offices in one form or another. Communities that want their government to be managed by a person with an extensive background in municipal management, a graduate degree in public administration, and a "passion for anonymity"[7] are more likely to get their wish by adoption of the council-manager form of government. That adoption, however, does not mean that the chief executive officer (i.e., city manager) will have no role in the policy process.

Drafters of the seventh edition of the *Model City Charter* would be well advised to consider the reality of the policy, if not the political, role of city managers. Many of the modifications contemplated or already made in the model charter would have the effect of heightening the political environment of local government.[8] Allowances for district election of council members and direct election of the mayor are two prominent examples. To survive in such an environment and to provide the policy assistance that councils increasingly demand, city managers must be more than mere technocrats. The survey results reported in this article suggest that city managers are making the necessary changes. It is time that the model charter recognize and legitimize this evolution, specifying among the powers and duties of the city manager the obligation to provide policy assistance as required by the council.

Notes
[1]Luther H. Gulick, "The New Model," NATIONAL CIVIC REVIEW, vol. 52 (December 1963), p. 584.
[2]A New Model City Charter," NATIONAL CIVIC REVIEW, vol. 74 (June 1985), p. 256.
[3]James H. Svara, in what is perhaps a more accurate depiction of reality, posits the existence of a four-category continuum depicting both the sharing and separation of responsibilities. Elected officials dominate "mission," share responsibility with managers for "policy and administration," and yield "management" to the managers. See: Svara, "Political Supremacy and Administrative Expertise," *Management Science and Policy Analysis,* vol. 3 (Summer 1985), pp. 3-7, and "Dichotomy and Duality: Reconceptualizing the Relationship Between Policy and Administration in Council-Manager Cities," *Public Administration Review,* vol. 45 (January/February 1985); *A Report to the Profession from the ICMA Committee on Future Horizons,* (Washington, D.C.: ICMA, 1979), which notes that the always fuzzy distinction between politics and administration has reached the point "at which both elective and administrative officials should concede that they have a shared stake in both policy and administration" (p. 17).
[4]For a more complete description of the study and its findings, see Charldean Newell and David N. Ammons, "Role Emphases of City Managers and Other Municipal Executives," *Public Administrative Review,* vol. 47 (May/June 1987), pp. 246-253.
[5]Deil S. Wright, "The City Manager as Developmental Administrator," Chapter Six in *Comparative Urban Research,* Robert T. Daland, ed. (Beverly Hills: Sage Publications, 1969), pp. 203-248.
[6]Wright, "The City Manager as a Developmental Administrator," p. 236. The data were gathered in 1965.
[7]*A Passion for Anonymity* is the title of Louis Brownlow's autobiographical account of his career as a public servant (Chicago: University of Chicago press, 1958).
[8]See "Working Paper III," unpublished working document of the Model Charter Revision Project, National Civic League, 1987.

The Emerging Agenda in State Constitutional Rights Law

Stanley Mosk

Stanley Mosk is the senior justice of the Supreme Court of California. He has served on that court since 1964. Prior to that he was attorney general of California for six years and earlier was a trial judge in Los Angeles. He is a graduate of the University of Chicago and has honorary doctorate degrees from six law schools.

ABSTRACT: Since the late 1960s, more and more state high courts have placed greater reliance on their own state constitutions in extending rights protections to individuals. Because many state bills of rights are more expansive than the federal Bill of Rights, state courts have often extended rights protections beyond those granted by the U.S. Supreme Court under its interpretation of the U.S. Constitution. As a result, one can speak of an emerging agenda of rights protection in state constitutional law. Among the important items on this agenda are privacy rights, education as a fundamental right, aid to religious schools, *Miranda* warnings, searches and seizures, self-incrimination, discriminatory peremptory challenges, obscenity, and freedom of speech, including free speech in shopping centers. Such state court activity suggests a revitalization of federalism, at least within the judicial sphere.

It may appear to be species of heresy to mention alternatives to the U.S. Constitution when Americans have so recently celebrated the bicentennial of that remarkable document. My only response is that human liberty is so fundamental that we must explore every avenue for its preservation. As Justice Robert H. Jackson wrote in 1952, "We can afford no liberties with liberty itself."[1]

There are times the U.S. Constitution does not meet all the convolutions of a problem. Under those circumstances, it may be expedient to look up to international instruments or down to state constitutions. Our attention will be devoted to the latter, but we should note that there have been times, and there will be more, when courts will rely on international documents that have the force of treaties for authority to protect individual rights. These include the Universal Declaration of Human Rights and subsequent international instruments prohibiting, among other vices, torture. These acts were employed as authority by the Second Circuit in a trailblazing 1980 opinion written by Chief Judge Irving Kaufman.[2] There are a growing number of cases in which at least reference is made to, if there is not reliance on, international human rights declarations.

In recent years, however, greater reliance has been placed on individual rights protections found in state constitutions. So much activity has occurred in this field that we can speak of an emerging agenda. By definition, any agenda is a compilation of items; consequently, there will be no opportunity here to delve into any aspect in length. The intention is to provide an overview of salient, emerging issues.

PRIVACY

Consider, for openers, the right of privacy. In courts throughout the land, that somewhat elusive concept is being urged and generally accepted. It must be placed high on any agenda.

It is significant that in many respects the Universal Declaration of Human Rights and the American state constitutions protect individuals in a similar manner and more expansively than does the U.S. Constitution.

For example, although the U.S. Supreme Court has on occasion found privacy to be among so-called penumbral rights, there is no specific guarantee of privacy in the federal Bill of Rights. On the other hand, in the Universal Declaration, article 12, there is this broad language: "No one shall be subject to arbitrary interference with his privacy, family, home or correspondence, nor to attacks upon his honour and reputation." Article I, section 1, of the California Constitution declares that among the inalienable rights are "pursuing and obtaining safety, happiness, and privacy." This kind of protection of privacy can be found in a number of other state constitutions.

Consider, for example, that a police officer or a public prosecutor may walk into a bank and, with no authority of process, demand to examine the bank records of a named individual or corporation. There is no constitutional violation here, and the U.S. Supreme Court in *United States v. Miller*.[3] Some state courts, however, have argued that a person's canceled checks, loan applications, and other banking transactions are a minibiography, that one reasonably expects one's bank records to be used only for internal bank processes, and that, therefore, an examination of them violates the state constitutional right of privacy, unless the records are obtained by a warrant or subpoena.[4] Does one reasonably expect privacy in credit card records or unlisted telephone numbers? Tune in later.

EDUCATION

To most of us, learning and knowledge are our most prized possessions. Yet the U.S. Supreme Court has never recognized education to be a fundamental right. Indeed, in *San Antonio Independent School District v. Rodriguez*,[5] the Court specifically held that education is not a fundamental right. The Court has never retreated from that position. In 1986, it reached a similar conclusion in *Papasan v. Allain*.[6] The Court has come no closer than *Plyer v. Doe*,[7] in which it applied a higher scrutiny standard to a statute that denied basic education to alien, undocumented school-age children; yet even under that standard, it reiterated that education is not a fundamental right under the U.S. Constitution.

Contrast that result with the growing number of states that have recognized the inherent value of public education. California, in its celebrated *Serrano v. Priest* case,[8] openly broke away from the U.S. Supreme Court's reticence and firmly declared that "the distinctive and priceless function of education in our society warrants, indeed compels, our treating it as a fundamental interest." Relying on state authority, particularly requirements of compulsory school attendance, the *Serrano* court quoted the credo of Horace Mann:

I believe in the existence of a great, immortal, immutable principle of natural law, or natural ethics—a principle, antecedent to all human institutions, and incapable

of being abrogated by any ordinance of man . . . which proves the *absolute right* to an education of every human being that comes into the world, and which, of course, proves the correlative duty of every government to see that the means of that education are provided for all.[9]

High courts in Connecticut, Michigan, Wyoming, Arizona, Mississippi, Washington, Wisconsin, and West Virginia have reached the same fundamental conclusion.

Aid to religious schools

The revival of religious fervor in the United States—and throughout the world—and the aggressiveness of the fundamentalist movement indicate future church-state conflict. In this area, U.S. Supreme Court cases have not been a model of clarity.

In *Everson v. Board of Education* (1947),[10] the Court upheld a New Jersey statute that authorized reimbursement of parents for fares paid by them to transport their children to public or nonprofit private schools, including religious schools, by carrier. In a 5-4 decision, the majority held that the legislation did no more than provide a general program to assist parents, regardless of their religion, to get their children to school safely and expeditiously.

The first case dealing with the constitutionality of providing textbooks for use in religious schools was *Board of Education v. Allen* (1968).[11] Under consideration was a New York law that authorized public school authorities to lend textbooks free of charge to all students in certain grades, including students in private schools. The Court invoked what has come to be called the child-benefit theory. It held that the financial benefit provided by the program was to the children and their parents rather than to the parochial schools and that no funds or books were furnished to the schools. Moreover, the Court held that books, unlike buses, are critical to the teaching process, that religious schools pursue both religious instruction and secular education, and that the record did not support the proposition that textbooks on nonreligious subjects were used by the parochial schools to teach religion. Still later, the Supreme Court declared that a law that confers an indirect, remote and incidental benefit on religious institutions is not for that reason alone unconstitutional.[12]

Trying to reconcile those cases with others, such as *Meek v. Pittenger, Wolman v. Walter, Levitt v. Committee for Public Education, Lemon v. Kurtzman, Walz v. Tax Commission*, and *Norwood v. Harrison*,[13] is an exercise in futility. In *California Teachers Association v. Riles*,[14] the California Supreme Court bluntly declared, "We are unable to harmonize the holdings of these cases."

The child-benefit theory has been criticized by several state courts on the ground that it proves too much. If the fact that a child is aided by an expenditure of public money insulates a statute from challenge, constitutional proscriptions on state aid to sectarian schools would be virtually eradicated. There is no logical stopping point. The doctrine may be used to justify any type of aid to sectarian schools because, as was stated in an Oklahoma case, "practically every proper expenditure for school purposes aids the child."[15]

It is impossible to predict how many states will rely on their own constitution to retain the traditional wall of separation, but some already have done so. Others will face the test in the near future. Many states have constitutional provisions more precise and sweeping than the First Amendment. Typical are these provisions in article XVI, section 5, of the California Constitution:

> Neither the Legislature, nor any county, city and county, township, school district, or other municipal corporation, shall ever make an appropriation, or pay from any public fund whatever, or grant anything to or in aid of any religious sect, church, creed, or sectarian purpose, or help to support or sustain any school, college, university, hospital, or other institution controlled by any religious creed, church, or sectarian denomination whatever; nor shall any grant or donation of personal property or real estate ever be made by the state, or any city, city and county, town, or other municipal corporation for any religious creed, church, or sectarian purpose whatever.

Nebraska, Oregon, and other states have similar constitutional provisions and thus have been more strict than the U.S. Supreme Court in enforcing church-state separation.[16]

MIRANDA

High on the constitutional agenda in the next few years will be *Miranda*[17] and what, if anything, to do about it. U.S. Attorney General Edwin Meese III has led a frontal charge against that bulwark of the Warren Court era. Will the Supreme Court capitulate?

Professor Yale Kamisar has written that the current Supreme Court believes that the *Miranda* ruling rejected "the more extreme position that the actual presence of a lawyer was necessary to dispel the coercion inherent in custodial interrogation."[18] Instead, the Warren Court settled for police-issued warnings that permit someone subjected to arrest and detention to waive his or her rights without actually receiving the guidance of counsel. Depending on one's viewpoint, says Kamisar, this is the *Miranda* case's great weakness or saving grace.

Attorney General Meese has taken a more extreme position, rejecting the right of suspects to terminate interrogation either by saying that they want to do so or that they desire to have the advice of a lawyer. Instead, the recent report of his office calls such persons uncooperative suspects and argues that the police

should be able to undertake persuasion to induce the suspect to change his or her mind and talk—translation: to confess.

Many observers doubt that the attorney general will succeed in this effort. The overruling of precedent prevailing for two decades or more is a slow process. It is usually accomplished in a succession of cases. It is seldom done from the bully pulpit or by press release.

In short, to paraphrase Mark Twain, the death of *Miranda* is exaggerated. Reversals of former precedent are not unprecedented, however. Remember the fate of *Lochner v. New York*, *Pace v. Alabama*, *Plessy v. Ferguson*, *Minersville v. Gobitis*, *Swain v. Alabama*, and others.[19]

When *Miranda* was announced in 1966, many states were reluctant to accept it. Some were dragged kicking and screaming into conformity, but conform they did. The question will be, if *Miranda* expires, will some states revert to their pre-*Miranda* policy of anything goes at the station house, or will they insist on some form of *Miranda* warning under state constitutional authority?

Unless the U.S. Supreme Court rules that a *Miranda* warning is forbidden—which seems inconceivable—many, if not most, states will probably adhere to the state rules that they adopted to conform to *Miranda*. It has taken two decades, but law enforcement officers in the states have become reconciled to giving appropriate warnings to suspects. Trial judges also understand that they must reject statements obtained from defendants who were not warned. Many of the state decisions have been based on state constitutions.

For example, in *Harris v. New York*,[20] the U.S. Supreme Court permitted statements obtained in violation of *Miranda* to be used for impeachment purposes. California and several other states, however, have held that if a statement offends *Miranda*, it is useless for all purposes. Here is a forthright declaration of state independence in *People v. Disbrow*:

> We therefore hold that the privilege against self-incrimination of Article I, section 15, of the California Constitution precludes use by the prosecution of any extrajudicial statement by the defendant, whether inculpatory or exculpatory, either as affirmative evidence or for purposes of impeachment, obtained during custodial interrogation in violation of the standards declared in *Miranda* and its California progeny. Accordingly, we . . . declare that *Harris* is not persuasive authority in any state prosecution in California.[21]

To the same effect are *State v. Santiago*, a Hawaii case, and *Butler v. State*, a Texas case.[22] Note this quotation from *Butler*: "*Harris*, of course, in no way obligates [state courts] to overturn prior decisions as a matter of state criminal procedure . . . Therefore, we cannot agree with the [prosecution's] contention despite the natural temptation to rush to accept the *Harris* rationale. The beauty is only skin deep."

SEARCH AND SEIZURE

Another hole was dug in the exclusionary rule by the U.S. Supreme Court in 1984. In *United States v. Leon*, [23] the Court announced the good-faith exception to the exclusionary rule: in the absence of an allegation that the magistrate abandoned his or her detached and neutral role, suppression of evidence from the prosecution's case-in-chief is, as a matter of federal law, appropriate only if the officers were dishonest in preparing their affidavit for a search warrant or could not have harbored an objectively reasonable belief in the existence of probable cause.

In addressing the question of the proper remedy to be applied to a concededly unconstitutional search, the Court answered by "weighing the costs and benefits of preventing the use in the prosecution's case-in-chief of inherently trustworthy tangible evidence obtained in reliance on a search warrant issued by a detached and neutral magistrate that ultimately is found to be defective."

The good-faith doctrine was expanded to include reasonableness in the *Garrison* case, decided in February 1987.[24] There the Baltimore police invaded the wrong apartment, but in a 6-3 vote Justice John Paul Stevens held for the Court that the validity of the search depended on whether the officers' failure was "objectively understandable and reasonable."

Several state courts, on state constitutional grounds, have declined to follow *Leon* and probably will do the same with regard to *Garrison*. All the cases to date have involved searches conducted pursuant to a warrant later determined to be invalid.

In *State v. Novembrino*, the New Jersey Supreme Court, in a lengthy opinion, refused to follow *Leon* because (1) its long-run effect would be to undermine the integrity of the warrant process by diminishing the quality of evidence presented in search warrant applications; (2) it would "ultimately reduce respect for and compliance with the probable-cause standard"; (3) it is inconsistent with the state constitution as interpreted; (4) there was no evidence that the criminal justice system was impaired by the requirement of probable cause; and (5) there is no satisfactory alternative to the exclusionary rule.[25]

The New York court, in *People v. Bigelow*, declined to follow *Leon* because it (1) frustrates the exclusionary rule's purposes; (2) places a premium on the illegal police action; and (3) provides an incentive for "others to engage in similar lawless acts."[26]

The Michigan court, in *People v. Sundling*, rejected *Leon* because (1) the magistrate's decision would, as a practical matter, be insulated from appellate review; (2) the exception would result in increased illegal police activity; and (3) the Court's claim that the exclusionary rule is not working is not supported—indeed, is contradicted—by the evidence.[27]

Justice James L. Robertson in Mississippi declared that the exclusionary rule is necessary to guarantee that magistrates "take seriously their responsibilit[y] to ensure that people are free of unconstitutional searches" and that *Leon* undermines the integrity of the judicial process.[28] The Wisconsin Supreme Court refused to employ *Leon* because the state constitution and prior Wisconsin court decisions interpreting it hold that the receipt into evidence of the fruits of an invalid search warrant violates the defendant's state constitutional rights.[29]

It would appear that if state courts can find other ways of rejecting *Leon* and retaining the rule of excluding illegally obtained evidence, they will do so.

Automobile searches

Motor vehicles present a particular problem for courts as they grapple with the boundaries of permissible searches. If a motorist is stopped by a police officer for a simple traffic violation, the motorist may be subjected to a full body search, and the vehicle may be searched, too. There is no constitutional violation here, the U.S. Supreme Court has said.[30] But Hawaii and other states have found such police conduct to be offensive to state constitutional provisions unless the officer has articulable reasons to suspect illegal conduct other than the minor traffic infraction.

Most courts have difficulty ascertaining the limits, if any, of automobile searches in light of more recent federal opinions. If a vehicle is stopped on mere suspicion, may the car be searched without a warrant? What about the glove compartment, trunk, or a closed container in the trunk? If the vehicle is a van with a bed, kitchen, closet, curtained window, and so forth, does it have the qualities of an automobile because it is mobile, or is it entitled to the protections of a home because one lives in it? These are areas in which the states are likely to reach independent and varying conclusions.

The right of police to inventory the contents of an impounded motor vehicle results in another conflict between U.S. Supreme Court and state court decisions. In *South Dakota v. Opperman*,[31] the Court held inventory searches of automobiles to be consistent with the Fourth Amendment. In a recent case, the Court justified the inventory as a means to protect the police and garage attendants from subsequent false claims of theft.[32]

Colorado, however, reached a different conclusion, as did California.[33] Because property could conceivably disappear prior to or during an inventory, both states believed that a simpler solution would be to lock and seal the automobile in a secure parking facility. The *Mozzetti* case was particularly egregious: the woman was not a criminal suspect, she had been in an automobile accident, and had been taken to the hospital. It is difficult to justify the police searching her car trunk and examining a closed suitcase on the back seat, all on an inventory theory.

SELF-INCRIMINATION

Another significant federal-state conflict arises over the use of a defendant's pretrial silence. All jurisdictions agree that, as held in *Griffin v. California*,[34] the silence of a defendant, under a claim of privilege against self-incrimination, may not be admitted in the prosecution's case-in-chief. There is some divergence, however, as to the use of such silence for impeachment purposes.

Jenkins v. Anderson[35] approved the prosecutor's use for impeachment purposes of a defendant's failure to surrender for two weeks, when he claimed on the stand that his act of killing was in self-defense. Most state cases agree on a theory that the silence must amount to an invocation of Fifth Amendment rights in order to be excluded.

After arrest, however, the dichotomy depends on whether *Miranda* warnings have been given. If so, *Doyle v. Ohio*[36] controls. Obviously, it would be unconscionable to penalize defendants for remaining silent after they have been told by the authorities that they have a right to refuse to talk.

If *Miranda* warnings have not been given, however, the U.S. Supreme Court held, defendants' constitutional rights are not violated by permitting them to be cross-examined about their pre-*Miranda* silence.[37] The Court reasoned that because there were no affirmative assurances as a result of the failure to give a *Miranda* warning, no fundamental unfairness would arise from allowing the defendants' silence to be used for impeachment purposes.

Courts in Washington, Connecticut, Alaska, New Jersey, Pennsylvania, Texas, and California have reached a contrary conclusion. The California court relied entirely on the state constitution. A fear was expressed in several of these state cases that to allow the defendant's silence to be used for any purpose would invite the police to dispense with *Miranda* warnings. These cases also expressed concern that silence used for impeachment would likely be used by the jury in determining guilt.

PEREMPTORY CHALLENGES

There is no better example of how the states can be laboratories for development of the law than the fate of *Swain v. Alabama*.[38] In that case, the majority of the U.S. Supreme Court held that there could be no limitations on the exercise of peremptory challenges. A modest concession was made if a defendant could demonstrate a long pattern of discriminatory use of the challenges. Such demonstration, of course, is impossible. How can a defendant, while jury selection is under way, demon-strate that the prosecutor had employed discriminatory tactics in some number of previous cases in which, of course, the defendant was not involved and in which the racial characteristics of previous jurors were not recorded?

California specifically rejected *Swain*.[39] The state court held that there could be a limitation on peremptory challenges if they were employed for a discriminatory purpose. The method of ascertaining the systematic exclusion of a cognizable group was described in detail, and if a prima facie case of discrimination was evident, the trial judge could call on the prosecutor to explain each of his or her challenges. If the prosecutor failed the test, the entire jury panel was to be excused and a new panel brought in to start proceedings over.

Massachusetts adopted much the same procedure, and a number of other states have acted similarly.

Last year, however, in *Batson v. Kentucky*,[40] the U.S. Supreme Court admitted that *Swain* is not workable and conceded that the use of peremptory challenges for racially discriminatory purposes must not be condoned. This ruling suggests that state courts can have a significant effect on the pattern of the law, even federal law.

OBSCENITY

A conflict is inevitable between national and state standards in the field of obscenity. Under the U.S. Supreme Court's *Miller* rubric,[41] material is obscene if (1) it depicts sexual conduct in a patently offensive manner; (2) the average person, applying contemporary state standards, would find that it, taken as a whole, appeals to a prurient interest in sex; and (3) taken as a whole, it lacks serious literary, artistic, political, or scientific value.

Recently, in the case of *State v. Henry*,[42] a proprietor of an adult bookstore was convicted by a trial court after his entire inventory was seized in a police raid. The Oregon Supreme Court reversed, declaring that its state constitution was written by "rugged and robust individuals dedicated to founding a free society unfettered by the governmental imposition of some people's views of morality on the free expression of others." Oregon's pioneers intended to protect freedom of expression "on any subject whatever," including the subject of sex. In rejecting the *Miller* rule, the court declared: "In this state any person can write, print, read, say, show or sell anything to a consenting adult even though that expression may be generally or universally considered 'obscene.' "

FREE SPEECH IN SHOPPING MALLS

A very interesting and important federal-state dichotomy is in the history of a not uncommon factual situation: a small orderly group of citizens undertakes to pass out leaflets, or solicit signatures on petitions, in a privately owned shopping center. The mall owners seek to prohibit that activity.

Obviously there is a built-in tension here between two constitutional guarantees. On the one hand, the citizens assert their right of freedom of speech and the right to petition their government for a redress of grievances. On the other hand, the shopping center owner asserts his right to control his private property and to exclude all activity not related to the business of the shopping center. In that conflict, which right is to prevail?

The Supreme Court of California held in 1970, in *Diamond v. Bland*, that unless there is obstruction or undue interference with normal business operations, the bare title of the property owners does not outweigh the substantial interest of individuals and groups to engage in peaceful and orderly free speech and petitioning activities on the premises of shopping centers open to the public.[43] This, of course, is subject to reasonable time, place, and manner restrictions.

On four occasions the shopping center owner sought certiorari and a rehearing from denial of certiorari. In each instance he was rebuffed by the U.S. Supreme Court, with no votes noted to grant. The California court, therefore, had every reason to believe that *Diamond v. Bland* was acceptable law.

Two years later, however, the U.S. Supreme Court took over an almost identical case from Oregon, and in *Lloyd v. Tanner*[44] held that the owners had the right to prohibit distribution of political handbills unrelated to the operation of the shopping center.

Back to the California Supreme Court came the owner in *Diamond v. Bland*. He asked to be relieved from the previous orders. A 4-3 majority of the court agreed that the state was bound by *Lloyd v. Tanner*.

In its original opinion, the court had relied on the First Amendment to the U.S. Constitution and on related federal cases. On this second round, I urged the same result under "unmistakable independent non-federal grounds upon which our earlier opinion could have been based," but a majority of the court retained consistency with federal law.

Five years later, though, in 1979, a new majority of the court decided in *Robins v. Pruneyard* that the free-speech provisions of the California Constitution offer "greater protection than the First Amendment now seems to provide."[45]

When the U.S. Supreme Court granted certiorari in *Robins v. Pruneyard*, the California court sensed doom to its theory of state constitutionalism. But the Supreme Court agreed with the California ruling, 9-0. Justice William H. Rehnquist wrote the opinion, which declared that the reasoning in *Lloyd v. Tanner* "does not ex proprio vigore limit the authority of the State to exercise its police power or its sovereign right to adopt

in its constitution individual liberties more expansive than those conferred by the Federal Constitution."[46]

CONCLUSION

No doubt there is growing interest in true federalism today. There was a time when states' rights were associated with Orval Faubus and George Wallace barring the entrance of blacks to public schools. We are long past that confrontational period.

Today, states' rights are associated with increased, not lessened, individual guarantees. There is every indication, particularly since *Pruneyard*, that the Rehnquist Court will defer to the states when they rely on state constitutional provisions.

At the top of any agenda for the bicentennial of the Constitution should be a consideration of James Madison's words in *Federalist* Number 45:

> The powers delegated by the proposed Constitution to the federal government are few and defined. Those which are to remain in the State governments are numerous and indefinite. The former will be exercised principally on external objects, as war, peace, negotiation, and foreign commerce; with which last the power of taxation will, for the most part, be connected. The powers reserved to the several States will extend to all the objects which, in the ordinary course of affairs, concern the lives, liberties, and properties of the people, and the internal order, improvement, and prosperity of the State.

Sound policy 200 years ago. Sound policy today.

NOTES

1. *United States v. Spector*, 343 U.S. 169, 180 (1952).
2. *Filartiga v. Pena-Irala*, 630 F.2d 876 (1980).
3. 425 U.S. 435 (1976).
4. *Burrows v. Superior Court*, 529 P.2d 590 (Cal. 1974).
5. 411 U.S. 1 (1973).
6. 92 L. Ed. 2d 209 (1986).
7. 457 U.S. 202 (1982).
8. 487 P.2d 1241 (Cal. 1971).
9. Quoted in *Readings in American Education*, ed. William H. Lucio (Chicago: Scott, Foresman, 1963), p. 336, italics in original.
10. 330 U.S. 1 (1947).
11. 392 U.S. 236 (1968).
12. *Committee for Public Education v. Nyquist*, 413 U.S. 756 (1973).
13. Respectively, 421 U.S. 349 (1975); 433 U.S. 229 (1977); 413 U.S. 472 (1973); 403 U.S. 602 (1971); 397 U.S. 664 (1970); 413 U.S. 455 (1973).
14. 632 P.2d 903 (Cal. 1981).
15. *Gurney v. Ferguson*, 122 P.2d 1002 (1942).
16. *Gaffney v. State Department of Education*, 220 N.W. 2d 550 (Neb. 1974); *Dickman v. School District No. 62C, Oregon City*, 336 P.2d 533 (Ore. 1962); *California Teachers Association v. Riles*, 632 P.2d 953 (Cal. 1981).
17. *Miranda v. Arizona*, 384 U.S. 436 (1966).
18. *Los Angeles Times*, 11 Feb. 1987.
19. Respectively, 198 U.S. 45 (1905); 106 U.S. 583 (1882); 163 U.S. 537 (1896); 310 U.S. 586 (1940); 380 U.S. 202 (1965).
20. 401 U.S. 222 (1971).
21. 545 P.2d 272 (Cal. 1976).

22. Respectively, 492 P.2d 657 (Hawaii 1971); 493 S.W. 2d 190 (Tex. 1973).

23. 468 U.S. 897 (1984).

24. *Maryland v. Garrison*, 94 L. Ed. 2d 72 (Md. 1987).

25. *State v. Novembrino*, 519 A.2d 820 (N.J. 1987).

26. 497 N.Y.S. 2d 630 (N.Y. 1985).

27. 395 N.W.2d 308 (Mich. 1986).

28. *Stringer v. State*, 491 So.2d 837 (Miss. 1986)

29. *State v. Grawien*, 367 N.W.2d 816 (Wis. 1985).

30. *United States v. Robinson*, 414 U.S. 218 (1973); *Gustafson v. Florida*, 414 U.S. 260 (1973).

31. 428 U.S. 364 (1976).

32. *Colorado v. Bertine*, 93 L. Ed. 2d 739 (1987).

33. *People v. Bertine*, 706 P.2d 411 (Colo. 1985); *People v. Mozzetti*, 484 P.2d 84 (Cal. 1971).

34. 380 U.S. 609 (1965).

35. 447 U.S. 231 (1980).

36. 426 U.S. 610 (1976).

37. *Fletcher v. Weir*, 455 U.S. 603 (1982).

38. 380 U.S. 202 (1965).

39. *People v. Wheeler*, 583 P.2d 748 (Cal. 1978).

40. 90 L. Ed. 2d 69 (1986).

41. *Miller v. California*, 413 U.S. 15 (1973).

42. 732 P.2d 9 (Ore. 1987).

43. *Diamond v. Bland*, 447 P.2d 733.

44. 407 U.S. 551 (1972).

45. 592 P.2d 341.

46. *Pruneyard Shopping Center v. Robins*, 447 U.S. 74, 81 (1980).

View From the Bench: A Judge's Day

Judge Lois G. Forer

Lois G. Forer is a judge in the Philadelphia Court of Common Pleas. This article is adapted from her book, The Death of the Law.

At 9:30 the court personnel begin to assemble. The crier opens court. "All rise. Oyez, oyez, all persons having business before the Court of Common Pleas Criminal Division come forth and they shall be heard. God save this honorable court. Be seated and stop all conversation. Good morning, Your Honor." The crier calls out the names of the defendants. Most of them are represented by the public defender. He checks his files. One or two names are not on his list. A quick phone call is made to his office to send up the missing files.

On one particular day when I was sitting in criminal motions court, three cases had private counsel. One had been retained by the defendant. The other two had been appointed by the court to represent indigents accused of homicide. Where are these lawyers?

As is customary, the court officer phones each of them and reminds his secretary that he has a case listed and he must appear. Several of the defendants are not present. The prison is called to locate the missing parties. The judge, if he wishes to get through his list, must find the lawyers and litigants and order them to come to court.

Frequently the prosecutor cannot find his files. When he does, he discovers that a necessary witness has not been subpoenaed. The case must be continued to another day. The other witnesses, who are present and have missed a day's work, are sent home. The defendant is returned to jail to await another listing. Often cases are listed five and six times before they can be heard.

On this day there were three extra-ditions. Amos R. is wanted in South Carolina. Seven years ago he had escaped from jail and fled north. Since then he has been living in Philadelphia. He married here and now has two children. His wife and children are in the courtroom. He is employed. Amos has not been in trouble since leaving South Carolina, where 10 years ago he was convicted of stealing a car and sentenced to nine to 20 years in prison. He had no prior record. In Pennsylvania, for the same crime, he would probably have been placed on probation or at most received a maximum sentence of two years.

Now he testifies that he didn't steal the car, he only borrowed it. Moreover, he didn't have a lawyer. When he pleaded guilty he was told he would get six months. This is probably true. Also, he was undoubtedly indicted by a grand jury from which Negroes were systematically excluded. All of these allegations would be grounds for release in a postconviction hearing, for they are serious violations of constitutional rights. But they are irrelevant in extradition hearings. The only issues that the judge may consider before ordering this man to leave his family and shipping him off to serve 18 more years in prison are whether he is in fact the Amos R. named in the warrant and whether the papers are in order. There is little judicial discretion. One is often impelled by the system to be an instrument of injustice.

This is the dilemma of a judge and of many officials in the legal system. Following the rule of law may result in hardship and essential unfairness. Ignoring the law is a violation of one's oath of office, an illegal act, and a destruction of the system. Some choose to ignore the law in the interests of "justice." Others mechanically follow precedent. Neither course is satisfactory. The judge who frees a defendant knows that in most instances the state cannot appeal. Unless

there is an election in the offing and the prosecutor chooses to use this case as a political issue, there will be no repercussions. But it is his duty, as it is that of the accused, to obey the law. If the judge is not restrained by the law, who will be? On the other hand, it is unrealistic to say, "Let the defendant appeal." In the long period between the trial judge's ruling and that of the higher court, if it hears the appeal, a human being will be in jail. One does not easily deprive a person of his liberty without very compelling reasons. Almost every day, the guardians of the law are torn between these conflicting pulls.

After hearing the life story of Amos R., as reported by the prosecutor, the young defender said, "Mr. R. wishes to waive a hearing."

I looked at the lawyer. "Mr. R., do you know that you have a right to a hearing?"

"Yes."

"Have you consulted with your attorney about waiving a hearing?"

"My attorney?" R. looks bewildered.

"Your lawyer, the defender," I pointed to the young man.

"Oh, him," R. replies. "Yes, I talked to him."

"How long?"

" 'Bout two minutes."

"Your Honor," says the defender, "I have spoken to the sheriff. There is no question that this is the Amos R. wanted. The papers are in order."

I search through the official-looking sheaf of documents with gold seals and red seals and the signatures of two governors, hoping to find a defect, a critical omission. At last I discover that Amos R. was arrested in New Jersey on a Friday night. He was not taken to Pennsylvania until the following Monday. It is 89 days that he has been in jail in Pennsylvania. The extradition hearing must by statute be held within 90 days of arrest. By adding on the three days he was in custody in New Jersey, I

From *The Washington Monthly*, February 1975. Copyright ©Lois G. Forer. Reprinted by permission of Curtis Brown, Ltd. Adapted from THE DEATH OF THE LAW, by Judge Lois G. Forer.

conclude that the 90-day time limit has not been met. Amos R. is once again a free man. This happy ending is unusual. Bureaucratic inefficiencies seldom redound to the benefit of the individual.

Prisoners of Bureaucracy

The next four matters are bail applications. All the defendants fit the stereotype. They are black males under the age of 30. Only one is in the courtroom. The others are in the detention center. It is too much trouble and too expensive to transport them to court for a bail hearing. I must decide whether to set free or keep locked up men whom I cannot see or talk to. If I don't release them, they may be in jail for as long as a year awaiting trial. The law presumes that they are innocent. I look at the applications. This is not the first arrest for any of them. For one there are records going back to age nine, when he was incarcerated for truancy.

"The defendant's juvenile record may not be used against him in adult court," I remind the prosecuting attorney.

"I know, Your Honor," he replies apologetically, "but the computer prints out all the arrests."

"How many convictions?"

The computer does not give the answer to that question.

One man is accused of rape. The record shows that his prior offenses were larceny of an automobile and, as a child, running away from home. The police report indicates that when the police arrived the defendant was in the complainant's apartment with his clothes off. He left so quickly that he abandoned his shoes and socks. The complainant admitted knowing him and gave his name and address to the police. No weapon was involved.

My usual rule of thumb is a simple one: "If he had time to take off his shoes, it wasn't rape."

Before releasing an alleged rapist from jail, possibly to prey on other victims, I want to speak with the accused. Although Lombroso's theory that one can tell a criminal by his physical appearance is out of fashion, I still want to see him, but he is not in the courtroom. Perhaps his lawyer, the defender, can give some helpful information. The defender, however, has never seen the accused. Someone else interviewed him on a routine prison visit. No one knows whether he has a family, a job, a home.

"Please have this defendant brought to court tomorrow and get me some information on him," I tell the defender.

He replies, "I'm sorry, Your Honor. I'll be working in a different courtroom tomorrow. There is no way I can find out about this man."

"We're dealing with human beings, not pieces of paper," I expostulate. "You are his lawyer. You should know him."

The young defender sadly shakes his head. "Your Honor, I work for a bureaucracy."

So do I, I remind myself, as I look at the clock and see that it is past 11:00 and there are 14 more matters to be heard today.

Four Up, Four Down

I refuse bail for a 14-year-old accused of slaying another child in a gang rumble. Will he be safer in jail than on the street, where the rival gang is lying in wait for him? I do not know. The boy is small and slender. The warden will put him in the wing with the feminine homosexuals to save him from assault. I mark on the commitment sheet that the boy is to attend school while in prison awaiting trial. But if the warden does not honor my order, I will not know.

A 23-year-old heroin addict tells me that there is no drug treatment program in prison. "It's just like the street. Nothin' but drugs," he says. I try to move his case ahead so that he can plead guilty at an early date and be transferred to the federal drug treatment center. He, like so many others up for robbery and burglary, is a Vietnam veteran. He acquired his habit overseas and now must steal in order to pay for his daily fix.

The next matter is a petition to suppress a confession. Court appointed counsel alleges that the defendant did not make a knowing and intelligent waiver of his rights when he confessed three murders to the police. Cornelius takes the stand and describes his life. His history is typical. He was sent to a disciplinary school at 11, ran away at 12, and spent a year in juvenile jail. At 17, there was a conviction for larceny and another period of incarceration. He is married, two children, separated from his wife. He is vague about the ages of the children. Cornelius works as an orderly in a hospital earning $80 a week take-home pay. At the end of each week he divides his money in two parts: $40 for living expenses and $40 for methadrine, which costs $20 a spoon.

Where does he buy it? On any corner in the ghetto. He steals the syringes from the hospital. His expenses are minimal except for the precious methadrine. He is riddled with V.D. He seldom eats.

While on a high, he shot and killed three strangers. Why did he do it?

"There are these voices I hear. They're fightin'. One tells me to kill; the other tells me not to. Sometimes I get so scared I run out into the street. That's when I'm in a low. But when I'm in a high, I feel I can walk in the rain without getting wet. I don't feel sad, I ain't lonely. When I'm comin' down from a high, I got to get another shot."

Now he is in a low—sad, soft-spoken, withdrawn, disinterested in his own fate. I see his skinny brown arms pocked with little needle scars. The psychiatrist says that when Cornelius is on drugs he cannot gauge reality. He could not understand the meaning of the privilege against self-incrimination and make a knowing and intelligent waiver of his rights.

The earnest psychiatrist explains patiently. I watch Cornelius, wraith-thin, sitting in withdrawn disinterest, lost in some dream of flight. Is he mad or are we—the prosecutor, the defense lawyer, the psychiatrist, and the judge? After five hours of testimony, I rule that the confession must be suppressed. There are dozens of eye-witnesses. The confession is not necessary to convict Cornelius. After this hearing, and before trial, a psychiatrist for the defense will testify that Cornelius is not mentally competent to stand trial; he cannot cooperate with his lawyer in preparing his defense. A psychiatrist for the prosecution will testify that when Cornelius has withdrawn from drugs he will be able to participate intelligently in his defense. The motion to defer trial will probably be denied. At the trial itself, one psychiatrist will testify that at the time of the shootings Cornelius did not know the difference between right and wrong and the nature and quality of his act. Another will testify that he did. Neither psychiatrist saw Cornelius at the time of the crimes. Both of them examined him in prison months later. They are certain of their opinions.

A middle-aged, white, epicenely soft man is next on the list. His face is a pasty gray. He mutters under his breath. He is accused of committing sodomy on three teenaged boys. Most of his meager salary he spent on these boys, and now they have turned on him. I order a psychiatric examination simply because I don't know what else to do. A month later the report is sent to me. It follows a standard format: facts (gleaned from the accused), background, diagnostic formulation and summary, and recommendation. This report states: "Probable latent schizophrenia. We recommend a full examination 60-day commitment." At the end of 60 days and the expenditure of hundreds of dollars, the doctors will decide that he is or is not schizophrenic, possibly sociopathic. A long period in a "structured environment" will be recommended. But what will the judge do? There are only two choices: prison, where he will be tormented and perhaps beaten by strong young thugs, or the street.

Lost in the Jailhouse

Most of the prisoners brought before me are young—under 30. I also see children who are charged with homicide. They are denied even the nominal protections of the juvenile court and are "processed" as adults. The 14-year-old accused of slaying another child in a gang rumble; the 16-year-old dope addict who, surprised while burglarizing a house, panicked and shot the unwary owner; the girl lookout for the gang, who is accused of conspiracy and murder. Many of these children are themselves parents. Can they be turned back to the streets? I refuse bail for an illiterate 15-year-old accused of murder and note on the bill of indictment that he be required to attend school while in detention. I ask the court-appointed lawyer to check with the warden and see that the boy is sent to class. But is there a class in remedial reading at the detention center? Who would pay for it? Not the overburdened public schools or the understaffed prisons. It is not a project likely to find a foundation grant.

A perplexed lawyer petitions for a second psychiatric examination for his client. The court psychiatrist has found him competent to stand trial but the lawyer tells me his client cannot discuss the case with him. Randolph, who is accused of assault with intent to kill, attacked a stranger in a bar and strangled the man, almost killing him. Fortunately, bystanders dragged Randolph away. I ask to speak with Randolph. A big, neatly dressed Negro steps up to the bar of the court. He speaks softly, "Judge," he says, "I'm afraid. I need help."

Randolph is out on bail. This is his first offense. He has a good work record. He is married, has two children, and lives with his family. It is Friday morning. I fear what may happen to him over the weekend. The court psychiatric unit is called.

"We've got people backed up for a

month," the doctor tells me. "Even if I took Randolph out of turn I couldn't see him until next week." When he does see Randolph it will be a 45-minute examination. A voluntary hospital commitment seems to be the only safeguard. But at least he will be watched for ten days. Gratefully, Randolph promises to go at once to the mental health clinic. What will happen to him after the ten-day period?

There is no time to wonder. The next case is waiting.

It is a sultry day. When the ancient air conditioner is turned on we cannot hear the testimony. When it is turned off the room is unbearable. At 4:45 p.m., I ask hopefully, "Have we finished the list?" But no, there is an application for a continuance on an extradition warrant. The papers from the demanding state have not arrived. It is a routine, daily occurrence.

I look around the courtroom. By this hour only the court personnel and a few policemen and detectives are present. "Where is the defendant?" I inquire. The prosecutor does not know. He is not responsible for producing him. The defender does not have him on his list. "Is he in custody?" I ask. We all search the records and discover that he was arrested more than five months ago. There is no notation that bail has ever been set. No private counsel has entered an appearance. A deputy sheriff checks and reports that he has not been brought up from the prison. The computerized records show that this man has never had a hearing. Hardened as we are, the prosecutor, the defender and I are horrified that someone should be sitting in jail all this time without ever having had an opportunity to say a word. Is he, in fact, the person wanted for an offense allegedly committed years ago and hundreds of miles away? Was he ever there? Is he a stable member of society? Has he a family, a job, a home? Is he a drug addict? No one knows. The papers do not indicate. No one in the courtroom has ever seen him. Each of us makes a note to check on this forgotten prisoner whom the computer may or may not print out for appearance on some other day in some other courtroom.

Nobody Waived Good-bye

The scene in criminal trial court is similar. Most of the cases are "waivers" and guilty pleas. The accused may waive his constitutional right to be tried by a jury of his peers and be tried by a judge alone. Fewer than five per cent of all cases are tried

by jury. In most cases, the accused not only waives his right to a jury trial but also to any trial and pleads guilty. Before accepting a waiver or a plea, the accused is asked the routine questions. Day after day defense counsel recites the following formula to poor, semiliterate defendants, some of whom are old and infirm, others young and innocent. Read this quickly:

"Do you know that you are accused of [the statutory crimes are read to him from the indictment]?

"Do you know that you have a right to a trial by jury in which the state must prove by evidence beyond a reasonable doubt that you committed the offenses and that if one juror disagrees you will not be found guilty?

"Do you know that by pleading guilty you are giving up your right to appeal the decision of this court except for an appeal based on the jurisdiction of the court, the legality of the sentence and the voluntariness of your plea of guilty? [The accused is not told that by the asking and answering of these questions in open court he has for all practical purposes also given up this ground for appeal.]

"Do you know that the judge is not bound by the recommendation of the District Attorney as to sentence but can sentence you up to —— years and impose a fine of —— dollars? [The aggregate penalty is read to him. Judges may and often do give a heavier penalty than was recommended. They rarely give a lighter sentence.]

"Can you read and write the English language?

"Have you ever been in a mental hospital or under the care of a psychiatrist for a mental illness?

"Are you now under the influence of alcohol, drugs, or undergoing withdrawal symptoms?

"Have you been threatened, coerced, or promised anything for entering the plea of guilty other than the recommendation of sentence by the District Attorney?

"Are you satisfied with my representation?"

All this is asked quickly, routinely, as the prisoner stands before the bar of the court. He answers "Yes" to each question.

The final question is: "Are you pleading guilty because you are guilty?" The defendant looks at the defender, uncertainly.

"Have you consulted with your lawyer?" I inquire.

"Right now. 'Bout five minutes."

"We'll pass this case until afternoon. At the lunch recess, will you please confer with your client," I direct the defender.

In the afternoon, the accused, having talked with the lawyer for another ten minutes, again waives his right to a trial. He has been in jail more than eight months. The eight months in jail are applied to his sentence. He will be out by the end of the year—sooner than if he demanded a trial and was acquitted.

The plea has been negotiated by the assistant defender and the assistant prosecutor. The defendant says he was not promised anything other than a recommendation of sentence in return for the guilty plea. But the judge does not know what else the defendant has been told, whether his family and friends are willing to come and testify for him, whether his counsel has investigated the facts of the case to see whether indeed he does have a defense. The magic formula has been pronounced. The judge does not know what the facts are. Did the man really commit the offense? Even if there were a full-scale trial, truth might not emerge. Many of the witnesses have long since disappeared. How reliable will their memories be? The policeman will say he did not strike the accused. The accused will say that he did. Friends and relatives will say that the accused was with them at the time of the alleged crime. The victim, if he appears, will swear that this is the person whom he saw once briefly on a dark night eight months ago.

The lawyers are in almost equal ignorance. The prosecutor has the police report. The defender has only the vague and confused story of the accused. The judge is under pressure to "dispose" of the case. There is a score card for each judge kept by the computer. The judges have batting averages. Woe betide those who fail to keep pace in getting rid of cases. A long trial to determine guilt or innocence will put the judge at the bottom of the list. The prosecutors and public defenders also have their score cards of cases disposed of. Private defense counsel—whether paid by the accused or appointed by the court and paid by the public—has his own type of score card. For the fee paid, he can give only so many hours to the preparation and trial of this case. He must pay his rent, secretary and overhead. All of the persons involved in the justice system are bound by the iron laws of economics. What can the defendant afford for bail, counsel fees, witness fees, investigative expenses? All of these questions will inexorably determine the case that is presented to the court.

The National Conference on Criminal Justice, convened in January 1973 by Attorney General Kleindienst, recommends that plea bargaining be abolished within five years. What will replace it?

At the end of a day in which as a judge I have taken actions affecting for good or ill the lives of perhaps 15 or 20 litigants and their families, I am drained. I walk out of the stale-smelling, dusty courtroom into the fresh sunshine of a late spring day and feel as if I were released from prison. I breathe the soft air, but in my nostrils is the stench of the stifling cell blocks and detention rooms. While I sip my cool drink in the quiet of my garden, I cannot forget the prisoners, with their dry bologna sandwiches and only a drink of water provided at the pleasure of the hot and harried guards.

Was Cottle really guilty? I will never know. Fred made bail. Will he attack someone tonight or tomorrow? One reads the morning paper with apprehension. It is safer for the judge to keep them all locked up. There will be an outcry over the one prisoner released who commits a subsequent offense. Who will know or care about the scores of possibly innocent prisoners held in jail?

This is only one day in a diary. Replicate this by 260 times a year, at least 15,000 courts, and 10 or 20 or 30 years in the past. Can one doubt that the operation of the legal system is slowly but surely strangling the law?

I must sit only three and a half more weeks in criminal court. But there is a holiday. So with relief I realize that it is really only 17 more days that I must sit there this term. Next year I shall again have to take my turn.

I am reminded of Ivan Denisovich. Solzhenitsyn describes Ivan's bedtime thoughts in a Soviet prison. "Ivan Denisovich went to sleep content. He had been fortunate in many ways that day—and he hadn't fallen ill. He'd got over it. There were 3,653 days like this in his sentence. From the moment he woke to the moment he slept. The three extra days were for leap years."

Women in State Government: Looking Back, Looking Ahead

As more and more women enter politics and seek careers in state elective and appointive offices, their presence and actions encourage other women to pursue public office. Moreover, there is growing evidence that women bring new perspectives to public policy and that women will work together to promote policies and candidates important to them.

Katherine E. Kleeman

Katherine E. Kleeman is a research associate at the Center for the American Woman and Politics (CAWP).

Not so very long ago, an early book on women in politics (Gruberg 1968, 192) observed:

Women have little part in the government of most states other than through their right to vote. Men are the movers; women are the ornaments. They have been accorded token recognition. Their appointments have usually clustered around certain activities regarded as "women's areas" — those dealing with juveniles, school affairs, health, welfare, and libraries. Men have to be reminded to appoint women; ordinarily, males do not think of females for government positions.

Just 15 years ago, the numbers of women in public office — to the extent that they were tabulated at all — were minuscule. To discuss women in state government would have required making assumptions and drawing generalizations on the basis of a tiny sample, or simply telling the (sometimes horrifying) stories of a handful who had somehow strayed into politics and managed to make their way into public office.

There was, for example, the time in 1972 when Maryland Delegate Pauline Menes chided the leaders of the House for failing to appoint women to important posts. The speaker responded by naming Menes chair of the "Ladies' Restroom Committee." When she tried to attend leadership meetings, Menes was barred on the grounds that her presence would "make the men feel uncomfortable (Alexander 1978, 3)."

Today the picture has changed for women in government, especially state government. While the numbers of women officeholders are still quite small in comparison with the proportion of women in the U.S. population, women have gained a foothold in the state capitals. Moreover, they are moving into leadership positions in the legislatures, winning statewide elective offices in increasing numbers and securing a growing share of state cabinet posts. Perhaps most significantly, they are now a visible presence and show signs of becoming a distinctive force in state government.

Where Are the Women?

The movement of women into elective and appointive offices has been most noticeable at the state level. Women hold 15.6 percent of state legislative seats in 1987, the highest percentage of women at any level of elective office and the latest step in a slow, but steady upward progression (see Table 1).

Similar growth has occurred in the numbers of women in executive posts. Women hold 14.6 percent of top elective statewide executive offices in 1987, and in mid-1986 women filled 17.9 percent of appointed positions in governors' cabinets.

Change in the presence of women in state government extends beyond the numbers to the range of positions they fill. A popular misconception holds that women serve only where

From *The Journal of State Government*, September/October 1987, pp. 199-203. Reprinted by permission of The Council of State Governments.

Table 1.
Women in State Legislatures, 1969-1987

Year	Women Legislators	Percent of Total Legislators
1969	301	4.0
1971	344	4.5
1973	424	5.6
1975	604	8.0
1977	688	9.1
1979	770	10.3
1981	908	12.1
1983	991	13.3
1985	1103	14.8
1987	1165	15.6

Table 2.
Women in Cabinet Posts, 1987

Functional Area of Appointment	Percentage Distribution of State Cabinet Positions Held by Women
Health/Social Services	17.2
Government Services/ Government Administration	7.9
Labor/Industrial Relations/ Employment Security	7.3
Finance/Budget/Taxation/Revenue	7.3
Community Affairs/Planning/Housing	5.3
Environmental Protection/ Natural Resources	5.3
Education	5.3
Aging	4.6
Human Rights/Civil Rights/ Women's Rights	4.6
State Personnel	4.6
Governor's Staff	4.0
Tourism/Recreation/Culture	3.3
Licensing/Regulation	2.6
Banking/Financial Institutions	2.6
Economic Development/Commerce	2.6
Energy/Utility Regulation	2.6
State	2.0
Transportation	2.0
Other	8.6
Total	100.0%

legislative seats are easiest to win, where the salaries are lowest, and where minimal professional staff is provided. In fact, women serve in every state legislature in the country; they hold 10 percent or more of the seats in all but 13 states, most of which are in the deep South. States such as Alaska, Maryland and Wisconsin, which offer substantial salaries and staff assistance to legislators, rank among the top 15 in the proportion of women lawmakers.

Similarly, women occupy positions along almost the entire range of state cabinet posts. While they are not exclusively concentrated in positions traditionally thought of as "women's jobs," their strong presence in the area of health and social services is notable (see Table 2).

Even the legislative leadership posts so far from women's grasp when Pauline Menes raised the issue are more accessible today. In 1987 women hold 122 (13.7 percent) of the 834 state legislative leadership positions available in both houses nationwide. Of the 2,021 committee chair positions, 214 (10.7 percent) are held by women. However, very few women occupy the most powerful legislative leadership posts. For example, there are two women House speakers and two women legislators are Senate presidents (in addition to three women lieutenant governors who preside over their state senates).

As women move into politics in increasing numbers, a growing portion of them are building careers in public leadership, assuming successively more visible and responsible positions, moving, for example, from state legislatures into statewide elected or appointed office. In New York Karen Burstein after election in the early 1970s to the state senate was appointed to the state Public Service Commission, later became civil service commissioner, and now holds a top-level position in New York City government. Harriett Woods of Missouri won a local council seat, then was elected state senator, and later became lieutenant governor. Both women bounced back from unsuccessful races for

Congress — Burstein for the House of Representatives, Woods for the Senate — to continue their state political careers. In Vermont, Madeleine Kunin began her career in state government in the legislature, moved up to lieutenant governor, and, after an initial defeat in her first gubernatorial race, returned to win two terms as governor. These women and many others — Joan Growe in Minnesota, Norma Paulus in Oregon and Hazel Gluck in New Jersey — provide models for women who would like to devote their energies and talents to state government.

Women Officeholders: What's Distinctive?

In many ways, women in state offices differ little from their male counterparts. Women are elected or appointed to do specific jobs, and, for the most part perform similarly to men in those jobs. But a growing body of anecdotal evidence suggests that differences may exist in the experiences women bring with them into office, the issues they choose, the style of management they employ, the information networks they establish and the formal and informal systems they develop to encourage other women.

The career backgrounds of women office-holders mirror those of American women in general, and differ significantly from those of male officeholders. While men in public office often have careers in law, insurance or real estate, the women are much more likely to come from traditionally female professions — teaching, social work, clerical work and health care. These "women's jobs" expose women to perspectives, problems and needs which most men seldom encounter. As public officials, women with these backgrounds may have very different approaches or interests from those of their male counterparts.

Until recently, it seemed unfair to look for systematic indications of women's distinctive impact or style. So few women held office, and so widely dispersed were the women who did serve that they could hardly be considered as a group. It made little sense to try to draw generalizations from their behavior or assess their impact. Only now is the Center for the American Woman and Politics undertaking the first major research project to examine the impact of women in politics. But signs and suggestions of that impact are already evident.

Much credit for the increased attention to what traditionally have been seen as "women's issues" belongs to the contemporary women's movement in general. The pressure from organized women's groups and the growing politicization of women across the country have carried new issues onto the public agenda and brought new perspectives to the awareness of public officials. But it also seems likely that some of that attention has come because women have been in positions of influence as lawmakers, cabinet appointees or statewide elected officials, and, increasingly, in a wide range of other positions throughout government and politics. The growth in public attention to issues such as child care, pay equity, reproductive rights, pension and insurance reform, family care leave, and flexible work schedules has paralleled the rise in women's political power.

The impact of a woman's perspective is evident in an illustration provided by a woman official who described a meeting with male colleagues to discuss state measures to conserve energy. One of the men suggested shifting all state employees to a four-day, ten-hour-a-day work schedule so that state office buildings could be closed on the fifth day. The men in the group thought the idea had merit; only the female appointee grasped immediately the implications for working parents who might have to find child care to cover the extra working hours. Women, by the nature of their life experiences, may bring such different perspectives to public life.

Women officeholders also pay special attention to the advancement of other women. Studies on "Bringing More Women into Public Office" showed that (Stanwick and Kleeman 1983, 16-17):

> The women who have chosen to enter public life make a statement simply by being there, telling the world that it is right for women to be leaders. Many women officeholders make that statement even more emphatically and explicitly by looking beyond themselves to other women who could join them in government, lending encouragement and aid to those women in a variety of ways.

The research demonstrated that women officeholders not only serve as role models and mentors for women moving up in leadership, but also take more concrete steps, such as (Stanwick and Kleeman 1983, 18):
• making special efforts to hire women when they are staffing their offices;
• speaking with groups of women to stress the importance of political involvement;
• meeting with individual women to share their political knowledge;
• actively seeking out and promoting women when they have opportunities to make appointments;
• lending their names and prestige to efforts undertaken by others on behalf of women.

In addition to these individual efforts, women in state government have joined in efforts to organize women officeholders, both in legislative caucuses and in statewide associations for elected women. About a dozen states now have caucuses of women state legislators, and a similar number have organizations for officeholders from all jurisdictions. Nationally,

---

. . . women serve in every state legislature in the country; they hold 10 percent or more of the seats in all but 13 states . . .

---

women lawmakers work together in two groups: the Women's Network of the National Conference of State Legislatures and the National Order of Women Legislators. Women elected or appointed to statewide office can turn to a networking group of their own, Women Executives in State Government. These groups serve several purposes: mutual support and encouragement, education on issues and political skills, informal exchange of information, and, on occasion, demonstration of political clout.

Three examples illustrate how women working together have been able to capitalize on their collective influence. In California, a network of Chicanas in the Los Angeles area decided that at least one of them should be in the state legislature. Together they researched which seats were open, determined which of them was best situated to run for that seat, and then threw their energies into getting Gloria Molina elected; she became the first Hispanic woman to serve in the California General Assembly.

In New Jersey, the Bipartisan Coalition for Women's Appointments was created just prior to the 1981 gubernatorial election for the purpose of pressing for high-level political appointments for women. When Thomas Kean was elected governor, the coalition provided to him and his staff the names and resumes of numerous women qualified for positions; it also issued a challenge to Kean to appoint a record number of women to his administration. Several of the women recommended by the coalition were appointed to important posts, including Jane Burgio, now New Jersey secretary of state, who felt that the coalition played a significant role in winning the job for her.

In 1987 women held 122 (13.7 percent) of the state legislative leadership positions available in both houses nationwide.

Women lawmakers in West Virginia showed the power of a women's legislative caucus when, in early 1987, they joined together to save a prenatal care bill. The bill had special urgency for women in a state with one of the highest infant mortality rates in the nation. The women's caucus first employed a variety of pressure tactics to force reconsideration of the bill by a Senate committee after the chairman sent the bill out with a negative recommendation. One woman senator threatened to stop all legislative business with a filibuster, while women members of the House pushed through a resolution asking the Senate to reconsider the bill, and outside advocacy groups organized a candlelight vigil in support of the bill. The bill finally passed, but the governor vetoed it, so the women organized once again to see that the veto was overridden. The legislation now stands as a monument to the collective energies of women within and outside the legislature.

Remaining Hurdles and Hopeful Signs

Women have yet to attain their full share of representation in state and other levels of government. Even the impressive gains to date have only begun to remedy years of women's near-total absence from positions of political power. While some obstacles to women's progress remain, other developments hold out hope.

Perhaps the greatest barrier to having more women in public office is the power of incumbency: the easiest way to win an elective office is to be the incumbent. Since so few women are already in office, there are few female incumbents to win re-election, and the most winnable

slots, open seats, are often hotly contested. Women must still struggle to win nominations for those coveted slots.

The good news is that when women are nominated, they are strong candidates especially in the realm of campaign funding, once one of the biggest barriers to women winning office. The most recent research suggests that women do about as well as similarly situated men — that is, a woman running for an open seat often can raise about as much money as could a man of her party running for an open seat in a similar district. Moreover, while there are still voters who resist women candidates in general, recent elections as well as public opinion polls indicate that the overwhelming majority of voters are not so prejudiced. By large majorities (which vary for different levels of office), citizens say that they would vote for a qualified woman nominated by their party; and in their voting behavior over the past 15 years, men and women have elected female candidates to virtually every office in government except the two highest, president and vice president.

Still to be overcome are some outdated attitudes among powerful men who remain skeptical of women's political ambitions. Former State Rep. Julie Belaga of Connecticut tells of her decision to seek the post of speaker after a man thought likely to pursue that job indicated his interest in another leadership position. When the man later decided to run for speaker, he was pitted against Belaga in the race. A journalist subsequently told Belaga that, when asked about the race, the man had said, "I didn't know Julie Belaga was so ambitious!" In his view, his desire to be speaker was appropriate and logical; for her to want the same thing was startling and, by clear implication, unfeminine.

Despite such attitudes, every year finds more women eager to gain state leadership posts. The 1986 elections saw more women candidates than ever before for every top state elective job; 57 women ran for the five top statewide executive positions in 1986, up from just 36 in 1974. (In several cases, women held both major party nominations for statewide offices; the most notable instance was the Nebraska gubernatorial race, but women nominees squared off in a number of contests for lieutenant governor and secretary of state and in several state legislative districts.) The number of women running for state legislatures across the country grows substantially with each election; just over 1,100 women ran in 1974, but more than 1,800 did in 1986. Once in the legislatures, women are seeking — and winning — more committee chairmanships and leadership jobs.

Essential to this progress is a growing community of political women. It is evident in the caucuses and associations already mentioned, and in the formal and informal support systems women officeholders and candidates have established to bolster one another. This new community gains strength from women in law, business and other fields who contribute to political action committees established to back women candidates, and from women's organizations that rally to support women's issues and women candidates.

Perhaps the most encouraging signs for the future come from the stories of the pioneering women who have overcome the barriers. These are women like Texas State Treasurer Ann Richards who was able to enter her first race for that job because a small group of women raised almost half a million dollars for her in two days. They are women like New Jersey Commissioner of Transportation Hazel Gluck, who has moved from a legislative seat to hold in succession three highly visible appointive posts. They are women like Julie Belaga, who was unsuccessful in her 1986 gubernatorial race in Connecticut but will surely be heard from again. And they are women like Vermont Gov. Madeleine Kunin, who has worked her way up from a legislative seat to

lieutenant governor, failing once in a gubernatorial race but running again and winning. Eight of the women currently serving in the U.S. House of Representatives earned their first political credentials in state legislatures, as did Associate Justice Sandra Day O'Connor of the U.S. Supreme Court. Such models and inspirations suggest a bright future for the women now moving into state government. □

Sources

Alexander, Marianne. 1978. *Report of a Legislative Internship Program of the Women's Caucus of the Maryland State Legislature*. New Brunswick, NJ: Center for the American Woman and Politics.

Gruberg, Martin. 1968. *Women in American Politics*. Oshkosh, WI: Academia Press.

Kleeman, Katherine E. and Kathy A. Stanwick. 1983. *Women Make a Difference*. New Brunswick, NJ: Center for the American Woman and Politics.

Technology Transfer in the Trenches

PAUL D. EPSTEIN *and* ALAN LEIDNER

Paul D. Epstein, principal of the consulting firm Epstein and Fass Associates, was formerly a productivity improvement manager for the New York Mayor's Office and the U.S. Department of Housing and Urban Development. Alan Leidner, former technology coordinator in the Mayor's Office, is now with the New York City Department of Environmental Protection. An earlier version of this article appeared in *Urban Resources*, Vol. 3 No. 1, © Division of Metropolitan Services, University of Cincinnati, 1986.

P ITY the poor public servant in a municipal bureaucracy who would like to try a new technique to get the job done better; who, God forbid, wants to purchase a new piece of equipment, something *different*, perhaps something a bit sophisticated that might be labeled "new technology" even if it has been around a few years and has worked elsewhere.

Our subject is no mogul of municipal power—no agency head in the public eye with the mayor's ear—but a middle manager, buried in the bureaucracy. It is rarely the head of a large organization who first proposes to introduce new technology. Because there are more of them and they are closer to day-to-day operations, more mid-level operations managers tend to be sensitive to opportunities for improvement. Such individuals are the key to introducing change in large organizations, but in government they find especially big obstacles in their way when they even think about new technology.

Obstacles to New Technology in Public Bureaucracies

The first obstacle a middle manager faces is *time*. The public manager conscientious enough to consider new techniques may well already be working overtime to manage a large workload with a poorly equipped, undertrained staff. Finding time to keep up with changing technology is extremely difficult; it often seems like a luxury to public managers. Even if a public official manages to keep current, who has the time to do the research and analysis to find the right product and the right application to improve an operation? And who has the time *and energy* to run the tortuous gauntlet required of anyone who wants to try something new in government, especially if it requires the expenditure of public funds? In local government a contract for a new form of goods or services will likely require the approval of a budget office, a city or county attorney's office, and a board or council of independently elected officials. They may all demand that their own political agendas be satisfied even if these agendas have nothing to do with the new product. If a vendor is doing business with a jurisdiction for the first time, as is likely for a new product or service, the vendor may be required to undergo special qualification reviews which add to the delays and frustrations of getting new technology adopted. Especially frustrating to the operations manager are reviews for social policy goals; though important to the community, they have nothing to do with the vendor's ability to perform on a specific contract.

> Mid-level managers are the key to introducing change in large organizations, but in government they find especially big obstacles in their way when they even think about new technology.

Since most direct operating managers have few, if any, support staff to maneuver a contract through the long approval process, they generally must first sell the idea of procuring new technology to a department head, chief appointed administrator, or an influential deputy who has the staff to assign to the project. Ironically, if the project succeeds the department head or assigned central staff may be more identified with the new technology, and better rewarded for success, than the operating manager who conceived the idea. Meanwhile, during the whole time-consuming procurement process, the operating manager runs the risk of appearing preoccupied by some cockamamie newfangled technology. The manager's reputation may suffer—he or she maybe perceived to be "not on top of things" because of this preoccupation. While actual job loss or a pay cut is uncommon being pushed to some lower level of authority with little chance for advancement is not. Thus the incentive structure works perversely against the innovating manager. Rather than "champions" or "change masters," as innovative corporate managers are called in popular management literature, government middle managers who insist on trying to innovate might better be called "kamikazes."

Numerous other obstacles to innovation persist. Two large ones are limited communication channels, and the lack of discretionary resources—either in the form of staff or funds—for experimentation. Government bureaucracies tend to be rigid functional organizations. Many departments and bureaus are like fiefdoms with their own formal and informal communications. Few channels exist for communication between fiefdoms, keeping managers from sharing experiences, finding common problems, and developing ideas and support for new solutions. Most formal cross-agency channels are set up in response to crises and are aimed at coordinating operations rather than stimulating innovation.

As for resources, there are no such things as risk capital or research and development funds in most government budgets. Only occasionally does a creative high-level manager hide one or two people in the budget to develop and try out new ideas. Staff without an explicit, narrowly defined function tend to be surgically removed by budget officers. There is no organizational culture to support the idea that managers should spend a percentage of their time, or dedicate any of their staff, to learning new techniques and keeping in touch with advancements in technology. The bureaucratic environment is unkind to the "dreamers" who can be most creative in finding new ways to apply technology.

Reprinted by permission from the March/April 1988 issue of *National Civic Review*, pp. 130-136. National Civic Review, 1601 Grant Street, Suite 250, Denver, CO 80203.

Techniques for Introducing New Technology

Despite all the obstacles to innovation governments don't stay in the dark ages forever. Some kamikazes survive to become innovators who guide new applications of technology into bureaucracies. The most effective are opportunists. They don't dive bomb whenever they learn about a new technology. They pick their shots—they're good at being in the right place at the right time. Sometimes they locate outside resources to test a new technology (which has become harder as federal grants have dried up). They can be quick to respond to deficiencies found by an auditor. They have even been known to try "innovation by humiliation" ("if Bedford Falls can do it, why can't we?"). Unfortunately, some opportunities only come in response to a crisis—sometimes a tragedy involving loss of life or limb.

Occasionally governments provide support mechanisms to help innovators find new technology and create opportunities for its adoption. These include the use of "technology agents" to stimulate technology applications, and various approaches to finding and sharing information and obtaining resources needed to make new applications possible.

The *technology agent* approach is extremely valuable in that it provides staff support that helps make all the other approaches work better. The model was developed in numerous small to mid-sized cities in the 1970s by Public Technology Incorporated (PTI), a nonprofit local government technology transfer organization, with the support of the National Science Foundation. The technology agent has free rein to seek out new technology—or new applications of existing technology—from any source, bring it to the attention of operational managers, help guide its adoption through the bureaucracy, and promote communication within the bureaucracy to stimulate sharing of ideas among agencies.

The technology agent is the rare bird in the bureaucracy who is allowed to be a dreamer—whose time really can be spent learning about new ways to do things. The position goes against the whole organizational psychology and is often fragile. Its value is hard to demonstrate to people who control budgets because the final application of technology is always accomplished by someone else, albeit someone who was assisted by the technology agent. A leap of faith is often required to understand the contributions made by the technology agent.

The Mayor's Office of Operations in New York supported a technology agent for about four years, but the position has been unfilled since the incumbent left two years ago. The Office of Operations has attempted to keep the function going on a part-time basis, but the idea of a technology agent has yet to be institutionalized citywide.

New York City's huge multi-service social services department initiated its own technology agent function some years ago with a small staff. This group grew and became institutionalized as the Office of Management Design (OMD), which evolved into a minicomputer/microcomputer systems development organization. While it has generated many valuable data processing applications, it lost the freewheeling style of a technology agent free to explore any type of technology.

Brave souls interested in advancing technology in government use two techniques: "spreading the word" (information sharing) and "begging, borrowing, and stealing" (obtaining resources). The emergence of cross-jurisdictional networks and information services supported by public interest groups and professional organizations has greatly enhanced information sharing. PTI, the National Civic League (NCL), the International City Management Association (ICMA), the National League of Cities (NLC), and others have supplemented their traditional forums for public officials with sophisticated information services for members. These include databases (some accessible on-line by subscribers) with information on products and services and on governments' attempts to solve particular problems and apply technologies. The National Civic League has CIVITEX, which contains profiles of community projects. (For more information on CIVITEX, see the "Cases in Community Problem Solving" department in this issue.) PTI's ANSWER service includes a staff to search numerous databases no single member government is likely to provide its managers. PTI-Net, the ICMA/NLC "Linus" service, and Control Data Corporation's LOGIN provide electronic mail and teleconferencing

capabilities to subscribers. Information services are most useful when managers and staff know about them and are encouraged to use them—hence the value of the technology agent or other staff whose job includes getting others to use these services. Information from these services can be crucial to establishing the credibility of new technologies with managers and budget officers. For example, a manager in New York City used information provided from prior successes to justify the purchase of "geotextile" material for site preparation for low load-bearing uses (e.g., playgrounds and landscaping) for city Housing Authority construction. The material saved the city over $1 million on the project by reducing the amount of excavation and refill needed.

Other information-sharing mechanisms include internal user groups (e.g., microcomputer users; users of a central computer system) and committees with representatives from similar functions in different agencies (e.g., a fleet management or vehicle parts committee). An immediate problem (e.g., frequent vehicle breakdowns) may keep such a group active until the crisis has died down. But continuous staff support is needed to provide new information and insure ongoing communication so the group will stay on track for long periods, and will adopt new technologies in non-crisis situations. Any group which provides new communication channels can aid a government's technological advancement, even if technology is not the group's primary focus. Some quality of worklife labor-management committees have stimulated technological breakthroughs. In New York's Sanitation Department, labor advocated replacing employees with industrial robots to paint vehicles. This change saved 14 per cent of the cost of painting each vehicle.

Progress is made in many local governments, but often slowly. As in any conflict, entrenched procedures and people are difficult to dislodge.

Obtaining resources for new applications of technology, particularly for technologies not yet thoroughly familiar to a jurisdiction, can be extremely difficult. At budget time the promise of new technology must compete with community needs and political demands that are much better understood by agency heads, budget officers, and elected officials. Federal seed money grants helped local governments experiment in the 1970s, but these grants have now largely dried up.

Some managers are frugal with the resources they control and use the savings to fund pilots of new applications that will not require extraordinary budgetary approvals. If the pilots work, they then try to justify larger-scale applications through the regular budget process. That approach assumes authority over at least a small amount of discretionary resources, an authority not available to most middle managers. Other public officials look to private foundations and corporations to provide the resources needed to test new technology. Local corporations can sometimes be convinced to provide "in-kind" contributions of expert staff time to help introduce a new technology.

Another way to obtain resources, particularly for highly competitive products, is the "free loaner" approach to testing new technology. New York greatly expanded the use of microcomputers in city agencies in this way. Once one vendor showed interest in lending office automation equipment to demonstrate its capabilities, other vendors were openly approached. Few wanted to be left out of this large potential market. As a result, loaned equipment was provided free to about a dozen agencies; many agency managers and staff learned firsthand how valuable this equipment could be. Larger agencies soon began purchasing microcomputers by the hundreds through the regular budgeting and competitive purchasing channels. Similarly, New York City's Department of Environmental Protection obtained free loaner equipment for a controlled test of computer assisted design and drafting (CADD) in its engineering divisions. They documented how much more productive this equipment could make their engineers, as well as what configuration best fit their needs. DEP used its test documentation to obtain $1.2 million in city funds to invest in new CADD equipment, which it is now using to great advantage.

Progress is made in many local governments, but often slowly. As in any conflict, entrenched procedures and people are difficult to dislodge, and the government sacrifice of kamikazes is a source of great frustration.

Variations Among Regions and States

The 50 state and approximately 8,000 local governments in the United States share many characteristics. They also differ in important respects. Diversity among regions and states is the subject of this unit.

The states and localities are all part of an overarching system of government whose center lies in Washington, D.C. Most state and local governments depend on higher levels of government for significant portions of their operating revenues. All operate in the context of a common national political culture and a common national economy.

The states share a common status in the American federal system. Each has a three-branch structure of government based on a written constitution and a system of local government that serves, in effect, to decentralize state governmental authority. Local governments have similar formal relationships with their state governments in that they are all "creatures" of their states.

For all their similarities, states and localities vary greatly. Alaska, the largest state in area, is nearly 500 times larger than Rhode Island, the smallest. California, the most populous state, has more than 50 times the population of Alaska, the least populous state. The city of New York, with about 7 million residents, provides a great contrast with those local government jurisdictions in rural areas in which the residents all know one another. The states and localities also vary in their economic activities and well-being; the ethnic, racial, and religious makeup of their populations; their history; their policies; and the voting habits and partisan attachments of their citizens. Thus, when we talk about "the states" or "local governments"—their problems, activities, capabilities, and weaknesses—we must bear their differences in mind.

Differences in state and local jurisdictions are often regionally based. That is, clusters of neighboring states (or localities) often exhibit common characteristics that vary from those characteristics held in common by other clusters of neighboring states (or localities). For example, the adjacent, oil-producing states of Texas, Oklahoma, and Louisiana have problems and opportunities different from those faced by states without substantial oil reserves such as Connecticut, Massachusetts, and Vermont. And the three cold-weather states just mentioned have sometimes found themselves in a situation quite different from such warm-weather southeastern states as Georgia, South Carolina, and Alabama that also lack sizable oil deposits. Sparsely settled Rocky Mountain neighbors such as Montana, Idaho, and Wyoming differ in significant

ways from highly urbanized, densely populated Middle Atlantic states such as New York and New Jersey.

Local governments also vary regionally. For example, as James Bryce observed in the nineteenth century (see unit 1), structures of local government differ significantly among New England, Middle Atlantic, and Southern states. Another example involves party organizations, which typically play more important roles in local and state governments in Middle Atlantic states than they do in West Coast states.

Not all differences among states and localities are regionally based, of course. Governments of populous states such as California, New York, and Texas have substantially more capabilities and responsibilities than governments of less populous states such as Alaska, Wyoming, and Vermont. The former have enormous tax bases and huge populations to service; the latter have smaller sources of revenue as well as responsibility for fewer people. It is one thing to design and administer programs to serve a state with 15 to 25 million people and quite another to handle programs for a state with only about a half-million inhabitants. The same point applies when cities with a million or more residents are contrasted with local governments serving only a few hundred citizens.

Selections in this unit convey some important differences among states and regions. Whether these differences outweigh common features of states and regions is a question of perspective, and reading the selections should help provide a basis for a more informed judgment on the matter.

Looking Ahead: Challenge Questions

What characteristics of your home state make it different from neighboring states? What characteristics does it have in common with its neighbors?

What region(s) of the country face(s) the biggest opportunities and biggest problems in the next 20 years? Why?

What distinguishes the locality in which your school is located from neighboring localities? What different problems are posed for the various local governments?

All in all, do you think that the differences among regions and states are more significant than the similarities? Or vice versa? Why?

Is there a region of the country to which you would like to move? If so, what is different about that region from the region in which you now live?

Unit 5

The New Regionalism

Neal R. Peirce and Jerry Hagstrom

E pluribus unum: one out of many; unity in diversity. For a half century in America, the emphasis has been on the "unum." Social security, federal labor law, the waging of World War II, the interstate highway program—all testified to the preeminent role of the federal government, buoyed by public support and fast-rising tax revenues.

Now the "pluribus"—a view of America state by state and in its great regional agglomerations—is staging a revival. A new regionalism has come to symbolize the post-federal era, when many of the crucial decisions are removed from the national capital.

A fraction of the reason may be political: the Nixonian and more recently Reaganite attempts to return more decision making to the state level. But no conscious regionalism affects federal policy making; indeed, of the country's eight regional economic development commissions, all save the Appalachian Regional Commission were abolished under President Reagan.

The new regionalism is driven instead by a combination of federal withdrawal, state-local activism and new decentralizing trends in American society:

● a decline in real (after inflation) federal aid to state and localities beginning in 1978 and accelerating rapidly under Reagan's budgets;

● the rise of stronger indigenous regional organizations, including the Northeast-Midwest Congressional Coalition and Institute, the Southern Growth Policies Board, the Western Governors Policy Office and the Center for the Great Lakes, all of them speaking strongly for their member states;

● higher-quality state and local governments as a result of one-man, one-vote legislative reapportionment, revised state constitutions and city charters, greater authority for governors, cabinet-style executive departments and higher degrees of professionalism within state, city and county bureaucracies;

● an explosion of neighborhood and other grass-roots activism, partially born of the "war on poverty" programs that developed through the 1970s and 1980s into locally based economic development organizations active in housing, commercial strip revitalization and job development programs;

● growing recognition of the central role of education—from kindergarten to university graduate levels—in reviving the U.S. economy, with a common national understanding that the principal impetus must come from state and local governments, not Washington;

● lengthy periods of national economic stagnation, reducing faith in federal macroeconomic policy and prompting state and regional business and political leaders to develop a generation of their own economic strategies, ranging from venture-capital initiatives to strategies to save troubled businesses by such devices as employee stock ownership plans;

● a dramatic realignment of the relative standing of regions, including the high-technology-fired revival of New England, the decline of manufacturing in the Great Lakes states, the spread of corporate headquarters outside the Mid-Atlantic states, the newborn diversification of the southern economy, the ebullient growth in the Mountain West and in Texas and the growing weight of California in both population and economic power.

The nation is now witnessing, John Naisbitt observes in *Megatrends* (Warner Books, 1982), "a tough new brand of economic regionalism, a geographic chauvinism that grows out of the unique problems and resources common to a group of states." Interregional conflict surfaced in the mid-1970s dispute over the allegedly disproportionate flow of federal funds from Frostbelt to Sunbelt states, in the Northeast's and Midwest's concern about the southerly and westerly flow of jobs and population and, above all, on the energy front. *(For background, see NJ, 2/12/83, p. 339; 2/2/81, p. 233; 3/22/80, p. 468.)*

Studies by the Advisory Commission on Intergovernmental Relations show that severance and other energy-related taxes have given such states as Texas, Oklahoma, Louisiana, Montana and Alaska a massive revenue boost, permitting them to improve their standards of living and economic competitiveness while imposing tax levels far below those of energy-poor states.

Parallel movements toward business decentralization appear to complement the trend, notwithstanding the spate of corporate takeovers and moves toward interstate banking in the early 1980s. "After limiting decision making to the inhabitants of top-floor offices for much of the past two decades," *Business Week* reported on April 25, "companies are now frantically trying to push it down to those who are closest to the marketplace, giving more autonomy to plant managers."

At the same time, birth rates of small businesses have skyrocketed. State and local economic development policies that once favored *Fortune* 500 firms now encourage small enterprises on the ground that they create more jobs.

No one—not the Census Bureau, not economists or political scientists—pretends to have a definition of U.S. regions that is beyond dispute. In this series, the states are divided into seven regions that reflect—as much as practical—common geography, historic and governmental ties and flows of business and political power. *(See box, this page.)*

The six-state New England region has been the most commonly recognized since Jedidiah Morse, in *The American Geography,* his seminal 1789 work on U.S. sections, noted that the states east of New York, with "the general name of New England," had "several things" in common, including "their religion, manners, customs and character; their climate, soil, productions, natural history, etc. . . . ."

The Mid-Atlantic region, from New York to Washington, D.C., encompasses the nation's greatest concentration of economic and political power.

The five states of the Great Lakes region are America's traditional industrial heartland, now fallen on particularly hard times.*

The 12-state American South, from Virginia, on the banks of the Potomac River, to Florida and around to Arkansas and Louisiana, experienced a second Reconstruction in the 1960s and saw its extraordinary post-World War II economic development peak in the 1970s. While Florida continues to boom in all seasons, other southern states now appear to be threatened by coal depression in the Appalachians and international competition for low-wage, low-skill manufacturing plants.

The Great Plains states, physically an immense swath through mid-continent, constitute the most static region, primarily agricultural, not terribly rich, not terribly poor. But Minnesota, on the region's northeast corner, remains a center of governmental experimentation. Texas and Oklahoma, while sharing much of the prairie culture, have been hotbeds of oil-driven development and new entrepreneurship.

The Rocky Mountain states, benefiting from mineral development, have begun to enjoy extraordinarily high levels of income, education and economic growth. At the same time, however, they fear for the future of their arid and fragile environment.

*As Pierce and Hagstrom make clear, the economic fortunes of different regions can vary as different sectors of the economy enjoy "boom" or "bust" times. For an update on economic and other developments in different regions of the country since this article was written in 1983, see other selections in Unit 5.

Seven Regions of the Nation

Here are the seven regions used in this series of reports and the states within each:

NEW ENGLAND

Maine	Massachusetts
New Hampshire	Rhode Island
Vermont	Connecticut

MID-ATLANTIC

New York	Maryland
New Jersey	Delaware
Pennsylvania	District of Columbia

GREAT LAKES

Ohio	Michigan
Indiana	Wisconsin
Illinois	

SOUTH

Virginia	Kentucky
West Virginia	Tennessee
North Carolina	Alabama
South Carolina	Mississippi
Georgia	Louisiana
Florida	Arkansas

PLAINS

Minnesota	Nebraska
Iowa	Kansas
Missouri	Oklahoma
North Dakota	Texas
South Dakota	

MOUNTAIN

Montana	New Mexico
Idaho	Arizona
Wyoming	Utah
Colorado	Nevada

PACIFIC

California	Alaska
Oregon	Hawaii
Washington	

The series concludes with the Pacific region, dominated by the "nation state" of California, so populous and economically powerful that it is the state that could most easily exist as an independent country. Along with the Pacific Northwest, Alaska and Hawaii, California is a trading partner and opening window to the trading world of Japan and the entire Pacific basin.

An Economic Role Reversal

For the past decade, the Sunbelt has been the big winner in the competition for jobs, industry and investment. But today, according to the authors, things are looking brighter for the Frostbelt.

Bernard L. Weinstein and Harold T. Gross

Bernard L. Weinstein and Harold T. Gross are, respectively, director and assistant director of the Center for Enterprising, an applied business and public policy research center in the Cox School of Business at Southern Methodist University, Dallas, Texas.

The shift of economic power from the industrial Northeast and Midwest to the nation's Sunbelt, thought to be permanent a decade ago, appears to have become transitory. In many resource-rich Southern and Western states, declining oil prices, among other problems, have plunged once robust economies into deficit. In contrast, state tax reforms, an improved national economy and a revitalized industrial sector have changed the face of a region once disparagingly tagged the "Rustbelt."

In a public policy climate less concerned with economic growth than with redistributing wealth, the back-to-back recessions of the early and mid-1970s fostered fierce regional conflict. In the competition for jobs, industry and business, the Sunbelt won big. Federal dollars poured into the Southern and Western states, in part because of the success of the Southern Growth Policies Board in arguing its case for federal support of its region's interests against the Northeast-Midwest Congressional Coalition.

By the early 1980s, however, regional economic changes had become more subtle, partly as an outcome of the rapidly changing political climate embodied in the Reagan administration's "New Federalism." But more importantly, the Sunbelt-Frostbelt wars have diminished into occasional skirmishes because many states in the Northeast and Midwest are returning to prosperity while much of the Sunbelt has faded into only a few "sunspots."

As a consequence mainly of structural decline in the refining, petrochemical, shipbuilding, automobile, textile and steel industries, 10 Sunbelt states have lost jobs since 1980, while seven Frostbelt states have posted employment gains.

New England and Texas, once regarded as the archetypes for the

The industrial Northeast, once plagued by deep recession and plant closings, has undergone an economic resurgence. Plants are once again operating at full capacity and employment in New England has increased dramatically.

Frostbelt and Sunbelt, characterize an economic role reversal that is typical of many other states. Between 1970 and 1980, when tens of thousands of jobless men and women headed for Texas seeking work and prosperity, the state's employment rate grew at 6.2 percent a year, compared to New England's 2 percent per year. While factories were shutting down in the country's industrial heartland, swelling unemployment rolls and hurtling states' economies into deep recession, manufacturing employment in Texas between 1970 and 1981 grew to more than four times that of New England. The personal income of Texans and New Englanders was additional evidence of relative prosperity and decline, with Texans earning some 3 percent more than their northern counterparts at the end of the decade.

Now, however, the tables have turned dramatically. Although population growth in Texas is today nearly double that of the New England states, the difference between the rates of growth in the two regions has narrowed considerably. The most telling indicator is the city of Boston, which grew by 1.8 percent between 1982

and 1984, while Houston's population declined by 1.2 percent.

Furthermore, in 10 of the 19 Sunbelt states, unemployment rates are higher than the national average. By comparison, there is only one New England state—Vermont—with a jobless rate above the national norm. The construction industry in Texas is virtually crippled. Housing starts in Dallas, the healthiest housing market in the state, were down 12 percent for 1985. In Houston, housing starts declined by 59 percent, while both San Antonio and Austin posted declines of over 30 percent. In Boston, housing starts were up 38 percent in 1985, and in New York they climbed 45 percent.

The recent drop in oil prices, some 60 percent since January, has exacerbated economic difficulties in Texas and other energy-producing states. State revenues are declining precipitously. In Oklahoma, which is facing a projected budget shortfall of $467 million in fiscal year 1987, Governor George Nigh has ordered a general freeze on hiring, state purchases and out-of-state travel. Governor Edwin Edwards of Louisiana recently ordered all state agencies to cut spending by

5 percent in order to avert a budget deficit in the current fiscal year. Because the fiscal year is two-thirds over, Louisiana state agencies will be slashing their budgets by roughly 15 percent for the remainder of the fiscal year ending June 30.

Perhaps the most dramatic fiscal impacts are being felt in the state of Texas. Taxes on the oil and gas industry make up about one-third of the state's anticipated tax receipts, and state officials estimate that Texas loses $100 million in revenue for every $1 decrease in the price of a barrel of oil. As recently as 1979, Texas recorded a budget surplus in excess of $2 billion. But in mid-February, comptroller Bob Bullock reported that the state is facing a $1.3 billion shortfall for the current fiscal biennium, which ends in August 1987. He also indicated that a 1988-89 state budget with the same rate of growth as the current one would create a $6.2 billion shortage. "I don't look for the situation to get much better," he says. "It's possible it might get much worse."

Bullock's comments are echoed by State Representative Stan Schlueter, chairman of the House Ways and Means Committee: "We built our budget for the last 10 years on the inflated price of oil while oil was going up. Now we have to pay the price as oil is coming back down."

Texas Governor Mark White, facing re-election and wanting to avoid calling a special session of the Legislature, has ordered all state agencies to cut their budgets 13 percent, which amounts to a 17 percent cut for the remainder of the biennium. Following suit, the Texas House of Representatives has cut its operating budget by 19 percent, part of which included the dismissal of 13 employees. And the Texas Senate, after an unusual election-year caucus, asked its administration committee to cut the Senate operating budget by 13 percent.

A few members of the Legislature, most notably Senator John Traeger, who is not seeking re-election, have urged the governor to call a special session after the May 3 primaries to

The sun sets on a drilling rig in Texas, where a steep decline in oil prices has caused a $1.3 billion budget shortfall.

raise $1 billion by increasing the sales tax from 4.15 percent to 5 percent. "If we are concerned about the future of the state of Texas, the hell with politics and everything else," states Traeger. "We better do something right away." House Speaker Gib Lewis, however, opposes a special session to consider raising taxes because of a lack of support among House members.

While Texas and other Southwestern states are squirming, Massachusetts and the New England region are basking in fiscal sunshine. "State revenues this year are running 15 percent ahead of last year's," boasts David MacKenzie, policy director of the Massachusetts Senate Ways and Means Committee. MacKenzie attributes his state's fiscal fortunes to a diversified and fast-growing economy coupled with a balanced revenue system that is not overly reliant on one industry.

"Because Texas does not have an income tax," argues MacKenzie, "state revenues don't grow in tandem with the state's economy." He also believes that Massachusetts' 5 percent tax on adjusted gross income has not been an impediment to business development or industrial relocation. "Businesses and individuals are much more concerned with property taxes than income taxes, and Massachusetts has reduced its property tax burden considerably in recent years," he says.

Not only are changing economic circumstances altering the budgetary outlooks for the Frostbelt and the Sunbelt, these economic shifts are occurring at a time when the intergovernmental fiscal system is being profoundly restructured. As the growth of federal aid to states and localities has slowed, state spending growth has slowed in turn. In fact, the 5.2 percent rise in state government spending during fiscal 1984 was the smallest increase in 23 years, according to the U.S. Census Bureau.

This can be partly explained by the fact that a national shift has occurred from an "old federalism," in which states looked to Washington to set the national agenda, to a "new federalism," in which states are more responsible for financing programs and creating a cushion against economic downturns, according to John Shannon, executive director of the U.S. Advisory Commission on Intergovernmental Relations.

So far, the states have responded well. According to its mid-season review of the fiscal 1986 budget, the Office of Management and Budget reported that the state-local sector posted a $10.4 billion surplus in fiscal 1984. But unlike the federal government, every state but Vermont faces a constitutional or statutory requirement to balance its budget.

Furthermore, the financial turbulence of the past several decades has made states assume—out of necessity—more fiscal responsibility as they witnessed the business cycle play havoc with their income and sales taxes, the tax revolt force repeal or reduction in state and local taxes, and "New Federalism" substantially reduce federal aid.

But the 1984 surplus posted by the state-local sector, coupled with the economic revival of many parts of the Frostbelt, suggests a promising fiscal outlook for some state and local governments during the remainder of the decade.

For the Sunbelt, however, the changing economic climate, characterized by the "deindustrialization" many thought was peculiar to the Frostbelt, promises fiscal hardship.

Are there lessons to be learned from the past 10 years? The rise and fall of the Sunbelt suggests to many economists that simplistic analyses and judgments about the economic health of the nation's regions should be suspect. The change in economic fortunes has undermined conventional perceptions of the Sunbelt as the "winner" and the Frostbelt as the "loser" in the competition for jobs, income and investment.

Texas and other fiscally pressed states in the Southwest might find themselves learning a lesson from New England. For decades these states have taxed their natural-resource based industries heavily while letting other sectors of the regional economy escape virtually untaxed. In retrospect this strategy was both inequitable and inefficient.

In today's environment of significant shortfalls and deficits, the energy producing states might do well to lower taxes on their traditional industries and begin to broaden their economic bases to avoid future economic crises.

The South

Halfway Home And a Long Way to Go

Acclaimed by many as one of the most moving and compelling public policy documents ever written, the South's new regional study has a message for leaders throughout the country.

Jesse L. White Jr.

Jesse L. White Jr. is executive director of the Southern Growth Policies Board. This article was adapted from remarks he made at NCSL's Assembly on the Legislature meeting in Montgomery, Ala. in March.

During the 1970s, the fabled "New South" seemed to become at long last really new, not just an Old South painted over. After 100 years as a prodigal region, this New South appeared to be coming home to the national family. There were glowing economic reports from the country's Sun Belt; blacks and whites were experiencing brotherhood there; and a Southern state had supplied a homegrown president of the United States.

But now it is 1986, and the prodigal South is still on the road. Despite a century of hard traveling since New South prophet Henry Grady, then editor of the Atlanta Constitution, pointed the way, today's South has come to another crossroads...still, as Governor Bill Clinton of Arkansas

says, "halfway home and a long way to go."

Why is the South taking so long to become fully at home in the modern global village? What has delayed the New South's transformation into the Promised Land it always seemed?

The 1986 Commission on the Future of the South, assembled every six years by the Southern Growth Policies Board, chose the words that began its report carefully. For behind them lay a century of history as fascinating and frustrating, as complex and familiar, and as hopeful and despairing as any history of a people could be.

The South underwent a profound transformation from 1930 to the mid-1970s. In 1930, the region had a per-capita income roughly half that of the United States, an agriculture-based economy, a society undergirded by a rigid racial caste system and averse to change, a highly provincial and domestic view of the region's economy, and a conservative philosophy that discouraged state investments in

education and social programs.

Several developments over the next 40 years turned the region around. First, the South developed a type of "industrial policy," which was to recruit branch plants of labor-intensive, low-wage manufacturing companies located outside the region with the promise of cheap and unorganized labor, abundant natural resources, an adequate infrastructure and public subsidies in the form of IDBs and tax abatements.

Second, millions of displaced agricultural workers simply left the region, headed mostly to the cities of the North. Third, a new era of federal policy, brought in by the New Deal, taxed and redistributed national wealth, often on the basis of need, which greatly benefited the impoverished South. And finally, the racial caste system was dismantled in the 1960s and '70s with the ending of all *de jure* and most *de facto* segregation.

These developments industrialized the rural and small-town South, exported much of its poverty to the

5. VARIATIONS AMONG REGIONS AND STATES

North, halted and even reversed the outmigration pattern and dramatically increased per-capita income to 86 percent of U.S. per-capita income in 1975, a far cry from the 1920 level of 50 percent.

And, all of a sudden, the "Sun Belt" was created in the national media and mind. It had come all the way from being, in FDR's words, "the nation's No. 1 economic problem" of the 1930s to the economic promised land of the 1970s. The first commission report in 1974 had the central theme of growth management—not economic development.

Ironically, almost as soon as the South acquired the reputation (believed by Southerners also) of being the land of milk and honey, the reality was already beginning to change.

The second commission report was issued in 1980. It was clearly a transition document, dealing with the growth management problems of Southern cities on one hand, and the implications of the energy crisis and alarming statistics on Southern children on the other. Prospects were still generally sunny, but storm clouds were gathering.

The old: Sturdivant Hall, completed in 1853, in Selma, Ala...

Photos: Alabama Bureau of Tourism & Travel

and the new: bustling Montgomery, Ala.

By 1986 it had become clear that the once-solid South was not at all solid anymore, that the region's economy had become highly complex, and that some segments were prospering while others were declining. It was impossible to ignore any longer the fact that within the region there were actually two Souths, and they were growing further and further apart. One was also, in the words of commission chairman William Winter, "that other South, largely rural, undereducated, underproductive and underpaid, that threatens to become a permanent shadow of distress."

Governor Bill Clinton of Arkansas, chairman of the Southern Growth Policies Board, followed the precedents of Governor Jimmy Carter of Georgia in 1974 and Governor Dick Riley of South Carolina in 1980 by appointing a 20-member blue-ribbon panel, the Commission on the Future of the South. It included former governors, a former U.S. senator, college presidents, business executives, a major newspaper publisher, state legislators, professors, leaders of non-profit organizations, a former lieutenant governor and a big-city mayor, among others.

His charge to the commission was "to produce a short, readable report to the people of the South which can be used by governors, legislators and other leaders to mobilize support for those public policies and public-private partnerships which will increase the per-capita income, reduce poverty and reduce unemployment for Southerners by 1992."

The commission organized itself into three working committees to deal with what it saw as the most strategic

The commission calls for cabinet-level strategic planning processes, consolidating the executive branch and enhancing the governor's authority, professionalizing legislatures, sorting out government roles and consolidating local governments.

development issues facing the South: human resource development, technology and innovation, and government structure and fiscal capacity. Five cross-cutting issues were also considered in all deliberations: equity, urban-rural differences, internationalization issues, infrastructure financing and quality of life. The three committees held seven public hearings and took testimony from 77 expert witnesses. They also received written testimony and input from many others.

The inquiry was supposed to yield at the end of the process a short, hard-hitting report akin to *A Nation at Risk,* the 1983 report on the state of the nation's education systems. During an intense and exhausting two days of round-table discussions, the commission distilled the mass of information into 10 strategic objectives and the outline for a report.

The final step was unprecedented: The commission hired a novelist, Doris Betts of the University of North Carolina, to write the final report. Working closely with staff and with two rounds of commission edits, Betts wrote *Halfway Home and a Long Way to Go,* acclaimed by many as one of the most moving and compelling public policy documents ever written. It is only 23 pages long and can be read in less than an hour.

The first four recommendations—providing better education, eliminating adult functional illiteracy, training and retraining the work force, and strengthening at-risk families—all deal with the gravest problem facing the South: the condition of the present and future labor force, particularly those in the bottom third of the social and economic system. By all measures of educational and social performance, Southern children and adults are at the bottom, a reflection of that historic reluctance to invest in education and social programs. And the South's predominant economic systems have been based on low-skill, low-wage workers—the sharecropper system of agriculture and labor-intensive, non-

durable manufacturing. As the commission report says, "decades after old economic systems have vanished, their high human costs remain."

Suddenly, it seemed, the earth shifted beneath the South and everything that used to be functional became highly dysfunctional, assets became liabilities and long-held beliefs became disbelief. Low levels of public investment had produced a labor force well suited for row-crop agriculture and low-skill manufacturing but ill-equipped for an economy based on services, information, automation and large-scale corporate farming. "In the South's long, even commendable, journey of progress, too many are left behind with education and skills which better prepare them to function in Henry Grady's Atlanta of 1886 than Andrew Young's of 1986," said the report. "These deficiencies in the labor force will be major choke points in the South's effort to adapt to technological change."

The four recommendations dealing with human resource development are aimed at producing an educated, skilled, flexible work force—in the words of economist Pat Choate of TRW, a "high-flex society." They involve sustaining for at least a decade the current momentum of education reform and funding, getting serious about reaching the millions of adult functional illiterates, revamping vocational education to meet contemporary needs and spending wisely on those social programs that will move the millions of at-risk families from fear and dependence to independence, strength and contribution to society and the economy.

The second set of objectives deals with some new thinking about the role of higher education. One is to strengthen the economic development role of higher education and another is to increase the South's capacity to generate and use technology. These objectives also arise out of the new competitive environment and business climate.

There was a strong feeling on the commission that the South was spending plenty of money on higher education in the aggregate, but that the region simply wasn't getting its money's worth. The trend during the 1960s and 1970s to elevate all institutions to university status and, in some states, create degree-granting branches, produced expensive higher education complexes filled with second- and third-rate institutions and very few centers of true excellence. The commission calls on states to rationalize their systems of higher education, to give institutions clear mission statements, to insist on higher quality and to establish clear measures of accountability.

Closely tied in with these objectives is the one dealing with technology, a relatively new area of concern for state policy. The South lags on almost every measure of technology—degrees granted per capita in science and engineering, per-capita patents, and per-capita spending on research and development. In this era of technological renaissance, the decisions made or not made now will determine whether the South will get its share of the global action. The commission calls on states to create regional centers of excellence in conjunction with world-class graduate programs, to upgrade graduate programs in science and technology, and to work through the Southern Technology Council to find regional approaches to getting technology from the laboratory to the market.

The last four objectives deal more directly with state economic development policies: Aim new economic development strategies at home-grown business and industry, enhance the South's natural and cultural resources, develop pragmatic leaders with a global vision and improve the structure and performance of state and local government.

The new economic development strategies, in essence, would call for an end to the South's old policy of industrial recruitment, and would concentrate state resources on creating an environment and a set of supports that would enable home-grown businesses to begin and succeed. They call for more assistance to entre-preneurs, stronger business-university partnerships and more sophisticated recruitment.

The objective dealing with natural and cultural resources meets head-on the old perceived tension between growth and environment. It is an im-portant statement because it basically asserts that environment and cultural protection and economic growth now support each other in this changed business environment. The emerging industries—business and consumer services, information-based business-es and tourism—all now require clean, enjoyable environments, livable cities and cultural amenities. A clean en-vironment also tops the list of criteria for many industrial locators.

Perhaps no objective is more important and more difficult to imple-ment than developing pragmatic lead-ers with a global vision. Development really does or does not occur at the local level; the distressed small towns that make it often have a small group of pragmatic, energetic leaders with vision. The commission calls on states to provide seed funding for leadership development programs based in schools and communities.

The final objective in the report also breaks new ground in asserting a rela-tionship between the structure of state and local government and the ability to implement sophisticated economic development policies. *Halfway Home* basically argues that the 19th century model of highly fragmented and weak executive branches and amateur legis-lative branches cannot formulate and implement long-term, sophisticated programs. The commission calls for cabinet-level strategic planning processes, consolidating the executive branch and enhancing the governor's

Regional Board Is Productive Tool

The Southern Growth Policies Board was established in 1971 as "a cooperative effort to develop, con-serve and put to best use the South's natural and human resources," according to its executive director, Jesse L. White Jr.

Governed and supported by state and local governments of the area, the board, according to White, is dedicated to the idea that by work-ing together for common goals, the Southern states can accomplish together what they cannot accom-plish individually.

Membership consists of five per-sons from each member state—a governor, a state senator, a state representative and two leading citi-zens. Participating states include Alabama, Arkansas, Florida, Geor-gia, Kentucky, Louisiana, Missis-sippi, North Carolina, Oklahoma, South Carolina, Tennessee, Virginia and the commonwealth of Puerto Rico. Also eligible to join are Dela-ware, Maryland, Missouri, Texas, West Virginia and the territory of the Virgin Islands.

Every six years, the board appoints a Commission on the Future of the South to draw up a set of regional objectives to be used as strategies for approaching regional problems, according to Arkansas Governor Bill Clinton, chairman of the board. The 1986 objectives were presented in the report, *Halfway Home and a Long Way to Go.*

"The South, though increasingly diverse, is still the most unified region in America, culturally, polit-ically, economically," Clinton says. "To earn full membership in the na-tional and global economy, we must embrace the premise that unless we all move forward together nobody's going very far; unless we all work for the common good there won't be any. Just as we share com-mon problems, we share common solutions to those problems. The changes in the last 10 years have produced a brand-new form of interdependence which requires the South to think regionally and globally at the same time."

—Sharon Randall

authority, professionalizing legisla-tures, sorting out government roles and consolidating local governments.

These objectives will not be inex-pensive to implement. "Can we afford to make high-priced changes when budgets are tight?" the report asks. "Can we afford not to?" In reality, it is talking about a generation of for-tunate, educated, working Southern-ers paying more than their fair share as they pay the double costs of past mistakes and future investments.

A more difficult cost, however, may have nothing to do with money, but according to the report, with the South's historic reluctance to change. "The familiar song says that old times in Dixie are 'not forgotten.' William Faulkner adds that in the South the past is not only not forgotten—it's not even past! History is to a people what memory is to an individual, and too often the Old South preferred the past, resting by the roadside swapping tales of yesterday, postponing changes until the weather cooled, the crops were in, or the moon was in the right phase."

As the report states: "To honor the past is one thing, to prefer it will cost us the future. We are carrying into that future as heavy a load of past mistakes as past glory. If part of the burden of history is a poor underclass now threatening to become permanently mired in poverty, if one of the South's surprises is how a wall of isolation, like Jericho's, has tumbled almost over-night, we must decide which parts of our past need to be preserved and which need to be discarded.

"As Robert Penn Warren has said, examination of the past should be done in order 'to find what is valuable to us, the line of continuity to us and through us.' Whatever the South failed at yesterday can be turned to success tomorrow; what it lost can be restored; what it dreamed can be made real... but change will prove tough and expensive."

The Two Souths

There are two Souths: the glassy, urbanized, Sunbelt metropolises where income and educational levels match or exceed the national average and where commuters zip home from downtown offices to bedroom communities along the interstates; and a rural South that includes some of the poorest sections of a rich country.

Politically, there are also two Souths: the South that Ronald Reagan has conquered, and the South in which Democratic governors such as Joe Frank Harris of Georgia and Richard W. Riley of South Carolina endure; the South where Republicans hold 12 of the region's 26 Senate seats and only 2 of its 13 governorships; the South in which Reagan, in his two bids for the presidency, won every state (except for Georgia's nod to favorite son Jimmy Carter in 1980) and in which Democrats control, usually by overwhelming margins, every state legislative chamber.

The story of the two Souths is spread across the map on this and the following page. For the 13 southern states, the map measures the falloff from the share of the vote Reagan received in 1984 to the tally for the most recent Republican gubernatorial candidate in each state. It charts the Republican Party's almost complete inability to transfer its successes at the federal level to the contests for state offices.

In only 30 of the 1,346 counties across the South—most visibly in Tennessee, the home of popular Republican Gov. Lamar Alexander—did the most recent Republican gubernatorial candidate win a higher percentage of the vote than Reagan did in 1984. In only 11 per cent of them—again concentrated in the outer southern states, principally Tennessee and North Carolina—did the Republican gubernatorial candidate run even within 10 points of Reagan's total. In 59 per cent of the southern counties, the Republican gubernatorial contender ran at least 20 points behind the President. Across the Deep South, the map is a sea of red and orange, symbolizing the Democrats' continued dominance in these crucial state races.

In yet another way, there are increasingly two Souths: a South of black Democrats and a South of white Republicans. Throughout the South, as throughout the country, blacks remain overwhelmingly Democratic, the party's most loyal voters. Over the past three decades, the allegiances of white southerners have shifted to the GOP, both steadily and in sudden bursts, in a trend that appears inexorable.

Consider: In 1952, more than 78 per cent of white southerners considered themselves Democrats, and only 19 per cent Republicans, according to University of Michigan researchers. By 1972, the Democrats' identification lead had diminished to 55-32 per cent. And in 1984, in the rush of Reagan's second landslide reelection, the GOP had reached virtual parity, trailing the Democrats only 46-43 per cent for the allegiance of white southerners.

Today, race is not the overt issue it once was in southern politics. But more than anything else, it was the fierce backlash against the federal government's pursuit of civil rights for black southerners that allowed the GOP to put down its first roots in the South. Today, "race still plays a role," said University of South Carolina political scientist Earl Black, the co-author of a forthcoming history of southern politics. "It's more indirect now. There is certainly less direct use of racial themes now. But there doesn't have to be a lot. There's just a gravitation [by race] to one party or the other."

With the cooling of racial tensions, pragmatic, moderate-to-conservative southern Democrats—symbolized by governors such as Riley and former Virginia chief executive Charles S. Robb—have been able to construct interracial coalitions to produce solid majorities. The continued success of Democratic southern governors in the 1980s has been one of the brightest spots anywhere for a party that has spent much of the decade in retreat.

Today, the Republican Party's fortunes in the South depend not on racial hostility but on urban propserity. Again

there are two Souths: a rural Democratic South and an increasingly Republican metropolitan South. But it is the Republican beachheads that are growing faster.

From 1977-82, 80 per cent of the region's job growth occurred in metropolitan areas, according to a study by the Southern Growth Policies Board. Per capita income grew 12 per cent faster in the metropolitan South than the non-metropolitan South from 1979-83. Population follows jobs and income. In the South during the 1970s, metropolitan areas grew 44 per cent faster than non-metropolitan areas, reversing the national trend. Through the early 1980s, the gap widened: The metropolitan areas grew twice as fast as the rural regions, where the traditional loyalty to the Democratic Party remains most powerful. And it is in those rural areas where the region's economic problems—the decline of such industries as textiles and farming—are most concentrated.

"Economically, there are two Georgias—metropolitan Atlanta, with a lot of growth and new jobs and population influx, and [the rest of the state] outside Atlanta, which relies on farming and light manufacturing and has a host of problems," said R. William Johnstone, campaign manager for Democratic Rep. Wyche Fowler Jr., who is challenging Sen. Mack Mattingly this fall.

This year, southern voters will elect nine Senators and eight governors. Each set of contests will measure the parties' relative strengths in the region.

On the federal level, where the Republicans have made their greastest strides, this election tests the GOP's breakthrough class of 1980. *(See NJ, 4/12/86, p. 864.)* In four of the South's nine Senate races, first-term Republicans are facing the voters for the second time. Six years ago, several of them were considered flukes: few people seriously thought that Republicans such as Mattingly or Jeremiah Denton of Alabama could be reelected without Reagan above them on the ballot. But today, both are leading against credible Democratic opponents. In a fifth seat currently held by Republicans, Sen. James T. Broyhill, appointed this summer to fill out the term of the late John P. East, is running a close race against former Gov. Terry Sanford; and with Rep. W. Henson Moore as its candidate in Louisiana, the GOP has an excellent chance to pick up an open seat in that state. Three Democratic Senators seeking reelection are considered safe.

These races may help determine control of the Senate, but the governors' races, if anything, may be even more crucial to the region's long-term balance of partisan power. Before the South can truly be considered a two-party battleground, Republicans have to begin winning governorships—the key to the lock on Democratic control of offices further down the ballot.

This year presents the GOP with a unique opportunity because popular Democratic governors are vacating four of the eight seats up for grabs. Those open seats represent the Republicans' best opportunity to match their federal gains at the state level—though they may also regain the governor's mansion in Texas, where Democratic Gov. Mark White has been dragged down along with the state's sinking economy. Hard times for the energy industry also color the Senate race in Louisiana and both the governor's and Senate race in Oklahoma.

Republicans still begin their campaigns at a disadvantage throughout the region. One problem is that the divisive national issues—taxes and spending, national defense, foreign policy—on which the GOP's positions appeal to traditionally conservative southern Democrats have little or no relevance in state races. Governors can play down or even avoid entirely such explosive issues as abortion and school prayer. The conversion of white southern evangelicals to Reagan's cause in the past two elections has been crucial to his success in the South. But for the religious Right, state races don't incite the same passions.

The GOP's other problem is even more fundamental: the ingrained voting habits of many southerners "who vote the way their daddy shot" in the Civil War, as Texas Republican political consultant Karl C. Rove puts it. Publicly, Republican candidates in the South are more likely to talk about Reagan than their party label.

It's for that reason that some Democrats hope that the Republican advance in the South will be blunted after Reagan, who has been phenomenally popular throughout the region, leaves the scene in January 1989. It is unlikely that any of the current leading Republican presidential contenders will evoke such emotions in southern voters, and many party insiders believe that the Democrats are certain to put a southerner on their presidential ticket in 1988.

But the growth of the Republican Party in the South, though slow in many ways, now traces back two decades. The demographic trends that underlie the party's success reach back well beyond Reagan and show all signs of continuing long after the President has retired to his ranch. Among young southern voters, the GOP is also strong. It appears inevitable that over time, the Republicans will grow more competitive in more southern races, and that the Democrats will have to be ever more resourceful to construct majority coalitions.

"I believe the trend is irreversible," said Mitchell E. Daniels Jr., assistant to Reagan for political affairs, "unless the Democrats undergo some sort of epiphany."

"Sweetheart, Get Me Re-Write. They've Indicted the Donut Dunker."

Eric Black

Eric Black is a reporter for the Minneapolis Star and Tribune.

America, to paraphrase a report I wrote in the fourth grade about Mexico, is a land of many contrasts. People in all parts of the country may watch the same TV shows and eat the same fast-food hamburgers, but some aspects of regional identities are too deeply rooted for even the combined power of the Ewing family and Big Macs to overcome.

My adopted home state of Minnesota, for example, offers a lifestyle for cross-country skiers, Lutherans, grain-dealers, and indoor baseball fans that's hard to match. But one sub-species for which the so-called good life in Minnesota is not so good is the investigative reporter. To really thrive, this group needs political scandals. Big, smelly scandals, and plenty of them. But Minnesota is suffering from a long-standing scandal shortage that shows no sign of easing.

We try harder. We protect our sources, follow up leads, ask the tough questions. But to no avail. Minnesota journalists are a cursed lot, doomed to inhabit a state in which tax dollars stand a pretty decent chance of being spent for the purpose for which they are intended, elections have a high likelihood of being won by the candidates who get the most votes, and public employees, more often than not, show up at the office on workdays.

We read enviously about chicanery in other states. New Jersey, for example, seems to offer what amounts to an affirmative action program for investigative journalists. Consider the following juicy episodes that occurred during March alone.

At the beginning of the month, New Jersey's senior U.S. senator, the formerly Honorable Harrison Williams, resigned in disgrace scant minutes before his colleagues would have expelled him for his conviction of bribery charges arising from the FBI's Abscam probe.

In the middle of March, William Musto, a 36-year veteran of the New Jersey legislature, was convicted of racketeering, extortion, and wire fraud. The charges stemmed from Musto's habit of accepting kickbacks from contractors who received building contracts from Musto in his capacity as mayor of Union City, New Jersey. The sum kicked back to Musto and his co-defendant was over $700,000.

As March was ending, a grand jury indicted Newark Mayor Kenneth Gibson, Newark City Council President Earl Harris, and former Councilman Michael Bontempo on 141 counts of conspiracy, fraud, misconduct in office, and theft by deception. The grand jurors decided that there was probable cause to believe that Bontempo, 81, had been paid $115,000 over the period 1974-1981 for his services as chief of security for the city water supply and that Bontempo had lived in Florida during most of that period.

For investigative reporters, March in Minnesota was a washout. There were absolutely no scandals of any kind. In the next month, however, two events occurred that will give you an idea of the sort of thing that inspires outrage around Minneapolis and St. Paul.

In early April, the Minneapolis *Star and Tribune* revealed that a city park board policy allowing a small number of elected officials and their guests to buy discount season passes for the use of municipal golf courses had been abused. And more than once some of the elected officials had lent their passes to friends, who brought their own guests to play on the courses. The park board voted unanimously to appoint a subcommittee to recommend a way to revise the policy in order to stop this abuse.

In mid-month, the paper broke another scandal wide open. A Minneapolis alderman attending a sports event had been allowed to park his personal car in a no-parking zone. Deputy Police Chief Leonard Brucciani, when confronted with the facts, admitted that he had told the officers working the game not to tag or tow the alderman's car.

5. VARIATIONS AMONG REGIONS AND STATES

The Minnesota investigative reporter has the advantage of writing for a readership with an astonishingly low threshold for indignation. This is part of the secret of the state's antiseptic politics. The merest whiff of impropriety and the press, public, and prosecuters swarm over the miscreant like flies on organic fertilizer. For example, as soon as the golf pass story broke, the *Star and Tribune*'s editorial cartoonist weighed in with a cartoon of a greedy, leering elected official and his golf clubs being carried on a throne by four overburdened taxpayers. The deputy police chief who allowed the alderman to park illegally acknowledged the seriousness of his transgression and begged for forgiveness. "I'll guarantee you, it isn't going to happen again."

Another example of high crimes and misdemeanors in the Gopher State: After a hotly contested 1980 race for a state senate seat from Minneapolis, both candidates were indicted by a Hennepin County grand jury for alleged violations of Minnesota's Fair Campaign Practices Act.

The allegations can be summarized roughly as follows:

The Republican candidate, Elsa Carpenter, sent out a letter that said: "Don't miss the opportunity to elect Elsa Carpenter the first woman to represent Minneapolis in the State Senate." Actually, in a 1979 special election, a woman had been elected to serve out the unexpired term of her late husband, who had been a state senator from northeast Minneapolis. Therefore, Carpenter's statement that, if elected, she would be the the first woman state senator from Minneapolis, was (gasp) *incorrect*. This "false campaign statement" constituted the first count of her indictment. Making a false campaign statement is a gross misdemeanor, punishable by up to a year in prison and a $1,000 fine.

The second count of the indictment, also an alleged false campaign statement, was based on another Carpenter mailing that stated: "But in order for Elsa to represent us, she needs money immediately. In fact, before the end of August, she needs $2,375 for brochures and lawn signs." The horrid truth was that at the time of the mailing, Carpenter's campaign chest held more than $2,375.

The third count alleged that Carpenter had offered "improper campaign inducements." It is illegal in Minnesota to offer voters anything of value in exchange for political support. But in brazen defiance of the law, Carpenter allowed some of her supporters to give a party, at which things of value such as coffee, tea, and actual ROLLS were profligately distributed to the public in a bald-faced attempt to buy votes. An improper campaign inducements rap is also a gross misdemeanor.

When I tell the story of Elsa Carpenter's indictment to friends from other cities, some of them just laugh and assume I am kidding around. But others, whose cynicism runs deep and who know I

WANTED

for serving tea & donuts

ELSA CARPENTER

alias
THE MINNESOTA DUNKER

never kid around, believe they see an explanation. Partisanship, they say. The grand jurors or the prosecutor must have been fierce backers of the Democratic Farmer Labor Party (the DFL is sort of Minnesota's version of Democrats, only more so). But if that were true, how can they explain the fact that Carpenter's victorious DFL opponent, Eric Petty, was indicted by the same grand jury?

The grand jurors nailed Petty for one false statement and one count of divulging that Carpenter was under investigation by the state Ethical Practices Board, a misdemeanor. The background and details of Petty's alleged false statement are awfully convoluted, so I will spare you from them. Suffice it to say that if it wasn't quite as minor a misstatement as the one that resulted in Carpenter's indictment, it was close.

The indictments, which were handed down in October 1981, received front-page play in the Minneapolis *Tribune*. They were dismissed three months later, but not before both politicians had been arraigned, booked and fingerprinted, had their mugshots taken, and spent an afternoon in the Hennepin county jail. Before being incarcerated, Carpenter's belt was confiscated, presumably so she wouldn't hang herself. Petty, who had a cold, was not allowed to keep his handkerchief.

Last August, as Minneapolis fire chief Clarence Nimmerfroh was planning a big lawn party at his home, he realized that the water level was down in the artificial pond he owns jointly with some neighbors. So, after checking with the city water department, Nimmerfroh had some of his men bring a city fire hose to his house. Accounts differ as to whether Nimmerfroh or the men actually hooked the hose up to a nearby hydrant, but without question, the chief did use the hose to fill the pond. He paid for the extra water, about $55 worth.

An outraged neighbor tipped off the press, the story made page one, and the next thing anyone knew Nimmerfroh's shocking abuse of office was the subject of this denunciation by Alderman Mark Kaplan: "He makes city government look crooked and that reflects on everybody in city government."

In late summer of 1977, a scandal rocked the administration of then-Governor Rudy Perpich. A state official accused the governor's office of the sin of "cronyism." That dread word appeared in news story after news story and put Perpich on the defensive.

What was the root of the problem? An official of the governor's manpower office alleged that two people, both of them members of the governor's DFL party, *were hired for state jobs after being recommended by the governor's office* and that the two were hired even though, in this official's opinion, there were more qualified applicants available!

"The system is debased when government starts to become an employment agency for friends and friends of friends," the Minneapolis *Star* editorialized.

The jobs in question paid $16,558 and $14,700 annually. The *Star* editorial noted that the jobs "are unclassified, which means that no civil service tests are required and no specific qualifications must be met to be employed. Those are circumstances that readily lend themselves to political abuse."

Plainly stung by the allegations, Perpich appointed a three-member panel to investigate. Later he decided to have all of the employees at the agency in question take tests to determine whether they were qualified for their jobs.

Chicago, the New Jersey of municipalities, offers an interesting contrast. The city's payroll boasts 16 relatives of Alderman Fred B. Roti. Roti's kin, as of last November, had annual salaries totaling $350,992. When asked by reporters if he could defend this, Roti did not suggest that an independent panel investigate. Instead, he replied: "What's there to defend? They're doing a day's work for a day's pay."

The highest-paid Roti relative on the city payroll was a son-in-law who had been a municipal painter before marrying Roti's daughter. After the wedding the young man suddenly was promoted to the $34,000-a-year job as general manager of maintenance at O'Hare airport.

When asked about the propriety of his son-in-law's rapid ascension through the ranks, Roti did not offer to have his protege take a test to prove he was qualified for the job. He replied: "He's my son-in-law. He's qualified. He's doing a good job."

Another big Minnesota story broke in November 1980. After a lengthy undercover investigation, using hidden cameras and surveillance

vehicles, the special WCCO-TV I-Team showed Minneapolis housing inspectors taking long lunch and coffee breaks, padding their mileage claims, doing personal errands on city time, and generally NOT WORKING HARD AT ALL.

The next week, the head of the inspections department was suspended because, according to the city coordinator, he should have known about the abuses. Two weeks later, two of the inspectors spotlighted in the I-Team investigation were fired, and eight others were suspended.

The reaction: "This waste of taxpayer's dollars on persons of this caliber is fantastic and bewildering," said a letter to the editor of the *Star* capturing the general sense of public outrage.

Back to Chicago in January 1978: After three months of operating a tavern called the Mirage with the help of hidden cameras and secret identities, a team of investigative reporters from the Chicago *Sun-Times* published photos and accounts of bribes solicited and accepted by the vast majority of the inspectors sent in to check out the place.

The fire, plumbing, building, electrical, ventilation, and liquor inspectors, plus one city clerk, took bribes ranging from $10 to $150 to overlook fire and health hazards at the Mirage. "That's one of the things about Chicago graft," said Zay Smith, one of the reporters who worked on the story. "Low prices, high volume." Those who didn't solicit bribes simply overlooked blatant code violations because they didn't take the time to do even a cursory inspection.

So widespread was the graft and incompetence that when the tavern operators/journalists found one honest cop who not only wasn't on the take but attempted to perform an honest inspection, it was page one news.

This suggests one reason why the Chicagos and New Jerseys of this world are not always heaven for the investigative reporter: virtue becomes the news because sin is so familiar. Even the slimiest, most festering of scandals get old when they are coming down the pike at a rate of three a month.

In the bloom of my idealistic youth, when I was a reporter in Arkansas, I frequently happened upon what I thought were great conflict-of-interest stories. A state senator who received a full-time salary from the Associated General Contractors, used his position to further all the pro-management, pro-construction bills he could and to defeat most of the pro-labor legislation that came along. The chairman of the House Banking Committee accepted a "consulting" job with a Little Rock bank, and so on.

But when I would breathlessly call my editors to describe the story, they'd reply, "So what?" or "That's been going on for years and everybody already knows it."

That's an answer you would never get in Minnesota. While the scandals may be minor and sometimes exaggerated, at least they're not ignored. That's good for the reporter—and what's more important, it's good for the citizens, too.

Cities and Suburbs

More than three-quarters of Americans live in cities or in surrounding suburban areas. In these densely populated settings, local governments face great challenges and opportunities. One challenge is to provide a satisfactory level of services such as policing, schooling, sanitation, water, and public transportation at a cost that taxpayers can and will bear. An accompanying opportunity is the possibility of helping to create a local setting that improves the lives of residents in meaningful ways. The challenges and opportunities occur amid a formidable array of urban and suburban problems: crime, violence, drugs, deterioration of public schools, racial tensions, financial stringencies, pollution, congestion, aging populations, decaying physical plants, breakdown of family life, and so forth.

Cities are the local government jurisdictions that generally exist where there is high population density. Major metropolitan areas generally have a large city at their center and a surrounding network of suburbs under a number of smaller local government jurisdictions. Smaller cities may be part of suburban rings, or they may exist independently of major metropolitan areas, with their own smaller network of surrounding suburbs.

Cities of all sizes generally provide more services to local residents than other kinds of local government jurisdictions. Thus, city residents generally expect their city governments to provide water, a sewerage system, public transportation, a professional firefighting force, public museums, parks and other recreational areas, and various other amenities associated with city life. By contrast, local governments in rural areas are not expected to provide such services. Local governments in suburban areas typically provide some but not all of them. With the greater range of services provided in cities come higher taxes and more regulatory activities.

Like cities, suburbs come in various shapes and sizes. Some are called bedroom or commuter suburbs because people live there with their families and commute to and from the central city to work. Others have more of an independent economic base. Local governments in suburbs have often emphasized "quality education" (i.e., good schools), zoning plans to preserve the residential character of the locale, and keeping property taxes within tolerable limits. Generally speaking, suburbs have a greater proportion of whites and middle-class people than cities have.

One problem facing suburban governments today stems from aging populations. Older people need and demand different services than the young families which used to occupy suburbia in greater proportions. It is not always easy to shift policy priorities from, for example, public schooling to public transportation and recreational programs for the elderly. A second problem is structural in nature and relates to the overlapping local government jurisdictions in suburban areas—school districts, sanitation districts, townships, counties, villages, boroughs, and so forth. The maze of jurisdictions often confuses citizens and makes coordinated and effective government difficult.

The goals of suburban local governments and the central city government in a single metropolitan area often come into conflict in such policy areas as public transportation, school integration, air pollution, highway systems, and so forth. Sometimes common aims can be pursued through cooperative ventures between suburban and city governments or through creation of metropolitan-wide special districts. Sometimes, through annexation or consolidation, a larger unit of general-purpose local government is formed in an attempt to cope with metropolitan-wide issues more easily.

Selections in this unit treat city and suburban governments and the problems and opportunities faced in metropolitan areas. Cities and suburbs, of course, typically face different sets of problems. Even so, it is important to note that not all cities face similar problems; nor do all suburbs.

Looking Ahead: Challenge Questions

Do you live in a city or suburb? If so, do you like city or suburban life? If not, what do you imagine are the key differences between city and suburban life?

Many people are pessimistic about the ability of local governments in major urban areas to cope with contemporary urban problems. Do you share their pessimism? Why?

Big city mayors are often highly visible politicians on the national scene. Have you heard of Mayors Ed Koch (New York), W. Wilson Goode (Philadelphia), Raymond Flynn (Boston), Thomas Bradley (Los Angeles), Henry Cisneros

(San Antonio), and Andrew Young (Atlanta)? Have you formed any impressions of the abilities of those mayors whose names you recognize? If so, what are your impressions?

Would it be desirable for suburban local governments to raise property taxes and provide better public transpor-

tation, more frequent garbage collections, and better recreational facilities? Why?

Would major metropolitan areas be better served if they each had only one metropolitan-wide local government, instead of the large number of local governments that currently exist in each metropolis? Why?

*The rapid growth of office space in suburbs
is creating "urban villages," which are confronting local governments with new
kinds of urban-planning problems*

HOW BUSINESS
IS RESHAPING AMERICA

CHRISTOPHER B. LEINBERGER
AND CHARLES LOCKWOOD

Christopher B. Leinberger is managing partner of Robert Charles Lesser & Co., headquartered in Beverly Hills, CA. Charles Lockwood is the author of a number of books on urban development issues.

SINCE THE END OF THE SECOND WORLD WAR URBAN planners and academicians have warned Americans that suburban sprawl is an evil to be fought with every ounce of our national energy. They have condemned cars as the cause of city-killing growth. They have idealized mass transit. Yet, other than business and political interests in city downtowns, few have paid attention to their cries. We Americans have allowed sprawl to happen. In fact, we have reveled in our low-density suburban housing, our automobiles, and our decentralized living.

Now it appears that the much-reviled postwar suburban sprawl, with its sea of split-level houses surrounding retail businesses and apartment complexes strung randomly along its highways, was merely a transitional phase between the traditional compact pre-war city and today's metropolitan area. Our cities are becoming groups of interdependent "urban villages," which are business, retail, housing, and entertainment focal points amid a low-density cityscape. Each urban village has its core—a kind of new downtown—where the buildings are tallest, the daytime population largest, and the traffic congestion most severe. And each urban village has its outlying districts, which may stretch as far as ten miles from the core.

Urban villages represent a dramatic restructuring of America's cities and suburbs—one that is already affecting how millions of Americans live and work. Almost every city is swept up in the urban-village phenomenon—not only fast-growing Sunbelt cities like Atlanta and Phoenix but also slow-growing older ones like St. Louis and Kansas City, and archetypal cities like New York and Baltimore.

The Urban Villages of Los Angeles

LOS ANGELES IS PERHAPS THE MOST EVOLVED EXAMple of the urban-village phenomenon. Although downtown Los Angeles has recently experienced an unprecedented boom in office-building, the metropolitan area has simultaneously given rise to sixteen smaller urban-village cores, among them Century City, Costa Mesa/Irvine/Newport Beach, Encino, Glendale, the Airport, Warner Center, Ontario, Pasadena, Universal City/Burbank, and Westwood.

One of the easiest ways to gauge the growth of Los Angeles's urban villages is to look at the downtown's market share of the metropolitan region's office space over the past decades. (Office space is used as a standard measure of changing patterns of urban development in this article, because the office is the "factory of the future." In parts of some metropolitan areas 40 to 60 percent of the people hired for newly created jobs go to work in office buildings—not only white-collar workers but also support staff like janitors and food-service workers and security guards.) Since 1960 downtown Los Angeles's share of the metropolitan office market has declined from 60 to 34 percent, as expansion has shifted to the faster-growing urban-village cores in the suburbs.

The Costa Mesa/Irvine/Newport Beach complex, in Orange County, provides a good example of how the urban-village phenomenon is reshaping greater Los Angeles. Until the early 1960s a series of small towns in a county whose total population was 868,000, the complex today is California's third largest downtown, as measured by office and business-park space. The first phase in the creation of the urban village's core was the construction of a regional shopping mall, as it has been in many other locations. In this case there were two—South Coast Plaza, in Costa Mesa, and Fashion Island, in Newport Beach, both of which opened in the early 1970s. Next developers completed modest two-story office buildings nearby for local professional firms, and light industrial facilities for aerospace and high-tech outfits.

In 1980 the population of Orange County reached

1,932,708, and jobs there numbered 1,670,100. The boom transformed the emerging Costa Mesa/Irvine/Newport Beach subcenter. Office space there now totals 21.1 million square feet—well behind downtown Los Angeles's 36.6 million square feet, but gaining fast on downtown San Francisco's 26.8 million. Both the architecture and the tenants of the new high-rises are often the equal of those of office buildings in Los Angeles and San Francisco. The urban village's new hotels include a Westin, a Meridien, and a Four Seasons. South Coast Plaza has more sales than any other shopping center in the country. It is projected that once an addition is completed later this year, the plaza's annual retail sales will surpass those for both downtown San Francisco and the "Golden Triangle" of Beverly Hills. South Coast Plaza has most of the exclusive shops found in those locations.

Many of Los Angeles's established urban villages are gaining their own identities. Los Angeles's aerospace industry is increasingly concentrated at the Airport and in Torrance. The entertainment industry, which has traditionally been located in Hollywood, is now moving over the Hollywood Hills to Universal City/Burbank. Los Angeles's insurance companies, traditionally found in the mid–Wilshire Boulevard district two miles west of downtown, have recently selected Pasadena as an insurance subcenter, because it is closer than the mid-Wilshire location to neighborhoods from which they can expect to attract clerical workers and is also close to an executive-housing neighborhood.

The insurance and financial industries are transforming Pasadena, a city of 128,500 residents eight miles northeast of downtown Los Angeles, into an urban-village core. Perhaps the best-known city of its size in America because of the annual Tournament of Roses Parade and Rose Bowl, Pasadena's history and image have long been conservative and "old money." However, by 1970 downtown Pasadena was marred by empty storefronts, fading turn-of-the-century resort hotels, and half-empty parking lots. Low-income, primarily black and Latino northwest Pasadena was troubled by crime, gangs, drugs, and welfare dependency.

In the early 1970s the I-210 freeway was completed, connecting the city to the rest of the San Gabriel Valley and eventually resulting in a spurt of office-building. Pasadena became a back-office employment center for insurance and banking offices that wanted to hire middle-class Angelenos living in the rapidly growing San Gabriel Valley suburbs. Since 1980 twenty-eight mid- and high-rise office buildings have gone up.

Because of all this office construction, the character of downtown Pasadena has changed radically. A shopping mall several blocks from City Hall, which opened in 1980, is among the most successful in southern California. Entire blocks of handsome 1920s and 1930s two-story commercial buildings have been restored, and restaurants, espresso bars, and shops are now moving into ground-floor retail space that had gone begging for many years.

On the edge of downtown, within walking distance of the new offices and shops, badly run-down single-family housing has been replaced by new condominiums and townhouses. Thousands of houses in nearby residential neighborhoods have been renovated as young families have discovered the city's turn-of-the-century architecture and tree-shaded streets.

Change has not come easily to Pasadena. Not all of the city is being renovated; residents of the still decaying northwest section fear that new construction will squeeze them out of the neighborhood. And the many new jobs have created traffic problems. Today about 60,000 people commute to work in Pasadena, whereas approximately 25,000 leave the city for jobs elsewhere.

Pasadena residents worry about the long-range impact of the downtown construction on the overall community. Why has Pasadena attracted back-office operations instead of professional and corporate tenants, which would be more in keeping with the city's lingering blue-blood image? Does Pasadena want more high-rise office towers of any kind? How will the growing traffic affect downtown Pasadena and the nearby reviving neighborhoods?

Why Suburbs Are Becoming Urban Villages

T HIS DEBATE OVER GROWTH IS BEING REPEATED IN neighborhood associations and city councils across the nation, in such widely dispersed locations as Walnut Creek, California; Princeton, New Jersey; Schaumburg, Illinois; and Bethesda, Maryland. In fact, attempts to control growth and traffic congestion are among the hottest issues in local politics today. And the reason is that the urban-village phenomenon is reshaping our cities. However, most people do not see the larger picture; they simply see the consequences. The phenomenon has occurred simultaneously in all kinds of cities across the nation, mostly for five reasons. Four of these have helped to create or further the postwar pattern of sprawl. When the fifth reason comes into play, it is easier to see why our metropolitan regions are coalescing into these sub-centers.

One reason for the growth of urban villages is that the nation's economy is shifting from a manufacturing to a service and knowledge base. The number of industrial jobs has declined from one third of all jobs in 1920 to one sixth today. The figure may drop to less than one tenth by the year 2000, with service and knowledge employment making up the difference, much as agricultural employment fell and industrial employment rose during the transition to an industrial economy in the late nineteenth and early twentieth centuries. From 1973 to 1985, while five million blue-collar industrial jobs were lost, the service and knowledge fields—which are as diverse as computer programming, the professions, retail sales, and fast food—accounted for all of the nation's employment growth (from 82 million to 110 million jobs). The Bureau of Labor Statistics reports that the number of service and knowledge jobs can be expected to grow by nine million in the next ten years. The shift to a service and knowledge economy has greatly accelerated the restructuring of our metropolitan areas by creating a need for much more office space. In eight years, from the beginning of 1978 through 1985, 1.1 billion square feet of office space was constructed in the United States—the equivalent of 220 World Trade Center towers.

People are willing to live near the office now, whereas they were reluctant to live near factories that were dirty, noisy, and visually unattractive. Traditionally the poor and the working class have lived near factory districts. Across the nation office buildings and high-tech business parks have appeared in middle-class and even exclusive suburbs, such as the horse country around Valley Forge, outside Philadelphia; Bellevue, near Seattle; and the Buckhead district, in the north Atlanta suburbs. In Newport Beach, California, south of Los Angeles, a new subdivision of homes costing from $300,000 to $2 million abuts a Ford aerospace facility doing research and small-component-part assembly for military contracts.

A second reason for the emergence of urban villages has been changes in transportation patterns. Business shipments have shifted from rail to truck and Americans have decided that they prefer automobile commuting to mass transit. With fixed-rail transportation, all shipments must go from central terminal to central terminal before delivery. With trucks, shipments can travel from door to door. Similarly, with automobiles, people can go from door to door whenever they choose, without having to pass through central stations and terminals at fixed times. By 1960, the first year that the U.S. Bureau of the Census kept track, 69.5 percent of all commuting trips were made by car. By 1980 the figure had increased to 86 percent.

A third reason has been recent telecommunications advances, notably the dramatic drop in long-distance telephone costs. More and more day-to-day work is being done over the telephone. Not only cheaper long-distance telephone rates but also overnight mail, telecopiers, Zap-Mail, and computer modems allow communication without physical proximity.

Fourth, it is cheaper for businesses to operate in urban villages than in cities. Suburban office, industrial, and retail rents are far lower than downtown rents are. Although construction costs are approximately the same in the two areas, land outside cities costs less—$10 to $50 per square foot in suburban office locations versus $50 to $1,000 per square foot downtown. The cost of building parking spaces is also lower in the suburbs, where most parking is located in above-ground structures or surface lots, both of which are much cheaper to construct than a downtown office tower's subterranean garage. The difference in land and parking-garage costs shows up in office rents—$15 to $24 per square foot per year for prestige high-rise suburban space versus $18 to $42 for comparable downtown space in most American metropolitan areas.

These factors might only have encouraged more suburban sprawl if another factor had not come into play: most

Americans like cities and the concentration of services that they provide. A critical mass of employment and housing is necessary to support desirable everyday services such as a good selection of shops, restaurants, and hotels. But this critical mass is achieved at well below the size of the pre-war downtowns. For instance, it takes about 250,000 people within a three-to-five-mile radius to support a modest regional mall and about 20,000 middle-class people within an equal area to keep a good restaurant in business. And it requires roughly 2.5 million square feet of offices (about fifty typical three-story suburban office buildings) to support a 250-room hotel.

Since people do not want to drive very far for these services, particularly office workers looking for lunch or business travelers needing a hotel, a degree of concentration much greater than that of a low-density suburb is necessary. Only so many potential locations have the necessary highway access and visibility to permit this concentration, a fact that has led to the focusing of postwar suburban sprawl into urban-village cores. When prime urban-village cores become congested, developers and employers hopscotch to outlying locations where land is cheaper and commuting is easier.

Thus our metropolitan areas have expanded tremendously. In the past twenty-five years, for example, metropolitan New York's sphere of direct influence has tripled in size. The metropolitan area extends as far north as New Haven, Connecticut, and into once-rural Dutchess, Ulster, and Sullivan counties, in New York State. On Long Island the metropolitan area now encompasses Yaphank and Brookhaven, in the middle of Suffolk County, and fades away just miles from the Hamptons. Metropolitan New York has swept southward past Princeton and into Ocean County, New Jersey, and Bucks County, Pennsylvania. In several years New York's suburban growth will collide with that of slower-growing metropolitan Philadelphia.

Los Angeles has always had an enormous metropolitan area; it was knit together before the Second World War by the world's largest trolley system. By 1960 metropolitan Los Angeles's sphere of influence stretched to Santa Monica in the west, Pasadena in the east, Long Beach in the south, and the San Fernando Valley in the north. Now metropolitan Los Angeles extends westward into Ventura County, east to San Bernardino and Riverside, and south across most of Orange County to span an area many times the metropolitan area's size twenty-five years ago. Other cities—among them greater San Francisco, Phoenix, Dallas, Houston, Boston, Chicago, Atlanta, and Washington, D.C.—are also expanding quickly.

As outlying urban-village cores become more urban, with their high-rise office buildings and hotels, increasingly sophisticated shopping, and high-density housing, the center cities are becoming more suburban. This emerging trend extends beyond the fast-food restaurants on downtown business streets and festive retailing complexes like South Street Seaport, in Lower Manhattan, and Harborplace, in Baltimore. Suburban-style shopping centers—where you buy children's clothes and household appliances, not just clever T-shirts and scented soaps—have recently opened in several American cities, and are doing quite well. Large, privately financed apartment and condominium projects have been built in cities without a downtown residential tradition, including San Diego, Detroit, Atlanta, and Los Angeles.

How Urban Villages Affect Cities

FEW CITIES HAVE BEEN TRANSFORMED BY THE URBAN-village phenomenon as rapidly as Atlanta, whose metropolitan region has a population of 2.2 million, having gained 90,000 residents last year and 78,000 the previous year. In 1980 downtown Atlanta was the metropolitan region's unchallenged center for all kinds of office employment. Although urban-village cores were emerging around shopping malls at the intersections of major highways, office space was limited. And neither in the appearance of the buildings nor in the quality of the tenants were the fledgling urban-village cores any match for the downtown high-rises. Most of the buildings were two-story wood-frame structures, and many of their tenants were banks and insurance companies renting inexpensive space for back-office operations.

By 1985—just five years later—this pecking order had changed completely. Downtown Atlanta had gained 4.3 million square feet of new office space, but Perimeter Center, at the I-285/Georgia 400 intersection, due north of downtown, had gained 7.6 million, and Cumberland/Galleria, at the I-285/I-75 intersection, northeast of downtown, 10.6 million. Many of the new buildings were gleaming, architecturally distinguished high-rises of the kind that once had been built only downtown. If present trends continue, the amounts of office space in both the Perimeter Center and the Cumberland/Galleria urban-village cores will easily surpass the amount in downtown Atlanta by 1990.

Downtown Atlanta, like downtown Los Angeles, is losing its metropolitan hegemony and becoming just another one of the region's urban-village cores. The urban villages around it, like those around downtown Los Angeles, are gaining distinct identities. Government, professional services, finance, wholesale trade, and the convention business are still in downtown Atlanta. However, as prestigious high-rises have been completed at Perimeter Center and Cumberland/Galleria, those areas have lost many of their price-conscious back-office banking and insurance tenants and have become instead favorite Atlanta locations for corporate headquarters and business services. Nearly every major accounting firm and many downtown law firms have offices in Perimeter Center and Cumberland/Galleria, the better to serve their clients. The regional corporate headquarters of Northern Telecom and HBO are in Perimeter Center.

Despite their importance as business locations, Perimeter Center and Cumberland/Galleria do not boast that tra-ditional downtown symbol, a soaring skyline of office buildings. The high-rises in these two urban-village cores are not clustered. Instead they are widely separated by parking lots and heavily landscaped open space. In keeping with the non-urban mood, the developers have even neglected to add sidewalks connecting the buildings, and most people use their cars instead of walking. From the top floor of a seventeen-story high-rise in Perimeter Center the view is mostly trees and lawns, not other office buildings. Like many (though not all) urban-village cores, these relatively low-density north Atlanta developments visually blend into the suburban landscape. Yet the explosive rise in the number of office workers and their cars at Perimeter Center and Cumberland/Galleria has affected once-peaceful residential neighborhoods, including the Spring Mill area, near Perimeter Center.

ONE SURPRISING RESULT OF PERIMETER CENTER'S boom has also been seen in suburban Dallas, Chicago, and Washington, D.C., and may be a trend. Residents of middle-class subdivisions near high-rise office clusters are banding together in corporations, getting their neighborhoods re-zoned for offices, and selling large "assembled" land parcels to real-estate developers, who either raze the houses or move them to new sites and build high-rises on the land. The suburban homeowners see the chance to leave an increasingly congested neighborhood where house prices are not keeping pace with those in comparable but quieter subdivisions nearby. Often they can sell their lots for twice what the homes on them are worth.

One such group formed three years ago in Spring Mill, a subdivision abutted on three sides by the high-rise office complexes of Perimeter Center. Randy Campbell, a former Spring Mill resident, recalls seeing a notice in a neighborhood newsletter in July of 1983 asking residents if they wanted to sell their property to office developers. "If you were interested," Campbell says, "you tore off a strip of paper on the bottom of one page, filled in your name, and sent it to the head of the neighborhood association. All but three or four of the 117 homeowners mailed in that piece of paper, so we got together in the community room of the Perimeter Mall. The average Spring Mill house sold for $70,000 to $75,000 then, but we learned that the half-acre lots were worth three times that figure to office-building developers. We didn't know how to go about the re-zoning or sale. So all the neighbors appointed a committee of five men and four women—small-business owners, several attorneys, a clergyman, an accountant, and a stockbroker. That was me."

For the next few months the committee met almost every night, learning about real-estate development and discussing strategy. By the end of the summer Alston & Bird, Georgia's largest law firm, had agreed to represent the homeowners on a contingency basis, and the firm drafted an option agreement to create Kingsborough–Spring Mill, Inc., a nonprofit corporation. By signing this option agreement a homeowner gave Kingsborough–Spring Mill's three-person board of directors power of attorney to accept a minimum of $225,000 in cash for his home, net after any expenses. It was understood that no deal would be final until the county commissioners changed Spring Mill's zoning from single-family homes to high-rise offices and multi-family units.

The night that Alston & Bird presented the agreement, in October of 1983, eighty homeowners signed it, and by January of 1984 the figure had risen to 114 of the 117. "Once the neighborhood was 'tied up'," Campbell says, "we looked for a buyer. They weren't knocking the doors down, because we wanted top dollar and all cash. As we explored various deals, all the neighbors wanted to know what was happening. So we prepared a newsletter almost daily, ran it off on our office copying machines, and stuffed it into everyone's mailboxes during our lunch hours."

In October of 1984 the board of directors located a buyer. "Albritton Development wanted to redevelop the twenty-seven-parcel Lake Hearn Place subdivision adjacent to Spring Mill," Campbell says. "But the Dekalb County commissioners rejected the re-zoning, reportedly because the project was too small, too piecemeal. So we made a deal with Albritton, which combined Lake Hearn's twenty-seven lots, the hundred and fourteen lots that we represented, and the three other Spring Mill owners that didn't join the neighborhood corporation. That made eighty-two acres—hardly piecemeal."

In June of 1985, however, the Dekalb County commissioners denied the re-zoning request for the site. Six months later Kingsborough–Spring Mill, Inc., the Lake Hearn Place homeowners, and Albritton Development sued the county commissioners. By last June the case had ended up in the Georgia Supreme Court, which ruled six to one in favor of the homeowners.

BALTIMORE IS ANOTHER KIND OF CITY BEING RE-shaped by the urban-village trend. Despite all the good news about Harborplace and the renovation of nineteenth-century row houses, the Baltimore metropolitan area is essentially stagnant. The population of the metropolitan area, as defined by the City of Baltimore and Baltimore County, declined from 1.53 million in 1970 to 1.44 million in 1980, and it is projected to drop to 1.40 million in 1990. Employment is growing only modestly—from 771,300 jobs in 1980 to 782,400 in 1985 and to 813,400 estimated for 1990. The Baltimore metropolitan area hardly seems like the place for a surge in construction. Yet there has been a boom in the outlying districts of Towson, Owings Mills, White Marsh, and perhaps most notably Hunt Valley.

Hunt Valley, twenty miles north of downtown Baltimore, was farmland until recently. Now it has a prestigious high-rise office and hotel core, which is surrounded by surface parking and low-rise industrial and office space. The low-rise industrial and office complexes came first, when well-to-do Baltimore businessmen decided to move their plants and offices closer to their homes in the north and northwest sections of the metropolitan area. After Hunt Valley was established as an employment center that offered low rents, the major landowner—McCormick Properties, owned by the family that owns the McCormick spice company—upgraded Hunt Valley by building high-quality mid- and high-rise office space and a Marriott Hotel. The PHH Group, Westinghouse, Burroughs, and Allstate Insurance promptly moved in. Now Hunt Valley is Baltimore County's top corporate address.

Even New York City has fallen under the sway of decentralizing urban-village development—which is surprising, considering that New York is the classic example of the traditional pre–Second World War city and that Manhattan has never been more prosperous nor its skyline more crowded with construction cranes. But although Manhattan gained 23.5 million square feet of office space from 1982 to 1985, during this short time its share of the metropolitan area's more than half a billion square feet of office space fell from 67 percent to 60 percent. This year, too, 7.6 million square feet is scheduled to be completed in Manhattan, bringing its total to 317.6 million—and 16.1 million square feet of office space is scheduled to be added to suburbs within a sixty-mile radius of Times Square, bringing the suburban total to 216.1 million.

In the past the typical new office building in New York's suburbs was part of the campus-like headquarters of a major corporation in Westchester County or southwestern Connecticut. Today, though, the exodus of corporate headquarters from Manhattan—to the suburbs or other parts of the country—has slowed. Now the typical new building is built on speculation, in an urban-village core such as Stamford or Danbury in Connecticut, the Route 110 corridor on Long Island, or Morristown or Princeton in New Jersey. One kind of tenant is a corporation's back-office operations or an entire division that can be separated from the Manhattan headquarters at considerable savings in rent, taxes, and business services but linked to the main office by computers and telecommunications.

As more and more jobs move to the suburbs (most of the metropolitan region's employment growth in the next decade is expected to take place not in New York City but in northern New Jersey), housing construction is booming in outlying towns. At Brookhaven, in Long Island's Suffolk County, 4,000 homes were built last year and another 8,000 are planned. At Dover, New York, a Dutchess County town of 7,200 residents northeast of Poughkeepsie, developers have filed proposals with the planning board for 1,200 new condominium units. The transformation is likely to be even more rapid at Chester, New York, fifty-five miles northwest of New York City. The population is 7,000, and the town board has received proposals for 3,000 new condominiums and homes.

In attractive communities near urban-village cores the prices of existing homes are rising fast, owing to the sudden demand from employees of relocated companies. That is one reason that metropolitan New York City experienced a 24.6 percent increase in the price of housing between the first quarter of 1984 and the same period in 1985. In Stamford, for example, a typical three-bedroom house now sells for at least $250,000.

The Princeton, New Jersey, area illustrates the impact of the urban-village trend on metropolitan New York. Seemingly overnight a metropolis-sized urban-village core has emerged several miles east of this tree-shaded college town on U.S. Route 1. It is estimated that by the mid-1990s the Princeton corridor will have 12 to 15 million square feet of office space—surpassing the amount currently in downtown Milwaukee, downtown Newark, or southwest Connecticut's I-95 corridor between Greenwich and Stamford. Two luxury hotels have opened in greater Princeton; a Marriott and a Radisson are planned. The number of housing units is expected to double, with over 25,000 scheduled for completion by 1990. If current growth projections prove to be accurate, greater Princeton will become New Jersey's largest city in ten years.

Housing for All Urban-Village Workers

NONE OF THE FAR-REACHING SOCIAL, ECONOMIC, and political issues raised by urban villages has a broader and deeper impact than housing. Urban-village cores generally arise at the outskirts of cities and grow in a limited number of directions. Nearly all of Atlanta's urban villages, for example, are in the northern suburbs, leaving the southern part of the city largely unaffected. Dallas is growing mostly toward the north and northwest. St. Louis, not exactly a booming metropolitan area, is heading west and northwest. The vast majority of America's urban villages, in fact, have one thing in common: they are growing in white, upper-middle-class areas. Executives and business owners usually make the decisions about office locations and industrial sites. Most of them are white and upper-middle-class, and they usually decide to bring their offices or industrial plants nearer their homes.

This arrangement is time- and energy-efficient for executives and business owners but not necessarily for clerical, light-assembly, and service employees, nor for the employees of the stores, restaurants, and gas stations near offices and plants. These workers cannot afford the executive-priced single-family houses, townhouses, and condominiums near most urban-village cores. They face a long—and often expensive—car or bus commute to the suburban or city home they can afford to live in.

The scenes in the parking lots of north Atlanta's Perimeter Center at 5:00 show the results of this geographical mismatch. Executives and professionals get into their Cadillacs and BMWs for the relatively easy drive home or a visit to one of the nearby "formula" restaurants for a drink. At the same time, many black employees are walking through the parking lots—Perimeter Center has few sidewalks—on their way to the bus stops, which are little more than a pole with a bus sign on top, planted on a flat, grassy spot that usually turns into mud when it rains. Atlanta's working-class black sections are south of downtown, fifteen to twenty miles from Perimeter Center, but the roads and bus lines to them don't follow a straight line. With one or maybe two transfers, many bus passengers endure a one-to-two-hour ride twice a day.

Suburban fast-food restaurants, hotels, department stores, car washes, and cleaning services are already experiencing a shortage of low-paid service employees. In some fast-growing suburbs businesses are offering bounties for new employees, raising the starting pay from the $3.35 minimum wage to $4.00 or more, and offering raises after several weeks rather than a year. One solution to the shortage is to bring affordable housing closer to the employment in the suburban urban-village cores.

This idea is one of the most polarizing issues in local politics today. Most suburbs have raised the drawbridge against housing for the poor and the working class, as epitomized by new guarded and gated "secure" communities. Affluent families do not want low-income housing in their one-acre-lot neighborhoods. Nor do they need to allow it. Our urban villages now encompass areas the size of many pre–Second World War cities. They have more than enough land for all kinds of housing—and socio-economic groups—if zoning boards permit affordable housing.

The key to truly affordable, non-subsidized suburban housing is allowing higher density, primarily in the form of rental apartments, so that fixed land costs are spread over more units. Building suburban apartments in smaller than average sizes, to reduce rents, should be permitted. Empire West, a Tucson developer, has built smaller than average apartments in the Southwest. Situated in 250-to-500-unit projects, the apartments range from 320-square-foot studios (equivalent to a 14-by-23-foot space), to 615-square-foot two-bedrooms (a 20-by-30-foot space). All apartments have complete kitchens, bathrooms, and closets, and are outfitted with scaled-down furniture.

These complexes usually offer the lowest rents in their local markets—typically from $225 to $400, at least $25 to $50 a month below rents for the cheapest conventional apartments. These rents fit the budgets of clerical employees, security guards, and maintenance workers who make less than $15,000 a year. Yet the complexes still offer "luxury" features like swimming pools, tennis courts, volleyball courts, and social events.

Of course, upper-middle-class suburbanites fight almost any kind of high-density housing. But attached housing complexes don't have to be built in affluent neighborhoods. They have been successful near commercial districts, where they create a buffer between a single-family-home neighborhood and an office-and-retail district. Another logical place for apartments is next to an urban village's commercial core. It seems likely that the vast surface parking lots of regional shopping malls will eventually be redeveloped as high-density housing and commercial buildings, with the cars going into above-ground or even underground structures. When these apartment and condominium developments are built near the shopping centers that form the focal point of so many urban villages, the members of more age groups and economic classes will be able to live near where they work and shop.

New Transportation Problems

IN MOST METROPOLITAN AREAS THE SUBURBAN RUSH hour now rivals downtown traffic, and in some surpasses it. The 1980 census reported that 27 million Americans commuted from one suburb to another, whereas only half that number traveled from suburbs to downtown cities. The imbalance has increased sharply since 1980, owing to the boom in suburban employment. Today's suburban highways are so overcrowded that once-easy five- and six-mile commutes take forty-five minutes of stop-and-go driving in locations as widely dispersed as north Dallas; Contra Costa County, east of San Francisco; and northern Virginia, near Washington, D.C. And the emergence of urban villages at the edges of the metropolitan areas—like Chesterfield, twenty-two miles west of downtown St. Louis—have brought bumper-to-bumper traffic to two-lane country roads that still run past farms and cow pastures.

Living up to its image, Los Angeles has the most heavily traveled freeways in the nation. The three busiest points on them are now near urban villages—miles from downtown Los Angeles and its four-level interchange, which once held the city's traffic record but has now fallen to fifth place. To reach their record-setting traffic levels, these Los Angeles freeways—like the slow-moving highways outside other cities—do not have a morning rush hour in one direction and an evening rush hour in the other. Commuter traffic now comes to a standstill at morning and early evening in both directions, and slowdowns occur frequently throughout the day.

Unfortunately, some city planners examining metropolitan-area congestion do not acknowledge the traffic near urban villages and repeat time-worn clichés about automobiles destroying cities. Others recommend the expansion of highways and mass-transit systems, but continue to think only of access to downtown, just as transportation needs soar in the suburbs. Still others recognize the rise of urban-village cores in the suburbs but propose transportation plans that are years behind the demand.

Planners and governments are working under a serious handicap in alleviating suburban traffic problems. Most urban-village cores are being created by private developers in a series of unrelated, uncoordinated decisions. To make matters worse, the process of formulating a transportation plan, gaining its approval, finding the funds, and completing the project is so time-consuming that traffic problems are bound to become painfully obvious before any action is taken.

How can government alleviate suburban traffic congestion near urban-village cores? The answer is not the construction of subways or elevated trains. Fixed-rail projects (unlike light-rail construction—for example, trolleys) justify their enormous capital expenditure and high operating costs "only when you have both trip originations and destinations highly clustered," according to Peter Muller, a professor of geography at the University of Miami and one of the earliest observers of the urban-village phenomenon. "We are building 1920s-style mass-transit systems for our 1990s metropolitan areas," he says.

One example of the gap between urban image and reality is Walnut Creek, California, near San Francisco, which has experienced considerable office and light-industrial development in the past decade. Although most of the new buildings are near the BART mass-transit station connecting the town to San Francisco, Walnut Creek now has such severe traffic congestion that last year it enacted an office-construction moratorium. Muller suggests that mass transit failed to help the town avoid traffic problems because the vast majority of the local workers commute by car regardless of a mass-transit option. "A great many of the people who ride the new fixed-rail mass-transit systems in cities like San Francisco, Atlanta, or Miami used to ride buses," he says.

Nonetheless, fixed-rail transit remains a gleam in many a downtown businessman's or politician's eye. Some proponents may imagine that it takes a subway for a city to be a city, and some may have in mind that the federal government has paid up to 90 percent of the bill in the past (though it will not in the future, if the policies of the present Administration remain in place). Even Los Angeles—the capital of California's "car kingdom"—wants to build an eighteen-to-twenty-mile "metrorail" subway system, at a cost of $3 billion. According to an official of the Southern California Rapid Transit District, the metrorail system "may come close to breaking even on an operating basis, but there is no way that it will pay for the construction of the system." Of course, this statement is based on predictions of operating cost and ridership. The reality of Atlanta's new MARTA fixed-rail system is that the fare box brings in only 35 to 40 percent of the annual operating budget, which would more than double if a reasonable amortization of the capital cost were included. Moreover, the proposed Los Angeles subway route serves downtown and only two of the sixteen other urban-village cores in the metropolitan region.

Even buses do not fully meet the needs of the emerging urban-village cores, because serving all the possible permutations between where people live and work would require too many routes to be economically feasible. In the new urban-village cores office and industrial buildings are not closely packed together, as they are in midtown Manhattan or Chicago's Loop; they are widely separated by parking lots and landscaped areas.

This lack of density means that only a few people will find it convenient to walk to any given bus or subway station, and that office workers must have a car during the day if they want to visit a client or go out to lunch. And where internal transit programs using buses and mini-vans have been tried, such as Tysons Corner, Virginia, and south of the Los Angeles International Airport, they have quickly failed for lack of patronage. In fact, even an official of the federal Urban Mass Transportation Administration asserts that conventional fixed-route transit systems will never carry more than a small percentage of non-downtown commuters. The official thinks that the only kind of mass transit with any chance of significantly decreasing commuter traffic is ride-sharing, and particularly car-pooling.

That leaves us with our automobiles. The new office complexes provide more room for cars than for the workers who drive them. The typical building allots approximately 200 square feet of space for each employee. The usual planning assumption is that one out of five workers uses a car pool or public transportation, and so a building will require four parking spaces for every 1,000 square feet of office space. Each parking space requires approximately 325 square feet for the space itself, ramps (if a garage, rather than a lot, is planned), and aisles. That means the developer must set aside 1,300 square feet of parking for every 1,000 square feet of office space.

Two years ago some of the nation's leading urban planners gathered in Scottsdale, Arizona, and searched for solutions to suburban traffic congestion. The planners expressed considerable disagreement, presented a myriad of solutions but little data to support the ideas, and were greatly concerned about finding the money to pay for any transportation improvements. The planners did for the most part agree on an approach to the problem: government working together with developers. This is already happening. In north Atlanta's fast-growing Buckhead urban-village core, for instance, developers paid $1 million toward a new $5.2 million bridge over a highway interchange. And in Montgomery County, Maryland, developers will pay half of the $109 million needed for road improvements around Germantown, an emerging urban-village core. Many developers favor this new spirit of public-private cooperation, because they realize that the alternative could be government-ordered construction slowdowns or moratoriums.

Planning for Urban Villages

LOCAL GOVERNMENTS CAN RESIST DEVELOPERS, BUT they can't resist them indefinitely or protect their communities from the bad effects of rapid growth. They are decentralized nineteenth-century entities trying to deal with far-reaching twenty-first-century issues. Greater Los Angeles, for instance, consists of well over a hundred cities and five counties. Metropolitan Atlanta has forty-six cities and seven counties. How can so many governmental jurisdictions possibly coordinate their actions to handle the amorphous growth of urban-village cores, which, like multinational corporations, know no loyalty to any single governmental body?

Real-estate developers most often deal directly with local governments. In this high-stakes game the developers hold many of the cards, because they can play one jurisdiction off another. Many local governments, in their desire to expand their tax bases, generate employment, and welcome "progress," try to entice developers with liberal zon-

ing, temporary tax abatements, and improvements to such things as roads and sewers at little or no cost.

Contrary to what their residents often think, well-to-do communities cannot totally control growth on their own, unless they are geographically isolated, like Santa Barbara, California. When a town is part of a metropolitan area, its fate is inextricably tied up with the region's, no matter how wealthy its residents or how stringent its growth regulations.

Even Beverly Hills finds itself relatively powerless to resist the relentless development pressures from Los Angeles, which almost completely surrounds the 5.7-square-mile city. Several years ago Four Seasons Hotels wanted to build a high-rise hotel on Wilshire Boulevard near Rodeo Drive, in the heart of the city's commercial Golden Triangle. The issues of building density and hotel-generated traffic congestion became so controversial that the city council refused to vote on the Four Seasons project and instead placed a hotel-development ordinance on the ballot. Last year Beverly Hills voters overwhelmingly defeated the ordinance, thereby eliminating the possibility that another major hotel will open in the city. That didn't stop Four Seasons. Earlier this year the company started construction on a 287-room, 15-story hotel on Doheny Drive and Burton Way, literally across the street from the Beverly Hills city line. Beverly Hills lost the new hotel's sales and occupancy tax revenues but will still be affected by the traffic.

What can local government do about growth pressures? Probably the best solution is the creation of strong, effective, multi-city and multi-county agencies, and perhaps even entire government structures, that correspond to the actual economic and psychological boundaries of a metropolitan area and its urban villages. Such broad-based government has already been pioneered by Indianapolis (Marion County) and Miami (Dade County.) This governmental reorganization is not easy, because it can involve jealously competing towns, townships, cities, and counties—not to mention states, as are involved in greater New York, Philadelphia, Washington, D.C., St. Louis, and Kansas City. But much as the number of school districts nationwide has shrunk from 100,000 in 1940 to 15,000 now, the number of planning jurisdictions can be brought down.

One possible first step toward the creation of more-effective local governments is metropolitan-wide zoning and planning boards that have real clout in granting zoning changes and allocating improvements to the region's physical facilities. Some metropolitan areas are already moving in this direction. In 1979 Phoenix—the nation's ninth largest city, according to the most recent census—took the revolutionary course of adopting the urban-village concept in its planning process. In 1985 the city finished its General Plan to guide the municipality's growth, and this established nine urban villages. "Each [urban village] would become relatively self-sufficient in providing living, working and recreational opportunities for residents," the General Plan said. The city also encouraged the "concentration of shopping, employment and services located in the village core."

Phoenix is using zoning approvals and planned allocations of money for physical improvements to try to match employment with housing. The city has clearly specified goals. In 1980 only two of the now defined urban villages had more than half as many jobs as people, indicating that they had moved beyond being bedroom communities. Phoenix hopes that by the year 2000 five urban villages will have more than half as many jobs as people, with the remaining four urban villages having between one fourth and half as many, clearly showing that jobs and people have moved closer together.

Elsewhere, developers, employers, and local governments have created transportation-management associations (TMAs) to find solutions to transportation problems. What are perceived locally as transportation crises have brought TMAs into existence in Baltimore's airport area; Warner Center, in Los Angeles's San Fernando Valley; north Dallas; and Tysons Corner, Virginia. According to Kenneth Orski, the president of Urban Mobility Corporation, which is a TMA proponent based in Washington, D.C., TMAs "fill a vacuum in suburban areas."

Besides organizing ride-sharing and van pools, promoting staggered work hours, and lobbying for government-funded capital improvements, some TMAs are expanding their role into child care, private police, and other services for their geographic areas. It is imaginable that TMAs, born of the traffic-congestion crisis, could mature into an echelon of government well suited to the realities of our emerging urban villages.

Considering what has happened so far, is the urban-village trend a good or a bad thing for our cities and our citizens? To a certain extent the question is irrelevant, because the trend is already so advanced that it is irreversible. But it is hard to imagine the ideal urban village as being anything but very good. The opportunity for all kinds of Americans to live, work, shop, and play in the same geographic area—while retaining easy access to other urban-village cores with specialized features that their own district lacks—seems almost too good to be true.

As the nation's cities reshape themselves along the urban-villages model, we must ask ourselves, What are the design features, housing policies, transportation solutions, and governmental structures that will make our cities and the lives of their residents more productive and satisfying? Unfortunately, the questions and opinions vastly outnumber the solutions and directions. A great deal of study, experimentation, and planning needs to be done—and done quickly—to help cities that are being rebuilt almost from scratch.

Snow White and the 17 Dwarfs: From Metro Cooperation to Governance

DAVID B. WALKER

David B. Walker is professor of political science, University of Connecticut, and former assistant director, Advisory Commission on Intergovernmental Relations. This article is adapted (with the editor's assistance) from his remarks to the November 1986 National Conference on Government in Kansas City. © 1987 by the National Municipal League.

SNOW White nearly lost her heart. But she overcame the hostility of her stepmother and was kept alive in the forest by a family of dwarfs.

Metro America is Snow White. Migration to suburban areas nearly took the heart out of her. Federal hostility toward taking a role in metro governance has driven metro America into a temporary disappearance from public view. The good news is that she is being kept alive by 17 distinct types of interlocal approaches, on a spectrum from intergovernmental cooperation to full regional governance.

Some view this spectrum as a path out of a dark forest of problems, toward a regional Camelot.

Increasing Need for Metro Approaches

The nation's metro areas are growing, and their problems along with them. Substate regionalism seeks to address problems that spill over the artificial boundaries of central city limits. As metro America expands, the substate regional drama is being played out in more arenas. Note these seven current trends:

1. More Metro Areas. More metro areas exist today (1982 data) than ever before, with a more than two-thirds increase since 1962.

2. More People in Metro Areas. Three-quarters of our total population is located there, compared to 63% in 1962. More people also live in suburban jurisdictions than previously—some 45% of total population compared to 30% two decades earlier.

3. Continued Metro Government Fragmentation. Growth in metro areas hasn't meant consolidation. More of the nation's local governments are located in metro areas now: over 36% of the 82,000 total as against 27% in 1972. The average metro area still encompasses about 100 governmental units, despite the slight increase in the percentage (48% of the total) of single county and presumably jurisdictionally simpler metro areas.

4. Increased Metro Diversity. Compared to their situation in the 1960s, metro areas are now more diverse in (a) population and territorial size, (b) the mix of private economic functions and the range of public services offered, (c) the respective position of central cities vis-a-sis outside central city jurisdictions, and (d) the kinds of jurisdictional complexity.

5. Advisory Disharmony. For officials seeking guidance from governmental gurus, theoretical harmony is more elusive than ever. More theories are in vogue as to how metro areas should be run. No wonder actual practice is more eclectic than ever before.

6. Reduced Federal Aid. Direct Federal aid to localities, from day care funds to revenue sharing, has been cut back year by year without a concomitant reduction in Federal regulations.

7. Reduced State Aid. Because non-educational state aid has been reduced without changes in state mandates and conditions, metro (and, though not the focus of this article, rural) communities' budgets have suffered a double whammy.

These metro area trends point to regionalism as a solution because it can (a) handle certain functions (usually of a capital-intensive or regulatory nature) on a multi-jurisdictional basis, (b) achieve economies of scale in providing various services by broadening the basis of fiscal support and the demand for certain services, (c) handle "spillover" servicing problems caused by rapid urban population growth and sometimes decline, and (d) confront the necessity for retrenchment by seeking more effective ways of rendering public services.

The 17 Approaches to Regionalism

Regionalism is a gold mine for officials seeking to solve local problems, and these 17 different miners may be put to work to extract the gold. These 17 approaches to regional service problems can be arrayed on a spectrum from the easiest to the hardest—from the most politically feasible, least controversial, and sometimes least effective to the politically least feasible, most threatening to local officials, and sometimes most effective, at least in the opinion of many in jurisdictions that have made these fairly radical reforms (see box).

Easiest Eight

The first eight approaches are the easiest:

1. Informal Cooperation. For many up against the wall, this is the easiest of them all. This approach is clearly the least formal, and the most pragmatic of the 17. It generally involves collaborative and reciprocal actions between two local jurisdictions, does not usually require fiscal actions, and only rarely involves matters of regional or even subregional significance. Although reliable information on the extent of its use is generally absent, anecdotal evidence suggests that informal cooperation is the most widely practiced approach to regionalism.

2. Interlocal Service Contracts. Voluntary but formal agreements

6. CITIES AND SUBURBS

between two or more local governments are widely used. Some 45 states now sanction them broadly. Survey data suggest a slight decline (4%) between 1972 and 1983 in their use, but well over half the cities and counties polled in 1983 had used such contracts to handle at least one of their servicing responsibilities. Metro central cities, suburbs, and counties generally rely on them to a greater extent than non-metro municipal and county jurisdictions.

3. Joint Powers Agreements. These agreements between two or more local governments provide for the joint planning, financing, and delivery of a service for the citizens of all the jurisdictions involved. All states authorize joint service agreements, but 20 still require that each participating unit be empowered to provide the service in question. Surveys indicate that the number of cities and counties relying on joint services agreements for at least one service rose from 33% in 1972 to 55% in 1983, making then slightly more popular than interlocal contracting, although usage closely parallels interlocal servicing contracts.

4. Extraterritorial Powers. Sanctioned in 35 states, extraterritorial powers permit all or at least some, cities to exercise some of their regulatory authority outside their boundaries in rapidly developing unincorporated areas. Less than half the authorizing states permit extraterritorial planning, zoning, and subdivision regulation, however, which makes effective control of fringe growth difficult. Because a number of states do not authorize extraterritorial powers, and because this approach does not apply to cities surrounded by other incorporated jurisdictions, this approach is less used than other techniques.

5. Regional Councils/Councils of Governments. In the 1960s, no more than 20 or 25 jurisdictions had created wholly voluntaristic regional councils. That figure had soared to over 660 by 1980, thanks largely to Federal aid and especially to Federal requirements (notably Section 204 of the Model Cities legislation) that required a regional review and comment process in all metro areas for certain local grant applications. Title IV of the Intergovernmental Cooperation Act of 1968 built on the Section 204 base to create a "clearinghouse" structure at the rural and urban regional as well as state levels. Local participation in regional councils still remained primarily voluntary, however, with jurisdictions resisting any efforts at coercion.

Regional councils, also known as Councils of Government (COGs) which rely so heavily on interlocal cooperation, assumed far more than a clearinghouse role in the late 1960s and 1970s. Thirty-nine federal grants programs with a regional thrust sometimes utilized COGs for their own integral parts of a strong state-established substate districting system, as well. Rural COGs tended to take on certain direct assistance and servicing roles for their constituents, while the more heavily urban ones usually served a

role as regional agenda-definer and conflict-resolver.

With the advent of Reagan federalism a reduction in the Federal role in substate regionalism occurred. Reagan's Executive Order 12372 put the prime responsibility for the A-95 clearinghouse role with the states, while providing a back-up Federal role (48 states picked up the challenge). Twelve of the 39 Federal regional programs were scrapped, 11 were cut heavily, nine lost their regional component, and six were revised substantially; only one was left fully intact.

To survive, COGs had to adapt and the overwhelming majority did so; less than one-fifth (125) of the 660 regional councils shut their doors. Some got greater state support both in funding and in power. Many others sought more local fiscal contributions and became a regional servicing agency for constituent local units. A majority of regional councils now serve as a chief source of technical services and provide certain direct services under contract to their localities. Some state functions have been transferred to regional council and many serve as field administrator of certain state-planned and fund services. All still perform some type of clearinghouse function and some assume specialized regional planning and other related functions under at least 11 Federal single-purpose grants and loan programs as of FY 1983.

Most COGs, then, reflect a greater "nativism," "pragmatism," and service activism than their predecessors of a decade ago.

6. Federally Encouraged Single-Purpose Regional Bodies. Single-purpose regional bodies came into being when institutional strings were attached to some 20 Federal aid programs (as of 1980). According to the 1977 Census of Local Governments, these federally encouraged special-purpose regional units numbered between 1,400 and 1,700 depending on definitions and classifications. A less rigorous, private, and meagerly funded survey identified more than 990 such bodies in 1983. Although the actual number as of 1983 was probably higher, by 1986 the total was probably a lot less, given the number of regional program revisions, budget cuts, and eliminations during the 1983-86 period. Single-purpose regional bodies now exist only in a few Federal aid programs (notably economic development, Appalachia, Area Agencies on Aging, Job Training, and metro transportation). Continued Federal fundings make them easy to establish and they play a helpful, non-threatening planning role.

7. State Planning and Development Districts (SPDDs). These districts were established by the states during the late 1960s and early 1970s to bring order to the chaotic proliferation of Federal special purpose regional programs. A state's own substate regional goals were a prominent part of the authorizing legislation (19 states) or gubernatorial executive orders (24 states) that established SPDDs. By 1979 18 states had conferred a "review and comment" role on their SPDDs for certain non-federally aided local and state projects. Sixteen conferred such authority for special district projects and 11 authorized SPDDs to assume a direct servicing role, if it was sanctioned by member governments or the regional electorate.

As a matter of practice, practically all SPDDs adhere to the confederate style of regional councils/COGs. Many regional councils have been folded into the SPDD system, although boundaries have sometimes changed. Approximately the same number of SPDD systems (43) exist today as in the late 1970s, although in the hard-pressed midwest funding problems have rendered some moribund. All of these states took on the devolved responsibilities under Reagan's Executive Order 12372 for the "clearinghouse function," as did five others. Over half fund their SPDDs but only five in a respectable fashion.

Although feasible, SPDDs are somewhat difficult because special authorizing legislation is required, state purposes and goals are involved, and the establishment of a new statewide districting system can at least initially appear threatening, especially to counties.

8. Contracting (Private). Contracting with the private sector is the only form of public-private collaboration analyzed here and is the most popular of all such forms. Service contracts with private providers are now authorized in 26 states—far fewer than their intergovernmental counterparts and usually with far more detailed

procedural requirements. Their use has clearly increased from the early 1970s to the present with scores of different local services sometimes provided under contracts with various private sector providers. Joint powers agreements and inter-local service agreements, however, are both more popular than contracting with private firms.

This approach rounds out the cluster of interlocal approaches that we term easiest. Contracting with private organizations has been placed last because authorizing legislation, especially non-re-

---

"Metro America is being kept alive by 17 distinct types of interlocal approaches, on a spectrum from intergovernmental cooperation to full regional governance."

---

strictive statutes, may be difficult to obtain. Moreover, the fears of public sector unions as well as certain public employees are aroused when local officials seek to contract services privately.

Middling Six

The middle cluster in the spectrum includes four institutional and two tough procedural approaches for new and usually broader territorial service delivery systems. These approaches present somewhat greater hurdles than those in the prior group but each is a more stable way to effectively align governmental and service delivery boundaries.

9. Local Special Districts. These districts are a very popular way to provide a single service or multiple related services on a multijurisdictional basis. Three-quarters of all local special districts serve areas whose boundaries are not coterminous with those of a city or country, a situation that has prevailed for at least two decades. Forty-one percent of all special districts were found within metro areas, making special districts the most numerous of the five basic categories of local government in metro America.

10. Transfer of Functions. This procedural way to change permanently the provider of a specific service jumped by 40% in a decade, according to a 1983 survey of counties and cities. The larger urban jurisdictions were much more likely to transfer functions than the smaller ones. Over three-fifths of the central cities reported such transfers compared to 37% of the suburban cities and 35% of the non-metro municipalities. Among counties, 47% of the metro-type counties transferred functions compared to only 29% in the non-metro group. Cities were likely to shift services, first to counties, then to COGs and special districts.

Despite its increased popularity, the difficulties involved in transfer of functions should not be overlooked. Only 18 states authorize such shifts (eight more than in 1974) and in half these cases voter approval is mandated. In addition, the language of some of the authorizing statutes does not always clearly distinguish between a transfer and an interlocal servicing contract.

11. Annexation. The dominant 19th century device for bringing local jurisdictional servicing boundaries and expanding settlement patterns into proper alignment remains popular. The 61,356 annexations in the 1970s involved 9,000 square miles and 3 million people. The 23,828 annexations in the first half of the 1980s affected one million citizens and 3 million square miles. Although the vast majority of these annexations involved very few square miles, they are an incremental solution to closing the gap between governmental servicing boundaries and the boundaries of the center city.

A look at the larger-scale annexations of the past four decades highlights a dozen municipalities that serve almost as de facto regional governments: Phoenix, Houston, Dallas, San Antonio, Memphis, San Jose, El Paso, Huntsville, Concord (Cal.), Ft. Worth, Omaha, and Shreveport. Most large-scale annexations have occurred in the southwest and west, thanks to the large amounts of unincorporated land on municipal peripheries and to pro-city annexation statutes. Students of public finance point out that central cities that were able to annex substantial land are usually in good fiscal shape since they have escaped the "hole in the doughnut" problems of central cities in the older metro areas of the east and midwest.

Annexation is limited by the nature of state authorizing laws

(most do not favor the annexing locality); its irrelevance in most northeastern states, given the absence of unincorporated turf in their urban areas; and a reluctance to use the process as a long-range solution to eliminating local jurisdictional, fiscal, and servicing fragmentation. Annexation, then, has limited geographic application and is usually used incrementally but when it is assigned a key role in a city's development, it can transform a municipality from a local to a regional institution.

12. Regional Special Districts and Authorities. These big areawide institutions comprise the greatest number of regional governments in our 304 metro areas. Unlike their local urban counterparts, these Olympian organizations are established to cope on a fully areawide basis with a major urban surviving challenge such as mass transit, sewage disposal, water supply, hospitals, airports, and pollution control. Census data show there were approximately 132 regional and 983 major subregional special districts and authorities in 304 metro areas in 1982, compared to 230 and 2,232, respectively, in non-metro areas.

Relatively few large, regional units have been established because they (a) require specific state enactment and may involve functional transfers from local units; (b) are independent, expensive, professional, and fully governmental; and (c) are frequently as accountable to bond buyers as to the localities and the citizen consumers.

13. Metro Multipurpose Districts. These districts differ from the other regional model in that they involve establishing a regional authority to perform diverse, not just related regional, functions. At least four states have enacted legislation authorizing such district, but they permit a comparatively narrow range of functions.

This option clearly ranks among the most difficult to implement, with metro Seattle the only basic case study. While multipurpose districts have a number of theoretical advantages (greater popular control, better planning and coordination of a limited number of areawide functions, and a more accountable regional government), political and statutory difficulties have barred their widespread use.

14. The Reformed Urban County. Because it transforms a unit of local government, a move frequently opposed by the elected officials of the jurisdiction in question, new urban counties are difficult to form. As a result, though 29 states have enacted permissive county home rule statutes, only 76 charter counties (generally urban) have been created.

In metro areas, however, three-quarters of the 683 metro counties have either an elected chief executive or an appointed chief administrative officer. The servicing role of these jurisdictions has expanded rapidly over the past ten decades or so. Since 1967, outlays for what used to be traditional county functions (corrections, welfare, roads, and health and hospitals) have declined, with expenditures for various municipal-type, regional and new federally encouraged services have risen commensurately. Overall, the range of state-mandated and county-initiated services have risen rapidly in metro counties, during the past two decades, which has necessitated a better approach to fiscal and program management.

"Informal cooperation is the easiest and probably the most widely practiced approach to regionalism. It generally involves collaborative and reciprocal activities, but not fiscal transactions."

In the 146 single-county metro areas this reform county option is excellent. However, since county mergers and modification of county boundaries are almost impossible, in the 159 multi-county metro areas the option is less valuable. It can only provide a subregional solution to certain service delivery problems, not a fully regional approach.

The Tough Trio

The hardest approaches to metro regionalism are the three general governmental options: one-tier or unitary, two-tier or federative, and three-tier or super-federative.

All three involve the creation of a new areawide level of government, a reallocation of local government powers and functions, and, as a result a disruption of the political and institutional status quo. All three options involve very rare and remarkable forms of interlocal cooperation.

15. One-tier consolidations. This method of expanding municipal boundaries has had a lean, but long history. From 1804 to 1907, four city-county mergers occurred, all by state mandate. Then municipalities proliferated but city-county mergers virtually stopped for 40 years. From Baton Rouge's partial merger in 1947 to the present there have been some 17 city-county consolidations, most endorsed by popular referendum. Among the hurdles to surmount in achieving such reorganizations are state authorization, the frequent opposition of local elected officials, racial anxieties (where large minorities exist), an equitable representational system, concerns about the size of government, and technical issues relating to such matters as debt assumption. Only one out of every five consolidation efforts has succeeded in the past 25 years.

Most consolidations have been partial, not total, with small suburban municipalities, school districts and special districts sometimes left out but the new county government generally exercises some authority over their activities. In addition, the metro settlement pattern in some cases has long since exceeded the county limits, so

> **"The hardest approaches to metro regionalism are complex consolidations and restructurings, which create new areawide levels of government, reallocate local government powers and functions and disrupt the political and institutional status quo."**

that the reorganized government may be the prime service provider and key player, but not the only one. This, of course, is another result of rigid county boundaries.

To sum up, one-tier consolidations have generally been most suitable in smaller non-metro urban areas and in smaller and medium (ideally uni-county) metro areas.

16. Two-Tier Restructurings. These seek a division between local and regional functions with two levels of government to render such services. These and other features, notably a reorganized county government, are spelled out in a new county charter that is adopted in a county wide referendum. The Committee for Economic Development advanced one of the most persuasive arguments for this approach in the 1970s. Metro Toronto, which created a strongly empowered regional federative government to handle areawide functions and ultimately led to some local reorganization by the merger of some municipalities, is a model for this approach.

The prime American example of this federative approach is Metro Dade County (Miami-Dade). Unlike the incremental reform approach of the modernized or urban county, a drastically redesigned county structure and role emerged from a head-on confrontation over the restructuring issue. Narrowly approved in a countywide referendum in 1957, the new Metro government's cluster of strong charter powers and its authority to perform a range of areawide functions were steadily opposed until the mid-1960s. Since then, its powers have grown and it is widely considered a success. Witness the extraordinary responsibilities Metro Dade assumed during the various waves of immigration since the early 1960s. The level of metro-municipal collaboration is better now than it was a generation ago, but tensions and confrontations are still part of the relationship—as they are in most federative systems. In my opinion, however, its survival is assured.

17. The Three-Tier Reforms. This is a rarely used approach, with just two U.S. examples. However, it deals with the special problems of multi-county metro areas.

The first example is the Twin Cities (Minneapolis-St. Paul) Metropolitan Council. Launched as a metro initiative and enacted by the state legislature in 1967, the Council is the authoritative regional coordinator, planner, and controller of large-scale development for its region which includes seven counties and a dozen localities.

It is empowered by the state to review, approve, or suspend projects and plans of the area's various multi-jurisdictional special districts and authorities; it is the regional designee under all federally

sponsored substate regional programs for which the area is eligible, and has the right to review and delay projects having an adverse areawide impact. Direct operational responsibilities do not fall within its purview but it directly molds the region's future development. Like any body that possesses significant power over other public agencies and indirectly over private regional actors, the Council has become somewhat politicized in recent years but its rightful place in the governance of the Twin Cities is not questioned.

The other three-tier experiment is the Greater Portland (Oregon) Metropolitan Service District (MSD), a regional planning and coordinating agency that serves the urbanized portion of three counties. Approved by popular referendum in 1978, the MSD supplanted the previous COG, and assumed the waste disposal and Portland Zoo responsibilities of the previous regional authority. The enabling legislation also authorized the MSD to run the regional transportation agency and to assume responsibility for a range of the functions, subject to voter approval, but these options have not been utilized. A 1986 referendum on a new convention center did pass and this task was assigned to the MSD. Unlike the Twin Cities' Council, the MSD has an elected mayor, an appointed manager, and an elected council of 12 commissioners, which provides a popular accountability that the Met Council has yet to achieve.

Both three-tier examples suggest how other multi-county metro areas might approach areawide service delivery and other metro challenges but they are arduous to achieve and not easy to sustain.

Summary Analysis

This probe of metro Snow White's current status suggests that she is alive and well, and is being looked after by her 17 regionable dwarfs:

1. Overall Growth in Regionalism. Virtually all of the various approaches have been on the increase. Since the early 1970s, the use of the eight easiest approaches has seen a net increase despite a reduction in the number of regional councils and federally supported substate districts. Meanwhile five of the six middling approaches grew markedly (the exception was the metro multi-purpose authority). Even the three hardest approaches have grown in use.

2. Multiple Approach Use. Very few metro areas rely on only one or two forms of substate regionalism.

3. The easier procedural and unifunctional institutional types of service shifts tend to be found more in larger metro areas while the harder restructurings usually take place successfully within the medium-sized and especially the small metro areas.

4. The expanded use of at least ten of the 14 easiest and middling approaches is largely a product of local needs and initiatives, as well as of a growing awareness of their increasingly interdependent condition.

5. Jurisdictional fragmentation has not been reduced as a result of restructuring successes, but even incomplete forms of cooperation are useful. Such approaches are used extensively; in a majority of metro areas they are the only feasible forms of regional and subregional collaboration.

6. Like much else in the American system of metro governance, the overwhelming majority of interlocal and regional actions taken to resolve servicing and other problems reflect an ad hoc, generally issue-by-issue, incremental pattern of evolution. However, most of the major reorganizations were triggered, at least in part, by a visible crisis of some sort.

7. The intergovernmental bases of substate regional activities remain as significant as ever. The states, which always have played a significant part in the evolution of their metro areas, must move into a new primary role if the federal role in this arena continues to erode.

Our Snow White would be ever so happy if her Prince Charming would gallop up soon, wake her from the slumber induced by her stepmother, take her out of the forest and—please—make room in the palace for 17 hard-working dwarfs!

Bibliography

Advisory Commission on Intergovernmental Relations, *Intergovernmental Service Arrangements for Delivering Local Public*

Service: Update 1983 (A-103). Washington, D.C., October, 1985.

_____, *Pragmatic Federalism: The Reassignment of Functional Responsibility (M-105).* Washington, D.C., July, 1976.

_____, *Regional Decision Making: New Strategies for Substate Districts (A-43).* Washington, D.C., October, 1973.

_____, *State and Local Roles in the Federal System (A-88).* Washington, D.C., April, 1982.

Bollens, John C. and Schmandt, Henry J., *The Metropolis, Fourth Edition,* New York, N.Y., 1982.

Florestano, Patricia and Gordon, Stephen, "County and Municipal Use of Private Contracting for Public Service Delivery," *Urban Interest,* April, 1984.

Hatry, Harry P. and Valente, Carl F., "Alternative Service Delivery Approaches Involving Increased Use of the Private Sector," *The Municipal Year Book—1983.* International City Management Association, Washington, D.C., pp. 199-207.

Henderson, Lori, "Intergovernmental Service Arrangements and the Transfers of Functions," *Municipal Year Book—1985.* International City Management Association, Washington, D.C., pp. 194-202.

Jones, Victor, "Regional Councils and Regional Governments in the United States," paper presented at the Annual Meeting of the American Society for Public Administration, Detroit, 1981.

Marlin, John Tepper, ed., *Contracting Municipal Services: A Guide for Purchase from the Private Sector,* Ronald Press, John Wiley & Sons, New York, 1984, pp. 1-13.

McDowell, Bruce D., "Moving Toward Excellence in Regional Councils," based on a paper presented at the New England Regional Council Conference in Portland, Maine on October 26, 1984.

_____, "Regional Councils in an Era of Do-It-Yourself Federalism," a paper presented to the Regional Council Executive Directors of the Southeastern States," March 20, 1986.

_____, "Regions Under Reagan," a paper presented at the National Planning Conference, American Planning Association, Minneapolis-St. Paul, Minnesota, May 8, 1984.

National Association of Regional Councils, *Directory of Regional Councils, 85-86,* Washington, D.C.

_____, *Matrix of Regional Council Programs, 1985-86,* Washington, D.C.

_____, *Special Report—No. 91.* Washington, D.C., January, 1984.

U.S. Bureau of the Census, *Local Governments in Metropolitan Areas* (1982 Census of Governments, Vol. 5-GC82 (5)). Washington, D.C.

U.S. Senate, Committee on Governmental Affairs, Subcommittee on Intergovernmental Relations, *Metropolitan Regional Governance,* Hearing, February 6, 1984. Washington, D.C.

Wikstrom, Nelson, "Epitaph for a Monument to Another Successful Protest: Regionalism in Metropolitan Areas," *Virginia Social Science Journal,* Vol. 19, Winter 1984, pp. 1-10.

Wirt, Frederick M., "The Dependent City: External Influences upon Local Autonomy," paper delivered at the 1983 Annual Meeting of the American Political Science Association, September 1-4, 1983.

Would We Know a Well-Governed City If We Saw One?

Harry P. Hatry

Harry P. Hatry is director of the state and local government research program at The Urban Institute. This is based on his presentation at the National Conference on Government in Cincinnati, November 1985. Publication of this article is made possible in part by a grant from the Shell Companies Foundation.

WOULD we know a well-governed city if we saw one? How should a city be rated? Results are the key. First and foremost, there should be evidence that the city's services are "good," that is, that they produce good results. There should be evidence that the *quality of life* is high, at least relative to other cities with similar characteristics, and that residents by and large have been pleased with services for the last few years. Another consideration is the condition of the community's streets, bridges, water and sewer mains, and buildings.

Further, how equitable are the services? How does the government treat its disadvantaged and minorities? Do those residents, often living in less attractive sections of the city, also feel that they are receiving adequate services in terms of the condition and cleanliness of their streets, recreational opportunities, human services, police and fire protection, etc., services that have resulted in decent living conditions?

Have taxes (property, sales, etc.) been reasonable, indicating an *efficient* city. Has that government avoided periodic budget emergencies, had a high bond rating, and, based on fiscal indicators, demonstrated *fiscal strength*?

In these three key results criteria—service quality, equitableness and efficiency—to be fair the city should be compared to places similar in age, area of the country, and basic demographics.

Unfortunately, most communities throughout the United States collect little information on the first two major criteria, i.e., service quality and equitableness. Residents, the media, and even public officials themselves seldom see such information. Few communities are making regular efforts to measure service quality and equitableness, although in recent years there has been considerably more interest. A number of city and county governments is attempting to do a better job on this key element of accountability.

Given the absence of information on service quality and equitableness, substitute criteria are often used to assess whether a city is well-governed or not. The use of these criteria is less satisfying and can even be misleading since a city could meet most or all of them and still not be achieving good service results. These substitute criteria are the following:

1. **Tranquility and the absence of squabbles (at least in public) among public officials.** Observers probably look first for the absence of confrontation and negative headlines in the newspapers. Cities with active warfare between the mayor and council or between the mayor and various community groups would generally be dismissed as not being well-run. The absence of scandals, prosecutions or claims of corruption involving city officials would likely be a prerequisite to a positive appraisal.

2. **Stability/continuity in office of government officials.** Frequent turnover in the highest levels of management, such as the city manager and department heads, is a negative. (Caution: in some situations, the chief officials may be doing a fine job of selecting, training and developing personnel. In such instances, the city might have more turnover among middle- and upper-level managers who may be offered substantial promotions in other communities.)

3. **Innovativeness.** Ah, innovativeness! This seems to be a favorite of observers. The frequent introduction of new, unusual projects is often taken as a sign of top-notch communities. It suggests that the government is not just a follower but also a leader. Innovativeness is probably the key indicator for most awards to public officials and communities. Though innovativeness is a good sign, it seems important to determine that the innovations have endured and that they provide major benefits to the community—not just that a city implemented an innovation.

4. **Participative management.** Participative management goes back decades, but in recent years it has begun to take off, especially as our country has shifted to become much more of a service economy. Thus, city evaluators have begun to look for employee-oriented management, the presence of labor-management committees, or some version of these such as quality circles, and high morale among government employees. Note, however, that the link between employee satisfaction and effective production has not yet been clearly established. We still find situations where autocratic management appears to work well, at least under certain conditions.

5. **Active public-private partnerships.** This is a big thing these days, a favorite topic for the current federal administration. Indeed, for many years many communities have attempted to leverage government funds with private sector resources in development activities to make their cities at least more physically attractive. These days we look for public-private partnerships relating not only to the physical infrastructure and economic development but also to human service activities, including school systems.

6. **Analytical budgeting and planning.** City evaluators, particularly those with technical backgrounds, look for some form of advanced budgeting and planning process such as program budgeting, zero-based budgeting, strategic (multi-year) planning, and the like, as distinct from the classic, line-item budget approach. The assumption is that such a process will help the government focus on what's important, on both its short- and long-term objectives and how these can best be achieved, playing down nit-picking and avoiding seeing the trees while neglecting the forest.

7. **Citizen input into government decisions.** Since at least the early '60s, citizen input has more and more become a criterion for good government. The belief is that well-governed communities should use citizen advisory groups, neighborhood advisory boards, or other means for regularly and systematically obtaining input from citizens that helps government officials select programs and policies. We in the United States have begun to believe that citizen input during elections is not sufficient. Between elections, citizens (who after all are the clients for the services of government) should be given opportunities to provide inputs to our public officials. The danger here is that officials will become too responsive, especially to the demands of select groups in the community at the expense of others, and will abdicate some of their responsibilities.

Each of these characteristics is good in a community. A government can, however, provide considerable opportunity for citizen input and never

Reprinted by permission from the May/June 1986 issue of *National Civic Review*, pp. 142-146. National Civic Review, 1601 Grant Street, Suite 250, Denver, CO 80203.

use it, or get overly selective input. A government can have a fine budget process and not make good decisions with it. A government may be very innovative but never maintain its innovations for long or achieve real benefits. The government may be very tranquil and stable yet be doing the wrong things or doing the right things in the wrong way.

Unfortunately, in local, state and federal governments only a small proportion of agencies, perhaps 5 to 10 percent, regularly assess the extent to which they are getting value for their dollars. Cities, counties and states seldom systematically examine the cleanliness and ridability of their streets, assess whether their health and social services have led to significant improvements for clients, or ask their clients—the citizens—for feedback on the helpfulness, timeliness and quality of services they have received.

Even more surprising, few cities measure on a regular basis and in a systematic way the efficiency (i.e., the productivity) with which services are delivered. (Efficiency and productivity here mean the amount of dollars and hours of employee time spent to achieve the amount of output produced.) The Urban Institute recently examined management-by-objective systems in city, county and state agencies, seldom finding objectives relating to service quality or effectiveness, or to service efficiency, productivity or even cost reduction. (On occasion, a department manager had an objective to stay within the city manager's budget, but this is not much of an incentive to save money, at least not without lowering the level of service.)

Yes, cities do obtain complaint data, and most appear to respond to complaints and other calls from constituents. But many citizens don't know how to complain, don't like to complain, or don't feel it would do any good, and this applies especially to the disadvantaged in a community. Yes, many officials travel about their jurisdictions, speak with constituents, and obtain a perspective on service quality, but this can be highly unrepresentative of conditions that exist throughout the whole community. Only a small number of cities or counties currently conducts annual or biennial surveys in order to obtain citizens' ratings of services. In the private sector, businesses periodically do market surveys and seldom take customers for granted. Peters and Waterman in their popular work *In Search of Excellence* reported that being close to customers and having a corporate belief in delivering quality service seemed to be highly correlated with successful businesses. Should not this also be the case with governments?

Recently, the Boston *Globe* reprinted a series of articles it originally ran June 16-21, 1985, on "City Services: Does Boston Deliver?" A team of reporters using a series of measurement procedures (in part developed at The Urban Institute) interviewed citizens and rated such factors as street cleanliness and park condition to generate information on the quality of city services. The disappointing element is that a newspaper had to do the measurement. The government was not doing it. This is not to criticize Boston; most cities are in the same situation.

The well-governed city in the decade of the 1980s will necessarily concern itself with entrepreneurship and the greater use of the private sector by the public sector.

Public services, as economists remind us, have for the most part been monopolies: meaning no competition and, thus, little incentive for the organization to improve its efficiency or the quality of its services. This perhaps explains the lack of regular measurement of efficiency or service quality by governments. Since California's Proposition 13 in 1978 and the new administration in Washington since 1980, however, there is clearly a drive toward the greater use of the private sector and business to help deliver government services. Without getting into the philosophical arguments pro and con, this new drive can be turned to almost everyone's advantage.

Public officials will need to become more entrepreneurial, to look at a broader range of options, and to try new approaches. This does not have to mean privatization. City personnel, both management and non-management, spurred by the new private competition, could become more motivated to cooperate and overcome bureaucratic inefficiencies that handicap them in delivering services. In Phoenix and Minneapolis, for example, city personnel are effectively improving procedures to make government more competitive with private sector options. Public sector agencies and their unions are naturally greatly concerned and opposed to anything that smacks of privatization. The answer may be for public agencies to become more competitive and be able to demonstrate their ability to deliver services as well as private organizations. A well-governed city may be able to accomplish this (see also pages 147 and 153).

With the growing complexity of modern society, including environmental threats, continued high rates of crime, influx of immigrants and refugees, and higher expectations, the demands on our cities will continue to grow. Over the next decade our less well-governed cities will need to break through to become well-governed cities and our currently well-governed cities to become even more so.

THE URBAN STRANGLER

How Crime Causes Poverty in the Inner City

JAMES K. STEWART

JAMES K. STEWART *is director of the National Institute of Justice. He was formerly commander of criminal investigations in the Oakland Police Department and a White House Fellow.*

The idea that poverty causes crime goes back at least as far as Aristotle, who called poverty "the parent of revolution and crime." But in the American inner city, the relationship is exactly the reverse. Poverty doesn't cause crime. Crime causes poverty—or more precisely, crime makes it harder to break out of poverty. The vast majority of poor people are honest, law-abiding citizens whose opportunities for advancement are stunted by the drug dealers, muggers, thieves, rapists, and murderers who terrorize their neighborhoods. These predators are not Robin Hoods of some 1960s ideal; they are career criminals who are destroying the labor and hopes of the poor and they are as oppressive as the most avaricious totalitarian regime.

The most obvious way that criminals prey upon the poor is by robbing them of their property—and sometimes their lives. According to the Bureau of Justice Statistics, 9.6 percent of households with incomes of less than $7,500 were burglarized in 1984. This was the highest victimization rate in the country, nearly twice as high as for households in the $25,000 to $30,000 range, and the poorest also suffer the highest victimization rates for violent crimes. Households with incomes in the $7,500 to $14,999 range suffer the highest median economic losses from personal crimes, including robbery, assault, and theft. Since poor people often cannot afford insurance, and since personal property accounts for almost all of their capital, the theft of a TV, furniture, or car can be devastating. Robberies of cash or checks—for rent, welfare, or Social Security—may at one stroke eliminate a family's ability to pay for home, food, or future.

The typical criminal does not rob from the rich to aid the poor; he steals from the helpless to help himself. There's a routine on "Mother's Day"—the day every week when welfare checks arrive in the mail—of criminals extorting or stealing checks from welfare recipients or looting them from their mailboxes. Automatic deposits or safe deposit boxes aren't necessarily safer, since a criminal who knows your weekly income can collect on penalty of physical assault.

The less direct costs of crime to the poor may be even more destructive. The traditional means by which poor people have advanced themselves—overtime, moonlighting, or education to improve future opportunities—can easily be obstructed by crime and fear. Why risk a late job or night school if the return home means waiting at deserted bus stops and walking past crowds of threatening teenagers? A secretary declines overtime opportunities if they extend into the evening because she fears being robbed between the taxi and her front door. A husband gives up night school rather than leave his wife and young children alone at home.

Crime lowers property values in inner cities, making it harder for poor people to accumulate capital and borrow money. Studies in Chicago by Mario Rizzo and Barton A. Smith have shown that for every rise of one percent in the crime rate, rents and home values drop by 0.2 to 0.3 percent. The result is disastrous for families saving and scrimping to build up some modest capital; only by moving can they improve their lot.

Renters, of course, may benefit from the decline in property values, but their gain is only temporary. If landlords have no incentive to keep up maintenance on their properties, both the quality and quantity of housing stock will deteriorate and renters will lose in the end. The vast stretches of vacant buildings in the South Bronx are probably due as much to crime as to rent control; even if landlords could raise the rents, no one who could afford the increases would want to live there.

Similarly, crime can destroy even the most attractive public housing projects, turning them into catastrophes for their tenants. With their long hallways, lonely elevators and stairwells, and absence of street life, public housing high-rises trap and deliver victims to their criminal predators; often they are more treacherous breeding grounds of crime than the squalid tenements they replaced. It was largely because of crime that the Pruitt-Igoe housing complex in St. Louis became uninhabitable and had to be demolished. The Cabrini-Green apartments in Chicago remain in use, but they are ridden with fear.

 Reprinted from *Policy Review*, Summer 1986, pp. 6-10. Policy Review, published by The Heritage Foundation. Reprinted by permission.

Crime strangles commerce and industry in the inner city, and therefore makes it harder for poor people to get jobs. Wherever people are afraid, the market cannot be free. And the high crime rates of poor neighborhoods prevent their residents from taking full advantage of the employment opportunities offered by America's market economy.

A number of economic features ought to attract capital to revive inner cities. Most poor neighborhoods are located in or near the center of our cities and therefore should be prime locations for commerce. The inner city usually provides easy access to railheads, highways, water, and power, as well as to a ready labor supply. It already has the infrastructure that is often missing from the suburbs and exurbs.

But crime in these neighborhoods builds a hurdle to economic development that investors cannot leap. As one recent National Institute of Justice study reports, crime and the *fear* of crime can influence entrepreneurs' investment decisions more than high taxes or labor costs. Crime is one of the major reasons why businesses restrict operations, relocate, sell, or close down. The Bronx was once an industrial center for injection molders in the plastics industry; crime was one of two main pressures (the other was energy costs) that drove the industry out.

A Buffalo business owner recently testified before Congress about a string of burglaries that had driven his father into early retirement. He said burglars stole "whatever they can get their hands on . . . Thanksgiving weekend they got us for about $3,000 worth of chicken products. . . . We have two separate alarm systems in our building and they are still getting it. We have fenced it in. We had guard dogs, two of them. They are cutting our fences at night and letting them out. It just never ends. This year alone we must have lost about $20,000 worth of products."

For those who stay in business, a high crime rate sharply raises operating costs. Another inner city Buffalo businessman removes the office equipment from his premises every night because of repeated burglaries. Added operating costs include insurance, which may become prohibitively expensive or even unavailable, and security investments, such as improved lighting and fencing. A typical inner city business might pay about $5,000 for a simple audible alarm system and $10,000 per year for a private security guard's salary. Such expenses can jeopardize the survival of small businesses—the strongest engine of employment growth.

Businesses in crime-ridden neighborhoods also may face higher labor costs to compensate employees for the higher risk of working there—or they may find it difficult to attract any employees at all. According to a study of two inner city Chicago neighborhoods funded by the National Institute of Justice, several industrialists were unable to staff additional shifts because of employees' fears for their safety.

Perhaps the most serious threat to business is that customers and suppliers are scared away. The Chicago study noted that "more than half of the businessmen in both neighborhoods reported that some or all of their suppliers had complained of feeling unsafe in the area." Cargo thefts were a familiar event, in which thieves "broke open the back door of the truck and quickly removed the cargo while the driver was stopped at a traffic light or waiting to deliver the goods at an alley loading dock." Auto theft from places of business was also common in these neighborhoods, including the theft of one customer's car while parked directly in front of the plant during a short business meeting.

Criminal Recycling Centers

Criminals can tyrannize poor neighborhoods because they are not significantly threatened by the criminal justice system. Only 20 percent of reported crimes are ever solved. And a large proportion of crimes—especially in poor neighborhoods—are never reported. Among households with incomes of less than $7,500, only 40 percent of burglaries and fewer than one-third of all household crimes are ever reported. In poor neighborhoods, people are usually reluctant to turn someone in, call the police, or testify in court. Their reticence is understandable, for local justice policy quickly releases criminal suspects and then delays their trials for months. Victims and key witnesses are therefore exposed to opportunities for intimidation by criminals or their confederates.

In addition, many inner city residents lack confidence in a criminal justice system that recycles convicted felons back into the community where they continue to prey upon victims. Fewer than 30 percent of those convicted of violent crimes and serious property crimes are sentenced to prison. Seventy percent are sent back into the community on "felony probation," a status which leaves them virtually without supervision. The majority of those on felony probation (65 percent) are rearrested for similar crimes within three years.

Because the poor have little or no mobility, there is no escape from these predators or from the totalitarianism of crime. Where criminal enterprises such as narcotics dealing, prostitution, and numbers are the chief income-producing activities, they choke off the growth of legal enterprises, while generating even greater numbers of related crimes in the community. And the street crime typical of poor neighborhoods—robbery, assault, larceny, burglary, drug dealing and use—has a profoundly debilitating effect on the economy.

A recent joint report by the Citizens' Crime Commission of New York City and the Regional Plan Association noted that the two "primary fears of pedestrians in urban public spaces" are "the fear of being suddenly and violently attacked by a stranger and the fear of being bothered by panhandlers, drunks, addicts, rowdy teenagers, loiterers, the mentally disturbed, and other disorderly people." The latter fear—the fear of what James Q. Wilson has termed "incivilities"—may be as powerful as the fear of more serious crime. Abusive or insulting language, harassment, drug use and sale, public drinking, and loitering teenagers are often interpreted as signs of more serious potential crime.

Of course, a panhandler who stands in front of the same store every day, a mentally ill person shouting at passersby, or a group of teenagers hanging out on a street corner are probably not plotting a crime. But when disorderly behavior reaches a certain density on the street, there is less of a deterrent to antisocial behavior. People feel insecure about working, shopping, eating, or strolling in the area. In Jamaica Center, in Queens, New York, a survey of office workers found that 60 percent left their buildings at lunchtime no more than once a week. Fifty-four percent avoided going through the local park during the day, even though it would have been more convenient to do so.

Such acts of avoidance eventually isolate people and empty out public places. They suggest how predatory crime and fear can damage the community in a way that extends far beyond personal injury and loss. As James Q. Wilson has observed:

> Predatory crime does not merely victimize individuals, it impedes and in the extreme case, even prevents the formation and maintenance of community. [It disrupts] the delicate nexus of ties, formal and informal, by which we are linked with our neighbors.

Neighborhood deterioration usually starts with an increased sense of fear and vulnerability. Commerce slows; people go elsewhere to shop and stay off the streets in the evening; stores put in alarms and bars in the windows; going-out-of-business sales increase, and as businesses change hands, the quality of merchandise declines and prices rise. Buildings get shabbier and some are abandoned. Disorderly street behavior increases. Investments and loans dry up. People who can afford to move out of the area do; schools deteriorate; and the whole community slides down the spiral of economic and social decline.

No urban redevelopment program can arrest the decline of inner city neighborhoods unless it is accompanied by a sharp reduction in crime. Billions of federal anti-poverty dollars have been poured into depressed inner cities without reviving them economically. The reason is that the people who live and work there are afraid and cannot make the most of the opportunities offered them. The natural dynamic of the marketplace cannot assert itself when a local economy is regulated by crime.

Enterprise zones will be no more successful in reviving inner cities unless they make security a top priority. Tax breaks can influence business locations, but they are of no avail to the company that cannot make a profit because its employees won't work overtime and its customers are afraid to visit. Crime is the ultimate tax on enterprise. It must be reduced or eliminated before poor people can fully share in the American dream.

Eradicating the Parasite

The best anti-poverty policy is a vigorous attack on crime in poor communities. Yellow fever was finally cured when attention was shifted from treating the dying patients to controlling the mosquito that carried the disease. Likewise, inner cities can be restored to economic health if we eradicate the parasite that infects them—crime.

A number of experiments around the country show that the spiral of commercial decline in a crime-ridden neighborhood can be stopped. The key is a dramatic reduction in crime.

In the early 1970s, a 40-block area in the East Brooklyn neighborhood of New York was home to about 200 businesses employing 3,000 people. But the area was deteriorating. By 1979, the number of businesses had fallen to 45, and they employed 1,500 people. The overwhelming reason given by businesses for leaving the neighborhood was fear of crime.

This is a familiar story of decline. A similar one could be told of neighborhoods in virtually every major American city. But in East Brooklyn Industrial Park, there is a surprising sequel. Between 1980 and 1982, the number of burglaries in the 40-block area fell from 134 to 12, the number of street robberies from 208 to 62. Signs of commercial vitality appeared. Twenty new firms have moved into the area and at least 40 others have expressed interest. A new office building of 60,000 square feet is under construction and other buildings are being renovated.

These and other changes were the fruit of a project by a private development company to increase security in the neighborhood. Working in collaboration with the New York City Public Development Corporation and the police and fire departments, the Local Development Corporation of East New York tore down abandoned buildings, fenced properties, put in burglar alarms, trained private security guards, patrolled the area, provided escort services for residents and businesses—and succeeded in persuading local businesses and residents to help pay for the project. The city contributed by repairing streets and putting in new lighting.

In Oakland, a security program was initiated in 1982 by a group of private developers. Clorox and IBM are among the major tenants of Bramalea Corporation properties who contribute about $300,000 annually to provide for a police enhancement program of the 40-block downtown business district. The program increased the police foot patrol in the area and added a mounted patrol, as well as more motorbike and motorscooter patrols—which create a greater sense of protection and accessibility to police than car patrol. The program also made a well publicized effort to curtail incivilities and disorderly behavior in the neighborhood.

Property crimes, which dropped nine percent citywide from 1982 to 1983, fell by 20 percent in this central area. Declines in strongarm robbery, purse snatchings, commercial burglary, and auto theft were particularly dramatic. But more important than the drop in crime was the greater sense of security and confidence people felt, indicated by the larger flow of orderly pedestrian traffic. One local businessman commented, "I don't hear about muggings any more." A bank manager noted that use of the bank's cafeteria dropped significantly (suggesting more workers were going out to eat in the neighborhood), and merchants reported greater lunchtime shopping by employees.

The improved security has been decisive in attracting and retaining businesses. IBM came into the neighborhood on the basis of the security program. One business owner noted, "If we didn't have the foot patrol and increased police presence downtown, I wouldn't be in business in Oakland."

A project in Portland, Oregon, to improve the security of the Union Avenue commercial strip also led to a significant reduction in commercial burglary, following improvements in street lighting and store security. Reversing a period of decline, businessmen reported that gross sales were holding steady or even increasing since the lighting and security changes.

Improved security is also the key to a remarkably successful urban project in Watts. The riots that destroyed parts of the Los Angeles community 20 years ago wiped

Poverty doesn't cause crime. Crime causes poverty—or more precisely, crime makes it harder to break out of poverty.

out marginal businesses and appeared to have killed off new business growth. New enterprises could not take root because crime made people unwilling to work, shop, or make deliveries in the area. Investors wouldn't touch the neighborhood, even with the prospect of capturing the market, because of the low customer traffic and risks of high losses.

> # Crime is the ultimate tax on enterprise. It must be reduced or eliminated before poor people can fully share in the American dream.

The first commercial enterprise of any kind to be built since the riots was the Martin Luther King, Jr. Shopping Center, which opened in 1984 at a location formerly called "Charcoal Alley" as a result of its fiery devastation in the riots. Estimated first year sales were about $45 million, or about $350 per leasable square foot—more than three times the average revenues of first-year shopping centers.

Though it was built in one of the most violent and crime-ridden areas of the city, no major acts of violence or vandalism have occurred there. "The success of the shopping center shows that you can make money and create jobs here without fear of the stereotype that says you can't do business in the ghetto because of crime," said Dr. Clyde Oden, a Watts physician who is president of the Watts Health Foundation.

Built by Alexander Haagen Development, the shopping center is designed to be an oasis of security where businesses can function and customers can do their banking and shopping without fear. The entire facility is surrounded by a wrought-iron fence like the one surrounding the White House. Inside there is a control center with closed circuit TV monitors. Private security guards trained by the developer patrol the shopping center 24 hours a day, and the center also has a Los Angeles Police field office.

The center has created jobs for local residents through its private security program as well as its stores. In the words of Grace Payne, executive director of a neighborhood job training and community counseling center, construction of the mall is "the greatest move that has been made for the people in this community to have jobs." Four smaller shopping centers have subsequently opened in the area.

Stimulating new business growth is the aim of a community redevelopment program initiated in 1984 by Pfizer

Corporation in the Williamsburg section of Brooklyn. One of the world's largest pharmaceutical companies, Pfizer operates a production and packaging plant in Williamsburg. It once shared the neighborhood with a number of breweries and other businesses. But by the mid-1970s, crime and the flight of area businesses had contributed to serious environmental decay. Buildings made unprofitable by vandalism and rent control were abandoned. People who could afford to, moved away, intensifying the poverty in the neighborhood. Crime was "the number one problem facing the plant that might have forced us out," according to Pfizer plant manager Tom Kline.

But Pfizer didn't want to leave Brooklyn, where it was founded 130 years ago. Instead, it embarked on a program to reduce crime and help redevelop the area. The company's goal is to attract seven manufacturing companies, employing 700 people, within five to seven years; some preliminary commitments have already been received. Pfizer's redevelopment plan also includes the building of 100 new two-family homes for owner-occupancy with rental units, to be built by private developers with assistance from city agencies.

Meanwhile, the Public Development Corporation of New York, with the assistance of Pfizer, has bulldozed, cleaned up rubbish, and fenced 100 lots in a five-block radius around the plant; Pfizer has invested in cameras and intercoms for the local subway platform. The city has provided another anchor business two blocks from Pfizer by opening a 400-bed hospital employing 2,300 people.

Real Social Security

The programs in Brooklyn, Oakland, Portland, and Watts show that, if security is provided, businesses can take root in even the most hostile environment. Reducing crime and its disruptive effect on community ties eliminates the largest and most devastating obstacle to development in many poor neighborhoods. And where businesses can develop, they encourage further growth and help create a community's cohesiveness and identity.

Crime is a hazard to everyone in our society, but it hurts the poor the most; the wealthy and the middle class can call upon private and community resources to cushion them from some of its dangers. The first step in any urban anti-poverty program must therefore begin with the reduction of crime. This means more vigorous prosecution of predatory criminals and more vigorous protection of people in poor neighborhoods. America is beginning to take the steps necessary to fight terrorism overseas; the time has come to fight the even more threatening terrorism in our own cities.

■ MANDELA REFERENDUM

Blacks in Boston Seek to Secede

ROGER HOUSE

Roger House is a staff writer for The Providence Journal/
Bulletin.

While Michael Dukakis does his best to downplay issues of race and class in the campaign debate, black communities in the capital city of his home state have proposed to secede and create a new Massachusetts city called Mandela, both as a practical response to the encroachments of speculators and gentrifiers and as a symbolic statement that race and class tensions in Boston are too ingrained ever to allow the comprehensive changes needed to bring about black empowerment and equality. Community residents will consider secession on November 8, when they vote on a non-binding referendum question.*

The movement for Mandela—after imprisoned South African leader Nelson Mandela—is an attempt by people at the grass roots to take control of their own affairs, and a declaration of the failure of integration and the liberal mentality behind it. But the significance of the secession proposal reverberates beyond Boston because the racism and neglect that have given rise to Mandela reflect the black-white tensions of inner cities throughout the country.

Mandela would contain a quarter of Boston's present population: Two-thirds would be black, one-quarter white

*On 8 November 1988, voters in six state legislative districts in Boston voted against "instructing" their state representatives to work for the creation of "Mandela." Of those voting on the issue, the proposal lost by a margin of about 2 to 1. The same proposal had been defeated by a margin of about 3 to 1 in November, 1986.

and the rest Latino and Asian, making it the most ethnically diverse city in Massachusetts. It would also be the only city in the state with a largely black population and political leadership. The new city would cover 12.5 square miles, or about one-quarter the land area of Boston, incorporating the central city neighborhoods of Roxbury, Lower Roxbury, Mattapan, Columbia Point, the Fenway and parts of Dorchester, the South End and Jamaica Plain. Downtown, Mandela would include the *Boston Globe* offices, the Boston Museum of Fine Arts, Northeastern University, Harvard Medical School and the Bay State Expo Center.

A tour of the wide commercial avenues in the area finds boarded-up apartment buildings, vacant lots littered with debris, check-cashing offices and other markers of urban destitution. But along the shady side streets are the features that appeal to speculators: Victorian houses with large yards and a view of the downtown skyline, small parks, historic cemeteries and landmarks dating back to the Pilgrims.

Ninety percent of Boston's black population lives in this section of the city, but skyrocketing housing and land values threaten to displace many families and convert the central Boston area to an affluent, predominantly white sector. In Roxbury, the hub of Mandela, one-bedroom apartments that were renting for $400 in 1985 are renting for $700 today; three-bedroom houses that were selling for $60,000 in 1985 are selling easily for $230,000 today. The boom in real estate is linked to Boston's expanding high-tech economy, the "Massachusetts Miracle" to some but a hoax to most black residents, who have been left out of the high-tech job market and are being pushed out of their homes by those benefiting from the tight housing market. This development has led secession advocates to contend that for black residents, "Mandela is the miracle of Massachusetts."

Although gentrification has hit nearly all of Boston's

ethnic neighborhoods, the black community is acutely affected because of the city's history of segregation. For the past forty years black residents have been restricted to central Boston neighborhoods through discriminatory rental and sales tactics and the brute force of urban renewal. The low rate of home ownership among black residents further compounds the problem. About 80 percent of the people in Roxbury rent, often from landlords outside the community.

The present housing crisis is only the latest assault against Boston's black community. Residents vividly recall the urban renewal process of the 1960s, which displaced most blacks from the South End in a series of razings initially touted as a means of improving the neighborhood. They remember the white community's vicious opposition to busing in the 1970s, and they lay the increase in crime in their neighborhoods over the years to the city's failure to police drug dealers in public buildings. Blacks say that city officials often encouraged white residents' opposition to school and neighborhood desegregation and argue that the city has tacitly condoned the banks' redlining of black neighborhoods.

The economic indicators tell another part of the story. In the area that would be Mandela, the unemployment rate is' about 20 percent. Some 30.5 percent of the families in Roxbury live below the poverty line, compared with 16.7 percent in the rest of the city. The neighborhood's per capita income level is about $2,300 less than Boston's overall average of $6,555. Some schools in the community have dropout rates of 50 percent, and activists say the mainly white teaching staffs are out of touch with the needs of black students.

This litany of woes highlights a structural condition that the new city of Mandela could not hope to reverse, at least in the short term. But the statistics do present, powerfully, the symbolic argument for secession: Roxbury and the surrounding areas are strongholds of the underclass, and in moving to secede from Boston that underclass is rejecting the legitimacy of white power, business as usual and a gradualist approach to equality.

"Control of land and territory for black people in the 1980s and 1990s is what jobs creation was in the 1960s," says Andrew Jones, a professional musician who lives in Roxbury. "America today has little concern for social justice or economic inclusion. In the 1990s, the black community that is unable to control its territory will not be able to survive. Mandela represents a logical extension of the civil rights movement, with a new approach to the goals of integration. This is not an attempt at militant separatism but the positive creation of the most integrated city in New England under a predominantly black power structure."

Jones, along with Curtis Davis, an architect for the state, founded the Greater Roxbury Incorporation Project (GRIP) two years ago for the purpose of putting the idea of secession to area voters. A first referendum was defeated, 57 percent to 20 percent, but GRIP is trying again, with a more developed plan and the help of another grass-roots group, Project FATE, for Focusing Attitudes Towards Empowerment. Their secession project has won the support of Byron Rushing and Gloria Fox, the black state representatives of

the Roxbury area, and of former state representative Mel King, who ran unsuccessfully for mayor in 1983 and who publicly discussed the possibility of secession in the 1960s.

GRIP and Project FATE contend that municipal incorporation will primarily give black residents the power to confront the community's housing crisis. With publicly owned land and buildings available for housing development, they say, the cost of construction and, consequently, the price of housing would be significantly reduced. A tax on new commercial property and on the profits of speculators would generate revenues to be put toward affordable housing, allowing realtors and speculators some profit while offsetting the inflationary effect of private development on neighborhood housing values.

Mandela sponsors would also raise land property taxes but cut building taxes. Large landholders would thus pay more whatever the condition of the buildings but, along with small owners, would no longer be financially penalized for making improvements. Furthermore, landlords would receive tax incentives for substantially improving deteriorating buildings and passing on to low-income tenants a modest share of the renovation costs. Proponents of Mandela also propose to institute rent control laws.

Boston Mayor Raymond Flynn and those black leaders opposed to Mandela argue that the best hope for the black community lies in positive change within the system. They point to Flynn's actions on housing development and neighborhood reinvestment; his Fair Housing Commission, which seeks to prohibit redlining; his embrace of affirmative action; and his openness to the views of black leaders.

Mandela supporters generally appreciate Flynn's efforts at a politics of inclusion, but such efforts hardly require gratitude; rightfully they should be part of any mayor's job. What's more, focusing on the support of Boston's chief executive ignores reality in at least two ways. First, municipal power is spread across an unsympathetic City Council, school board and bureaucracy, and across a business and labor community that is outside Flynn's influence. For example, although Flynn has supported a program for the integration of public housing in white areas, one City Councilman is rallying his community to oppose the program, saying that it discriminates against poor whites. The racism that so pits blacks and whites with similar class interests against one another is the second, rock-bottom reality.

Blacks on either side of the issue have been careful in their criticisms, not liking to display disunity to Boston whites. "While Mandela has shed light on the black community's problems and gotten people involved, what the activists are offering are promises," says the Rev. Mickarl Thomas, pastor of the Charles Street A.M.E. Church. "Mayor Flynn is offering concrete changes and access. We don't want to lose that." In this respect, Thomas and other black mainstream leaders agree with a spokesman for Flynn who pointed out that although black activists would like to see radical change, the reality is that political and business empowerment is "a process and not an event."

Planning a city can hardly be described as an "event," though, especially since even if the referendum is approved November 8, it would take years for the measure to pass through the Massachusetts Legislature and years more for the new city to be finally created. What is at issue here is fundamentally a philosophical matter.

"Our mainstream leaders are suffering from a pathology of doubt, and are unable to imagine a city where black people govern themselves," Jones says. He and fellow Mandela advocates argue that those leaders are retarded in their political development because of their position in the white establishment. With the development of a black middle class and skilled work force, they say, it is time for the people to set the pace for their "leaders." Indeed, a recent *Boston Globe* survey shows residents identify the activists as legitimate community leaders in greater numbers than they do the traditional black representatives. Still, the activists cannot dismiss the result of the 1986 referendum or the objections of people like Ronald Homer, president of the black-owned Boston Bank of Commerce, who asserts that then "the man on the street was saying he doesn't want to create a new city."

The low rate of black voter participation and an aggressive misinformation campaign waged by City Hall both contributed to that result. Furthermore, many voters opted to withhold their support until they could learn more about the impact of secession. GRIP notes that 14,000 of the 60,000 who cast ballots left the referendum question blank. To recruit supporters this time, activists have been educating voters, explaining the proposal through the media, door-to-door visits and neighborhood forums. They have also dealt more seriously with practical aspects of the plan, having sought technical assistance from the Lincoln Land Institute in Cambridge on public finance strategies and from the University of Massachusetts in Boston on the black community's prospects for economic growth.

One of GRIP's more intriguing ideas involves the acquisition of municipal buildings; equipment like police cruisers and fire trucks, schoolbooks and chairs; and even money and debt from Boston. Many of these items would come from the "divorce settlement" of Boston's assets, an issue that would surely be decided by the courts were the referendum to win. GRIP reasons that historically the Mandela area has contributed through its labor and its tax dollars to the development of Boston. Therefore, residents of the proposed Mandela, like a partner in a divorce, have equity in Boston's property and a right to ask Boston to divide its assets. City officials decline even to discuss the possibility.

GRIP recognizes the weaknesses in its overall plan, particularly with respect to improving essential services. Advocates have been unable to draw up a budget for the estimated cost of sanitation, police and fire services, saying that Boston will not release the number of man-hours, equipment needs and maintenance costs of providing such services within the borders of the proposed city. Boston says it does not maintain that kind of information. As for running the school system, the Boston School Department depends largely on state and Federal money, and those funds are calculated according to the economic need of students. Barring a drastic and discriminatory change in the criteria for distribution, Mandela would inherit a large part of the subsidy now going to Boston. But Boston officials argue that those funds have been won through hard lobbying and that Mandela proponents should not bet on receiving much of Boston's share.

"Mandela would be a poor city, dependent on state funds," warns Ronald Homer, alluding to the problems of economic development and the possibility of a white political and business backlash if Mandela becomes a reality. The statements of city and state officials about preventing Mandela from inheriting Boston subsidies and the like could be interpreted as veiled threats, and there is the potential for white business flight from the proposed city. Advocates admit the possibilities but view the backlash argument largely as a scare tactic. Mandela could successfully challenge in court any discriminatory changes in the way state subsidies are distributed, they say, and the new city's prime location, growth of the area economy and lack of available land nearby insure a relatively stable commercial base. According to GRIP, any backlash would occur during the early phase of municipal incorporation and involve small businesses that could move easily; large companies have too much capital invested in the area to relocate capriciously. And the flight would stop once businesses realized that the new city was not a threat. Mandela would also aggressively recruit businesses—particularly minority companies—to set up shop.

Whatever one thinks of secession and the efficacy of such procedural politics for dealing with structural problems, the concept, especially in a symbolic sense, does pose a serious challenge to the community, the city and even the country. Twenty years after the civil rights movement, America remains a land of deep racial and class tensions. At the very least the debate over Mandela forces blacks and whites in Boston to confront that issue in their city. For blacks, the debate offers a healthy exercise in grass-roots democracy and a chance to assess their current status and future role in society. Whether they ultimately decide to secede, blacks can only benefit from a process that encourages practical thinking about local control, social justice and the means to achieve them.

Finances and Economic Development

- **Revenues (Articles 41-43)**
- **Economic Development (Articles 44-46)**

Like all governments, state and local governments need financial resources to carry out their activities. State and local governments rely on a variety of revenue sources, including sales taxes, income taxes, and property taxes; user charges (for example, motor vehicle registration fees and college tuition); lotteries; and grants of money from other levels of government. But despite this diversity of funding sources, the overall financial situation of state and local governments is often far from satisfactory.

Conspicuous attempts to curb spending at all levels of government have been made in recent years. Most prominent among such measures was Proposition 13, passed by California voters in a 1978 referendum. Proposition 13 put ceilings on local government property taxes and, in turn, affected the programs that local governments in California could offer. The Proposition 13 tax revolt soon spread to other states. By now, measures designed to limit government spending have come into effect in states and localities across the country. At the national level, a constitutional amendment has been proposed and legislation has been passed in attempts to make it difficult for Congress to pass an unbalanced budget.

Unlike the national government, state and local governments get a sizable portion of their revenues from intergovernmental grants. The national government gives money to state and local governments with various conditions attached. Money can be given with virtually no accompanying "strings" or with considerable limitations on how it can be spent. Similarly, states provide state aid to local governments under varying sets of conditions. Governments providing financial grants, of course, exercise control over the amount of funds available and the conditions attached to such funds. This, in turn, can cause considerable uncertainty for governments relying on grant money. As should be apparent, intergovernmental relations and state and local finances are areas which overlap considerably.

The financial situation of state and local governments differs from that of the national government in other important respects. The national government has considerable ability to affect the national economy by controlling the money supply and by budgetary deficits or, at least in

theory, budgetary surpluses. By contrast, most state and local governments are legally required to balance their budgets. For those not required to have balanced budgets, it is difficult to borrow money for large and persistent budget deficits. The fiscal crises of New York City and other local governments during the 1970s showed that lenders will go only so far in providing money for state and local governments whose expenditures are consistently greater than their revenues.

Both the national government and state and local governments seek to promote economic development. New industries employ workers who pay taxes and thus increase government revenues. What is new on the state and local scene is the energy and persistence with which states and localities compete with one another to attract industries to their areas.

Finances are a complicated but critical aspect of state and local government. The first section of this unit treats taxes, lotteries, and related revenue-raising matters. The second section focuses on economic development activities by state and local governments.

Looking Ahead: Challenge Questions

Approximately how much money do you (or your parents, if you are not a full-time wage-earner) annually pay to local, state, and national governments, respectively? Is this an easy question to answer? Why or why not?

Property tax, a tax on the value of real estate and buildings, is a primary source of revenue for local governments. Do you think people who live in rented apartments or houses avoid property taxes? Why or why not?

Why do you think that the national government has assumed more and more of the burden for raising revenues for all three levels of government?

What do you think is the best means for state and local governments to raise revenues: property taxes, income taxes, sales taxes, lotteries, user charges, or something else?

Do you think that measures such as Proposition 13 in California and Proposition 2 1/2 in Massachusetts are desirable? Why or why not?

The Quake Didn't Quit

Ten years ago, Californians started a nationwide tax revolt by adopting Proposition 13. Now they may ease the spending limits, but the cross-country aftershocks continue.

JERRY HAGSTROM
AND NEAL R. PEIRCE

SACRAMENTO—Ten years ago this June, Californians set off a nationwide governmental earthquake with Proposition 13, the initiative that swallowed the Golden State's property tax increases. Moving eastward, the tax revolt soon smothered property and income tax rates and over-all state and local spending across 50 states and set the fiscal tone for the Reagan presidency.

Now, a decade later, millions of California voters appear to have tired of rutted highways, poorly performing schools and other fruits of government on the cheap. Practically everyone agrees that Proposition 13 checked runaway government spending and triggered long-overdue economies, but public opinion polls suggest that many Californians now believe enough is enough. Chances are relatively bright for at least one measure on the June 7 primary ballot that would release the state from some of the strictest spending limits.

Political liberals and unionized public workers who were rattled by Proposition 13 and its aftershocks should not rejoice too quickly, however. Even its strongest critics now say that the tax revolt movement has earned a respectable—and seemingly permanent—place on the political landscape and represents one of the major U.S. political movements of the 20th century. And this year, antitax activists in several other western states are gathering signatures for new initiatives, whether California backslides or not.

Proposition 13's chief proponents still defend it, even if a principal effect has been to undermine local control by shifting decision making from city councils, county supervisors and school boards to the state Capitol here. "I'm very proud to have been part of Proposition 13," Paul Gann, one of its authors, recently told

California Journal. "I think that the thing we were trying to say was, number one, to make it possible for people to retain their homes. Number two was that we want less government, not more government."

"Proposition 13 has in large measure done what it was supposed to do—suppress the sharp increase in property taxation that was occurring and make pressures tighter on local budgets," said state Sen. Quentin Kopp, an independent who backed it as a member of San Francisco's Board of Supervisors.

Even public-sector unions that originally saw Proposition 13 as the devil's work incarnate now put forth a more sophisticated analysis of why it and its clones were passed. "The tax revolt is the wrong answer to the right question, 'Why are my taxes so high?' " said Iris J. Lav, assistant director for economic policy of the American Federation of State, County and Municipal Employees (AFSCME), the biggest labor union representing public workers. Often, tax revolts are a legitimate signal that something is dramatically wrong with a state's or locality's tax structure or government performance, Lav said. In retrospect, she said, Proposition 13 seems to have been more a reaction to unfairly high local property taxes and to the state's budget surpluses than an indiscriminate attack on government and unions. And this year's tax limitation campaigns in Colorado, Montana, Oregon, South Dakota and Utah, she said, reflect severe economic problems in states that depend on tax receipts from the ailing energy, mining and timber industries.

Property taxes remain the most important source of local government finance. But they have declined as a percentage of per capita income in nearly every state, according to the Tax Foundation in Washington. In their place have come higher

sales tax rates, increased dependence on state income taxes and a host of ingenious user fees and nuisance taxes.

Twenty states have imposed state spending or revenue limits since 1977 through initiatives or legislative action. Proposition 2½ in Massachusetts, which was passed in 1980 to curb high property taxes, helped bury that state's "Taxachusetts" reputation.

Perhaps more important, the mere threat of a revolt in other states helped hold down tax rates and government spending. "The tax revolt did have a lot of effect beyond the states that had initiatives," said Steven D. Gold, director of fiscal studies for the National Conference of State Legislatures (NCSL). "It's been tougher to raise taxes in this decade than in the '60s or '70s."

Proposition 13 also foreshadowed the popularity of Ronald Reagan's anti-inflation, antigovernment presidential campaign in 1980. And a case can be made that the distrust of official decision making shown in the initiatives ultimately surfaced in the 1985 Balanced Budget Act, which authorized automatic spending cuts, if needed, to meet deficit-cutting targets.

Like that federal law, many of the states' tax cut measures have loopholes and exceptions. But even when modifications prove necessary, the public still seems to support such measures. "People are willing to tax themselves, willing to spend more public funds," said Roger King, a lobbyist for the County Supervisors Association of California. "But they want to know exactly what it's for because they don't trust the politicians that make those decisions."

CALIFORNIA CASE

No other state's tax revolt has been as

dramatic as California's. But then, no other state's tax crisis was as big. In the 1970s, the value of homes in California skyrocketed as a result of inflation and relentless demand for housing. Local officials made no real effort to reduce property tax rates, and by 1978, California's property tax bills were denounced as 50 per cent higher than the national average. The Legislature, meanwhile, was sitting on a massive surplus but seemed unable to devise a tax reduction scheme.

Then Gann and fellow Los Angeles businessman Howard Jarvis came up with Proposition 13. (Jarvis, who died in 1986, had a belligerent battle cry: "Death and taxes are inevitable. But being taxed to death is not inevitable!") Frustrated home owners quickly embraced its simple, straightforward provisions to reduce property taxes to 1 per cent of market value based on 1975 assessments (later changed to 1979 assessments) unless the property is sold. The measure also made it very difficult to impose new taxes at the local or state level.

California's establishment—from the Bank of America to labor unions to leading newspapers to the League of Women Voters—opposed Proposition 13. But it brought out 6.6 million voters, almost 750,000 more than the 1976 presidential primary attracted, and 64.8 per cent of them voted yes.

Under Proposition 13's mandate, property tax bills were slashed by 57 per cent, and cities, counties and school boards lost $7 billion in property tax revenue. Then-Gov. Edmund G. (Jerry) Brown Jr. declared himself a "born-again tax cutter" and began to work frantically with the Legislature to distribute $4 billion of the surplus to cities, counties and school boards. The Legislature also cut state taxes by $1 billion and indexed the state income tax so that inflation would not lift taxpayers into higher tax brackets.

Even that was not enough. In 1979, amid fears that high inflation could still fuel increases in government spending, Gann collected signatures for another initiative, Proposition 4, which was passed easily. It limited state, county and local spending by a formula based on the U.S. inflation rate, plus an adjustment for population growth.

A decade after the tax cuts began, a range of studies have painted a fairly clear picture of what's happened to California. State and local tax revenue per $1,000 of personal income fell from No. 4 in the nation in 1976 to No. 25 in 1986. According to the Tax Foundation, California property tax bills rose only 8.2 per cent from 1976-86 compared with a national average of 74 per cent—and a high of 286 per cent in the District of Columbia. California's property tax collections, ranked by $1,000 of personal income, fell from No. 4 in the nation to No. 32.

The impact on schools was dramatic: Per-pupil spending declined, dropping California from No. 21 in the nation in 1977 to No. 26 in 1988, and class size rose to the largest in the 50 states. And, in this state where people are almost totally dependent on the automobile for local transportation, per capita highway spending slipped to No. 50 in the nation.

County officials believe that of all units of government, they have suffered the most under Proposition 13. Under California law, counties must administer and partly pay for state programs as "providers of last resort" for those who need public aid or medical care. Since 1972, the state has been required to pay for programs that it orders local governments to deliver, but county officials contend that the Legislature ducks its obligation by not fully reimbursing the counties.

Before Proposition 13, counties helped pay for mandated programs by increasing property taxes. But since Proposition 13, county officials say, they have had to find the money by slashing other programs. The two major trouble-causing mandates, they say, are welfare and criminal justice. Despite the strong growth of California's economy, welfare caseloads have risen because of depressed conditions in some rural areas and the continuing migration of poor people from other states and other countries. And every level of government has felt the impact of rising crime rates and stiffer sentences. California's prison population, according to *Golden State Report*, rose from about 27,000 in 1981 to about 72,000 this year, with 81,000 projected for 1989. In many counties, the only public buildings put up since Proposition 13 have been jails.

In remote agricultural counties such as far-northern Shasta and Tehama, the situation reaches crisis proportions: Shasta closed its libraries; Tehama does not have enough sheriff's deputies. Some rural counties have become so irate over their tax straightjacket that they're challenging the state's authority: The supervisors of Butte County, along the spine of the Sierras, voted to cut back state-ordered spending to 1978-79 levels. County Judge Reginald Watt ruled the county's action unconstitutional but said the state cannot order the county to run the welfare program unless the Legislature gives it the money to do so, saying, "There is a real and present danger that . . . the county of Butte will be reduced to little more than a puppet." The issue of the legality of state-mandated programs, Watt has said, sets the stage for a "county versus state battle of the century."

The counties charge that they have lost their property tax base while cities monopolize the sales tax; unlike cities, counties cannot raise taxes or impose fees without the Legislature's permission. Leg-

islators retort that county officials have failed to broaden their economies and build up their sales tax bases. "Counties are seen as nags," said state Sen. Kopp. "There's relatively little sympathy that's translated into legislative relief."

All local officials in California have complained that the substitution of state aid for local property taxes has resulted in a massive transfer of power to the state. The public's loss of interest in city and county government was described by a 1987 California Legislative Budget Committee analysis, which concluded that so many decisions are made at the state level that "citizens no longer have a stake in local government."

Proposition 13 also has caused disparities between long-term home owners and recent buyers because it allows reassessments of houses each time they are sold, and so recent homebuyers pay taxes several times higher than their neighbors' taxes. The newcomers—executives from other states and immigrants from Asia and Latin America—find California housing costs daunting. "While Proposition 13 support is part antigovernment and part property tax revolt, it is also part drawbridge mentality," said state Sen. John Garamendi, a supporter of higher state spending. "We're seeing an anti-newcomer attitude," Garamendi said, "which could have a devastating impact."

Mervin Field's California Poll in February showed that 70 per cent of Californians disapproved of Proposition 13's dual property tax formula. But 60 per cent were not in favor of legislation suggested by Gann to roll back all property tax assessments to pre-Proposition 13 values. The rollback would have reduced property tax receipts by as much as $2 billion annually, necessitating increases in other taxes or reductions in service.

The California Poll also showed that Californians no longer think their government is too big. The survey showed that they are almost evenly divided, 48-43 per cent, over whether they prefer a smaller government with fewer services or a larger government with more services. In 1980, 60 per cent favored a smaller government. The new poll also showed, however, that 55 per cent still favor a tax rebate rather than allowing additional spending if the state collects more tax money than it is now permitted to spend.

Two propositions on the June ballot would change the current appropriation limit. Proposition 71, backed by education groups and public employee unions, would alter Gann's formula by substituting the California inflation rate for the national rate and growth in school enrollment for general population. California's inflation rate is higher than the national average because the state's economy is booming. And the influx of immigrants with big families has caused school enrollments to rise faster than the general population.

Proposition 72, an alternative, is sponsored by Gann and would exempt gasoline taxes from the state revenue limit and dedicate all state taxes on gasoline to transportation: It would also make the state set aside a reserve fund of 3 per cent of the budget each year. Gov. George Deukmejian opposes that initiative and instead is backing a $1 billion bond issue, also on the ballot, to finance more highway and other transportation projects.

MASSACHUSETTS STORY

In the aftermath of Proposition 13, tax cut initiatives were launched across the nation. Some lost and some won, but none had as much impact as Proposition 2½ in Massachusetts. If any state shocked the nation more than California by cutting taxes, it was notoriously liberal, pro-union Massachusetts.

The Bay State's establishment opposed the tax revolt, including Michael S. Dukakis, who, after his first term as governor, had been defeated by fellow Democrat Edward J. King in 1978 and was then teaching at Harvard University. But the citizens' tax movement got help from the Massachusetts High Technology Council, which said that what was good for traditional businesses was not necessarily good for high-techers. Young engineers came to the state to be educated, the council argued, and wanted to settle near its fine educational institutions, but they were being lured away by states with lower taxes.

Government and union leaders opposed the plan to limit property taxes to 2.5 per cent of assessed valuation, but the high-techers and Citizens for Limited Taxation, the grass-roots group that originated the measure, prevailed. The task of coping with Proposition 2½ fell to the legislature and King, but when Dukakis returned to the governorship in 1983, he, like Brown in California, found himself spending money on local programs that he had hoped to spend on state programs.

By almost all accounts, Proposition 2½ is commonly accepted in Massachusetts today. Local officials complain much less than their California counterparts about its effects, though they are concerned about the future impact of its restrictions. "Massachusetts is a bit different from California in that Massachusetts did not have limitations on state revenue growth," said Helen F. Ladd, an expert on the state's government who is now a professor of public policy at Duke University. Massachusetts did not have a big surplus when Proposition 2½ was passed, Ladd noted, but "has benefited from quite significant revenue growth at the state level."

"Proposition 2½ has been both good and bad," said Ed Moscovitch, executive director of the Massachusetts Municipal Association. "The property tax in Massachusetts really was too high. By forcing a reduction in the property tax, 2½ created a crisis and forced the state to come up with aid financed by broad-based income and sales tax. Overdue cuts were made in local budgets; Prop 2½ made them easier to accomplish. By and large, it's been done so far without unacceptable cuts in services."

Under Proposition 2½, Moscovitch noted, local school committees lost their autonomy. With enrollments falling, local governments stepped in, firing teachers and closing buildings. Some officials grouse about the loss of local authority. But Barbara Anderson, executive director of Citizens for Limited Taxation, notes that since Proposition 2½, "the state cannot mandate programs unless it's willing to pay for them." Property taxes, she said, should "pay only for things that relate to property. Using it for education is just bizarre. The level of aid should be brought up to the point that the state is funding education while the cities and towns control the education process—no strings attached."

Among the prices paid for Proposition 2½, Moscovitch said, was the deferral of essential maintenance on roads and public buildings. Looking to the future, he said that "enrollment in elementary grades is rising—there are 20 per cent more 1-year-olds than 7-year-olds"—and localities face such challenges as putting their pension systems on a sound basis. "Now expenses are rising more quickly than available revenue," he concluded.

Proposition 2½'s major problem, in Moscovitch's view, is its 2.5 per cent ceiling on yearly local budget increases. "If the economy is growing 7 or 8 per cent," it's not unreasonable to ask the government to grow 7 or 8 per cent per year," he said. Many localities have held elections to override Proposition 2½, and about half have succeeded, he said. But it's easier, he suggested, to get an override for a new facility than for meeting over-all cost growth. The towns likely to override, he noted, are small and rich: "I'm afraid that in 10 years, the larger, poor towns in the commonwealth will have a crisis in public services and education."

Anderson, however, is leery of more taxes. In 1986, her organization successfully mounted an initiative to set a state tax revenue limit. And in the midst of Massachusetts's current budget battle, Anderson has urged big budget cuts, saying that politicians "have a lot of nerve suggesting even a minor tax increase."

STATE LIMITS

The Massachusetts tax limit is only the latest result of a movement that preceded Proposition 13. Colorado, New Jersey and Tennessee set such limits before the Californians were gathering signatures. But Proposition 13 had immense, nationwide psychological impact.

By 1986, 17 additional states had passed such limits, either on revenues or on spending, by initiatives or legislative action. In 1978, Arizona, Hawaii, Michigan and Texas passed limits. In 1979, Louisiana, Nevada, Oregon and Washington followed suit, and California passed the Gann initiative. In 1986, just as liberals thought that the fever had passed, Massachusetts voters supplemented Proposition 2½ with a tax revenue limitation initiative, and in 1987, the New Mexico Legislature put a lid on growth in the state's salaries and wages.

As with Proposition 13, the Gann limit on California state revenue has proved most important among the states. In 1987, California found itself obliged to rebate $1.1 billion to taxpayers; individual checks ranged up to $272. But such western states as Colorado, Idaho and Montana, having embraced revenue limits in the era of Proposition 13 fervor, found themselves in trouble when their energy and commodity-based economies declined.

But the bigger story has been the tax revolt's suppression of tax increases, combined with conservatives' preference for sales taxes over income taxes, the NCSL's Gold said. Throughout the decade, he noted, states have been willing to raise income taxes for only two reasons—"to avoid a deficit due to a weak economy or to put money in the schools." There were no tax increases in 1979–80, and 12 of 16 states that raised income taxes in 1982–83 rolled them back in 1984–85. Sales tax increases almost all stuck, he noted. Two other factors contributed to the antitax or low-tax climate of the 1980s, Gold suggested: indexing, which was passed by 10 states, and tax-cutting competition between states, which resulted in reductions in high marginal income taxes.

After a decade of battles, there are now tax revolt "establishments" on each side. Taxpayer groups are active in most or all of the 24 states that have the initiative process and in virtually all other states through the legislative process.

The tax revolt counterattackers are also staying active but have changed tactics. After the passage of Proposition 13, AFSCME, other unions and pro-government citizens groups formed a coalition, Citizens for Tax Justice, to find out why Proposition 13 had been so successful. Today, the groups work with government administrators and local businesses to oppose the revolt and force politicians to make tax burdens fairer, especially for the poor. They also favor tax relief for the elderly and oppose "unfair" tax breaks for business.

Few tax initiatives were passed as the 1980s wore on, and some—in Michigan and Ohio, for example—met spectacular defeat. Californians said no when Jarvis, in 1980, sought to halve income tax rates.

There has also been a rise in the approval rate for public works bond measures.

The public's willingness to pick and choose among initiatives has reassured those who thought that voters could never evaluate these proposals, said Karen M. Benker, a former National Association of State Budget Officers analyst who now

works in the Colorado budget office. "The more extreme the cut, the less likely the initiative is going to pass," Gold added. "The more moderate measures, limiting expenditures to growth or income tax indexing, almost always pass. But the tax revolt is like a big fire. There are still some embers out there, and if gasoline is poured on them, it flares up again."

GOING FOR BROKE

The lottery craze
makes for lots of losers

FRANCIS J. FLAHERTY

Francis J. Flaherty, a member of The Progressive's Editorial Advisory Board, writes on legal issues from New York City. Funding for this article was provided by a grant from Essential Information, Inc.

May the fours be with you!" So goes a *Star Wars*-style television commercial for Pennsylvania's state lottery.

Whatever the luck of the nation's gamblers, the force is certainly with the promoters of government-sponsored gambling. With ever more states operating lotteries each year, the annual take approaches $12 billion, according to the Public Gaming Research Institute of Rockville, Maryland. The game craze has turned into a cash machine that is the predominant new revenue source for state governments in the 1980s.

The odds are the lottery is here to stay. About two-thirds of the public solidly backs its use, and politicians have found it a potent source of patronage and a painless way to raise money. A state's take from a lottery—ranging from 25 to 42 per cent of the gross—is counted on to fund a variety of state programs. And the IRS has even come up with a new tax form—Number 5754—exclusively for lottery winners.

The private sector also perceives the lottery to be long-lived and lucrative. Bally Corporation, the major supplier of equipment for games now in operation in twenty-two states and the District of Columbia, has spent hundreds of thousands of dollars lobbying for new lotteries in states that lack them. In 1985, Scientific Games, the leading lottery-ticket maker, topped its 1984 figure of one billion tickets sold to state lottery commissions.

A sprawling peripheral industry has sprouted as well. A player seeking guidance can shell out a few dollars for Dr. Robert Hieronymous's *How to Pick Your Personal Lottery Numbers* or any one of dozens of similar books. For a few more bucks, the player can join such groups as the Happy Players Club or One to Won and be supplied with computerized picks. Zealots can subscribe to *Lottery and Gaming Review* or *Lottery Advantage* for analyses of the game, while more casual devotees can open their local newspapers to lottery columns like the half-page "Will Wynn" featured in the *New York Daily News*.

All this buildup has taken little more than twenty years. Around the turn of the century, a series of scandals led to the abolition of lotteries in every state of the union. But in 1964, New Hampshire initiated the new round of government-sponsored lotteries, and the ball was rolling again.

Big as the game is now, its backers plan an even bigger future for it. Congress mulls over no fewer than four bills proposing a national lottery to deal with the Federal deficit; optimists say it could net up to $100 billion in five years. The states of Maine, New Hampshire, and Vermont launched the first regional lottery last September. California started a game in October that was expected to become the biggest such revenue-raiser in the nation—and promptly sold thirty million one-dollar tickets in the first two days. New York Governor Mario Cuomo wants to expand his state's game to include a sports lottery. The imaginative city officials of Ishpeming, Michigan, even tried to use a parking-ticket lottery to encourage scofflaws to pay their fines, but the state attorney general said their scheme was illegal.

The lottery is a regressive and inefficient tax that promotes addiction to gambling, seduces the poor into purchase of a bogus American Dream, turns states into sleazy shills for a game with infinitesimal odds, and provides ample opportunity for corruption.

As the late Texas Congressman Wright Patman noted, "Gambling is actually the most regressive form of taxation that can be devised. It is designed to pick the pockets of the poor."

Boardwalk Casino Blues

(Las Vegas News Bureau photo)

THE MAIN EVENT—Casino gaming remains Las Vegas' main attraction, despite the ever-increasing number of non-casino diversions available in and around the city. The latest innovation in games of skill and chance are coin-operated computerized games. Hi-tech gambling, though popular, will never replace live action, as these players at the Lady Luck Casino in downtown Las Vegas would agree.

The whole thing is a joke," Gene Wallace says bitterly. He grew up in Atlantic City and owns a men's clothing store near the city bus terminal. Every working day, he breathes the exhaust fumes as tour buses carry thousands of tourists past his Atlantic Avenue shop. "The only people benefiting from casino gambling are the casinos themselves," he remarks.

He is not alone in his thinking. Ten years after an overwhelming majority of New Jersey voters bet that a get-rich-quick solution known as legalized casino gambling would revive a dying Atlantic City, frustration is common among the handful of merchants who have hung on, the city's steadily declining population, and even some casino executives.

Back in 1976, though, the press and public were quick to accept the unremitting stream of promises made by gambling advocates, believing that Atlantic City would be transformed into a money-making mecca, a Las Vegas by the sea. Indeed, the group that led the

legalization campaign called itself the Committee to Rebuild Atlantic City.

It has turned out otherwise, and the resort is hardly the example the 1976 New Jersey Casino Control Act anticipated, when it called legal gambling a "unique tool of urban redevelopment."

The casinos have invested $2.7 billion in the city and now lure twenty-eight million free-spending visitors annually, but the business section of town is sagging and depressed. The eleven casino hotels employ 40,000 people, but joblessness in Atlantic City exceeds 10 per cent and is much higher in the cold months when tourism falls off. A quarter of the residents live below the poverty line.

The casinos tower above the resort as glitzy, gaudy symbols of success and high style, but a short distance away from the high-rollers and hype are idle working-age people. The back streets resemble the South Bronx: one supermarket, no legitimate movie house, shuttered bars and restaurants, and a disastrous housing sit-

uation. This state of affairs led Joel Jacobson, a member of the New Jersey Casino Control Commission, to describe the city as "eleven Taj Mahals in a war zone."

The lack of new housing for long-time residents and casino employees is a major disappointment of the gambling experiment. Speculators made millions buying and selling littered lots and crumbling tenements in a process that has allowed land to stagnate and its value to rise to the point where construction of low-income and even moderately priced housing is out of the question for legitimate developers. Yet the casinos, with their sophisticated lawyers and connections, assembled prime real estate along the ocean front and bay.

Unrealized expectations have put the casinos on the defensive. In their behalf, they say that like any business they are responsible to the city only insofar as they create jobs, pay taxes, and perhaps exercise their charitable impulses. The casinos wish to be viewed as catalysts of

civic improvement, not limitless sources of money and answers to perplexing municipal problems.

"A casino," says Thomas Carver, president of the Atlantic City Casino Association, "is not a golden goose laying golden eggs." In November 1984 the Atlantis Casino Hotel filed for bankruptcy, the first to do so.

Atlantic City has turned into a company town, vulnerable to shifts in the economy and the threat that nearby communities are considering legalized gambling.

"You know what these [casino] people fear most is competition," Joel Jacobson told a group of Rutgers alumni. "They worry about the Catskills or North Jersey or even Coney Island. I wonder if that isn't why they'd rather not hurry to fix up Atlantic City. It's much better for them if every other town looks at that

one and says that they don't want that to happen to them."

Actually, Jacobson doesn't believe in conspiracy theories. But even if he did, Atlantic City doesn't need a conspiracy. It's doing badly enough on its own. If nothing else, the city's sad fate should be viewed as a warning, a red flag to the many well-intentioned communities that are thinking of betting their futures on casino gambling.

—ROBERT A. POLNER

(Robert A. Polner reported for The Press of Atlantic City and now writes for The Record in northern New Jersey.)

Lottery officials see it differently. They vigorously dispute the contention, according to a recent report by the Florida attorney general's office, "that poor people bet more heavily on lotteries." To the contrary, they echo the statement by Washington State's lottery director that "it's the middle class who plays."

Indeed, data can be cited to show that lotteries are not primarily the province of the poor. Colorado lottery officials, for example, analyzed the claim forms filled out by winners and found "the typical lottery player is a middle-aged man who makes $30,000 per year and has at least a high-school education." The Florida report also discloses that Arizona lottery players average $27,000 in annual income; Maryland's, $15,000 to $21,000; New York's, $25,000 to $30,000, and Vermont's, $17,000.

Yet these are *average* incomes that include the earnings of many people at or below the poverty level who also play the lottery. More important, a California Senate study concluded that poor lottery players spend a greater proportion of their incomes on the game than those who are better off. And therein lies the proper measure of regressivity.

In Connecticut, players with annual incomes below $5,000 buy 5.3 per cent of the lottery tickets but earn only 1.3 per cent of the state's income. And Connecticut is not unusual. "Nationwide," says the Florida report, "the poor bought lottery tickets at 2.8 times their income share" during one surveyed year.

According to Daniel Suits, a Michigan State University professor of economics, the lottery is two-and-a-half to three times as regressive as the sales tax. The Federal Commission on the Review of National Policy Toward Gambling reached a similar conclusion in 1976.

Evidence abounds that the poor spend more than they can afford on lotteries. The Federal Commission found, for example, that during the recession of the 1970s,

Michigan not only had the country's highest unemployment rate but also its most lucrative lottery. Last August, as the day approached for picking the winner of New York's celebrated $41 million game, the airwaves and news columns were full of tales of homeless people collecting bottles and cans to come up with a dollar for a ticket.

The lures of the jackpot prey upon others, as well. A teen-ager in Erie, Pennsylvania, spent $6,000 on lottery tickets and tried to kill himself when he lost. A New Jersey man who spent $1,500 a week on the lottery enrolled in a hospital treatment program for compulsive gamblers. A Michigan woman was charged with dozens of counts of criminal fraud for allegedly forging checks to finance her thousand-dollar-a-day lottery habit.

The California Senate's study cited research suggesting that "lotteries can increase compulsive gambling by as much as 10 per cent."

Nonetheless, these players continue to risk the dangers of addiction for a pipe dream. Indeed, the chances of winning big money in a lottery are barely more than nil. In New York's $41 million jackpot, the largest to date, the odds against buying the lucky ticket were an unsporting 6.1 million to one. While casinos and race tracks keep 5 to 25 per cent of their takes, state lotteries keep as much as 60 per cent for profits and costs—prompting the irreverent to rename them "looteries." As one gambling counselor says, "You stand seven times better chance of getting struck by lightning than you do of winning a million dollars in the lottery."

Lottery officials add insult to the injury of long odds with their deceptive descriptions of lottery prizes. For example, the $40 million that an Illinois man won in a 1984 lottery was actually worth less than $8 million at the time of the award. The talk of $40 million ignored the tax pay-

ments he would owe as well as the fact that the prize is paid out over twenty years.

A man in Arizona recently won $1 million. When he found out about the twenty-year installment plan to pay out his winnings, he was so enraged that he sued the state for fraud. He did not win the case.

The lottery is not an efficient way to raise revenue. Traditional taxes cost a penny or two per dollar to collect, but lotteries can cost up to seventy-five cents per dollar of revenue. The prizes account for something between 40 and 50 per cent of the gross take; administration, promotional campaigns, and vendors' fees gobble up 10 to 25 percent. No more than half—and often much less—of lottery revenues ends up in state coffers.

About half the states with lotteries deposit the income in their general funds. In the others, where such revenues are earmarked for some special purpose, deception often crops up once more.

In New York, for instance, 45 per cent of lottery revenues are set aside by law for education, but the education budget is fixed. If lottery revenues go up, the state cuts back on other monies slated for schools; the amount spent on education remains constant. In effect, then, large lottery revenues translate as more money for *other* state programs—programs often less politically palatable than education.

The spectacle of the state as bookie also rankles. Jasper S. Wyman of the Christian Civic League of Maine said last August that government by jackpot only "lowers the entire moral tone of government." Iowa Governor Terry Branstad agrees. It is inappropriate, says Branstad, for a state "to be in the business of enticing and encouraging people to go out and gamble."

Deaf ears met both remarks. The tri-state lottery Wyman railed against began operations last September, and the Iowa version opened for business in August.

In the rush to promote government gaming, states risk corruption and infiltration by organized crime. A year ago, former New Jersey lottery commission chairman Reese Palley pleaded guilty to falsifying evidence in a state ethics commission investigation of charges that he sought private business from companies with state lottery contracts. In 1980, Pennsylvania was plunged into scandal when a televised $1 million drawing was found to be fixed. Three lottery directors in Ohio have resigned following allegations of political patronage and kickback schemes.

Lottery lovers dismiss these problems. Talk of the game's regressiveness as a revenue-raiser is off base, they say, because the lottery is not a tax at all. People "don't have to play if they don't want to," says Duane Burke, president of the Public Gaming Research Institute. Thomas Jefferson, too, was persuaded by this reasoning: Lotteries, he said, "lay taxation only on the willing." Advocates add that spurning lotteries because people may not play them prudently smacks of paternalism.

One thing is certain: Political realities favor lotteries. Even if the games are inefficient compared to traditional taxes, they are popular and politically achievable, unlike tax increases. As a Connecticut official told *Newsweek*, "People seem less annoyed at losing their hard-earned money on the lottery than losing it in the form of taxes."

Defenders insist that the long odds and the dangers of corruption are not fatal flaws. They say states could offer more, but smaller, payouts to increase bettors' chances. They also say states could monitor more vigilantly against criminal infiltration, though monitoring and reporting provisions in current laws are taken seriously in few states.

Best of all, say advocates, the lottery is fun. It lets people dream of vast riches, laugh and cry with winners and losers, and feel the thrills and chills of the chase for cash. The lottery has provided America with a real-life soap opera.

The nation cheered for the unemployed Jamaican house painter who raked in $5.9 million in the Pennsylvania lottery a while back. And it grieved for the Michigan woman who turned from winner to loser in a few days several years ago: Told that she had won $200,000 in the lottery, she soon learned that officials had held her finalist's number upside down, reading her losing "9" as a winning "6."

There is no end to the poignant tales. The son of a foundry worker nets $40 million in the Illinois lottery. A group of immigrant factory workers in the Bronx split one of the three winning tickets in the $41 million contest. A Pennsylvania man in 1972 buys a ticket that wins $1 million, only to lose it when his wallet is swept away by Hurricane Agnes—and then to find the wallet and ticket two days after the statutory deadline for claiming the prize.

But the critics of bettor government are steadfast—and rightly so. Lotteries may be the most popular form of gambling in the United States, and they may ease the financial burdens of government. But they simply saddle the poor with an unfair share of public expenses. Thomas Jefferson notwithstanding, the lottery exploits the American Dream and turns the state into a purveyor of slim hopes for Shangri-La to those with no other chance at financial security.

TAXING THE POOR

One of the fundamental aims—and results—of federal tax reform was to lower the taxes of the poor. Should states pursue the same goal?

Steven D. Gold

Steven D. Gold is director of Fiscal Studies for NCSL. A book on tax relief for the poor will be published by NCSL.

"The tax system should not be an additional burden to those who are struggling to escape from poverty; insofar as possible, those below the poverty line should be freed from taxation altogether." These are not the thoughts of a disciple of Karl Marx. They are the words of President Ronald Reagan, as he presented his tax reform proposals to Congress in May 1985.

Lowering taxes of the poor was an integral part of federal tax reform as it wended its way toward passage. The U.S. House of Representatives provided more relief than proposed by the president, the Senate went beyond the House and the conference bill that finally passed was more generous to the poor than previous versions of tax reform. To judge by congressional rhetoric, tax relief for the poor—six million low-income households were taken off the federal tax rolls—was something in which to take considerable pride.

Why did this happen? Alan Murray, a *Wall Street Journal* reporter on tax reform, says "the Reagan administration was embarrassed by studies showing that the taxes of the poor had been rising sharply," and that "tax relief for the poor was an inexpensive way to balance big tax rate reductions for high-income households."

All of this could have important implications for the states as they grapple with how to respond to federal tax reform, because poor people have paid considerably more taxes to state and local governments than they have to the federal government before it lowered their taxes. According to a recent study by economists Howard Chernick of Hunter College and Andrew Reschovsky of Tufts University, for example, income, sales and property taxes in a representative state amounted to 13.3 percent of income for poor households in 1986, while federal income and Social Security taxes averaged less than 3 percent of their income.

Besides, state and local tax systems are nearly all regressive, meaning that they claim a bigger share of income of the poor than of families with higher income. The main reason for this regressivity is heavy reliance on consumption taxes, like the general sales tax and excise taxes on tobacco and gasoline. The personal income tax, which is normally progressive, plays a much smaller role in state-local tax systems than in the federal revenue system. It represents only 20 percent of state-local tax revenue compared with 45 percent of federal revenue.

What accounts for the striking contrast between tax relief for the poor at the federal level and the heavy burdens imposed on them by state and local governments? At least four considerations come into play.

- **Hidden burdens.** States didn't explicitly set out to tax the poor at a higher rate than other taxpayers; it occurs because of the way poor people spend their money. The property tax is the largest revenue source at the state-local level, and it hits the poor hard because housing consumes a lot of their income, and a big share of the property tax falls on housing. Likewise, the poor typically spend virtually every cent they receive while families with higher incomes can afford to save some of their income; the result is that consumption taxes (which do not fall on savings) take a bigger share of income from the poor.

- **Ease in designing relief.** It is easier to relieve the income tax than other taxes because poverty is defined by low income. Targeting income tax relief to people with low incomes is a relatively simple matter. Property or sales tax relief is more complicated, requiring refundable tax credits if it is to be provided efficiently. A refundable credit is one that goes to people whose income tax liability is zero.

- **Poverty is a federal concern.** A widely held theory is that fighting poverty is more the federal government's responsibility than that of state and local governments. Rationales include the federal government's ability to transfer income from wealthy to low-income states and the possibility that redistributive state-local policies might cause people to "vote with their feet," with the affluent moving away from jurisdictions that place a high priority on helping the poor. While this argument is often used in relation to spending programs and state income taxes on the affluent, it is seldom applied to tax relief for the poor.

- **Political clout.** After most states enacted property tax relief programs for the poor (primarily the elderly poor) in the late 1960s or early 1970s, political interest in relieving their state-local tax burdens decreased. Advocates for the poor at the state level focused their attention primarily on spending rather than tax programs.

This could be about to change. One reason is that federal tax reform raised the visibility of poor people's taxes. Concern about the poor waxes and wanes. In 1963, for example, poverty suddenly became a major national issue, leading to the initiation of the "War on Poverty," but in the late 1970s and 1980s poverty fell a long way from the top of the national agenda. While combating poverty is still not a high federal priority, reducing taxes on the poor is. A second reason why the impact of state taxes on the poor may receive more attention in the years ahead is that federal tax reform stimulated formation of a new coalition of advocacy groups that previously had not paid much attention to tax issues. The major accomplishments last year in Washington, D.C. demonstrated that tax policy can be a tool for helping the poor, and this lesson is being carried over to the state level.

The Center on Budget and Policy Priorities in Washington, D.C. played a key role in developing the case for federal tax relief for the poor, and it is not turning its attention to the states. Robert Greenstein, the Center's director, observes that three years ago few if any groups were very concerned about the federal tax burden on the poor, but that situation changed rapidly in 1984 and 1985. "Our hope is that a similar development will occur at the state level, and we can already see some initial signs that it will," he said. Among the groups that are expected to get involved at the state level are affiliates of the U.S. Catholic Conference, the Children's Defense fund and the National Women's Law Center.

Citizens for Tax Justice (CTJ) recently published a report condemning states for taxing the poor more heavily than the affluent. CTJ's executive director, David Wilhelm, hopes that the "revelations" in the study will "wake up" the public about the unfairness of state taxes. His group is also shifting its priorities from the federal to the state level.

Legislators who want to reduce taxes paid by the poor have a variety of options, which can be divided into those affecting the income tax, the property tax, the sales tax and all taxes at once. The various approaches differ considerably in terms of their pros and cons.

New Mexico has the only relief provision that attempts to encompass all of the taxes paid by the poor. Its Low Income Comprehensive Tax Rebate (LICTR) is intended as a device for re-

moving the regressivity of all state and local taxes for the poor; that is, making the tax system proportional below the poverty line. LICTR provides tax rebates to taxpayers with incomes under $10,000, with the rebates increasing as income decreases and family size grows. This program, which costs about $6.80 per capita, considerably reduces the tax burden on the poor, but this level of funding is inadequate to eliminate regressivity completely.

This year most attention will probably focus on income tax relief because state income taxes are directly affected by federal tax reform. One approach that some states will take is to increase personal exemptions, as the federal government has done. This is not an efficient method of providing relief to the poor, however, because while it does help the poor, the bulk of its benefits goes to the non-poor. Jerry Miller, executive director of the National Association of State Budget Officers, urges that it not be discounted because it is considerably more progressive than an across-the-board tax rate cut.

A second approach is to boost the standard deduction. This helps low- and moderate-income households disproportionately because they are not likely to have sufficient deductions to itemize. States could enact a standard deduction that is the same regardless of income (or establish a minimum standard deduction) rather than the percentage standard deductions that many of them currently have.

A tax credit that phases out as income rises is a third alternative. For example, in 1985 North Carolina created a credit that is $25 per return if income is under $5,000, $20 if income is between $5,000 and $10,000, and $15 if income is between $10,000 and $15,000. California and New York are among other states with vanishing tax credits targeted at low- and middle-income levels.

A fourth approach is to establish an earned-income tax credit like the one the federal government provides. The federal credit is for 14 percent of earnings up to $5,714, with a maximum benefit of $800. It phases out gradually once income exceeds $9,000, so that no benefit is received when income reaches $17,000. Wisconsin had such a credit pegged at 30 percent of the federal credit until it was repealed as part of a broad tax simplification in 1985.

A final way of providing tax relief is to establish a no-tax status below which no taxes need be paid. Last October, for example, Massachusetts passed a law freeing all joint returns with an income under $12,000 from tax liability. Mary-

land says that if no federal return is required, no state income tax return need be filed either. (Unless carefully designed, such provisions can create a "notch" where tax liability jumps hundreds of dollars when income increases slightly.)

According to a 1983 Census Bureau survey, the poor pay more than 10 times as much property tax as they do state income tax. The most efficient way of relieving the poor's property tax is a circuitbreaker—a state-financed property tax credit whose value decreases as income rises. Renters as well as homeowners normally benefit from these programs, with some proportion of rent being treated as constituting property taxes. About 30 states have such credits, but only nine circuitbreakers cover other than senior citizens. States could relieve the poor's property taxes by liberalizing circuitbreaker formulas and/or expanding eligibility.

Seven states have refundable credits (three of which are just for senior citizens) that offset part of the regressivity of the sales tax.

Another reason why tax relief for the poor may be more urgent now is that the ranks of the poor have been growing. In 1985 there were about 33 million persons below the poverty line nationwide, more than in any year during the 1970s, when the number never exceeded 26 million. The poor population shot up during 1979 and the recessions of the early 1980s and has declined only slightly since then. This year the poverty line for a family of four will be approximately $11,586.

The composition of the population below the poverty line also needs to be taken into account. Improvements in federal programs such as Social Security and Supplemental Security Income (SSI) have sharply reduced poverty among the aged. The poverty rate among seniors is 12.6 percent, slightly less than for the entire population. But contrast, in 1959 the poverty rate in this group was 35.2 percent, more than 50 percent higher than for the general population. Poverty among children, on the other hand, is more than 43 percent higher than average; more than half the children in households headed by females are poor. The biggest recent increase in poverty has been among the working poor, the very group affected most by federal tax reform.

These developments have implications for designing tax relief provisions. A program to relieve the poor's tax burden that's limited to senior citizens will not help 90 percent of the poor. On the other hand, it makes sense for the benefits of a program to be sensitive to the number of children in a household, and for single-parent households to receive more favorable treatment than single persons.

An important theme that runs through the analysis of ways to provide tax relief for the poor is that its cost can be held relatively low by targeting it carefully. Some programs that are sold as ways of helping the poor—such as exempting food and utilities from the sales tax and boosting personal income tax exemptions—may represent good policy for other reasons, but they should not be viewed primarily as ways of alleviating the tax burden on the poor because most of their benefits go to people whose income is well above the poverty line.

Will many states follow the federal lead? Most states that reduce taxes will probably take some sort of action to help the poor, but it is too early to tell how much. State Senator Fred Kerr of Kansas says legislators are troubled by the fact that many households with income between $6,000 and $12,000 will owe state income tax but not federal income tax. While some tax relief will be considered for them, the bleak state fiscal situation limits what can be done. Missouri state Senator Wayne Goode is also sympathetic to the plight of the poor but says that "in Missouri, we need all the revenue we can get," so he is not enthusiastic about anything that reduces Missouri's already low tax level.

In the competition for limited state funds, tax relief for the poor *by itself* is often not a strong contender compared to alternatives with strong constituencies, but it may enhance the attractiveness of a general reform package because it can balance tax relief for other groups. That's what happened in Washington, D.C. last year, and it could occur in many states in 1987 and the years to come.

A Few Devices for Relieving Taxes

States can choose among a large number of devices for cutting the taxes of the poor. Here are some examples:

• A property tax circuit breaker. Iowa's circuitbreaker is one of the easier ones to understand. Eligible households (mainly senior citizens and the disabled) receive credits according to this sliding scale:

If income is	Rebate is equal to
Under $5,000	100% of property tax
$5,000–5,999	70% of property tax
$6,000–6,999	50% of property tax
$7,000–7,999	40% of property tax
$8,000–8,999	30% of property tax
$9,000–11,999	25% of property tax

Rent is treated as though 25 percent represents property tax payments, so renters are covered as well as homeowners. Applications are taken by county treasurers, who turn them over to the state, which then audits the applications and reimburses local governments for the reductions in property tax bills resulting from the circuitbreaker.

• An income tax credit. California provides an income tax credit that eliminates tax liability for most of the poor and gradually phases out as income rises. Benefits vary for single, head of household and joint returns. Here is the schedule of benefits for joint returns and certain widow(er)s with a dependent child. (This was the formula for 1986. Income levels are adjusted annually for inflation.)

If adjusted gross income is	Credit equals
Under $11,280	100% of net tax
$11,280–13,040	80% of net tax
$13,040–14,800	60% of net tax
$14,800–16,560	40% of net tax
$16,560–18,320	20% of net tax
Over $18,320	0% of net tax

• A comprehensive tax credit. New Mexico has the only provision of this type. Tax refunds depend on a household's gross income and the number of personal exemptions it claims, so larger families receive greater benefits. The largest payment is $375 for a household with income between $2,000 and $2,500 having six or more exemptions. If such a household has an income between $6,000 and $6,500, its rebate would fall to $150. With an income between $9,500 and $10,000, it would receive just $10, and nothing if its income is higher.

• A rent credit. Oregon has a program designed to help poor seniors who do not own their own homes. This rental assistance refund program, restricted to households with incomes under $5,000 headed by someone who is 58 or older, pays all gross rent in excess of 40 percent of income, up to a $2,100 maximum.

• A sales tax credit. Last year Kansas changed its credit that offsets the regressivity of the sales tax. Previously it offered a $20 credit to all senior citizens and disabled persons with incomes under $10,000. It extended eligibility of families with dependent children under the age of 18 and boosted the credit, placing it on this sliding scale:

If income is	Refund is
Less than $5,000	$40 for head of household $30 for each additional member
$5,000–10,000	$30 for head of household $25 for each additional member
$10,000–13,000	$20 for head of household $15 for each additional member

—*Steven D. Gold*

THE STATES' GLOBAL HUSTLERS

Martin Tolchin
and Susan Tolchin

Martin Tolchin is a correspondent in the Washington bureau of *The New York Times.* Susan Tolchin is a professor in the School of Government and Business Administration at George Washington University.

O n the streets of downtown Tokyo, state officials from Virginia, Indiana, California, Florida, New York, Georgia, and a host of other states regularly greet each other. The same people also meet each other in Hong Kong, Singapore, and Brus-

sels, but unlike most reunions of Americans abroad, these encounters are strictly competitive. The officials are prowling the streets of foreign capitals on the same mission: to lure foreign investors to the United States—preferably to their state. As the competition for the foreign dollar

Statesmanship: Above, Governor John Carlin delivering some Kansas sirloin to a customer in a Tokyo supermarket in 1986.

heats up, legions of state officials travel the globe, selling the superiority of their state as a home for foreign investment.

All trade-related activities on the state level, including foreign investment, have expanded rapidly over the past 20 years, signaling a new era in business development. As the only non-controversial trade issue, foreign investment has benefited from inattention, emerging virtually untouched by negative publicity or legislative oversight. These factors have combined to make foreign investment a top priority of some of the nation's leading governors, who have recognized the immediate benefits of their states' overseas recruitment efforts and moved quickly to reinforce and expand them. Foreign investment means an infusion of fresh capital and new jobs, in that order, and the message has emerged loud and clear.

The enthusiasm of the governors has made all the difference. With a singularity of purpose uncommon to the public arena, the states moved so quickly and aggressively that they assumed almost total dominance of the issue. No one questions the fact that the states now lead the nation in shaping foreign investment policy—unimpeded and quietly encouraged by the Federal Government. They earned their new role through sheer tenacity. They provided the leadership, dictated the parameters of the issue, and persuaded their legislatures to allocate resources earmarked for recruiting foreign capital.

This new wave of state activity has revolved around job creation, a theme of such paramount importance that it is sounded repeatedly by governors, mayors, and state development officers. Simply put, foreign companies bring jobs, and jobs are the political bread and butter of state leaders. The linkage between opportunities abroad and jobs at home is forged again and again with concrete actions that are quickly implemented. In fact, when unemployment soared between 1978 and 1980, states responded with the first major expansion of their overseas offices; the next burst of activity followed the recession of 1982.

The search for investment opportunities soon shifted its focus from Western Europe toward Japan and other Far Eastern countries. This turn toward the East was spurred by the increasing difficulty of attracting European firms, particularly from countries whose unions regarded investment in the United States as a threat to their jobs. The Japanese high rate of savings provided a reservoir of available funds, and the U.S. consumer market and high interest rates provided an enviable investment opportunity.

In the quest for investment and the jobs that followed, the states operated as individual entrepreneurs. They competed vigorously, treated other states as their enemies, and guarded their secrets closely. Inevitably, bad feelings

> In their zeal to lure foreign capital to their states, the nation's peripatetic governors may be stepping on each other's toes—and hurting some domestic producers.

abounded as one state emerged victorious in the competition for the Honda plant, the Nippon-denso distributorship, or the U.S. headquarters of the Bridgestone company. Georgia resents Tennessee, while Virginia accuses her neighbors of "giving away the store."

The results are mixed. The increase in foreign investment has indeed brought jobs and other benefits to many parts of the country and helped many local economies—some of them already flattened by foreign competition—to rebuild. Once foreign multinationals commit themselves

AP/Wide World Photos

Rudy Perpich of Minnesota, one of the most successful governors at bringing home the foreign-investment bacon.

to a region, many become ideal citizens: active in community affairs, anxious to integrate socially, and eager to contribute to local projects. They make it a point to hire as many Americans as they can and to keep their own foreign nationals to a minimum. (Actually, foreign companies have little choice; U.S. immigration law forces them to adopt this policy.) Some companies even promote Americans to top executive posts, and in a few rare cases—such as the Yokogawa electronics plant in Georgia—claim they would eventually like to hand their American subsidiaries over to American chief executive officers. Yokogawa's record of promoting foreign nationals in other countries indicates the likelihood of their transferring top executive power to American leadership.

Watching states scramble for the foreign dollar raises the question of how this trend fits into a larger context. What are the ultimate consequences for the United States if 50 states make their own individual agreements with foreign governments and foreign multinational corporations? Does this put America, the only industrialized country that allows such separatist tendencies to flourish, at a competitive disadvantage in the global economy? As a world power?

It can be argued that the states are, in effect, conducting a form of foreign policy on their own, unhampered by either executive-branch leadership or Congressional oversight. This is neither a conspiracy nor a ploy; the states are acting honorably and, in their view, in the best interests of their citizens. In many instances, the effects are positive for the economy of the state and negligible for the country. But what if a state lures a foreign manufacturer whose presence threatens a domestic manufacturer in another state with extinction? What if a foreign government is subsidizing a U.S. investment, sustaining a company's losses until the market is cornered and domestic competitors are driven out of business? Or what if that foreign manufacturer acquires, through its new investment, proprietary technology vital to U.S. security or industrial stability? These scenarios are not fantasy; they represent real situations with long-term effects that are uncertain at best and potentially catastrophic.

The crux of the matter is that virtually no coordination exists at the Federal level, which means there is no serious ongoing assessment of the long-term implications of this important trend. In fact, quite the reverse is occurring, with the Federal Government—in the spirit of the New Federalism—tacitly encouraging the states to continue their solo flights. The positive side of this new configuration of state-Federal power is that it reflects the success of the New Federalism: the Federal Government in a quietly supportive role, building the capacity of the states to develop their own programs.

Other issues flow from this central question. In the heated competition for foreign investment, the states go head-to-head, offering a smorgasbord of inducements to potential clients—tax holidays, bonds, low-cost loans, free advice, roads, sewers, and other public improvements. The cost to the taxpayer, states argue, is more than justified by the influx of new business. But to what extent are the states giving away too much? Some critics argue that the states would spend considerably less if they coordinated instead of competed with each other. Still others argue that the factors drawing investment to the United States have little to do with incentives. Companies invest primarily to avoid protective tariffs, to corner market share, and to reduce transportation costs. Weighed on that scale, new sewers and tax holidays may be inconsequential to multinational corporations, as well as unnecessary expenditures for hard-pressed taxpayers.

States view foreign markets and foreign investment the way Americans used to view the frontier: as an opportunity for economic expansion as well as an outlet to reverse economic decline. The governors play the role of ambassadors in the effort to open up new frontiers of foreign economic policy, an area once dominated by the Federal Government. They see themselves as staving off the devastating effects on their states of imports, job layoffs in the manufacturing and lumber industries, and the country's trade deficit.

Diplomatic and cooperative on the surface, they compete fiercely behind the scenes in a high-stakes game that brings $10 billion and 300,000 new jobs into the United States each year. In New England, for example, according to research by a Federal Reserve analyst, Jane Sneddon Little, 20 percent of all investment activity in the early 1980s was conducted by foreign nationals, most of them in the high-tech field; transactions of at least $6.7 billion took place between 1979 and 1983.

The governors are clear about their new role and the reasons that led them to it. At the annual convention of the National Governors' Association Conference in 1985, John Carlin, then Governor of Kansas and president of the association, spoke of the "real role for the governors and the state government in the international arena." The rapid entry of state governments into international trade and investment activity was regarded as a necessity, since the Federal Government was doing little to meet their needs. As reported in *The New York Times*, Carlin emphasized that the governors would not be getting into the political quagmire of Federal tariffs; the states were too diverse to agree on a common position. What was left, exports and foreign investments, was relatively free from controversy and Federal regulation.

Power loves a vacuum, and the governors took to their new role as international supersalesmen with enthusiasm. Governor Rudy Perpich of Minnesota, a Democrat, campaigned on a platform in 1982 to improve the state's economy by attracting foreign investment. A former dentist and international businessman, Perpich had the experience and commitment to fulfill his promises; within two years, 15 foreign companies were involved in setting up plants or sales offices in his state, while serious inquiries from more than a hundred others were discussed.

Perpich branched out on several fronts and penetrated the traditional isolationism of the Midwest. He set up a 30-member trade office in the state capital, began building a world trade center in St. Paul, held seminars in northern European cities, and traveled the globe seeking investment opportunities. He also restructured the state incentive system to make investment opportunities more attractive to foreign investors. "If they invest in a depressed area, we buy down the interest rate," he said in an interview. The state also subsidizes wages, offering to pay the first $5 an hour for six months if investors hire the unemployed.

"We had a hard time attracting foreign investment," recalled Perpich at the annual winter governors' conference in 1985. He analyzed the predicament in terms of the complacency of his constituents. The citizens of Minnesota, lulled into a false sense of security about the economic health of their state, failed to recognize the economic urgency confronting them. "Nobody cared," Perpich said. "Minnesota has a good internal market, its own agriculture, high tech in the cities, the Mayo Clinic medical complex,

and abundant natural resources. But now the situation has changed. The strength of the dollar is killing our agriculture; Canadian lumber is hurting us; and the technological drain is returning to haunt us."

In his efforts to bring foreign investment to Minnesota, Perpich found himself forced to make as big a sales pitch to Minnesota as he did to the foreign companies he was trying to attract. What made it easier, he said, was that the cultures of the companies he had targeted were compatible with the ethnic origins of the state. "We concentrate on Scandinavians," said Perpich. "Our people are Scandinavian." Under Perpich's leadership, Minnesota was one of the first states to break free from the isolationist pattern typical of many Midwestern states, concentrating on northern Europe, a region that had not, up to that point, been heavily involved in the United States. "We think they feel more comfortable with us," said William Dietrich, director of the Minnesota trade office.

Following the Minnesota pattern, national preferences have also played a part in other areas, where, according to Jane Sneddon Little's research: "some clustering does occur . . . 40 percent of Canadian investments are in the Mid-Atlantic, while 40 percent of Dutch and one-third of German and Belgian investments are in the Southeast. Similarly, about one-third of Italian, Swedish, and Japanese investments are in the Mid-Atlantic, the Great Lakes and the Far West respectively."

Geographic proximity also plays a part in site selection—witness the preference of the Far

Two for tea: Harry Hughes, then Governor of Maryland, visiting Beijing with a state delegation in 1980. They met with Vice Premier Deng Xiaoping.

AP/Wide World Photos

Tennessee waltz: Former Governor Lamar Alexander, left, at a Tokyo hotel in 1982, with Takeishi Sakai of Nihon University and Charles E. Smith of the University of Tennessee. They signed an agreement for student exchanges.

Eastern investors for the Far West—along with previous migration patterns: the "Italians in the Mid-Atlantic, the Swedes and Germans in the Great Lakes, and the Japanese in the Far West," writes Little. Investors also like to hire workers from their own ethnic group and may already have relatives or business contacts in a region.

While cultural affinities may play a crucial role in attracting investors, when domestic companies feel threatened those ties don't count for much. "Foreign investment was just starting to come in," recalled Governor Perpich, "when I brought a $90 million cheese plant into Little Falls. People are fighting it. The smaller creameries feel it will put them out of business." He also complained that a certain resistance to foreigners put a crimp in the incentives he was able to offer: "As soon as it's foreign, someone blows the whistle, and we can't give them UDAGs [Urban Development Action Grants from HUD]."

In Minnesota, foreign investment took another interesting turn: It forced domestic business out of its lethargy, in one case literally to protect its turf—the state racetrack. After several Scandinavian banks began negotiating to buy the racetrack, the state's own banks sat up, took notice, and finally filed their own bids. "They didn't have their act together before the foreign banks started eyeing the track," said Governor Perpich.

Ultimately, the key to attracting foreign investment rests with the quality and effectiveness of a governor's leadership. In state after state, the same pattern prevails: The governor persuades the legislature to provide the dollars that fund the state's trade office; it is the gover-

nor's clout that impresses foreign investors and the governor's willingness to circle the globe in search of foreign investment that gives a state the edge over other states.

In the race for foreign dollars, some governors stand out for their ability to recruit foreign business. Perpich is one of the most successful. During his term as Governor of Tennessee, Lamar Alexander led the nation in recruiting Japanese business. Before Ohio's banking crisis occupied so much of his time, Governor Richard F. Celeste traveled extensively in Asia and Europe, bringing home an impressive payload of foreign investment. After attending an international conference in West Germany, he returned with two companies: the Kosmos brewery for Youngstown and Roxane Laboratories for Columbus, an extensive complex that will house the pharmaceutical company's U.S. headquarters and its manufacturing, warehousing, and distribution facilities together in one location. Illinois has also reaped a string of recent successes: Twenty companies from Hong Kong, more than 30 from Taiwan, and 40 from South Korea have located offices in Illinois.

Encouraged by the success of their competitors, prodded by the political necessity to produce jobs, and reinforced by their national professional groups, many other governors have directed their energies to the job of recruiting investment.

Harry R. Hughes, who traveled to Japan to seek investment during his term as Governor of Maryland—once with the Baltimore Orioles baseball team—applauded the results. "It has created a lot of jobs," he said. "We've encouraged it. With only one exception, all foreign

Why, Oh Why, Oh? Governor Richard Celeste, center, greeting foreign representatives at last year's International Trade Exhibit at the Ohio State Fair.

direct investment in Maryland is in the form of joint ventures with American companies." Typically, foreign companies investing in Maryland follow a three-step pattern: First the company sets up a sales division, then a service branch, and, finally, a manufacturing plant. More than 440 foreign investors have located their companies in Maryland, producing more than 45,000 jobs. They are credited with reducing the state's already low unemployment rate of 5.8 percent by two points.

The governors' contention that jobs result directly from foreign investment is supported by Commerce Department data indicating the exact number of jobs traced to foreign-owned property, plants, and equipment. The top five states in 1985 were Texas, California, New York, Alaska, and Louisiana, in that order, with Texas claiming 212,159 jobs from $37.9 billion in foreign investment.

Recruiting foreign investment is only half the job; the governors must also work hard at keeping those companies in the state. That means protecting them politically from occasional onslaughts by the Federal Government as well as challenges from their competitors in other states. In effect, foreign investors find themselves in an enviable position, enjoying the same political benefits as their American counterparts and occasionally, as in the case of the Japanese company YKK, given preferential treatment.

YKK, the world's largest manufacturer of zippers, is also Georgia's largest foreign investor. It has made an investment of more than $200 million and hired a labor force of 1,000 workers at its Macon plant and 140 at its office in Marietta, according to George Dubuc, deputy director of the International Division of the Georgia Department of Industry and Trade.

YKK is thriving in Georgia, thanks to the help of a former governor, George Busbee. It was Busbee who interceded with President Gerald Ford when a complaint was filed against YKK with the International Trade Commission (ITC) by Talon, a domestic zipper manufacturer, ironically also located in Georgia. Talon argued that foreign zippers were hurting domestic manufacturers. Before filing its petition in 1975, Talon executives offered to sell the company to YKK, but the Japanese company refused, fearing such an acquisition would violate the antitrust laws. At that time, YKK had 60 percent of the world market and 60 percent to 65 percent of the U.S. market.

The case before the ITC resulted in a tie vote in 1976 and went to the President for a final decision. At that point, Governor Busbee actively interceded on behalf of YKK. John D. Welsh, then director of the Georgia Department of International Trade, went to Washington to read the Governor's testimony. "We said YKK were good citizens," he recalled in an interview. "Talon also had a plant in north Georgia. They wrote a letter to Busbee saying they would never vote for him again. He answered them with the statement that their comments were duly noted.

"The petition was up before the ITC when Henry Kissinger paid a visit to Georgia and stayed at the governor's mansion," Welsh continued. "Busbee warned Kissinger that the case would jeopardize foreign investment coming into the United States. The President came down in favor of YKK."

Busbee's intervention in the YKK case showed how far a governor would go to defend a major foreign investor, even at the expense of an American investor in the same state. Clearly, YKK was the larger company, with more jobs at stake, more growth potential, and more to contribute to the state's economic base. Perhaps most important, YKK's experience would influence future foreign investment in Georgia. The Governor's decision showed the high priority he placed on foreign investment, a priority shared by many of his fellow governors who would follow his example. It also showed the linkage between recruiting foreign investment and the political vigilance required to insure that investment's future in the United States. The pattern was set, with the governor in the role of chief lobbyist for foreign investors. It worked well in encouraging foreign investors to locate in the United States; they learned from experiences like that of YKK that they could count on a friendly political environment.

The new global-state relationship in investment politics was not trouble-free. Many governors often returned home from foreign travels to face criticism from angry constituents who objected to having their tax money spent on "pleasure" trips. "States have the problem of the occasional failure in political communication," said Marsha Clark of the National Association of State Development Agencies, a national resource and support group for the states. "Governors must defend themselves against charges of junketing. The common perception is that it is a luxury." To a lesser extent, governors also find themselves fielding criticism for spending money for state offices abroad—offices that recruit foreign investment and seek outlets for their products.

When the level of criticism is sufficiently intense, the states respond in a manner often detrimental to their long-term interests. John Y. Brown, then Governor of Kentucky, caught in the political turbulence, made the mistake of closing his state office for foreign investment, a decision he later regretted. Forced to make large cuts in social programs, Brown pacified his critics by promising to give up "what's nearest and dearest to my heart, international development." Ultimately, "this damages the states," explained Clark. "The continuity of presence is very important."

U.S. governors say that foreign investment has produced political controversy in only one area: farmland. It is ironic that only in agriculture have Americans objected to the threat of foreign domination, while fully accepting foreign investment in manufacturing, banking, urban real estate, and securities. The nation's agrarian heritage, deeply rooted in Jeffersonian democracy, goes further than any other factor in explaining why Americans find the loss of their land more

threatening than foreign purchases of their banks or factories. Even today, land remains a symbol of personal ownership. More Americans can identify with owning a farm than owning a bank or a factory.

In Maryland, for example, local residents opposed German land purchases. "We had some political flak several years ago with the foreign purchases of eastern-shore farmland," recalled Harry Hughes, then Governor. "Germans bought land as working farms and pushed the price of land up. A bill came up in the State Legislature requiring 51 percent ownership of land [by a U.S. citizen]. It didn't get anywhere."

The controversy over farmland crested in the late 1970s and early 1980s; with the steep drop in the price of agricultural land, the issue appears to have died down. Nevertheless, many states still restrict foreign ownership. Minnesota, for example, has a law forbidding foreign purchases of land that is vigorously opposed by the Governor, who calls it "not rational."

Another dimension of the controversy, according to a state official who lived through it, was simple racism. "My personal judgment," this official said, "was that this was not an issue when Europeans were buying, only when non-Caucasians—Japanese, Saudis, etc.—were involved. It was important as an expression of prevailing sentiment."

Any foreign investment that produces radical changes in the market is bound to produce controversy. Initially, agricultural-land purchases created resentment when farmers found the prices so inflated they couldn't afford to buy land for themselves. By 1986, the price of farmland had declined so markedly that many farmers welcomed any investors, foreign or American; in fact, during the last days of debate on the tax reform bill, farmers opposed the repeal of a tax break for foreign land purchasers.

In Utah, a similar controversy surfaced in real estate. "The investment came in too fast," said Governor Norman H. Bangerter, himself a former real estate developer, "faster than we could assimilate it. There are now heavy vacancies which have depressed the inner city and commercial rents in Salt Lake City. There's been too much development, too fast." One of the biggest developers was Adnan Khashoggi, a Saudi Arabian investor and international arms dealer, whose TRIAD corporation built an industrial park and an office complex in the city. By early 1987, the project had collapsed, and TRIAD faced 47 lawsuits from creditors demanding more than $100 million. Khashoggi reportedly threatened not to pay the company's debts, blaming TRIAD's problems on unfriendly treatment from city officials. He subsequently filed for Chapter 11 bankruptcy protection.

Despite the flooding of Salt Lake's real estate market, Bangerter views foreign investment with cautious optimism. "I have some concern that foreign investment may stop, as well," he continued. "We have to be wary. We shouldn't be overly dependent on foreign investment."

Junketing, inflated property values, and fears of absentee farm ownership seem minor, however, in view of the pockets of political protest that emerge when foreign investors threaten American-owned businesses. Especially when those investors are supported by the American taxpayer. In Wisconsin, dairy farmers lodged a strong protest against an impending investment by an Irish company that planned to build dairies in Georgia with the aid of tax-free industrial development bonds.

The cross-purposes of state and Federal policies were never so stark. As reported in *The Washington Post*, Georgia's farmers were under pressure from the Federal Government to reduce milk surpluses. They agreed to cut their state's milk production by 22 percent, taking 24,000 cows out of production. At the same time, Macon County officials were busy selling $4.5 million worth of bonds to help the Irish company, Masstock International, set up a $35 million operation that would grow to 20,000 cows within a few years. It was a wonderful deal for Masstock: The company benefited from tax-exempt bonds that would reduce their borrowing costs by 2 percent to 3 percent; they would pay no tax on income from the bonds; and their investors could look forward to the future protection of their investment by Federal price supports, which—thanks to regional differentials—kept Georgia's prices higher than in other parts of the country.

The controversy pitted Americans against one another. Macon County officials, backed by their Governor, Joe Frank Harris, a Democrat, argued that it was not fair to discriminate against the Irish investor for a dairy crisis that was 20 years in the making. They claimed that the Irish investment meant jobs for farm workers and benefits for the local economy.

American dairy farmers, led by their representatives in Congress, felt otherwise. "What is happening in Georgia makes no sense," said Senator Robert W. Kasten Jr., a Republican from Wisconsin. "We are paying family farmers to leave the dairy industry through the buy-out program at the same time as we're paying foreign corporations to get into dairying through tax subsidies and price supports. It's an affront to dairy farmers and taxpayers and must be stopped."

Joined by Representative Tony Coelho, Democrat from California and former chairman of the House Agriculture Subcommittee on Livestock, Dairy, and Poultry, Kasten vowed to protect American farmers. Although bipartisan, their efforts met roadblocks from Reagan Administration appointees in the Agriculture Department. "We are in favor of free markets," said Richard Goldberg, Deputy Under Secretary of Agriculture. "This Administration believes the Government should not interfere with an individual's right to open or expand a business."

Faced with such disarray among states and between the executive branch and Congress, foreign investors find it easy to drive a wedge into American markets. By the time policy-makers discern a pattern of disadvantage and attempt to remedy it, it is often too late; the investor is solidly established, with all the political protection of an American business.

Moving west across the country, one finds more criticism of foreign investment, ranging from Utah Governor Norman Bangerter's balanced caution to the firm opposition of former Governor Richard Lamm of Colorado. The Western states bristled under their prior status as economic colonies of the East and, some say, regard foreign investment as a new form of colonization. In addition, analysts note that the Western states' lower unemployment rate makes them less eager for new jobs than states in the South, Midwest, Middle Atlantic, and Northeast. The Western states can afford to be futurists, they say, and take a longer view of what is happening to the country as a whole, in contrast to the more myopic perspective of the majority of the nation's states. The exceptions are California, which tends to view itself closer commercially to the Pacific Rim countries than it does to many parts of the United States, and states such as Idaho, whose economies were especially hard hit by the decline in agricultural exports.

Speaking for several of the Western governors in a *New York Times* article, Lamm sharply criticized the shortsightedness of the states' new international independence and said he feared where it was leading the country. During his term in office, Lamm was one of the only governors who did not recruit foreign investment, although he remarked that his inaction—and overt hostility—did not seem to have had any effect in discouraging the rapid incursion of Japanese investment in Colorado. Lamm warned: "There is a strong sentiment on the part of the Western governors that there is something really wrong here. I do not want Japanese coming in and buying up American technology. I do not want them in our state. I don't want the Arabs owning our banks or the Japanese owning our means of production. It terrifies me."

"The governors can play a real role," Lamm continued, "but we're being outnegotiated on everything. The Japanese want it both ways. They're screwing us. They have a different set of values. What's mine is mine, and what's yours is negotiable." Lamm argued that his fellow governors' lack of foresight on the issue of foreign investment would haunt the United States for years to come. "Politicians fight the last war. This is tomorrow's issue emerging."

Then Governors Bruce Babbitt of Arizona and Robert Kerrey of Nebraska shared Lamm's concern and agreed to put the issue on their agenda for a 1985 summer meeting in Honolulu. "Foreign investment is a great concern of mine," said Kerrey. "Technology drain is a major issue. Reciprocity is a major concern. They bring in jobs and money when they come in to invest, but we find ourselves importing their product. The trade deficit creates a major employment problem for us at home."

As a group, the governors have brushed aside warnings that the growing level of foreign investment may restrict domestic production and eventually worsen the budget and trade deficits. For them this scenario reaches too far into the future and is eclipsed by the immediate stimulating effect that foreign investment has had on the economies of their states. With such heady successes, it is reasonable to assume that the states will continue their aggressive campaign for foreign investment, making impressive inroads into the global economy. In that context, the national perspective, national needs, and national interests can expect to remain secondary for a long time to come.

DELAWARE INC.

Fifty bucks - credit cards accepted - will put you in business.

L. J. Davis

L. J. Davis is a contributing editor ⸱
Harper's *magazine.*

On Jan. 3, 1986, the readers of the Asian edition of The Wall Street Journal were treated to an arresting full-page advertisement. Topped by a smiling photograph of S. B. (for Shien Biau) Woo, the Lieutenant Governor of Delaware, who is also the state's highest-ranking elected Democrat, the highest-ranking Chinese-American official in the United States and a physicist, the ad posed two questions. "Are you thinking of investing in the USA?" it asked. "WHY NOT DO AS THE AMERICAN DO!" The wily Americans, Woo's text explained, incorporated their companies in the benign business climate of Delaware, established trusts there and founded Delaware banks and holding companies.

Shortly after the ad appeared, Woo himself was in the Orient, personally extolling the virtues of his state. With the Delaware Secretary of State, Michael E. Harkins, in tow, the Shanghai-born official traveled to Taiwan, Hong Kong, China, Indonesia, Singapore and the Philippines, tirelessly drumming up business with the help of a bilingual pamphlet that resembled something dreamed up by the National Lampoon back in the days when it was funny. "We Protect You From Politics," ran one passage. "By incorporating secretly, in the event of an emergency in your home country, such as insurrection or invasion by a hostile power, you company can temporarily or permanently move its domicile and be protected by the laws of The State of Delaware (for additional fees)." The text went on to explain the many and subtle beauties of Delaware

trust law, described the state as an investor's paradise and expounded on the wonders of the Port of Wilmington, a major point of entry for bananas and Volkswagens.

Strange as Woo's campaign may have seemed to an American, it worked. In the United States, Woo may be virtually unknown outside his adopted state, but in the Far East he is famous, and many doors fell effortlessly open before him. "We all know a lieutenant governorship isn't worth a hill of beans," he says, "but they don't." If all goes according to plan, Delaware will shortly become the proud possessor of the only steel mill in the Western hemisphere partly owned by the Peoples' Republic of China.

Meanwhile, half a world away, Delaware's Governor, Michael N. Castle, was a man with all the delightful problems that accompany a booming economy and a healthy budget surplus. His state has long been known, not always favorably, as a corporate haven, a kind of American Leichtenstein—"a pygmy state," fumed the late William L. Cary, a former chairman of the Securities and Exchange Commission, "interested only in revenues."

As recently as January 1988, the state lived up to its reputation when it passed legislation requiring anyone raiding a Delaware corporation either to acquire a whopping 85 percent of its stock in a single transaction or to suspend such efforts for a tedious three years. The precise effect of this legislation is unclear, especially because the S.E.C. immediately challenged its constitu-

tionality, but it's typical of Delaware's tradition of tender concern for the well-being of its corporate children.

It is not a concern widely shared by other states in the Middle Atlantic region. Indeed, sympathetic observers of what is often called "the Delaware design" have long been known to express amazement that large, sophisticated neighbors like Pennsylvania and New York haven't found a way to compete with Delaware for the incorporation business. "Surprisingly," notes one legal study, "much of the difficulty of these large states appears to be . . . because of their legislatures." The large states persist in viewing corporation laws as complex moral and political problems rather than—as in happy Delaware—a way of making everybody rich.

Delaware has long boomed as a corporate venue; it now booms in other ways as well. The unemployment rate, at 3.3 percent of the work force, is the second lowest in the nation; only New Hampshire's is lower. Indeed, Delaware has become a net importer of labor, with more than 21,000 out-of-state commuters, most of them from Pennsylvania, Maryland and New Jersey. Downtown Wilmington, only a decade ago dominated by the stone mass of the Du Pont Building, the vacant lots of failed urban renewal schemes and a huge junkyard, now boasts a new skyline whose crown jewels are the 12-story Hercules Plaza (the junkyard still visible from its windows), the handsome mirrored facility of the Chase Manhattan

Bank and the new 23-story Manufacturers Hanover Plaza.

In just seven short years, Delaware in general and Wilmington in particular have become a major financial center, a development that has brought the state some 15,900 jobs, 9,616 of them directly involved in the operations of out-of-state institutions like Manufacturers and Chase—jobs that would once have been domiciled mostly in New York. Moreover, Wilmington is the nation's largest depository of privately owned gold, largely because Delaware charges no sales tax on precious metals transactions—nor, for that matter, on anything else.

The absence of a Delaware sales tax is comparatively old hat. Of more interest is the fact that the state averaged an annual revenue growth of 7.7 percent over the past five years—more than double the rate of inflation—despite four consecutive cuts in the personal income tax that reduced the annual bite to an estimated 4.1 percent. Some have called the state a supply-side miracle. Others, perhaps more temperate in their judgment, suggest that the Delaware miracle is what happens when conservative Republicans like Michael Castle and Pierre S. du Pont 4th end up in the Governor's office.

In many ways, they are less ideological than pragmatic. Their policies have reflected the concerns of the well-educated professional class—the members of the state's unusually powerful bar association, the Ph.D's from Du Pont, the executives in the booming banks—that forms such an important part of the Delaware constituency. Like many of their generation and accomplishments, Delaware's Governors have been liberal on matters of civil rights, pragmatic on social policy, deeply concerned about education and fiscally conservative. "In Delaware, there isn't a lot of difference between the Democrats and the Republicans," says Governor Castle, who used the occasion of his latest State of the State message to utter some fairly tart words about the Federal Government and its abdication of its responsibilities. "I'm more of a Governor than I am a Republican."

Delaware may not be easier to govern than, say, New Jersey, but it's certainly very different. In a state with 644,000 inhabitants occupying only 1,982 square miles—"Three counties at low tide," says Castle, "and two counties at high"—obtaining a consensus is fairly easy. "Everybody knows everybody else," one official explains. This doesn't necessarily mean that everybody is interested in looking after everybody else. "I'm not very proud of it, but we have

the highest infant mortality rate in the country," Castle says. Delaware also has one of the highest rates of black teenage pregnancy, and its welfare benefits are the second lowest in the mid-Atlantic region, after West Virginia. "The Delaware miracle?" says the Rev. Otis Herring, the president of the Ministers' Action Council. "I wait to see it."

Surrounded by the dark paneling and antique china of the executive conference room on the 12th floor of the Carvel State Office Building in downtown Wilmington, Castle and his aides contemplate their handiwork and discuss a dilemma. With money pouring into the state coffers from the economic boom, Delaware sailed out of fiscal 1987 with an unencumbered surplus of $85 million. Castle wants to devote the money to long-term projects, to his new highway trust fund, to his welfare reform, to his overcrowded prisons and environmental programs.

Unfortunately, the legislators in the state capital of Dover also want to spend the money. "Day-care centers," says Castle. "People want to put their names on buildings. This whole day-care thing has gotten out of hand." At the same time, there is talk around the big table of granting a tax break to venture-capital firms. 'I don't see anything wrong with giving a tax break to a business that isn't even here yet," says Castle, ending the debate. Someone points out that the whole question is moot, since Delaware will be at the bottom of the Atlantic Ocean in a mere 7,000 years. "Yeah, well," says Castle. "That's the trouble with us politicians. We always think in the short term."

Down on the 11th floor, Lieutenant Governor Woo contemplates the handiwork resulting from his 1986 swing through Asia. Woo's office estimates that the Lieutenant Governor's efforts have led to an annual $1 million in incorporation fees from Oriental companies. The Ambassador of the People's Republic of China came to call; Wilmington and Ningbo, a port city near Shanghai, were designated as "Friendship Cities," and the Lieutenant Governor was on the lookout for some Ningbo shipping business. With Woo pinch-hitting as interpreter, a local company won an important polypropylene contract from the People's Republic, and a refinisher of 1840's furniture landed a $1.5 million joint venture to build a furniture plant. And while Woo is looking forward to a rich harvest of Hong Kong flight capital in anticipation of the British pull-out from the colony in 1997, in the short run he can look forward to restarting the moribund

'I don't see anything wrong with giving a tax break to a business that isn't even here yet,' says Governor Castle.

Phoenix Steel Corporation mill using money advanced by a Hong Kong investor together with the China International Trust and Investment Corp., the second largest financial institution in the People's Republic.

IT WAS IN DELAWARE, IN 1802, on the banks of the Brandywine River, that Eleuthère Irénée du Pont de Nemours erected his first gunpowder mills and laid the foundation of the nation's largest chemical company. Evidently a man of iron nerve, he built his personal mansion overlooking his works, the most explosive site in North America. Soon, however, the estates of his heirs were spread all over the northern arc of the state, and the du Ponts occasionally seemed to harbor the illusion that they owned the place.

With 25,400 employees, the Du Pont company easily remains the largest in the state, far ahead of Hercules Inc., the chemical and plastic concern (2,700), the British-owned ICI Americas Inc. (3,600) and the General Motors plant (4,200). "Until the out-of-state banks began to come in around 1981," says one local banker, "three institutions ran this state. One was Du Pont, of course. Another was the Wilmington Trust. And the last was the corporate law firm of Richards, Layton, & Finger." The firm's legendary Aaron Finger, who died in 1969, was regarded as one of the most formidable corporation lawyers in the United States, a voice that was respected, sometimes feared, and often heeded. And thereby hangs a tale.

Once, in Delaware and many other states, the life of a corporation was limited to a specific term (in Delaware, 20 years, after which it had to be incorporated again) and for highly specific purposes. The method of incorporation was via a special act of the Legislature, which offered rich possibilities for bribery. In 1875, the Legislature passed a general incorporation law that permitted the founding of corporations "for religious, charitable, literary and manufacturing purposes, for the preservation of animal and vegetable food, building and loan association, and for draining low lands."

Then, in 1896, New Jersey adopted its own incorporation statute, the most liberal in the land. In New Jersey, a corporation could be eternal. It could carry on operations anywhere it pleased, it could merge and consolidate its operations as it pleased, and within the bounds of the law it could revise its charter by a simple vote of its board of directors, without consulting the pesky and unpredictable stockholders.

Needless to say, companies raced to New Jersey; by 1902, its income from filing fees and the franchise tax was so great that it abolished the property tax. Delaware, quick to sense an opportunity, was not far behind with its own General Corporation Law of 1899, which was ballyhooed as even more liberal than New Jersey's, to say nothing of cheaper, but Delaware was wasting its breath. New Jersey remained the premier incorporation state until 1913, when the outgoing Governor, Woodrow Wilson, persuaded the Legislature to outlaw trusts and holding companies.

Most of Wilson's law was repealed in 1917, but by then the damage was done; Delaware, which had nothing against trusts and holding companies, also had most of the business. By 1929, corporate fees and taxes provided 42.5 percent of state income. Still, nothing lasts forever. By 1945, with more than 30 other states having liberalized their own corporate statutes, only 16.3 percent of Delaware's revenue came from the corporations it sheltered. By 1955, the figure was down to 7.2 percent.

Clearly, something had to be done. In 1967, when corporate filings had reached a new low, the General Corporation Law was revised under the guidance of a committee put together by the Secretary of State's office. It was an unusual but very tidy arrangement, rather as though the nation's defense contractors were to draw up the military budget. Few dissenting voices were heard in Delaware. "You can't trust the Legislature to do a lot of things," says former Governor du Pont, "but you can rely on it to keep the corporation law up to date." With a little help from its friends, of course.

SHOULD YOU DECIDE TO INcorporate in Delaware, the state makes it easy for you with a booklet entitled, appropriately enough, "Incorporating in Delaware." It comes complete with handy foldout forms, and it is a gold mine of useful tips. Should you be at a loss for a precise reason for incorporating in Delaware — or if you have reason for lying low when the subject is raised — the booklet suggests that you simply state: "The purpose of the corporation is to engage in any lawful act or activity for which corporations may be organized under the General Corporation Law of Delaware."

The minimum filing fee is $50. For an additional $100, the state will incorporate you on the day you hand in your papers; $50 gets you incorporated within 24 hours. "We respect your privacy," Woo's pamphlet reminds us. "You don't have to tell us the details of your business; you don't have to list who's on your board or who's holding office; and you don't have to use your name and address — just use your Delaware agent's."

The job can be done in a matter of moments. "The fact is," says Carolyn McKown, the vice-president of Corporate Agents Inc., a Wilmington specialty firm, "it's real easy to get incorporated in Delaware, no matter how you do it. We can do an incorporation in about three minutes." Buying a used car should be so simple. "No waiting!" trumpets the C.A.I. advertisement in the state booklet. "Just call us toll free ... and our friendly, professional staff will form your corporation while you are on the telephone via our direct computer link to the Delaware Corporation Department. (Have your VISA or MasterCard ready.)"

Once you have received your certificate, the advantages accrue immediately. For example, you can hold meetings of your anonymous board by telephone, saving yourself much bothersome expense. Your profits, if earned outside Delaware, will be exempt from state taxation. You can pay dividends, if any, out of either your annual profits or your accrued surplus from past operations. (New York allows dividends to be paid only from the surplus, meaning that you have to establish a track record. Delaware is uninterested in your track record.)

Other states allow outraged stockholders to sue board members for glaring misjudgment, an increasingly common (and successful) practice that has led insurance companies to withdraw their protection — which

in turn has caused many candidates to decline the honor of a company directorship, creating a small crisis in the nation's boardrooms. In 1986, however, Delaware allowed its corporations to reimburse their directors for many kinds of court-ordered money damages, which solved the problem quite nicely.

Moreover, if a charter is properly written, companies can change their by-laws without stockholder approval, a handy power to have when defenses are being put in place to repel a raid. And when it comes to corporate raiding, Delaware is by no means immune to those irrational moralisms and political acts that so bedevil the Legislatures of its larger neighbors. In 1987, when the Texas oilman T. Boone Pickens Jr. was trying to accumulate an ominous block of stock in the Boeing Company, long a loyal Delaware corporation, he uttered many eloquent words about the state and even traveled to Wilmington. ("I was surprised that he was so charming," says Governor Castle.)

Around that time, the thinking of the Legislature in Dover was sharpened when Hercules Inc. abruptly sold its share of a joint venture for $1.5 billion — meaning that Hercules, with all that money on its books, was now itself a prime takeover target. In January 1988, the incorporation statute was amended to forbid any holder of 15 percent of a Delaware company's stock from effecting a merger for three years unless the board of directors approved, two-thirds of the stockholders overrode a negative board decision or the raider managed to acquire 85 percent of the company's unencumbered stock in a single purchase.

Still, anyone can make laws, and states seeking a share of the Delaware pie have amended their incorporation laws in a so-called "race to the bottom line" as they strive to accommodate the needs of corporate America and, not incidentally, pick up some of Delaware's handsome fees. Notwithstanding, companies have continued to flock to Delaware, whose continued pre-eminence in the field resides largely in the hard-to-duplicate depth and expertise of its powerful legal profession and, not least, in its unique Chancery Court, modeled on a royal institution that was abolished in most of the rest of the United States at the time of the Revolution. "I think a lot of my predecessors were Anglophiles," says the present Chancellor, William T. Allen, only the

19th person to have occupied the post in nearly 200 years.

His decisions — like those of his predecessors — will be cited by courts and lawyers far from Wilmington as the definitive word on the subject. Everything that happens in the Chancery Court is potentially worth millions of dollars to the arbitrageurs who bet heavily on the outcomes of the various battles, which accounts for the fact that the Chancellor's diminutive and almost makeshift courtroom—it seems to have been furnished from the catalogue of a third-rate store specializing in providing liturgical furniture to impoverished storefront churches—is sometimes thronged with local lawyers in the pay of the nation's investment community.

At crucial moments, the lawyers bolt for the phones; at least one lawyer has been known to boast of reporting to his masters directly from the courtroom, by means of a concealed cellular phone. Yet for all the vast sums involved, no Delaware judge has ever been convicted of corruption. "I think it's because we're so small," says Allen. "If somebody started getting rich as this job, the rest of us would notice."

In the midst of the slightly hallucinatory Delaware miracle, it's easy to forget that it was not always thus. In 1978, Irving S. Shapiro, then the chief executive officer of Du Pont, flatly advised other companies not to locate in the state. For one thing, the personal income tax was a confiscatory 19.8 percent. "When I first came to the Legislature in 1963," says State Senator Herman Holloway Sr., "we used to hope that a du Pont would die so we could balance the budget with the inheritance taxes."

To Pierre du Pont, who was elected Governor in 1976, the problems were enormous, but the causes were simple. "In 1976, we were the classic liberal basket case. High tax rates. Second highest unemployment rating in the country. Lowest bond rating. When I first got here, I wondered if I could actually run this place. When I was a Congressman in Washington and we needed money, we always said we could take it out of the Defense budget. But Delaware didn't have a defense budget."

Du Pont, an improbably handsome patrician Republican of the bluest blood, immediately adopted a classic remedy. "I decided I could only do two or three things a year, but I was going to get them done," he says. High on his list were balancing the budget and cutting taxes. "Pete du Pont is a little like Mike Dukakis," says a banker close to the situation. "He got lucky. He can take credit for someone else's success."

What happened next is a little confusing, at least in its details; victory has many fathers. Du Pont, his first tax cut on the books, was deep in his 1980 re-election campaign when the Chase Manhattan Bank came to call. "They wanted to move in their credit-card operation," says the banker. "They said they could live with our situation, but they needed the usury law [the state law that set a cap on interest rates] repealed. They did not meet with a good reception." Other Wilmington businessmen persuaded Chase officials to pay calls on the Governor and on Irving Shapiro of Du Pont. Mr. Shapiro regarded the Delaware usury laws as absurd.

In early 1981, with Governor du Pont safely re-elected and the future tax cuts therefore assured, the Legislature passed a remarkable law called the Financial Center Development Act. The new law permitted out-of-state banks to set up shop but prohibited them from engaging in retail banking that could take away customers from local banks—a move that assuaged the anxieties of Wilmington Trust. It also required them to bring in at least $25 million in capital within their first year of operation and to hire at least 100 employees. But it offered them a remarkable tax advantage. A bank generating less than $20 million in income within the state boundaries would pay a tax of 8.7 percent, while a bank that earned more than $30 million would pay only 2.7 percent on anything over that amount.

Business flocked in. Chase was joined by Manufacturers Hanover, Chemical Bank, Citicorp, Bankers Trust Company, J. P. Morgan & Company, E. F. Hutton & Company, J. C. Penney Company, Montgomery Ward & Company and the Bank of New York; other banks moved in operations from as far away as Michigan and Texas. E. F. Hutton established a trust company; J. C. Penney and Montgomery Ward set up consumer-credit operations. "We had no idea it was going to be so successful," says governor Castle. In Wilmington and its suburbs, construction boomed. In a state the size of Delaware, the prospect of 10,000 new banking jobs and 7,000 new jobs in support industries, many of them held by minorities, was no small event.

"Electricity in Delaware costs roughly half as much as it does in New York," says William E. Pike, the executive vice-president of Morgan's Delaware operations. "We have found that Delaware productivity is 20 percent higher per employee, at a minimum. There's a completely different political environment here. In New York it sometimes seems that the environment is not very hospitable. In Delaware, they couldn't have been more welcoming and helpful. You can't move Wall Street to Delaware, of course, but there's no reason to keep all those back office operations in lower Manhattan."

What does it all mean? To former Governor du Pont, whose Presidential ambitions are clearly not dead but sleeping, the Delaware miracle is a triumph of sound conservative principles and supply-side economics. He regards the Delaware model as easily exportable to other states, once they come to their senses.

Others are not so sure. "I don't understand supply-side economics," says Irving Shapiro, now a lawyer with Skadden, Arps, Slate, Meagher & Flom, "and I don't think Pete du Pont does either. But as a businessman I can tell you it doesn't work." To some, the Delaware phenomenon is a result of luck, good timing, a regional boom (especially in financial services) and increasingly predatory tax policies in other states. "We are a very small place with a very large industrial base and a long head start in corporation law," says one local banker. "You can't duplicate that sort of thing. I can't believe how complacent everyone is."

Civic Strategy
for Local Economic Development

ROSS GITTELL and NANCY KELLEY

*Ross Gittell and Nancy Kelley are co-directors of the Community
Revitalization Project at the Center for Business and Government, John
F. Kennedy School of Government, Harvard University.*

Little systematic study has been made of the steps communities go
through in attempts to improve and manage their economies. Discussions of community economic development have been dominated
by economists and political scientists who too often ignore or discount
local factors and lack a multidisciplinary approach to the problem.

We believe practitioners in all sectors can gain from greater knowledge
about the ingredients and stages of recent revitalization efforts in mid-
sized industrial communities. Such information yields practical insights
about what local interests can do to alleviate economic dislocation and
provides guidelines for fashioning state and federal programs to assist
such efforts.

Important aspects of economic revival can be addressed from the
local level. Over the past three years as directors of The Community
Revitalization Project at Harvard University we have grappled with that
topic by asking: What aspects of its economic life can a community
effect? What positive roles can local leaders and institutions play? How
may a community determine the extent and nature of its economic
problems and the best ways to cope with them?

Specifically, we explored the mechanisms associated with recovery
efforts in three once-industrial communities that had experienced dramatic economic dislocation and are now at different stages redevelopment. The foci of our investigation are Lowell, Massachusetts, the
Monongahela Valley in Pennsylvania, and Jamestown, New York. Using an "analytic microscope" we conducted extensive interviews and
collected data in the field, to uncover the essential components of local development and community revitalization.

In this article — the first of series for the NATIONAL CIVIC REVIEW —
we provide an overview of our findings to date including brief economic
histories of three of the communities. We highlight the components
of local economic development that relate most closely to the theme
of this issue, the role of participatory groups in civic life.

The Communities

Lowell, Massachusetts, the Monongahela Valley in Pennsylvania, and
Jamestown, New York are now at different stages of economic development. Each has faced difficult problems in the past and confronts somewhat different ones today.

Lowell

Of the three communities, Lowell is at the most advanced state in
its revitalization. Lowell has a population of 93,000 and lies northwest
of Boston, near the Route 128 high-technology complex. Lowell has

frequently been cited as the "model city" for community revitalization
in Massachusetts and New England.

Lowell was the second planned industrial community in the U.S. (after
Paterson, N.J.); its growth and development were closely tied to the
introduction of the power loom and the industrialization of textile
manufacturing, because of its cheap and abundant supply of water power channeled from the Merrimack River into canal systems throughout the city, and its ample supply of immigrant labor.

Lowell's attractiveness to textile manufacturers declined after 1900
as steam and electricity replaced water power as inexpensive sources
of energy, and labor unrest forced mill owners to relocate to the South
where wage rates were lower and energy less expensive.

Economic depression first hit in the early 1920s. Manufacturing employment in the city fell almost 50% from 1924 to 1932. Unlike many
other communities, Lowell saw no post-depression or post-World War
II recovery. Instead, it experienced a long period of economic and demographic stagnation. While the nation grew rapidly from 1920 to 1970,
Lowell's population actually declined from over 112,000 to less than
95,000. In the early 1970s the city reached its low point with a jobless
rate near 13% — the highest in the nation among cities of over 50,000
residents — and the average family income just above the poverty line.

Over the next ten years, business, banking and political leaders developed and implemented a strategy for change and economic development based on a vision for Lowell provided by Pat Mogan, the former
Superintendent of Schools. Mogan's concept called for celebrating
Lowell's industrial past to build a new industrial future. Related economic development efforts were led by U.S. Senator Paul Tsongas, a
Lowell native and former councilman. Senator Tsongas was instrumental
in mobilizing local consensus behind the venture and helping to formulate an action plan to commit substantial public and private financial and human resources and to develop the necessary organizational
capacity.

By the early 1980s Lowell's economy had improved substantially by
any traditional measure of economic vitality. The unemployment rate
had dropped below three percent, among the lowest in the nation for
cities of comparable size. Several major high-tech firms, including Wang
Industries, had located there. A $20 million urban National Park, the
first of its kind, had been completed. The downtown mill and retail
districts had been renovated and retail sales were growing faster in Lowell
than in any other Massachusetts city.

Despite its highly publicized success, Lowell's public and private sector
leaders were heavily criticized by local community groups. As in many

Reprinted by permission from the May/June 1988 issue of *National Civic Review*, pp. 213-223. National Civic Review, 1601
Grant Street, Suite 250, Denver, CO 80203.

local development efforts, initial revitalization activities focused on business and downtown development. From 1975 to 1985, 83% of public and private funds devoted to the project (over $141 million), were invested in the central business district. Meanwhile, surrounding neighborhoods presented a sharp contrast to Lowell's revitalized downtown. Only two blocks away in the Acre, a low-income neighborhood comprised mostly of immigrants, whole blocks of housing stood decaying with missing windows and burned-out floors.

Community groups in Lowell took action. They felt that they had been excluded from the decision-making process and denied many of the benefits of economic recovery. The Coalition For a Better Acre devised a strategy to obtain funds to revitalize housing in the area. They circumvented the city government and local public and private sector leaders, who ignored their complaints, and worked closely with members of Governor Michael Dukakis's staff and a private insurance company. Their purpose was to persuade city officials and local developers to secure financing and a federal grant for new housing in the Acre neighborhood.

Eventually, Lowell's public and private sector leaders were forced to accept housing and neighborhoods as essential components of community revitalization. They also accepted the Coalition for a Better Acre as a legitimate participant in future economic development decision making.

Jamestown

Jamestown, New York is a smaller and more isolated community than Lowell. Jamestown has a population of 36,000 and is located 70 miles southwest of Buffalo.

Like all our study communities, Jamestown has a long manufacturing tradition. In the last half of the 19th century, its economy benefitted from the new crafts and skills brought to the region by an influx of Swedish and Italian settlers. The city flourished around the production of lumber and wood products, and wood and metal furniture.

Since 1950 there has been a steady decline in manufacturing employment and a dramatic change in its composition. Most significantly, jobs in the furniture, lumber and wood product industries declined over 63 percent.

Struggle to Retain and Attract Industry

Jamestown engaged in an ongoing struggle to retain existing factories and attract new ones. To date, the most significant efforts have focused on fostering labor-management cooperation (led by former Mayor Stan Lundine, now New York's Lieutenant Governor) and, more recently, developing a vision and strategy for Jamestown's future by an active economic development committee of community leaders, funded by local foundations.

Labor-Management Relations

Stan Lundine's campaign in the early 1970s aimed to address what was then perceived as the fundamental problem in the community—conflict between labor and management that resulted in Jamestown's having the most work days lost due to strikes per worker of any U.S. city. Under his guidance, the antagonists came to recognize their shared concerns and to cooperate in a Jamestown Area Labor-Management Committee (J.A.L.M.C.) with notable results. Not only were existing jobs saved, but new industries, most significantly Cummins Engine with 500 employees, were attracted to the area. The J.A.L.M.C. was the first of its kind and has served as the model for similar ventures elsewhere.

Unfortunately, Jamestown was unable to sustain this momentum due to several factors, including Lundine's move to Congress. The labor-management committee slowly lost its ability to serve as the institutional vehicle to promote on-going economic development efforts. Meanwhile, Jamestown's economy has continued to decline. Industrial employment in 1980 was 3,800, one-third the 1950 total. The downtown retail district suffers from a high vacancy rate, and housing conditions continue to deteriorate, with over 75 percent of the housing stock having been built prior to 1940.

The heads of locally based foundations have refused to sit still as their community experiences a slow but steady decline. Last year a group of local foundations collaborated to fund an economic development

steering committee with multiple objectives. Its principal mandate is to develop a plan and vision for Jamestown's economic development. Other objectives include grooming committee members as community leaders and the group itself as an on-going mechanism for processing development proposals and systematically implementing them.

It is too early to predict the effect of Jamestown's young economic development committee. To date it has apparently revived community interest in revitalization issues and provided a means for involving area youth in community development efforts.

The Monongahela (Mon) Valley

By comparison with Lowell and Jamestown, the communities of the Monongahela Valley are still in the primary stages of economic revitalization. Located southeast of Pittsburgh, the Mon Valley occupies 140 square miles along the banks of the Monongahela and Youghiogheny Rivers. The Valley encompasses more than 38 separate governments, including three counties and three governing councils. Over 270,000 people live in the area.

Economic prosperity in the Valley has historically revolved around the steel industry, dominated mainly by one company, U.S. Steel (now USX). From the turn of the century to the early 1960s, many Mon Valley communities prospered. As the U.S. economy expanded, demand for iron and steel products grew. Steel from the Valley built the Empire State Building, the Hancock Building and the Golden Gate Bridge. Local steel workers became the highest paid industrial workers in the world.

The precipitous decline of the American steel industry is well documented. Since 1973, jobs in the industry have dropped from 540,000 to 180,000. More than 25 steel companies have gone bankrupt, over 50 have terminated operations, and more than 500 facilities have been closed down—many of them in the Mon Valley cities of McKeesport, Homestead, Clairton and Duquesne.

Residents in the area have felt themselves helpless victims of economic events beyond their control. Many Valley communities lost more than 50 percent of their populations in less than 20 years. One recent local survey unofficially estimated the household head unemployment rate at 55 percent. Until 1987, many people looked for a revival of steel to bolster the Valley economy. Now that dream is largely dead.

Sustained economic vitality depends on committed local individuals engaging in an on-going process of education, discovery, and continued innovation and adjustment over time.

Despite the economic devastation, some hope now comes from other quarters. Under the direction of Mike Eichler, the area LISC (local Initiatives Support Corporation) coordinator, an effort to apply traditional community-organizing and capacity-building strategies to economic development activities across the Valley is taking shape. Supported by the Allegheny Conference (a group of Pittsburgh-based corporate and banking leaders who initially combined energies to revitalize downtown Pittsburgh in the 1950s), the Heinz Foundation and the Pittsburgh Foundation, Eichler has helped form the Mon Valley Development Team. This team consists of two groups: organizers, who can encourage potential community-based leaders to become involved and assume leadership positions in local development efforts; and technical experts, with training in law, urban planning, public policy and finance, who assist in locally based development projects and help communities set up development corporations while training local leaders.

This unfolding strategy is based on the principle that local people with a sustained interest in their communities represent the most reliable base for economic recovery. It also assumes that enduring economic vitality requires more than an injection of state and federal money, but ongoing, locally based initiatives (a special form of "self-help").

Benefits from the Mon Valley Development Team are already apparent. Communities across the Valley are beginning to demonstrate skill at initiating and implementing their own modest, but tangible programs. This experience demonstrates the importance of taking small, positive steps and building local capacity at the start of the revitalization process.

Overview of Findings to Date

Our observations in these three communities indicate that, contrary to much conventional wisdom, local communities can significantly affect their economic future. Sustained economic vitality depends on committed local individuals engaging in an on-going process of education, discovery, and continued innovation and adjustment over time. Communities must continuously update their assets and liabilities and redefine their unique qualities, capabilities and areas of comparative advantage. Effective development strategies evolve over time and adapt to changes in the external environment over which a community has no control.

The process of economic development involves far more than disparate efforts to attract industry, prevent a local plant from closing, or attempts to garner state and federal assistance. Although such factors may be important components of an overall economic development strategy, they are not sufficient in and of themselves.

We have uncovered several essential "ingredients" for sustained local economic vitality. Three of these merit special attention here—*leadership;* a *vision* for the future; and development of local professional and *organizational capacity.*

Leadership

In all three communities this factor proved critical, especially at the initial stages of the development process. In Lowell, Senator Paul Tsongas came forward as the leader in revitalization efforts. From his position on the Senate Banking Committee in 1975 he accused the local banks of failing in their obligations to the city and got them to commit 0.5 percent of their savings account assets to a pooled city economic development fund. In the Mon Valley the lack of community-based leadership is one reason why Allegheny county and state initiatives have not been successful. Effective local leadership is required to raise awareness of a problem, mobilize citizens for collective action, and to lead the community through the various stages of the development process.

Effective local leadership is required to raise awareness of a problem, mobilize citizens for collective action, and lead the community through the various stages of the development process.

Community leaders in economic development efforts can come from a wide variety of local institutions—the school system, foundations, and community-based organizations, as well as more traditional sources such as government, private corporations and development agencies.

Leaders are often the first to publicly recognize a problem and/or an opportunity, and propose a plan of action. A crisis situation—for example, a plant closing or a local strike—can be used by emerging local leaders as an opportunity to offer proposals for change and put themselves at the forefront of local development efforts. In Jamestown, Stan Lundine helped conceive the idea of bringing labor and management together in a Jamestown Area Labor-Management Committee. He publicly declared that labor-management conflict was causing industry to leave and ruining the community.

Community Vision

As a first step leaders help form a vision for some political or economic unit called a community. (Identifying precisely what governmental unit represents a community is often problematic. The definition of community presents a major problem because the relevant population affected by the problem can shift with time and circumstances.) Visions, as we define them, are general strategies in community economic development. Examples from our study include making the community a model for labor-management cooperation—Jamestown's vision in the early 1970s—or celebrating and reviving a community's industrial past—Lowell's vision.

Community visions with the greatest potential for enduring success capture multiple targets (including dimensions that do not appear in most traditional economic development plans such as improving social and educational services and increasing citizen participation). These "other" objectives of local development, as we see in the Mon Valley, should be viewed not only as ends in themselves but also as necessary means to achieve sustained economic vitality. In Jamestown's recent "visioning process," members of the economic development committee recognized that the future vitality of their community depended on retention of young people as well as care of the elderly.

As a first step leaders help form a vision for some political or economic unit called a community . . . Visions, as we define them, are general strategies in community economic development.

In order to be widely accepted and a source of motivation, a vision must be consistent with the community's history and identify something that is unique, or perceived to be unique about the place. Thus the vision-forming process must therefore include a frank assessment of local assets and liabilities and an appreciation of community heritage. Often, as the people in Lowell learned, the potential for growth lies dormant and unrecognized by citizens whose perceptions are shaped by a depressed physical environment. Documentation of resources may suggest new and creative ways of viewing the city. In this way, Lowell's crumbling textile mills and canal waterways, became major assets, as perceptions and opportunities changed during the revitalization process.

A more thematic and general vision can facilitate essential consensus for the effort. If the vision is too narrow (e.g., attracting new industry, *only*) it may alienate significant community segments which perceive little or no benefit for themselves. A development program should capture the imagination of the community at-large and engender the belief that all members can gain from its implementation.

Organizational and Human Capacity

The basis for collective effort to achieve change provided by a vision and strong local leadership must be supported by *organizational capacity* at the local level to focus collective energy and implement resulting action plans. We found that the most successful development efforts are orchestrated by what we refer to as single core organizations.

The core organization serves as the centerpiece and coordinates all economic development efforts. It must focus on "doing development deals," packaging projects and formulating programs to increase both public and private investment in the community—the implementation phases of any strategy. These activities must follow priorities identified in the vision.

A core organization can have various forms. In Lowell the city planning department plays this role. In Jamestown the core organization is a private, nonprofit Industrial Development Agency. In the Mon Valley, the Mon Valley Development Team is attempting to fill a serious void and become the temporary core organization for communities throughout the Valley. Eventually, the Mon Valley Development Team aims to transfer its skills to local groups which will perform core functions for their communities.

Ideally, core organizations should possess a diverse set of resources and expertise. It is critical that communities develop sufficient professional expertise of their own to implement a plan and coordinate intersector and inter-governmental efforts. The lack of indigenous professionalism of the Mon Valley presented a dilemma. Without it, all the state and federal programs designed to aid the troubled communities in the Valley were virtually impotent. On the other hand, it is a resource few communities admitted they needed. The Mon Valley Development Team was formed to explicitly address the problem of expertise.

Expertise, once fashioned, can improve a community's long-run prospects more than one-shot development grants or industry-attraction programs. Since development skills are usually learned on the job and transferred from one individual to another, expertise lodged in a stable core organization can reinforce the economic development process by providing continuity. During the 1970s Frank Keefe, now director of the Massachusetts Department of Administration and Finance, was a staff member in Lowell's city planning office. One of his colleagues in the city planning department, Jim Milanazo, went on to head the department before he became executive director of the Lowell Plan (a private, nonprofit development corporation designed to assist the community in setting longer-term objectives). Milanazo's successor, Peter Aucella, like Milanazo, started as a staff member in the department. Thus, core organizations are important not only for what they formally do—development deals—but also as vehicles that can provide continuity by training tomorrow's community professionals and leaders.

The formation of local organizational and human capacity is too often ignored in economic development initiatives. More prudent stewardship of resources—both public and private—would channel more investment towards building human and organizational capacity, thereby helping communities develop visions for the future while enhancing the ability to turn visions into effective plans and actions.

Conclusion

The experiences of Lowell, Jamestown and the Mon Valley demonstrate the value of local initiatives in economic development and provide some guidelines for other communities. Local initiatives will not prevent economic upheaval and change, but they can help to uncover opportunities and problems, enabling communities to respond more constructively to circumstances outside their control.

In this article we have highlighted the importance of broad participation in development efforts and better management of the economic development process. In future articles we will focus on other vital aspects of local economic development, including the role of leadership in development organizations, how to turn a vision into a plan of action, and how to engender collaborative effort between the public and private sectors.

Policies and Policymaking

- Privatization (Articles 47-48)
- Health, Education, and Welfare (Articles 49-53)
- Other Policy Areas (Articles 54-56)

One only has to look through a daily newspaper to realize the multiple and diverse activities in which state and local governments engage. Indeed, it would be an unusual American who, in a typical day, does not have numerous encounters with state and local government programs, services, and regulations.

State and local governments are involved in providing roads, sidewalks, streetlights, fire and police protection, schools, colleges, day-care centers, health clinics, job training programs, public transportation, consumer protection agencies, museums, libraries, parks, sewerage systems, and water. They regulate telephone services, gambling, sanitation in restaurants and supermarkets, land use, building standards, automobile emissions, noise levels, air pollution, hunting and fishing, and consumption of alcohol. They are involved in licensing or certifying undertakers, teachers, electricians, social workers, child-care agencies, nurses, doctors, lawyers, pharmacists, and others. As these incomplete listings should make clear, state and local governments affect many, many aspects of everyday life.

Among the most prominent state and local government functions is schooling. For the most part, public elementary and secondary schools operate under the immediate authority of local school districts. Typically headed by elected school boards, these districts are collectively responsible for spending more than 100 billion dollars a year and have no direct counterparts in any other country in the world. State governments regulate and supervise numerous aspects of elementary and secondary schooling, and school districts must operate within the constraints imposed by their state government. In addition, most states have fairly extensive systems of higher education. Tuition charges are higher at private colleges than at state institutions, and taxpayers make up the difference between what students pay and actual costs of operating state colleges. While the national government provides some aid to elementary, secondary, and higher education and involves itself in some areas of education policies, state and local governments remain the dominant policymakers in the field of public education.

Crime control and order maintenance make up another primary state and local government function. Criminal statutes, police forces, prisons, traffic laws (including drunk driving laws and penalties), juvenile detention centers, and courts are all part and parcel of state and local government activities in the area of public safety. Presidential candidates sometimes talk about crime in the streets and what to do about it, but the reality is that state and local governments have far more direct involvement with this policy area than the national government does.

Singling out education and public safety in the preceding two paragraphs is not meant to slight the many other important policy areas in which state and local governments are involved: planning and zoning, roads and public transport, fire protection, provision of health care facilities, licensing and job training programs, and environmental protection, to mention just a few. Selections in this section on policies and policymaking should provide greater familiarity with various activities of state and local governments. They should also provide a feel for interactions between states and localities in carrying out policies and programs in particular areas.

The first section of this unit focuses on privatization. It raises the issue of what services state and local governments should provide through public revenues and how such services should be provided. The second section treats the policy areas of health, education, and welfare. The third section covers other policy areas.

Topics in this unit of the book can be viewed as the consequences of topics treated in earlier units. Intergovernmental relations and finances, parties, voters, interest groups, and governmental institutions all shape the responses of state and local governments to policy issues. In turn, policies that are adopted interact with other components of state and local politics and modify them accordingly. Thus, the subject matter of unit 8 is an appropriate way to conclude the book.

Looking Ahead: Challenge Questions

List all the occasions in a typical day in which you come into contact with state and local government services, programs, regulations, and the like. Compare your list with a similar list of daily encounters with the national government.

Identify some policies pursued by your state government or one of your local governments that you consider undesirable. Identify some desirable policies, too.

Do you think it is fair that parents who send their children to private or parochial schools still have to pay property taxes to support public schools in their school district? What about people without any children? Should they have to pay taxes to support public education? Why or why not?

Do you think that your state's system of higher education is satisfactory? Why or why not? Do you think that students attending state colleges should have to pay tuition? Or should state colleges be free in the way that public elementary and secondary schools are?

Is it right for state and local land-use regulations to restrict how private citizens can use property that they own? Do you approve of the power of state and local governments to take property away from citizens through *eminent domain*?

What do you think is the single most important service that state governments are primarily responsible for providing? Local governments? The national government?

If you were an elected state government official, on what policy areas would you concentrate your efforts? If you were an elected local government official?

Privatization Is a Means to "More With Less"

JOHN R. MILLER and CHRISTOPHER R. TUFTS

John R. Miller is a partner with Peat Marwick Main & Co. in New York City, and National Director of the firm's Government Services Practice. He is a member of the board of directors of the National Civic League. Christopher R. Tufts is a senior manager in the Washington, D.C. office of Peat Marwick.

America's industrial leaders have come to realize that to be competitive in the global economy they must demonstrate to the buying public that their products represent the best value. Such mode of economics-based decision making is now being applied by taxpayers to the goods and services produced by government. Taxpayers and consumers alike are demanding the best quality and value for their hard-earned dollars.

Companies realize that in order to win in the marketplace and make a profit, they must "accomplish more with less"—fewer people, less money, less time, less space and fewer resources in general. To be competitive and profitable, many companies are adopting "downsizing" business strategies. Key components of downsizing include: productivity and quality improvement programs; mergers, streamlining operations; and divestiture of businesses in which they are not competitive. These strategies must be balanced by more creative management.

Government has a comparable challenge. Faced with public demand for increased or improved services in a period of diminishing resources and a changing pattern of accountability, government officials must also develop innovative solutions to win public confidence. This article discusses the concept of downsizing government and specifically focuses on privatization of service delivery as one alternative.

Downsizing

Government downsizing is the selective application of a broad range of management and cost reduction techniques to streamline operations and eliminate unnecessary costs. These same techniques can be applied to the development or expansion of government service, as well as to maintaining service levels, improving quality, and reducing existing government service cost. In all cases the objective is the same: Identify practical solutions and implementation plans that best serve the public through more effective management and delivery of government services, while saving or avoiding unnecessary costs.

Downsizing alternatives can be grouped into five major categories:

- Productivity and quality improvement programs;
- Consolidation (intra-and inter-government cooperation);
- Privatization;
- Program reduction;
- Program abandonment.

The objective of "accomplishing more for less" is most frequently achieved by exercising a combination of downsizing alternatives. For example, a government may initiate a productivity and quality improvement program in its health services; consolidate, through a multi-jurisdictional agreement, to provide shock trauma medical treatment; contract with the private sector to provide drug prevention programs; attempt to reduce the demand for service through the imposition of user fees for ambulance service; and eliminate minor injury treatment services at government hospitals. Each potential opportunity for downsizing must be approached creatively to ensure the public still receives the best service at the lowest possible cost.

Privatization As a Downsizing Choice

As many corporate leaders are retrenching to do better what they do best, so too must government be willing to do the same. Peter Drucker, in his book *The Age of Discontinuity,* called for "reprivatization" of many government functions, saying "The purpose of government is to make fundamental decisions and to make them effectively. The purpose of government is to focus the political energies of society. It is to dramatize issues. It is to present fundamental choices. The purpose of government, in other words, is to govern. This, as we have learned in other institutions is incompatible with 'doing.' Any attempt to combine governing with 'doing' on a large scale paralyzes government's decision-making capacity."

One downsizing alternative for government to consider is to competitively engage the private sector to produce goods and services that are readily available from many commercial sources. Although the current impetus for privatization is largely pragmatic, the guiding political philosophy behind it is as old as the nation itself. Americans have long alternated between the Jeffersonian and Hamiltonian philosophies of government. However, the new momentum for privatization transcends political and ideological boundaries, and is rooted in the determination of creative government managers to develop innovative solutions to serve the public interest.

Today a broad and growing consensus recognizes that privatization, properly implemented, is a viable and legitimate response to a wide range of philosophical and practical concerns. Experience is showing that the private sector can indeed provide many services rendered by government with equal or greater effectiveness, and at lower cost. Consequently, privatization is likely to exert a powerful influence over the shape of political and economic institutions in coming years.

What is Privatization?

George W. Wilson, Distinguished Professor of Business and Economics at the Indiana University School of Business, defines privatization on a philosophical plane. He writes, "The broader and more relevant meaning of privatization must refer to nothing more or less than greater reliance upon market forces to generate production of particular goods and services."

In practical terms, privatization is a process by which government engages the private sector to provide capital or otherwise finance government programs, purchase government assets, and/or operate government programs through various types of contractual arrangements.

As privatization usually occurs in combination with other downsizing initiatives, so too do many privatization transaction involve a combination of methods. For example, private sector capital financing, using such vehicles as leveraged leasing, lease purchases, and turnkey contracts, is frequently accompanied by operation of government programs through one of four types of arrangements: franchises, grants, vouchers, or contracts.

Privatization is nothing new. It can be traced to the first Bank of the United States which served as the Federal government's fiscal agency and principal depository of the Treasury and was owned by private shareholders. When the Federal government wanted to deliver mail to its citizens west of the Mississippi, it contracted with 80 horseback riders and spawned the Pony Express. The Homestead Act gave settlers government-owned land for a small fee if they would cultivate soil for a fixed period.

In the last decade, privatization has expanded from capital construction and professional service contracts to traditionally in-house administrative and public service programs. The majority of governments now contract for at least some legal, medical, engineering, technical and other professional services. Indeed, state and local government spending for public services performed by the private sector rose from $27.4 billion in 1975 to well over $100 billion in 1985. The trend toward privatization will continue to grow even though the growth rate for state and local governments appears to be slowing.

State governments, though less active than local governments with privatization, are experimenting in many areas. The state of California alone in 1985 wrote 7,000 contracts, worth over $2 billion, to carry out administrative or public service functions, including mental health, corrections, and a full range of administrative services.

Objectives of Privatization

What are the primary objectives of privatization? They are:

• To improve the use of scarce resources by reducing the costs of providing public services, particularly where private enterprise is strong and government is assured of more effective services at lower costs;

• To modify the role of government from that of a primary producer of goods and services to that of governing;

• To enable government to meet responsibilities that might otherwise be abandoned because they are too costly;

• To reduce the debt burden;

• To limit tax rates.

Privatization of government services should be considered:

• When government's operations are unrelated to the central function of governance. Examples of governance are legislative, judicial, and certain financial activities (e.g., rate setting, debt issuance, revenue policy);

• When current government service is in direct competition with services operated by the private sector;

• When the cost of an existing government-provided service exceeds the available or projected resources;

• When current government operations are inefficient and/or service is of poor quality and all remedial actions have resulted in insufficient improvement.

Privatization Successes

As already noted, privatization transactions cover a wide range of services. The following are examples of applications of various types of privatization.

Fire Protection. Rural/Metro Fire Department Corporation, a privately-owned company, serves half a million people in Arizona (one-fifth of the state's population), and 100,000 more in Tennessee. Rural/Metro Corp.'s $4.3 million contract with Scottsdale, Arizona for 1987-88 averages out to $36 per capita per year, compared with an average of $50 for public fire departments in similar cities. Scottsdale's fire insurance rates are average.

Ambulance Service. Newton, Massachusetts, estimates saving nearly $500,000 by privatizing its ambulance service while at the same time increasing ambulance availability and coverage.

Street Light Maintenance. The City of New York is divided into eight service areas for the provision of street light maintenance. All eight are competitively bid. No single company can "win" more than two service areas.

Legal. In Los Angeles County, Rolling Hills Estates broke off a contract it had with the County Prosecutor to handle all its cases, mostly involving violations of building and other town codes. Rolling Hills Estates now pays a private law firm to act as Town Prosecutor.

Grounds Maintenance. The school district of Rye, New York, recently contracted for grounds maintenance with a private company at an estimated savings of $34,000.

Prisons. The Dade County Jail is run by the Corrections Corp. of America, which runs several correction facilities throughout the United States, including two for the United States Immigration and Naturalization Service in Texas. Some interesting questions arise in privatizing corrections. Who chases escapees? Who is liable for the prisoners and their actions? Is prisoner rehabilitation compatible with profit? (Court decisions so far indicate that *both* the government and private contractor are liable for the actions of private guards.)

Fleet Maintenance. The city of Philadelphia contracts for the repair, maintenance and replacement of its motor vehicle fleet at an estimated savings of more than $4 million over the past four years.

Health Care. In Corsicana, Texas, the Navarro County Hospital was old, losing money, and about to lose its accreditation. To put it in shape, $12 million was needed. The county turned it over to the Hospital Corporation of America, which built a new hospital right next to the old one. The former hospital cost taxpayers $50,000 a year to operate. The new one is paying taxes of over $300,000 a year. In a similar vein, in 1983 the city of Louisville, Kentucky turned over the operation of a teaching hospital at the University of Louisville to the Humana Corporation. This hospital now benefits from the advantages of mass purchasing, gained by being part of Humana's 85-hospital chain.

Public Defender Services. Shasta County, California, reported a $100,000 per year savings in indigent-defense court costs by contracting its entire public defender program to a private firm run by a former member of the district attorney's staff in a association with six full-time lawyers, three secretaries and a part-time investigator. The switchover was prompted by a study that showed Shasta's in-house Public Defender's Office was about one-third more costly than contract services would be.

Data Processing. Orange County, California, whose population has doubled to over two million since 1973, estimates that it has saved more than $3 million over the past 12 years by hiring a private firm to run its computer center. "Without automation and the professional know-how to use the computers efficiently," said Howard Dix, manager of the center's operations, "the county would have faced an explosive growth in costs for personnel and facilities."

Privatization Failures

Let us now look at some failures in privatization, and the pitfalls they illustrate.

Two towns in Ohio hired a private security firm to provide police protection. The equipment provided was totally unacceptable. Both towns fired the private company and hired the guards to be public police officers.

In another case, a city contracted for trash pickup at one cent per household per month less than the city could provide the service. The company could not work that cheaply. Within months, the company was raising cash by selling equipment given it by the city. At Thanksgiving and Christmas, garbage piled up faster than the company could collect it. A new company took over the contract. Said the mayor of the city, this "case makes me a lot more cautious. It was false economy to take a bid that was low by one cent per household per month."

New York City's Parking Violations Bureau scandal is a sore reminder of what can happen in contracting for services. Several public officials and business people pled guilty to, or were convicted of, serious crimes involving contract corruption. Two contracting corporations, without admitting any guilt concerning the alleged bribes, reached an out-of-court settlement with the city wherein the companies paid $600,000 in damages.

In a New Jersey city, private trash haulers bill residents directly. As local landfills close, the haulers' costs rise dramatically, and they in turn raise the rates they charge. Complaints to the haulers have been unavailing, and the reaction of some residents is to cancel service and dump their own garbage illegally in any open space. This has precipitated a limited health emergency. City officials are now considering eliminating use of the franchised haulers and instituting municipal trash collection, even though it will require raising property taxes.

How To Accomplish Privatization Transactions

To avoid the pitfalls of the failure examples, a careful process should be followed. The process should begin with analysis of privatization alternatives (franchises, grants, vouchers, and contracts) relative to the current delivery methods practiced. This analysis should examine implementation feasibility, technical performance, and costs. Its objectives are to determine which services may be privatized, select the most appropriate privatization method, and develop a scheduled work plan for implementation of the privatization transaction.

In order to meet these objectives, a multi-disciplined team approach should be followed. At minimum, this team should consist of personnel with technical experience in the function under review; legal, personnel, fiscal, and contracts staff; and political advisory and independent review support. The team approach provides the appropriate balance of expertise to ensure that all issues are identified and practical solutions are formulated. In addition, the use of political and independent review advisory support will assist in building the necessary consensus and commitment to change among all constituent groups. Most important, the team approach provides appropriate balance between program, fiscal, and political considerations.

Implementation Feasibility Analysis

Implementation feasibility analysis is the study of the political, legal, market, government operations, and other factors of each privatization option relative to the status quo, to anticipate the difficulties in accomplishing each option. The team approach provides the appropriate expertise to identify issues and barriers and develop solutions to minimize the impact of the issues and eliminate the barriers. The objective of the implementation feasibility study is to develop action plans identifying the specific objectives, scope, process, responsibilities, and timing for implementation of each service delivery option. The implementation feasibility study must address:

Political Barriers. Are the current coalitions of beneficiaries, near beneficiaries, service providers, government administrators, officials, political activists, unions and general populace amenable to change? How do you build the coalitions necessary to support the change process?

Legal Issues. What are the statutory, regulatory and tax law barriers, incentives, and/or requirements for privatization? What modifications to union agreements or ongoing contracts are required? What is the impact on liability?

Market. Is the private sector market mature or developing? Has the private sector shown interest through unsolicited proposals, industry studies, or research by industry experts? How capable is the private sector of providing quality goods or services? Is there a sufficient number of qualified bidders to ensure competition and provide the government a favorable risk/reward ratio? Does the private sector perceive a favorable risk/reward ratio? What is the private sector track record in government contract performance?

Government Operations. Will privatizing selected functions disrupt continuity of operations? How will the affected employee be treated? What effect will privatization have on accountability? Who will monitor the private sector? How, and with what frequency will the private sector be monitored? What performance measures will be used to determine whether performance standards have been met? How will the government control the quality, timing and cost of delivery of services to be privatized? What are appropriate penalties (or incentives) to ensure compliance with performance standards and service requirements?

Other Factors. Who will have control over the staff, equipment, and facilities? Are the resources available to do the necessary analysis, conduct the planning, preparation, and execution of privatization transactions?

Technical Performance Analysis

Once a government has examined the implementation feasibility of the privatization options, it needs to compare the overall implementation difficulties anticipated against the total benefits to be derived. Each option must be evaluated in terms of technical performance criteria including, but not necessarily limited to: availability, quality and effectiveness, risks, and program impacts. Through review of historic experience within and outside the jurisdiction, demographic and geographic studies, and/or the performance of pilot programs, analysis can be performed to evaluate each option. Criteria should be weighted and each alternative scored to determine the optimal anticipated technical performance option. At a minimum the criteria should include:

Availability and Costs to Citizens. Will individual consumers obtain improved choices of supply and service levels? Will all consumers including disadvantaged groups or geographically remote regions be served? If user fees are charged, will disadvantaged users be able to afford the level of service they need? Will the service cost to all consumers be fairly distributed? Will the overall cost to citizens increase?

Quality and Effectiveness. Will government objectives be achieved more effectively? Will the quality of service improve?

Risks. Will service disruptions be more likely? What contingencies will be required? A risk analysis that quantifies the technical, implementation, and cost risks associated with each of the alternative delivery options provides a comprehensive and disciplined approach towards reducing uncertainty and focuses the attention of the team on the most critical issues.

Program Impacts. What synergies or benefits will be derived? Will the government benefit from new technology? What impact will there be on the operations of other departments, especially if the program or service is for internal government use?

Cost Analysis

Since privatization is heavily influenced by cost, a thorough costing, economic, and pricing analysis must be performed for each option. The purpose of this analysis is to estimate potential savings, assess the economic impact, determine specific costs, and establish pricing requirements. The three types of studies most frequently performed are:

Financial Feasibility Studies. A determination of the current and future gross and net costs or savings of the planned privatization transaction in relation to the costs of the current method of operation.

Cost Benefit Analyses. A determination of the costs of new methods of providing services or doing business, compared against the benefits of the alternatives, to identify the methods that are the most cost-responsive.

Cost and Pricing Studies. An identification and examination of the direct, indirect, fixed, variable, opportunity, and oversight costs associated with a privatization transaction for different levels of service; a definition of what will happen to total costs as the service levels change;

and the recommendation of pricing strategies and/or prices to achieve desired utilizations, cash throw-offs, and/or rates of return.

For each study the first step should be to determine what constitutes cost, where the data should be obtained, how costs should be calculated, and how costs should be projected for future years. For a cost comparison between government service performance and a service contract between government and a private vendor, the major cost elements to examine include:

Government Performance Costs

• Personnel costs: basic pay (salaries or wages), other entitlements (e.g., night differential, hazardous duty differential), fringe benefits (e.g., FICA, pension, workers' compensation), other (e.g., overtime, uniform and meal allowances);

• Materials and supplies costs: costs of raw materials, replacement parts, repairs, office supplies, and equipment, necessary to provide a product or perform a service;

• Overhead costs: operations overhead (e.g., supervision) and general administrative overhead (e.g., personnel, data processing, legal);

• Other specifically attributable costs, such as rent, utilities, maintenance and repairs, insurance, depreciation or use charges, travel;

• Additional costs, unusual or specific circumstances that occur only under government operation or don't fit other categories.

Contractor Performance Cost

• *Realistic* contract price: the contractor must be able to deliver the service at the quantity and quality desired at the bid price, and still make a reasonable profit, for a contract price to be realistic;

• Start-up costs (e.g., learning curve);

• Contract administration costs, including execution of quality assurance monitoring, payment processing, negotiation of change orders, and contract close-up;

• Conversion costs (e.g., disposing of expendable items, retraining, severance pay, lease termination penalties, conducting the privatization transaction);

• Additional costs (e.g., lost volume discounts).

Cost Advantage Based on the Above Costs

The cost advantage is defined as the difference between the total government performance cost and the total contractor performance cost, adjusted for additional or lost tax revenues. Because of the risks involved in implementing such a change, public managers should generally look for a major cost advantage before shifting to new modes of service delivery, to avoid being caught short like the city that changed to contracted trash pickup for only a one cent per household cost differential.

Selection and Implementation

Having completed implementation feasibility, technical performance, and cost analyses, a government manager can select the preferred method of service delivery. Privatization can be one of several downsizing alternatives available to government managers. It is not a panacea for challenges facing government managers. If analysis shows that government provides a service more efficiently and effectively than the private sector, it should continue to do so. Privatization offers an opportunity to introduce the cost-saving, creative, service-generating aspect of competition into the public arena. It is important that public managers retain both decision-making and ultimate responsibility for public services. It is they who must decide what services will be privatized and who will provide them.

Not all methods of privatizing will benefit all parties or work in all situations. The concept works best when public managers carefully examine public assets and services to determine which could be replaced by private functions, thoroughly evaluate private sector competition, assemble representatives from all affected parties to agree on alternatives and solutions, and analyze the combination of tactics to satisfy a broad range of constituents. The key is to develop a workable mix of program and fiscal alternatives.

Privatization is an appealing concept because it offers governments flexibility in meeting their public responsibilities and, at the same time, presents entrepreneurs with a new set of challenges. Entrepreneurs, as George Gilder notes in his book *The Spirit of Enterprise,* are "engineers of change." The challenge to public managers today is to identify and manage change.

Privatization
Presents Problems

HARRY P. HATRY

Harry P. Hatry is Director of the State Policy Center, the Urban Institute, in Washington, D.C. This article is adapted from a presentation at the American Political Science Association Annual Meeting September 4, 1987 in Chicago, Illinois, as part of the session on "The Politics of Privatization."

Admittedly, public officials should periodically consider options for greater use of the private sector for delivering their services. This is good public policy and good public management.

But public officials should also examine existing instances of private sector delivery and consider the option of switching *back to public employee delivery.* This is also good public policy. For a number of reasons, private delivery can become inefficient or have quality problems.

The Best of Times, the Worst of Times—to Contract

Our work at The Urban Institute indicates that the appropriateness and success of using a particular privatization option is *highly situational.* Success depends on many factors that are individual to the particular public agency, in the particular location and at the particular time. Success of a privatization approach depends on:

• The current level of performance of the current delivery system. A government agency may indeed be delivering the service quite efficiently and with good quality—leaving little room for improvement. (As hard as some people find it to believe, often public employee delivery *does* work very well.) In other situations, the service may be inefficient or of poor quality. This is the situation that provides the mayor opportunity for successful change.

• The way the option is implemented. Without good implementation even the best ideas will go away. For example, in a switch to contracting, the quality of the request-for-proposal process is key to assuring that a capable contractor is selected. And a sound, sustained contract administration and monitoring process is essential to assuring that contractor performance remains up to par.

Threat of Privatization is Often Enough

I believe that the major advantage of the privatization movement is not that the private sector can reduce costs or improve service to a great extent, but that consideration of privatization encourages public officials and public employees to innovate and to break down obstacles to improving public employee efficiency.

Increasingly, examples occur where employees and their unions agree to changes, such as reductions in the size of garbage collection crews, when faced with a city council threat to contract the service.

Other governments have introduced procedures that involve direct competition between public and private agencies. In the "Phoenix Model," public agencies such as the City of Phoenix Public Works Department submit proposals that compete directly with bids received from private firms for services such as garbage collection and street sweeping. (The City Administrative Services codified this in January 1985 as "Management Procedure: Procedure for Preparing Cost Estimate City Services Under Consideration to be Performed by Private Industry on a Contractual Basis.")

In a third approach, Kansas City, Phoenix and other cities have split their work, such as garbage collection, into districts, some of which are served by private contractors (if they win) and some by public employees. The city reports on comparative costs, encouraging competition between public and private service providers.

Private Isn't Necessarily Cheaper

Lower cost with improved efficiency is the most frequently given reason for contracting. I am not convinced, as some others are, based on the evidence thus far available, that privatization lowers costs in most instances. Hospital care is one of the few areas that has been extensively studied in recent years. A University of California study of contracting the management of public hospitals in a number of counties in California did not find evidence that the contractors had achieved cost savings. The study did find evidence that the private firms were better at securing revenue. [1] Last year's National Academy of Sciences study of private versus public hospital care found that "studies of hospital costs that control for size (and in some cases for case mix and other factors) show for-profit hospitals to have slightly *higher* expenses than not-for-profit public and private institutions." [2]

The Urban Institute recently worked with two states (Delaware and Maryland). In three of the four programs that the states considered for a change to contracting, we found that state employees were likely to achieve costs similar to or lower than the private sector. In one, food service for inmates of Delaware's prisons, we surveyed ten other states that had contracted for inmate food service. Six reported higher costs with contracting, three lower, and one reported about the same costs. Delaware's own current costs appeared to be similar to those expected if the service were contracted. The department is still considering contracting, its motivation being the difficulty in hiring prison kitchen supervisors and, secondarily, the desire of some prison administrators to reduce the administrative headaches in arranging for meals.

Columbia University's classic 1970's analysis of solid waste collection costs found higher *average* unit costs for public employee delivery than for contractor-delivered service. [3] But it also found that the most expensive delivery method was delivery by franchised firms— firms that dealt directly with households and not through a government. The more recent Ecodata study of Los Angeles County also private vendors were, on average, cheaper. In all these comparisons, however, averages hide the fact that in some cities the unit costs were lower for public employee delivery than in some contracted cities.

Vouchers, while often an excellent way to give consumers more choice, do not necessarily involve lower costs. It depends on how the government sets the value of the vouchers. Hennepin County (Minnesota) in

Reprinted by permission from the March/April 1988 issue of *National Civic Review,* pp. 112-117. National Civic Review, 1601 Grant Street, Suite 250, Denver, CO 80203.

its trial of day care vouchers found that total costs increased when it switched to vouchers.

It is dangerous to generalize as to the success of privatization options. There will be situations where a switch will be worthwhile and cases where it won't be.

Three Important Potential Problems With Privatization

Three major potential problems in privatization, are almost always raised by public employee unions. While these problems are acknowledged by advocates of privatization, they are often treated too casually, as if they were easy to overcome, only minor inconveniences. These three problems are: 1. potential for corruption; 2. possibility of reduced quality of service; and, 3. possibility of reduced access of disadvantaged citizens to services.

Corruption. High financial stakes introduce great temptations to individuals to engage in illegal action. We have frequent examples—New York City's Parking Violations Bureau; recently, in the District of Columbia, in all sorts of contract awards; and, over the years, the City of Chicago has had its share of problems. The American Federation of State, County and Municipal Employees (AFSCME) has taken great pains to document numerous instances of hanky-panky in public sector contracting.[4] The possibility of corruption can be reduced by establishing sound procurement procedures, and in the case of divestiture, by installing appropriate regulations. Nevertheless, the threat remains.

Possible Reductions in Service Quality. Again, when substantial payments are involved, a natural temptation is to do whatever is necessary to maximize profitability and skimp on quality to save dollars, particularly in for-profit organizations. This temptation becomes even greater when a firm gets into financial difficulties. This sometimes happens even with private nonprofit organizations. The principal protections against poor quality are performance contracting and adequate performance monitoring. The need for these protections has been noted by both proponents and opponents of privatization. A classic example of this problem is recent shoddy aircraft maintenance in deregulated airlines facing major financial problems. Some airlines have been assessed large fines for inadequate maintenance.

However, it is much easier to say that monitoring is needed than to provide it. Most government contracts I have seen in recent years have very weak or non-existent performance requirements. To make matters worse, performance monitoring of contracts is very sparse.

Possible Reduced Access to Services for Disadvantaged. The incentives to private firms—particularly for-profit firms—are to avoid clients for whom securing payment for services is likely to be difficult, and to avoid clients who may be particularly difficult and expensive to help, such as disadvantaged clients.

This problem has become particularly acute in the delivery of medical services. Persons without medical insurance or other funds have reportedly been turned away from private hospitals and even from emergency room care. The National Academy of Sciences study cited earlier concluded that access is a major national concern. The study found that for-profit hospitals served fewer uninsured patients and had a smaller proportion of uncompensated care than non-profit hospitals. The researchers felt that although the percentage differences were small among the types of providers, they could nonetheless "translate into large numbers of patients: Data from four of five states demonstrate that not-for-profit hospitals provide two or three times as much uncompensated care, on average, than for-profit hospitals. (Both types provided less uncompensated care than public hospitals.)"[5] Debate continues about what laws and regulations should be introduced to encourage or require private hospitals to admit patients regardless of their ability to pay, particularly emergency-care patients.

This problem can be alleviated through contractual and statutory requirements and the provision of subsidies. Alleviating the problem, however, will often reduce the benefits of privatization.

Conclusion

Privatization should be viewed as neither panacea nor poison. It is simply one tool available to public officials. Before they attempt to apply it universally, there are points they should remember:

• The success of privatization is highly situational, dependent on local circumstances and how well the new approach is implemented.

• Periodically consider options that involve greater use of the private sector.

• Periodically consider switching *back* from *private* delivery to *public* delivery.

• Give serious attention to the three potential problems of privatization-corruption, reduced service quality, and reduced access of the disadvantaged to services.

Perhaps the main virtue of the privatization movement is that it encourages public employees to improve their own productivity in order to help ensure their own competitiveness in the face of privatization. Increasingly, the message to the public sector is that if a service has problems in efficiency or quality, the agency needs to "shape up or be shipped out." The net result should be less costly and higher quality services for all the public.

Notes
[1]William Shonick and Ruth Roemer, *Public Hospitals Under Private Management: The California, Experience,* Institute of Governmental Studies, University of California, Berkeley, 1983, Chapter 5.
[2]Bradford H. Gray, Editor, *For-Profit Enterprise in Health Care,* National Academy Press, Washington, D.C., 1986, p. 93.
[3]Barbara J. Stevens and E.S. Savas, "The Cost of Residential Refuse Collection and the Effect of Service Arrangement," Graduate School of Business, Columbia University, September 1976.
[4]See, for example, John D. Hanrahan, *Government For Sale,* American Federation of State, County and Municipal Employees, Washington D.C., 1977.
[5]*Ibid.,* p. 116.

Safety nets for the poor

Isaac Shapiro

Isaac Shapiro is the co-author of individual studies of state safety nets and a national overview of state safety net policies just published by the nonpartisan, nonprofit Center on Budget and Policy Priorities.

The need for state action is underscored by the persistence of large federal budget deficits which make it unlikely the federal government will make dramatic changes or provide substantially increased funding for safety net programs in the years ahead.

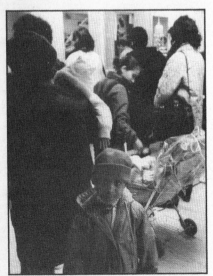

A child waits in the welfare line with his family.
Photo courtesy
New York Department of Social Services

We often speak of the safety net of federal programs designed to provide cash, medical and other assistance to the poor, but in reality no single safety net exists for the United States.

More accurately, there are 51 safety nets — one in each state and the District of Columbia. What is often overlooked, at least at the national level, is the substantial influence of state decisions on how well — or badly — the safety nets protect the poor. For example, states can be solely responsible for determining the level of cash assistance to poor households, eligibility for Medicaid and unemployment insurance and the amount of state taxes the poor must pay.

Because of state control, the 51 safety nets differ vastly in quality. For example, under a major federal-state assistance program, Aid to Families with Dependent Children, maximum benefits for a three-person family total $1,416 a year in Alabama. The same family in California would receive $7,596 a year. In many states, two-parent families are not eligible for cash assistance programs or Medicaid, while in other states they are eligible. The percentage of jobless who received unemployment insurance in 1986 ranged from a low of 16.6 percent in Virginia to a high of 65.7 percent in Alaska.

Are the safety nets adequate?

To determine the adequacy of the 51 safety nets, the Center on Budget and Policy Priorities, a nonpartisan organization in Washington, constructed a set of 10 standards against which to measure them. It is within the authority of the states to meet all the criteria, with the possible exception of the standard for unemployment insurance coverage. Federal decisions have substantial influence on the extent of unemployment insurance coverage.

The standards do not require especially generous levels of support. The standard chosen for AFDC benefit levels — that a state's maximum benefit be equal to half the federal poverty line — is rather modest. Another modest standard calls for a state's Medicaid income eligibility limit to be equal to or greater than 75 percent of the poverty line. Though the standards are fairly lenient and somewhat arbitrary, testing state policies against them should, nevertheless, provide some context for assessing the adequacy of these policies.

Safety net standards

• States set the level of AFDC benefits. *Standard: Maximum AFDC benefits for three-person families that are equal to or greater than half the poverty line* (19 states met this standard).

• States have the option to provide AFDC coverage to two-parent families with an unemployed primary earner. *Standard: Have an AFDC-Unemployed Parent program* (28 states).

• States decide whether and how much to supplement the basic federal Supplemental Security Income grant. *Standard: State supplemental SSI benefits of more than $15 per month for an individual* (21 states). Six states supplement SSI

 From *State Government News*, June 1988, pp. 14-15, 25. Reprinted by permission of the Council of State Governments.

benefits by less than this standard, with a range from $2 to $15 a month, but such assistance levels provide relatively insignificant amounts of aid. The median state supplement in states that meet the standard is $56 a month.

• General assistance programs can provide cash assistance to needy households who do not qualify for AFDC or SSI. State general assistance programs are subject to no federal requirements. *Standard: A state general assistance program that is not restricted solely to the disabled and elderly* (eight states).

• States set Medicaid income eligibility limits, subject to some federal requirements. *Standard: A Medicaid income eligibility limit for a three-person family equal to or greater than 75 percent of the poverty line* (11 states).

• Under the Sixth Omnibus Budget Reconciliation Act option, approved by Congress in 1986, states can make all pregnant women and young children in poverty eligible for Medicaid. *Standard: Adoption of the option* (25 states).

• States can adopt a "Medically Needy" program that allows them to set Medicaid income eligibility thresholds above that of AFDC and SSI and to extend benefits to households whose income after medical expenses are deducted is below the Medicaid income eligibility threshold. *Standard: Adoption of the Medically Needy program for families and the elderly and disabled* (35 states).

• States have substantial discretion in determining eligibility for basic unemployment insurance benefits. *Standard: More than two-fifths of the unemployed receiving unemployment insurance* (eight states).

• Income taxes tend to be the method of raising revenue that is least burdensome on the poor. Other state taxes, such as sales taxes, tend to be highly regressive; they take a much higher proportion of income of low-income households than of high-income households. *Standard: At least 40 percent of state revenue collected through income taxes* (16 states).

• Local property taxes comprise nearly three of every four dollars of local taxes. They tend to be the most burdensome of all taxes on poor households. Renters as well as homeowners pay property taxes because landlords generally pass along most or all of their property taxes in rental charges. State tax provisions (often known as circuit breaker programs) can provide substantial property tax relief to low-income households; benefits are typically provided as tax credits and are generally phased out as income rises. Thirty-one states offer such tax breaks, but most are limited to households with an elderly or disabled person. *Standard: A property tax break that is not restricted to households with an elderly or disabled person* (10 states).

The majority of states do not pass these relatively easy tests and many states fail by a wide margin (Table 1).

• Thirty states meet three or fewer criteria.
• No state meets all 10 standards.
• Four states meet none of the criteria; another seven states achieve only one of the 10 standards. Of these 11 states, six are outside the South.
• Less wealthy states generally score lower on the test than other states, but even some relatively wealthy states fare poorly. For example, Colorado, Florida, Nevada, Ohio and Virginia all have above-average levels of per capita income, but meet two or less standards.

A small amount of attention

A farm wife's letter to Sen. Bill Bradley (D-NJ) in August 1987 told the tragic cost of poverty.

"In 1983 . . . I became pregnant . . . We were a small farm family and having suffered two devastating drought years we were also literally broke. Nonetheless, I wanted my baby very much.

"I went to the county Health Department and practically begged for someone to 'at least take my blood pressure.' I was told that they no longer do that. So . . . I thought, well, everthing will be all right. I just couldn't afford to see a doctor.

"At 28 weeks gestation, I gave birth . . . at the local emergency room. My baby girl weighed two pounds, four ounces and was the most pitiful sight. . . . After almost five months hospitalization and thousands of dollars on Medicaid, we brought home a four pound, eleven ounce baby.

"If only I could have received a small amount of medical attention."

From *A Children's Defense Budget FY 1989: An analysis of our nation's investment in children.* Copyright 1988 by the Children's Defense Fund, Washington, D.C.

Table 1
States and the Safety Net

Number of Standards	States Meeting Standards
Zero	Alabama, Indiana, South Dakota, Texas
One	Georgia, Louisiana, Mississippi, Nevada, New Mexico, North Dakota, Wyoming
Two	Arizona, Arkansas, Colorado, Florida, Idaho, Kentucky, Missouri, Montana, Ohio, South Carolina, Tennessee, Utah, Virginia
Three	Hawaii, Illinois, Nebraska, New Hampshire, Oklahoma, West Virginia
Four	Alaska, Delaware, District of Columbia, Iowa, Kansas, North Carolina
Five	Maine, Maryland
Six	Oregon, Washington
Seven	Connecticut, New Jersey, Pennsylvania, Vermont, Wisconsin
Eight	California, Minnesota, Michigan, New York, Rhode Island
Nine	Massachusetts
Ten	None

- Only 13 states meet more than half of these criteria.

State innovations

Although in many ways states provide less support to the poor than they did in the late 1970s, some states have recently taken steps to strengthen their safety nets. Thirteen states have followed the federal lead by removing the working poor from the income tax rolls. Others have responded to the rise in the nation's infant mortality rate with comprehensive prenatal care programs for low-income families. Still other states have initiated welfare-to-work programs for low-income families — such programs, when designed specifically to improve employment prospects of the hardest to employ — have met with modest success. These and other state anti-poverty policies warrant consideration by all the states.

State choices can mend safety nets

This examination of state safety net policies suggests a range of areas exist where modifications in policies could substantially improve the situation of the poor. The need for state action is underscored by the persistence of large federal budget deficits which make it unlikely the federal government will make dramatic changes or provide substantially increased funding for safety net programs in the years ahead. In some areas, such as state-initiated comprehensive prenatal care programs for poor and near-poor pregnant women, some states already have taken the initiative to mend their safety nets. If the safety nets are to be strengthened substantially, such efforts will need to be intensified.

Variations among state programs are often justified on the grounds that they reflect the need to tailor policies to the unique problems and situations in each state. For example, job training programs should be tailored to local economies and education policies benefit from local participation by parents.

But when it comes to the dramatic variations among benefit programs for low-income people, such considerations are less convincing. Instead, the extent of variations in state poverty policies appears to stem principally from differences among states' philosophical commitments and financial abilities to aid the poor. In some states, there is less public support for government policies to alleviate poverty. In addition, some states are less able than others to afford more extensive assistance to poor people.

Nevertheless, it is not readily apparent that philosophical and financial differences justify the magnitude of the current variations. Differences of such great scope make a strong case for increased federal standards, often accompanied by greater federal funding. An enhanced federal role — especially in areas relating to basic benefits for poor families — could reduce the probability that benefits would vary so much across the states and the status of many poor families and children would not depend so much on where in this nation they happen to live.

At the same time, while such federal actions could strengthen the state safety nets, action by the states remains crucial. Given the current political and budgetary climate at the national level, the federal government is unlikely to establish large-scale sweeping changes in poverty policies. For well into the future, the choices made by the states are likely to remain of paramount importance in determining the quality of the safety nets for our nation's poor. □

Where's the safety net?

In Washington D.C., a young mother of two children with health problems said: "For AFDC mothers or even single mothers on general public assistance, there is no counseling — job counseling or personal counseling assistance — for transition (into employment), and some will say 'I don't want to risk getting out there getting a job for three months or six months. I might end up being totally on my own with no assistance.' They will be out of the safety net. It is unfair for people to expect people on welfare to give up that safety net when people on jobs are looking for that safety net as well."

From *How the Poor Would Remedy Poverty*. Coalition on Human Needs: Washington, D.C.

INQUIRY LINE

Q What approaches have the states used in setting child support guidelines?

A Under the federal Child Support Amendments of 1984, the deadline for the states to develop objective guidelines for child support settlements was October 1987.

Researchers from the Texas Child Support Enforcement Division identified three approaches to determining guidelines. First, the cost-sharing approach, where the actual cost of raising one or more children is estimated. The parents share those costs in proportion to their incomes. This approach has been criticized for ignoring various added costs for dual households. Washington uses cost-sharing in determining support awards.

Second, the income-sharing approach, where the combined income for both parents above subsistence needs is divided between the two households, theoretically equalizing the standard of living for the custodial and non-custodial households. This approach has been criticized as a return to alimony for the custodial parent. Supporters note that it is impossible to raise the standard of living for the children without affecting that of the custodial parent. Delaware has used this method of setting awards since 1979.

The third approach, child support as a state-administered tax, had not been used by any state when the Texas study was conducted. Wisconsin has since enacted support/tax guidelines under which the non-custodial parent of one child must pay a straight 17 percent of his or her income in child support regardless of the custodial parent's income. The percentage increases with the number of children involved. This approach has been criticized as unfair and overly burdensome to the non-custodial parent, who may be unable to afford care for the children during visits or even to afford remarriage.

—Ruth E. Spencer, intern, States Information Center.

The States Information Center (SIC) inquiry service can help you locate relevant information quickly and responds to requests by phone or letter. The service is confidential and free to state officials and staff. Write or call: The Council of State Governments, States Information Center, Iron Works Pike, P.O. Box 11910, Lexington, KY 40578, (606) 252-2291. □

The Changing Balance in State and Local Power To Control Education

A restructuring of federal, state, and local relations is ceding considerably more control of education to the states. This spurt in state activity comes at the end of a decade of steady growth in state control. Mr. Kirst, guest editor of this special section, speculates on the new state initiative.

Michael W. Kirst

MICHAEL W. KIRST (Stanford University Chapter), guest editor of this section on the changing role of the states, is a professor of education at Stanford University and a member of the Kappan *Board of Editorial Consultants.*

CONCERN ABOUT the quality of American education has virtually exploded in the last year and a half. There may or may not be a rising tide of mediocrity, but we are certainly riding the crest of a wave of state initiatives in public education.

This brief period of national interest in education — which will probably last no more than three years — has been characterized by an intense response on the part of the states. For example, the Education Commission of the States (ECS) reports that as many as 290 high-level state commissions are now studying the quality of public education. It is not unusual for the governor, the state legislature, and the chief state school officer to have their own separate commissions in the same state. And these commissions have been responsible for a great deal of change. As of 1 August 1984, *USA Today* reported:

• Tougher high school graduation requirements have been approved in 35 states. In California, where requirements had been left to local districts, a new law requires 13 credits for graduation. One credit equals one year of coursework. By 1986 Florida will require 24 units of credit for graduation — up from 18 — including three years of math and science. In Florida, one unit equals half a year's coursework.

• Textbooks and curricula have been revised in 21 states. A major study now in progress is looking for ways for groups of states to establish cooperative textbook purchasing policies, which would give them the combined leverage needed to force publishers to produce more demanding books.

• Longer school days and years have been tested in 16 states. North Carolina is entering the second year of a pilot program that lengthens the school year from 180 to 200 days.

Even more changes lie ahead. Maine, Illinois, Wisconsin, Missouri, and Washington have major studies of education under way. Most such studies have led to increased funding for the schools, especially for teacher salaries. States that have already boosted school aid in 1984 include Tennessee, $350 million; New York, $500 million; Alaska, $20 million; Texas, $2.8 billion (over three years); Arkansas, $148 million; and California, $1.2 billion.

Many states were already considering major "reform" legislation before the recent spate of highly publicized national reports. Indeed, this recent wave of reform comes hard on the heels of the aggressive state initiatives that began with the passage of the Elementary and Secondary Education Act of 1965. The most striking feature of state/local relations in the last 20 years has been the growth in state control over education. Today, the organizations of professional educators and the local school organizations are making suggestions for only marginal change. And under the Reagan Administration, the federal role has been restricted to cheerleading and sponsoring small pilot programs.

These trends promise a restructuring of state and local relations that will cede considerably more control of education to the states. However, this new state/local relationship will include an enormous range of variation in the aggressiveness with which states take control — from the highly aggressive states, such as California and Florida, to the least aggressive states, such as New Hampshire and Colorado.

The recent spurt in state activity comes on top of the steady growth in state control throughout the 1970s, when states began to get involved in such things as school finance reform, categorical programs, school improvement efforts, minimum competency testing, and civil rights regulations. But it was not until the 1980s that state governments provided the majority of the current operating funds for education. (John Augenblick's article in this issue traces the growth of the states' role in school finance and outlines interstate variations in fiscal control mechanisms.)

But dangers attend aggressive, broad-based state action in the area of educa-

From *Phi Delta Kappan*, November 1984, pp. 189-191. Reprinted with the permission of Phi Delta Kappan and the author.

tion. States change policy through statutes and regulations, which have a standardizing effect. Moreover, the new focus of state policy making is no longer on peripheral groups, such as the handicapped or minority students; instead, it is aimed at the core of instructional policy, including what should be taught, how it should be taught, and who should teach it.

In a recent article, Douglas Mitchell and Dennis Encarnation posit seven mechanisms that states can use to control education policy: 1) structural organization of the schools, such as district consolidation and electoral policies of school boards; 2) policies on generating revenue that determine who will pay how much for the schools; 3) policies on resource allocation, such as categorical grants or school finance equalization formulas; 4) definition and accreditation of the instructional program; 5) training and certification of personnel; 6) testing and assessment of school progress; and 7) the development and selection of curriculum materials.[1] The reforms of the past two years focus more closely on the last four of these mechanisms.

STATE REGULATIONS cannot be easily adapted to the diverse contexts of local school sites, however. Indeed, state goals are sometimes in conflict with one another. For example, state policies designed to attract and retain high-quality teachers are clearly in conflict with state policies designed to insure that a certain minimum amount of content is covered in all classrooms in a state. Outstanding teachers are attracted to a profession that offers independence and an opportunity to be creative; they are not attracted to requirements that align their classroom content to the items on a statewide test.

State mandates work better for some policy changes than for others. For example, state mandates can move local policies toward higher academic standards through state curricular requirements and tests. But other objectives, such as increasing the amount of homework, are best encouraged through state technical assistance rather than through a state mandate requiring a specified number of hours of homework each week.

An aggressive stance by the states on these instructional issues forces policy makers to make tradeoffs and seek some balance between state and local control, between strategies that insure compliance and strategies that offer technical assistance.[2] More regulation in curricular areas might be accompanied by deregulation somewhere else — perhaps in state categorical programs. Moreover, state education agencies often lack specialists in

The same set of state-level political actors is leading the current wave of reform as led the wave of school finance reform in the 1970s.

curriculum and instruction who are capable of providing needed technical assistance to local educators. For example, in 1982 the department of public instruction in California had 10 nutritionists and 12 child-care-facility specialists on its staff — but only one half-time specialist in mathematics. The staffs of state agencies are now being reorganized to provide instructional leadership rather than administration of categorical programs. But this change cannot take place overnight.

The states appear to be playing such a large role in instruction in 1983-84 because of a lack of initiative and power at the local level and in the professional organizations. Local school boards, administrators, teachers, Parent/Teacher Organizations, and taxpayers are playing purely reactive roles. Nor have statewide organizations of school boards or of administrators devised their own specific plans and urged their states to monitor the results of implementing them in the local districts. Perhaps these organizations lack the capacity for policy analysis that the states have built in the years between 1965 and 1980.

We are witnessing a major change in the relationship of the states to the schools. State mandates are now far more common than technical assistance. Karen Louis and Ronald Corwin write:

> SEAs [state education agencies] are likely to support those aspects of school management programs that will receive public support even if these are not known to be most effective for reaching official goals. Technical assistance and related programs supported on research evidence are not especially popular at the policy level — either in Washington or in the state legislatures. Legislators (and sometimes senior state agency staff) do not necessarily understand the need for technical assistance to support local change efforts.[3]

The same set of state-level political actors is leading the current wave of reform as led the wave of school finance reform in the 1970s. The initial influential actors are legislators, governors, and business interests. The traditional education interest groups — teachers, administrators, and school boards — have been used primarily as consultants. Specific items have been modified to take account of their objections, but the overall strategy and the omnibus legislation have been developed by state-level actors.

It is noteworthy that the increasing state control of the past decade has not been limited to such traditional high-control states as California and Florida. The high tide of state intervention in local instructional policy is also washing over such one-time bastions of local control as Virginia and Louisiana.[4] Michael Killian's article in this special section provides a fascinating case study of Texas, a state in transition from strong local control to strong state control.

National movements and widespread coverage in the media have played a crucial role in the current wave of reform, just as they did in school finance reform and in the minimum competency testing movement. Between 1982 and 1984 the idea of increasing college entrance requirements spread to more than 25 states without any federal mandate or organized interest group lobbying for its passage. Political leaders discovered that a proposal simply to spend more money for education or to raise teacher salaries was not going to pass state legislatures. But more money *combined with reform* turned out to be a winner, as shown in Texas, where the state taxes were increased by the largest amount in history in the summer of 1984. Will such reform bills lead to remote control of local instruction by state agencies? In this issue, Larry Cuban and Michael Killian argue that it will.

Indeed, many of the new state initiatives focus on curriculum mandates, particularly graduation requirements. Local considerations can influence the curriculum at the local level, and many of the reformers feel that granting local districts too much leeway in setting curricular requirements could deprive some students of an opportunity to study essential subjects in sufficient depth. Indeed, the variable that best predicts high school achievement on a test is whether or not students have had a chance to study the topic being tested.[4] Many legislators believe that the public interest is best served by insuring that all students in a state have a chance to study crucial curriculum content. For example, California officials contend that science receives too little time in the elementary grades (about 40 minutes total per week), so they have added science to the statewide tests. In their article in this special section, Beverly Anderson and Chris Pipho document the explosion of new state tests and analyze the potential for state tests to steer the local curriculum.

THE RECENT SPATE of reports on the state of education nationwide is indicative of a loss of confidence in the ability of local authorities to provide high-quality education. Consequently, state legislatures have felt compelled to step in and preempt local discretion, and the actions that the states have taken as a result have been directed at the heart of the instructional process.

Discontent about the effectiveness of schools has led states to prescribe stricter, more uniform standards for teachers and students. Yet the literature on effective schools suggests that the most important changes take place when those responsible for each school are given more responsibility rather than less. While centralization may be better for naval units, steel mills, and state highway departments, the effective schools literature suggests that it is more important that principals, teachers, students, and parents at each school have "a shared moral order."[5]

The reports on the state of education nationwide indicate a loss of confidence in the ability of local authorities to provide high-quality education.

Why is the new wave of state influence taking this centralized course? For one thing, higher statewide standards do appear to be consistent with other parts of the effective schools literature. For instance, higher standards do seem to indicate that clear instructional objectives exist and that the content and outcomes of schooling have been specified. But new state curricula that specify the grade level at which particular math concepts must be learned (e.g., the Texas proposal) create rigid timetables that seem likely to destroy the kind of school climate that usually characterizes effective schools.

The articles in this special section of the *Kappan* offer a variety of perspectives on the growing role of the states in controlling local schools. During the past decade, state control has grown and has become more focused, while there have been very few attempts to expand local discretion. The next decade promises to be an exciting time for U.S. education. We hope that this special section will help policy makers achieve an appropriate balance.

1. Douglas Mitchell and Dennis Encarnation, "Alternative State Policy Mechanisms for Influencing School Performance," *Educational Researcher*, May 1984, pp. 4-11.
2. For an overview of this issue, see Lorraine McDonnell and Milbrey McLaughlin, *Education Policy and the Role of the States* (Santa Monica, Calif.: Rand Corporation, 1982).
3. Karen Louis and Ronald Corwin, "Organizational Decline: How State Agencies React." *Education and Urban Society*, February 1984, p. 180.
4. Decker Walker and Jon Schaffarzick, "Comparing Curricula," *Review of Educational Research*, vol. 44, 1974, pp. 83-112.
5. See Chester E. Finn, Jr., "Toward Strategic Independence: Nine Commandments for Enhancing School Effectiveness," *Phi Delta Kappan*, April 1984, pp. 518-24.
6. For a rating of state centralization and an overview of the evolution of state education policy making, see Michael Kirst and Frederick Wirt, *Schools in Conflict* (Berkeley, Calif.: McCutchan, 1982), pp. 187-252.

Bring Back the Orphanage

An answer for today's abused children

Lois G. Forer

*Lois G. Forer, a former judge, recently retired from the state
Court of Common Pleas in Philadelphia.*

April sat on the witness chair clutching a Cabbage Patch doll. Her blue eyes blazed with hostility. In clear, precise language, accurately relating dates, times, and places, this ten-year-old girl described the repeated acts of sexual abuse to which she was subjected by her stepfather for two years. The incidents occurred in the presence of her mother. She said that her maternal grandfather had tried to kill her stepfather but his shotgun misfired. When called to the witness stand, the grandfather, an old wino, mumbled incoherently. The mother, who has an IQ of 72, was unable to say more than "yes" or "nope" or "I dunno" in response to questions. April has an IQ of 146. No one knows the identity of her natural father.

This trial lasted four days. It was heartbreaking and distasteful. But the aftermath was frustrating and appalling. I convicted the stepfather of statutory rape, involuntary deviate sexual intercourse, and contributing to the delinquency of a minor and sentenced him to 19 to 38 years, the maximum the law allowed. I could not convict him of rape because April had not resisted. As she explained, the guidance counselor at school and the family therapist to whom the stepfather had taken her told her to obey her father, that he knew what was best for her. Even with time

off for good behavior and the eagerness of the parole board to make room for new convicts, the stepfather will probably remain in prison until April is 18 and, I hope, can protect herself.

But what will become of her in the important remaining years of her childhood and adolescence if she lives with her retarded mother and drunken grandfather? After sentencing, I began a long, fruitless quest to have April placed in a safe and suitable environment. I implored every public and private agency involved in child welfare to find her a suitable home. I was told it was impossible. There was a shortage of foster homes and insufficient funds. Moreover, it is the policy of both governmental and private agencies to keep families together. The child's caseworkers assured me that April's mother was receiving counseling. But no amount of counseling will increase the mother's intelligence or alter her promiscuous habits.

* * *

Tyrone was beaten so severely by his father, Robert W., that the neighbors called the police. Robert is a prize-fighter trainer. He repeatedly struck Tyrone with a doubled-over electric cord. A doctor at the hospital where Tyrone was treated testified in court. He described several deep, bloody wounds on the eight-year-old boy and presented X-rays of healed fractures and a diagram of the youngster's body showing the location of more than 70 scars of old and recent beatings. Robert testified that he was just "disciplining" a bad boy. Tyrone's evil conduct was wetting the bed.

"Robert is not a criminal," his lawyer argued. "He was just reprimanding his son." The prosecuting attorney recommended family counseling and probation rather than prison. Whether Robert was in prison or not, Tyrone would have to live with his mother, who had testified that Robert was a good and loving husband and father and Tyrone was incorrigible. Again, no agency would even attempt to find placement for Tyrone. The family should be kept together.

* * *

Tony has no scars. Neither of his parents was arrested. They came to court voluntarily in a custody battle. They were divorced when Tony was four years old. He is now nine. The father tells Tony his mother is a whore, an evil woman. The mother tells Tony his father will kill him, his stepfather, and his half-brother. Tony twitches and stammers. He has attempted suicide twice. He is failing in school although he is a brighter than average child. Neither parent will consent to his hospitalization and no psychiatrist would give a professional opinion that Tony's mental health was endangered by remaining with his mother and stepfather. Without such evidence, I could not order the institutionalization of Tony. The rights of the family cannot be violated.

I gave Tony a paper and pencil and asked him to write a story while he was waiting in the anteroom during my conference with his parents. Tony wrote: "Dear God, Please help me."

These are but a few of the thousands of abused, neglected, and homeless children I have seen during my 16 years on the trial bench in Philadelphia and when I was a practicing lawyer. These children are white, black, and Hispanic. Some are brilliant, others mildly retarded. They range in age from newborn to 16 and 17 years. What they have in common is that all desperately need a safe, permanent home.

My experiences are not peculiar to Philadelphia. Unfortunately, this is not a local problem but a national epidemic. Thirty states reported increases of more than 50 percent in child abuse between 1980 and 1985. The National Committee for Prevention of Child Abuse reports that in 1986 at least 1,300 children in the United States died from neglect or abuse. In 1986, 2.2 million cases of child abuse were reported nationally. It is likely that ten times that many occurred but were not reported, although every state has a law requiring doctors, hospitals, and others who suspect child abuse to report it and protects them for doing so. Undoubtedly, 1988 will see an even greater number of mistreated children as teenage pregnancies, drug and alcohol abuse, homelessness, and economic and housing problems escalate.

These deaths and thousands of cases of continuing abuse occur not because social workers are uncaring (although some are) and not because judges fail to treat child abuse as a serious crime (although some do) but because there are no places for these children to live. For at least the past quarter-century Americans have been captivated by two concepts that have become accepted public policy: deinstitutionalization and preservation of the family. Both are worthy goals pursued to unworthy ends.

I suggest that it is time for us to demand that government provide permanent, well-run orphanages for the more than two million abused children who are de facto orphans. It will be costly. However, we are spending billions in futile efforts to prevent child abuse, to find adoptive and foster parents, and to pay them for the temporary, uncertain, and largely unsupervised care of helpless children in foster placement. We are also paying for inadequate shelters for tens of thousands who spend their childhood in a limbo of uncertainty, waiting in vain for a home. There is a high statistical probability that many of these abused children will become delinquent teenagers and adult criminals. The money we save on their early care will be spent on "correctional institutions" later. If this is to be the decade of the child, we cannot ignore those in the greatest need, abused and abandoned children.

Therapy for rapists

At mid-century deinstitutionalization and the preservation of the family were appropriate responses to real evils. Many mental institutions had become warehouses offering little therapy and less chance of release. Commitment procedures were lax. Many families were glad to be rid of problem members, such as spouses who drank, forgetful elderly parents, and rebellious, nonconforming teenagers. Institutionalization was their first resort, not their last. Mental health experts embraced their mission of treating allegedly mentally ill persons with unbounded optimism, often against the patient's will and with little regard for their rights.

In the 1970s, the promise of quick cures for behavioral problems through psychogenic drugs, the spiraling costs of institutions, and a belated concern for patients' rights sparked the movement for deinstitutionalization. Between 1963 and 1980, almost 400,000 persons were released from mental institutions in the naive expectation that "community-based care" would adequately provide for them. But fewer than 800 of the planned 2,000 community treatment centers were established. The result has been an enormous in-

The Flight of Michael and Tabitha

Tabitha has been in a juvenile detention center for months while cadres of public employees and social workers in private agencies search for a home for her. Tabitha ran away from home after she was raped by her father. Tabitha, who is 15, has no prior court record. She is now charged with delinquency, the crime of running away. The rape occurred on the night of her graduation from junior high school. After she had come home from a school party and gone to bed, she awakened and went to the kitchen for a soda. Her father grabbed her and raped her on the kitchen floor. He did not dispute her testimony but stated that he was drunk, Tabitha was in her nightgown, and Tabitha's mother had been confined to bed for three months with a difficult pregnancy. All of which, he thought, justified his conduct. I sentenced the father to two-and-a-half to five years in prison to be followed by five years' probation. When I pronounced the sentence the mother screamed at me, "Who is going to take care of me and my children? Tabitha can take care of herself."

I knew the mother would have a difficult time making ends meet and that Tabitha would have a miserable time living with her mother, who blamed Tabitha for the family's economic difficulties. The father, who is a skilled worker, earned much more money at his regular job than in prison. I permitted him to be allowed work release. He must sleep in the prison but can work during the day. His wages, less a small deduction for his maintenance, are paid to his wife. But despite my efforts, no one could find a home for Tabitha.

The last report of the father's probation officer was that the father has been a model probationer since his early release from prison. He has his old job back and is living with his family.

"How is Tabitha?" I inquired. He told me that Tabitha had run away some time ago.

Before the rape Tabitha had been a reasonably good student. She had missed almost a semester of high school while she was in detention, charged with running away. For several months after her release, she attended school and signed her own report cards. No one knew where she was living. Then she quit school and vanished into the anonymity of the city. In Chile, children who have been snatched by the military are called the "disappeared." The world is rightly enraged over a society in which children can disappear and be lost forever. Less dramatically, thousands of American children simply vanish each year. The school system strikes them off the roster. The police list them as missing but no one looks for them.

* * *

Michael N. III, 16, is the scion of a prominent family. He discovered that his father was looting the trust funds established for Michael and his sisters by their grandparents. When Michael confronted his father with the facts, the father beat Michael severely and locked him in the cellar. Michael made his escape with the help of the gas man who came to read the meter. Michael was charged with running away and the theft of his grandfather's watch that Michael attempted to pawn. Michael claimed that the watch had been given to him. He remained in custody until his eighteenth birthday because there was no other facility for him and Michael refused to go home. He did not graduate from high school because there was no equivalent schooling in the detention center.

—L.G.F.

crease in the number of street people, in the arrest and imprisonment of former inmates who are unable to function in society, and an overload on available resources.

The principle of deinstitutionalization extended to the field of child care, where it is a given that institutions are bad and that private homes are good. We cling to the notion that institutions for children are Dickensian places of evil and cruelty. However, even in Victorian times there were good orphanages. Leslie Thomas, who grew up in an orphanage established in the nineteenth-century by an English reformer, wrote a well-known memoir about his life there, *This Time Next Week: The Autobiography of a Happy Orphan*. After the death of his parents, Thomas spent ten years in this orphanage. He attended public school where he was prepared for his career as a writer.

In nineteenth-century America, almost every community had publicly supported orphanages resembling what we now call group homes. Children lived there and attended the local public schools until they reached adulthood. Anne Whitt Thompson of Gaithersburg, Maryland, wrote a letter to *The New York Times* in 1987 stating in part, "I lived in two orphanages and three foster homes growing up in North Carolina, and I can say nothing but good about my life in orphanages. We did not wonder where we would eat or sleep, because the orphanage was our home...." Girard College in Philadelphia was established in the 1800s as an orphanage. Many of its graduates became leading citizens, prominent in industry, government, and the arts. They look back on their days there as happy, secure, and fulfilling. This was a wealthy, well-run institution.

Of course, not all orphanages were like these. Before I went on the bench, I prosecuted the director of a church-sponsored orphanage where children were physically and sexually abused and another privately operated rural orphanage where children were hired out to work on farms like indentured serfs. The director pocketed the children's wages. There have been real evils in orphanages, but abuse and mismanagement are not peculiar to them, nor are such conditions inevitable.

In addition to deinstitutionalization, another belief that took hold in the mid-twentieth century was that mental health professionals and social workers should decide the adequacy of parents. This resulted in families on welfare being held to unreasonably high standards of parenting. Well-meaning psychiatrists and psychologists saw their role as determining the proper environment for a child. In an influential book published in 1973, *Beyond the Best Interests of the Child*, authors Joseph Goldstein, Albert J. Solnit, and Anna Freud wrote: "How, the question becomes, can the law assure for each child a chance to become a member of a family where he feels wanted and where he will have the opportunity on a continuing basis not only to receive and return affection but also to express anger and learn to manage his aggression?" This was obviously an impossible goal. But professional hubris led many to believe that psychoanalytic theory could provide the correct answer to child placement. Many poor children were removed from imperfect but not abusive parents and institutionalized. In response to this undesirable practice, theory changed, and it is now established policy to keep families together no matter how undesirable the family situation is.

A new profession arose to implement this goal, namely, family therapists. Some family therapists are licensed psychiatrists and psychologists. Many are not. Some are former school teachers and social workers who call themselves family therapists. Others are individuals with no formal training and little experience who set themselves up in business as family therapists. On the whole, it is a profitable occupation. Schools, courts, and hospitals refer troubled families to such persons for treatment. I have had many cases involving physical abuse, incest, and other crimes against children in which the conventional wisdom dictates: "Keep the family together. Order therapy."

In one case, the family had been "in treatment" with a family therapist for more than a year after the father had been convicted (before another judge) of having sex with his 12-year-old daughter. The father then was before me in criminal court charged with statutory rape of his ten-year-old daughter. These two unhappy little girls were failing in school. The prosecutor, the court psychiatrist, and, of course, defense counsel all urged probation with family therapy for the father. With the consent of the parties, I met with the family therapist who had been treating them. He told me that the mother refused to have sex with her husband but that the therapist was getting her to change her attitude. He urged me not to incarcerate the man.

"It's my duty to protect the girls," I told him.

"But I am keeping the family together," he indignantly replied.

In my opinion, this was not a family that should be kept together. If the man had molested a girl who was not his daughter, no one would have objected to a prison sentence.

Foster failures

Of course there is a middle ground between institutions and families: foster homes. But it's a solution that's never proven adequate. Although extensive and expensive public relations programs to recruit foster families have been in effect for several years, they have not produced enough foster families to meet the need. Few sensible persons will agree to take care of a strange child 24 hours a day, 365 days a year, for pay of less than $5,000 with no vacation or sick leave and no fringe benefits. In 1987, the American Public Welfare Association reported that 33 states paid only between $200 and $300 a month per child for basic foster care. With the exception of a small number of saintly souls, foster parents are like all other people who work for a living. They want good pay, reasonable hours, and good working conditions. The pay for foster parents is attractive only to those who have no other options.

Whether foster placement is or is not preferable to institutions, it must be recognized that there are simply not enough foster parents to care for all the infants and children who need homes. In New York City the demand for foster care placements jumped 29 percent from 1985 to 1986, according to the Children's Defense Fund. In Illinois, there was a 32 percent increase in the number of children entering care from 1986 to 1987. But the number of licensed foster homes in Illinois dropped from 3,597 in June 1984 to 2,790 three years later.

Some 1,000 children from newborn to two years old in New York City are in hospitals as "boarder babies." Many have been abandoned. Others have drug-addicted mothers. It is unlikely that any of these children will be adopted. They will be shifted from hospital to hospital, wherever a bed is available. Often the diagnosis of a child will change to meet the admission requirements of the institutions, not the needs of the child. I have seen

Two-year-old Joseph Huot died after being placed in the foster care of a convicted rapist. Police have charged the foster parents with murder.

many children who have been diagnosed at different times as retarded, emotionally disturbed, and "predelinquent" in order to find a bed somewhere for a homeless youngster.

After the public outcry about the death of little Matthew Eli Creekmore, who was kicked to death by his father in Seattle despite repeated intervention by state workers, more than 5,000 children were removed from abusive homes in the state of Washington. But authorities could find foster homes for only 3,800.

And there is no assurance that foster placement will provide even a modicum of care, security, or permanence for the child. Public institutions are answerable to the public. They can be inspected regularly by public officials. Committees of private citizens can act as overseers and keep a careful eye on the operations of such orphanages. It is difficult and expensive for social workers to inspect at frequent intervals all foster homes.

An audit of the New York State Division of Youth by the state comptroller disclosed that children have been placed with foster parents who were emotionally unstable, suicidal, violent, and financially unable to provide the youths with a clean place to live and necessities such as drinking water. In 1987, Judge Daniel D. Leddy of New York Family Court told *The New York Times*, "It's gotten to the point where we're sending kids home to bad circumstances because foster care is such a terrible alternative."

Two-year-old Joseph Huot died of brain injuries in January, two months after being placed in the foster care of a convicted rapist. Philadelphia police have arrested the foster parents and charged them with murder. Huot was placed in the couple's care (his parents separated and his grandfather could no longer care for him) despite the fact that the foster father, 26-year-old Walter Hairston, had pleaded guilty seven years earlier to rape, aggravated assault, and burglary. Police said Hairston falsified his application with Catholic Social Services, deleting his criminal record. The Hairstons received $18.55 a day to care for Huot, who doctors said died of "shaken baby syndrome," which occurs when the brain strikes against the skull. Though Huot family members began reporting their suspicions of child abuse in November—after spotting bruises on the child's back—doctors said they did not suspect abuse, and state social workers ruled the family's claim unfounded.

I saw a different example of the failings of the foster care system when Edward came before my court. Though he was only 16, Family Court decided he was incorrigible and he was transferred to be tried as an adult. Edward's juvenile court file consisted of two thick volumes. His problems had first landed him in court when he was seven, when his father was murdered and his mother, a drug addict, disappeared. The court psychiatrist's report stated: "Edward grieves for his father. He misses his mother. He needs a warm, supportive home and intensive counseling." Edward remained in juvenile detention for more than six months while efforts were made to find him a foster home.

Mrs. S., his first foster mother, had two children of her own. In addition to Edward she had three other foster children. It was a noisy, impersonal household. Mr. and Mrs. S. did not abuse Edward. They fed him and gave him a bed in a room with two other boys who complained that Edward cried at night. The school teacher reported that Edward did not pay attention in class. Mrs. S. told the social worker that a neighbor had accused Edward of stealing her pocketbook. Delinquency charges were filed against Edward and he was back in the detention center. When the theft charges came up for trial the neighbor did not appear. The court entered an order: "determined," a concept peculiar to some juvenile courts. The child cannot be found guilty because there is no evidence. But in order to give the child the benefit of juvenile court supervision, the court does not dismiss the charges. With this record, it was even more difficult to find a foster home for Edward. Who wants to take in a thief even if he is only ten years old?

The second foster mother also made a living out of this occupation. She increased her meager profits by scrimping on the food and clothing she provided for the children and pocketing some of the allotment, a not uncommon practice. When Edward complained, she beat him. He ran away, earning a second delinquency charge. On the street he ate from garbage cans and stole. He was caught and placed in the detention center again. Two more charges: runaway and theft. He ran away from the center and was caught while attempting to steal a candy bar. Two more charges of delinquency. The Family Court then sought a "secure facility," that is, a jail, for Edward. Finally it was decided that Edward was beyond the rehabilitative powers of the juvenile court system and that he should be treated as an adult offender.

For nine years Edward had been under the control and supervision of the juvenile court and the welfare system. The only schooling he had was a few months while he lived with the first foster family and an occasional hour or two in the detention center. Somehow Edward did learn to read. Although he was examined and evaluated three times by court psychiatrists who all recommended therapy, he never received any. So far as I could see Edward had not failed the juvenile court system; it had failed him.

The orphanage option

There is an alternative to this deplorable situation: group homes for abused and abandoned children—orphanages. In 1964, Dr. Karl Menninger, the famous psychiatrist, established the first Village for homeless children. The impetus came from a judge. As Dr. Menninger explains, a judge asked him, "Dr. Karl, what the devil can I do with this boy? Where can I put him? He has done no crime, he has no disease, but he doesn't have dependable parents and he is on my hands. These foster placements keep jailing and ditching the children so often."

There are now 16 Villages in Kansas and Indiana. The children who live there have been neglected, abused, or abandoned. No child needs to leave the Village until he or she has reached adulthood. When I visited one of the Villages in Topeka, they were having a wedding. A young man who had spent his adolescence in the Village came back to his "home" to be married.

Compare this experience with the life of Bill, who has been in foster care in New York City for five years and has had to move ten times. Bill told a reporter for *The New York Times*, "I've had so many social workers I can't remember them. They say, 'All right, we're gonna help you.' But then they go against you. They're always on your back. It's like Rambo against the Vietcong."

Most communities do not have a children's Village. Some cities have a few group homes, but not nearly enough to meet the need. And few are more than temporary shelters. Judges who see abused, neglected, and abandoned children often have no option but a temporary detention center in which delinquents are also housed.

When I was running a law office for indigent children funded by the Office for Economic Opportunity in the 1960s, we encountered this situation daily. Once when a judge was about to commit a child to juvenile jail even though the youngster had not committed a crime, I protested.

He replied, "The parents won't keep him. There is no place that will take him. Will you take him to your home?"

All institutions are not bad; all families are not good. Neither are all foster parents good or bad. There is really no way of knowing. Caring foster parents rarely make the headlines; those who kill and abuse do.

When Elizabeth Steinberg of New York City was beaten to death by her adoptive father, or Matthew Eli Creekmore died in Seattle despite repeated intervention by state workers, these deaths were headline news. Such cases tear the hearts of Americans. "How can such things happen in a civilized country?" people ask.

We can do better. Bring back the orphanage.

Where the Fight Will Be Fought: AIDS and State and Local Governments

In the United States, AIDS will present unprecedented challenges to state and local governments — the bodies responsible for the protection of public health.

Richard Merritt and Mona J. Rowe

Richard Merritt is a senior research associate at the Intergovernmental Health Policy Project, 2011 E Street, N.W., Suite 200, Washington, D.C. 20006. The project recently established the State AIDS Policy Center.

Mona J. Rowe is a senior research associate at IHPP and co-author with Caitlin Ryan of *AIDS: A Public Health Challenge*.

In the United States, AIDS is the subject of unparalleled media attention and the target of millions of federal dollars in research funding and public-health efforts. But, despite the furor at the national level, it is little understood that control of the AIDS epidemic and the many social and ethical considerations associated with the disease are very much a state and local responsibility.

Constitutionally, states have been charged with the protection of public health. Moreover, state and local governments — not the federal government — have assumed primary control over public education.

States license and regulate health-care professionals and facilities. State and local governments often provide residual financial coverage or access to medical services for those who do not qualify for federal assistance or cannot obtain private health insurance. And states set the terms and conditions by which health and life insurance companies do business.

By the end of 1984, when AIDS had already claimed thousands of lives, only a handful of states regarded AIDS as a significant public-health or public-policy problem. Less than three years and many thousands of deaths later, however, almost every state has come to realize some of the awesome consequences that this disease can bring.

During the 1987 legislative sessions, more than 550 AIDS-related bills were introduced and discussed in 47 of the 50 states. This represents almost a 100% increase over 1986.

Four-fifths of the states have seen the formation of an AIDS task force, commission, or advisory body whose purpose has been to review the state's current policies and recommend changes to the governor and/or legislature. Another measure of the growing involvement of the states is their increasing willingness to appropriate state general revenues for various programs and activities aimed at curbing the transmission of the virus.

Since fiscal year 1984, states have allocated more than $239 million in general revenues to AIDS activities — starting at $9.3 million in 1984, increasing to $27.5 million in 1986, and reaching $126.3 million for 1988. Generally, the level of state-only funding has increased as the number of states with expanding AIDS problems has grown.

For example, in fiscal year 1984, five states allocated their own money for AIDS programs. In 1988, 30 states will be appropriating general revenue funds to combat the disease. If Medicaid funding is added, states will spend about one-third of what total federal expenditures for AIDS programs will be in 1988.

It is widely acknowledged that, until a cure or vaccine for AIDS is discovered, the only realistic means for controlling the spread of infection and AIDS is through prevention and education. More specifically, the objective is to notify those at risk of infection of the

The authors wish to acknowledge the assistance of Caitlin Ryan in preparing this article.

From *The Futurist*, January/February 1988, pp. 19-24. The Futurist, published by the World Future Society, 4916 St. Elmo Avenue, Bethesda, MD 20814.

means for reducing or eliminating their risk of exposure to the virus.

A number of public-health education strategies evolved once a test for the presence of the AIDS virus was developed. One of the most important educational strategies has been the offering of test-linked counseling.

These testing/counseling services, financed mostly by federal funds, encourage those who have practiced high-risk behavior (specifically, unsafe sex or the sharing of unclean needles) to come forward to be tested, on an anonymous basis if they wish. Those tested are then advised of the results of their tests and counseled on how to reduce their exposure risk if their tests are negative and how to reduce the risk to others if their tests are positive.

Public-health officials note that far too much attention has been devoted to the test itself as the important variable in modifying behavior, whereas, they argue, it is really the appropriate counseling that leads to the kinds of risk-reduction behavior that is desired.

AIDS Testing

The existence of the AIDS-virus test has spawned a number of controversial issues, such as whether testing should be voluntary or mandatory and who should be tested.

The overwhelming consensus in the public-health community and, at least so far, in the political community is that prevention and educational efforts can be best achieved through voluntary means. The argument is that compulsory measures, such as mandatory testing, would tend to be counterproductive to public-health goals by keeping those most at risk of infection from coming forward to be tested and counseled.

Clearly, those who practice high-risk behavior should not feel that they will disadvantage themselves by coming forward for testing and counseling. This is why meaningful protections of confidentiality and enforceable safeguards against discrimination are essential prerequisites for a successful public-health response. Although most

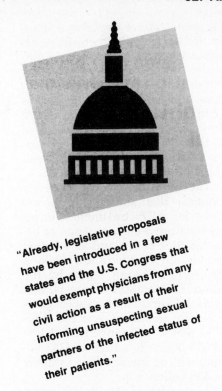

"Already, legislative proposals have been introduced in a few states and the U.S. Congress that would exempt physicians from any civil action as a result of their informing unsuspecting sexual partners of the infected status of their patients."

states have relied on existing confidentiality protections found within long-standing public health, communicable disease, sexually transmitted disease, or general medical record statutes, several states have enacted new, strengthened provisions to deal with AIDS.

One area of growing controversy involves the reporting of AIDS virus (HIV) positive test results to state health officials. While all confirmed diagnosed cases of AIDS are reported to the U.S. Centers for Disease Control and the state health departments, reporting of HIV infection is required by only 13 states at this time. The majority of these states require that some form of identification be given to receive the test result. A growing number of states, however, are considering reporting test results without personally identifying that information, to improve the quality of the data collected at the state level about the disease.

AIDS and Confidentiality

One growing controversy is whether physicians and other health providers have a responsibility to inform spouses or sexual partners of individuals who test HIV positive. Traditionally, the ab-

solute confidentiality of the physician–patient relationship has been sacrosanct, but, given the possible life-and-death consequences of HIV infection, many believe that the patient's right to privacy should not serve as a pretense for inflicting harm on others.

The American Medical Association, in its recent policy recommendations on AIDS, said that "physicians who have a reason to believe that there is an unsuspecting sexual partner of an infected individual should be encouraged to inform public-health authorities. The duty to warn . . . should then reside in the public-health authorities as well as the infected person and not in the physician to the infected person."

Already, legislative proposals have been introduced in a few states and the U.S. Congress that would exempt physicians from any civil action as a result of their informing unsuspecting sexual partners of the infected status of their patients.

Mandatory Testing for AIDS

Approximately 20% of all the AIDS bills introduced over the past two years have related in one way or another to mandatory testing. And while many call for required testing of prisoners, prostitutes, and hospital patients, the overwhelming number of testing bills have focused on premarital AIDS testing. In 1987, bills requiring marriage-license applicants to be tested for AIDS were introduced in 35 states.

While this issue has garnered much publicity and legislative attention, premarital testing has thus far received little support. Only Illinois, Texas, and Louisiana have managed to enact legislation, and the Texas law may not go into effect. All other bills were either defeated or carried over until the next year's legislative session. Three states — California, Virginia, and Hawaii — amended their bills to require that, in lieu of testing, applicants for marriage licenses be provided information about AIDS and where they may be tested for AIDS if they so desire.

A few states have begun to require that individuals in certain high-risk groups be tested on a routine basis. For example, prisoners are being (or will be) routinely tested in Colorado, South Dakota, Nevada, and Idaho. In 1988, Oregon intends to start testing certain individuals convicted of drug-related or sex-related crimes. Prostitutes are routinely tested for HIV infection in Nevada, the only state that has legalized prostitution, while Florida will require under its sexually transmitted disease law that convicted prostitutes be

"Florida will require under its sexually transmitted disease law that convicted prostitutes be tested. And all pregnant women with high-risk characteristics will be tested in Florida."

tested. And all pregnant women with high-risk characteristics will be tested in Florida.

Policy makers who generally oppose mandatory testing are beginning to ask questions about the success of the voluntary approach. For example, one legislator in New York asks: Can we honestly say that the voluntary approach is working when we know that the number of people in New York State infected with the AIDS virus is estimated to be 300,000–500,000, but only about 40,000 people in that state have been tested?

The Cost of AIDS

The cost of caring for AIDS patients can be extremely high, given that most of the costs of AIDS care are associated with hospital stays

for acute care of opportunistic infections. Currently, there are no reliable estimates as to what the ultimate costs of AIDS services will be, either on an individual-patient level or in the aggregate. Estimates of inpatient hospital costs range from a low of $40,000 to a high of $140,000, based on an average survival time of 18 months between diagnosis and death.

The U.S. Public Health Service predicts that annual health-care costs for AIDS treatment will increase from a current range of between $1.2 billion and $2.4 billion to between $8 billion and $16 billion by 1991. A recent study by the Rand Corporation suggests that the total cumulative medical costs for AIDS treatment over the 1986-1991 period will range from a low of $15 billion to a high of $113 billion, with an intermediate estimate of $38 billion.

Regardless of the discrepancies in cost estimates, there is little doubt that Medicaid will play an increasingly important role in financing medical aid and other services for AIDS patients. If Rand's intermediate cost estimate is correct, spending on AIDS services could account for about 3% of Medicaid program costs by 1991, or 13% if its most pessimistic scenario occurs. It is estimated that, at any given time, 40% of all AIDS patients have some of their care covered by Medicaid.

Although for many of those with AIDS the Medicaid-eligibility process has been abbreviated, gaining eligibility is not always tantamount to obtaining access to care. Many states have reported that those with AIDS have had difficulty in finding nursing homes that would accept them.

A few states, such as Wisconsin and Florida, have tried to overcome these barriers by offering enhanced reimbursement to providers on the justification that the care provided to AIDS patients is more intense and complex and therefore more costly than the average nursing-home patient. Other states are dismantling regulatory barriers that restrict nursing-homes from accepting AIDS patients, supporting the development of specially desig-

nated nursing-home beds to care for AIDS patients, and developing intensive education programs for nursing-home staffs.

Models for AIDS Care

Given the variability and episodic nature of the disease, AIDS patients usually require a continuum of care, from intensive acute-care services to various non-medical, mostly social, services such as transportation, housing, and personal care.

Significantly, a 1986 report esti-

"San Francisco General Hospital's AIDS-specific outpatient unit provides testing, referral, comprehensive medical treatment, mental-health and substance-abuse services, and a range of psychosocial support services."

mated that about half of those diagnosed with AIDS were fairly mobile, self-sufficient, and in need of outpatient care only. Data from San Francisco indicate that only 6% of those with AIDS are classified as inpatients in one of the city's hospitals.

San Francisco's provision of medical and social services to those with AIDS has been touted as a model for other cities. The San Francisco model is an integrated, community-based delivery system that provides a continuum of care to persons with AIDS. San Francisco General Hospital's AIDS-specific outpatient unit provides testing, referral, comprehensive medical treatment, mental-health and substance-abuse services, and a range of psychosocial support services. Social workers are available to assist AIDS patients with such critical problems as gaining eligibility for public assistance and securing housing and transportation. The hospital has an AIDS unit for inpatient needs and accounts for about one-third of the total number of AIDS-related patient days in the city.

This integrated, case-managed approach is largely the reason that San Francisco's inpatient costs and hospital lengths of stay are among the lowest in the nation. Supporting its success, however, is a large, unmatched corps of volunteers that helps keep costs down. Experts feel that without such volunteerism it will be difficult to equal San Francisco's success.

A different approach is exemplified by New York's initiative of designating certain hospitals to serve as centers for the care of AIDS patients. The objective is to increase the access of those with AIDS to essential health care and community resources and to address patient needs not being served by the existing health-care and social-services delivery systems.

The designated-center concept also provides for or arranges a full continuum of services that may be required by an AIDS patient. Under the plan, designated AIDS centers qualify for a higher Medicaid-reimbursement rate for providing or brokering a broad range of comprehensive services. The concept also involves the use of system-wide and regional planning.

The New York Department of Health has designated three hospitals as AIDS centers so far, expects to approve five more soon, and is considering applications from a number of other facilities.

Still another alternative involves the use of home-based and community-based waiver services by state Medicaid programs. Under this approach, Medicaid pays for a wide range of care delivered at home and in the community for patients who might otherwise be institutionalized. By law, states can

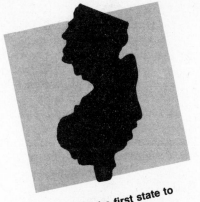

"New Jersey is the first state to receive a waiver specifically for AIDS and ARC patients. Under the terms of the three-year waiver, the state expects to serve approximately 3,000 patients at a cost of about $68 million in Medicaid funds."

target their home-based and community-based services waiver at AIDS and AIDS-related complex (ARC) patients or can offer these services to all Medicaid recipients as an optional service.

In applying for the special AIDS waiver, states must provide assurances that per capita Medicaid expenditures for the specified group will not increase as a result of the waiver. Moreover, in implementing the statute, states must also implement a cost formula which ensures that total Medicaid program expenditures will not increase with the waiver.

Although there are currently over 70 general home-care and community-care waivers in effect, New Jersey is the first state to receive a waiver specifically for AIDS and ARC patients. Under the terms of the three-year waiver, the state expects to serve approximately 3,000 patients at a cost of about $68 million in Medicaid funds. Other states with such waivers include New Mexico and North Carolina; several other states are developing applications.

Paying for AIDS Drugs

One major unknown has to do with the overall impact on cost of care by introduction of antiviral drugs. Retrovir (or AZT), the only FDA-approved antiviral so far, has shown promising results in prolonging the survival times among certain AIDS patients. Preliminary data suggest that the use of AZT can mean reduced medical costs for many AIDS patients, primarily because of fewer opportunistic infections and fewer hospitalizations.

Nevertheless, the cost of the drug itself is high — $8,000 to $9,000 annually — and its use can lead to serious side effects that are costly to treat. Hence, the cost effectiveness of reimbursing expensive drug therapies such as AZT is still unclear.

Despite these ambiguities, as of June 1987, 44 states had decided to pay for the costs of AZT for AIDS patients who qualify for Medicaid coverage. Only two states with significant incidences of AIDS — Florida and Texas — have decided not to cover the drug.

Health and Life Insurance

One of the most difficult questions is to what extent, if any, states should intervene in the underwriting process for health and life insurance by regulating the conditions under which the industry can use HIV tests for underwriting purposes.

An absolute exclusion of test information runs the risk of driving insurance companies out of the market — some companies fear a large number of AIDS-related health claims, while others believe they should be able to assess claim risks for AIDS as they would for any other disease. On the other hand, giving insurance companies complete freedom may lead to blanket exclusions from coverage for those at risk of HIV infection and even those perceived to be at risk of infection. This in turn could lead to a growing class of uninsured — for which the state may have to assume ultimate responsibility.

Currently, four states and the District of Columbia have taken specific legislative action to restrict the conditions under which insurance companies may require applicants to be tested for AIDS. Several other states are using the regulatory process to create some safeguards against discriminatory requests for and applications of AIDS tests and test results and to enhance the confidentiality of medical information. Still others are using guidelines recommended by the National Association of Insurance Commissioners.

A significant number of states, however, have taken no action at all. Thus, the prevailing practice is for companies to require blood tests from applicants for expensive or individual health and life insurance policies. Many that test positive will be denied coverage, and others will forgo coverage because they are unwilling to take a test.

One partial solution to this dilemma is the establishment of a State Health Insurance Risk Pool. A risk pool usually comprises all health insurers (except those with self-insured plans) doing business in the state. The pool offers a comprehensive health insurance plan to individuals who, because of poor health or a chronic affliction, are high risks and cannot obtain coverage through the private marketplace. Such pools work by spreading the excess financial risk of covering otherwise uninsurable individuals among all health insurers in the state.

Health Insurance Risk Pools are currently authorized in 15 states. However, to date, only two of the top 10 states most affected by AIDS and HIV infection have a state risk pool — Florida and Illinois.

The establishment of risk pools will address at least one major concern about permitting insurance companies to require applicants to take a blood test for their exposure to AIDS — i.e., what health-insurance alternatives should be available for those who test positive. However, the premiums for getting insurance under a risk pool are expensive, and only one state has decided to offer a premium-subsidy program.

Another safeguard states may use is their existing statutory or regulatory authority to prohibit insurers from canceling, not renewing, or increasing premium rates on a person's existing life or health insurance policy because of a post-

"Four states and the District of Columbia have taken specific legislative action to restrict the conditions under which insurance companies may require applicants to be tested for AIDS."

issue change in the subscriber's health status. West Virginia has passed a bill specifically prohibiting insurers from canceling or failing to renew the accident and sickness insurance policy of any insured individual because of a diagnosis of AIDS.

AIDS and the Law

Recently, considerable attention has been given in the media to various isolated episodes of individuals who are aware they are infected with the AIDS virus but nevertheless continue to behave in ways that endanger the public health — either by trying to donate or sell their blood or engaging in unsafe sexual practices without informing their partners of their infection.

Such episodes, while small in number, have raised public anxieties and led to demands for legislative remedies. Already, some states have responded with legislation prohibiting those with a known HIV infection from selling or donating blood, or from having sexual intercourse with another person unless they have informed the person of their status.

A different approach involves the application of targeted or limited isolation or other restrictions on an individual's freedom. Connecticut recently revised its public-health statute to allow for the detention of individuals with a communicable disease who refuse

or fail to conduct themselves in a way that prevents the transmission of the disease. Several other states, upon examining their public-health statutes for their ability to protect against such situations, concluded that the statutes were outmoded and, for the most part, failed to provide appropriate civil-rights protections.

As a result, several states have amended their laws on communicable disease or sexually transmitted disease to authorize the quarantining or isolation of an individual, but only after adherence to strict due-process protections. Most states already have this ability as part of their broad authority to protect public health. The real issue for states is how broad their existing powers are and whether they can be exercised in a way that will protect individual freedom while protecting public health.

AIDS and Public Policy

Trying to forecast the nature of public policies related to AIDS five years into the future is a perplexing task, given the number of unknowns about the disease. However, the following observations are based on an assumption that current government projections regarding the future incidence and prevalence of HIV infection and AIDS are essentially accurate. Hence, a cumulative total of more than 270,000 AIDS cases will have occurred by the end of 1991. Also, by the end of 1991, there will have been a cumulative total of more than 179,000 deaths from AIDS in the United States, with 54,000 of those occurring in 1991 alone. Another important assumption is that the vast majority of AIDS cases will continue to come from currently recognized high-risk groups.

Since the scientific establishment agrees that a vaccine for AIDS is at least 5-10 years away, we must rely on the only approach available — education.

One has to believe that we will learn a great deal over the next five years about which educational programs and other interventions are the most effective at modifying behavior. One also must believe that the general public will begin to take those educational messages more seriously as they come more and more into contact with friends, relatives, business associates, and colleagues who are suffering from the disease. Targeted education will be stressed, especially for minority groups hit hardest by AIDS. An increasing number of states have already heeded the U.S. Surgeon General's advice and are mandating AIDS education in schools.

Provider reluctance or refusal to care for persons with AIDS or ARC

"West Virginia has passed a bill specifically prohibiting insurers from canceling or failing to renew the accident and sickness insurance policy of any insured individual because of a diagnosis of AIDS."

will continue to be a major problem. Reluctance will be manifest throughout the health care delivery system, from emergency personnel and private practitioners to hospital workers, nursing-home administrators, and home health aides.

States may be forced to adopt a number of practices, combining the use of both incentives and regulations, to overcome such resistance. Increased reimbursement to cover the full costs of treating an AIDS patient may be sufficient incentive for some institutions. With others, states have already begun to use their licensure or certificate-of-need authority to persuade some institutions, as well as individual health-care providers, to accept AIDS patients. Special state scholarship programs may also be needed to attract interns and resi-

dents to hospitals with a high volume of AIDS patients.

State and local policy makers — both elected and appointed — will play a significant role in defining the nature and extent of what our societal responses will be to the AIDS threat. Whether most will resist the temptation to play to the fears and anxieties of their constituents for political gain remains to be seen. One hopes that most will follow the example of one official, who said, "It is the job of the elected official not to repeat back the fears of the public but rather to lead so that the fears expressed are appropriate to the risks that exist."

Public Health Care Challenges

Perhaps more than any other disease, AIDS holds the U.S. health care financing system up to the mirror, reflecting in sharp detail all its inadequacies. Even before the AIDS crisis, states were engaged in finding solutions to improving financial access to health services for a growing population of uninsured and underinsured. The growing number of ARC and AIDS cases will certainly compound the problem by adding a new subset to the uninsured population.

State Medicaid programs, most of which will continue to face considerable pressure to control costs, will have to find more creative and effective ways of organizing and delivering health-care services for AIDS patients. At the same time, the Social Security Administration will most likely expand the definition of what constitutes a diagnosis of AIDS, increasing significantly the number of individuals who may qualify for Medicaid assistance.

States will see to it that the private sector assumes some share of the increased financial responsibility for AIDS patients. The most likely response will be through the enactment of health insurance risk pools. States are likely to offer some partial subsidies of the premiums of those who fall below a certain income level.

Realistically, Medicaid expansions, risk pools, charity-care subsidies, and the like will take a state only so far. Unquestionably, many

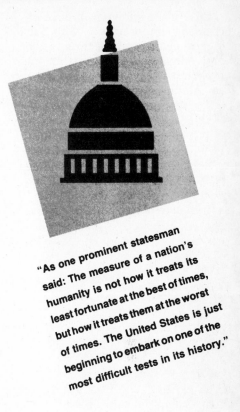

"As one prominent statesman said: The measure of a nation's humanity is not how it treats its least fortunate at the best of times, but how it treats them at the worst of times. The United States is just beginning to embark on one of the most difficult tests in its history."

people will still find themselves uncovered.

Some argue that these cost and access pressures will lead to a more rational — and therefore national — health care financing program. A more likely scenario — at least for the next few years — has the federal government providing the states with additional financial resources, such as block grants or matching grants under Medicaid, or reducing insurance regulations, allowing states to require self-insured health plans to participate in health insurance risk pools.

The health care delivery model of the future will necessarily combine both inpatient and outpatient services with a comprehensive network of complementary, nonmedical services that enable individuals to maintain themselves outside of the acute inpatient setting. Most likely, dedicated AIDS treatment centers will serve as the focal point for managing patients' medical and social needs. New antiviral drugs and improved treatment practices will mean an increased need for noninstitutional alternatives for the care and maintenance of persons with AIDS.

Case management will have increased importance, with its biggest challenge in securing alternative living arrangements for the homeless with AIDS. Nonetheless, as AIDS affects an increasingly large proportion of the indigent population before it spreads to other groups, the public-health problem of trying to maintain access to quality health care will only grow.

If the scenario projections prove false and AIDS manages to spread widely beyond the current high-risk populations, no social or political institutions will remain unaffected. Despite this gloomy thought, it bears repeating that most state and local governments are not powerless to affect the outcome of this public-health crisis. Most states still have low numbers of citizens with AIDS and therefore have time to formulate policies and programs. These states are also in a position to benefit from the experiences of some of the high-prevalence states.

The next five years will demand extraordinary leadership from our public servants and tolerance and trust on the part of the public. As one prominent statesman said: The measure of a nation's humanity is not how it treats its least fortunate at the best of times, but how it treats them at the worst of times. The United States is just beginning to embark on one of the most difficult tests in its history.

Drunk Driving: The Highway Killer is Back

Barbara Bellomo

Barbara Bellomo is a staff writer for State Legislatures.

A dramatic increase in alcohol-related traffic fatalities in 1986 could force states to consider once again passage of even stricter laws to get drunks off the road.

In the early '80s, the states rushed to pass more than 900 laws aimed at reducing what had become an alarming and continuous increase in alcohol-related deaths on the country's streets and highways.

The result of this increased public awareness of the national menace of drunks behind the wheel—spawned in large part by such groups as Mothers Against Drunk Driving (MADD)—was a decline in alcohol-related traffic deaths from 1982 to 1985.

But in 1986, fatalities related to drinking and driving rose by 7 percent, causing concern among traffic safety experts and anti-drunk-driving groups, some of which urge wider enactment of laws that have proven effective and others who call for stricter law enforcement and tougher sentencing.

"We've made inroads in reducing drunk driving, but now we're slipping back," says Barry Sweedler of the National Transportation Safety Board (NTSB). "The issue has lost the glamour it had in the early '80s."

Dr. Ralph Hingson of Boston University's School of Public Health believes that public pressure is essential in keeping the issue alive in legislatures in light of the sharp increase in drunk-driving-related deaths.

"There's no doubt that there was tremendous progress in the early '80s. It was unprecedented," he said. "The drunk driving laws and all the public discussion surrounding them were great, but it's almost like we found the key and now we're throwing it out. We have to stay on top of it."

After steadily declining since 1982, deaths caused by drunk drivers are on the rise again.

How effective have those tough drunk driving laws been?

The American Bar Association and the National Transportation Safety Board recently evaluated state laws to determine what works most effectively to keep drunk drivers off the road. Successful initiatives include:

• Allowing police officers to confiscate drunk drivers' licenses at the time of arrest;
• Requiring judges to impose mandatory sentences for first and multiple offenders;
• Restricting or eliminating plea bargaining;
• Sobriety checkpoints;
• Raising the minimum drinking age to 21; and
• Enacting dram shop laws.

The most effective deterrent, according to the studies, is "roadside administrative revocation," which allows law enforcement officers to take away a drunk driver's license on the spot. Nearly half the states have such laws.

The NTSB acknowledges that while some people will continue to drive even without their license, most will drive less, or at least sober, until their court date. Many DUI offenders, before they even get to court, are arrested a second time for the same offense. Yet in states that don't have automatic revocation laws the second arrest will often show up as the driver's first offense.

License revocation in all 50 states continues to be one of MADD's national goals. Norma Phillips, national president, says, "Most citizens value their drivers' licenses. [Revocation] also has a psychological effect on people. It hits home that what they've done is unacceptable behavior."

John Grant, executive director of the National Commission on Drunk Driving, believes that tougher drunk-driving legislation—including automatic revocation—has had the greatest impact on social drinkers, who understand the consequences of drinking and driving. And Senator Rod Monroe of

Some judges are using public humiliation as a tactic for reducing drunk driving. In Tuscarawas County, Ohio, Judge Edward O'Farrell issues special-colored license plates to first-time DUI offenders. And in Sarasota County, Fla., Judge Becky Titus requires offenders to place bright red and gray bumper stickers on their cars, so that other drivers know that they have been convicted of driving drunk.

Oregon says that while repeat offenders in his state sometimes continue to drive under suspension, the new laws have had an effect on social drinkers. "It has produced an awareness. Even at political functions you see lots of non-alcoholic drinks being served now."

Most criminal justice specialists agree that automatic revocation is a tool in fighting drunk driving, but they argue that it does little to deter hardcore repeat offenders who often are alcoholics. They believe that the emphasis of the anti-drunk-driving campaign should focus on problem drinkers instead of the social and moderate imbibers who may get in a scrape only once, if ever.

Sweedler believes that repeat offenders pose the biggest challenge to law enforcement. Revocation legisla-

tion is important because "it still reduces their driving if not their drinking problem." But he adds that the Safety Board urges states to require an evaluation of an offender's drinking problem before sentencing.

"If he's an alcoholic, sending him to an alcohol education program isn't going to work, and committing someone who went out one night and had a little too much fun to a six-month program is inappropriate as well. We must match treatment with the problem," he says.

While evaluation is key to handing down an appropriate sentence, both the bar association and the National Transportation Safety Board agree that mandatory sentencing of repeat offenders is

critical in getting drunk drivers off the roads.

MADD members regularly monitor courtroom proceedings in drunk driving cases, because, according to Phillips, "When we are present in court to offer the victim support, you see judges handing down stricter sentences."

Ohio Judge Edward O'Farrell, who recently appeared on ABC's Nightline with Ted Koppel, is one judge who consistently is hard on drunk drivers.

O'Farrell achieved notoriety for his practice of ordering first-time offenders to sport canary yellow plates on their cars that help to alert police that they are DUI offenders. In addition, he imposes a mandatory 15-day sentence, six-month license suspension and a $750 fine. If the offense involves an accident or injury the penalty goes up considerably. O'Farrell says his intent in the beginning was "to shock the hell out of people."

"The number of people dying in my county has plummeted because of my intractable position that no matter who you are, you're going to jail if you drink and drive," he says. Last year, there was one alcohol-related traffic fatality among the 85,000 residents of Tuscarawas County, O'Farrell's jurisdiction.

Phillips believes "the laws on the books aren't worth the ink they're written in if they are not enforced. Judges still have discretion (with mandatory sentences). But they must hand down more swift and sure penalties because only the threat of jail will deter drunk driving."

Senator Monroe says his primary focus is to see that the drunk driving legislation he has sponsored in the past "is properly enforced." He attributes the leniency of many judges to their view that "DUI cases are minor offenses" that clog already overburdened courts.

"Drinking is part of the macho West—a test of manhood in some people's eyes. When judges grew up, everyone drank and drove," he said. "Some are very strict, but others don't feel it is that serious. They have a tendency to wink at it and impose minimal fines."

Monroe charges that judges in his district routinely refer teen-agers arrested for drunken driving to a two-hour alcohol education program, even though a law he authored gives them the latitude to confiscate the licenses of drunken drivers under 18.

Mandatory sentencing can get drunks off the road and into treatment or behind bars, but only when states restrict or eliminate plea bargaining in drunk-driving cases, the NTSB and bar association studies state. When plea bargaining is allowed, the association argues, there is often no record of a driver's first DUI offense, allowing repeat offenders to continually receive lighter sentences.

In addition, the ABA's report found that, "It (plea bargaining) eliminates many options for appropriate action by the justice system to reduce future risk. By failing to charge an offender with drunk driving, the system is prevented from accurately identifying the risk that individual presents if he

commits a subsequent offense."

While some critics believe the criminal justice system is slacking off on drunk drivers, in many states there simply is not enough room in jails to hold them.

"Judges are frustrated because there are very few meaningful sanctions for second offenders—jail space is very precious in this state," says Oregon Representative Dick Springer.

A number of criminal experts believe that incarceration can be an effective deterrent, but alcohol treatment must be provided to effectively reduce drunk driving. Jailing drunk drivers with criminals is inappropriate, they argue.

Arizona and Massachusetts are among a few states where lawmakers have appropriated funds to their corrections departments to build minimum security facilities strictly for DUI offenders. Other states are looking at alternative punishments to relieve overcrowded prisons and jails and to respond to the concern that jail is a place for criminals, not alcoholics.

One of the tougher alternative punishments for repeat offenders is automobile forfeiture, already on the books in Alaska and New York. Alaska Representative Niilo Koponen has sponsored legislation that would make forfeiture mandatory. Although New York also has a forfeiture law, judges there rarely invoke it. But the state has generated $22 million through a statewide program that collects county fines from DUI offenders. The revenue is used to provide funding for the state's anti-drunk-driving campaign.

Five states have enacted legislation allowing judges to require repeat offenders to install a breathalyzer device in their cars that locks the ignition if the driver's alcohol level is over a specified limit. Oregon is the most recent. Its one-year experiment, the Ignition Interlock Pilot Program, requires judges in 11 counties to order the device for repeat offenders who need to drive. To obtain an occupational or hardship license, the driver must have previously received alcohol treatment, carry insurance and have the breath tester.

"It's an electronic probation officer," Representative Springer, the law's sponsor, says of the device.

Another effective deterrent, according to the NTSB and the ABA, are sobriety checkpoints. Twenty-five states have established them, and a number have landed in court as a result. Civil liberties groups, arguing that checkpoints are unconstitutional, have successfully brought suit against them in California, Oregon and Pennsylvania. The California Supreme Court later reversed its ruling, stipulating that law enforcement agencies must give the public advance notice of the checkpoint's location and must use systematic selection criteria.

The Pennsylvania Supreme Court recently outlawed random sobriety roadblocks, saying they were set up at "such unlikely times and places" that citizens were being stopped unjustifiably by police. But like California, the court upheld their legality, imposing similar restrictions on law enforcement departments. Last September, Oregon banned the use of checkpoints.

Despite constitutional challenges, the NTSB maintains that roadblocks are cost effective and a strong deterrent to drinking and driving.

Alcohol-related fatalities among teen-agers 15 to 19 are a real concern. Deaths in this age group were significantly higher in 1986 than in 1985, according to John Grant of the National Commission on Drunk Driving. He attributes the increase to the fact that automobiles are more accessible, fuel is cheaper and "kids drive with more abandon and less responsibility."

However, Boston University's Hingson theorizes that the anti-drinking movement had little impact on this group because "it was before their time. The number of new laws geared toward drunk driving reached its zenith in 1985 and evidence shows it may be tapering off. That's a bad sign for a high risk group such as teen-agers who are just entering the driving pool."

Preventing alcohol-related fatalities among teen-agers has spurred many states to enact legislation targeted specifically to those under 21. With the exception of Wyoming, every state has raised the drinking age to 21 (some with a nudge from Congress, which threatened a loss of federal highway funds without it). State troopers across the country say the laws have already saved many lives.

Maine recently lowered its maximum permissible blood alcohol content to .02 percent for drivers under 21. The new law deals a double blow—a fine is imposed for drinking under age and driving privileges are suspended for one year. Rhode Island has introduced legislation that would lower its legal blood alcohol limit to .04 percent for teen-agers.

As part of its national lobbying effort, MADD is urging all states to lower their maximum blood alcohol limit to .10 percent. But the American Medical Society says that even at .05 percent a person is too impaired to drive. Forty-two states have .10 percent maximum levels and Oregon and Utah have lowered their limits to .08 percent. Colorado recently introduced a bill that would lower the legal limit from .15 percent to .10 percent.

To date, half the states have enacted strong liability legislation—which the studies consider to be effective—aimed at bars and restaurants that serve drinks to intoxicated patrons, and Maine, Oklahoma and Texas are among several states that require or encourage training programs for bartenders to learn how to identify customers who have had too much to drink.

Grant says that drunk-driving legislation in and of itself is not a panacea. He theorizes that the key to getting drunk drivers off the streets and highways lies in a coordinated approach by states.

"Enforcement and implementation of the laws has been the biggest challenge. We don't need any new laws. We need to implement the ones we have.

"Everyone must do their part from judges to more active police enforcement to better court interpretation of what the law says. Education and prevention in the work place and the schools are a big part of it, too. And it's vital that the media keep the issue alive," he says.

The battle over land use:

A second wave emerges

John M. DeGrove

Dr. DeGrove is director of the Florida Atlantic University/Florida International University Joint Center for Environmental and Urban Problems.

A second wave of growth management initiatives by states is underway, but this time concerns about infrastructure and not the environment are the driving force.

A new movement emerged in a number of states in the early 1970s which became known as the "quiet revolution in land-use control." Land use had traditionally been the almost exclusive province of local governments. But concern for the environment was the powerful issue that brought states into the prickly political thicket of land-use controls in the first half of the 1970s.

The confident prediction by many observers, however, that the environmental movement had peaked by 1975 and states would not continue to move into the land use/growth management field has proved in the 1980s to be far off the mark.

A second wave of growth management initiatives by states is underway, but this time concerns about infrastructure and not the environment are the driving force.

State land use laws

In the 1970s, citizens formed environmental pressure groups — at the local, state and national level — alarmed at the increasingly obvious destruction of natural resources, especially land and water, by poorly planned development projects.

Environmentalists, convinced that local governments either could not or would not protect the environment, turned to the states for help. The result was a series of state laws regarding land use and growth management that increased the involvement of state government in a series of important ways.

Hawaii was a forerunner of these new laws. The state passed legislation in 1961 establishing a State Land Use Commission charged with zoning all land as urban, agricultural, conservation or rural. The primary purpose was to protect the state's agricultural lands from unplanned urban encroachment.

Vermont followed in the 1970s by adopting Act 250, the state land use and development law. The object of the law was to establish a regional and state agenda for reviewing projects within the context of protecting Vermont's environment.

California and Florida were next in the state land-use parade. California tried for three legislative sessions to pass a coastal planning and management law. When the third effort failed in 1972, a citizen initiative known as Proposition 20 was approved by voters and thrust California into the coastal growth management business.

In Florida, a severe drought in 1970 and 1971 gave broad support to environmental concerns. The state legislature in 1972 passed a series of laws which placed growth management responsibilities for land and water management with the state. The effort was extended in 1975 by the passage of the Local Government Comprehensive Planning Act. The act mandated the adoption of a comprehensive plan by all of Florida's cities and counties, but provided little state review.

Oregon in 1973 embraced the most comprehensive effort at managing growth with the passage of Senate Bill 100, establishing a Land Conservation and Development Commission. The commission was charged with developing and adopting goals and policies to protect Oregon's farmlands. The key tools were the development of local government plans and land devel-

opment regulations. All of Oregon's 241 cities and 36 counties were required to develop plans consistent with the policies and goals of the state commission.

In 1974, Colorado and North Carolina joined the parade. Colorado passed House Bill 1041 which featured a relatively weak state role in land use, but gave local governments the opportunity to strengthen their own growth management activities. North Carolina surprised itself and others by approving a relatively strong Coastal Area Management Act which established limited state review of areas of environmental concern and required all coastal counties and cities to develop plans consistent with state policies. Other states during the first half of the 1970s took less comprehensive actions, typically to protect wetlands and other areas of critical state concern.

A second wave

In the mid-1980s, a second wave of growth management initiatives arose. These new efforts stood in sharp contrast to the growth man-

The most powerful force driving states to address and re-address growth management in the 1980s was a growing alarm by citizens and government officials at the inability to keep infrastructure abreast with the pace of growth.

agement laws passed in the first half of the 1970s. The most powerful force driving states to address and re-address growth management in the 1980s was a growing alarm by citizens and government officials at the inability to keep infrastructure abreast with the pace of growth. By far, the largest source of concern involved poor transportation systems. Freeway gridlock and seemingly endless waits at traffic signals fueled the growing concern that inadequate infrastructure was eroding the quality of life. Legislators, governors, mayors and county commissioners recognized most

growth did not pay for itself. New strategies, ranging from impact fees to taxes, were required.

Florida, in 1985, became the first state to pass a sweeping set of growth management laws that required local governments to develop comprehensive plans and land development regulations consistent with state goals. The legislature also mandated the adoption of Comprehensive Regional Policy Plans by Florida's 11 regional planning councils.

Many of the mistakes of Florida's effort in the 1970s were corrected. Local plans were to be reviewed and approved by the State Land Planning Agency based on a minimum criteria developed by the agency and approved by the legislature. Substantial funding to local governments was provided by the state to help with the cost of drafting plans and land development regulations. The most powerful new policy was the provision that it would be unlawful for a local government to approve new developments unless the infrastructure was in place concurrent with the development. Put simply, the state and all participants must stop the deficit financing of growth caused by the build up of large infrastructure backlogs and begin paying the cost of growth as it occurs.

The bold action by Florida highlighted the force of new state initiatives in growth management. Citizens and elected officials have become alarmed that a failure to "pay as you grow" is diminishing the quality of life. The explosion of state action in the 1980s to set policies and implement tools for managing growth may have been led by Florida, but was quickly followed by a number of other states, including Maine, Massachusetts, New Jersey, Vermont and Virginia. In California, local growth management initiatives are sweeping the state. City and county growth control programs also are increasingly evident in other parts of the nation.

The New Jersey Legislature approved the State Planning Act in January 1986. The act establishes a State Planning Commission staffed by the Office of State Planning. The law included a broad range of goals aimed at protecting the quality of life of New Jersey's citizens amidst strong economic growth. A draft state development and redevelopment plan was ready for public scrutiny by January 1988. Its focus was balancing development and conservation objectives with the demands of infrastructure. The process called for the final adoption of the state plan and the preparation of local plans by municipalities and counties. Consistency between state and local plans was to be achieved through negotiations between all parties.

In Vermont, Gov. Madeleine Kunin in September 1987 established the Governor's Commission on Vermont's Future and charged it with preparing a report on how Vermont could best manage its growth. The commission presented its report to the governor on the last day of 1987. On Jan. 12, the governor devoted her entire State-of-the-State address to the establishment of a new system for managing state growth. All towns and newly constituted regional agencies would be required to develop comprehensive plans. The local plans were required to be consistent with regional plans, which in turn would

be consistent with state guidelines drawn from those recommended by the commission and adopted by the legislature. New funding for the planning effort also was proposed, featuring a doubling of the real estate transfer tax (about 3 million new dollars). The funds would be divided between support for the planning process and additional funding for the Housing and Land Conservation Trust Fund. The governor's recommendations were well received and as of early April, an act to encourage consistent planning, House Bill 8779, had passed the House. The Senate Natural Resources and Energy Committee was still drafting its version of the bill at press time. The infrastructure issue was a key in the discussion that led to the proposals.

About two years ago, Maine also began serious consideration of statewide planning and growth management legislation. A special legislative commission heard testimony from a large number of state groups and by mid-February the commission's report became the basis for the proposed Comprehensive Planning and Land Use Regulation Act. The proposed legislation would mandate that local governments develop land-use regulations. The legislature is considering whether to require a state review of the local plans to determine their consistency with state objectives. The legislation also would encourage towns to plan for and provide infrastructure to support the impacts of development in a timely manner. The legislation is still in committee, with the major issue being the extent of state involvement in the planning process.

The Chesapeake Bay experience

The growth management initiative in Virginia is the exception to the rule that concern for infrastructure is the driving force in the new wave of state growth management initiatives in the 1980s. The Chesapeake Bay Preservation Act creates a nine-member Chesapeake Bay Local Assistance Board. The board is charged with developing criteria for defining the Chesapeake Bay preservation areas and for developing a second set of criteria for use by local governments in making land-use decisions within preservation

Agricultural runoff is a problem for estuaries.
Photo by M.E. Warren
Courtesy of Chesapeake Bay Foundation

areas. Counties, cities and towns will establish the geographic areas to be protected, subject to state criteria. Local governments also must develop and enforce zoning, subdivision and other regulations to protect the water quality of the Bay. The board also is charged with assuring local land development regulations are consistent with board criteria and other provisions of the act. The act's importance goes beyond Chesapeake Bay because it allows local governments outside Tidewater, Va. to use provisions of the act. Thus the powers of all local governments in Virginia to manage growth is strengthened by the law.

A number of other states are considering growth management actions. Some, such as Massachusetts and New Hampshire, already have drafted legislation. Others, such as Georgia and South Carolina, have named growth management commissions, but have yet to propose legislation. In all such instances, a concern with managing growth to achieve balance between development and infrastructure has been at the heart of the issue. Growth management has emerged in the 1980s as a major policy question for state governments and more states can be expected to take action as the 1990s approach.

Infrastructure in Trouble

Joseph M. Giglio

Joseph M. Giglio, senior managing director of Bear, Sterns & Co., Inc., chaired the National Council on Public Works Improvement.

One measure of a nation's well-being is the quality and extent of its public works. Public health depends on water supply and sanitation facilities. Social, political and economic integration rely on highways and transportation services. Even in less measurable ways, public works shape society.

Of all public services, infrastructure may be most taken for granted. When tap water runs clear, traffic flows easily, cities are clean, buses and trains operate on time, and the like, no one notices. But, when roads are clogged or sewer plants pollute, public and media attention often comes only after the real damage already has been done.

Congress, recognizing that safe and productive public works are vital to the nation's defense, economy and well-being, passed the Public Works Improvement Act of 1984, P.L. 98-501, establishing the National Council on Public Works Improvement to assess the condition of public infrastructure.

The Council found that the nation's infrastructure is inadequate to sustain a stable and growing economy. The Council's two years of study are summarized in "Fragile Foundations: A Report on America's Public Works," given to President Reagan and Congress Feb. 24, 1988. The Council analyzed the condition of the nation's infrastructure, going beyond previous reports, and presented options for solving problems.

The Council found an overall decline in the level of investment in our nation's infrastructure in the past two decades. For the economy to continue to grow, the Council called for a renewed investment in the nation's infrastructure. This investment requires a comprehensive effort by all levels of government to solve our large, but manageable infrastructure problems.

The size of the nation's existing infrastructure investment is huge. The public works categories studied by the Council represent a capital stock of $1 trillion and represent 10 percent of the nation's total capital stock. Public spending on these facilities exceeds $100 billion annually or nearly 7 percent of all government spending. Public works are a major source of jobs, employing some 7 million people in construction, operation and maintenance. Yet to keep America competitive, capital spending on public infrastructure needs to increase by 100 percent.

Infrastructure report card

Some types of infrastructure are in better shape than others. For example, water resources and aviation are in reasonably good condition, while mass transit and hazardous waste treatment facilities are dangerously near collapse. The Council graded eight categories of public works using the motif of a report card.

Highways — C plus. Although the decline of pavement conditions has been halted, overall service continues to decline. Spending for system expansion has fallen short in high-growth suburban and urban areas. Many roadways and bridges should be replaced.

Mass Transit — C minus. Productivity has declined significantly. Mass transit is overcapitalized in many smaller cities and inadequate in large, older cities. Systems face increasing difficulty diverting people from automobiles and are rarely linked to broad transportation goals.

Aviation — B minus. Service is declining in the face of increasing airport and airspace congestion as a result of deregulation. The building of trust fund balances limits the expenditure of revenues for capital expansion and worsens the air situation. The air traffic control systems needs upgrading.

Water Resources — B. Navigation and flood control projects perform well, but some are costly and inefficient. New legislation could increase local costs so much that only wealthy communities receive aid. Project implementation is slow, cumbersome and bureaucratic.

Water Supply — B minus. While regional performance varies,

From *State Government News*, July 1988, pp. 8-9. Reprinted by permission of the Council of State Governments.

water supply stands out as an effective, locally operated program. Many public water systems suffer from pricing below costs, inability to meet purity standards or source contamination. Storage and distribution systems are deteriorating in some older cities and supplies are limited in some parts of the West and Eastern coastal cities.

Wastewater — C. Despite a federal investment of more than $44 billion in treatment plants, water quality has not improved as much as expected. Many secondary systems are inefficiently designed.

Solid waste — C minus. Environmentally acceptable alternatives to landfills are being developed. Tougher environmental standards mean more rigorous monitoring, but safe facilities are expensive to build and public opposition is strong to new facilities.

Hazardous waste — D. Despite a five-fold increase in funding for cleanup of toxic sites since 1986, a massive backlog of poisons and projects remains. More effort needs to be made to reduce the amount of toxic waste produced.

Greater investment needed

Many of these problems stem from a lack of monetary investment in public works. Total public spending on infrastructure dropped from 3.6 percent of the gross national product in 1960 to 2.6 percent in 1985, with capital spending declining from 2.3 percent to 1.1 percent of GNP. Moreover, spending on operations and maintenance of public works has not kept pace with costs. The state and local capital investment in infrastructure peaked at $34 billion in 1972 and federal spending at $25 billion in the late 1970s. If our infrastructure is to support the increased demands of the public and industry in coming years, this trend must be reversed. Industrial use of infrastructure will increase by 30 percent over the next decade, according to an estimate by the U.S. Department of

Commerce. A sound infrastructure is essential to long-term economic growth. Economic efficiency and public health are linked inextricably to adequate transportation, water quality and waste disposal. Governments' investment in infrastructure affects the private sector's investment. For every public dollar spent on building and maintaining roads, streets and bridges, the private sector spends $15 to move people and goods, while for every public aviation dollar, the private counterpart is $9.

The Council endorsed four principles to serve as a guide in revitalizing infrastructure.

A larger share of the cost of public works should be paid by those who benefit.

The federal government should be a partner in financing public works, including allowing flexible block grants to localities. The administration and Congress should remove unwarranted limits on the ability of state and local governments to use tax-exempt financing for infrastructure projects.

States should develop comprehensive infrastructure finance strategies. States should revise laws that restrict local infrastructure investments. State spending on infrastructure dropped from 32 percent in 1970 to 23 percent in 1985. State spending of $25 billion annually is less than one-third of the non-federal government spending on public works.

Local governments should make maintenance of public works a budgetary priority. Attention to details of maintenance will result in fewer major renovations and increase the lifespan of public works.

The Council agreed that no single approach is adequate to ensure the vitality of America's infrastructure. Rather, a broad range of measures is needed.

The state role

For the nation to meet its infrastructure needs, states will have

to actively pursue a greater capital investment and efficient use of infrastructure funds. To do so, states must work with all levels of government.

State and federal officials must work to assure capital is accessible. Strong state lobbying at the federal level is essential to maintain and to increase the ability of state and local governments to obtain low-cost tax-free financing. States must fight to protect their right and the right of localities to borrow tax free for infrastructure. If states are silent on these issues, the federal government will continue to restrict state access to capital through tax constraints.

States also need to have rational capital budgeting processes. To build and strengthen public works, states must accurately assess needs and plan spending increases. In addition, state budgets must include a system of planned maintenance and repair for existing public works. States must plan for the upkeep of infrastructure. In this way, infrastructure projects will have longer useful lives and the effectiveness of every dollar spent will increase.

Government investment in public works can be supplemented by greater reliance on user fees. User fees could finance more than half of our current annual infrastructure needs. As general funds grow tighter, user fees represent a reliable and available source of infrastructure funding.

Each of these components depends on increased cooperation of federal, state and local governments with private businesses and citizens. The nation's infrastructure problems cannot be solved without a cooperative approach. Only by combining our efforts can the nation rebuild its fragile foundations and create an infrastructure able to support future economic growth. □

The Myths of Mass Transit

"Whether we consider buses or trains, urban public transit systems offer inferior service, both in quantity and quality."

San Francisco cable car.

Catherine G. Burke
Associate Professor, School of Public Administration, University of Southern California, Los Angeles

MASS transit is an idea whose time has passed. It is costly, ineffective, inhumane, wasteful of energy, can not serve our real needs for transportation, and helps to increase congestion and air pollution. If all this sounds shocking and absolutely wrong to you, be assured you are not alone. One of the most widely believed myths in our society is that the problems cited above are created by the automobile and can be solved by mass transit.

Letting go of cherished beliefs is one of life's most difficult undertakings. There are some things we simply "know" are true, and we refuse to be confused by mere facts. Such cherished beliefs are myths—stories whose origins are forgotten, but which ostensibly relate to historical events which are usually of such character to explain some practice, belief, institution, or natural phenomenon.

These myths are so widely believed that they are assumed to be common knowledge and are rarely questioned. Even when contrary facts are presented, they are quickly forgotten and the myths prevail. Part of this has to do with a natural human characteristic not to abandon a theory, even when it has problems, at least until a better theory appears. Another part of the reason, however, may have to do with potential beneficiaries should the myths prevail and the public invest large amounts of money in mass transit systems.

Before examining the myths in detail, some definitions of terms may help. For many people, the term mass transit can refer to any type of public transportation. The idea of mass transit, however, implies the movement of large numbers of people (masses) at the same time along fixed routes. Today, it is best confined to rail rapid transit, whether subways, elevated trains, or ground-level trains which are separated from other types of traffic. Such systems serve internal transportation needs of an urban region and usually include commuter services as well as intra-city services.

Public transportation, on the other hand, can include not only mass transit (rail systems), but also buses (large and small), taxis, moving sidewalks, people movers, elevators, personal rapid transit, and other means of transporting people and goods. Their common characteristic is that they are available to the public at large, rather than involving private ownership and usage provided by the automobile or bicycles.

Thus, it is perfectly possible to believe in the necessity for public transportation while at the same time opposing mass transit or other particular forms of public transit because of service quality, cost, or other problems. As with all public projects, it is not enough to argue that something is good or it is bad; what is needed is an examination of the purposes to be served by a particular project, the most effective means to achieve those purposes, and the costs and benefits to be achieved.

Although over-all costs and benefits are important, it is also important to disaggregate the costs and benefits to find out specifically who benefits and how much, who pays and how much. Public policies which are promoted without such examination are unlikely to have long-term success or public acceptance. They will be based on myths, not on fact, and their ultimate failure will make it even more difficult to institute innovative policies which show much greater promise for success.

Myth 1: We once had adequate public transit systems in our cities and these were destroyed through a conspiracy of large corporations—National City Lines, General Motors, Firestone Tire and Rubber, Standard Oil, and others.

This myth is one of the most pernicious, because it assumes things were better in the past and, if we could only return to what we had, things would be good again. It is also one of the most persistent myths, since there is considerable evidence to support it. Part of the evidence comes from fond memories of the Big Red Cars in Los Angeles or the streetcars which provided good service in many cities in the early part of the 20th century.

There is also a Supreme Court case—*United States v. National City Lines et al,* 341 U.S. 916 (1951)—which indicates that National City Lines was incorporated in 1936 to purchase transit systems in cities where streetcars were no longer practicable and convert them to motorbus operations. To raise capital to make such purchases, a plan was devised to procure funds from manufacturers whose products would be used by the operating companies. This was the basis of the conspiracy wherein National City Lines and the other defendants were convicted of monopolizing the markets.

For those who would like to build new rail systems today, it is attractive to assert we once had good rail systems which were destroyed for narrow profit motives. The evidence, however, does not support the conspiracy theory. Rail transit systems began having serious financial difficulties during and just after World War I. Rail systems which had been built to support real estate ventures could no longer be maintained, since the land was long since developed and the profits realized. Real estate development began to take place between the rail lines, making the rail service inadequate for many people. Beginning in 1912, people turned to the convenience of the auto and—despite hard times, wars, and energy crises—the trend has not

changed. By 1919, one-third of the rail operating companies were bankrupt.

The death of street railways

The first competitors to the rail systems were the jitneys—private autos which offered fast and flexible service for a nickel. Many people financed their first car by traveling along streetcar lines picking up waiting passengers for a quicker and more convenient trip. Some jitney operations apparently attracted up to 50% of the peak-hour electric rail ridership. The situation of the urban transit industry became so serious that Pres. Wilson appointed a Federal Electric Railway Commission after World War I to investigate it. The solutions offered by the industry were to restore corporate credit by reestablishing their monopoly, to ban the competition (jitneys), and to raise fares.

The transit industry got what it wanted, but it was not enough to save the street railways. The trend toward autos accelerated. Within transit operations, the trend toward buses began in the 1920's, as some jitney operations were taken over by the street railways and placed on schedules using buses rather than rail lines. Buses offered a number of advantages as track construction and maintenance were eliminated: one mechanical failure did not shut down an entire line and buses could be rerouted if demand shifted or if a street were blocked due to construction or some other emergency.

The critical factor leading to the conversion of street railways to buses and to the further decline of the industry may have been the Public Utility Holding Company Act of 1935. In 1931, over 50% of the street railways and over 80% of the total revenue passengers rode bus or streetcar lines controlled by the power holding companies. The original street railways had been drawn by horses, and the new electric companies bought out the street railways in order to convert them to electricity and develop a market for their generating capacity.

Even during the Depression, most of these holding companies could make a reasonable profit through their electric, gas, lighting, and other ventures. In 1935, however, the Utility Holding Company act was passed, which required these firms to divest themselves of their urban transit operations. During the legislative hearings on the act, the power trusts did not mention the subject of transit, and one can assume they were anxious to get rid of these unprofitable operations without incurring the wrath of local communities, which might jeopardize their more lucrative franchises.

It was at this point that National City Lines and the other "conspirators" entered and played a significant role in

offsetting the contraction of capital for transit modernization caused by the 1935 act. Clearly, they also had a profit motive, and the chance to write off ancient, obsolete equipment still carrying high book values was an important attraction for outside capital.

Later, in the 1950's, when the National City Lines case led to another major loss of capital backing from suppliers, this, coupled with the loss of patronage, made it unprofitable for large holding companies to remain in the transit business. Public ownership became essential to keep the transit systems operating. Thus, it seems clear that economics, not conspiracy, destroyed the street railways. The abandonment of streetcars probably prevented the financial collapse of the industry.

Almost overnight an industry with high fixed costs of maintenance of way, generation of power, and, in some cases, engineering and construction of rolling stock, found itself buying standardized products from a limited group of manufacturers, as well as relieved of the problem of maintenance of right of way. The motor bus brought other significant savings. In many cities, two-man streetcars were replaced with one-man buses. . . . [The companies] were able to close down unneeded depots, sell excess real estate. . . .[1]

Myth 2: Rail rapid transit can promote high-density growth and high land values in the concentrated central city districts.

The idea is that rail systems can counteract the multi-centered urban areas such as Los Angeles and Houston and move us toward more concentrated patterns such as New York or San Francisco. Urban density is assumed to be good and urban sprawl bad. Even if one prefers density (and it is quite clear that many do not), it is not certain that rail systems can cause more dense development. In Toronto, there are indications that the development that took place along the Yonge Street subway would have occurred anyway due to the city's high rate of growth in the 1950's. The rearrangement of development that took place was accomplished as much with zoning as with transit development.

Whereas some claim the billion-dollar construction boom along Market Street in San Francisco was caused by BART, others believe the growth in San Francisco was due to its service-type economy and would have taken place with or without BART. In Houston, Dallas, and Denver, which rely solely on automobiles and buses, even greater expansion in high-rise central office building has occurred.

Urban sprawl may also be a product of rail transit development, since these

[1] L.M. Schneider, *Marketing Urban Mass Transit* (Boston: Harvard University Press, 1965).

systems best serve those who work in the central city and live in distant suburbs. These are usually the more affluent members of society who reach the train by auto. Rail systems make long-distance commuting tolerable and the land boom that has taken place around San Francisco (especially Contra Costa County) offers some evidence of this pattern.

In situations of little growth, or even decline, as in many of our large central cities, it seems likely that growth in some areas will reduce demand in other areas. Whether these increases and declines offset each other is uncertain from existing information. Aggregate estimates of costs and benefits frequently fail to reveal that values are being transferred, rather than created.

Even where growth is assumed, a major rail network may not have major impact on development. Washington Metro officials estimate that the number of jobs in downtown Washington, D.C., will increase from 500,000 in 1974 to 750,000 in 1990. At the same time, jobs in Washington suburbs are expected to grow from 500,000 to 1,500,000, despite the building of the $8,000,000,000 fixed-rail system.

One reason for this is the low diversion rate from automobiles to trains. BART reduced the number of cars on most heavily used lines by five per cent. In Chicago, the Dan Ryan expressway train line carries less than 20,000 people per day in rush hours, while the adjoining freeways carry 160,000. Experience is consistent that diversion from automobiles is equal to about one year's increase in vehicle counts. Much of the diversion to rails comes from people who rode in buses or carpools before or from those who could not travel before (latent demand). This puts considerable strain on bus systems, since the trains frequently compete for their most profitable lines.

Myth 3: Rail rapid transit systems can reduce home-to-work rush hour congestion. The low diversion rates cited above indicate why rail systems can not have major effects upon rush hour congestion. New rail systems may even increase central city congestion.

If a high-rise office building is erected in the central city in order to house economic activity that might otherwise have been located in a diffuse pattern, only some 15% of the employees can ordinarily be expected to use the rail facility to reach it. The other 85% use the streets, either in buses, in automobiles, or on foot.[2]

Myth 4: Rail rapid transit systems can help alleviate air pollution problems. To the extent a concentrated pattern of

[2]G.W. Hilton, *Federal Transit Subsidies: The Urban Mass Transportation Assistance Program* (Washington, D.C.: The American Enterprise Institute, 1974), p. 101.

development does occur, it may act to concentrate pollutants from automobiles, making air pollution worse. Vehicles moving at low speeds and stopping frequently produce four times the pollutants than are emitted by vehicles moving freely on an expressway.

Even if there were no increase in congestion, rail rapid transit can have only negligible effects on over-all pollution. This is partly due to the low diversion of people from their autos and also due to the controls on automobiles which attack the problem directly by reducing their polluting qualities.

Myth 5: Rail rapid transit systems can reduce our energy requirements, especially petroleum energy.

Based on the operating energy required per passenger-mile, rail systems appear to be real savers of energy. Such appearances vanish, however, once trains must be run at less than full capacity. Under typical operating conditions, full capacity is met for, at most, 20 hours per week during rush hours. At other times, trains must still run, and new rapid rail systems such as BART in San Francisco or the Washington Metro are actually energy wasters, rather than savers.

The principal reasons for this waste are the widespread use of low-occupancy private automobiles to gain access to the system, the attraction of people from more energy-efficient forms of public transportation, and the high use of energy to build the system and to operate stations—46% of the energy which will be consumed by BART over the next 50 years was consumed before the first train was run. Most recent studies suggest the best opportunity for energy savings is to improve the energy efficiency of the automobile. According to a 1977 study prepared for the Senate Committee on Environment and Public Works, "Rail rapid transit offers little aid to the nation's effort to save fuel."

Why rail rapid transit does not work

Myth 6: Mass transit can provide good service for a large (or significant) portion of the population, especialy the transit-dependent such as the poor, elderly, young, physically handicapped, and others without easy access to the automobile.

The main reason rail rapid transit systems can not work well for these people is the same reason it can not work well for anyone else. Our cities are now multi-centered urban regions with housing, commerce, and industry scattered over large areas. Both residence and employment are becoming increasingly dispersed, modifying the demand patterns for urban transportation. The causes of these patterns are multiple and varied. It is too simple to say they have been caused by the automobile, though the auto clearly has permitted such development which began long before the auto came on the scene.

As people became more affluent, they had more choices in housing, and the early street railways allowed urban expansion in roughly star-shaped corridors. Later, the development of electric motors made land-extensive horizontal factories in outlying areas more economic than the vertically organized steam-powered factories in the central core. Telephones removed the need for hand-delivered messages between offices and also allowed people to communicate with those who lived in more distant neighborhoods. Trucks freed manufacturers from the need to be near a central rail system, and these factors plus the lower cost of land and taxes in outlying areas made greater dispersal of industry attractive.

Government housing policies regarding zoning, taxation, and financing of home purchases also encouraged the move to the suburbs. With the expansion of both housing and industry, many jobs, especially industrial jobs, are now found outside the central city. In perhaps the extreme case, Los Angeles, only 6.6% of all jobs are found in what passes there for a central business district. Even a concentrated city such as New York has lost over 600,000 jobs since 1969, many of them to outlying suburban areas.

Since rail systems tend to best serve those in the suburbs who wish to travel to the central city, poor people who live in the central city and need to get out of the city to industrial jobs find the train systems offer little or nothing. Other needs for mobility (roughly 75% of all urban trips) can not be easily met by train systems—the needs to go to market, to visit friends, to reach a doctor, or to get a recreation area. Granted the auto-dominant system we now have offers little for the transit-dependent, the mass transit systems proposed for our cities will do little to alleviate their problems.

Myth 7: Mass transit systems will save travel time.

It is assumed that cutting travel time will attract riders to mass transit systems. Therefore, stations are placed at least a mile apart, and frequently more than a mile apart. Thus, there are few points of access to and egress from the system. The 71-mile BART system has only 34 stations. the larger Chicago system has 150, and Boston has 70. While this may reduce the time on the train, total trip time becomes longer as it takes more time to get access to the system and more time to get from the system to one's final destination. It is total trip time, however, which is most important to the consumer. Waiting time and other out-of-vehicle activity are very onerous to potential customers.

Myth 8: Mass transit systems will result in lower costs for transportation in cities.

The costs to build urban rail systems is extremely high. The most recent construction for the Washington Metro is running roughly $100,000,000 per mile. Nonetheless, despite high capital costs, proponents of rail systems claim operating costs are much lower than for, say, bus systems, The evidence for this is quite the contrary, with the all-bus Southern California Rapid Transit District showing much lower costs than other big city systems which have rail transit as part of their operations. In San Francisco, costs of the BART system exceed not only those of buses, but also those of subcompact and even standard autos.

With all these difficulties, it is not surprising that rail transit systems are viewed with little favor by their users. Around the world, rail systems are declining in ridership as more affluent people seek more convenient alternatives. Rail systems also decline because of their inflexibility. As cities develop and change, the rail systems can not be moved to accommodate the change. The growth of low-density rings around metropolitan areas discussed earlier is part of this problem. Another factor is the growth and development of new attractions. A considerable portion of the decline in use of the New York subway system can be attributed to its lack of service to attractions that have been built in the 50 years since its completion. A new sports complex, airport, or other major traffic generator is unlikely to be served by existing rail lines.

Despite all these problems, rail systems have enjoyed considerable support in major cities and in the Federal government (prior to the Reagan Administration). Much of the support comes from downtown business interests, which want increased property values, and the consultants and contractors who will design and build the system. Big-city mayors (who get much of their support from downtown business interests) also support these systems. A number of observers attribute this to a kind of boosterism—a city isn't really a city unless it has a rail transit system.

Some people seem to have an emotional attachment to trains—a predisposition to rail transit because of a childhood fascination. "They don't have to have a reason for wanting it, they just want it." For local politicians, there is also a desire for a visible accomplishment—something that can be pointed to with pride during the next election.

Environmentalists have been important supporters of train systems. Many of them have fought the road gang for years and they "know" rail systems are the answer. They genuinely believe these systems will reduce energy consumption, air pollution, and congestion, as well as help the transit-dependent and improve the over-all quality of urban life.

A significant segment of the public apparently agrees with them, at least on the issue of air pollution. A poll taken in Los Angeles prior to a 1974 vote on a rail transit proposal indicated an overwhelming proportion of voters felt it would reduce smog. This was not enough to gain a favorable vote on the proposal, however, perhaps because another poll in the same area indicated 86.8% of the respondents believed Los Angeles needed a new transit system, but only 4.7% said they definitely would ride it.

Finally, there are the rapid transit districts. Their support has come primarily from the downtown business groups and the consultants and contractors who build rail systems. The transit districts appear to respond to this support by offering rail solutions time and again. Until recently, such systems offered the promise of Federal money, and such money would give more power to the transit districts, more jobs, and more income for the technostructure of the agency.

Alternative approaches

First, it must be recognized we have an auto-dominant system, not because people are perverse, but because this system offers more people greater mobility and access to the goods of our society than any transportation system in history. It is the very success of this system which has created difficulties for society as a whole and for those who can not or do not wish to use it.

Whether we consider buses or trains, urban public transit systems offer inferior service, both in quantity and quality. Riding on these systems is usually slow and often a dehumanizing experience. Crowding and crime both take their toll. Given this situation, our best strategy is to alleviate and ameliorate the problems of the auto-dominant system while, at the same time, we attempt to create new transit systems which can better meet our needs.

To reduce petroleum consumption, we do not add one per cent of the people to public transit, we reduce the size of the automobile and increase its fuel efficiency—something which the high cost of petroleum is already bringing about. Automotive air pollution can be attacked through better engine design and by changing to non-polluting fuels. Public policies to encourage the use of methanol (which can be made from any organic matter, including garbage) could help reduce petroleum usage and contribute to pollution control.

Auto safety can be improved through the use of roll cages and fuel tank bladders such as those which protect race drivers. Their additional weight could be offset by using lighter materials elsewhere.

Congestion can be reduced through improved traffic controls, as well as such social devices as flex-time. We can also make better use of existing systems by encouraging paratransit—carpools, vanpools, jitneys, subscription buses, and shared taxis.

Often overlooked as public transit, taxis can provide important service, especially if we support the move to computerized dispatch, as has been done in a number of European cities. For a cost of roughly $5,000,000, we could develop a central computerized dispatch system for a city like Los Angeles which would greatly improve the productivity and profitability of all taxi companies as well as enable them to provide superior service. For those who can not afford taxis, it would be far less costly to subsidize taxi rides and it would provide far better service than rail systems.

Such short-term solutions could meet immediate transportation needs and also help attack the ancillary problems associated with our present transportation system. In the long run, we must develop new technologies which will fit the multi-centered and dispersed shape of our cities. Elsewhere, I have argued that Personal Rapid Transit (a small automatic electric vehicle system) shows the most promise for meeting our individual and societal needs for a cost-effective, energy-efficient, non-polluting, and aesthetically attractive transportation system.[3] It is my belief that work on such a system should begin now; in the meantime, we should make every effort to meet today's transportation needs with systems which are low in capital cost and which promise a high return in both service and costs. We should avoid systems with high capital costs which lack flexibility and are vulnerable to changes in values, the physical dimensions of cities, working hours and patterns, and human failures such as strikes, criminal violence, and civil disturbance.

Mass rail rapid transit offers the highest costs and the least flexibility. It is truly an idea whose time has passed. If the Reagan Administration sticks to its intention to cut off funds for rail rapid transit, it will be doing all of us a favor. By saving money which would otherwise have been wasted on expensive and ineffective rail systems, we can begin to work to improve our auto-dominant system. We can also begin to explore and develop new technologies which will improve upon the present system and offer us better service, greater opportunities, and a better quality of life.

---

[3]C.G. Burke, *Innovation and Public Policy: The Case of Personal Rapid Transit* (Lexington, Mass.: D.C. Heath, 1979).

Index

Credits/ Acknowledgments

Cover design by Charles Vitelli

1. Early Commentaries
Facing overview—Greater Boston Convention & Tourist Bureau. 31—Florida Department of Commerce/Division of Tourism.

2. Intergovernmental Relations
Facing overview—WHO photo by Kalisher.

3. Voting, Parties, and Interest Groups
Facing overview—Vermont Development Agency.

4. Government Institutions and Officeholders
Facing overview—State of Connecticut, Department of Economic Development/Dominick J. Ruggiero. 83–86—Nebraska State Historical Society.

5. Variations Among Regions and States
Facing overview—New York State Department of Commerce, Albany. 137-138—Alabama Bureau of Tourism & Travel.

6. Cities and Suburbs
Facing overview—United Nations photo by Yutaka Nagata. 167—Department of Housing and Urban Development.

7. Finances and Economic Development
Facing overview—Florida Department of Commerce/Division of Tourism. 179—Las Vegas News Bureau. 180—David Suter. 185, 186, 188, 189—AP/Wide World. 190—Steven Harrison, courtesy Ohio Department of Development.

8. Policies and Policymaking
Facing overview—Bay Area Rapid Transit photo. 230—New York Department of Social Services.

We Want Your Advice

ANNUAL EDITIONS:
STATE AND LOCAL GOVERNMENT 89/90
Article Rating Form

Here is an opportunity for you to have direct input into the next revision of this volume. We would like you to rate each of the 55 articles listed below, using the following scale:

1. **Excellent: should definitely be retained**
2. **Above average: should probably be retained**
3. **Below average: should probably be deleted**
4. **Poor: should definitely be deleted**

Your ratings will play a vital part in the next revision. So please mail this prepaid form to us just as soon as you complete it.
Thanks for your help!

Annual Editions revisions depend on two major opinion sources: one is our Advisory Board, listed in the front of this volume, which works with us in scanning the thousands of articles published in the public press each year; the other is you—the person actually using the book. Please help us and the users of the next edition by completing the prepaid article rating form on this page and returning it to us. Thank you.

Rating	Article	Rating	Article
	1. The Federalist No. 17		30. Technology Transfer in the Trenches
	2. The Federalist No. 45		31. The New Regionalism
	3. The American System of Townships . . .		32. An Economic Role Reversal
	4. Local Government: Observations		33. Halfway Home and a Long Way to Go
	5. Nature of the American State		34. The Two Souths
	6. Federalism: The Linchpin of Liberty		35. "Sweetheart, Get Me Re-Write. They've Indicted the Donut Dunker"
	7. The States Make a Comeback		36. How Business Is Reshaping America
	8. A More Favorable Court: States Fare Better on Preemption		37. Snow White and the 17 Dwarfs: From Metro Cooperation to Governance
	9. The New Federalism Hasn't Meant Less Government		38. Would We Know a Well-Governed City If We Saw One?
	10. The State of State-Local Relations		39. The Urban Strangler: How Crime Causes Poverty in the Inner City
	11. Mixed Electoral Systems: The Newest Reform Structure		40. Blacks in Boston Seek to Secede
	12. I Was a Chicago Ward Heeler		41. The Quake Didn't Quit
	13. The Arms Race of Campaign Financing		42. Going for Broke
	14. Buying State Access		43. Taxing the Poor
	15. Populism Revived		44. The States' Global Hustlers
	16. Civic Strategies for Community Empowerment		45. Delaware Inc.
	17. Electoral Accountability: Local Recalls		46. Civic Strategy for Local Economic Development
	18. Reinventing the Legislature		47. Privatization Is a Means to "More With Less"
	19. Party Politics: The New Chamber Game		48. Privatization Presents Problems
	20. Fifty Years Without a Conference Committee		49. Safety Nets for the Poor
	21. The Decline and Fall of Town Meeting		50. The Changing Balance in State and Local Power to Control Education
	22. Practicing Political Science on a Local School Board		51. Bring Back the Orphanage
	23. Strategies for Leaders Who Do Not Have a Lot of Power		52. Where the Fight Will Be Fought: AIDS and State and Local Governments
	24. Change Masters for the States		53. Drunk Driving: The Highway Killer Is Back
	25. From Dreamers to Doers		54. The Battle Over Land Use: A Second Wave Emerges
	26. "City Managers Don't Make Policy": A Lie; Let's Face It		55. Infrastructure in Trouble
	27. The Emerging Agenda in State Constitutional Rights Law		56. The Myths of Mass Transit
	28. View From the Bench: A Judge's Day		
	29. Women in State Government: Looking Back, Looking Ahead		

(Continued on next page)

ABOUT YOU

Name_____ Date_____

Are you a teacher? ☐ Or student? ☐

Your School Name _____

Department _____

Address _____

City _____ State _____ Zip _____

School Telephone # _____

YOUR COMMENTS ARE IMPORTANT TO US!

Please fill in the following information:

For which course did you use this book? _____

Did you use a text with this Annual Edition? ☐ yes ☐ no

The title of the text? _____

What are your general reactions to the Annual Editions concept?

Have you read any particular articles recently that you think should be included in the next edition?

Are there any articles you feel should be replaced in the next edition? Why?

Are there other areas that you feel would utilize an Annual Edition?

May we contact you for editorial input?

May we quote you from above?

ANNUAL EDITIONS: STATE AND LOCAL GOVERNMENT 89/90

BUSINESS REPLY MAIL

First Class   Permit No. 84   Guilford, CT

Postage will be paid by addressee

The Dushkin Publishing Group, Inc.
Sluice Dock
DPG **Guilford, Connecticut 06437**

No Postage
Necessary
if Mailed
in the
United States